Informing Statecraft

Informing Statecraft

Intelligence for a New Century

ANGELO CODEVILLA

THE FREE PRESS
A Division of Macmillan, Inc.
NEW YORK

Maxwell Macmillan Canada
TORONTO

Maxwell Macmillan International
NEW YORK OXFORD SINGAPORE SYDNEY

The Free Press
A Division of Simon & Schuster
1230 Avenue of the Americas
New York, NY 10020

The Free Press and colophon are trademarks of Simon & Schuster Inc.

Manufactured in the United States of America
10 9 8 7 6 5 4 3 2 1

Library of Congress Cataloging-In-Publication Data
Codevilla, Angelo
        Informing stagecraft: intelligence for a new century/Angelo
Codevilla.
        p.   cm.
        Includes bibliographical references (p.   ) and index.
        ISBN: 0-7432-4484-2
        1. Intelligence service—United States.   2. Intelligence service.
    I.   Title.
    JK468.I6C58   1992
    327.1273—dc30   91-46172
                                                CIP

For information regarding special discounts for bulk purchases, please contact Simon &
Schuster Special Sales at 1-800-456-6798 or business@simonandschuster.com

Coniugi Dilectissimae

Contents

CONTENTS

Preface

Conflict is an ineradicable part of international affairs. Knowledge of friends and enemies can be decisive in conflict. In statecraft such knowledge is called "intelligence." This volume explains the principles of intelligence—the nature of the business. Although written by an American from the point of view of the United States, this book is not exclusively about American intelligence. Rather, it compares the tasks that American intelligence has performed, and may be called on to do in the future, to both the enduring standards of the craft and the circumstances of time and place. It offers an understanding of intelligence by which one may judge the performance of all intelligence systems, each in its own circumstance. But it is naturally focused on democratic systems, and on the impending turn of the century. Rather than the Millennium the year 2000 will most assuredly will bring troubles of its own, different from those of previous decades and less predictable. To deal with this new world, the major elements of U.S. intelligence will have to be rethought and rebuilt. This volume provides an understanding of the basics of the craft upon which U.S. intelligence may be rebuilt.

This book is the fruit of many years' experience at various levels of government and intelligence service, as well as of much academic reflection. I received my first security clearance in 1966 at age 23 when, during a break from reading Xenophon and Machiavelli in graduate school, I worked for the Bendix Aerospace Systems Division on Air Force contracts to study Soviet military tactics. Three years later, I was a U.S. Navy officer aboard ship, assigned to the classic military intelligence job: Pass information collected in the course of ship's operations up the line, and sort the information coming down the line, for each of the ship's departments. At sea, as well as during a tour of duty at the Fleet Intelligence Center, Atlantic, I observed that modern intelligence replayed ancient scripts with new technology.

Back in civilian life, I wrote my Ph.D. dissertation on French political culture, talking with mayors, secretaries, soldiers, and priests about things important to them. I then taught political science—both international conflict and political philosophy. In the meantime, as a Naval Reserve officer, I received the standard training in counterintelligence investigations and counterinsurgency, and served a tour of duty as an intelligence briefer for the Chief of Naval Operations.

When I joined the U.S. Foreign Service my first assignment, as a regional analyst in the Bureau of Intelligence and Research, afforded me a worm's-eye view of the process by which intelligence flows into Washington and is distilled for policymakers. My next job, on the staff of the U.S. Senate Select Committee on Intelligence, gave me a unique bird's-eye view.

For a variety of reasons, the thousands of individuals involved in the hundreds of tasks that make up U.S. intelligence live out their careers as specialists and do not know about each other's jobs. Even the top staff of the Director of Central Intelligence is the sum of specialists. Only a handful of top executives ever get to look at the whole of intelligence, and they are so burdened by day-to-day decisions that they hardly think about it. Fewer than a dozen staffers on the intelligence committttees of the U.S. Congress, however, are privileged to look at *all* fields of intelligence simultaneously, without actually having to micromanage *any* of them. Even fewer take advantage of the opportunity they have to reflect on the nature of the business. I was one of these people.

Between 1977 and 1985, as the personal representative of Senator Malcolm Wallop (R-WY), the ranking member (and subsequently Chairman) of the Subcommittee on the Budget, I had to scrutinize the two-foot-high stack of justifications for all the U.S. intelligence agencies' requests for money. A senior bureaucrat in the office of the Director of Central Intelligence might specialize in, say, three inches' worth. I read that mass of stuff not only to do my job, but also with an academic bent to understand intelligence—what makes it work well, and what makes it work badly. The fact that I was moonlighting by teaching courses in classical and modern political theory reinforced my perspective. I asked Aristotle's simple questions of officials throughout the intelligence community: What is the purpose of this activity? Why do you do this rather than something else? Do you do this for the sake of that, or vice versa? By what criteria do you judge your products good or bad? I was astounded at how little thought had been given to decisions that affected thousands of careers, billions of dollars, and in fact the nation's future. All too often the answers to my questions were "We've always done it this way" and "How insulting of you to ask!" I thought that the best, as well as the most interesting, way to do my job was to do the thinking that the bureaucrats were not doing.

The job of the Senate Intelligence Committee also involves refereeing the countless quarrels within the intelligence community. Any senior bureaucrat who wanted to push a program or foul up one he disliked would try to meet and "lobby" members of the committee staff. As such I found myself learning far more than I wanted to about the pros and cons of individual covert actions; the consequences of legislation, regulations, and policies; and so on. Since reputations are at least as important in the intelligence community as elsewhere, I found myself lobbied on historical matters as well, and got competing explanations about who was right and wrong about this or that intelligence estimate, the great missile accuracy controversy, the great Nosenko controversy, and many lesser ones. As I listened I asked Why is this good? Why is this bad? All too often I had to answer my own questions.

I shared my reflections with my colleagues on the Intelligence Committee in classified form. I also presented them in unclassified form at a variety of conferences, and as a series of seven chapters in edited collections on intelligence.[1] In 1980, while serving on President Reagan's team to prepare the transition of control of the U.S. intelligence community to his administration, I was the principal author of the team's classified report to CIA Director-designate William Casey. Recent books have conveyed the bureaucrats' view that they felt threatened by that report, and by me personally.* The actual document is classified far above TOP SECRET, only one copy exists in the CIA's bowels, and the "old boys'" caricature of it is based on fear, not knowledge.

I returned to academic life in 1985. Yet even my full-time affairs with history and philosophy have not excluded intelligence: I have taught, among other topics, a classified course on intelligence at the U.S. Naval Postgraduate School. My most recent book War: Ends and Means (with the late Paul Seabury) shows the role of intelligence in warfare. The present book is the refinement of thoughts on intelligence that have been developing for 25 years. Today, as ever, I treat intelligence as part of the perennial art of politics.

In sum, mine is the perspective of an academic who has been as far "inside" as one can get, who is not part of the anti-intelligence lobby, but who, emphatically, is no "insider." And there is the rub. The reader will quickly notice that this author is not in awe of U.S. intelligence, nor of the people who have run it. Over

---

*See John Ranelagh, The Agency: The Rise and Decline of the CIA, pp. 659–671, and Bob Woodward, Veil, p. 60. Both books obviously depend heavily on the opinion of CIA "old boys," especially those of an elderly Washington aristo named John Bross. Both books' descriptions of the transition team's report are outright caricatures.

the years at countless conferences, through correspondence and personal contact, I have noted that many U.S. intelligence officials (and former officials) who react with *schadenfreude* when radicals accuse them of being murderers and threats to the American Way of Life have lost their composure when anyone has questioned their competence. Instead of replying with facts and reasons to argue that what they did was the best that could have been done in the past, and a reliable guide to success in the future, they have attacked the questioner. The attack is usually three-pronged: First, this person must be revealing classified information. Second, this person does not know the whole story, and we who do know it are forbidden from commenting, except to say "You're wrong." Third, this person's demeaning tone precludes a rational exploration of some admittedly valid points. So, in practice, the three points boil down to one: Leave the field of intelligence to the "old boys."

One prominent "old boy" commented on this book's manuscript as follows: "Major changes [in U.S. intelligence] are overdue, but they will have to come from initiatives taken by the President, the Secretary of Defense, and the DCI. Congress cannot do it. Nor can public pressures." In other words: Thought by outsiders on this subject is inherently illegitimate. This "old boy" argued only one point of mine, the proposition that U.S. intelligence would benefit by hiring fewer people cast in the mold of bureaucrats. He wrote: "The kinds of people Codevilla wants in intelligence work are difficult to attract. And even if they did join, the environment of any bureaucracy soon compels them to engage in many dysfunctional practices." In other words, if the needs of bureaucracy conflict with the needs of the job, by all means choose bureaucracy. One could not ask for a clearer statement of Mosca's Iron Law.* After accusing me of violating the espionage laws (though CIA cleared my manuscript†), he opined "I believe I know more than a Congressional staffer could learn." Perhaps the "old boys'" knowledge of their own activities is a better basis than mine for serious thought about the nature of the business. But in fact the "old boys" have produced no book that both asks fundamental questions and answers them from a broad historical perspective.

This book's aim is precisely to remove intelligence—at least intellectually—from the grip of bureaucrats. The essence of bureaucratic thinking is to turn all questions into "What does this mean for the agency, and for us who define our

---

*Regardless of the purpose for which any organization is established, it will, sooner or later, serve the personal advancement of its leaders.

†When I accepted a job with the U.S. Senate Intelligence Committee in 1977, and again when I was appointed to the 1980 presidential transition team, I agreed to submit all my future writings that touched what I learned therefrom to the Central Intelligence Agency for security review. I have complied fully with that agreement.

worth by our association with it?" In a 1977 Washington debate, I was cast as the defender of intelligence against one of the leading demonizers of the subject. A former intelligence official rose from the audience and, mixing rage with disbelief, sputtered at me "But . . . you don't give a *damn* about the CIA!" I confess that I do not—nor even about the FBI, which I esteem more highly. Bureaucracies ought to be seen dispassionately as means, not ends.

This volume, unlike any other book on intelligence, does not take the CIA, the KGB, the Mossad, or any other bureaucracy as the point of departure. This is not an insider's brief for or against any current intelligence mission, technological capability, or specific individuals. Though it contains facts of which few have been aware, it is not an exposé of secrets. Many books that are ostensibly on intelligence are actually partisan tracts on the Cold War. We ask of the events of the Cold War the same questions we ask about events in the Peloponnesian War: What can they teach us about intelligence? This book applies knowledge of the intelligence business, from the four corners of the earth and from times both ancient and modern, to the new world taking shape before us.

The three parts herein explain the subject of intelligence from three radically different points of view, the convergence of these considerations producing a level of understanding that could not be achieved by a single treatment. Part I sketches the outlines of the subject while highlighting its critical role in successful statecraft. It explains what intelligence is, what happens to states that have good intelligence and to those that don't. Wide-ranging illustrations suggest that there are many paths to success and failure, but that the craft of intelligence is governed by underlying principles, and the key is to adapt them to circumstances. I then try to sketch the world of the turn of this century, a world pregnant with many kinds of conflict. Any government that wants to navigate it safely will need intelligence. Any and all who are concerned with the long term—public utilities no less than armies, navies, or intelligence services—base their plans on a vision of the future, explicit or implicit. Explicit visions are preferable because they allow planners to keep clear in their own minds the reasons why they are doing things. Such clarity enables a more responsible readjustment of plans when circumstances turn out different than expected.

Part II shows that the United States' apparatus for collecting information, for countering hostile intelligence, for analyzing information, and for conducting covert action grew from the postwar period to the present with little thought of matching what we *could* do to what we *had to* do. The U.S. has done as well as it has *despite* its intelligence. Mounting evidence points to a mismatch between the world of the 1990s and the U.S. intelligence system being prepared to deal with it. Here our field of vision narrows to match the restricted perspective of the people who have run U.S. intelligence without reference to the principles of intelligence. We explain, in their own terms, what they thought they were doing. Note however that, with notable exceptions, the practices of U.S. intelligence usually failed, even when judged on those terms. U.S. intelligence is worth our attention both because it is ours, and (more to the point) because all too often its practices have been excellent, albeit mostly negative, illustrations of the principles of intelligence.

Part III explains the principles of the intelligence business, drawing on a broad range of exemplary successes and failures. We break down each of the elements of intelligence—collection, counterintelligence, analysis, and covert action—into *their* components and show not just what works and what doesn't, but why. From the fundamentals of the craft we draw, piece by piece, a theory of intelligence, and clarify its relevance to the situation of the 1990s. Intelligence can neither replace responsible policymaking nor compensate for misfortune. Yet competence in intelligence can help any government, including that of the U.S., to pick its steps with skill and foreknowledge.

This book is not a set of recipes for "doing it right," but rather a guide to rigorous thought about the various problems of intelligence. Ever since select committees of the U.S. House and Senate issued multivolume reports in 1976 on the misdeeds of U.S. intelligence, a debate of sorts has occurred in the United States (and to a lesser extent elsewhere as well) about what intelligence agencies ought and ought not to do. In the 1990s the Congress, for better or worse, seems committed to substantial changes in the $30 billion-per-year edifice that is U.S. intelligence. This volume takes the debate back to basics. It develops intellectual criteria for judging the controversies of the past 15 years, and suggests that the intelligence issues that stir the U.S. government are small potatoes for the most part, compared to the ones it ought to face.

Stanford, California
September 1991

Acknowledgments

Senator Malcolm Wallop (R-WY) nominated me to the staff of the U.S. Senate Select Committee on Intelligence in 1977. Judge Laurence Silberman asked me to join him to prepare the presidential transition of 1980 for the U.S. intelligence agencies. I thank these admirable men for stimulating my interest in this subject.

Ever since 1979, it has been my privilege to discuss intelligence matters with an extraordinary group of scholars and intelligence officers from much of the world under the auspices of the Consortium for the Study of Intelligence, organized by Roy Godson. Nowhere else, ever, have there been such penetrating, wide-ranging discussions of intelligence. I will always be in Roy Godson's debt.

I thank Noreen O'Connor and Robert Harrington of The Free Press for their steadfast efficiency. But this is Erwin Glikes' book. He commissioned it, and made the crucial decisions.

I am grateful to the scholars who read and commented on the manuscript: Louis Dillais, Philip Fellman, Lewis Gann, Robert Gates, the late Paul Seabury, and Richard Staar.

My research assistant, M Carling, produced the manuscript while gently introducing me to computer-aided research.

This book was written at the Hoover Institution. No other place on earth provides so much academic freedom, so much intellectual and material support. Any shortcoming of a book produced at Hoover must be the author's fault.

PART I

Intelligence and Our Time

1

The Nature and Importance of Intelligence

When the five Intelligences all occur together
And none know of the method,
This is called the Divine Web,
It is the treasure of the Ruler.
            – *Sun Tzu, The Art of War*, Fifth Century B.C.

Intelligence is an instrument of conflict. It consists of words, numbers, images, suggestions, appraisals, incitements. It consists also of truths that enlighten or mislead, or of outright falsehoods. Because it is immaterial, intelligence cannot wound. But its use has led to the killing or saving of millions.

Because intelligence has been practiced by saints as well as by monsters, by dictatorships as well as by democracies, by primitives, sophisticates, Westerners and non-Westerners, one is tempted not to consider it as a single art.* But closer

*The information-based strategy that Saint Dominic used in his campaign against the Albigensian heresy at Montsegur in Languedoc, southern France, in 1215 is similar to that of

examination shows that it *is* a single art, and that its principles can be abstracted from circumstances.

The best way to begin seeing the "form" of intelligence through its various manifestations is to break it down into its four functional components: collection, counterintelligence, analysis, and covert action. Hence this chapter answers the question "What is intelligence?" in four parts. Starting with a close look at what "collection" is we record historical instances of exceptionally instructive successes and failures at observation, espionage, interception of signals, and so on. Counterintelligence, analysis, and covert action receive the same treatment. We focus on the consequences of doing well the jobs we describe, and of doing them badly. Success and failure in conflict usually are reliable indicators of when a job is done well and when it is not. The rest of the book explains what constitutes doing the job well, what does not, and the connections between particular aspects of the art and success in conflict. This chapter explains what each element of intelligence consists of, and why it is important.

Implicit in our description of the four elements of intelligence is the existence of a fifth: the art of using each only in proper combination with the others, and all in the service of policy. Intelligence, after all, never exists purely for its own sake.

Collection

It is a commonplace to equate being well-informed with "having the facts." Thus, for many, intelligence boils down to getting basic facts about geography, political institutions, armies, or economies, facts about who is doing what at any given time, and technical facts about the features of machines.

Open information about basic features of a foreign country can be more useful than a prized spy's hot "scoop" or precise observations of enemy weapons. Just about any fact can be of great importance, or no importance, depending on the use to which the recipient puts it. What is useless to one customer will be precious to another who has the insight and the will to use it.

Take Hannibal's victory at Cannae (216 B.C.), one of the key battles of the

Gen. Jacques Massu in the Battle of Algiers against the insurgent Algerian National Liberation Front in 1958. See Steven Runciman, *The Medieval Manichee*, pp. 130–147, and Jacques Massu, *La Vraie Bataille d'Alger*. On the other hand, the American CIA and the Soviet KGB have been so radically different in the role they have played in society and in their methods of operations that they are hardly in the same business at all. See Roy Godson, "What Is Intelligence?" in K. G. Robertson, ed., *British and American Approaches to Intelligence?* pp. 2–37.

Second Punic War. Hannibal had led Carthaginian troops through Spain and southern France, and across the Alps, and by a combination of concentrated force and tactical genius was dismantling Rome's empire. Rome's General Fabius had publicly announced his strategy: Shadow the Carthaginian invaders, watch them decrease in strength, watch for opportunities, but do not bring Hannibal to battle. The Senate grew tired of Fabius and replaced him with his chief critic, Varro. Hannibal had followed the debate from afar, much as someone today might follow press reports. The events in the Senate did not convey information about what the new Roman commander would do in any given situation—only that Varro had an incentive to prove that he had been correct in criticizing Fabius. Hannibal provided an opportunity for that state of mind, and Varro fell for it.[1] In hands less skilled than Hannibal's the information might have proven no more useful than climatological tables. For that matter, climatological tables showing that, after October, military operations in Russia require winter clothing, shelter, food, etc. evidently proved quite useless both to Napoleon in 1812 and to Hitler in 1941.

Everything else being equal, facts are useful, and the more the better. But because everything else is seldom equal, facts are mixed blessings. It is possible for a political leader or a military commander to choose the right course of action with little (or in spite of) information. Thus Pericles set Athens' successful strategy for the first half of the Peloponnesian War on the basis of general principles alone. So sure was he of these principles that he exhorted his people not to be distracted by opportunities to depart from them. If the fundamentals are all-important, the flow of facts can only be a bother. Consider also that one and the same Soviet military term encompasses both the concept of air defense and of antimissile defense.[2] Knowledge of this tiny "static" fact is quite enough to allow an analyst to doubt masses of data organized on the assumption that the Soviet air defense network was extraneous to the Soviet antimissile defense program. Nor do masses of facts guarantee good judgments, either about intelligence or about action. This argument is akin to that of the role of material possessions in happiness: A bare minimum is necessary for life. More usually helps, but not necessarily.

Whether a fact turns out to be useful or harmful also depends on timeliness, volume, intelligibility, and inherent relevance. Thus in October 1962, after the first photographs from the U-2 reconnaissance aircraft had confirmed the presence of Soviet ballistic missiles in Cuba, President John F. Kennedy had all the substantive knowledge he would ever have on the Soviet missile presence there. Yet Kennedy delayed the decision to confront the Cuban missile situation until he got close-up photographs. These additional photos cost not only the life of one pilot, but also a week's time. As it turned out, the loss of time was not

5

harmful, because the Soviet missile crews did not rush their work to completion. Had the Soviets readied their missiles to fire, the U.S. might well have found the better pictures a poor substitute for timelier action based on poorer ones.

The volume and format of information can overwhelm its relevance. The National Security Agency (NSA) of the United States intercepts untold thousands of conversations every day in most areas of the world. Especially during crises, U.S. decision-makers are flooded with intercepts, or reports about them. As the U.S. tried to figure out whether or not the Soviets would invade Czechoslovakia in 1968, and later whether Egypt would strike Israel in 1973, these reports quite simply "muddied the water" and "[challenged] the ingenuity of even the most experienced all-source analyst searching for meaning and patterns in a mountain of material."[3] The conversations reported were relevant. There were just too many.

But if the facts are irrelevant, they are a total drag. Every intelligence officer attached to an operational unit (whether military or political) has experienced going through "the traffic" with mounting anger at how very little useful information there is in the mass of paper through which he must wade. This is not an exclusively modern phenomenon. Whenever a government has been willing to pay for information, its spies or listening devices have produced it. But much more than money is required to collect relevant information. Let us see what it takes to collect several kinds of facts, and how important they are.

STATIC FACTS

The geography, climate, demography, culture, political and economic institutions, and biographics (Who's Who) of any given country change so slowly as to be considered static. The Soviet practice of placing false maps of itself in the world's libraries was an exception. All nations have deliberately spread some knowledge about themselves to the world. Pericles once claimed that Athens had no secrets[4] (though it kept foreigners away from its shipyards). How is static information gathered, and how useful is it?

First consider observation. The United States produces precise maps of the earth's magnetic field in the north Polar regions. They are essential to the accuracy of U.S. ballistic missiles. Observation from well-known satellites also allows the U.S. to inventory much of the world's military establishment: ships, guided-missile silos, tanks, airplanes, and physical structures. Even during the most glacial of times, observation of Soviet newspapers and television yielded information about sensitive matters. Indeed, historian Robert Conquest wrote an excellent account of the purges within the Soviet intelligence services of the 1930s—surely as secret a subject as there ever was—strictly from the highly censored Soviet press accounts of who was appointed to which job, when, and of who was tried and convicted of what.[5]

6

Yet the fruits of observation are often spurned. The Stalin regime's advertising of its purges, including newsreels of prosecutor Andrei Vishinsky's cynical behavior, was not enough to convince President Roosevelt's principal adviser, Harry Hopkins, that Stalin was anything but the hope of the world.* By the same token, during the 1970s a dour Shi'ite cleric named Ruhollah Khomeini wrote and broadcast tirades against the Shah of Iran from Paris. These tirades openly promised that should Khomeini come to power in Iran he would institute a regime much like that which he did in fact institute in 1979. Yet this static, open information proved useless not just to the U.S. government, but also to such renowned analysts of Iranian affairs as James Bill.[6] Perhaps the principal reason why these facts were overlooked is that the people who received them were intellectually incapable of understanding the role played by religion, even in a purely instrumental way.[7]

Contrast Rome's Emperor Vespasian in A.D. 70. His spiritual appreciation of Judaism was probably no greater than James Bill's appreciation of Islam. But Vespasian knew enough about Judaism to realize the significance of the Sabbath, and to attack the Jews on that day. In 1968, Ho Chi Minh launched his bloodiest offensive against South Vietnam on the holiest day of the year—Tet, the lunar New Year. Abandoning his ancient faith did not dull Ho's mind to the significance of faith.

Sometimes static facts are so closely protected that they can *only* be collected by espionage. Foremost among them are biographic facts: Who is *really* who in a given regime? This is the case in totalitarian dictatorships and wherever political parties control jobs throughout the bureaucracy, as well as in economic and social institutions. In Mexico and Italy, as well as in Third World and Communist-ruled countries, the answer to the question "Who is he?"† should include the name of the person who put him in his position, the names of those

---

*For example, after the Yalta conference of February 1945, Hopkins wrote: "In our hearts we really believed a new day had dawned, the day we had for so many years longed for and about which we had talked so much. We were all convinced we had won the first great victory for peace, and when I say we, I mean all of us, all civilized mankind. The Russians had proved they could be reasonable and farsighted and neither the President nor any one of us had the slightest doubt that we could live with them and get on peaceably with them far into the future. I must, however, make one reservation—I believe that in our hearts we made the proviso that we couldn't foretell how things would turn out if something happened to Stalin." Sherwood, *Roosevelt and Hopkins*, p. 870. The Soviet government considered Hopkins an agent of influence, albeit unwitting. Christopher Andrew and Oleg Gordievsky, *KGB: The Inside Story*. Note that Hopkins' views of the Soviet Union were quite conventional in the U.S. foreign policy establishment.

†Throughout the book, when I use the words "he" and "him" without reference to specific individuals, they could refer to women as well as men. It is nonsense to ask "who is he or she?" Nor are human beings "it."

he has placed, and the resources he controls by virtue of his unofficial ties. This sort of information can be *inferred* through résumés. But it can only be *discovered* by asking questions discreetly.

The most important of "static" biographics concerns the *forma mentis* of political actors—i.e.: What kind of people are the leaders of country X? What really moves them? What are they capable of doing, and what are they not capable of doing? In 1978 the world's intelligence services expected the Shah of Iran to order his elite guard, the "Immortals," to shoot the mobs that were lapping at his throne. But these services did not know the extent to which Western liberalism had shaped the Shah's mind and sapped his will, because they lacked reports from someone who had overheard the Shah's unguarded conversations *and* who was sensitive enough to understand their implications.* Similarly, in 1989 the world's chanceries gazed at revolutionary happenings in the Soviet bloc and, hampered by a similar lack of basic data about their intellectual and moral structures, asked themselves whether communist rulers would shoot. The closest thing the West had to "inside information" on their thinking, however, was a book written almost a decade earlier by a Soviet émigré.[8]

Intercepted messages are quite useful sources of information about some basics (e.g., the number and location of enemy antiaircraft radars comes from the interception of those radars' signals). But to build a picture of the "statics" of a foreign country through intercepts may be compared to the FBI's attempt in the 1960s to understand the Rev. Martin Luther King's political affiliations by audiotaping his hotel rooms.

Cultural "Statics"

The U.S. government did not lack information on the structure and objectives of the North Vietnamese government. Nor, for that matter in January 1968, did it lack information that North Vietnam had made preparations for a big offensive. But since the U.S. government figured correctly that such an offensive would be militarily disastrous, it mistakenly assumed that it would not be launched. This failure stemmed from the deeper failure to understand a way of living and thinking very different from that of American liberal democrats. This is old news. During the second century B.C., as Rome conquered Greece, the Greeks could not accept the fact that the Romans viewed treaties as akin to marriage, while the Romans quickly developed undue contempt for the Greeks'

---

*There exists an explanation of the Shah's behavior from the standpoint of psychology. Marvin Zonis, *Majestic Failure*. But analysis of someone's mind by someone who does not know him is no substitute for listening to his unguarded thoughts.

habit of shifting alliances. No amount of factual information could bridge the gap in cultural understanding.[9]

DYNAMIC FACTS

Facts on tactical situations speak for themselves more clearly than facts on underlying states of mind or conditions. Nevertheless, they still do not speak univocally.

Consider facts collected by observation. In 1983 as the U.S. Congress was debating aid to the "Contra" forces fighting the communist Nicaraguan government, the debate hinged on Nicaragua's supply of weapons to Salvadorean guerrillas. To prove that Nicaragua was fueling the war in El Salvador, the U.S. Air Force showed a congressional committee infrared night photos of boats leaving a Nicaraguan harbor and landing crates on a Salvadorean beach controlled by Salvadorean guerrillas. One congressman, however, said the photos proved nothing because they did not show the contents of the crates. Another, in reply, asked ironically whether they might be filled with lingerie.

Observation is a faultless source of dynamic facts—but only after they have assumed their full character. Traditionally, the number-one means by which military forces obtain intelligence about the capacity and intention of opposing forces is to engage them. Thus Gen. Douglas MacArthur claimed that his reason for sending thin U.S. armored columns toward Chinese troop concentrations on the Yalu River border in November 1950 was to discover the true intentions of China, and to "spring the trap" if the Chinese had set one.[10] Be that as it may, Chinese troops flooded across the Yalu, and China entered the Korean War. "Reconnaissance-in-force" is applicable to political matters as well. Hence the practice of diplomatic "probes" and "tests": "If they don't balk at this, it must mean they're really interested." Obviously, *fore*knowledge of dynamic facts is preferable. But although observation cannot supply foreknowledge, diplomats and military commanders are constantly on the lookout for facts that indicate what foreign leaders are preparing to do before they have to learn the truth the hard way.

This makes some sense. Just as one may safely deduce that a hunter armed with a rifle rather than a shotgun wants to shoot deer rather than ducks, it is entirely reasonable for any government to take another government's deployment of silo-killing missiles as evidence of that government's intention to open hostilities with a disarming strike. On the other hand, which observed events one takes to be the harbingers of other events that have not yet happened is quite arbitrary. Hence that subdiscipline of collection known as "indications and warning" is fundamentally subjective. That is why so many attacks throughout history have surprised their victims despite abundant information. Thus "confidence-building measures" by which armies exchange "observers" at each others' maneuvers, for example the 1987 U.S.–Soviet Stockholm agreement in the context of the CDE (Conventional Defense Europe) conference, are at least as likely to help the aggressor lull his victim to sleep as they are to warn the victim. Such observers see what is presented to them. What do they notice? There is no certain relationship between their observations and future events.

That is why espionage is so important as a means of collection of dynamic facts. Stalin, according to Alexander Orlov, used to tell his intelligence officers not to bother with observations that required interpretation, but rather to get at the secrets in the enemy's safes.[11] And indeed in the fall of 1941, as Stalin was fighting for the life of his regime, Richard Sorge, a Soviet spy in the German community in Japan, was able to obtain documentary proof of a most important dynamic fact: Instead of joining in the Axis' war against the Soviet Union, Japan was going to expand southward and eastward. Sorge's report allowed Stalin to transfer an army to the crumbling Moscow front, just in time to hold off the Germans until the real reinforcements arrived—the cold months of January and February 1942.* Soviet spies have indeed managed to put themselves where they could warn their masters of impending enemy moves or nonmoves. In the U.S., State Department official Alger Hiss was in a position to provide President Roosevelt's agenda at the Yalta Conference in 1945.

But historically the U.S. has also drawn enormous benefit from spies reporting "dynamic" facts. In December 1777, as George Washington's Continentals began to huddle for the winter at Valley Forge, Pennsylvania, the British forces occupying Philadelphia were planning to finish them off. But one of Washington's spies, an old lady named Lydia Darragh, overheard some British officers talking about their route of march, and told Washington. The ensuing American ambush at Whitemarsh ended the threat to Valley Forge.[12] A few months earlier, in the Hudson Valley, another American spy, working as a tailor in the entourage of British Gen. John Burgoyne, provided American Gen. Horatio Gates with the information that led to the American ambush at Bemis Heights and eventually to General Burgoyne's surrender at Saratoga—the turning point in the Revolutionary War.[13]

Of course spies have sometimes been terrible guides to dynamic events. David Kahn argues that spies usually are unreliable, and cites the fact that "After the Allied D-Day landings on Normandy, the Germans analyzed 173 spy reports on it. They found only 8 percent were right. Of the remainder, 59 percent, or

---

*Sorge had made that point before, but Stalin had not acted. Perhaps Stalin believed Sorge in October because of greater corroboration from signals intelligence. But surely by October 1941 the Wehrmacht's proximity to Moscow was a powerful incentive to believe any information that would justify putting more Soviet bodies between himself and the Germans.

almost three out of five, were wrong, while 14 percent were partly right, 15 percent were not checkable, and 4 percent too general to be of any value."[14] But the reason why espionage was counterproductive in this case is that the spies had been captured and "turned." This is not always so.

Interception of messages had always been an important means of finding out what other people are doing. Thucydides tells of soldiers being stationed on hills to watch for fire signals between widely separated parts of enemy forces. Xenophon tells of the elaborate system of mail-opening on the major roads of the Persian Empire. In our time the size of armies, the wide geographic spread of political relations, and the development of electronic communications have meant that leaders signal and coordinate dynamic events through electronic messages and, hence, that the interception thereof can be the primary means of collection on such events. During World War II, Britain was able to read a high percentage of the messages through which Germany ran its war. It is difficult to overestimate the worth of this. Since World War II the growing advantage of methods of encryption over methods of decryption has gradually shifted the focus of communications intelligence. One focus is toward getting the electronic keys to encryption systems (e.g., the materials that former U.S. Navy CPO John Walker sold to the Soviet Union.) Another is to somehow get the message, before it is encrypted, through any of a variety of approaches including the placing of sensors near the encryption machine. The U.S. did this to the Soviet *Kommandatura* in Vienna soon after World War II, and the Soviets may have done it to the U.S. Embassy in Moscow until the late 1980s.

TECHNICAL FACTS

Technical facts partake of both static and dynamic elements. Knowledge of the performance of equipment and the resistance of defenses is more important in our time, when technical parameters change swiftly, than it was in antiquity, when they changed slowly. Many kinds of military actions make sense only given precise knowledge about the performance of enemy equipment. What route shall airplanes take over enemy territory? If the pilots do not have precise data on the location of enemy radars (their power, resolution, and susceptibility to available electronic countermeasures), they will not know when they might be detected, or when to take evasive action. Such information can be collected through various technical means of direct observation.

Since a nuclear weapon is not a magic wand but possesses a certain yield and accuracy, one must know the hardness of its intended target. Here collection is usually indirect. Photography gives data on the design of silos and shelters. Then replicas are built, and their resistance to overpressure is tested with explosives. This process can give quite good results and makes possible rational targeting.

Allocating ammunition for tanks or antitank weapons without hard facts about

11

the hardness of the target tank is irresponsible. The best collection consists of getting hold of the tank. In World War II the U.S. had to get this kind of data the hard way, by combat contact. By then, however, U.S. mass-production lines were rolling, and so U.S. equipment often remained inferior until the end of the war, at the cost of incalculable casualties. This is why nowadays the U.S. government rejoices when it can test a Soviet tank that the Israelis have captured or bought.[15] Likewise, making torpedos, and drawing up the guidelines for shooting them (i.e., the angles from which it is possible to intercept, say, an enemy submarine) without knowing the maximum speed and acceleration of enemy subs would be irresponsible, because a torpedo must be able to overcome the target's speed. Information about the maximum speed of submarines can be gained by observation, but must be constantly updated.

Espionage is generally a more effective method of obtaining technical data than is observation. The United States' knowledge of the earliest Soviet atomic bombs, gained by analyzing isotope products picked out of the stratosphere following Soviet nuclear tests, provided an order-of-magnitude estimate of the yield, and a guesstimate about how the fissile material was brought to critical mass. By contrast, the Soviet Union's knowledge of the earliest U.S. atomic bombs, gained through spies Klaus Fuchs, Harry Gold, and Julius Rosenberg well *before* the bombs exploded, yielded precise technical data that cut years from the Soviets' development program. During the 1970s and 1980s, while the products of elaborate U.S. observations of Soviet missiles, aircraft, and such were estimates of performance, Soviet intelligence was able to send human beings to purchase the plans, the hardware, and in some cases even the tools, for manufacturing U.S. technical components. Because of human intelligence, Soviet guidance systems run on ball bearings manufactured by U.S. made equipment.[16]

Interception of messages with regard to technical facts is something of a hybrid between observation and espionage. The clearest example of this is the interception of telemetry—the transmission of data on performance from equipment being tested, back to the engineers who are running the tests. But even the most comprehensive telemetry, while it gives many clues to the details of design, cannot be compared to the usefulness of a blueprint. Even if one assumes (as one should not) the capacity to intercept and decode any and all electronic messages, one is still compelled to recognize that complete guides to the construction of technical equipment are not transmitted over the airwaves. There is simply no reason to transmit them, and every reason not to.

THE IMPORTANCE OF COLLECTION

Since success or failure in war and diplomacy depend on how facts are interpreted and used, it is impossible to establish a causal relationship between collection and events. Nevertheless, the correlations are as impressive as they are unsurprising.

The 1775 victory of Massachusetts Minutemen at Lexington and Concord, which encouraged the American colonists to believe that the British Redcoats could be beaten in open combat, would have been inconceivable but for the observers who signaled Paul Revere via a lantern code reminiscent of those of the Peloponnesian War that the British were coming—and by land to boot. General Sam Houston's devastating surprise attack on the superior (but sleeping) forces of General Santa Ana near Texas' San Jacinto Creek was made possible by a host of frontier skills. But among them was surely the Texans' capacity to observe the Mexicans' movements without being observed. On the other hand, failure to keep the enemy under constant observation nearly caused ancient Syracuse to be captured by Athens in the first major battle of the Peloponnesian War's decisive Sicilian campaign. The Athenians' expeditionary force, encamped in the nearby city of Catana, had sent a double agent to inform the Syracusans of a (fictitious) opportunity to catch the Athenians asleep in their camp. In the absence of Syracuse's observation of the Athenian camp, this ploy had the intended effect of drawing the Syracusan army out of the city. The Athenians were able to position themselves along the Syracusans' return route. They won the ensuing battle, and only their irresolution prevented a possibly decisive victory.

In our time, heat-sensing "DSP" satellites 22,300 miles above the earth "stare" at the broad zone of the Soviet Union where ballistic missiles are deployed, ready to register and transmit information concerning the hot exhaust plumes of any and all Soviet missiles launched.* This is more relentless observation than that of the low-orbiting photographic satellites. Within the U.S. government the importance of DSP is unquestioned, and one of the Pentagon's main worries is that those high-flying observers might be blinded. Yet a moment's reflection is enough to conclude that the importance of DSP is directly proportional to the United States' possession of policies and equipment to actually do something useful in case the satellite reports an attack. After all, there is a difference between intelligence and voyeurism.

What difference can a spy in the enemy camp make? How different might the second half of the twentieth century have been if Richard Sorge's espionage had not facilitated Stalin's transfer of troops from Siberia to Moscow? How different might the Soviet Union's behavior have been in the world circa 1949–50 had its

---

*DSP stands for Defense Support Program. The full name is meaningless, and most of the people who work with the satellites would have to think twice if it were used, which it never is. The name is DSP. For further information see *Aviation Week and Space Technology*, 20 February 1989, p. 34; and Angelo Codevilla, *While Others Build*, pp. 103, 153, 172, and 192.

acquisition of the atom bomb been postponed until after Stalin's death? Would there have been a Korean War? Would there have been the suppression of Eastern Europe and the political assault on Western Europe? In another case with far-reaching implications, historians may never know precisely what information Felix Bloch did or did not convey to the Soviet Union in the 1980s. Bloch was in a position to know that the United States' proposal to remove U.S. intermediate-range nuclear forces from Europe had been made because the U.S. was confident that the Soviets would not accept it. Bloch was in a position to know that the U.S. had no plans for actually carrying out such a withdrawal without pulling the rug out from under the conservative European (mainly German) politicians who had sold Europe on the necessity of deploying U.S. missiles on the Continent. Without espionage, the Soviets might well have suspected that U.S. policy was bluff. But only with precise knowledge of what the U.S. was and was not prepared to do could Gorbachev call President Reagan's bluff as confidently as he did at Reykjavik in October 1986.*

Not having a spy in the enemy camp means never knowing for sure—about what is being prepared for the future, but also about the true meaning of what has happened in the past. Not having a spy means relying on observation, with all its invitations to self-deception. The entire history of U.S. intelligence with regard to the Soviet Union, with its decades-long controversies among intelligence analysts over Soviet intentions, illustrates that reading tea leaves is not healthy. But there are many other illustrations just as vivid. In 1939–41, during the 21 months of the Nazi–Soviet pact, Stalin did not have a spy in a position to tell him about Operation BARBAROSSA. To be sure, as June 1941 approached, the evidence of a possible German invasion of the Soviet Union piled high on Stalin's desk. On June 21, 1941, Richard Sorge reported from Tokyo that the attack would come the following day. But evidence planted by Hitler that Germany was only planning an ultimatum to achieve marginal concessions was also piling up. Lacking "ground truth," Stalin put himself in Hitler's shoes and accepted the most rational explanation he could. It almost cost him his life.

Intercepted communications can be even more important than espionage. In our time, a "break" into the codes that protect the communications between the farflung parts of a military and diplomatic establishment is the equivalent not of

*Mikhail Gorbachev proposed removing all intermediate-range and shorter-range nuclear weapons from Europe. When the U.S., embarrassed, went along, Germany's Chancellor, Helmut Kohl, and his Minister of Defense, Manfred Wörner, had to argue against the utility of nuclear weapons. This embarrassing reversal set West Germany on the path to denuclearization and neutralism—until the political roof fell in on Communist Eastern Europe in the autumn of 1989. But at the beginning of 1989 it seemed that Gorbachev had achieved a master-stroke at Reykjavik. See Angelo M. Codevilla, *The Cure That May Kill: Unintended Consequences of the INF Treaty.*

one but of a thousand spies, all ideally placed, all secure, and all reporting instantaneously. During World War II, spies could not possibly have told Britain about the time and place of virtually all German military operations, the daily location of U-boats, and German reactions to British deception efforts. Yet these were the daily fruits of Ultra, the program that in effect duplicated at Bletchley Park the Germans' army, navy, air force, and foreign-office cipher machines. Sometimes British commanders saw their German opponents' orders before the Germans themselves did.[17] Ultra was possible only under the technical conditions of the 1930s and 1940s. No breakthrough is likely to ever be so total again. Nevertheless, regardless of the means employed, or of the extent of the break, to read an opponent's messages is to read his mind.

Analysis and Production

Once in a while a fact—a picture, a message, an event—is so clear in its import that an intelligence service transmits it to policy-makers without analysis, and the policy-makers find its meaning self-evident.* But even in such cases the key is knowing the difference between facts that can be treated that way, and facts that cannot. That screening itself is analysis. And, of course, the policymaker who receives the fact must fit it into his image of the world. This too is analysis. Usually, however, analysis is more than that. Intelligence produces masses of data, the import of which is clear only to people educated to understand it. The whole point of an analytical establishment is to make sure that certain kinds of data get into the hands of those to whom it will mean the most.

Suppose, for example, that during the same year (1) an obscure Soviet scientific publication mentioned that an efficient technique had been found to strip protons and electrons from streams of accelerated subatomic particles, (2) that a European physicist returning from an international conference told his intelligence service that several Soviet specialists in subatomic particle accelerators scheduled to come to the conference were too busy to do so, and (3) that U.S. satellites had photographed construction of large vacuum chambers at a Soviet site where subatomic particle accelerators had been known to exist. Any analyst worthy of being assigned to cover directed-energy weapons should have written for his superiors an item headlined "Soviets May be Preparing Neutral

---

*The category of "self-evident truths" is elastic. First note that any proposition is meaningful only to those who understand its terms. The truths of mathematics are self-evident only to mathematicians. Second, the meaning of most human events depends largely on what people subsequently make of them. The death of a tyrant may bring the end of his regime, or it may not. Third, although one need not go as far in skepticism as did Talleyrand upon hearing of the death of the Russian ambassador ("I wonder what his intention was"), one must bear in mind the ubiquity of deception in human affairs.

Particle Beam Weapon for Use in Space." The item should have explained what is self-evident to the analyst: Stripping charged particles from beams produces neutral ones, which are useful in space because they cannot be bent by the earth's magnetic field. To associate vacuum chambers with particle accelerators may be for the purpose of testing beams in a simulated space environment.

How do disparate facts become focused conclusions? What are the consequences of good and of bad analysis? Regardless of whether the job is done by professional intelligence analysts in some ministry, by a military commander under fire, or by a high government official, governments must somehow deal with a flood of reports that do not speak for themselves. The task has not changed across the centuries, nor does it vary across continents and cultures: Sort the important facts from the trivial; clarify murky reports and fit them into a meaningful picture, making sure that they get into the right hands; and try to answer the new questions that these raise. The task is essentially the same regardless of whether the subject is static (the capacity of a foreign economy or military establishment, or the health of a foreign regime) or dynamic (figuring out what a regime or an army is doing and preparing to do), or even technical (determining the capacity of foreign equipment).

Hovering over every part of the analytical process are two nemeses. First, there is not likely to be enough data to draw an unchallengeable conclusion. After all, analysis is what you do when you don't know for sure. Second, since the data concern human struggles, it is likely to have been biased precisely in order to deceive the analyst. In addition the analyst, being human, comes fully equipped with bias, misplaced interest, and preference for pleasing over truth-telling. In addition, he is probably not as expert in the field as he should be. History is full of instances in which analysts nevertheless cut through fog, picked nuggets out of slag heaps, and essentially turned on the lights. It is also full of analysts who could not (or would not) see opportunities or disasters under their very noses—in short, who turned dim light into darkness.

SELECTION: WHO IS INTERESTED?

On any given morning, thousands of officers and officials of every nation around the world fulfill a ritual as ancient as government itself: They read, or listen to, reports from various intelligence sources. These senior soldiers or bureaucrats are (or fancy themselves) busy, and generally jealous of their prerogatives. So most of them refuse to be burdened by the opinions of their underlings. They want to see "all" the reports that have come in, and they want them "in their original form." But no human being, Nebuchadnezzar the Babylonian no more than a president of the United States, can absorb all the information flowing into the nerve center of a vast country. The trick is to select only topics that one knows or is seriously studying. Expertise is the great divide.

Consider first what it takes to understand basic facts about foreign countries. Julius Caesar, like most generals of his day, was his own intelligence analyst, and received agent reports directly. Caesar was a good analyst: His books on Gaul, Germany, and Britain are conclusive proof that he understood the reports well enough to put together portraits of the lands and peoples against which he operated that were both accurate and useful guides to military operations. At the opposite extreme was President Jimmy Carter, who in 1979 declared that the Soviet Union's invasion of Afghanistan had taught him more about the Soviet Union than he had learned during his entire life prior to that event. One may wonder how Carter, despite his passion for facts, profited from them. His successor, Ronald Reagan, was no more Caesar-like as an analyst. Reagan liked intelligence briefings in video format in which predigested facts were arranged like decorations on a cake.

Serious interest and serious mind are the real prerequisites for being able to make sense of raw data. Acquaintance with a subject over time sometimes diminishes ignorance, and may sometimes even substitute for an able mind. That is why the odds against Caesar-like analysis are high in the case of the average U.S. subcabinet officer who flips through his daily three-inch stack of "raw" reports in some 20 minutes (and spends only 18 months in his job).

The most obvious disadvantage of ignorance is that one simply misses the importance of data. Thus in 1979, as the Sandinista rebels entered Nicaragua's capital in triumph, one of their first acts was to close down *El Pueblo*, the publication of the Maoist Frente Obrero, as well as the mimeographs of the *Revolutionary Marxist League*, the local Trotskyite affiliate. This widely reported fact was meaningful only to the few who knew that such people are threatening to no one in the world except orthodox Stalinist communists.[18] By taking such an interest in little Trotskyite and Maoist rags, the Sandinistas had made their Stalinism self-evident—but only to those who understood the culture of Marxism–Leninism. Ignorance also makes it easier to force one's own assumptions onto the data. Hence, as Sandinistas marched into Managua, U.S. intelligence analysts (seasoned "area experts" no less than writers for *The New York Times'* editorial page) saw them through the optic of American Liberal culture as pluralistic democratic reformers.

Perhaps the sturdiest kind of ignorance stems from disinterest. The most outstanding contemporary example is the contemporary Western elites' lack of interest in religion. This results in an educated incapacity to take seriously reports dealing with religion from the Middle East, the former Soviet empire, or indeed anywhere. Failure to take the professed faith of Arab Muslims as a door through which one can enter their minds has led to superficial stereotypes. For lack of better understanding, those who write for the Pentagon, the State Department, or the CIA, just like those who write for the newspapers, describe Shi'ite

Muslims either as madmen for whom life means nothing, or as people who use a peculiar language to cloak nationalism or greed. In either case, one need not bother trying to understand "them" on their own terms. If one disregards creeds, one will find it easier to interpret the struggles between Ukrainian Uniate Catholics, Russian Orthodox Christians, and Soviet communists. But one will misunderstand those struggles.

Far from being an American disease, educated incapacity also afflicted the Spartans in the Peloponnesian War. For two decades Spartan troops had been raiding Athenian territory and Athenian allies and then, in true Spartan fashion, returning home to plant the next year's crops. Sparta always had the option to cut off Athens' access to the mainland, but never realized the importance of doing so because the Spartans lived by the stereotype of Athenians as men of the sea for whom unfettered access to the mainland meant nothing. It took the Athenian defector Alcibiades to make the Spartans see how important that access was to Athens. In our own time Hitler was so blinded by his racial theories that he saw America as containing only 60 million people racially fit for war.[19] It cost him his life.

In technical matters, acquaintance and analytical competence are more likely to go together. Consider Leonid Brezhnev's capacity to understand facts about ballistic missiles. Stalin named the young Brezhnev to oversee the program for developing long-range ballistic missiles. Brezhnev also was Khrushchev's choice as chief political commissar for the new strategic rocket forces, established in 1958. In short, Brezhnev spent some 30 years in the missile community. He spoke its language. He was briefed on virtually all Soviet and American successes and failures. He heard more than a generation's debates about how to build and how to use missiles. He saw people in the business "pull fast ones" on each other, and perhaps pulled a few himself. If he had not been running the Soviet Union, he might not have been a bad choice for chief analyst of ballistic missile intelligence. By contrast consider not former movie star Ronald Reagan, but his Secretaries of Defense Caspar Weinberger and Frank Carlucci, who scarcely had the occasion to *see* a ballistic missile before taking office. How could they be expected to make sense of reports on Soviet missile tests? Someone else would have to do that, and these high officials would fulfill their responsibility by choosing the people to whose advice they would listen.

With regard to dynamic facts, however, it is more difficult to pass the buck. Prior to World War II the British government, not illogically, funneled all available facts about Hitler's Luftwaffe to the Royal Air Force, and heeded its opinion on the subject. But according to the official history of British intelligence in World War II, the RAF not only grossly overestimated the number of German aircraft, especially bombers. It also totally misjudged the function of the Luftwaffe.[20] The RAF thoroughly believed that modern air forces must consist primarily of heavy bombers designed to inflict a knockout blow on the enemy's capital.* This was the RAF's own "air power" doctrine, even though the RAF never acquired the requisite planes to carry it out. Prior to the outbreak of war these analytical shortcomings may have been explained by German deception, such as the practice of concentrating all available bombers at airfields that hosted foreign visitors. Yet the misestimates continued well into the war, despite the Germans' demonstration that they would use the Luftwaffe to clear the way for normal military operations. The RAF simply interpreted every German raid, including one on the far northeast coast of England, as a preparation for the knockout blow on London. In this case Britain missed a vital sign that Germany was weakening the RAF's capacity to resist an invasion of Norway.[21]

By the same token, on May 6, 1940, on the eve of the German offensive that shattered the Western front, Britain simply disregarded a reconnaissance photo of the Germany–Luxembourg border showing concentrations of armor on the edges of the Ardennes forest, and a report on the next day that 400 tanks were in the area. It was British War Office policy that forests were not good tank country. The generals were the experts. But their expertise was such as to prevent them from realizing what would have been self-evident to the uninitiated.

The foregoing is not an argument against expertise. On the contrary, it suggests that the expertise must be specific to the subject at hand. Plato argues that only an expert thief can understand thievery.† But of course the trick lies in precisely matching the analyst to the task.

MAKING SENSE OF THE DATA

Compiling estimates on the strength of armies, productivity of economies, and the like is more complex than adding numbers. Among the grossest examples of static analysis was Nazi Germany's estimate of the United States' capacity for producing war material. In 1939–41 the Germans quite simply noticed that the United States' Gross National Product was about $100 billion, the military budget was less than 2 percent of that, American recruits were training with wooden rifles, and conscription was just barely acceptable to a Congress absorbed with a decade-long Depression. How could such a nation possibly play a major role in Europe, especially since it would likely be fighting for its Pacific

---

*The RAF's (and later the U.S. Air Force's) belief that air power is decisive is supposed to rest on the theoretical ground laid out by Italy's Gen. Giulio Douhet in his 1921 book Il Dominio dell'Aria. But two facts argue against this. First, Douhet's book is based on his experience in the Libyan campaign of 1912, and concludes that air power is decisive in the desert—not universally. Second, according to Lidell-Hart, though many RAF officers had heard of Douhet, virtually none had read him.
† Knowledge of perverse practices, argues Plato, is necessary but not sufficient to understand perversion. The perspective of virtue is essential. Republic, Book III, 409.

territories against Japan? No wonder that on December 11, 1941 Hitler gratuitously declared war on the United States. The Germans' "bean-counting," however, neglected all the moral factors that, by 1943, had *doubled* America's GNP and raised the military's share to about 50 percent. By contrast, on the night that disarmed, depressed, disunited America entered World War II, Winston Churchill was convinced that the world's mightiest economic power had decisively stepped out onto the scene. Charles de Gaulle went even further, telling his associates that the essential issue—who would win the war—had just been settled. Churchill and de Gaulle did not have figures different from those the German analysts had. Hitler misunderstood the moral character of Americans. They got it right. The lesson here, as in the failure of static economic analyses everywhere, is that in human affairs even static facts must be analyzed with an eye to underlying dynamics.

Bean-counting itself, however, is not as straightforward a proposition as might appear. One must first define the beans—that is, ask "What will I accept and what will I not accept as belonging to the category of the thing I am counting?" Then one must estimate the relationship between the beans seen and those not seen. If one fails in either of these preliminary steps, the raw numbers may well prove worse than useless. Thus when the generals of Thucydides' time received information that they faced a given number of enemy troops, they always asked how many were full citizens of the main enemy city. And how many were from the city on whose territory the battle was to be fought. These two categories could be expected to fight much harder than either mercenaries or the contingents from faraway cities. Modern military analysts also know that not all ground force divisions or aircraft or ships are created equal. So they use a variety of devices to give their numbers some usefulness. Alas, some of these—e.g., the British term "front-line aircraft" applied to the Luftwaffe in the 1930's—were themselves the source of obfuscation. As we will see later, so have been the host of terms that in our time have arisen out of the arms-control process.

The relationship between the seen and the unseen necessarily is the stuff of conjecture. As long-time military analyst Amrom Katz has written, "We have never found anything that the Soviets have successfully hidden." His point applies not just to concealment but also to the inherent difficulty of, in effect, making an inventory of vast continents with regard to things that are not always readily apparent or whose characteristics are ambiguous.[22] Take chemical weapons. Given that the principal difference between a chemical weapons factory and a pharmaceutical factory lies in the content of vats at any given time, an analyst's count of a country's chemical warfare potential amounts to both more *and* less than simple addition. Even massive amounts of data do not radically alleviate this difficulty. After World War I the Allied powers had the fullest access to Germany's military-related industry. Yet complete information did not prevent them from drawing the wrong conclusions about German rearmament until it was too late.[23]

The problem of extrapolation is even more acute in political analysis. Perhaps the quintessential problem of politics ("Who speaks for whom?") is many times harder to handle when it concerns clandestine or semiclandestine movements. In the Soviet Union of the early 1990s, where dozens of movements with the most varied inclinations struggled half-publicly, half-clandestinely, where the Communist Party went from ruling absolutely from above to exercising influence under various guises, analysts who tried to build a political roadmap of the country had to work with reports that were by nature not just fragmentary but even anecdotal. In such situations the light—or the darkness—must come from within the analyst.

The problem of clarification of data arises more specifically with regard to technical matters. Often given as little as a photograph and a couple of observations of performance, the analyst must compile a report on a weapon, describing its threat specifically enough to help one's military to do something about it. Ideally, the military intelligence analyst would have the actual foreign weapon in his hands, and, having tested it to his heart's content, he could fruitfully search the files for indications of how the enemy might use it. The armed forces themselves would provide the final analysis by using the weapon in simulated combat. Failing that, and given enough data, the analyst might work with weapons technicians to build a replica of the weapon, which could then be tested. With less data the analyst can infer some characteristics from others— e.g., a submarine hull built of titanium rather than steel might reasonably be expected to produce a 50 percent improvement in the ship's operating depth, while a report that the instrumentation on a test of a missile guidance system has improved in accuracy reasonably leads to the conclusion that the accuracy of the guidance system itself may have increased by the same proportion. By the same token, naval analysts use long experimental experience in the design of ships' hulls to gauge a foreign ship's maximum speed and sea-keeping capacity from photographs of the hull.

Of course, as the quantity and specificity of the data in the analysts' hands decreases, and given the constant demand for specific answers to technical intelligence questions, there is a sharp increase in the room the analyst has to insert his own assumptions, and in the incentive for him to do just that. Regardless of what he has to work with, however, the analyst produces a report which policymakers and military men often read as if it came directly from the enemy's safes.

The need to shed light on data is most urgent with regard to dynamic events. But here the analyst is at his greatest disadvantage: The data is sketchiest, the opportunities for deception and self-deception are greatest, and the time is shortest. Sometimes this quicksand comes well-disguised as solid ground. As Persia's King Xerxes was conquering Greece during the fifth century B.C. he overwhelmed the city of Athens. Its people fled to ships and took refuge on outlying islands. The Athenian fleet was outnumbered by over two to one. Xerxes received accurate information that it was concentrated near the island of Salamis and that the Athenian commander, Themistocles, would give battle there to protect the refugees. What else was there to know before rushing in to destroy it, thus removing the last barrier to ruling Greece? Had Xerxes analyzed the situation further, he might have noticed that the waters dividing Salamis from the mainland were too narrow for him to bring his superiority to bear, and asked whether perhaps Themistocles had a plan in that regard. But Xerxes, looking only at the hard facts before him, lost the battle, the war, and nearly his life.

In a similar vein, even after the Shah of Iran left his country in January 1979, intelligence analysts throughout the world had one very solid reason for doubting that the regime would suffer a total reversal. There could be no doubt about the absolute loyalty to the regime of the Shah's own guard, the "Immortals," nor about their eagerness to kill its opponents, and their invincibility should they set about doing it. But as it turned out, a fact less well known, and of far less obvious significance, intervened. Lt. Gen. Robert Hauser, the U.S. government's emissary to the senior Iranian generals, convinced them to order the Immortals to stand down. At Hauser's suggestion, the generals negotiated with the Revolutionary Mullahs for a place in the "moderate" government that the U.S. was sure Khomeini would establish. The result: Most of the generals were killed.[24] Some of the luckier ones wound up driving cabs in Washington, DC. It is easy to sympathize with the analysts who did not know of General Hauser's mission. But even if they *had* known, how (especially in such a crisis) could they have taken into account the possibility that the Iranian generals would set aside their normal prudence and figuratively put their heads into nooses?

It is also difficult to blame the German analysts who, in 1944, were fooled into accepting the existence of the fictitious First U.S. Army Group (FUSAG) in southeastern England, supposedly poised for the invasion of Calais. The Germans had substantial, multisource evidence for their conclusion, including reconnaissance photos of (fake) tanks, and lots of intercepts about landing craft being sent eastward, not to mention agent reports. Had the German analysts had time, the fraudulence of many of the facts might have become apparent. For example, had a German photoreconnaissance plane overflown the area of the fake Army Group after a windstorm, it might have brought back pictures of ruined papier-mâché armaments. Something like that happened in the 1970s: A U.S. satellite which had been counting submarines under construction at Soviet shipyards passed over after a windstorm and found what had been counted as a submarine to be bent in the middle. The analyst realized that it was a sub-shaped balloon, and christened it "rubber ducky."[25] The difference between good and bad analysis here was that time gave the weather and photo reconnaissance the chance to combine.

On what, then, can the analyst rely when time is short and facts are ambiguous? He can rely on his knowledge of the character of the people he is observing. This is not to say (as some do) that the analyst can safely assume that the patterns he has observed will continue.[26] Rather, the analyst who understands his subject can interpret the latest events as evidence either that established patterns will be followed or that they will be broken.

Machiavelli tells the story[27] of Pope Julius II, who boldly captured the tyrant of Perugia, Giovanpagolo Baglioni, in 1506 simply by making a show of force with his army, and then walking unarmed into Baglioni's well-armed fortress. The pattern of Baglioni's behavior hardly suggested that he would respect spiritual authority. After all, Baglioni kept his own sister as a mistress, and had killed his own relatives. But Julius knew the difference between cheap depravity and the grand kind, and judged that Baglioni did not have it in him to do something as momentous as killing a pope.

Delivering the Product

Intelligence has done all it can when it delivers the best possible report that the facts allow to the right person at the right time. An enduring myth in America is that in 1941 enough fragments of information were floating around the U.S. government to indicate that Japan would strike Pearl Harbor on December 7, but that the alarm was not given because there did not exist a mechanism for bringing these fragments together into a form that would compel an "Aha!" Hence the creation of the CIA. But in fact, though integration of information is always a Good Thing and might well have helped in December 1941, the historic record shows that on December 6 and 7 there was enough univocal information in one place for the correct judgment to be made in time, and that the effective cause of the surprise was quite strictly the failure to *deliver* that information to someone who would act on it.

A single item of information told the entire tale. On December 6 the Navy intercepted, deciphered, and translated 13 parts of a 14-part cable from Tokyo to the Japanese Embassy in Washington, DC, replying negatively to the United States' conditions for improving U.S.–Japan relations. At 5 A.M. (Washington, DC time) on December 7 the final section was deciphered. It instructed the Japanese Ambassador to break off negotiations. Then came a separate message instructing the ambassador to deliver the message to the U.S. Secretary of State at 1 P.M. Washington time—7 A.M. in Hawaii—and to destroy the Embassy's code books and cipher machines.

To the analysts this looked like the war would start at 7 A.M. Hawaii time and they acted accordingly. By about 8 A.M. (2 A.M. Hawaii time) they began rushing the intercept to every top decision-maker they could. They reached the Chief of Naval Operations, Adm. Harold Stark, in midmorning, and by about 10:30 A.M. the Secretaries of State, of War, and of the Navy were deliberating on the message. Nobody called Hawaii. Army Chief of Staff Gen. George Marshall was harder to get hold of, took his time getting to the office, and read from the top to the bottom line. Then, at 11 A.M., with less than three hours to go before the bombs fell, *he* sent his warning to Hawaii—by routine teletype. The messenger at the Hawaiian end routinely put the envelope in a mailbox. It was delivered to Gen. Walter Short at 2:40 P.M., Hawaii time, as 3,000 Americans lay dead and the pride of the U.S. Pacific Fleet rested on Pearl Harbor's bottom.

This was failure—but not a failure of intelligence. The collectors instantly analyzed, and even managed to deliver. But the high officials who received the product did not order action. They did not even pass the buck fast enough so that the commander in physical danger could decide for himself whether or not to act.[28] Once again intelligence and military commanders bore the blame for the shortcomings of policy-makers.

The elaborate arrangements within the world's intelligence systems (in the U.S. very elaborate indeed) for delivering briefings, producing various kinds of intelligence studies, warnings, reports, and so on are intended to prevent the sort of thing that occurred at Pearl Harbor. The essence of all those arrangements is the concept that someone who occupies a given position is to receive all of the information available, from throughout the intelligence system, that may be relevant to that position. Theoretically, that concept is unexceptionable. In concrete circumstances, however, two factors intervene. First, the providers of intelligence—the spymasters, the interceptors and decoders of signals, the photointerpreters—are jealous of their sources and methods. Also, each of these providers does not want the worth of his product second-guessed, and does want the honor and the power of presenting important facts to top policy-makers. The offices where "all-source" information is supposed to be analyzed become little more than dumping grounds for second-rate information while the "hot stuff" gets passed to the top through special channels. The most outstanding example of this practice was Nazi Germany, of which David Kahn says: "Each unit refined its information, passing it either through special evaluating agencies, as with the military, or through the general bureaucracy, as with the Foreign Office. Then the jealous ministries, the arrogant Party officials, the proud warlords of the high commands all scrambled to bring their tidbits to the Führer."[29] The line of argument employed in such end-runs everywhere is: "Never mind this or that all-source assessment. Here is the real scoop that no one knows about but we."

Second, the various *users* of intelligence—the armed services and the diplomatic corps—all realize that the power to state officially what foreign conditions are like is at the same time the power to determine military budgets and foreign policy. That is another reason why navies claim peculiar right to be the final judges on naval matters, diplomats on diplomatic matters, and so on. The first and second kinds of jealousies, perhaps combined with the prejudice for or against certain policies on the part of those in charge of routing intelligence information, can make nonsense of the most rational delivery system.

ANALYSIS AND FUTURE INTELLIGENCE

Anyone who tries to answer questions on the basis of fragmentary information naturally notices that the information often raises more questions than it answers. The analyst's first recourse is to the files, but these seldom suffice. Effective intelligence services, therefore, rely substantially on analysts to specify which facts are needed, and to give the collectors hints on where and how to look. Thus the Soviet Union's acquisition of Western technology was steered by thousands of analysts who figured out what would be most useful to fill the holes left by previous acquisitions, and scoured Western trade publications for signs of precisely whom to contact, and where.

It is routine for analysts everywhere to "go back" to the collectors for more facts. Indeed their doing so is the beginning and end of what intelligence schools call the "intelligence cycle." One important difference among intelligence systems, however, lies in how far out of their way collectors are willing to go to get the additional facts. This author has heard CIA officers utter a complaint that must be commonplace among the world's intelligence collectors: "We've gone back to our sources and pressed them [on this or that] but they just don't know. We can't squeeze blood from stones." The complaint is usually justified as far as it goes. But it avoids the main issue: If *these* sources can't get the facts we need, why not develop entirely new ones? Developing new kinds of sources, however, is surely the hardest of all jobs in collection. On the other hand, what is the point of collecting facts other than the ones the analysts really need? Nevertheless, unless the analyst is the head of his country's government, or is very well connected with him, he will not be able to command the collectors. At most times and in most places the collectors' intellectual and bureaucratic flexibility is low. So they will develop new sources and methods only when forced to.

Counterintelligence

Definition

While any intelligence service collects and analyzes facts, while it tries to meddle in other governments' internal affairs, those other governments' intelligence services are trying to steal *its* secrets and meddle in *its* affairs, as well as to penetrate *its* operations and skew *its* analyses. So, unless an intelligence service is able to counter these hostile efforts, its government can have little confidence in the service's information and judgments. At worst the government will have few secrets, and its intelligence service can become the tool of foreign powers that are more adept at counterintelligence. Hence, while intelligence services must busy themselves with a host of things, a part of them must be constantly devoted to collecting and analyzing facts about other intelligence services—in short, to doing counterintelligence. But this also involves *doing* things to foul them up, such as planting false agents among them, feeding them false or disruptive information, arresting their agents, and so on. Counterintelligence, then, not only looks and thinks, but also acts, both because it must protect the services' own observations and thoughts, and because its actions may be valuable in and of themselves.

Counterintelligence often is confused with security—that is, merely with protecting secrets and protecting against subversion. Yet whereas the objective of security is to cut and prevent all contacts between hostiles and those who are to be protected the objective of CI is to engage hostile intelligence, control what it knows, and if possible control also what it does. In principle, neither security people nor CI people deny the validity of the others' approach, but CI people think of security as flatfooted cops, and the latter think of the former as game-playing spooks.

It is easy to confuse CI with a host of other intelligence activities—collection, analysis, covert action—because good CI does everything that a full-fledged intelligence service does, and takes a hand in everything the rest of the service does. Adequate attention to hostile intelligence services is a prerequisite for making one's own collection, analysis, and covert-influence activities succeed. In all that it does, CI is engaged in a contest with its opposite numbers: Will it be the manipulator or the manipulated? In all that it does, CI must play both defense and offense. Defense means guarding the integrity of one's own operations. Offense, while employing a variety of means, has one culminating purpose: deception. Successful CI can be a significant strategic asset.

MANIPULATORS AND MANIPULATED

Anytime two manipulators work against one another, the question must be asked: Who is exploiting whom? Whenever one "runs" a foreign agent, especially if he is an intelligence officer, one must ask for whom he is really working. If the agent volunteered or defected, one must ask doubly hard. We have already mentioned that most German agents in Britain during World War II were sending home only the reports that the British Double Cross committee wanted sent. These agents had been well-trained. They were loyal to Germany. But they had been caught and given the choice of dying or cooperating.

26

Similarly, Leopold Trepper, the famous "conductor" of the "Red Orchestra" of Soviet spies in German-occupied Europe, was a devoted communist. Nevertheless, when the Gestapo arrested him in Paris in 1942 he did not hesitate to offer his professional services to his captors—until he escaped in 1943. During his captivity he acted as a double agent (working for Germany while pretending to work for the Soviet Union), but might well have been a *triple* agent, perhaps transmitting his messages with some code indicating to the Soviets that he was under German control. An agent is valuable because he tells you the truth about the enemy. A double agent is doubly valuable because he tells you about the enemy while letting you lie to the enemy. A triple agent is trebly valuable because in addition to the services of a double, he is the channel through which the enemy tells you lies that you already know to be lies, and which therefore disclose his deepest intentions. Those who understand that the answer to the question "To whom does this source belong?" should always be open will prosper. Those who do not, get into trouble.

Fear of being manipulated, however, can be paralyzing. Thus, Christopher Andrew reports that in 1983 Michael Bettaney, an employee of Britain's counterintelligence agency, MI-5, stuffed an envelope into the mailbox of Arkady Guk, the KGB's chief-of-station (called by the Soviets "rezident") in London, containing information and an offer to spy.[30] Guk thought this offer too good to be true, and passed it up. Meanwhile, Guk's deputy, Oleg Gordievsky, who *was* a British spy, informed MI-5, and Bettaney was arrested. Because of excessive skepticism the Soviet Union lost a chance to recruit its first spy inside MI-5 in a generation. In 1968, however, the KGB resident in Washington accepted a similar offer, and reaped John Walker, the most important spy of the age. By contrast, in 1918 insufficient attention to the possibility of being manipulated lost British intelligence whatever chance it might have had of overthrowing the fledgling Bolshevik regime. British diplomat Robert Bruce Lockhart conspired with a variety of anti-Bolshevik elements who were so thoroughly penetrated by Lenin's Cheka that by far the most fearsome elements of their conspiracy, subversion of the Red army, were part of the Cheka's stage management to draw Lockhart in. The point here is that normal prudence, rather than axiomatic acceptance or rejection, is the soundest approach to the constant contest of CI.

Information gathered or transmitted through technical means is also subject to manipulation from all sides. In both World War I and World War II the Germans suffered greatly because they assumed that their techniques for enciphering made their communications secure. In 1917, Germany continued to send diplomatic messages through overseas cable networks that passed through London, including Foreign Minister Zimmerman's telegram to Mexico

City proposing a German–Mexican alliance against the U.S.[31] But the British Navy's codebreaking agency, known as Room 40, had already solved the German code. Britain used the Zimmerman telegram to ignite the American people's always-smoldering anxiety about extrahemispheric powers interfering in Mexico, and to help draw the U.S. into the war. In World War II, Germany had put its faith not so much in its codes as in the complex machines—Enigma and Geheimschreiber—that periodically fed new sets of variables into complex arrangements. But once the British got the machine, they were able to reconstruct each new set of variables and read the messages. Because German intelligence did not give sufficient credit to British CI, German arms suffered countless losses. Had the Germans been so humble as to concede the possibility that their mail was being read, they could have sent deceptive messages. The manipulation might have been mutual rather than one-sided.

Manipulation is the operational essence of covert activities. But if the manipulators want to make sure that they themselves are not being manipulated, they had better check independently on what their partners are doing, and why. In 1920–22, when British and French intelligence began to cooperate with the self-described agents of a vast anticommunist conspiracy within the Soviet Union, the former naturally feared that the KGB* might be trying to dupe them, just as it had done in 1918 in Moscow. So they paid close attention to the judgment of impeccably anticommunist Russian émigrés, and to the corroborating evidence that the agents brought with them, including newspapers smuggled out of Russia that were full of reports of the conspiracy's activities. Alas, the newspapers were fake and the émigrés deluded. But because British and French intelligence had no agents *independent* of those involved in the operation, checking on those who were, they delivered millions of gold coins, as well as lives, into the KGB's control. Because the KGB won this counterintelligence battle, the outcome of the entire operation was a foregone conclusion.

DEFENSE AND OFFENSE

Counterintelligence has two "ultimate weapons": an agent near the top of the hostile service's CI, and the capacity to read the other side's message traffic. These weapons promise in full measure what lesser penetrations yield only in

---

*The term KGB (Committee for State Security) denotes herein the organization instituted at Lenin's orders on 20 December 1917 with the acronym VChK and called the Cheka. It underwent eight changes in name (GPU, OGPU, MGB, et al.) while exercising essentially the same functions before adopting in 1954 the name it bears today. From the beginning, "Chekists"—as they have never ceased to call themselves—have received their pay on the twentieth of the month.

part—knowledge of what the other side knows. Such knowledge serves purposes both offensive and defensive. It helps to know which agents or operations the enemy is running against one's self, as well as to secure the success of agents or operations that one is running against the enemy. Counterintelligence always plays both offense and defense simultaneously. Moreover, whether any item of knowledge, any penetration, is useful for either offense or defense, or becomes an asset for a hostile service, depends entirely on whether "they" know that "we" know. One of the standard jokes about intelligence goes: "They know. It's all right—we know they know. No, they know we know they know. It's all right—we know they know we know they know"—and so on, *ad infinitum*. But in real life such chains are finite, and the most useful kind of knowledge about the enemy is knowledge of which the enemy is not aware.

Defensive CI at the very least means watching those whom the enemy is likely to recruit, either by surveillance or by recruiting agents among them, so that if some enemy does try to recruit them one will be able to identify him and neutralize him. Dictators routinely have their CI services watch all those who are close to them, listen in on their conversations, recruit agents among them, and let everyone know that this is going on. Thus they hope to preclude plots against themselves. The knowledge generated by this sort of CI is a valuable tool for controlling the dictator's inner circle. Those who do this well get to die in bed, like Joseph Stalin. Nicolae Ceauçescu similarly infiltrated his inner circle and his army. But he died before a firing squad, apparently because a superior network within his army, one apparently loyal to the Soviet Union, decided to take advantage of the revolutionary mood in Eastern Europe in December 1989 to sweep away Ceauçescu's entire security apparatus by *force majeure*. The total collapse of the East German state in November and December 1989, despite a CI service that had forced perhaps one-twentieth of the adult population to become informants, shows even more clearly that information can only help to *aim* the government's guns and intrigue. When the government loses the will to shoot, or the enemy overwhelms intrigue, the world's best CI is no shield at all. The collapse of the Soviet security establishment's *coup de régime* in August 1991 occurred apparently because the KGB's Alpha force, the very people whom the regime had counted on to kill its enemies, refused orders to storm the Russian Parliament. If the guardians of the CI service refuse to perform guard duty, what good are the service's other products?

Even nondictatorial systems use defensive CI to run tests to find out how penetrable their security is, and even the most liberal societies have placed informants in groups thought to have relationships with enemy powers. No one suggests that when cases of espionage arise there should not be investigations of what the enemy has learned, how the information loss occurred, and how further loss might be prevented. But this amounts to closing the barn door after the horses are out. In 1944, Nazi Germany did not help itself greatly when it executed Adm. Wilhelm Canaris, the head of its foreign intelligence agency, the Abwehr, who had been passing information to the British through most of the war; nor did Britain help itself significantly by assessing the wreckage of its intelligence service after Soviet spy Kim Philby capped his meteoric rise through its ranks by retiring in Moscow. The point here is that purely defensive CI, like purely defensive strategy in any field, is no way to play the game.

Offensive CI means somehow getting inside the hostile service. The easiest (but shallowest) penetrations are dangles. One intelligence service places someone in whom it has confidence where he will appear to be an attractive recruit for the hostile service. If the hostiles "bite" they will take into their outermost circle someone whose eyes and ears belong to other masters. Once he is accepted, the dangle will be able to report to his service at least which questions the hostiles have asked him. If all goes well, the hostiles may use the dangle in other operations, or involve him in discussions. Of course the dangle can pass misleading information to the hostiles. Offensive CI also means "turning" enemy agents, as the British "turned" the German agents. Physical coercion is the standard method, although French accounts of double-agent operations during the Algerian War also contain instances of turning by sexual seduction. Turning can also be effected without the agent knowing about it. That requires monopolizing the agent's sources of information, quite simply allowing him to steal a planted item of "information" therefrom. Thus, in 1959, French Gen. Jacques Massu's CI service allowed several known agents of the Algerian FLN to steal lists of "French agents" inside the FLN. These people, however, were among the FLN's most effective leaders. The resulting internecine warfare served the French cause well.[32]

Even more offensive is the recruitment of hostile intelligence officers, or (what amounts to the same thing) "running" hostile officers who have changed their allegiances but are still at their post. History is so full of high-level intelligence officials who actually worked for the other side that one is forced to conclude that whether or not top intelligence jobs *attract* the disloyal, they surely offer *incentives* to disloyalty. Certainly a high intelligence officer can be certain of making his biggest possible mark on the world by providing information to a hostile service. He can also command a high price for his services. Thus in 1902–13 Col. Alfred Redl, chief of Austro–Hungarian intelligence, was a Russian agent; Wilhelm Canaris, chief of the German Abwehr in World War II, worked for the British; Kim Philby, who was almost head of Britain's MI-6, worked for the Soviets; and two heads of West German counterintelligence really worked for East Germany. A service so penetrated is capable neither of offense nor defense. The hostiles may chose to arrest or to "feed" every agent it sends. Every agent who goes against it goes equipped at least with a road map to the secrets he seeks, and at best can be sure that he will be protected.

The other side of the coin, however, is that defectors or recruited agents from within hostile services are mortal dangers because it is most difficult to discern on which side they are really working. The higher the rank of the "penetrator," the more helpful he is, the easier it is for him to act as a "triple," and the greater damage he could do. That is why some intelligence services have flat rules against ever divulging anything whatsoever to anyone who was ever an officer in another service. Thus the KGB always treated Kim Philby with tongs though he had proved his devotion by his entire career. From 1963, when he defected to Moscow, until he died in 1989, Philby, though he lived in excellent style in Moscow, was never allowed to take part in the KGB's work. He visited KGB headquarters only once, and continued to be known as "Agent Tom." This is extreme medicine, but it is a sure cure for the disease. On the other side of the ledger, during the Peloponnesian War the Spartans were so delighted with the very important information and advice that the Athenian defector Alcibiades had brought them that they took him into their counsel—after which Alcibiades betrayed them to the Persians *and* to the Athenians. As we will see, U.S. intelligence has raised the most disturbing questions about itself by making Soviet defectors parties to its internal affairs. The most fearsome swords have two edges.

The double-edged character of CI applies to intelligence machines as much as it does to intelligence officers. The principle is simple: A microphone inserted into "enemy headquarters" (be this a foreign embassy, a military operations center, or a gang's hideout) can be devastating. But if the foreign ambassadors, the military planners, the gangsters know about the microphone, they can play-act in front of it and prepare nasty surprises for those who believe what they are hearing. Thus during the Vietnam War, the U.S. Army, at the urging of Secretary of Defense Robert McNamara, dropped a series of sensors along the routes that North Vietnam was using to infiltrate its men and supplies into South Vietnam. The sensors worked fine in the technical sense. But after the North Vietnamese found them (as the Americans should have expected them to, but did not), they drove trucks around and around some of them, and diverted trucks away from the others, in order to give the Americans precisely the wrong information on which to base the next set of air raids. Thus American bombs would fall on jungle, while the North Vietnamese trucks would roll undisturbed.

DECEPTION

The point of the contest for privileged knowledge is that the winner gets to deceive the loser. Deception, in turn, is the greatest of strategic goods. Because it can ensure that the enemy's strength is wasted while one's own strength is matched against the enemy's weakness, deception can make the weak strong, and make the strong unchallengeable. In a close contest it is the easiest way of tipping the balance.

During the American Revolutionary War, as British troop-carrying ships were heading toward Newport, Rhode Island, to overpower the small American garrison there, Gen. George Washington saved the garrison with his pen and a low-level agent. Washington wrote what appeared to be a set of orders for his forces in what is today Orange County, New York, to prepare to attack New York City in the absence of a significant part of Gen. DeWitt Clinton's troops. A man well-known as a Tory farmer delivered the letters to the nearest British officer, saying he had found a packet lying on the road. The officer, noticing the content, rushed them to General Clinton, who quickly used fire signals along Long Island Sound to recall his ships. Clinton credited good intelligence with averting an American attack on New York. In fact, he had been had.

Two thousand years earlier, Hannibal immobilized the Romans' superior forces just long enough to pull his army from a box canyon. When night came, Hannibal had bundles of sticks tied to the horns of his army's cattle herd, and set afire. The Roman generals saw a crazy, hurried movement of lights. Fearing a trick, they ordered their troops into defensive formations, blocking the valley floor. Meanwhile, Hannibal's army was marching out single-file along the rim. No agents were involved, but rather the manipulation of the equivalent of today's satellites and other sensors. The Romans saw what they saw, much as today's aerial cameras might report an event. The deception consisted in Hannibal's calculation that perception of the event would freeze Roman power.

During the last days of October 1956, when the Soviet Union decided that the Western powers would not intervene on behalf of the Hungarians who had revolted and driven out Soviet occupation troops, and hence that it could safely crush the revolt, the Soviet commanders knew that they would enjoy overwhelming military superiority in the coming fight. Nevertheless, they chose to begin the fight with a politico–military decapitation of the rebels. Janos Kadar, a Hungarian double agent under the control of Soviet Ambassador Yuri Andropov, lured the rebels' political leader, Imre Nagy, and their military leader, Pál Maléter, to a negotiating session where both were arrested, and executed soon after. Thanks to this deception, the Red Army faced semiorganized opposition rather than an organized (albeit small) nation. In similar manner, the Soviet invasion of Afghanistan, which would have succeeded anyhow through overwhelming force, involved only the KGB Alpha force's killing spree at the Presidential Palace because the Soviets had infiltrated their own men into position whence they could cripple the movement of the Afghan Army by, among other things, removing the rotors in its vehicles' engines. Soviet troops who looked like Afghans and dressed in Afghan uniforms drove right up to the palace.

The confrontation between Hitler's Germany and the Western allies in 1944 was straightforward: The Allies would try to invade somewhere in northern France. If the Germans could concentrate their forces at the point of landing faster than the Allies could build theirs up there, the Germans would win, and the Western theater would continue to be a place for relative rest and recreation. If the Allies managed a faster relative buildup, a deadly threat from the West would soon match the one from the East. The Allies' best chance in the race was to get a running start while the Germans stood still. The best way to achieve this was deception. That deception, in turn, required mastery of every channel through which the Germans were receiving information about Allied intentions. And the mastery was achieved: German agents (under British control) reported that the Allies would land along the Pas de Calais, not Normandy. German airborne reconnaissance photographed massive armaments (decoys) on the British coast opposite Calais, while intercepted signals as well as newspapers carried news (including wedding announcements) to support the existence of forces there. Finally, the Germans knew for a fact that for every Allied bombing raid in Normandy there were two somewhere else. But all these facts lied. Considering that the success of Operation OVERLORD was a close call, the deception might well be counted as having made the difference.

OPERATIONAL SECURITY

To see ourselves as others see us, to look at every move we make from the standpoint of someone who might want to take advantage of it, is the beginning of prudence. To ask "How do I know that?" and "What is there about the way I came to know this matter that could have biased my view of it?" is the foundation of such certainty as prudent men permit themselves. In philosophy, to address such questions is called epistemology. In intelligence it is operational security. It involves watching one's own activities to see who else is watching them, and testing both one's own sources of information and one's own conclusions. These precepts are old and universal. The classic Indian manual of statecraft, the *Arthasastra*, prescribes the "invisible watchman," and counsels that any information gathered be "tested by intrigues."[33]

Although good operational security (Opsec) does not guarantee the success of any intelligence operation, faulty Opsec almost surely guarantees worse than failure. The German Abwehr, for example, practiced operational security on its own spies in Britain to some extent. In the case of the agent code-named Hektor, they noticed his tendency to report what he thought they wanted to hear. So they asked him to check on a (nonexistent) factory that supposedly had been spotted by aerial reconnaissance south of Worchester. When Hektor supplied data about the factory, he destroyed his credibility.[34] But such successes on the part of the Abwehr were kept small by Britain's superior Opsec. Most of the data that the British fed the Abwehr through double agents was tailored to correspond to what the Germans could observe.

The Allies ran their operations against Germany conscious that the Germans were watching. The Germans received a variety of data about the Allies' preparations for the invasion of North Africa in December 1942. During October the American OSS, through double agents, briefly managed to convince the Germans that the invasion would take place near Dakar, Senegal—two thousand miles away from the true target, the Algerian coast. Although the evidence of Allied preparations farther north quickly dispelled that illusion, the Allied buildup was designed so that its observable features would not reveal the destination of the operation. This was relatively easy to do with materiel: British ships concentrated at Gibraltar, where they had a variety of options, while American ships sailed to the invasion directly from America. As regards the diplomats and agents who were trying to smooth the invasion's path with French authorities in North Africa, the U.S. government seems to have acted on the sound Opsec assumption that they were penetrated, and did not inform them of the precise location of the landings until the last moment.[35]

The elaborate operational security arrangements oriented against Germany served not at all against the Soviet Union. The tiny number of people cleared to know about Britain's biggest secret, the Ultra decryptions of German communications; the provision that people thus cleared could not be put into positions where they might be captured; the rule that information obtained through Ultra could not be used without a "cover" that would lead the Germans to look elsewhere to explain their loss—none of these things prevented British communist John Cairncross from giving the Soviets stacks of Ultra intercepts, plus the "keys" to help the Soviets do the job themselves. While the British (and Americans) were terribly careful about German sympathizers, they were downright cavalier about communist sympathizers. The point here is that *Opsec arrangements are not primarily technical in nature.* Rather, they depend on arraying specific defenses against specific threats. *One must ask: Secure against whom? For what purpose?*

Now consider the famous "midnight ride" of Paul Revere on April 18, 1775. How did the Minutemen know that Paul Revere was carrying accurate intelligence about British intentions to seize their weapons magazines—that he was neither an enemy agent nor a dupe? (After all, Revere was a friendly neighbor to British Major Pitcarin). They knew because for two years Revere and his committee of safety, known as the "Mechanics," had been keeping track of British troops; because during those years the members had tested each other innumerable times; and because the latest test had occurred just three days before, when Revere had warned Sam Adams and John Hancock that the British were after them. If Pitcarin had suspected Revere of being an American agent, he could first have tested Revere by making remarks about (fictitious) British plans. Then, if the Americans acted as if those plans were real, his suspicions of Revere would have been confirmed. *Then* he might have told Revere about plans for a march on Lexington and Concord, causing the Americans to reveal themselves. Later, armed with that intelligence, small squads of British Redcoats could then have plucked the Americans from their farms, one by one. But the Americans' intelligence was more secure than that of their foes.

This was true throughout the Revolutionary War. George Washington, while he guarded his information closely, often gave the impression of carelessness: He would leave sheaves of papers full of information about his strength, his plans, and his sources lying around headquarters. Of course these were false. Since he could not guarantee that the British could not penetrate his entourage, at least he could raise the odds that a penetration would serve his purposes rather than Britain's.

THE STRATEGIC SIGNIFICANCE OF CI

How many lives have been saved or lost because of counterintelligence? If one reads the classic of Persian statecraft, the *Shah Nameh (Book of Kings)*, one might conclude that heads, battles, and kingdoms are hardly won or lost any other way. To be sure, in oriental cultures, double-dealing and deception do seem to be the rule.* Modern totalitarian states and Third World regimes (Iraq, Iran, Syria, Libya, Cuba, Angola, etc.) also seem to depend substantially on spying and counterspying. Indeed, the Soviet KGB (neé Cheka, December 20, 1917) is the institution that transformed Russia into the Soviet Union, drove it through its development, sustained it in its old age, and survived its formal disestablishment remaining a major factor in the country's political life. Because the Soviet Union was neither a Rechtsstaat nor a place where people prospered by productive labor, but rather a place where all privilege came from political connections and was secured by fear, it has rightly been called a "counterintelligence state."[36] Because the KGB and its priorities continue to be important to the Soviet Union's successor regimes, knowing about it is essential to dealing

---

*See Adda Bozeman, *Politics and Culture*. Note that when Britain and France expanded their empires into Asia and Africa, they found it necessary to govern substantially through espionage, just as the empires that had governed those regions since time immemorial had done. Rudyard Kipling's *Kim*, a novel of the nineteenth-century Anglo–Russian "great game" over Afghanistan, illustrates the extent to which espionage and counterespionage were part of imperial government.

successfully both with it and with those regimes. The same applies to the intelligence services of Third World regimes and to Western conspiratorial movements whose moral–political structures are similar to those of Soviet communism.

Thus the fact that in 1921–27 Lenin's Cheka and Stalin's GPU helped win the battle to decide how the West would interpret the Soviet regime (a mortal enemy or a progressive outfit "with whom we can do business") helped the regime to survive when it might well have perished. During World War II, when the Soviet Union hung between destruction and the spectacular gains that would follow from German defeat and Western acquiescence at its expansion, the Soviet Union's mastery of the CI contest helped produce precisely the Western attitudes that Stalin needed. The most clamorous example was that NKVD agent H. P. Smolka (alias Peter Smollett) put himself in position to be asked to undertake, on Winston Churchill's behalf, a project "to counter the present tendency of the British public to forget the dangers of communism in their enthusiasm over the resistance of Russia." Smolka was able to turn that into a campaign that argued to the British people that anti-Bolshevism was a Nazi plot.[37] Thus also the fact that, in the 1960s and 1970s, the KGB won the battle against Western security services for access to Western technology, was one of the reasons why by the 1980s the Soviet Union fielded armed forces roughly on a technical par with those of the West despite the fact that the overall Soviet economy was operating on the technical plane of the Third World.[38] During the revolution that began in 1990 the Soviet government marshaled the support of Western governments in a series of attempts to counterbalance total rejection by its own peoples. Inferior in so many other ways, the Soviet state used its superiority in intelligence to try to even the scales.

Disparity in understanding can be achieved by raw disparity in knowledge as well. This was the case at the battle of Midway, in May 1942. The U.S. had partially broken the Japanese Navy's code, and was able to piece together Admiral Yamamoto's plan, which in part involved laying a reconnaissance screen of submarines around Pearl Harbor to shadow the U.S. fleet as it sailed to the defense of Midway Island. Admiral Nimitz moved the U.S. fleet out before the Japanese subs arrived, and so Yamamoto did not know where his enemy would be. But Nimitz knew where Yamamoto was. He also knew that a well-advertised northward movement by elements of the Japanese fleet was a ruse. This disparity of knowledge, plus Nimitz's excellent sense of timing in launching his main attack, was enough to overcome an eight-to-three deficit in aircraft carriers, an eleven-to-zero deficit in battleships, and a serious deficit in quality of aircraft and experience of crews.[39]

In sum, it matters less whether a disparity of knowledge or understanding is created by a double agent, by a microphone or other sensor unknown to the party observed (or known to the party observed, unbeknownst to the observer), by an intercepted message, or by careful analysts working against less-careful ones. The result is always that *when one side's intelligence loses the contest in quality control, it becomes a net liability.*

Covert Action

In 1952 the U.S. government coined the term "covert action" to denote some of the less-than-blatant ways in which it was interfering in the internal affairs of other countries. *Covert* meant that the actions were not meant to be entirely secret. And indeed, while watching or listening to someone may be kept secret, anyone who is acted upon will know it. Rather, covert actions were meant to be *covered* by some stratagem so that they would not necessarily be attributed to the U.S. government—i.e., the U.S. government might avoid taking responsibility. Obviously the government invented only the term, and not the reality to which it refers. Interference in the affairs of other countries long predates the discovery of America. In truth the very purpose of foreign relations is to interfere with other countries, and statesmen long ago developed a variety of tools—some more blatant than others—for doing so. There is no precedent for putting the more secret of these tools into a special category, or for assigning them exclusively to an intelligence agency. As we shall see (Chapter 6), in recent years the U.S. government has issued executive orders setting forth procedures by which the CIA alone may use this (inherently undefinable) category of tools, even to the point of prohibiting it from soliciting another government to do things not authorized according to proper U.S. government procedures.

American legalisms, however, are a bad place to begin understanding this sort of thing. The world does not live by U.S. executive orders. And, in fact, neither do Presidents of the United States. Quite reasonably, U.S. Presidents have not limited themselves to the CIA when trying quietly to exercise influence abroad. In 1984 the White House admitted to having used the State Department secretly to finance the election campaign of El Salvadorean political parties opposed to Conservative candidate Roberto D'Aubuisson.[40] Two years later the President revealed that he had used the staff of the National Security Council on secret diplomatic missions to Iran and Central America.[41] In 1991 the State Department secretly brokered the exile of Ethiopia's dictator, Colonel Mengistu, in exchange for the Ethiopian rebels' peaceful occupation of Addis Ababa.

Nor is this sort of thing merely recent. In 1978, Army General (later Ambassador) Vernon Walters published a book detailing how "five Presidents" had used him on "silent missions."[42] Some of these ventures were wise, others foolish. Some succeeded, others failed. But neither wisdom nor success have been related to the use of the CIA, or of other instruments. The first point here is that the effort is foredoomed to define *whom* a chief executive officer may use to convey urgings or cautions, or money, or deals. The second is that the category "covert action" is inherently amorphous. How secret does an act have to be to qualify? Secret from whom? And for how long? Perhaps the term confuses more than it explains, and so should never have been coined. But even if it had not, there would still be the need to understand activities that lie at the juncture of intelligence and state power.

FUNDAMENTALS

First consider the ambiguous relationship between covert activities and intelligence. The standard advice to spies is to be inconspicuous—but action is by nature conspicuous. A secret "agent" will be secret at best for one action. As soon as he acts he will invite hostile CI to check on everyone with whom he has ever dealt. So, once a government finds a secret friend in an influential position in the enemy camp, it faces a problem: Should it use the friend to help get things done, or as a source of information? It would be nice if a country had entirely separate networks of confidential contacts in the enemy camp, one for information and the other for action. In practice, however, the two often overlap. One reason why they do is that the people who act as sources often do so precisely because they want to cause things to happen. All history teaches that information flows to governments that are in the process of acting—successfully. Finally, note that influencing foreign governments is intelligence-intensive work. It requires precise knowledge of who in the target government would be receptive to what threat or blandishment; it requires cover; and it requires protection against hostile CI. And in fact throughout history intelligence people (though by no means they alone) have been involved in influence work. Hence we include this topic in our discussion of intelligence. We label it "covert action" despite the term's lack of precision because we write for an audience that has adopted it.

Second, although we hardly claim that the world runs on covert action, and indeed we believe that writers on intelligence make altogether too big a deal of it, we believe that it is necessary to understand covert action in order to understand statecraft in our time. The modern American view of international relations as totally bound by law but utterly devoid of objective moral standards, in which intrigue is exceptional, is a peculiar evolution of Wilsonian secular religion. Its call for total respect of sovereignty, open diplomacy, and recognition of UN resolutions as positive moral standards would have astonished the Americans of *The Federalist Papers* for whom "secrecy and dispatch" were principles of statecraft,[43] but for whom moral standards were universal and objective.

For different reasons the modern American view of international relations is incomprehensible to most modern regimes. Communists recognize no law, no good, common to themselves and their enemies. They explicitly reject the nation–state as the organizing principle of political life, and have historically conducted their international relations at least as much through unofficial channels as through official ones. Regimes in the Muslim world (much of Africa and Asia) have been reverting to pre-Western and often pre-Muslim traditions in which the nation–state is nonexistent and conspiracy is the primary route to political power. The most dynamic political forces in this vast region blame the nation–state for the people's troubles. Europe, Latin America, and "Westernized" Asia are heirs to the modern statist tradition that views governments on the international scene as leviathans above any law but their own. Everywhere, when conflict looms, scruples against skullduggery recede. Thucydides tells us that whereas before the Peloponnesian War cities seldom fomented revolts among each others' serfs and minorities, in the latter stages of the war they did it consistently.[44] Whereas prior to the Reformation European ambassadors had behaved like lawyers, in its aftermath they behaved like subversives.[45] So covert action is pervasive. Why then is intrigue effective when so many expect it? The difference, it seems, lies not in the depth of statesmen's cynicism, but in that of their understanding.

Herein we introduce intelligence-based intrigue by explaining the advantages that governments get from doing it well, and the disadvantages they incur by doing it badly or not at all.

Conspiracy Matters

Pace conspiracy theorists, most of the world's great events occur for reasons and through means that are largely in plain sight. But, oh, the exceptions! The Bolshevik regime in Russia—perhaps the most significant development of the twentieth century, and surely among the greatest tragedies of mankind—was incubated with the help of the Tzar's secret police, and introduced into Russia by an act of the Kaiser's military intelligence service. It devastated its host populations through its own secret service and, in its old age, lived only by the fear and confusion that its secret service could sow.

Before World War I the Tzar's secret police, the Okhrana, had thoroughly infiltrated the Russian Socialist party.* The Okhrana's strategy for weakening

---

*The Okhrana's files are available to researchers at the Hoover Institution, Stanford University. Also see Bertram Wolfe, *Three Who Made a Revolution*, Ch. 31; and Stefan Possony, *Lenin the Compulsive Revolutionary*. There is legitimate controversy over whether the Okhrana ever succeeded in recruiting Stalin as an agent. It certainly did succeed in recruiting Roman Malinovsky, who became the Bolshevik leader in Parliament.

socialism was to foster a split between the moderate Menshevik and the extremist Bolshevik factions. This proved to be easy because it happened to coincide with the Bolsheviks' own strategy of claiming to be the sole representatives of true socialism. The Okhrana also judged that the most fractious Bolshevik personality, Lenin, would be the best insurance against a broad leftist anti-Tzarist coalition. So it smoothed his path to becoming the boss of the Bolsheviks by arresting some of his rivals. The Okhrana got all it bargained for, and far more.

So did German military intelligence. When the Tzar's regime collapsed in February 1917 and was replaced by a weak parliamentary regime, Germany's intelligence chief, Colonel Nicolai, saw a chance to win World War I by a deft maneuver. The new Russian government was committed to carrying on the war. But its hold on the country was shaky. Moreover, it had allowed political freedom. There was in Zurich a disciplined group of Russian Socialists, led by the zealot Lenin, who since August 1914 had advocated that Russia get out of the war. Perhaps, reasoned Nicolai, if this group were injected into the Russian body politic they would tip the internal balance in favor of peace. If Russia did get out of the war, Germany's Eastern front would disappear, and a million German troops could tip the delicate balance on the bloody Western front before the Americans arrived to tip it in the other direction. Sound thinking if ever there was. Shipped to Petrograd in a sealed train, like a germ in a hypodermic needle, Lenin not only tipped the balance—he overthrew the government. He not only pulled Russia out of the war: Through the Treaty of Brest–Litovsk, he gave up Poland as well as substantial parts of Byelorussia and the Ukraine. German troops flowed west (though not as many as previously planned—after all, Germany wanted to hold down its new Eastern conquests) and Germany's spring 1918 offensive nearly won the war.

But of course Lenin's regime had its own dynamic. Within three years its agents were fomenting riots in Berlin. In the following decades its own secret police slaughtered some 20 percent of Russia's population, while convincing Westerners that they could "do business" with the Bolshevik regime. The Soviet services also whipped together the armies that occupied Germany for the second half of the twentieth century. The point here is that although the consequences of covert action—like those of overt action—often are unforeseeable, they can nevertheless be quite significant.

INFLUENCING POLICY

Intrigue by well-placed agents can (among other things) reduce the price to be paid for hostile policies, gain allies, keep neutral a country that might otherwise enter a war as an enemy, or even make for deep cooperation beneath a cover of enmity. In the mid–1930s, as the German National Socialist regime built up its armaments and rallied the German people to anti-British sentiments, Adolf Hitler sent "Putzi" Hänfstängel, his favorite "pop" pianist, to ply the British social circuit with the good news that, despite what Hitler seemed to be doing, the British upper classes could count on him as a friend. This argument, which would not have stood a chance in the open, flourished in what was a hothouse atmosphere. So delighted were British aristocrats to see a National Socialist who ate with knife and fork that they eagerly supported a policy of appeasement of Hitler.

In the 1620s an equally simple plot also paid big dividends. Diego Sarmiento, Count of Gondomar, Ambassador of Catholic Spain to the Court of England's Protestant King James I, built a wide net of secret "pensioners" (recipients of regular payments from the Spanish treasury) among high-ranking English personages. The lists of pensioners fell into the hands of King James—who, however, did nothing about them, since he himself was Gondomar's biggest friend in London. As a result of Gondomar's work, King James resisted strong domestic pressures for England to come to the aid of the Protestant Netherlands in their rebellion against the Catholic King of Spain. James even arrested some of the anti-Spanish activists in London.[46] Thus a quiet (though by no means secret) relationship that went against the grain of England's natural foreign-policy proclivities overcame them.

Now note the relationship between the state of Israel from its inception in 1948, and Iran, until the Iranian revolution of 1978. Israel quite simply had the equivalent of excellent diplomatic relations with this Muslim country, including help in extracting Jews from neighboring Arab states, and assistance in infiltrating agents into them. The Shah of Iran was happy to do all this—on the condition that the relationship be kept secret.

What role, then, does secrecy play in influencing the policies of foreign governments? Quite simply, it is a means of dealing with some members of the foreign body politic while avoiding having to deal with others. Secret relationships are a means of playing some members of a government against others, or of dealing with an entire body politic under false pretense. Good relations with Israel were quite acceptable to the Shah of Iran and to those in his entourage who were oriented to the West or to ancient Persian traditions. They would have been unacceptable to many Iranian Muslims. And, in fact, in 1978 the Ayatollah Khomeini used the Shah's relationship with Israel to whip up popular rage against him. The secret had never been total. So long as there had not been a powerful political movement to exploit it, it sufficed that the affront to the Muslims not be blatant.

Similarly, Gondomar could not possibly have convinced the English Parliament to abandon the Netherlands to Spain's tender mercies. But he could convince the King, and was able to protect his achievement by "painting" those Englishmen who pressed for England to fulfill its natural role as opponents of the King and as warmongers to boot.* As for making hostile acts seem friendly, or friendly ones hostile, the art consists of telling the audience what it wants to hear, with a voice that is as close to its own as possible.

AFFECTING BODIES POLITIC

Governments can radically affect foreign bodies politic. The Romans used to say that introducing into a Greek city a set of the writings of Democritus—a materialistic, hedonistic author—had an effect on the ensuing battle equivalent to adding a legion to the attacking force. The Romans were of course commenting on the inherent consequences of ideas, and not about the means of propagating them. Even more forcefully, Machiavelli called language the ultimate weapon because changes in the terms in which people think not only can win a quarrel, but also erase the memory of it or render it irrelevant.[47] During the wars of the Reformation, the several governments of Europe actively fostered the growth of their religious denominations in their opponents' realms. Napoleon used as a potent weapon against his enemies the secular idea that political boundaries ought to follow ethnic and cultural ones. In the ancient duchies, principalities, and republics of Germany and Italy—even in millenarian Venice—thousands of people responded by forming conspiratorial nationalist groups. Napoleon benefited, and the partisans of *ancien régimes* suffered.[48]

A government that does not try to convince the world that right lies on its side gives up more than a potential advantage. Its passivity will help lead its own people to accept any ideas that might be coming from the other side. Thus between 1963 and 1975 the U.S. government suffered virtually a social revolution in part as a result of the widespread conviction of the American people that it was fighting in Vietnam *against* a just cause. And why not? It seldom spoke as if the government of North Vietnam was evil, and never suggested that the Americans who were loudly vilifying their country—quite in coordination with the North Vietnamese[49]—were anything but admirable folk. The world heard only one full-hearted, consistent set of arguments.

In some circumstances the most direct way, short of war, of changing a

---

*By a similar token note that upon the signing of an arms-control treaty with Mikhail Gorbachev in December 1987, President Ronald Reagan remarked that domestic opponents of the treaty, who tended to be habitual supporters of his, had accepted "that war is inevitable" while Mr. Gorbachev was a partner in peace. *New York Times*, 4 December 1987. Regardless of the merits of the matter, Mr. Gorbachev achieved the remarkable feat of splitting the U.S. President from a sector of his supporters.

foreign government (and perhaps of opening the way to systemic change) is to help someone inclined to carry out a *coup d'état*. Those inclined to such things are sometimes encouraged by foreign help in the enterprise, by the possibility of foreign refuge in case of failure, and by the promise of foreign help in consolidating a victory. And indeed the standard practice of tyranny from antiquity to our own time calls for the new tyrant to provide himself with foreign guards and enforcers. Thus the most sought-after commodity by aspiring politicians in the Third World of our time is not the good will of international moneylenders, but rather the good will of those states that export effective Praetorian guards and secret police systems. Until its demise, the world's most prestigious exporter of this commodity was East Germany. Its satisfied customers ranged from Ethiopia to tiny Grenada. Cuba, Libya, and the Palestine Liberation Organization are also in the business of assisting and preventing *coups d'état*. As we shall see (Chapter 6), the U.S. government was in the coup business until the early 1960s. Nominally it is still in the business of training the security forces of friendly leaders. But its product line lost luster in 1981 when its primary beneficiary, President Anwar Sadat of Egypt, was assassinated.

The most common way for one government to affect the long-term fortunes of another is to acquire and build up special relationships with influential groups within the other's body politic. Later (Chapter 11) we will explain the several ways—secrecy is only one of them—by which such operations are covered. For now suffice it to say how privileged Leonid Brezhnev was in 1978 to sit at a banquet in the Kremlin and tell 150 specially selected leaders of American business, among them David Rockefeller of Chase Manhattan and Donald Kendall of Pepsico, "I am looking around this hall and see that our contacts have really become a system."[50] Brezhnev was referring to the transformation of the perceived self-interest of individual American businessmen (for deals that the Soviet leadership could make sweeter than private customers might) into a powerful, mutually supporting, unabashed, bipartisan lobbying group within the U.S. for making politico–military concessions to the Soviet Union.

A limit-case of foreign support is that which Nazi Germany provided to the Sudeten German minority in Czechoslovakia. The German government took up the Sudeten people's grievances (real or manufactured) with the Czech government, and pressured the Czech cabinet virtually to include the Sudetens' leader, Konrad Henlein, as a member. Of course the National Socialists had built the Sudeten political organization in their own image. They were the main source of money, arms, and strong-arm tactics within the Sudeten community. Under the circumstances, it is inconceivable that an anti-Nazi could have challenged Henlein for the leadership of the group. Thus the Sudeten Germans became a mere hammer with which Berlin effectively smashed Prague. In the long run they suffered as much as the Czechs did. For similar reasons in our time Palestinian Arabs, especially on the West Bank of the Jordan River, have been "supported" and "protected" by Arab governments who want to show their peoples how anti-Israeli they are, and by a Soviet government eager to convince the Arabs that it is their friend, whereas the U.S. is not. Thus the West Bank is awash with money by which various somewhat competing foreign patrons woo the allegiance of local residents, as well as with fear of the assassinations by which they try to secure that allegiance.

Covered Warfare

It is hard to find examples of wars in which one side or the other doesn't try to "raise" armed activity behind enemy lines. (Usually both do.) Some groups are perennially disposed to fight, seeking only the opportunity—namely, that the oppressor be principally occupied elsewhere, and that a friendly power be willing to supply arms and hope. Readers of Thucydides learn to anticipate the words of Spartan or Athenian envoys to city after city (or minority group) in the enemy's sphere of influence: "This is your chance. . . ." In 1754, when Britain and France fought for primacy in North America, France "raised" the Indians against both the British and their American colonists. So the British and Americans together fought the French and Indian War. A decade later, when these colonists began to make trouble for Britain, the British raised the Indians against *them*. And so in 1776 when the Americans declared their independence and fought the Revolutionary War, they fought against both the British *and* the Indians. In our own time, Iraq's Kurdish minority has been raised by Americans, Iranians, and Turks. History shows that while those who do the raising usually benefit somewhat thereby, the ones raised usually are left to their oppressors' even harsher mercies.

Covered warfare also occurs in time of peace. Indeed it is difficult to draw the line between the building-up of one's own groups inside a foreign country and the waging of war against it. Does one draw the line at violence? How does one consider demonstrations intended to intimidate the host government into self-defeating policies? How about a little violence, attributable to "the situation" but not quite to the group being sponsored, and certainly not to the country that sponsors the group?

The basic point is obvious, and applies to all kinds of covert action—even the gentlest. It is convenient to enjoy the fruits of one's actions against an enemy who somehow cannot even use the losses he suffers to rally his own forces. However, because war is the one activity least susceptible to being hidden (especially from those against whom it is being waged), it raises most inescapably the question: What covers it, and from whom?

POWER OF THE WEAK, BREATH OF THE STRONG

The commonplace view that covert action is the weapon par excellence of the weak states is true, but misleading. First, covert action works for the weak not insofar as they are weak but insofar as they are smart. Second, it works even better for the strong than it does for the weak. The equation of covert action with weak states gained currency in the 1950s when Egypt's General Nasser publicly argued that he had found the sure-fire recipe for striking the enemy with impunity. He told his senior officers:

> There is one method which reveals all and another method which reveals little and conceals the rest. We know now that Egypt can achieve much by the second method. . . . The great advantage of indirect warfare is that our enemies cannot answer back. If we ordered our armies to capture the oil pumping stations whose pipes run through Jordan, Syria, and Lebanon and to cut off their flow, this would unite the entire world against us; but if we sent a commando unit to blow up those pumping stations, we would achieve the same result and the Great Powers would watch us with their hands tied. . . . Irregular warfare costs us little and costs our enemies dear.[51]

Nasser evaluated his environment correctly: By that time, for a variety of reasons, the leaders of the U.S., Britain, and France had invested so many hopes, so much praise, so much political capital in the leaders of the so-called nonaligned states—Egypt's Nasser, Ghana's Kwame Nkrumah, Indonesia's Sukarno, India's Nehru, the people whom Paul Johnson termed "the Bandung generation" after the Indonesian resort where they held a much-publicized meeting in 1955—that nearly two decades would pass before they would allow themselves to notice the barbarism, squalor, and rank hypocrisy of "nonaligned" regimes. Against opponents more willing to call enemies by their name and to treat them accordingly, Nasser's formula would have brought disaster. In fact the various "covers" in which he clothed his covert acts against Israel availed him nothing, because Israel simply exacted more than the proverbial eye or tooth for every injury. In that case, Nasser's maxim held in reverse. But against the Western powers Nasser was correct.

Nasser's formula contains a core of generally applicable truth: If a weak country operates beneath the threshold where its enemies recognize danger, it can achieve a lot. Take Col. Muammar al-Qaddafi's Libya. Here is a regime that has virtually no assets. Most of its 3.6 million people live as their ancestors did centuries ago. Qaddafi's regime—a police state in which the good life is reserved for the dictator's friends—could never attract a mass following. The regime's vast oil wealth has filled hundreds of desert acres with the latest Soviet military equipment, protected against all hazards of storage except obsolescence. Still,

Libya became a major force in Africa, and perhaps beyond, through covert action.

In Chad, in November 1990, Libya sponsored the victory of its client, Idriss Deby, against the regime of Hissène Habré, who in 1986 had beaten back a Libyan invasion with the help of France and the U.S. In 1985 Libya had paved the way by sponsoring the overthrow of Sudan's pro-Western President Jaffar Nimeiri. In 1990 Libya moved its air and air-defense forces to the Sudanese–Chadian border to cover the swift arrival of Deby's troops, who were riding in Toyota land cruisers that Sudan had purchased from Japan with Libyan money and landed on the Red Sea coast. Deby's troops were armed with Milan anti-tank guided missiles purchased from Europe. Only Western intervention massive enough to overcome Libyan air defenses could have saved Habré. Since the West was otherwise occupied with Iraq, that intervention was not forthcoming.

In Burkina Faso (Upper Volta) Libya had an ally that, like Sudan, was gained with conspiracy and kept with money. In Liberia, Qaddafi provided the insurgent forces of Charles Taylor with material superiority, and challenged nearby Nigeria with the prospect of a full-scale war if it wanted to deny Taylor victory. Meanwhile, Qaddafi offered to pay Nigeria to wash its hands of Liberia. In Cameroon, the government complained that some students were using Libyan money to organize strikes and riots. By late December of 1990, reports were circulating in Cameroon's capital of Youndé that cadres of Idriss Deby's army had slipped into the country and were waiting for the right moment to overthrow the Cameroonian government. In Senegal, the heart of Francophone Africa, Libya was supplying weapons, including rocket-propelled grenades, to the Diola tribe, and supporting its separatist claims. Similarly, it was supporting the Touareg tribe's revolt against Niger and Mali.

Interestingly enough, the leaders of these countries under attack, far from retaliating against Libya, publicly gave in to the demands of pro-Libyan elements. The reason is the cover under which the Libyan operations took place, namely Libya's accusation that these governments were insufficiently Islamic and insufficiently supportive of Iraq's fight against the West. The cover was well-chosen. By 1990 the Islam that had spread far south of the Sahara to become Black Africa's dominant religion had less to do with the spiritualism of the Koran than with resentment of the corrupt state structures bequeathed by Western colonial powers. The African masses, full of resentment at their daily deprivations, were looking for a savior. Iraq's Saddam Hussein presented himself as just that, and by early 1991 pro-Saddam mobs of hundreds of thousands were heard in the capitals of the Muslim world. Even the well-entrenched leaders of Morocco and Egypt, where there is little Libyan subversion, were making pro-Iraqi noises.* Imagine then the predicament of heads of state like Senegal's President Abdou Diouf, who had to wonder how to keep their people from flocking to the Libyan-supplied rebellions and into Libyan-led mobs around their palaces. In the long run, it is impossible to imagine a state as fundamentally weak as Libya dominating a significant part of the African continent. But in the short run, by judicious use of covered warfare, Muammar Qaddafi made Africa shake.

Now consider how the strong may use covert action. In December 1984, according to several accounts, a Shia Muslim faction in Beirut kidnapped several officials of the Soviet Embassy, in the same fashion that dozens of Western citizens had been kidnapped and held hostage to press some demand on their government. Although the identity of the individual kidnappers was unknown, the faction which had taken them claimed credit. Within days, so goes the story, some officers of Syrian intelligence, acting on the Soviet Union's behalf, kidnapped a member of that faction. The following day his family received his severed genitals, and word spread in the neighborhood where he had lived that if the Soviet officials were not released immediately, Syrian forces would turn that neighborhood into another Hama—Syria's third largest city, large parts of which the regime of Hafez Assad turned to rubble in 1981. The Soviets were released forthwith. The set of severed genitals were effective, only as a reminder of a much more ominous reality.

*Morocco's King Hassan, who in August 1990 had sent troops to join the U.S.-led expedition against Iraq, was proclaiming his solidarity with "brother Iraq." Even Egypt's President Hosni Mubarak, who perhaps had the most to lose from further gains in Saddam's popularity, felt obliged to declare that he had nothing against him and looked forward to working with him once Iraqi troops had left Kuwait.

2

A New World Disorder

The future lasts a long time.
– *Charles de Gaulle*, War Memoirs, *Vol. III*

As the 1990s began, the world seemed anything but boring. The biggest intellectual splash in the U.S. in 1989 had been made by a U.S. State Department official's article suggesting that history had ended, all the really important issues before mankind had been settled, and boredom would be the greatest inconvenience for the remainder of time.[1] But of course history had not ended at all. Rather, by 1991 it seemed as if someone had hit its "fast forward" button. The revolution of 1989–91 freed Eastern Europe from 45 years' subjection to the Soviet Union and began a process of dissolution in Moscow the end of which no one can foresee. But by no means did this abolish war (or even the fear of war), nor did it preclude radical changes in the character of nations, nor new combinations of nations. On the contrary, the revolution of 1989 seemed to encourage peoples everywhere to make major changes. All dreams became possible. But so did all nightmares: Within two years the U.S. had fought two wars—with Panama in 1989 and with Iraq in 1991. In August 1991 the world watched a military coup in Moscow and wondered about the Putschists' intentions with regard to nuclear weapons. Nevertheless, today, as in the post–WWI period, those who write on conflict are obliged to make a case for what should be obvious: that the future may well bring as much high-stakes conflict as the past. This chapter shows how the U.S., and indeed any nation, will require intelligence to deal with both the threats and the opportunities of the 1990s. It also describes in general terms the circumstances for future intelligence operations.

A *Legacy of Disorder*

Since World War II the U.S. government has made "stability" its highest, indeed its overriding, goal. It has assumed—contrary to all teachings of history—that long-term stability is possible. Hence the U.S. government has been the most avid consumer of "end of history" theories. The proposition that the collapse of communism in Eastern Europe and its loss of nerve in the Soviet Union portended a "new world order" based on U.S.–Soviet cooperation quickly became the sort of Washington dogma that one challenges only at one's own risk. This is not so new. During World War II (if not earlier), President Franklin D. Roosevelt and some in his administration imagined that Stalin was shaping the Soviet Union into a reliable partner with which the U.S. could lead the world to perpetual peace and progress. This was the basis of the United Nations system, and the attempt to divide the world into spheres of influence at Yalta. This dream survived the Cold War, the Korean and Vietnam wars, and the Soviet global offensive of the 1970s, and again came to dominate the U.S. foreign policy establishment in the late 1980s. Thus in 1990, even as the peoples of Eastern Europe were trying to rid themselves of *all* Soviet troops, the U.S. government expressed gratitude to Soviet dictator* Mikhail Gorbachev for signing an agreement to permit equality between U.S. and Soviet troops in Europe. As the peoples of the Soviet Union—in polls, in demonstrations, and in elections—expressed the desire to be rid of the Soviet Union, the U.S. government supported the Soviet government against its people, in the hope that a "reform communist" regime could deliver "stability." When the KGB and the Army attempted a takeover in August 1991 to preserve the Regime, the U.S. government opposed the takeover in the name of the Regime. But the coup's failure brought an unmistakable revolution against communism that must eventually establish a new order.

---

*Fashionable as it is to refer to Mikhail Gorbachev by his self-appointed title of President, the salient fact is that he was never elected except by the Communist party, refused all opportunities to expose himself to election, and spent the bulk of his energies guarding his power against contenders who were elected. This was the focus of conflict in the Soviet Union after 1989. The closest thing to an inside account is Eduard Shevardnadze *The Future Belongs to Freedom*. The trials of the perpetrators of the August 1991 Soviet *coup d'e'tat* scheduled for 1992 promised to shed further light on Gorbachev's role.

Communism was never a basis for order, and its collapse is an unavoidable fountain of disorder. Communism resolved no problems. Wherever it ruled, it paved over political life, killing or suppressing some aspects and forcing others (e.g., patronage politics) to express themselves through its mechanisms. It exacerbated enmities between ethnic groups by distributing benefits according to quotas. It ruled minorities alternatively through both quislings and foreigners. Borders of ethnic republics were drawn to ensure conflict. Occasionally it suppressed entire groups. "Nationalism" was actually a criminal offense in the Soviet Union. Communism suppressed religion in general, and dealt with particular religious groups by setting them against one another. Hence its legacy is anti-Semitism and every other kind of intolerance. Communist policies toward economic life, far from obviating class conflicts, established hundreds of categories of people who held peculiar economic privileges by virtue of their connections with the regime. Because most people had and enjoyed material goods in ways incompatible with the welfare of their neighbors, economic life became a source of hate. And so it was in every field of life. On the international scene, too, communist practice was true to Marxist ideology and brought nothing but conflict. Hence, as communism loosened its grip, ancient grievances mixed with new ones in an explosive mixture.

The fall of communism brought no new order because communism collapsed from within. It was not pushed out by coherent political forces willing and able to impose their own vision. The proximate cause for the collapse was the communists' waning will to murder. Once the subjects of communist countries became aware that they would not be killed in large numbers, at least for merely acting as if their governments did not exist, the future of communism was sealed. Despite predictions by Western governments and the press in 1989–91, neither Czechs nor Serbs nor Russians were at all interested in "socialism with a human face." They wanted to be rid of everything reminiscent of socialism.

The biggest problem was how to actually do away with the millions of government officials, bureaucrats big and small, teachers, soldiers, policemen, factory bosses, and fawning intellectuals—all of whom had gotten their jobs through the communist connection. But while this problem remained unsolved, while communists retained impressive armaments in the Soviet Union and important privileges throughout Eastern Europe, it complicated the resurgent political agendas of the former communist empire. What kind of country will we be? Who shall rule, and to what ends? Yet it isn't as if society had survived intact and that once the communist overlay cracked it sprang up whole. Like green grass, society could not stay healthy under the concrete, and it could not resume life as if nothing had happened. So, quite literally, communism's loss of nerve meant that everything was up for grabs, and in a not-so-benign environment.

Would Germany remain tied to the West as it had since the days of Konrad Adenauer (1946–1953), or would it follow the role of a powerful mediator between East and West traced out by Otto von Bismarck in the nineteenth century and rechampioned by German socialists in the 1970s and 1980s? Which of the many strains of Russian nationalism would become important? How would Russian nationalism deal with the powerful police and military forces left over from communism?

So for the peoples of Eurasia the stakes of politics both national and international did not decrease in 1990. Arguably they became greater than ever. Dreams of a future without familiar tyrannies were troubled by nightmares comparable to those of communist rule. Thus, while Armenians cheered the receding tide of communism they rued the rising tide of an Islam that had been even more cruel to them than communism. Much as Poles had worked and prayed to be rid of Russian influence, they cast a wary eye at the reunification of a Germany that had killed almost as many Poles as had the Russians.

For the United States, too, the stakes of European politics did not drop. After all, the revolution of 1989–91 did not destroy the impressive fruits of a generation of Russian weapons manufacturers any more than it repealed geography. The revolution put into question who would control the massive Russian military apparatus, and opened a vast range of political possibilities in Europe. The United States' interests in Europe, however, remained the same: To prevent its domination by any power hostile to the U.S., and to prevent a war which might involve the United States. But whereas prior to 1990 these interests might have been threatened by the decision of the Soviet Politburo alone, after 1990 any number of conceivable events might have touched off a war, and any number of Russian factions might have bid for power. In the longer run, the reunification of Germany raised all the specters of an earlier age.

The collapse of the Soviet Union as a power willing to sponsor communism around the globe also had revolutionary effects outside of the Eurasian continent. In the Middle East the Syrian government, which was bristling with Soviet armaments and nursing hegemonic ambitions from the Mediterranean to the Persian Gulf, quickly realized that, without Soviet backing, it could never again afford to go to war with Israel. So it merely annexed Lebanon. On the southern tip of Africa, the white South African government realized that its opponent, the African National Congress (ANC), had exchanged the Soviets' powerful patronage for that of Western radical-chic elements. Hence the government dared an ANC that had lost its military option to engage in open political competition. All of this portended peace. But in the Mid-East Iraq, having bled Iran for a decade, bet that it could make itself the suzerain of the Persian Gulf. In the Indian subcontinent, where the shortening Soviet shadow left India somewhat weaker vis-à-vis Pakistan, Muslim militants in Indian

Kashmir dared raise to violence their campaign for unification with Pakistan. All these conflicts and prospects for conflict represented as many temptations for those in control of military power in Russia. In short, the revolution of 1989–91 did not turn lions into lambs; much less did they cause them to lie down together peaceably. It simply cut down on one among many sources of supply for immemorial quarrels.

The number of these quarrels, however, seemed to increase. Since moral suasion played no bigger role than in previous times, order would be the result of conflict, force would be the final arbiter, and the instruments of conflict—including intelligence—would be worth cultivating.

Constant Interests

The United States, like any other regime in history, intuitively knows that it is more likely to prosper if its neighbors are both similar to it in character and well disposed toward it. For a continent-size nation in the twenty-first century, the world is a single neighborhood. During the post–World War II period a commonwealth of free, peaceable, prosperous nations developed from Berlin and Helsinki in the East, through Toronto and San Francisco to Tokyo, and to much of the Pacific rim in the West. It was a true Pax Americana. The maintenance and expansion of that vast zone of congeniality is essential to the United States, regardless of who might threaten it or why. As General de Gaulle used to say, "The future lasts a long time." While it is impossible to know what will threaten one's interests, it *is* possible to know those interests.

So, both within and outside the boundaries of the former communist empire the revolution of 1989–91 left standing the traditional *intellectual* tasks of international politics: To distinguish friends from enemies, and to discover what people are really after, what tools they have at hand, and how they may be preparing to use them. Sometimes regimes that are alien in every way (e.g., Haiti or the Central African Republic) are of no concern, while other entirely congenial ones, like Germany, are of the greatest concern because their size and potential for good or harm are very great. Mexico is in a special category for the U.S.—sheer size and physical proximity make any major events there inherently interesting. The intellectual part of statesmanship requires intelligence in both senses of the word.

Responsible statesmen also have no choice but to know about the military forces that can affect their country. The revolution of 1989–91 turned few potentially hostile swords into plowshares. For a variety of interesting reasons, communist rulers chose not to use the military power at their disposal, and by-and-large passed from the scene. But, contrary to euphoric belief, the guns they had chosen not to use did not become irrelevant. Rather, there was a lively contest for control of the means for violence. In Romania the secret police

(*Securitate*) fought against the armed forces for control of society. In the aftermath of Nicaragua's electoral revolution of 1990, the conflict between the Sandinistas' armed forces and the former Contra army was the fulcrum of public life. Similarly, the future of the Soviet Union hinged on the split within the Soviet KGB and Soviet armed forces, between those who prefered to think of themselves as Soviet and others who preferred to think of themselves as Russian. Guns are fearsome or not, depending on who controls them. That is why there is no substitute for knowledge of the character and plans of those who control them. In sum, the world of the 1990s early on proved the need to understand international conditions that, on balance, would seem to be more difficult to fathom than in previous decades.

In parts of the Third World, where narcotics traffickers have become powerful, the gathering of intelligence is as dangerous as ever it was in the communist world. In parts of Mexico, Peru, and Bolivia, in most of Colombia, and in areas of Burma, narcotics traffickers have set up veritable regimes. They are well-supplied with money and arms, and conduct violent anti-espionage operations as a matter of course. In 1991 the Colombian government found a mass grave near a camp used by narcotics traffickers and guerrillas, containing bodies of some 300 people whom the guerrillas had considered disloyal. The breakup of transnational communism has left any number of groups around the world with arms and the knowledge of how to use them to make a living, but without political purpose. There is every reason to believe that while some of these groups (e.g., Colombia's M-19) will enter legitimate life, others will manufacture new reasons for continuing violent lives and, if anything, become even more important in their countries. Such groups have always been difficult intelligence targets and are not likely to become more accessible.

Conditions of Intelligence Operations

In Chapter 9 we will discuss how one may gather intelligence in this new environment. Suffice it to say here that while outside of the former communist world the revolution of 1989–91 hardly affected the conditions in which human beings gather political and military intelligence, *within* that world the changes were enormous. In a nutshell, the number of potential sources increased while the transfer of the East German state security service's files to a united, NATO-allied Germany, and the rise of anti-communist governments in most of Eastern Europe and Russia, were a massive blow to Soviet counterintelligence. Disaffected and demobilized military men swelled the rank of potential Western recruits. But while the number of officers from the KGB's satellite services in Eastern Europe who sought to defect to the CIA or to other Western intelligence services increased after 1990, it was but a small proportion of the number of high-level operatives in Eastern Europe. Most sought to disappear.

The KGB itself weathered the storm without apparent major losses until, after the failure of its leaders' attempt to take over the country in August 1991—a failure caused by a split within the KGB—the agency was put under new management. Its future was up for grabs. Still, the former Soviet Union and Eastern Europe are awash in people who know what they are doing in this field. Hence, while it is reasonable to expect a flood of defections it is also reasonable to expect competent performance by those CI units that remain intact. Nevertheless, political processes that had been impenetrable became, if not transparent, then certainly vulnerable to human intelligence. If we add to this the fact that the revolution did not affect the long-standing trends that had been changing the character of technical intelligence and reducing its short-term value for the U.S., we must conclude that the revolution surely increased the relative value of human intelligence.

The revolution had a very different sort of impact on covert action. The Communist parties of Eastern Europe and the Soviet Union shot all their bolts in attempts to discredit their internal opposition and succeeded only in isolated cases. In short, the effectiveness of *political* action within the empire had depended on fear of *police* action. In 1990 communism's internal bag of tricks was nearly empty. Only vis-à-vis the West did the Soviet covert action campaign show success (see Chapters 10 and 11). Indeed the Soviet regime continued to be effective abroad as it was dying at home.

In the Third World, the withdrawal of East German CI experts from African communist regimes had a significant effect; however, it had no effect at all on the CI services of Mid-Eastern and Asian affiliates of the Soviet Union. The reason for this is that the competence of Syrians, Cubans, Afghans, Yemenis, and others in the feigning of loyalties and the testing of evidence and loyalty never depended either on communist ideology or on foreign advisers, but rather on old traditions.

Let us now look at some of the most important parts of the world to see precisely why they will be the proper focus of intelligence into the twenty-first century, and what sort of threats and opportunities intelligence officers will have to investigate, and the conditions in which they will have to do it.

The Soviet Union

The Military Factor

In 1990 the Soviet Union became a nuclear-armed Lebanon, 11 time-zones wide. That is, it ceased to be the most centralized polity in the world and became a geographic area in which factions of every kind battled—some to win power over the whole state, others over only a part, some for privilege or booty, others for revenge or self-preservation, and yet others to escape the fray altogether.

Among the most serious potential conflicts is that between the armed forces and the KGB over a variety of long-standing grievances, but also for exclusive control of the some 30,000 nuclear weapons that make up the world's largest nuclear stockpile. The great struggle within the Soviet armed forces seemed to be for control of the unified command while a variety of civilian groups sought out like-minded men in uniform. When Boris Yeltsin became president of the parliament of the Russian Republic in 1990 he began to ask military men to think of themselves as Russian rather than as Soviet. Evidently enough answered his call so that, in August 1991 some Soviet units defected to him, while others refused orders to move against the Russian Parliament. In Leningrad the local military commander was talked out of using force against the people. Leaders of other Soviet republics have similarly appealed to their co-nationals. It remains to be seen to what extent and under what circumstances those appeals will be answered.

The Soviet military, especially its strategic rocket forces, remain capable of destroying most of the U.S. military in a first strike. But whereas prior to 1990 command over the armed forces—although flowing through both military and KGB channels—had a single point of origin, after 1990 Westerners and Soviets alike had to ask which armed unit would be loyal to whom, and for what purpose. Given the quantity and quality of Soviet military equipment, these are high-stakes questions. They can be answered only through intelligence.

In a Lebanonized Soviet Union, resorting to armed force is to be expected, and there is no guarantee that it would be directed only against internal opponents. Poles, Iranians, Ukranians, Germans, to mention but a few immediate neighbors, as well as Americans, are inescapably interested in knowing about any Russian military preparations against anyone, including other Russians.

Consider first a possible war between the Russian armed forces and the KGB. There are ample material and psychological bases for such a war. Since 1917 the KGB (under a half-dozen previous names) has been the principal means of coercion in Soviet society. It ran the Gulag, carried out the purges, and starved, shot, and otherwise killed some 40 million human beings.* Its Third Directorate, which controlled and purged the armed forces on behalf of the Communist party, is particularly hated by military officers. At the height of its power the KGB had some 400,000 uniformed troops, armed with tanks and aircraft, including the "black beret" troops that drove over civilians in Lithuania in 1991

---

*R.J. Rummel, in his book *Lethal Politics*, documents that the number of murders attributable to the Soviet regime ranges from a minimum of 28 million to maximum of 127 million with the most probable number being about 57 million. The precise figures are less important than the fact that there is hardly a family in Eurasia without a grudge.

as well as the "Alpha force" that carried out the Afghan coup of 1979. After August 1991 the bulk of these troops, the border guards, were transfered to the Army. The location and allegiance of units specially trained to deal with internal challenges to power and, in the last resort, to put down revolts within the military is of the utmost interest. In the pre–1991 Soviet system, the KGB was perhaps the foremost center of power and social privilege. It is surely the base on which Yuri Andropov and his protégé Mikhail Gorbachev rested their power. But the KGB is also the most hated of institutions in Soviet society, and in the 1990s it sat inescapably in the line of the rest of society's fire. It was easy to foresee any number of incidents in the 1990s—a crippling strike by railroad workers, an attempt to crush ethnic separatists, a fight between authorities of the Russian Republic and the central bureaucracy—that might start such a war. Army troops would be likely to side against the central bureaucracy, while the KGB would support it. The armed forces might also fight to wrest nuclear weapons from the KGB's control while the KGB might try to wrest the launch systems from the armed forces' control. Then of course there is the possiblity that any ethnic group, or subgroup, might fight another. As in Lebanon, it is impossible to tell which other wars one war will spawn.

It is important to know the people and the organizations that might coalesce as opponents, as well as to keep track of changing war aims and tactics. Knowledge of each side's character should be the basis of U.S. decisions about whom to favor. Should the U.S. decide to tip the balance in favor of either side in such wars, possession of satellite intelligence about troop deployments would allow the U.S. to pass information to one side or the other. Also, possession of intelligence about how the war might threaten, say, neighboring Iran or Sweden would allow the timely building of international coalitions to protect them.

As of 1991, *pace* the conventional wisdom in Washington, it was clear that intelligence about the Soviet military would be as important in the future as it had been in the past, for the sufficient reason that even as the Soviet regime (not to mention the Soviet economy) was collapsing, the Soviet military's superiority in relation to the rest of the world's armed forces had not disappeared. While military production throughout the Western countries had declined steadily since 1985, and the U.S. military budget had dropped some 15 percent over that period, and while in 1991 the only discussion in the U.S. was about how much lower the next drop would be, in the Soviet Union production of nearly all military goods was hovering at several times that in the U.S., and in most cases above the levels of all NATO countries combined.[2] Even if all military production had ceased in 1991—which it did not—Soviet military equipment was enough to overawe the world for years to come. The Soviet military seemed to be on autopilot, insulated from the regime's crash, and waiting for some authority, any authority, that would make use of it.

Throughout the 1980s the balance between the U.S. and the Soviet Union as regards the equipment that "covers" all military missions, namely long-range missiles and antimissile devices, continued to shift in the Soviet Union's favor. Whereas in 1980 the Soviet Union had about 4,000 warheads possessing the combination of nuclear yield and accuracy to destroy the United States' (roughly) 2,000 missiles, bombers, missile-carrying submarines, and command centers (a ratio of 2 to 1), by 1990 the Soviet Union had some 7,000 such warheads, for a ratio of 3.5 to 1, and U.S. cutbacks were continuing to raise this ratio. In other words, while the Soviet Union's purely military options against the West had shrunk in some respects—conventional forces—they had expanded as regards the "queens" or "trump cards" of modern war, namely strategic missile forces and anti-missile devices. Indeed these forces were the only truly world class assets that the communist regime bequeathed to its successors.

Although it is a grave error to reduce military questions to ones of Sovietology, whether or not "the Russians" will "come" or whither they will go is primarily a political question. In any case the most interesting questions about Soviet political and military matters can be plumbed to their depths only through intelligence. Soviet military options were such that any reasonable human being would want to have as much advance knowledge as possible of whether whoever controlled Soviet military forces had decided to use them. Any reasonable military strategist would also want a plethora of details about these forces, in order to maximize his chances of dealing with them successfully.

The Soviet Intelligence and Security Services
Circa 1990 the balance of power *within* the KGB shifted from the Second Chief Directorate (internal security) to the First Chief Directorate (foreign espionage). The First Chief Directorate had nearly quadrupled in personnel during the previous 15 years, and its long-time leader, Vladimir Kryuchkov, took his top management team with him when he became head of the entire KGB in 1989. Kryuchkov was close to Mikhail Gorbachev both personally and politically. Christopher Andrew and Oleg Gordievsky called both men "realists."[6]

Perhaps Gorbachev valued the KGB's successes abroad. By 1990 every indication (see Chapter 4) was that the KGB was doing better than ever at acquiring Western technology. Indeed, because by 1990 the perception of the Soviet Union as a threat had declined in the West, access by Soviets—and hence by the KGB—to Western societies had increased dramatically. Seven to ten thousand KGB professionals were now abroad at any one time (some three and one-half times the number of CIA officers abroad), in addition to the Eastern European officers, many of whom (for all practical purposes) joined the KGB after their countries changed regimes.[7] Within the U.S., there were perhaps

1,500 identifiably Soviet KGB officers, and possibly several dozen KGB officers who managed to pass themselves off as Americans. The KGB's covert-action campaigns abroad were prospering too. While the Soviet regime was running up the white flag of surrender with regard to its economic and political principles, and eagerly sought not just help but also advice from the West on how to reform itself, the KGB stepped up its covert attempts to portray the West, especially the U.S., in monstrously unfavorable terms—as international purveyors of the AIDS virus and slaughterers of South American babies for organ banks. Given that some of the Soviets traveling to the West ostensibly for advice on how to dismantle communism have been close to the KGB all their lives, it is clear that the KGB was spearheading the regime's effort to make the western world into a pillar of support for itself while nevertheless maintaining enmity toward it.

Just as clearly Mikhail Gorbachev increased the KGB's importance *within* the Soviet regime (not that it had ever been small). Established on December 20, 1917 for the "revolutionary settling of accounts with counterrevolutionaries," the KGB was the *sine qua non* of the regime. Without the terror sown by Feliks Dzerzhinsky's "men in black leather jerkins"—the estimates of murders in the first year *start* at a quarter-million[8]—the regime would never have established itself. Without the KGB's collectivization campaigns, which cost at least 20 million lives, the Soviet regime would not have taken on its fully totalitarian character. During most of the regime the KGB was the principal management tool of the Party leadership. The fact that it often worked through other state institutions—e.g., the Armed Forces' Main Political Directorate or the Interior Ministry—cloaked but did not detract from its power. In the late 1980s, as the regime's vitality ebbed along with its control over society, the KGB became the principal prop of the regime's old age. By 1990 there was no doubt that the KGB had become the most significant institution in the regime. Mikhail Gorbachev ordered it (even as Lenin had) to force the state's products (especially food) into the state's distribution system. A KGB general, Boris Pugo, took over the Interior Ministry, and KGB troops took charge of the streets. Much as in the case of the Praetorian Guard of the Roman emperors, it became difficult to tell whether the KGB served the Soviet dictator or the other way around. In July 1991, one month before the KGB was to exercise its Praetorian option on him, Mikhail Gorbachev introduced Kryuchkov to the President of the United States as the guarantor of his regime and its commitments.

Relations between KGB and military units became more important than ever. Historically the KGB's Third Directorate, which controlled the Soviet armed forces, was especially careful to infiltrate and dominate the military intelligence service, the GRU—and always to know what was on the minds of military leaders. Even more important to the KGB was the allegiance of the various militarized police forces in the country. Thus it thoroughly infiltrated those attached to the Ministry of the Interior. In the end, though, the KGB relied on its own. Of these the most fearsome and most reliable was the Alpha force, of Afghanistan fame.

The survivors of the eight-man junta who, on August 19, 1991, set aside the vacillating Mikhail Gorbachev and set about to destroy the chief threat to the Soviet regime, the freely elected government of the Russian Republic, will dispute who among them was the leader. But there can be no mistaking what they chiefly relied on: The Alpha force of the KGB would be the spearhead of some 15,000 special troops who would have killed Boris Yeltsin and his entourage as well as other elected officials throughout Russia. But, to Kryuchkov's surprise, the Alpha force refused his orders. In Leningrad, the militarized police of the Ministry of the Interior obeyed its local chief and supported the democratically elected mayor, an ally of Yeltsin. The junta collapsed as it sought shelter under Gorbachev's irremediably clipped wings, Kryuchkov was arrested, Boris Yeltsin emerged as the most powerful figure in the empire, and Yeltsin appointed Vadim Bakatin to head the KGB with a mandate to reform it.

What Bakatin meant to do with the KGB, and whether or not he would succeed, was not clear. It was clear only that 280 million people would stand a chance of dismantling the Soviet Union only to the extent that they dismantled the very thing that had held it together. The list of questions was as long as it was obvious: Would the new government try eventually to rid itself of everyone in the KGB? Could it? If it did not try, would the old guard be a reservoir of subversion within the new Russia? Why would the new government want to keep *any* remnant of the KGB? Against which domestic enemies does it wish to use it? Which foreign countries does the new government regard as threats? Does the new government intend to inherit the Soviet Union's role as the global enemy of the United States, does it wish to adopt it in a milder vein, or will it utterly reject it?

Over the years, perhaps decades, before the Russian Revolution of 1991 produces its definitive results, personages from throughout the former Soviet Union will present themselves to the West in a variety of ways which may or may not represent the truth. The West has one reliable way of checking: Find out what the personage's relationship is to the old KGB or to the new Russian intelligence service and, of course, find out what that service's agenda is. These certainly are classic tasks of intelligence and counterintelligence.

Soviet Politics

Up to 1989 the rigid structure of the Communist party defined the role of every individual in society. Thus politics in the Soviet Union, although hidden by the inaccessibility of its top participants, was relatively easy to infer. At the top of the CPSU, politburo members struggled for primacy by acquiring the right to hire and fire chunks of the Party and governmental apparatus below them. Subordinate officials would try to do the same thing in turn with respect to their subordinates, while trying to retain as much autonomy as possible with regard to their patrons and protectors. That this was a latter-day feudal system was never clearer than when Mikhail Gorbachev began to dismantle it. In December 1986, when Gorbachev replaced Dinmukahmed Kunayev, the Party chief of Kazakhstan, with an ethnic Russian more responsive to the Center, riots involving hundreds of thousands of people shook Kazakhstan's capital, Alma Ata. Why? Because Kunayev's replacement had disrupted the network through which the entire region's patronage and privileges had flowed. This system, broken beyond repair by 1989, *was not replaced by any other*. In its attempts to take control of the country the Center resorted more and more to self-defeating means. In 1991 the Center collapsed. But the feudal bonds that held 280 million people from Minsk to Vladivostok remained. The system's manifold well-armed dukes and privileged baronets were on their own. The fate of each, how long the people would have to live with the rubble of the old system, and what would replace it were difficult questions that interested the whole world.

When Mikhail Gorbachev took power in 1985 he apparently thought that the deteriorating economy, the growing sullenness of the population, and the increasingly unresponsive party apparatus could be set right by a campaign of discipline, including showy purges of bureaucrats. But Gorbachev vastly overestimated the reservoir of goodwill for the regime among the population, and was driven to more and more radical attempts to secure the population's assent to his rule and support for his purges. Like his predecessors (and like tyrants in general), he threw the burden for the people's horrid lives onto his colleagues and predecessors, and asked common people to criticize them. Criticism of the Party would make it easier for Gorbachev to fire unresponsive apparatchiks and replace them with his own. But Gorbachev overdid it. At first this criticism, *glasnost*, could only be practiced, as it were, with a license and against specific targets. But it got out of hand; people acquired the habit of telling the truth. Hence, in the process of purging the Communist party and seizing power over it, he destroyed its authority. He had gained undisputed possession of the best cabin on the Titanic. He built representative institutions at all levels of society, but gave them only the power to talk. He tried to protect the authority of the KGB, the armed forces, and the government, and indeed in a series of constitutional changes he replaced the dictatorship of the Communist party with the dictatorship of the organs of control. But once the people were free to talk they quickly lumped these institutions with the Party.

The communist nobles, the so-called Nomenklatura, found themselves in a quandary. They held all the wealth and privilege in the land. They held the guns. But, especially after the East European revolutions of 1989, they dared not shoot at the angry waves of people who would sack their privileged stores and shout abuse at them, at workers on strike, or at conscripts who refused induction. The few occasions on which the government used a little violence against anticommunist forces (Tiblisi, Georgia in 1989; Baku, Azerbaijan in 1990; and Lithuania in 1991) convinced its leaders that while a little would not be enough to quell the spirit of rebellion, a lot would be the equivalent of shooting inside a munitions bunker. Moreover, ever since the late 1980s more and more of the Nomenklatura had begun to hedge their lives' bets. By 1990 there were popularly elected mayors in Moscow and Leningrad, as well as leaders of various republics—above all, Russia's Boris Yeltsin—who were ready to take advantage of any missteps the government might make. Many of these people, whom the government regarded as traitors, were very much *inside* the Communist party. With one foot on the government side and another in some sort of opposition, these members of the Nomenklatura were better equipped to face the future than those at the very top.

By 1991 those at the top, other than Mikhail Gorbachev, were high officials of the "organs of control"—the KGB, the Army, and the Ministry of the Interior. Their agenda was quite simply to preserve the Soviet Union by some sort of violent crackdown on the opposition. By mid-1991 the Soviet mass media were back under control. But the freely elected Yeltsin was the nub of the problem. Gorbachev's indecision with regard to this problem was the occasion for his "organs of control" to take over on August 19, 1991. When the "organs'" leaders failed to muster an armed force willing and able to storm the Russian parliament (and some Soviet units that had come to its defense), their fate was sealed and so was Gorbachev's. The leaders of the coup had been the only domestic constituency he had left. Not Gorbachev, but Gorbachev's main competitor, Yeltsin, had defeated them. After August 1991 Gorbachev represented nothing that anybody wanted. He had been truly the last Soviet man.

The revolution, however, was just beginning. None of the Nomenklatura made any efforts to stop crowds from toppling statues of Lenin. Indeed in Azerbaijan, the Ukraine, Kazakhstan, the communist presidents of Union republics declared independence from Moscow and tried to present themselves as nationalists. Azerbaijan's president, Ayaz Mutalibov, called a snap election and got himself elected democratically. There was every chance that these men had noted the success of Serbia's President Slobodan Milosevic in causing his people to forget that he is a communist, to tolerate his and his friends' rule, by waging war against neighboring nationalities. The Soviet Nomenklatura's strategy was obvious: Change labels and adopt causes as required, become a nationalist or a technocrat, make whatever alliances may be required, but hang on to power and privilege. In the absence of a serious campaign to find and root communist careerists out of positions of power and privilege, these people stood a good chance of "ruling from below" for a generation.

The Soviet economy had never been an adequate provider of goods and services. By 1985 per capita consumption of meat had not risen above the level of 1913, the last prewar year under the Tzar. But the Soviet economy had worked reasonably well for 70 years as a producer of social control and as a dispenser of favor. It might have continued to do so indefinitely had Gorbachev, beginning in 1986, not radically decreased jailings for "economic crimes," had he not allowed a limited free market which drained materials and labor from the official economy, and had he not filled the air with officious blessings for "change." So from circa 1987 on, a chronic economic malaise became an acute degenerative disease. Food and other goods disappeared from the state's distribution system as state enterprises and private individuals appropriated what they could and exchanged it as best they could outside the state's control. This was not so much a collapse of economic life—people still worked and ate—as an abandonment of the Soviet economic system, a very real, if very unofficial, privatization.

Even prior to the collapse of the center in August 1991, the world's press was full of "plans" for restructuring the Soviet polity and reforming the Soviet economy. Western governments yearned for the chance to send billions of dollars. Western economists flooded the East with advice. There was no shortage of Soviets eager to act as conduits of Western money and prestige. But the fundamental fact of political and economic life in revolutionary Russia, Ukraine, et al. was precisely that nothing had been settled beyond the smashing of old symbols and a top-level purge. The new rulers of Russia and the other republics had yet to decide to what extent and in what ways they wanted to preserve or extinguish the old regime's baronies. Considering that there were scarcely any power bases in the country except these baronies, and that innumerable ties of friendship and interest bound these leaders to them, these would be difficult choices. In practice, plans for the future would have to wait. In the meanwhile, every decision by a Western nation to give any aid, or pursue any initiative, through any particular person in the former Soviet Union would inevitably strengthen some and weaken others in their struggles to deal with the past and build the future.

Everything is possible in the former Soviet Union—the annihilation of enmity to the West or the successor regime's assumption of the Soviet Union's old role as the chief threat to peace. Free and productive societies may result as easily as a kind of morass dominated by interest groups left over from the former regime. Russia could grow into the West, or stagnate as the "India of the North." Peace amongst diverse peoples is as possible as war. Everything depends on which people and what agendas predominate. Naturally, discovering just what may be the agenda and connections of any given actor on the Russian political scene will require digging beneath his press releases, while understanding the facts thus gathered will require analysis. In sum, revolutionary Eurasia had become an underfed, overarmed, underscruped continent that, while it offered hope in the long run, could affect the world in the short run only through its surplus of awesome weapons and desperate men. Intelligence would be essential for monitoring the communist compost pile, and for dealing with the very powerful, very noxious elements that might come out of it.

Europe

In the early 1990s the world finally learned how unfounded (or at least how premature) had been the obituaries of Europe's importance. In 1990 Europe began to deal with an agenda that had been overshadowed since the 1930s by the onslaught of communist and National Socialist totalitarianism—namely, European integration. World War I had destroyed, probably forever, European nation–states as entities that inspired the near-religious devotion of the educated classes. So, in the 1920s, even as state-worship flourished in Germany and Italy under the impulse of half-educated Fascists, young German and French technocrats (the most prominent of whom was Jean Monnet) began to plan for a European common market and for political harmonization. After the holocaust of World War II, the most ardent supporters of these ideas became the leaders of their countries: Robert Schumann in France, Konrad Adenauer in Germany, and Alcide de Gasperi in Italy. All were from the border areas of their countries, and all were conservative Catholics. They established the Council of Europe, the Western European Union, and the Coal and Steel Community, and fathered the European Economic Community—a long process intended to complete economic integration of Europe by January 1, 1993.

Moderate socialists such as Monnet and Jacques Delors have been mainstays of economic Europeanism. But the political element of European integration was always held back by the existence of a strong left-wing socialist tendency in Germany, and to a lesser extent throughout Europe, that put good relations with the ruling Communist parties of the East ahead of a European integration. In 1949, the looming united Europe seemed to Kurt Schumacher, Germany's Socialist leader, "clerical, conservative, capitalist, and creating a monopoly." Besides, there hung over any Western European arrangement the ominous possibility that an eventual reunification of Germany would wreck it all. But in 1989–90 the Communist parties of Eastern Europe collapsed into tiny rump groups, left-wing socialists in the West reduced their involvement in international affairs, and Germany was reunified within the framework that Adenauer had envisioned. This put on the table all the questions about the future of Europe that had been simmering since the 1920s, and did so for Eastern as well as Western Europe.

But the answers to these questions were by no means self evident. The biggest of all concerned Germany. Public opinion polls in 1990 showed that even though Germans did not question their country's growing integration in "Europe," perhaps a plurality wanted their country to be disarmed and unconnected with the international projects of any other nation—in short, as Joachim Maitre put it, "to drop out of the game." There surely was no will at all in Germany to be responsible for great things in the world. Nevertheless, there was a very widespread desire to have an unspecified "special relationship" with the East. Involvement without responsibility raised the possibility that Germany might be party to the struggles of others.

As Adenauer had pointed out, Germany's size and location made it impossible for it to be neutral. If it were weak it would be the plaything of Russia and the West, while if it were strong it would, as in Bismarck's time, be a heavy object sliding from side to side on the European balance, with bad consequences for all. That is one of the reasons why Adenauer wanted to integrate Germany with Western Europe. But most German socialists early in the 1990s, although they did not want a divorce from Western Europe, demanded the right to have extramarital liaisons with the East. Hence there was every reason for Westerners to fear that Germany might be a conduit for economic or military aid to this or that Russian faction, or that it might be tempted into a new Rapallo. Of course there was also every reason to hope that a united Germany would help to fulfill the European dreams of Schumann, Adenauer, and de Gasperi.

What path *would* Germany choose? For the U.S. that question touched on nothing less than the very reasons why it entered two world wars and kept a million military dependents on the European continent for half a century. Quite starkly, Germany's choices could spell either victory or defeat for what had become quite literally the secular goal of U.S. foreign policy.

To monitor Germany's choice, foreigners could not count simply on observation of its overt actions. As we shall see, it is a rule of thumb that to use intelligence on free countries, especially friendly ones, is both wasteful and inappropriate. Yet even free democratic countries sometimes hide important things from their friends. Thus in the 1960s, 1970s, and 1980s, West Germany never revealed even to its partners in the Common Market—who had both a financial and a political stake in the matter—how much money or by what means it was giving to communist governments in the East. In the 1980s, West Germany never revealed to its NATO allies its cooperation with the Libyans and Iraqis, who were respectively building plants for the production of poison gases and nuclear reagents. These matters were so hotly disputed by Germans themselves that all agreed to shut their allies out of their domestic debates. In the

1990s, Germans are sure to guard ever more jealously their concrete decisions with regard to the holders of Russian military power, and to various Eastern suitors of its own economic involvement. Only through intelligence may interested foreigners obtain timely understanding of how Germany is throwing its considerable weight around Europe.

In addition, the Germany of the 1990s is full of people (Easterners as well as Westerners) who had served as agents of East German intelligence, and whose past renders them vulnerable to blackmail. The German government does not seem to want to know how deeply it had been penetrated, and wants to sweep an unpleasant past under the rug. This means that other governments will be dealing with at least some Germans who—willingly or under duress—may be hostile agents. It will be impossible to understand Germans adequately without secret insights into their secret world.

Intelligence, too, will be required to understand how the formerly communist countries of Eastern Europe are developing. After all, each of those countries bequeathed to Europe many thousands of people for whom fighting Western interests had been the highest point of their lives, and who might continue to serve hostile governments or organized crime either for money or because of blackmail. What, if any, roles would such people play into the twenty-first century? A *priori* one might hypothesize that some would act as agents for Russian factions, and perhaps broker Russian influence. So intelligence would be necessary to understand the extent of their influence. Early in the 1990s the lands of the former Soviet empire aspired to full membership in "Europe," and people therefrom presented themselves as anticommunist. Only a few might be expected to be hostile agents. Many more might have retained some of the conpiratorial style of communist politics and be serving who-knows-what agenda. Things in Eastern Europe will not always be as they appear. This is essential to remember as the U.S. considers how the countries of Eastern Europe manage their relationships with Russia. Vast reservoirs of anti-Russian and anticommunist feelings cannot be expected wholly to overcome the need for these countries to somehow accommodate Russian power. But they can be expected to push such accommodations into secret channels.

Indeed, much in Eastern Europe will remain murky. At the threshold of the 1990s the dismantling of socialism had hardly begun. Most people were still employed in state-owned enterprises, were still turning out low-quality goods, and were still consuming similar goods made by their neighbors. More importantly, the formerly communist countries had not begun to establish either property rights or nondiscriminatory access to business and professional success. In sum, people in those countries lived dependent lives. In such situations the meaning of politics is to be found where people's privileges are won or lost—that is, below the surface. Answers to the most important question in politics ("Who is he, and where is he coming from?") would have to be pursued by investigating people's connections, not just with political parties and factions but also with various interests, both domestic and foreign. The fact that the fortunes of individuals in the semidependent states of Eastern Europe can be determined by foreigners who pick them as intermediaries means that the potential for intrigue and disorder—historically high in those countries—may be higher than ever. When dealing with the "sick man of Europe," there will be no substitute for human intelligence.

China and East Asia

The 1990s were even likelier to bring civil war to China than to Russia. When Chinese army tanks literally crushed the students who had been demanding democracy in Beijing's Tienanmen Square in 1989, only superficial observers (including the U.S. government) concluded that the Communist party had reimposed control. In fact, the 1980s had seen a decline in the Communist party greater than that which occurred in the Soviet Union. Throughout this period, Deng Xiao Ping made and unmade Party Secretaries at will. He did so from his power base as head of the Defense Council (Gorbachev himself was to shift his base to the Defense Council at the end of the 1980s). Deng and his group had used the Party as a tool for governing. But by May and June 1989 Deng was receiving requests from the Party that he allow it to move toward democracy.

When Deng sent the army to Tienanmen Square, he did it as much to control the Party as to crush the students. However, when the army went in, it openly took upon itself a brand-new, supervisory role in domestic politics. After June 1989 the army became the not-so-shadowy government of China, and the Party became its front. But, of necessity, that government became regional and local, with army commanders increasingly assuming the role held by warlords in former times, and army officers deeply involved in business. Early in the 1990s the various regional commands were even collecting tolls or tariffs on goods entering their jurisdiction. But the army itself had not become totally regionalized. This mixture of local army power with the presence of nonlocal army elements virtually ensured that any major social disruption would result in clashes *between* Chinese troops. Tienanmen Square would prove to be the last occasion when the Chinese army acted united.

A warlords' China at the turn of the twenty-first century must interest the U.S. just as it did at the turn of the twentieth century. Vacuums of power and civil wars alike draw foreign involvement. The Japanese and Russians have been drawn into China before under such circumstances, and might be again. The means (and above all the ends) of such involvement are seldom scrutable except through intelligence. It is fruitless to speculate what such involvement may bring. But it makes much sense to understand it both from the Chinese perspective and from that of the potentially intervening powers.

Except for likely involvement in China and Siberia, the future of Japan should be scrutable without resort to secret collection. Japan is an open, democratic nation, and it ill suits Americans to conjure up the image of a "yellow peril" that may somehow impoverish the United States through "unfair" economic competition, and toward the monitoring of which U.S. intelligence should devote major attention. Just as democratic politics must be understood in terms of the decisions of millions of voters rather than in terms of the cabals of a few, economic affairs cannot be understood in terms of industrial espionage and clever schemes to capture markets. Economic espionage—e.g., Japanese securities firms that obtain information on U.S. Treasury auctions by hiring well-connected ex-employees of the Federal Reserve—can make individuals rich. But its effect on nations is marginal. Economic success or failure depends on the capacity of companies to produce items that millions of consumers will freely choose over competing products. Japan may or may not become wealthier than America in the long run. But so long as its instruments are economic, it must get that wealth the old-fashioned way—earning it by providing goods and services that Americans and others prefer. Economic success depends on the education of the labor force and the wisdom of management. To believe that it depends in any substantial way on intelligence is both ignorant and unwise.[9]

Might danger arise from Japan? It might, in the same way that it might from Germany. Just as Germans cannot help but become involved in Eastern Europe and Russia, Japan must surely become deeply involved in Siberia, China, and Southeast Asia. In the 1990s the world's second largest economic power would no longer be encumbered by memories of a lost war. The ends and means of that involvement will be openly debated. Beyond that, any Japanese moves in Asia and the Pacific that might threaten the U.S. would first appear as *political* arrangements (with governments or factions in the area) that the Japanese might try to keep secret from Americans. Thus the best early-warning system that the U.S. might devise, other than sensitive attention to open developments in Japanese society and politics, is likely to be knowledge of the intelligence services of whoever controls Vladivostok, Manchuria, Vietnam, the Philippines, and the like, as well as of Japan itself. While spying on allies is almost as bad an idea as spying on democratic countries in general, spying on intelligence services (i.e., counterintelligence) is usually in order.

In sum, at the turn of the twenty-first century, East Asians in general will be either wealthy or eager to imitate their wealthy neighbors, and very much ready for fundamental political change. For Americans, physical and electronic access to the region should pose few if any problems. But, as we will see below (Chapter 5), Americans will have very serious problems understanding what they see and hear.

Mexico and Latin America

What happens in Mexico is of more immediate importance to Americans than what happens in Europe or Asia. Since the Mexican War of 1848 the U.S. has not had to live with a hostile border. The prospect that the Mexican border might become hostile led President Lincoln to threaten war against France, and helped President Wilson to lead America into World War I. It is no exaggeration to say that America's willingness and capacity to involve itself overseas depends substantially on the enjoyment of friendly borders. By the 1990s, the border itself had become a swath hundreds of miles wide in which people from both sides blended inextricably. The prospect of a U.S.–Mexican free-trade agreement only speeded up the human contacts. Moreover, by about the year 2010, perhaps one out of ten Americans will be of recent Mexican origin and will reflect to some extent whatever developments occur in Mexico. Since Mexican politics was not about to become democratic—and indeed since Mexico contains several semisovereign fiefdoms within its government as well as semisovereign drug enterprises within its borders—intelligence would continue to prove essential to understand what events in Mexico might mean to the U.S.

By 1990, 42 percent of Mexico's 90 million population were under 15 years of age. Just over half the population lived in slum-shackled cities. Mexico City had become the largest city in the world (14 million), overflowing the Valley of Mexico. Since the 1920s the country had been ruled by the Institutionalized Revolutionary Party (PRI) a self-selected group who legitimized their power by staging fixed elections, who ruled by co-opting all who would be co-opted, and who beat up or killed those who refused. The PRI had once been led by able politicians who had sunk deep roots in labor, business, education, etc. But in the 1970s control of the Party had passed to university-trained apparatchiks. They tended to split along ideological lines: some, like the followers of Jose Lopez Portillo (1975–1982) and Cuauhtemoc Cardenas, were socialists, while others, like Carlos Salinas de Gortari (1988–1994), were free-market liberals. At the same time, much of northern Mexico was being effectively assimilated into the American way of life, and millions of young Mexicans were simply going to live in America. Clearly, in the 1990s, Mexico was going to change radically. But how?

The Eurasian revolutions of 1989–91 reduced the influence of the left on Mexican developments. The desire to enlist the rest of the world in an anti-American struggle had always been a large part of the Mexican left's mentality. In the 1980s some leftists desirous of stopping the liberal pro-American trends in the country, heartened by the nearby presence of communist Cuba and pressed by an expansive communist Nicaragua to the south, dreamed of a coup against their PRI rivals, and of governing Mexico with support from the Soviet Union. But in 1990 the communist Nicaraguan regime fell, and Cuba's Castro became stranded when the Soviet Union collapsed. So the Mexican left was thrown back entirely on its own resources. Moreover, President Salinas worked effectively to reduce those resources, arresting some of the country's leading labor and administrative figures for enjoying what had once been the bread and butter of the PRI: using state funds and property to build private clienteles and private armies. Nevertheless, the patronage beneficiaries of the PRI's left wing knew very well that the transformation of Mexico into a free-market system governed by fair elections would destroy their livelihoods. Given Mexico's custom that every President hand-picks his successor, the Mexican left's obvious path was to organize the PRI bureaucracy against the President (no easy task) while organizing possibly violent "mass support" for their moves among their impoverished clientele. President Salinas' evident determination promised that he would succeed—unless something like a coup stopped him.

Thus Mexican politics early in the 1990s promised either to turn Mexico into a better neighbor for the U.S. than ever, or to convulse it into civil strife, the only good feature of which would be its lack of international connections. Since developments in Mexico would depend substantially on nonpublic activities by Mexican politicians, it would be essential for the U.S., or indeed for anyone else who tried to understand them, to employ the techniques of intelligence.

Intelligence would also be needed to deal on the retail level with the consequences of greater turmoil in Mexico. No doubt some of the protagonists of civil strife would try to build support for their cause north of the border, and perhaps violently to neutralize opponents there. Civil strife, or an unfriendly regime, may also increase the flow of illegal drugs across the border. That flow is controlled by groups of growers and traffickers who are outside the government's control, in part because they exercise influence within it—much as with Italy's mafia.

We do not mean to imply that even outstanding intelligence on Mexico or Latin America could somehow "fix" America's drug problem. Even if the flow of illegal drugs into the U.S. were stopped completely, those Americans intent on altering their mental state would turn to domestic synthetic drugs. Intelligence would help the U.S. not so much to kick its drug habit as it would to monitor the political effects of the drug trade on Mexico and Latin America. These effects have been great. Colombia, for example, is a country with a GNP of $40 billion into which foreign drug customers have poured some $15 billion per year. The impact of this money has been proportionate to what almost $2 *trillion* would do if placed in the hands of organized crime cartels in the United States. It is a tribute to the decency of the Colombian people that they have not succumbed entirely to this foreign-financed cancer. Nevertheless, going into the 1990s Colombia had to be understood not so much in terms of electoral politics as of the relationship between the private armies of the two main drug cartels, the private armies of two leftist guerrilla movements that finance themselves through drug profits, and public officials (the foremost question about whom was their possible relationship to drug money). Colombia in the early 1990s had not succumbed entirely, as had Panama in the 1980s. But in the 1990s the drug billions would continue to finance the establishment of armed centers of power throughout northern Latin America that at the very least would be independent of governments, but in most cases nevertheless would influence them. So long as some Americans continue to finance the drug lords, the U.S. government will have no alternative but to try to understand the shadowy, violent worlds that they helped to create on our doorstep.

The Middle East

The United States' interests in this region remained unaltered heading into the 1990s. But while political geology changes very slowly in this part of the world, its morphology changes as rapidly as the desert sands shift. This area remained vital because oil continued to be essential to both Western Europe and Japan. Because the Middle East is the geographic axis between Europe and Asia, control of its waterways by any hostile power from either outside the region or within (e.g., Iran or Iraq) immediately threatens the security of southern Europe and the oil lifelines to Japan. The security of the world's principal oil exports is the major reason why the U.S. risked war with the Soviet Union when it threatened Iran in 1946, and Israel in 1973. It is also why U.S. naval forces went into combat in the Persian Gulf in 1987 and 1988, and why in 1990–91 the U.S. staged by far the largest invasion that the region had ever experienced (though surely the briefest). It is also one of the main reasons why the U.S. supported the Afghan Mujahedeen against Soviet forces for ten years.

The Arab–Israeli conflict and the Gulf remained the two main foci of U.S. concerns. Throughout the area from the Gulf to Morocco, Islamic fundamentalism and political radicalization were on the rise as Western ways continued to lose prestige. But Islam offered no coherent principle of political life, and there were important differences and hostility among Islamic Shiites and Sunnis, as well as among Islamic nations. Military power itself became the organizing principle of life in the region.

In the 1980s, as Iran and Iraq bled one another, Syria had emerged as a significant military power in the Arab world, thanks to massive infusions of Soviet armaments. But by the end of the decade, Russia's self-absorption reduced Syria's international cover, its supply of spare parts, and hence its power. In the 1990s two nations could be counted on to dominate the area militarily—Israel and Iraq. The Iraqis had both the means and the will to replace Saudi Arabia as the arbiter of Gulf affairs. The Israelis had the military capability to prevent any one Arab state from dominating the region, but lacked any political way of pursuing that goal. Only the U.S. would have those means in the 1990s, as before.

Politically, the basic institutions in the region would be unlikely to change. Outside of Israel, most of the area's states have been ruled by authoritarian elites influenced by transnational forces. Diverse Palestinian, Islamic, Marxist–Leninist, and even Westernized elements have crossed national boundaries and jockeyed for influence with military governments. In most states, power has remained, and could be expected to remain, in the hands of a single ruler backed by military and security services.

So the military and security services must be key determinants of the outcome of the struggle for power both within the states of the region and in the region as a whole. Much depends on where the military and security elites were trained. The Egyptian, Saudi, Turkish, and Omani military and security services, having been trained (and equipped) by the U.S. and Britain, will be well disposed to the West, while Syrians and Iraqis will be otherwise oriented. The Israelis, of course, are very close to the U.S., and have enjoyed a working relationship with Egypt since the early 1980s. Yet the security services and the military in most of the region are inherently suspicious of the U.S. (as indeed of most outsiders). By any measure, the politics of the region will be as conspiratorial, as opaque to surface scrutiny, as requiring of secret intelligence, as any politics anywhere in the world at any other time in history. But the Middle East will be less accessible to Western intelligence throughout the 1990s than ever before.

The Middle East gave the world the first major politico–military conflict of the 1990s—and intelligence (as we again will see in Chapter 7) played a major role in it. On August 2, 1990 Iraq invaded Kuwait, seizing its money and oil. By so doing Iraq made itself the dominant military power in the Persian Gulf, and put itself in the position of dictating the world's price for oil. Overnight the world faced the nightmare of the 1970s: an enemy in control of the world's oil tap. Only the identity of the enemy was different. After the Gulf War of 1990–91 the Mid-East was more disorderly than it had ever been, and no source of order was on the horizon. American firepower had destroyed much of Iraq's military hardware, but Iraq's dictator, Saddam Hussein, retained enough to crush popular rebellions against his regime. His ferocity helped to restore a bit of the prestige that he had gained by standing up to the United States for six months, and oil revenues soon began to bolster his regime in other ways. In a nutshell, although Saddam's ambitious plans had suffered a serious setback, he remained the driving force in the region. Worse, Saddam's strategy remained viable.

That strategy had been nothing less than to take advantage of the Islamic masses' resentment against the super-rich royal families of the Persian Gulf, and their relationships with infidel foreigners, in order to gain something like leadership of the Islamic world. This strategy had two pillars: Iraq's military power, and the shaky political bases of regimes in the Islamic world. After the war those regimes proved none the firmer. Iraq or another dictatorial regime in the region can be counted on to try this strategy again as soon as it musters enough military power.

Intelligence will be indispensable to monitor the confused tickings of this time bomb. In Iraq, we were certain to see a replay of the process by which the German military outwitted the on-site inspectors who were trying to implement the disarmament provisions of the Treaty of Versailles—except of course that purchasing arms, which Iraq is likely to do, is much easier to conceal than manufacturing them, which is what Germany had to do, *and* except for the fact that modern arms are easier to conceal than those of the 1920s. Iraq appeared also sure to evade the UN's controls over its oil sales by selling (at some discount) through middlemen—therein another challenge to intelligence. But all these paled in comparison with the challenge of figuring out whether Iran or Syria was preparing to try to reap—albeit somewhat differently—the same prize for which Saddam reached. The basic conditions were there: Mobs ready to cheer those who promise them blood and booty, and target regimes who rely on the twin thin reeds of mercenaries in their own armies plus Western intervention. Perhaps early warning would make it possible to deal with such threats with less than a deployment of half a million men.

CAN U.S. INTELLIGENCE COPE?

Sound knowledge of a disorderly world, rather than faith in a trouble free, post-end-of-history "new world order," will best fit nations to thrive in the twenty-first century. However, U.S. intelligence was not equipped, either materially or in human terms, to cope with the challenges, or to exploit the opportunities, of the new century. Why not is a long story. As we tell it, we will enter a world delimited by the intellectual horizon of a particular generation and class of Americans who became entirely absorbed by the US–Soviet Cold War. We will lose sight of the principles of intelligence. But the checkered record compiled by American intelligence between 1947 and 1990 will naturally lead us to ask, "Does intelligence have to be done that way?" This in turn will lead to a deeper look at the principles of intelligence.

PART II

Why U.S. Intelligence Won't Do

3

Vain Spying

Not only can't they cheat on arms control—they can't even use the phone to cheat on their wives without our knowing it.

— A CIA "Old Boy"

We have never found anything that the Soviets have successfully hidden.

— Amrom Katz, Rand Corp.

Collection has taken up the vast bulk of the money that the U.S. has spent on intelligence. Occasionally, especially in the realm of technical spying, U.S. collectors have performed spectacular feats. Routinely refugees, defectors, U.S. diplomats, the world press, military intelligence, and foreign governments—including unfriendly ones—have given the U.S. a reasonable amount of information on the basis of which to conduct statecraft and plan military operations. On the whole, the U.S. has not suffered from a lack of facts. Yet the U.S. intelligence collection system has shed little light on the world's most important secrets.

Overt Spies

The CIA's Deputy Directorate for Plans (since renamed Deputy Directorate for Operations) set the tone for the CIA just as in Gen. William Donovan's wartime Office of Strategic Services (OSS)* the clandestine branches, Secret Intelligence (SI) and Special Operations (SO) had set the tone. In the CIA, as in the OSS, the clandestine services made little effort to be clandestine. By their nature, SO's activities were not clandestine at all (see Chapter 6). SI ran its spies primarily into Nazi-controlled Europe. The operatives who did this, from Allen Dulles to William Casey, were not "secret agents" because they did not work undercover. For example, when Allen Dulles set up shop in Bern in November 1942, a newspaper article announced his arrival and his function.[1]

Allen Dulles' and William Casey's "penetration" of Germany consisted of receiving reports from disaffected Germans, not of jumping into the Reich and seducing bureaucrats or cracking safes. The OSS did send Americans into German-occupied France. But these men—the "Jedburgh" teams—were in uniform, and were accompanied by Frenchmen who had good contacts with the Resistance.[2] They were more like scouts operating in advance of the U.S. armed forces than like today's popular image of intelligence officers. When Allied armies approached Germany itself, a variety of Germans, displaced persons, and prisoners of war volunteered to cross or be dropped behind the lines to fulfill the same role. Most OSS espionage agents were Frenchmen or Germans who were willing to rejoin family and friends in enemy-controlled territory, and send back such information as would be evident to any observant person in the area, or from traitors. These "agents" were close to the fighting fronts in both space and time. Their success in gathering sources, and their relevance to the war, were both low when they were far behind the lines, but increased dramatically as victorious American troops approached their area of operation. (By contrast, in the Far East, where no Japanese volunteered to supply information, the OSS was hardly in the espionage business.† The OSS certainly did not try to send American officers to Japan under assumed identities to tease out or steal information.)

Thus, the *idée fixe*, so powerful at CIA, of the gentleman spymaster who steals into the enemy's backyard and skillfully suborns traitorous moles in the enemy camp has no basis at all in the history of the real OSS. Real OSS

*OSS had also included a Research and Analysis Branch (R&A) which many in Washington thought more valuable than SI and SO. Some of R&A's leaders, and all of their outlook on intelligence, eventually ended up in CIA, where they struggled for the primacy of their point of view vis-à-vis the clandestine service. (See Ch. 5.) But during the early years of the CIA, just as in the OSS, research and analysis played second fiddle to the clandestine services.

†One rare exception was Operation RUTH in Bangkok. An OSS operative lived clandestinely in Japanese-controlled Bangkok and was fed reports from Thai officials on developments in Japan (by Thai officials in Japan).

spymasters, following the tradition of British intelligence, lived by the rule that they themselves should neither masquerade as natives nor steal documents, but rather that they themselves should recruit and manage the people who do such things. They expected that such people would seek them out. And why not? All their lives when these wealthy, powerful Anglo–Saxons had traveled abroad they had been thronged by people who wanted to deal with them. Hence, like the British, both OSS officers and their CIA "clandestine" successors have almost advertised their presence in the belief that "It's the walk-in trade that keeps the shop open." How would walk-ins know who the American intelligence officers were if they kept their identity secret? However, while OSS personnel in Italy or neutral countries occasionally strayed from this rule, adopted secret identities and became spies themselves, the CIA from the outset has been much stricter in separating the roles of case officer, the American full-time career employee of the CIA, and the agent—a foreigner whose "case" the officer manages, and who is paid to spy. The CIA clandestine image notwithstanding, the CIA case officer is a daggerless bureaucrat in bureaucrat's clothing. The agents wear the cloaks, and some have had daggers.

The Deputy Directorate of Operations (DDO) has always been organized much like the U.S. State Department, and CIA clandestine officers lead lives similar to those of Foreign Service officers. At CIA headquarters in suburban Langley, VA, the DDO is organized by geographic divisions (Africa, East Asia, Mid-East, etc.). The division chiefs supervise local branches, i.e., "country desks." These in turn supervise "stations" in each country in which the U.S. has an embassy. Each station has a chief, who serves directly under the U.S. ambassador. But the station chief runs a separate part of the embassy, and is primarily responsible to CIA headquarters. Almost like the ambassador or the captain of a ship at sea, he runs his own show.

The station chief is not a "spook" who spies while pretending to be a waiter, a businessman, or a butterfly collector. If he is not an outright public figure in the country to which he is accredited, he is almost always well-known for who he is in the host capital's social circles. Sometimes he develops a famous relationship with the chief of the host government, much to the envy of the U.S. ambassador. Thus, for example, in the 1960s station chief Ray Cline was famous in Taipei for his drinking bouts with Chiang Ching Quo. In 1976, however, station chief Richard Welch was assassinated in Athens after his name was published by an anti-CIA group in the U.S. But the two events were not necessarily related because Welch had been as public a figure as any other station chief.

The post of CIA station chief is prized because it entails gracious living, high-level contact with foreign intelligence chiefs, and the chance to direct the work of many case officers. To be a station chief is the culmination of a successful career, or the first step into the highest reaches of the CIA. With few exceptions, important officials in the DDO have been station chiefs, as has a high percentage of officials in other divisions of the CIA. Unlike intelligence services abroad, CIA does not co-opt into its top ranks people who had been successful in other professions. Rather, it believes that only career people can do the job. Two out of three career officers who rose to the post of Director of Central Intelligence — Richard Helms in 1964, and William Colby in 1973 — had been station chiefs.

To be a station chief in a given country a CIA officer need not speak either the language of that country or the language of the people his station is trying to recruit or run. Hugh Montgomery, station chief in Rome in the 1970s, was atypical in that he mastered not just Italian but several of its dialects. Few station chiefs get beyond receiving-line greetings, and most can't even do that. However, the chief must be able to fit in with the leading personages of the Directorate of Operations.

The case officers, like the station chief, are assigned to the embassy under "cover" as diplomats, or as the representatives of some other U.S. government agency. Like their chief, the case officers seldom are fluent in a foreign language. Unlike the chief, most case officers are not ostentatious about their CIA jobs. Like other embassy employees, they are supposed to overtly gather information on local politics, economics, etc. But while they are doing these things, and after hours as well, they are supposed to use their special training to spot, assess, and recruit secret sources of information. Occasionally they are supposed to "dry-clean" themselves — that is, make sure they are not being followed, melt into the local scene, and secretly meet with agents or pick up and leave messages for them.

Like other embassy officials, the case officers are transferred to different countries, or back to Washington, every few years. Only very rarely do they spend their entire career working on one country or subject matter. They are expected to be generalists whose skills are applicable almost anywhere in the world and to any subject matter from nuclear physics to labor relations.

In some countries many U.S. case officers are "declared" to the intelligence services of the host government. But even the undeclared ones usually become well-known. In the postwar world the State Department's policies made it relatively easy to "spot the spooks." Embassies have been staffed by local employees, who note who works in the few rooms off limits to them. The interpreters are especially well-positioned to tell who does what job. In addition, the State Department used to reserve specific designations for the CIA employees that it "covered," in order to preserve the title Foreign Service Officer (FSO) unsullied to designate its own cadre. Real FSOs are listed in the Department's "stud book." One need but compare embassy rosters — especially positions like "second secretary, political section" — with the "stud book." In the

1970s a whole rash of books and magazines appeared identifying many CIA officers by taking advantage of these bureaucratic distinctions.

A small and decreasing percentage of CIA case officers have served under nonofficial cover (NOC), as American businessmen, academics, or journalists. Because—for reasons of safety—the NOC program was always restricted to noncommunist countries, the U.S. did not have its most clandestine officers where it needed them most. NOC officers also suffered several hardships. They would have to work hard at their cover jobs but, like officers who lived in the indulgent climate of the embassy, they were judged on the number of reports they produced. Moreover, NOCs could not shop at embassy commissaries, buy cars at diplomatic discounts, or, of course, live in embassy housing. But they have been paid the same salaries as their "official cover" brethren. Add to this the fact that NOCs were looked down on at promotion time, and one can see why the NOC program at CIA withered.

The job of the CIA personnel abroad is to recruit and run agents. Whether the embassy is in South America, Europe, or Africa, CIA case officers have had Soviet, Chinese, and other communist (or "hard target") officials as their first priority. The recruitment of one Soviet agent was enough to make a case officer's career. Then came those people—mostly local communist officials— who were likely to have access to the Soviet or Chinese government. Then came the members of the power structure of local governments. Last, but not least, have been those with access to other people who may affect the lives of Americans, such as terrorists, drug traffickers, or leaders of private economic centers of power.

THE SOVIET AGENT

From the beginning, the CIA concentrated on recruiting as many "moles" as highly placed as possible in the Soviet Union and other communist countries. Since then, however, the few thousand CIA case officers on the job have come up with only a handful of Soviet agents at any given time, and most of these were "walk-ins." CIA case officers soon found communist countries to be "harder" than any intelligence targets in history. Even the wartime Germany against which most of the OSS veterans had worked had never restricted its citizens' freedom of travel, or checked identities, or maintained counterespionage networks so pervasively as did communist-ruled countries. By the time the OSS began focusing on Germany late in 1944, physical devastation and looming defeat had broken down Nazi security as dispirited Germans were rushing to curry favor with the prospective victors. By contrast, Soviet security was outstanding. Moreover, the Soviet Union exported its security system—surely its only world-class export—to all of its client regimes. The least of the members of the "socialist commonwealth," tiny Nicaragua and Grenada, proved to have security many times tougher than the Nazi state against which the OSS had worked. Prior to 1989 the Soviet state also successfully projected an aura of invincibility that frightened most of its subjects into passivity or cooperation. Of course a flood of refugees had fled communist rule, but those leaving were predominantly from the ranks of the oppressed—not the oppressors. Most of the communist officials who defected simply wanted to get out, and were reluctant to "defect in place" and act as spies. Indeed, until 1990, of the many Soviets who defected to the West, few believed they were joining the winning side.* So spying behind the Iron Curtain proved to be more like spying against wartime Japan.

Nevertheless, at first the CIA tried to send agents into the Soviet Union and Eastern Europe in the same way that it had sent them into the Reich. The purposes were similar: military reconnaissance, and warning of enemy movements. The U.S. expected the Soviets to attack in Europe, and to carry the war into Soviet territory. Hence the first priority was to put teams of native agents near every major Soviet airbase, equipped with radio sets and with instructions to send a warning in case the bombers were getting ready for massive operations. In 1947 the U.S. actually succeeded in parachuting dozens of such teams in, with fake documents, and a few teams actually established themselves. Attempts continued until 1954. The second priority was to send teams of agents "in" to join resistance forces, which would serve as bases for the collection of information. In the postwar period there was no shortage of armed resistance groups in the Soviet Union, especially in the Ukraine. So the U.S. equipped willing nationalists with radios, gold, and instructions, and sent them back.

Not surprisingly, most such moves ended in disaster, only partially due to communist security. Just as important, Soviet agents Blake, Philby, Burgess, Maclean, and Blount—inside British intelligence (with whom the CIA had shared the secrets of these operations)—betrayed a large proportion of them. But CIA learned the full reasons for the disasters only long after events had taught a perhaps excessive lesson: Never again try to send truly clandestine collectors into communist countries. Besides, by the mid–1950s fear of Soviet attack had waned, and the U.S. was acquiring airplanes, cameras, and antennas

---

*The memoirs of defectors, e.g., Arkady Shevchenko's *Breaking with Moscow*, Ion Pacepa's *Red Horizons*, Stanislav Levchenko's *On the Wrong Side: My Life in the KGB*, Ilya Dzhirkvilov's *Secret Servant*, John Barron's rendition of Victor Belenko's recollections in *MiG Pilot*, never voiced confidence in the collapse of communism. Instead they speak of frustration and injustice as the immediate incentives for leaving. The memoirs of the most famous of internal defectors, Whittaker Chambers' *Witness* (1954), explicitly expressed the view that the West was doomed. But communism was so evil that Chambers rejected it despite its rosy prospects.

for reconnaissance and early warning. The CIA gratefully handed over the job of simple observation of military events to technical collectors (mostly military). By 1954 the Soviets had also crushed the last armed resistance movements. There was no further need for illegal agents to deal with them.

The late 1940s taught another lesson as well. United States Embassy personnel in communist countries could hardly look twice at local residents without getting them into trouble with the secret police. Thus communist security cut CIA's "legal" access to ordinary citizens as well as to officialdom. The CIA soon found that the only Soviet and East European citizens whom its officers could meet were people whom the communist governments specifically allowed to meet with them: embassy personnel and members of other Soviet official delegations. Even here, meetings were largely restricted to official occasions. Most were perfunctory. United States case officers could not "crash" Soviet residences for confidential contacts. When meaningful contacts did occur, the Soviets initiated them. *Faute de mieux* the CIA has had to make the best of such limited contacts. Sometimes, in frustration, CIA officers would telephone every Soviet official and, to their amazement, make a formal pitch for collaboration, cold. Such conversations were very short.

The CIA's strategy for obtaining spies from "hard" countries, emerged from this harsh environment. It focuses on their "installations" abroad, i.e., their embassies and missions. The first step is to gain biographic data. This gives some idea of who in each mission possesses what information. The second is to learn what, if anything, might lead any given individual not to reject out of hand the question "Will you work with us?" Biographic information about each Soviet stationed abroad (his background, habits, professional interests, career, hobbies, thoughts, etc.) also serves to give any potential recruit the impressive impression "We know all about you and your friends." Case officers also seek to become personally acquainted with their "targets." As they deepen their own knowledge they gain the target's confidence—never mind that the target may be a case officer himself, and be trying to return the favor. CIA officials welcome this game of wits.

Through meetings, and possibly social acquaintance, the case officer assesses his target. Perhaps he is resentful for not having risen higher in his bureaucracy. Perhaps he is one of the many whose families have suffered at the hands of communists. He may be religious, or he may be greedy. He may be moved by the strangest motives. The case officer's job is to discover those motives and use them. Thus it was that in the early 1960s the CIA found a Soviet for whom stamp collecting was the *summum bonum*. The case officer, the station chief, and sometimes even CIA headquarters then decide on a "manipulative ploy" to exploit the particular vulnerability. In the case of the philatelist, the CIA arranged for him to learn that one of the two very rare stamps needed to make his collection into something of international fame was for sale nearby. When the man spent his life's savings to buy the stamp, the CIA had reason to believe he would do even more to get the second one. The case officer then offered him the other one—along with the chance to "work with us" by clandestinely delivering the information to which the Soviet had access. The ploy worked, and the target became an agent. After a productive career, he physically defected to the U.S. He and his stamp collection lived happily ever after.

Such outright recruitments, though they are the prime objectives of case officers, are rare. By far the greatest number—and virtually all the important sources who have worked for CIA—offered their services without being solicited. The walk-in trade has kept the shop open. But because not all walk-ins have come fully prepared to become dedicated agents, the case officer who first works with the walk-in must sometimes use manipulative ploys to turn a tentative contract into a firm relationship. This is when thorough knowledge of "the installation" (the embassy or trade mission) to which the "walk-in" is attached can pay off.

By giving the impression "We know all about you," the case officer can establish a relationship of psychological superiority. Such knowledge is also the most immediately available basis on which to question the walk-in. If he does not tell the truth about people and events with which the case officer knows he is familiar, then there is little basis either for accepting him as a defector who is buying his way in with valuable information, or for developing him into an agent. If he seems to be genuine, then the case officer does his best to persuade him to go back to his regular job "for a while" and to meet with him only under clandestine conditions. That is, he makes him into his agent. He finds out what kind of information the agent has access to, and teaches him how to photocopy and deliver it. The CIA considers both recruits and walk-ins as the normal fruits of its clandestine service's efforts, and handles its agents irrespective of how they came to be such.

CIA's Idea of the Agent

The CIA, following in the footsteps of the OSS, regards every foreigner who takes the first step to becoming an agent not as a potential ally whose apparent newfound friendship is to be nurtured, but rather as a traitor who has proved his essential weakness and henceforth must be trapped by blackmail or by financial or psychological addiction. The CIA recognizes that its case officers may be inclined to "fall in love" with their agents—that is, to think too highly of them or to become overly concerned for their well-being. But agency policy is that the case officer is, in the jargon, a "scalp hunter" who must turn a contact into an agent wholly dependent on him. The agent is supposed to be, or to become, like

Aristotle's natural slave, without purposes of his own or the capacity to think for himself. Only when that happens can he be a true controlled American source.

Even when agents don't want money, the CIA foists it upon them to press them into the mold or just to "strengthen their motivation" for cooperating, and steps up the pressure for them to commit themselves to compromising acts. Individuals who want to exchange information for U.S. assistance on specific projects are particularly distrusted. The agency might work with them, but only as a last resort. Similarly, when the agent says that he is betraying his government because he believes that it is on the wrong side of the great moral divide while America is on the right side, CIA policy is not just to doubt whether he means it (which is only prudent), but to assume that such words cannot possibly have any meaning. The agency has always been proud of its cynicism, regarding it as a mark of sophistication and in accord with modern "value free" social science.* Individual case officers have very different relationships with their agents. And indeed few agent cases actually work like this.† But this perspective on agents is the ideal, and it has affected all CIA human operations.

CIA officials see themselves as American patriots. But they do not believe that the American way of life, or the triumph of American policy, are objectively any better than their opposites. They are neither better nor worse—just ours. CIA officers, like their State Department counterparts, literally do not understand how anyone could switch political allegiances because of a rational judgment about better and worse. So, believing that men are moved by lower motives (money, fear, etc.), the CIA seeks to develop weaknesses into "handles" by which to steer the potential agent. Of course the CIA case officers do not reject agents who claim to be moved by higher motives. But they consider such agents less manageable, and hence less reliable.

The epitome and logical conclusion of this way of looking at agents was the CIA's Mk Ultra program of the 1950s and 1960s, a series of experiments with drugs intended to develop a means of testing the motivation and reliability of agents without ever having to make value judgments. The ultimate objective of Mk Ultra was the development of drug-aided techniques for turning the agent

---

*The central tenet of modern social science is that, in Max Weber's words, "values" are rationally inscrutable, "demonic" choices. No preference is better than any other. See Max Weber, *Wirtschaft und Gesellschaft*. In English see *From Max Weber: Essays in Sociology*, edited by Hans H. Gerth and C. Wright Mills; and Max Weber, *The Sociology of Religion*. The best critiques of this philosophical position are Eric Voegelin, *The New Science of Politics*, and Leo Strauss, *Natural Right and History*.

†One veteran case officer deliberately *lowered* the pressure on recruits to commit themselves, by building "reflection time" into his recruitments. Tom Gilligan, *CIA Life: 10,000 Days with the Agency*, p. 183. Gilligan wanted to make sure that the recruit really wanted to cooperate of his own free will. But this is the opposite of the recommended procedure.

into a wholly dependent controlled tool—a value-free spying machine disguised in a human body.*

Ideology aside, the basic problem in running agents is keeping the relationship between agent and case officer secret from the KGB and other hostile intelligence services. This ruled out face-to-face meetings in communist countries. In such countries, even the safest form of communication, "dead drops" (leaving messages in crumpled cans in predesignated hiding places such as hollow trees), was very dangerous because surveillance was near-perfect. So the CIA normally chose to wait until the agents were reassigned to the West. The CIA instructs agents to "dry-clean" themselves of surveillance, and go to a home or office clandestinely owned or rented by the CIA, called a "safe house." There the agent can be closely questioned, often while hooked up to a polygraph "lie detector" machine.

In the way it contacts and instructs the agent, the CIA must walk a fine line between getting the most out of him and endangering him. Since the purpose of the relationship is "productivity" (causing the agent to deliver as much important material as he can), the CIA follows the standard rule of espionage: Instruct the agent to take or copy things only in ways that will not be noticed, and not do anything that will bring suspicion on oneself—such as obtrusively seeking access to more secrets than one already has.

Nonagents, Refugees, and Émigrés

During the late 1950s, the CIA's scrambling for human intelligence on the Soviet Union briefly led it outside what it deems the normal bounds of agent operations. Khrushchev's "thaw" was making it possible for thousands of Western tourists to visit at least some parts of the Soviet Union, and Soviet citizens were no longer punished for casual contact with foreigners. The CIA reasonably sought to exploit this new access. American (and sometimes foreign) businessmen, professors, and tourists whose travel plans came to CIA's attention received invitations to ask certain questions, photograph certain locations, remember certain details. In addition, the CIA would train and dispatch its own "tourists" on all-expense-paid "vacations" in the USSR. This effort yielded— besides masses of biographic data—close-up pictures of manufacturing equipment, serial numbers of vehicles (indicating manufacturers' output), good accounts of the balance of power and policy direction within various ministries,

---

*One reason why the CIA investigated the use of drugs in espionage was the supposition that the Soviet Union had been successful in these techniques. But in fact the Soviets never showed any interest in them. See *Final Report of the Select Committee to Study Governmental Operations with Respect to Intelligence Activities*, U.S. Senate, 94th Congress, 2nd Session, U.S. Government Printing Office, 1976.

the state of the art within Soviet professions, and so forth. The few thousand reports that came out of the tourist program did not make the Soviet Union into an open book. But the very size of the superficial sample it took did remove the Soviet Union's human reality from the "other side of the moon" category.

But of course the various tourists were not agents. Neither were the Soviets with whom they dealt. None of the operations had a chance of developing potentially willing contacts into moles. The CIA officers felt less like the managers of deep penetrations than like travel agents. So the leadership of the clandestine service was eager to get out of the business. Besides, the U-2 was providing basic data on industries, roads, bridges, new apartments, and so on. The CIA briefly considered putting some of its own personnel undercover deep enough to roam the Soviet Union as tourists, or creating a cadre of part-time case officers among those academics and businessmen with regular contacts in the USSR. But instead, by the early 1960s, the CIA decided to shrink the tourist business into the Domestic Collection Division (DCD)—a division of DDO officers stationed in major U.S. cities who interview Americans who travel to the Soviet Union or receive Soviet visitors. Some of the DCD's programs in science have been spectacularly successful. But the DCD has always been out of the CIA's mainstream, in terms of thinking as well as of careers.

U.S. case officers also spent some time interviewing some of the numerous refugees and émigrés who somehow made their way through the Iron Curtain. Such people have surely provided far more human intelligence than all the secret agents. No budgetary comparison has ever been made of the amount of information received from émigrés and refugees per dollar spent on gathering it, versus the amount of information received from "controlled sources" per dollar spent on the "clandestine services." Our informed guess is that the cost/benefit ratio would favor the refugees. True, refugees could not promise a running account of the future. Also, they seldom occupied high-ranking positions, or possessed the confidence of the greats of the communist world. For these reasons, CIA case officers sometimes likened the job of interviewing them to sifting through mounds of refuse. They did the job while holding their noses, wishing they were "out there" doing "real" human intelligence. Hence they seldom exhausted the knowledge of the people they interviewed.*

Defectors, those who illegally left their countries and sought refuge in the West, also were a valuable source of information. Hundreds of officials in the Soviet bloc and other countries of priority interest to the U.S. defected to the West. Most were officials from ministries of foreign affairs or trade. As many

---

*A few CIA military specialists came to value the émigré sources, even though they were looked down on by other CIA colleagues for doing so.

as a third were intelligence officers from the foreign directorates of the KGB and other services. The CIA isolated the defectors to protect them from their former employers and to protect the U.S. from them in case they turned out to be infiltrators. But of course isolation limited the defectors' usefulness. The CIA debriefers often did not know, or sometimes even care to ask, the questions that would tap a defector's expertise.

Anyone who has ever talked with defectors could not help but have noticed their resentment at the attitude of their CIA debriefers. With due allowance for wounds to exaggerated egos, one still finds remarkable Czech Gen. Jan Sejna's (defected 1968) report of the CIA's refusal to listen to his accounts of his dealings with the Soviet Defense Council.[3] He tried to tell the CIA how the supreme Soviet organ for politico–military decision-making coordinated various programs and offensives within the Warsaw Pact, and how high Soviet bureaucrats talked with one another about important matters. They wanted him to talk about "the organization of Czech army rifle platoons." How different was U.S. military intelligence's treatment of General Sejna. They brought him his favorite Czech beer and took seriously his accounts of his liaison with the Defense Council. Yet, as we will see below, the military have been progressively excluded from U.S. human intelligence.

One reason for the underutilization of defectors is that handling them was not prized work in the CIA. Usually it fell to substandard case officers or to those near the end of unremarkable careers. Most of the handlers themselves saw their job as looking after misfits. Nevertheless, in the earliest postwar years, the "huddled masses" of émigrés and defectors who were eager to tell everything they knew (rather than the rarer-than-hens'-teeth, laboriously recruited spies, or even the official "walk-ins") were by far the most productive human sources. They gave bits and pieces about which factory was producing what, about the basic intentions of communist regimes, and about the facts of life there. On the whole, their views turned out to be more accurate than those of the haughty people who spurned them.

The Communist Satellites

Early CIA case officers in Germany and Austria were besieged by throngs of East European refugees and émigrés who begged to be sent back to their home country to spy for America. Of course some of these were sent by communist security services and, according to Harry Rositzke, who was in charge of such operations at the time, communist security services "were able to learn the identities of Western cross-border agents even before they were dispatched."[4] This could have happened only because in these operations the CIA did not use serious security precautions, such as isolating one agent from another, and contacting agents only clandestinely. In fact, agents reported to central office complexes—where case officers could comfortably handle a high volume of cases and produce volumes of reports—not healthy for operations. Be that as it may, no one claims that these cross-border operations yielded anything but experience. In Rositzke's words: "The first generation of CIA operations officers was learning its trade by doing. . . ." They also yielded dead East Europeans, who had thought of themselves as the vanguard for serious Americans rather than as guinea pigs for sorcerers' apprentices.[5]

Like early "illegal" operations into the Soviet Union, these forays into Eastern Europe were designed primarily to gather short-term tactical intelligence that might be useful during war, and their abandonment was speeded both by the receding prospect of war and by the advent of better technical means of gathering tactical military intelligence. But the CIA never attempted to use the thousands of willing East European recruits as long-term penetrators of their societies, their governments, or their Communist parties, or even as means of contacting those relatively well-placed East Europeans who from time to time offered themselves as agents. The CIA seems to have had an ironclad rule: "Real" agents, i.e., moles (not the riffraff expended in cross-border operations) can be courted and handled only by "classic" American officers posing as diplomats.

Within the satellite countries of Eastern Europe, hatred for communism and Russians—often extending into the ranks of Party officials—provided the CIA with an inexhaustible supply of potential agents. As in the case of Soviets, nearly all East European agents have been walk-ins. The rate of positive responses to "pitches" made was always very high. Only operational difficulties (identifying and, above all, secretly communicating with, the agent) kept the number of actual agents down. Some provided exceptionally accurate information on the most important of topics. For example, in 1981 Polish Col. Ryszard Kuklinski gave the United States the Polish–Soviet plans for crushing the Solidarity trade-union movement through martial law.[6] It was not his fault, and was no reflection on the value of Humint, that he was not listened to.

Similarly, when China and North Korea came under communist rule in the late 1940s the fledgling CIA found no shortage of refugees, deserters, and the like willing to go back into communist-held territory and report on troop concentrations as well as political conditions. Rates of attrition were high. But these agents kept the U.S. abreast of local political conditions and of troop deployments. John Ranelagh, reflecting the views of CIA "old boys," says that the agency failed to warn both of North Korea's invasion of the South on June 25, 1950 and of China's entry into the war that November. Harry Rositzke correctly points out that "no agent forecast" the precise time for the offensive. But the U.S. had been literally saturated for months with reports from line-crossers and refugees that a big offensive was coming—and, indeed, the

Director of Central Intelligence, Adm. Roscoe Hillenkoetter, delivered a warning of the impending attack to Secretary of State Dean Acheson, who signed for it. All of this was duly reported to Congress.[7] The Chinese forces' crossing of the Yalu was also not "called" to the day. But a Soviet deserter who had been working for the CIA as a line-crosser had reported they were preparing to attack.

In this case the CIA had done its job, but top policy-makers failed to listen. Perhaps they would have listened to reports from more socially elevated sources. In subsequent years the CIA too would fall into the habit of believing people according to their social position.

Free World Communists

Communist officials in the free world could not isolate themselves behind security forces, could not kill or imprison disloyal colleagues. CIA case officers could approach them safely. Hence, around the world but especially in Europe, the CIA recruited more agents in this category than in any other. Of course, CIA case officers, known as Americans and usually not fluent in the language, could seldom approach Communist party members directly to find out who would be amenable to a pitch. Nor, at least in the early years, did they know enough about communism and the controversies within it to recognize what might cause someone to defect. But the CIA people were personally close to local noncommunist leftists who had good personal contacts among communists and who, in those years, were happy to serve as scouts for the Americans. And of course there was no shortage of potential recruits. Every Soviet outrage produced fresh crops of disaffected communists: In 1948 the Prague coup; the sacrifice of Greek, Italian, and French communists; the campaign against independent communism in Yugoslavia; the purges of Jews. In 1951 the trials and executions of Czech communists (including Rudolf Slansky). The 1953 workers' revolt in Berlin. The crushing of the Hungarian revolution in 1956. And the constant clashes between the interests of the Soviet leadership and those of local Communist parties—not to mention the Sino–Soviet split. Add to that the attrition that any organization experiences through personality clashes and dashed ambitions; take into account that Communist parties are big targets that sit in the same places for years; subtract the physical and economic coercion that Communist parties in power can exercise; and it is easy to see why finding agents inside free-world Communist parties was like shooting fish in a barrel.

Sometimes a little subtlety was required. The American case officer might ease the communist recruit's bartered conscience a bit by asking him to report, if he wished, only on the "Soviet stooges" in the Party, not on the "real" comrades to whom the recruit might still feel loyal. If the local communist was particularly nationalistic, the American might disclaim interest in the affairs of his country and ask only about the Party's relationship with the Soviets or Chinese. Or, if the communist recruit was anti-American, the affair might be run through a local noncommunist leftist. In short, the agency accommodated the variety of its sources' motivations.

This meant that the CIA learned about free-world Communist parties just about everything it wished to know, and often more than its analysts were capable of understanding. In other words, any mistakes that CIA reports contained about free-world Communist parties were not due to a lack of sources. For example, the depth of the CIA's information about the Italian Communist party is beyond doubt to any reader of the memoirs of William Colby, station chief in Rome in the mid-1950s. The book shows, among other things, how the Soviet Union financed the Italian Communist party. This knowledge was anything but hard to obtain; even novice academics had it.[8] Yet, despite knowledge of the many detailed ways in which the Communist party controlled the Socialist party, Colby in particular and the CIA in general wildly underestimated the strength of the Communists' hold on the Italian Socialists. It is almost as if the facts had come so easily that the CIA had not bothered to understand the nature of the beast it was examining.

The Free World

The tenuous link between familiarity and understanding was especially evident outside the "hard target" countries. Like U.S. diplomats, case officers based in friendly countries became acquainted with the host governments' officials, leaders of the opposition, the press, and so on, in order to gather information about them and to exercise influence on them. Like other Americans in the postwar period, CIA officers were beset by friendly foreigners. At the highest levels, ———, ———,* and others like them became personal friends of CIA case officers. Unlike diplomats, however, U.S. case officers tried to mold these contacts along the lines of their relationship with clandestine agents. They made the relationships as confidential as possible and paid as many of these sources as would accept money. Thus U.S. case officers sent back to Washington reports on the views of a usually broad and deep sample of the leadership of open societies. But of course these sources were anything but controlled. It was out of the question to submit them to polygraphs and psychological ploys. So, the reports from such "agents" did not differ—except perhaps in time—from the statements that these sources gave to the press. Not surprisingly beginning in the mid-1950s CIA reports from free-world sta-

---

*Deleted at the request of the Central Intelligence Agency.

tions more and more took on the character of press and diplomatic reporting. The CIA was in effect competing with the press, and more often than not losing.

One reason for this was biased coverage. Human beings who report on struggles are hard put not to prefer the company, and the success, of some over others. All professional reporters try to counter their biases by making sure they spend time with and "put themselves in the shoes of" those they don't like. They know how easy it is to be "captured," and try to discount the personal favors and comforts they receive from those they do like. But diplomats in general and, it seems, CIA case officers in particular, have been less successful at this than newspapermen. First, because their reporting is not public, they are not as readily called to account for their biases, nor are they subject to letters to the editor or competing coverage. They are also part of a bigger organization, the U.S. government, where an "office view" can thrive with less challenge than in a less insulated private organization. Indeed "office views," bias, and "government policy" melt into one another. Thus during the postwar period there was within the U.S. government virtual unanimity that the salvation of the world lay with the "noncommunist left." There was no one to challenge the predilection of Colby and his staff to choose people they liked as sources of information. No surprise, then, that (for example) the reporting from William Colby's Rome CIA station was a replay of the views of the left-wing sector of the noncommunist Italian left. The same happened virtually everywhere.

Also, U.S. officials often have been more restricted in their movements than have reporters. It is the diplomat's *déformation professionnelle* to stick close to the host country's Establishment. For example, in the Shah's Iran, the government did not approve of U.S. officials spending time with (and giving legitimacy to) the opposition. So, few U.S. officials, including intelligence officers, got to evaluate the opposition personally, much less recruit agents within it. This logic applied with far greater force in communist countries. During the 1970s in the Soviet Union, U.S. embassy officers stayed away in droves from dissidents (and encouraged private American citizens to stay away) because, as U.S. Ambassador Malcolm Toon told me, "Our valuable relations with those who count here would suffer." This may or may not be wise diplomacy. But it is bad for an intelligence system based on official cover. By similar token, U.S. policy during the Afghan–Soviet war that began in 1979 was that, to discourage speculation about U.S. assistance to the Mujahideen, no officers of the U.S. Embassy in Pakistan were allowed to meet with any Mujahideen. This ensured that the U.S. government's information on the subject was second-hand.

Another reason for the low quality of reporting from places where sources were abundant was the CIA's policy of rewarding officers for the *quantity* of their reports. One poignant account by a conscientious officer bemoans the practice of "splitting one really good report into three acceptable ones." The "numbers game" caused more serious distortions as well: "Agents were being recruited that [sic] were not really needed, exposing them and the organization to risk; focus was shifted from the difficult, important targets to easier, nonvital ones . . . the same individuals were used time and again to get to Soviet targets, making the counterintelligence job easier for the KGB and increasing the long-term risk to recruited Soviets; Agency counterintelligence standards were lowered to increase the prospects of recruitment."[9] In other words, bureaucratic imperatives corrupted the mission.

Finally, in the free world, as elsewhere, the CIA too often insisted that agents transfer their loyalty to the case officer, to the U.S., or to money. But just as it is unnecessary for someone who is willing to report on the state of, say, religious opposition to the Egyptian government to transfer his loyalty to the United States, so it is unnecessary that he transfer it to the case officer, and indeed unnecessary that he betray the religious opposition to the Egyptian government. Case officers found by bitter experience that, especially when the U.S. government was lightly involved in a foreign situation, the most successful approach was that of the newspaper reporter: neither to control the source nor to be controlled by it.

Vietnam

The CIA flooded Vietnam with case officers, and reaped reports from hundreds of thousands of human sources through a dozen major programs. The Saigon station alone had as many as 1,900 indigenous employees at one time. Each of South Vietnam's four military regions had a sizable CIA base, and each province had a staff. If one were to judge by the quantity of reports, one would have to conclude that the CIA had total human coverage of Vietnam. In fact "the numbers" are as unreliable a guide to the CIA's performance as they are to that of the rest of the U.S. government in Vietnam, and for the same reasons.

Begin with the most basic Humint function in war: interrogating prisoners. The CIA built regional and provincial interrogation centers, of standard design. The interrogators were Vietnamese. The supervisors were CIA employees who spoke no Vietnamese. But neither worked from files that identified the prisoners, or the units and locations to which they belonged. Hence the Vietnamese used the interrogation centers for extortion and sadism, while the CIA officers filed useless reports and gnashed their teeth. When one CIA man introduced files and "wiring diagrams" as bases for questioning and as repositories for the answers, the CIA greeted this re-invention of the wheel as a radical innovation.[10] The same officer also hit upon the revolutionary idea of interviewing defectors and deserters in depth to build files on Vietcong organizations and Vietnamese units.

Then there was the Census Grievance Program. Every week in every province, CIA officers would give bundles of cash to Vietnamese employees who ostensibly would travel to outlying villages to pay individuals who supposedly received intelligence under the guise of listening to peasants' grievances. In theory, these middlemen would not pocket the money, but rather would use it to pay their sources. The results were nearly worthless, as were those of a similar "infiltration" of the Rural Development Program. The PHOENIX program, for its part, was supposed to consist of a sharing of intelligence by various Vietnamese bureaucracies at the provincial level, from which identification of Vietcong cadres would be made. But since the Vietnamese agencies were notoriously jealous, and since the U.S. paid for quantities of enemy cadre identified, little intelligence was shared, and too many identifications were made *post hoc propter hoc* when Vietnamese Provincial Reconnaissance Units would bring in the bodies.

Here and there individual CIA officers learned Vietnamese, built files, recruited agents in particular villages or units, and passed the information in ways that led to effective military operations. But, in general, a generation of CIA officers, much like their military counterparts, played the numbers game. The CIA officers "punched" their career "tickets" and thousands of Vietnamese pocketed money. Ironically, the bulk of the reports thus generated proved most useful to the North Vietnamese, who got them basically intact when they overran the U.S. Embassy in Saigon on April 30, 1975. One of the reasons that the files were intact is that, until the last days, CIA station chief Thomas Polgar apparently believed human intelligence reports that the North Vietnamese would be amenable to a negotiated settlement of the war.[11]

Terrorism and Drugs

Collecting information on terrorists and narcotics became of some concern only in the late 1960s and 1970s. Managers and case officers for the most part applied the same techniques they used in collecting on other hard targets. With rare exception they operated under official cover. There was no special training or special recruiting of case officers who could blend in with the terrorist groups and their state sponsors, or narcotics traffickers, and their coconspirators in governments in Asia, Europe, and Latin America.

Collection on Palestinian terrorism began after the 1967 Arab–Israeli War, when the newly formed PLO and other Palestinian groups became close collaborators of the Soviet Union and Palestinians started attacking U.S. personnel, aircraft, and installations. At first, developing agents in the Middle East was relatively easy. The U.S. was a major player in the region and some Palestinians wanted contact with the U.S., to make their case against Israel. Others wanted money. Also, the PLO and other groups were not very security conscious. Over time, U.S. influence in the region declined, particularly after the Arab oil embargo of 1973 and the Islamic revolution in 1978. The PLO received counterintelligence and security training from Soviet-bloc security services. They were taught how the CIA and other services were recruiting among them, and the basic security practices that could neutralize much of this effort. The Palestinians in turn trained young militant Shi'ites from Iran and Lebanon, as well as Marxist–Leninist groups from Nicaragua and Western Europe.

Also in the mid–1970s the CIA virtually stopped talking to people who participated in terrorism, lest it be held responsible for terrorist actions. Case officers were held "responsible" for their agents' behavior, as if every agent were really "controlled." The ultimate example was the CIA's contact with Christian Lebanese who were seeking to penetrate and fight radical Palestinian and Shi'ite terrorism in Lebanon. When, on March 8, 1985, some of these Lebanese planted a bomb to kill Sheik Fadlallah, the spiritual leader of Hezbollah, and instead killed 80 people in a neighboring building, Bob Woodward of *The Washington Post* claimed that the bombing was a U.S.–Saudi CIA plot.* Since the only people who can provide specific information on terrorist acts usually are themselves involved in terrorist activities, the CIA was in a bind. Moreover, the CIA's case officers hardly spoke the same language as those who lived cheek-by-jowl with bombs and knives. To some extent this was compensated for by liaison relationships with the Israeli and French intelligence services, which were not so constrained and who mounted a major effort to penetrate the terrorist groups.

Also in the late 1960s, the Directorate of Operations began to take an interest in narcotics trafficking. But despite the fact that Seymour Bolten, one of the U.S. government's premier experts in the field, became an adviser to the Deputy Director for Operations, the Directorate did not develop case officers especially fit to penetrate drug rings. Instead it relied on U.S. law-enforcement agencies— especially the Drug Enforcement Agency—and on information from foreign police organizations.

Changing Fundamentals

In the postwar period the power, wealth, and majesty of the U.S. inspired countless people to try to bring Americans to *their* side in their quarrels. They would rush to the most officious-looking American they could find and tell him things that they hoped would lead mighty America to come and relieve their

---

*Bob Woodward, *Veil*, p. 397. The notion that the CIA is responsible for car bombings in Beirut is on the same level as the notion that the CIA is responsible for corruption in the Philippines—or for cold weather at the North Pole.

distress. As America's postwar majesty waned, however, so did the flood of eager recruits.

Thus, for example, beginning in 1959, as Fidel Castro began to kill, imprison, seize, and arm in Cuba, the U.S. had multitudes of agents and subagents in that country. Throughout 1962 the CIA was flooded with agent reports of Soviet missiles in Cuba, and for that very reason—coupled with a firm U.S. policy after the Bay of Pigs (1961) not to be drawn into Cuba—the CIA tended to discount the reports in part as motivated by the desire to "get" the U.S. to overthrow Castro. After the Cuban missile crisis of 1962, as the U.S. government arrested Cuban exiles who were attacking the Castro regime from the Florida Keys and the Tortugas, and as Castro's people-control measures took hold, the Cuban people realized that there was much less to be gained than lost by trying to give information to the U.S. Hence, the flow of human intelligence from Cuba dried to a trickle, and that trickle came under Castro's control.

In sum, despite wide disparities in details, the fundamental story of U.S. human intelligence in the postwar world has been not unlike that of U.S. human intelligence in World War II, in that (the purest of mercenaries aside) people have been willing to serve as agents insofar as they have perceived America as fighting their battles.

Liaison

The U.S. and British intelligence communities have worked together so closely over the years that they are almost one body. There are few secrets between them, and neither undertakes any espionage against the other. Although no other service is as close as the British, the U.S. has had written or unwritten information-sharing arrangements not only with NATO countries, Israel, and Australia, but also with such friendly regional powers as Guatemala and Thailand. Especially when the CIA was just getting started, but even in later years, liaison with Britain and France allowed the CIA indirectly to tap a pool of case officers in places like the Persian Gulf and Southeast Asia, where the CIA had no experience and could scarcely afford to develop it. In addition, case officers who knew the language and fit in with the culture of their target areas could always be expected to gain far more access than Americans.

But since liaison is a two-way street, it has worked best when the U.S. and the host government have acted as if friendship and a community of interest existed. The problem of community of interest has overshadowed all others, including security. Despite the uncovering of dozens of high-level penetrations in the intelligence services of Britain and Germany,* U.S. intelligence officers deal

---

*The fall of the East German regime in 1989–90 provided proof of the very great extent to which the West German government's intelligence had been penetrated by the East. At one

with Britons and Germans with respect, and act as if no one in the U.S. government had ever given the relationship between the countries and the services a second thought. The British reciprocate fully. The Germans have not shared information gathered in the course of activities that would displease the U.S.—such as sales of poison gas technology to Libya and Iraq, and certain commercial activities in Eastern Europe. But the CIA scarcely takes notice. By contrast, although the CIA has had far less proof of leaks from French intelligence, the CIA's liaison with France is at arms' length because the U.S. government has never taken France entirely seriously as an ally. Perhaps for the same reason the CIA's liaison with Italy is even more distant, and at times the CIA station chief's relationship with the chief of the Italian external intelligence service (always a General and until 1989 a veteran of World War II) has sunk to "I'm trying to teach that boy to be a spy."[13] No need to be surprised at French and Italian reticence to share secrets.

One of the commonplaces of those close to U.S. intelligence in the 1970s and 1980s was that foreign intelligence services had become reluctant to share their secrets with the CIA out of fear that the CIA would "leak," either through U.S. congressional oversight or through the Freedom of Information Act. I have spoken with any number of foreign intelligence officials over the years, and have indeed heard expressions of reticence about liaison with the CIA, but seldom on grounds of insecurity of information. The principal causes touched the core of the relationship: friendship, community of interest, and reciprocity.

Prior to 1974, for example, James Angleton handled the U.S. end of the intelligence relationship with Israel out of his office in the counterintelligence staff of the CIA. There was nothing logical about the arrangement, except that Angleton loved Israel, and the Israelis knew it.* The Israelis also knew that there were plenty of officials in the U.S. government and U.S. intelligence who favored their Arab enemies. But they trusted Angleton to make sure that nothing Israel gave the U.S. would wind up favoring the Arab cause, and that Angleton would make sure they got any information from the U.S. that would help them.

---

time even the director of the Office for the Protection of the Constitution, West Germany's chief counterintelligence agency, was an East German agent. Indeed, Klaus Kuron, who was in charge of double agents for the West German BND, confessed to having been an East German double agent himself. *New York Times*, 11 October 1990. p. 1.

*Liaison relationships normally are handled by the geographic divisions of the Directorate of Operations. There is much to be said for that. On the other hand, handling liaison through CI channels tends to prevent liaison from becoming penetration of one's own service, and helps it to become a tool for penetrating the other service. But that is not why Angleton had the Israel account. Thomas Powers, paraphrasing a common (and correct) opinion, says that "Where suspicion of Arab motives was concerned, Angleton made Golda Meir seem trusting." Powers, *The Man Who Kept the Secrets*, p. 289.

The difficulties in the relationship began when Angleton was replaced. By 1982 there was enough of an admixture of pro-Arab sentiment in U.S. policy, and in those in charge of the U.S. end of the liaison, that Israel refused to turn over pieces of Soviet armament gained in the course of its invasion of Lebanon. The CIA sent Deputy Director John McMahon to negotiate. But since McMahon was known to be aligned with "progressive" and pro-Arab people in the agency, it is not surprising that he was greeted coldly.[13]

The public argument of those in the CIA who cooled the relationship with Israel is that the U.S. simply cannot give Israel information about the location of Arab terrorists or key Arab military facilities gained through satellites because the Israelis are likely to use it to kill people, as they did in 1981 when they used U.S. intelligence about an Iraqi nuclear reactor to bomb it.* This author recalls Deputy Director Bobby Ray Inman expressing heartfelt rage to Congress over Israel's action. He called it a "breach of faith" with the U.S. The Israelis countered by asking what else they should use the information for. And they retorted by not telling Americans the scope of their agent operations. Besides, why should Israel give the U.S. government information about terrorists if the U.S. will not act on it? And, since the U.S. will not volunteer information, why not bargain on a case-by-case basis? On this path, of course, lies the ruin of intelligence liaison.

In 1986 a young U.S. Naval Intelligence analyst, Jonathan Pollard, took it upon himself to supply Israel with reams of information from U.S. intelligence files. In the growing climate of U.S.–Israeli mistrust, the U.S. government prosecuted, and the court sentenced Pollard as if he had endangered American lives by spying for the Soviet Union. Clearly, friendship and hostility are easier to manage than equivocation.

Military Humint

Throughout the postwar period the U.S. armed forces' capacity to recruit and run agents declined steadily. No one denies the abstract proposition that the U.S. military must have the capacity to run precursors, line-crossers, and stay-behinds in wartime, and *should* be able to run agents in peacetime (if only to gather information of specific relevance to potential military operations); and also that military commanders ought to run agents at *any* time into any organization that threatens physical harm to, subversion of, or espionage against their unit. But in the absence of war, and given the military's increased reliance on technical battlefield intelligence, the CIA has used its primacy in the field of human

---

*In the wake of Iraq's August 1990 invasion of Kuwait there was much retrospective gratitude in the U.S. government toward Israel for this act. But in 1981 there was much bitterness in CIA over what the Israelis had done and over how they had, indirectly, involved the U.S.

intelligence to virtually deprive the military of any serious agent-handling capacity, with the exception of the physical safety of military units in their peacetime deployment areas.

In Vietnam the U.S. military's human intelligence showed few bright spots. The brightest was the Special Operations Group. It sent soldiers to spy directly on North Vietnamese units as they infiltrated South Vietnam, and to capture prisoners therefrom. Some of its noncommissioned officers "went native" and thus were able regularly to recruit useful agents. In general, military espionage was directly proportional to the proximity of small-unit actions. Large American military units got their human information either from their Vietnamese counterparts, from the CIA, or from their own intelligence units. Since these units (much as with CIA case officers) consisted of people who did not know the language or the country, and whose motivation was to turn in a sufficient *quantity* of reports until the time would come to be transferred back to the real world, the standard military espionage product in Vietnam was worthless.

Until the mid–1970s the U.S. Army in Germany maintained networks of several hundred German and East European native agents who infiltrated anti-U.S. groups, tried to identify East German, Czech, and Hungarian agents, and gathered significant amounts of information about the Warsaw Pact forces facing them. The Army also recruited agents who would "stay behind" in case of a Soviet invasion, and even a few agents inside Soviet and East European armies. Until 1976 the U.S. Navy maintained Task Force 157, a group of naval officers who sometimes worked undercover to recruit agents in ports visited by Soviet ships, who would then try to buy or steal Soviet secrets, place sensors near the ships, photograph key parts clandestinely, or even spot Soviet naval personnel to recruit as spies. Since the mid–1970s, however, Navy human intelligence has been removed from positive collection and restricted to investigating reports of espionage and criminal activity. The Army has not gone quite that far, but almost.

In 1980, after the Ayatollah Khomeini had captured the entire U.S. Embassy staff in Teheran, the U.S. government mounted EAGLE CLAW—a military rescue operation. This operation required knowledge about the habits of those guarding the hostages, about who was likely to be in landing zones at what time, etc.—in short, information that could only be gathered by people on the ground. This is the sort of information that does not require "moles" in the government, but rather the presence of agents who could mingle with local crowds. But the CIA had never recruited agents among what one might call "average" Iranians. Nearly all of the CIA's Iranian agents—officials in the Shah's regime—had fallen along with that regime, and CIA officers in Iran were prisoners. So the U.S. armed forces had to assemble quickly some daring Persian-speakers as infiltrators to gather the basic data for the mission.

Afterward, the Army tried to develop a group of intelligence collectors who could be infiltrated into foreign areas ahead of military operations. This outfit was called Intelligence Support Activity (ISA). But the CIA argued within the executive branch and to the Congress against funding the ISA. Some elements in the Army also opposed it as a foreign body within the Army. Finally the excuse for disbanding ISA was that in order to familiarize its officers and men with foreign areas and keep up their language skills, the Army had sent them on foreign vacations with their wives. What makes sense operationally is often the kiss of death bureaucratically—and the other way around.

In 1981–83 the Department of Defense also proposed a project, code-named MONARCH EAGLE, to form a cadre of military officers who would be stationed abroad under a variety of covers to recruit agents with access to military information. Thus American military case officers undercover in a hypothetical Guinea might have befriended a member of the Soviet military assistance mission in that country. But although CIA Director William Casey supported the project (as did some others, including Robert Gates, who would later become his deputy), both of the Deputy DCIs of the period, Bobby Ray Inman and John McMahon, worked with opponents to kill it. MONARCH EAGLE was finally reduced to a plan for allowing some military officers to serve tours with CIA.

In sum, although the military retained substantial authority to gather battlefield intelligence, including taking and interrogating prisoners, peacetime military Humint in the U.S. has been reduced to a theoretical proposition.

THE WIDENING MISMATCH

How well did this system work? How did its performance change as the years passed?

The Soviet Target

The perhaps *ten thousand* CIA case officers who have worked on the "hard target" over the years have beaten their heads against a pretty solid wall. There is little reason to believe that their activities have had any effect whatever on the decisions of perhaps two dozen lower- to mid-level Soviet officials to serve the West "in place," and of scores of other Soviet officials to defect. Now and again American hard-target espionage *has* paid concrete dividends: The Southeast Asia division of the DDO was able to buy the operating manuals of the Soviet SA-2 antiaircraft missiles against which U.S. pilots had to fly during the Vietnam War.

It seems, however, that as time has passed, the value of U.S. human intelligence—never of national significance—has declined. GRU Maj. Vladimir Popov, who "walked in" to the CIA in Vienna in 1952, was the first and perhaps the most valuable penetration of the Soviet government the U.S. ever had.[14] For six years he photographed and transferred GRU documents, and told the U.S. of the GRU agents he knew. He was invaluable if only because he was our only window into an otherwise dark world. He also caused much turmoil inside the GRU. But, according to his case officer, this greatest of American "moles" saved the U.S. only about a half billion dollars' worth of military expenditure[15]—an inconsequential amount. Nor did Popov's information help the U.S. to make significant moves in international affairs. Yet, for every Popov, who told the U.S. the truth, there has been a proven liar, and some of these liars have had some pretty bad effects on the U.S.

Indeed, there have been fewer and fewer agents/defectors like Popov, whose every report checked out, and more like Anatoli Golitsyn, whose imprecise information did as much harm as good; or like Yuri Nosenko, whose stories about himself were self-contradictory; or like Vitaly Yurchenko, whose revelations "blew" Soviet agents whose usefulness had already ended. In other words, it seems that the U.S. has had more and more reason to wonder about the *bona fides* of the sources as well as about the intrinsic worth of the information. Most important for our purposes here is that the agent-handling skills of American case officers probably did not affect the number, the value, or the reliability of the few Soviets who defected either in place or outright.

In a few cases the skill of American case officers was key to maximizing the usefulness of the walk-in. Even in the early years, when significant numbers of case officers had been foreign-born or the children of immigrants, only a handful knew Russian or East European languages well enough to converse intelligently with walk-ins. When need arose, such people were rushed to the scene—and often did a good job, showing a sense of balance between getting as much production as possible out of the agent, and not endangering his safety. The CIA handled Popov this way. Our point here is that the CIA's agent-handling performance has been better when cases have been handled in an extraordinary manner by people picked especially for the job than when they are handled in the normal routine, by regular people. *There is little reason to believe that if twice the number of CIA officers had been sent to U.S. embassies there would have been twice as many Soviet agents, or the same number twice as good,* or that if only half the number had been sent, the number of agents would have been cut in half. There is no reason at all to believe that more officers would have meant either better handling or significantly more useful information.

But the bottom line is that the recruited agents, walk-ins, and émigrés who provided the bulk of the human information gave the U.S. only a taste of what human intelligence is supposed to provide: the inside scoop on how the other side views its own strengths and weaknesses, and on what it plans to do next. If we ask: What would we have done wrong that we did right, or done right that we did wrong, if we had to steer U.S. policy without the clandestine service, wholly by open and diplomatic sources? The answer in both cases is that secret human intelligence has made little difference for good or for ill. Here is one among many examples.

Before 1957, when the U-2 spy plane began to photograph wide areas of the Soviet Union, the United States' knowledge of the number of Soviet tanks, airplanes, and such was based on inferences from sketchy reports. For example, the grossly mistaken conclusion reached in 1956 that the Soviets would soon have 1,000 jet bombers flowed directly from the (accurate but understandably fragmentary) report of a U.S. air attaché about the number of bombers he had seen fly over Moscow's annual May Day parade. The Soviets, in a maneuver reminiscent of Mussolini, had simply flown all their available bombers over Red Square several times. But the report of the flyover fit well with other fragmentary human reports about lots of new construction of aircraft factories. These reports too later turned out to be correct. But in the absence of specificity, intelligence analysts fell prey to a prevailing anxiety and drew the reasonable but mistaken conclusion that Soviet factories were disgorging huge numbers of bombers. Later, when U-2 photography drew the connection between the new factories and ballistic missiles, the lack of access to secret documents and secret conversations allowed a brand-new, updated fear of the moment to conclude that the Soviets were producing large numbers of intercontinental missiles. In fact the factories were producing some 1,000 intermediate-range missiles intended at that time solely for the European theater of operations.

The conclusion that the Soviets were building ballistic missiles to support operations against Europe should not have been difficult to reach. The human reports certainly led to it, as did other Soviet military preparations and published Soviet military doctrine. But these bits of evidence were not enough to overcome the various fears then in vogue. To do that, intelligence would have had to come up with *a specific, confidential, high-level avowal of the link between the great Soviet aerospace buildup of the late 1950s and the European theater.* Since human intelligence had not penetrated deeply enough for that, there obviously existed a mismatch between what it could deliver and what was required to turn on the lights in the minds of American decision-makers.

Human intelligence at its best is associated with the name of Col. Oleg Penkovsky, a walk-in to British intelligence in 1961 who was comanaged by the CIA. The handling of Penkovsky was the dramatic apotheosis of the CIA's image of itself: His major contribution is said to have been that, before the Cuban missile crisis of 1962, he told the U.S. precisely how few intercontinental ballistic missiles the Soviet Union really had, and how little confidence they had in them. This allowed President Kennedy to face down Nikita Khrushchev, confident that the Soviet Union would not make war. The CIA published a book purporting to be the Penkovsky papers, and basked in the glory of the case for two decades.[16]

But there is both more and less to the story. Penkovsky did indeed provide the correct number of Soviet missiles. But by that time, the first generation of U.S. photographic intelligence satellites had already documented it, and the Soviet Union was aware of the fact that its missile bases had been overflown by U.S. satellites. Also, shortly before the Soviets announced his arrest, (shortly after the missile crisis) Penkovsky provided reams of Soviet plans for the construction of missiles in the future. Can one expect more from a classic mission of espionage? Alas, what the Soviet Union actually *did* in the field of ballistic missiles during the 1960s turned out to be diametrically different from what the Penkovsky documents *said*. According to the Penkovsky papers, the Soviets had conceded to the U.S. perpetual superiority in missiles. They would not even try to match, much less exceed, the number of U.S. missiles. Nor did they see missiles as instruments of strategic fighting, but rather as instruments of mindless destruction and deterrence. Penkovsky's information was one more reason why U.S. intelligence analysts continued to misinterpret Soviet missile construction throughout the 1960s and most of the 1970s. Why the discrepancy? Perhaps Soviet authorities changed their minds about missiles after Penkovsky, or perhaps they had fed Penkovsky false material just before arresting him, or perhaps Penkovsky had been a plant all along. At any rate, after all is said and done, this greatest coup of U.S. human intelligence looks smaller as the years go by.

The standard rejoinder is that the record of U.S. espionage looks bad because, by the nature of the intelligence business, only failures come to light, while successes must remain buried. There is some little truth to this. I am aware of some agents who have not come to public attention, and would not be surprised if a few important ones had existed of whom I have no knowledge. In practice, however, the CIA has waited the barest minimum—and sometimes not even that—to rush its successes into the policy debate and thence into the news media. In the 1960s the CIA subsidized the publication of *The Penkovsky Papers*. In 1985, within weeks after Vitaly Yurchenko, a high-ranking KGB officer, offered himself to the CIA, the CIA was crowing to *Newsweek* magazine about its coup.[17] Washington insiders have long known that no part of the U.S. government is as solicitous about its image in the media as the CIA. Few agencies are so riven by internecine quarrels in which both sides impugn the other's judgment to enhance their own image. The CIA's "family jewels," dossiers compiled by various U.S. intelligence factions on what their intramural friends have done right and their opponents have done wrong, have long since found their way to Congress and the press. The most secretive form of advertising consists of CIA boasts at interagency meetings that someone's position is wrong, and that CIA knows better because of an especially sensitive source about whom it can say nothing. The source quickly becomes a legend within the government, and soon prestigious journalists cite it in hushed tones at the best Washington dinner parties. Then it becomes a weapon of personal aggrandizement, mutual recrimination, and, finally, of literary contention. In the author's experiences over two decades, this cycle has played out innumerable times.

Most important, the record is public in terms of the "dogs that did not bark"—the instances in which the U.S. made policy without knowledge of the Soviet leadership's thoughts. This of course is the main point. The U.S. has had to deal with the most vexing aspects of its relationship with the Soviet Union without the help of spies, whether recruited or walk-ins. How far did Khrushchev mean to carry his threats to close off access to Berlin? Did the Soviet Union intend to abide by the 1958 nuclear test moratorium? What was the Soviet Union's intention in entering into the series of negotiations on strategic armaments that began in 1969? Did the Soviet leaders intend to use their missile force to destroy American missiles or to destroy cities? What precisely did Brezhnev intend in 1972 by entering into the relationship of détente with the U.S.? How did his intentions compare with Henry Kissinger's? How did the Soviet leadership react to Kissinger's vision that the commercial part of détente would so enmesh them that they could no longer afford to harm the interests of the United States? Just what did Gorbachev mean to accomplish internally? Why did his announced plans change so often? Why did he turn the levers of government over to hard liners who then turned on him? What is Boris Yeltsin's private view of the usefulness of military force? How would the Soviet armed forces react in a revolutionary situation? The U.S. intelligence community turned out literally thousands of pages of analysis on these subjects. *If there had been good espionage, ten-page reports would have done nicely.* In 1989–1991, U.S. human intelligence sources added nearly nothing to press reports of the collapse of communism—and what they added was misleading.

Soft Targets

Whereas clandestine officers vied with professional Kremlinologists and Sinologists in arranging sparse tea leaves into their favorite dreams or nightmares, when it came to the rest of the world they competed with the press, diplomats, businessmen, and academics for scoops. CIA training, procedures, and equipment supplied no special edge. Thousands of careers were made reporting on soft targets like Chile and Iran. But despite very high-level contacts, clandestine reporting did not warn the U.S. government of major changes in such countries.

POSTWAR SPYING INTO THE TWENTY-FIRST CENTURY

How then would this system of human intelligence function in the turn-of-the-century world that we have outlined? In a nutshell, the United States' spymasters-in-the-guise-of-diplomats would be baffled by the new difficulties and would be too inflexible to grasp the new opportunities. The human intelligence mismatch of the 1990s boils down to this: An unspecialized, homogeneous corps of would-be spymasters chasing potential sources who are increasingly heterogeneous and who have fewer incentives than ever to serve the United States. This mismatch is not a mere prospect, but a growing reality.

The CIA has already hired most of the case officers that it plans to use in the 1990s. The typical officer was brought up in a nice American suburb during the 1960s and graduated barely in the top half of his class from a typical American college in the 1970s and 1980s. He has never done manual labor, and has never been personally close to anyone who has lived by it. He has never had to struggle for his next meal, and has never known anyone who has. He has no idea of life under arbitrary power. He has never served in the armed forces, much less has he known danger. He has traveled abroad as a tourist, but has never lived or transacted business abroad. His upbringing did not acquaint him with passion of any kind. It taught him to distrust the notion that anyone can believe in anything. He does not attend church or synagogue, nor does he argue about religion. He is a pleasant fellow, neither aggressively patriotic nor aggressively anything, and is uncomfortable with anyone who is. His education did not make him an expert in any field, such as chemistry or computers. But his lack of technical training does not mean that he has a classical education, either. He does not know the history, the language, or the politics of any part of the world. Nor does he know a line of business, like cars, or printing, or garment manufacturing. He is not independently wealthy. He has been an employee of the CIA, and has been around the State Department. This case officer, who is much less potent than his postwar predecessors, has a much tougher row to hoe than they did.

This case officer will have a hard time meeting and getting along with his potential source. Not only can he not, say, live as a mechanic in Ruritania and get a job fixing cars for the secretaries of a hypothetical foreign military mission. (His forebears couldn't either, but they didn't have to.) He is unlikely even to be able to recruit a mechanic to act as his source, because he is unlikely ever to have had a meaningful conversation with any mechanic. He literally does not speak that language. If he tries to frequent places where mechanics congregate, he is sure to stick out like a sore thumb, much as George Bush in the 1984 electoral campaign inadvertently pointed to his patrician upbringing via a maladroit imitation of the average American.* For precisely the same reasons, our case officer cannot expect to "get in" among scientists, or professional politicians, or soldiers, or stockbrokers, or priests. If by luck he manages to enter such circles, he is not likely to understand what he sees. After all, while a scientist is attuned to the vagaries of the world of science and can instantly recognize the types of people there (the passionate risk-takers, the bean-counters, the entrepreneurs, the careerists, etc.), all its inhabitants will look alike to our case officer. As an unspecialized bureaucrat, our case officer will be able to get to first base only with unspecialized bureaucrats.

Consider also his cultural limitations. There are a few people in America who have passed themselves off as Muslims and literally risked their heads on their knowledge of Arabic and Islam by going on the pilgrimage to Mecca, the *Hadj*. There are many more Americans who can blend into Mexico, and even some who can talk shop with Chinese farmers. But such people don't get hired by the CIA. Spanish is the mother tongue of perhaps 25 million Americans. Yet the CIA has been unable (read *unwilling*) even to staff its Mexico City station with people who speak Spanish—never mind people who speak and have a "feel" for the Spanish of Mexico City secretaries. The same goes for any other field in any other nation. Serbian physicians, Thai soldiers, Japanese athletes—each group speaks its own language. But none of these languages are spoken at or by CIA.

The Soviet Succession

In the territory of the former Soviet Union, CIA case officers will miss opportunities. In 1991 political, social, and economic life involved more and different kinds of people than ever, organized into any number of groups and factions with views, leaders, and plans peculiar to *them*. Some are more accessible than others. The great Soviet enigma broke into any number of enigmas, *each* of which must be penetrated.

But this sort of penetration has little in common with that which the CIA has ever tried. During the Gorbachev era the CIA focused on the circus master who opened the lions' cages long after the lions were roaming the grounds. It failed to penetrate Gorbachev's Politburo, and would not have gained much insight into the gathering Soviet storm if it had succeeded. But the techniques it employed are quite irrelevant to "penetrating" various kinds of Russian or Ukrainian nationalists, Army cabals, or connections between interest groups and politicians. The barrier to this sort of political intelligence is less the KGB than the natural reticence of Russian managers, Ukrainian or Georgian factory workers, and so

*Bush referred to his debate with Geraldine Ferraro, a woman vice-presidential candidate, as "kicking a little ass."

on, to talk seriously about sensitive matters with a U.S. diplomat who has no reason to be talking to them other than to report to the U.S. government, who has nothing in common with them, and who doesn't really know how to hold up his end of a conversation with them. By contrast, people from around the world, the U.S. scientists who have been meeting with members of the Soviet Academy of Sciences for a variety of reasons, journalists, economists, political scientists, businessmen, tourists, even pollsters, have gotten earfuls of political information from nationalists, religious groups, industrial workers, and others.

Turmoil means factions, and factions mean people willing to "tell" on other factions. But if CIA case officers in the former Soviet Union remain who they are and stay where they are, anyone who is willing to talk to them about the secrets of his competitors will have to put himself through a lot of trouble: go to Moscow; worm himself into the narrow social circles frequented by U.S. diplomats, find out which of the diplomats really are intelligence officers, and then open up to them. But alas the people best placed to do this are not upstart secretaries to factional leaders, but rather purveyors of disinformation. Thus the CIA is poised to discourage the right kind of walk-in business, and to encourage the wrong kind.

The post Soviet regimes' loosening of restrictions on travel—not to mention their encouragement of increased business contacts—have already *reversed* the postwar situation in which U.S. officials had a near (though near-worthless) monopoly of contact with the Soviets. In the 1990s unofficial contacts will increasingly dwarf official ones. But U.S. intelligence officers were not among those businessmen, churchmen, lawyers, physicians, scientists, labor leaders, and the like who took advantage of the Gorbachev thaw to establish relationships with people unconnected with Gorbachev.

The new difficulties that will baffle CIA spymasters in the former Soviet Union add up to this: many interesting people who are willing to say interesting things but are inaccessible to traditional U.S. case officers, while those who are accessible to them are perhaps the least interesting and most controlled people in that vast land. Thus in the 1990s CIA human intelligence on the former Soviet Union promises agents whose reports will be both less useful and more likely to be contaminated by disinformation than the sources of just about any private researcher. In the 1990s human intelligence may well answer key political questions about post–Soviet society—but not through an intelligence system like ours.

The New China

The problem of human intelligence in China lies less in getting people to talk (not to mention getting Westerners into the country) than it does in simply finding one's way around a huge society where non-Chinese are naturally objects of curiosity. Virtually every sector of Chinese society—agriculture, manufacturing, transportation—welcomes foreign experts, who as a result establish innumerable relationships. The television news magazine "20/20" was even able to put reporters and a camcorder into a Chinese forced labor camp. In the future, the extent to which relationships will be permitted will depend on the increasingly powerful local army commanders. The integration of Hong Kong and the opening of special economic zones means that millions of Chinese living in relatively unrestricted circumstances will be able to travel freely throughout China. Yet, as U.S. intelligence is now constituted, CIA officers will not be among the flood of travelers in the China of the 1990s. To be useful in the byways of that enormous country they would have to have the kind of sociopolitical roadmap that does not now exist. Indeed their first job would be to draw one up. Instead, CIA case officers will remain in official U.S. installations —they and their few agents, fixed targets for Chinese surveillance.

U.S. intelligence, following U.S. policy, has mistakenly regarded Chinese politics as monolithic, grounded in the perceptions of U.S. intelligence collectors based in the embassy who talk with the top levels of this monolith. But in the fractured reality of Chinese politics in the 1990s the action will not be at the center. When a general, or another personage in one of China's farflung corners, gathers a following, or when a particular social category, such as students or policemen, organize a mass movement, U.S. intelligence will know neither the leaders nor the followers. Events, not intelligence, will answer the question "Who are these people, and what do they want?" As when Eurasian communism collapsed, the U.S. government will be a spectator after the fact in one of the great dramas of mankind.

The Third World

Mexico and the Philippines, two countries important to the U.S. in the 1990s and so different in so many ways, are similar as objects of human intelligence. American citizens have a myriad of family connections and business investments in both countries. Though it is not always safe to ask pointed questions in either country, travel in both is unrestricted. In the 1990s, the politics of both nations should be permeable by Americans. In the past, especially in the Philippines, more people were volunteering to be agents or informants for the U.S. government than the U.S. could possibly accept. In the 1990s, the U.S. for the first time will have to seek out informants who are motivated by something other than the desire to obtain U.S. help in their struggles. Since the information will not be coming from the top of factions, our corps of spymasters who wait for government officials (or at least factional leaders) to come into their offices won't do. Nor is this corps fit to seek out clandestine contact with people who are engaged in politics at lower levels. Since these countries' political systems rely heavily on patronage, much of the political activity below the top takes place in nationalized industries, in labor unions, among government contractors, etc. But the CIA officers do not know who owes his job to whom. They do not have a political roadmap. And even if they had one, they could not approach their targets quietly and sympathetically because they don't speak their language, and because they stick out like sore thumbs.

India, Brazil, and other growing regional powers will challenge American collectors because the sources of information on their military industries and political purposes will be both diverse and deeply indigenous. These countries are more like empires than like banana republics. They are sophisticated enough to build nuclear weapons and space systems. Yet today, for example, the U.S. has next to no information about the state of assembly of India's nuclear weapons, never mind about specific plans for their use. By the turn of the century, when Indian nuclear stocks will be larger, the premium on a thorough knowledge of India's nuclear program will be greater. The Indian technical community is permeable, if only because it is so dependent on professional contacts with the West. But India's nuclear secrets will remain safe as long as attempts to run agents into that program come from the faraway world of diplomacy. By the same token, the Indian military buildup is highly specialized and spread all around the subcontinent. It is not realistic to expect some agent recruited at the top to give the U.S. access to the Indian military's many pieces.

Access to the pieces—i.e., to individuals—will also be the key to political intelligence, since the trend in both India and Brazil will be to empower more different kinds of human beings than ever before. There is one exception to this rule, however: Given the growing importance of the military in both countries, understanding their politics will require agents spread throughout their military forces. United States military attachés can provide *some* information on military politics. But to do a good job the U.S. would need collectors sympathetic with the local military but under cover deep enough to allow them to run actual covert agents. Occasional escorted trips to Indian military bases by white or black American attachés won't do.

The Islamic world will present a straightforward problem: With few exceptions (Bahrain and postwar Kuwait) it affords far fewer opportunities for contact with Westerners (especially Americans) than only a generation ago. This broad trend, though not motivated by desires to counter Western intelligence, is surely having that effect. In the 1990s, embassy-based collectors will have the kind of access to Saudi Arabian society that they did to Soviet society in the days of Stalin. But while Muslim society is closing itself to Westerners, it will not be immune to worldwide increases in international travel and economic relationships. Islamic countries will be perhaps more permeable than ever to non-Western foreigners. Certainly the oil states import every kind of human being, from the menial laborer to the supplier of luxury goods, to the purveyor of high technology. So while Indian or Brazilian businessmen or arms merchants will range freely through, say, Iraqi society, American intelligence officers will be restricted to official relations with the most disciplined sectors of that society. In times of turmoil, when human intelligence is most valuable, they will be obvious targets for even further restrictions, for expulsion, or for disinformation.

How will the CIA deal with Black Africa's increasing blackness—and with the U.S. government's increasing irrelevance on the continent? American administrators of food aid, American scholars, American tourists (in East Africa) and businessmen (in Nigeria), will have as much access as ever; perhaps more. African students returning to their countries from the U.S. will be even more valuable points of contact than ever. Nor will there be any shortage of political maneuvering on which to gather intelligence. But since the politics of Black Africa tend to be tribal, with a heavy dose of conspiracy, people involved in it will be reticent to be seen in the company of whites in general, Americans in particular, and official representatives of the U.S. government most of all.

In sum, then, the U.S. human intelligence system that already exists to deal with the world of the 1990s will not do because it will not furnish American collectors enough access to sources, and because it will not provide American collectors who possess the personal qualities needed to make use of those sources.

Technical Collection

THE SOVIET FOCUS

The questions that U.S. military commanders asked in the immediate aftermath of World War II were not so different from the ones they had asked about Axis forces a few weeks before: Which units are facing us? What have they got? What are their plans? The very same radio intercepts that had helped to track the remnants of Axis power now tracked the Soviet units in front of them. But whereas, in the latter part of World War II, U.S. reconnaissance planes had been able to overfly the enemy at will, now the Soviets made it clear that they did not want their forces overflown. Even American aircraft going to and from the U.S. garrison in Berlin would have to stay in specified corridors. So the U.S. was limited to turning its aircraft-borne cameras sideways to make maximum use of high-altitude flights along the borders and corridors of Soviet-controlled territory. These flights also carried antennas and recording devices to intercept whatever electronic signals were emanating from Soviet territory. All of this gave the U.S. marginally acceptable answers to tactical military questions about Soviet forces immediately across the line. But in those years technical collection shed little light on the interior, and hence on strategic questions.

The Border Strategy

For the first ten years of the postwar period, then, the United States' strategy for technical collection was to place cameras and antennas near the borders of the communist empires. This often involved flying U.S. airplanes directly toward Soviet border installations, so that the Soviets would activate their fire-control radars as well as the communications nets that serviced antiaircraft guns and interceptor squadrons. The U.S. planes, however, would turn away before getting to the border, having recorded the Soviet emissions. On other occasions U.S. aircraft would actually penetrate the borders and cause real scrambles— whose electronic manifestations they would record. On yet other occasions they would try to fly quietly along the borders just to listen to normal traffic. On a half-dozen occasions in the late 1940s, U.S. RB-29s flew from Alaska through Siberia and out to Japan, photographing and listening as they went. Once, in 1955, at the urging of the United States, a British crew flew an RB-50 from Scandinavia down along the Volga to the Caspian Sea and to Turkey. It landed safely, but full of bullet holes.[18] During this two-year period the U.S. also sent RB-57s, RB-66s, RB-69s, and P-2s on such missions, losing some two dozen aircraft. To the maximum feasible extent, the U.S. also ringed the Soviet empire with electronic listening posts: Iran, Norway, Turkey, Italy, Pakistan, Japan, and Korea all hosted U.S. intercept equipment, the complexity of which grew every year. Ships too carried antenna farms outside the three-mile limit of the empire's territorial waters. Not until 1968, when the North Korean Navy seized the U.S.S. *Pueblo* and its crew, was such a ship bothered.

This "border collection" provided some excellent data. The combination of pictures of a Soviet air defense radar's "dish," along with a recording of that radar's emissions, gave enough information for positive identification as well as accurate assessment of the radar's power, frequency, and resolution. This in turn was enough to guide development of sophisticated and very effective "penetration aids" for U.S. bombers. Also, a variety of devices recorded conversations and messages among Soviet commands. For many years, beginning in 1947, the U.S. was able to read even some of the encoded traffic because of a brilliant technical insight. CIA officers had noticed that as American cipher machines transmitted coded traffic, they also radiated the "clear" version for short distances, especially along cables. Thus CIA and British intelligence dug under the cable coming out of the Soviet command post in Vienna, and recorded its messages in both the "clear" and coded versions. This of course allowed the U.S. to reconstruct the code and thus to read some encoded messages from other Soviet sources that the U.S. managed to record. Until the late 1950s this provided solid knowledge of how Soviet forces operated, and promised early warning of plans for major attacks.

But the "border" approach did not allow much recording of messages from the interior of the Soviet Union. The major exception was the "take" from the antennas set atop the U.S. Embassy in Moscow. This allowed the recording of all broadcast communications, and of some telephone and teletype traffic, in and out of the Moscow area. In addition, by the 1960s, when the Soviet leaders acquired radio-telephones—as yet not encoded—for their limousines, the U.S. could listen in. In 1971, however, a Jack Anderson newspaper column told the world about this activity, together with its code name, "Gamma Gupy." By this time the Soviets had long since developed the equipment to encrypt such traffic, and "Gamma Gupy" instantly became useless.[19] Moreover, Soviet codes had evolved so far that the "key" obtained a generation earlier had long since become useless. Indeed, U.S. communications intelligence against the Soviet Union since the 1950s was something of a cyclical race: As the U.S. (none too secretly) gained the capacity to record a particular link, the Soviets either encoded it or shifted interesting traffic to secure links.

MODERN OVERHEAD COLLECTION

The first major American step beyond the borders was the U-2 aircraft, which first flew over the Soviet Union in 1957 at 80,000 feet. Soviet radars had it on screen, but neither Soviet fighters nor surface-to-air missiles could reach it. The Soviets were aware that the airplane could theoretically photograph and listen in on all broadcasts and beams near its flight path. They wished they could camouflage the military installations and silence the "clear" transmissions in its path, but this was impossible, since the plane never flew predictably. This problem ended in 1960, when the Soviets perfected the SA-2 missile that shot down the U-2. The satellites that the U.S. launched in the early 1960s—both photographic and electronic—were more intrusive than the U-2, because they passed over part of the Soviet Union every day. But they were also predictable. Hence the Soviet government instituted a program to warn all sensitive installations in the country to alter their operations during the time of their exposure to the satellites. While this practice did not prevent satellites from taking pictures and recording signals, it surely took much of U.S. technical collection about the Soviet Union out of the category of "secret intelligence."

Indeed at the very outset of the space age President Kennedy's decision to wrap in secrecy the basic facts of U.S. satellite reconnaissance (and their pictures) had nothing to do with enhancing their ability to collect, but rather was intended to weaken potential *domestic* challenges to policy.[20] No one was proposing to publish the details of the frequencies which our electronic satellites were optimized to intercept, or the operating manuals of our photographic "birds." But why not publish pictures that the Soviets already knew had been taken? Kennedy decided that, to the extent that data from satellites was widespread, to that very extent the president and those "in the know" would lose the authority that comes from the presumption that they are privy to special knowledge. Kennedy, and the presidents who followed him, all valued technical intelligence about the Soviet Union in large part because it would support their policies ("soft" or "hard") with regard to the Soviet Union, which they deemed important to their political success. Most specifically, technical intelligence was essential to arms control. Any president who engages in arms control must be able to assure the voters that *he* knows what the other side is doing *and* that he knows this better than any of his domestic opponents of the right or left.

Optimization: Arms Control or Military Operations?

Almost from the outset of the space age the history of U.S. technical collection has been closely intertwined with that of arms control. From the end of World War II throughout the years of "border collection" of the U-2, and even as the first photographic satellites were being designed, the U.S. collection strategy assumed that the next item gathered would be equally useful for any and all possible purposes of the U.S. government, from accommodation to military confrontation. Clearly this cannot be so. But many years would pass before anyone would officially suggest that it is not.

In the crucial years 1958–1963, this misperception was due to a fortuitous confluence between the technology of the first-generation, space-based intelligence, and the technology of the military threat *du jour*, the first-generation ballistic missiles. Arms-control enthusiasts wanted to know how many Soviet missiles were where, so that they could negotiate about them, while the people in charge of targeting U.S. strategic forces wanted to know the same information, in order to drop atomic bombs on them before they could be launched. In those days each missile had to be laboriously assembled on a launch pad that took months to build. In those days also, imaging satellites would drop "buckets" of film every few weeks, and could deliver comprehensive mosaics of the missile deployment areas along the trans-Siberian railroad every couple of months. Hence there was sound reason to expect the interaction between missile technology and surveillance technology to yield adequate warning of new missiles, as well as their accurate location. The U.S. military also wanted the pictures to show as much detail as possible, in order to estimate the damage that

111

the missiles could do, while arms controllers wanted detail in order to specify what they were negotiating about. All of this produced joint demands for more and better pictures of deployment areas as well as calm confidence that the intelligence situation was and would forevermore be well in hand.

But as the second generation of intelligence satellites was being designed, the question "For whose purposes shall they be optimized?" gently arose. Those in charge of war plans did not care so much about the quality of the pictures. They wanted lots of pictures of lots of countryside as often as possible, to make sure that no Soviet missile could remain untargeted. The scientific and technical intelligence people cared less about quantity, or about comprehensiveness, or even about timing. They insisted that the pictures they got be very good, suitable for careful study. The arms controllers were in the middle. They wanted lots of pictures of pretty good quality. But since they preferred pictures of known deployment areas, they agitated against spending resources for photographic "fishing expeditions." Thus the arms controllers were able to broker conflicting demands on the satellite designers regarding coverage, quantity, and quality.

The CIA's Herbert Scoville (former Deputy Director for Science and Technology) and those who have followed his lead (e.g., William Burrows, author of *Deep Black*) have written that U.S. technical collection is simply whatever the state of the art allows, and that arms controllers and war planners make of it what they can. Only the second part of the proposition is correct. Rather, U.S. technical collection is the result of consistent technical choices based on the supposition that space intelligence is essentially part of U.S.–Soviet cooperation and that ballistic missile warfare will never happen.[22] Military operations people do the best they can with information optimized for nonmilitary purposes.

The idea was simple: The U.S. and the Soviet Union had climbed onto a technological–strategic plateau that stretched out indefinitely, and which neither had an interest to transcend. Both could "destroy" one another, but neither could protect itself. Intelligence from space would help both sides to target their missiles on each others' cities, to realize that their own cities were targeted, and to realize that the other side's missiles were as invulnerable as their own. Space-based intelligence would reassure each side that the other was not trying either to protect its own population or to threaten the other side's missiles. Of course, each side would respect the other's space-based intelligence assets. In other words, space-based intelligence was to be not an instrument of conflict but the handmaiden of the strategy of "assured destruction," (assumed to be "mutual") codified in the SALT treaties, which U.S. negotiator Raymond Garthoff describes as "incipient cooperative strategic planning," and which was supposed to last forever.

Imaging Satellites
During the 1960s, the U.S. built two separate series of imaging satellites, one for low-resolution wide-area coverage, and the other for high-resolution "spot" imaging. The military targeters were the primary customers for the former, while the scientific and technical analysts and arms controllers were the primary customers for the latter. The high-flying, low-resolution series culminated in the KH-9. One (or at most two) would be in orbit at any given time. Each bird would last as long as a year in orbit, and would drop a bucket of film every few weeks. Over a year, it might produce one cloud-free frame of film of every part of the Soviet Union. The low-flying, high-resolution series culminated in the KH-8. Like the KH-9, the KH-8 would drop several buckets of film during its lifetime. It would be programmed to take close-ups of ships, planes, missile silos under construction, and whatnot. But both the high- and low-resolution birds often were redirected to what turned out to be the principal mid-to-high-resolution mission: the constant monitoring of missile deployment areas for purposes of arms control, as well as for the ubiquitous Indications and Warning.

By the early 1970s the U.S. was developing a new satellite, the KH-11. While the KH-11 was more versatile than all of its predecessors, it was optimized for monitoring places already known to be interesting. The KH-11 was almost as good as the KH-8 on resolution. But instead of passing film through its focal plane, that plane was occupied by a set of electro-optical sensors. The signals from these sensors are relayed to a ground station near Washington, DC, and the images reconstructed by a computer in near-real time. Thus the number of images that the KH-11 can send back is limited principally by the electrical power available through solar cells, and by the capacity of the equipment for processing the images—and of course by the satellite's location. Above all, the KH-11's capacity is limited by the small quantity that exist, which is determined by price. By 1990 each copy cost the better part of $1 billion over its lifetime.

From the late 1960s to the late 1970s, although neither mission was pursued to the satisfaction of its advocates, there was still a balance between high resolution (in the KH-8) and wide-area coverage (in the KH-9). But the decision in the late 1970s to rely solely on a few highly expensive copies of the KH-11 effectively gave up the balancing act. Henceforth U.S. reconnaissance would monitor with high resolution the roughly 4,000 Soviet strategic targets already known to be interesting, and especially the 2,000 targets useful for arms control. Inevitably this decision minimized "fishing expeditions," not just over the Soviet Union but over the rest of the world as well—even though the KH-11 itself (*if one disregards its price*) was better suited for fishing expeditions than its predecessors. But of course the price meant that only one or two would be in orbit, and that its capacity would be too precious for fishing expeditions. By the end of the 1970s a high-level committee (called COMIREX) would resolve the conflicting requests from throughout the U.S. government for the services of only *one* KH-11 in orbit. Known targets got priority, and searches for targets indicated by other sources came in second. Hunches need not be brought to the table. Constant surveillance had long ceased to be a goal.

Another set of U.S. government decisions in the late 1970s (as reported by *Aviation Week*'s Clarence Robinson, *The New York Times*' William Broad, William Burrows' *Deep Black*, and Bob Woodward's *Veil*) were made to develop the next generation of U.S. imaging satellites further, along the line of the KH-11. The satellite itself was modified to include an infrared focal plane for imaging at night. An entirely separate satellite named LaCrosse, using radar to produce images through clouds, was first planned in 1978, and launched a decade later. It can gather and transmit even fewer images than the KH-11, and of course a radar imaging system *ipso facto* advertises its own presence as well as much of its capacity. It is the antithesis of secret intelligence.*

By the end of the 1980s the U.S. had in fact accomplished a coherent program with regard to imaging systems. A tiny handful of very expensive satellites took surface pictures day in, day out, regardless of darkness or clouds, of places already known to be interesting. But the U.S. had given up any thought of viewing places that the Soviet Union did not expect to be viewed, much less of doing so without the Soviets knowing it.

This choice was entirely consistent with the logic of the U.S. position at U.S.–Soviet arms control talks since the 1960s. In a nutshell: U.S. negotiators have sought Soviet forces whose numbers, capacity, and location would be known in advance and verified by U.S. satellites built to notice and count the external features of known, fixed objects. Alas, U.S. decisions about both intelligence and policy ran diametrically counter to the logic of Soviet military developments: The Soviet Union built increasingly mobile strategic forces whose changing performance has been less and less clearly related to their observable characteristics. And the rest of the world (one need only mention the Persian Gulf) followed suit. By 1990 the U.S. regretted the imaging systems' lack of flexibility.

Electronic Collection
Satellites gave U.S. intelligence a new—and expensive—means of putting antennas into position to intercept signals. Hence the question "Which signals

*Note however that Robinson and those who have followed *Aviation Week*'s usually authoritative lead refer to a new satellite, the KH-12, which is supposed to embody not just all imaging capabilities but various kinds of signals intelligence as well. In reality there is not and never was a KH-12. Robinson mistakenly aggregated all the latest capabilities into a single "composite."

most interest us?" was inescapable from the beginning. The lion's share of the funds went to exclusively peacetime functions, notably arms control: intercepting telemetry from Soviet missile tests, and attempting to forecast the appearance of new test models by intercepting the telephone and teletype traffic transmitted by microwaves from locations associated with the development of strategic weapons. Lesser shares went to exclusively military purposes: identifying and keeping track of Soviet "emitters," e.g., fire-control radars and command-post radios. Of course there was a sizable gray area, and any given item of intelligence may be used for several purposes at once. But the big, expensive electronic satellites were undeniably optimized for peacetime.

The U.S. wanted Soviet missile telemetry not only for purposes of arms control but also in order to gauge the military threat to which it is exposed. To this end, in 1973 the U.S. supplemented its listening stations in Norway and Iran with a "big ear" at geosynchronous orbit (22,300 miles above the equator) code-named Rhyolite. This system (revealed to the Soviets by convicted spies Boyce and Lee) has been updated and renamed several times.[22]

The advantage of space-based over ground-based telemetry collection is that no horizon hides the telemetry transmitted by the first stage of a missile, which is the best indicator of the missile's launch weight and throw weight. Through telemetry it is possible to figure out how much a missile can carry, how reliable it is, and how accurate it is. Hence telemetry tells something about the state of the art of the missile, as well as how many and perhaps what kinds of places are vulnerable to it. But it really does not help anyone to do anything *about* the missile. To do that, as we will see in Chapter 9, one would need very different kinds of information. So it is important to note that the decision to collect every bit of telemetry from every test, and to analyze it for all it's worth, was not made to satisfy any *military* requirement. From the military point of view, only a bare minimum of telemetry information is usable. The rest is a kind of voyeurism. The precise telemetric calibration of a missile's characteristics, however, was currency for the arms-control bargaining table.

Access to communications is potentially the most useful of all intelligence, especially in case of war. Hence from the very outset of the space age the U.S. has supplemented its land, air, and sea-based listening posts by placing devices to record communications on a wide variety of spacecraft. But a number of technical factors and bad choices—and Soviet espionage—have reduced the performance of U.S. communications intelligence, Comint.

Space-based Comint has some inherent peculiarities. Although low-orbiting satellites can place a recording device reasonably close to the source of a radio beam or of a broadcast, the satellite zips through the beam (or through one of its side "lobes") too fast to catch meaningful conversations. (For similar reasons, low orbiters were never serious options as platforms for recording telemetry; most of the time they would not be "in view" of the source). So, serious space-based Comint had to await the development of antennas both large and sensitive enough to pick up signals from geosynchronous orbits *and* light enough to be lifted that far. Although the Rhyolite satellites first launched in 1973 had a secondary capability to pick up communications, not until 1978 was a satellite, code-named Chalet, parked in a geosynchronous orbit, where it wandered amongst the tails of microwave communications beams originating in the Soviet Union and elsewhere.

Like most of the land-, air-, and sea-based legs of the Comint network, Chalet operated on the "vacuum cleaner" principle. It would intercept all of the flood of signals coming its way, and then use various criteria to select a minority of channels worth recording. Some of these alerted the U.S. to the movement of military units, and other operationally useful information. There was also some "strategic early warning" of weapons already in progress but not yet out for satellites to photograph. But Chalet and its successors did not add much to the *operational* Comint already being gathered by ground stations and airplanes. The principal reason that the U.S. spent billions to expand its communications intelligence into space was quintessentially one of peacetime strategy: to monitor the intentions of the Soviet government. Not incidentally, the prime item on the U.S.–Soviet agenda was arms control. As we shall see, they did a lousy job.

To deal with Soviet military "emitters," other U.S. satellites had to do two jobs requiring somewhat different approaches: First, to record the signals of radars from the interior of the Soviet Union (from the small ones that guide surface-to-air missiles, to the stadium-size Pechora, Pushkino, and Hen House radars that guard the country against ballistic missiles), U.S. satellites had to be able to spend more than the few minutes over them that a low orbit would provide. Yet no antenna at geosynchronous orbit could pick up the signals well enough to analyze any of them. So the U.S. took a hint from the Soviet Molnya satellite, and built a generation of electronic intelligence satellites that fly in highly elliptical orbits (known in the trade as Molnya orbits), and which therefore spend small amounts of time flying low and fast over the South Pacific and the rest flying high and slow relative to the Soviet Union. This management of time-over-target also makes it more difficult to turn on the radars only when the satellites are not in view.

Second, to keep track of where *mobile* Soviet emitters (such as fire-control radars on antiaircraft guns, or the communications equipment of military command posts) are at any given time, the satellites need only glimpses—but they need them often. Hence the U.S. built several generations of small, numerous, low-orbiting satellites that well nigh cover the earth and flash their simple finding (e.g., "Emitter A is in location X") to the U.S. via relay satellites. These small satellites, because of their coverage, can be enormously useful to American military commanders in wartime because they would be practically the only means of continuously targeting moving forces—assuming the latter turned on their electronic equipment. (They proved useless during the Gulf war because Iraqi forces were stationary.)

In addition, the U.S. technical collection system includes the aforementioned satellites at geosynchronous orbit known as DSP, whose infrared telescopes register the hot exhaust plumes of Soviet missiles. In the early days, these satellites could merely warn that an attack was coming. Over the years, improvements in technology have given them an increasing capacity to track each missile and tell where it is heading. Most recently, the U.S. has chosen not to fit DSP satellites with on-board data-processing systems that would allow them to communicate this data directly to antimissile systems, and thus to serve as part of antimissile defenses. DSP technology is inherently useful for antimissile operations. The fact that it is not used for that purpose is not its fault.

In addition to DSP there are also high-altitude satellites, known as Vela, that watch for the flashes of nuclear bombs exploded in the atmosphere or in space. This of course is strictly for the purposes of monitoring the 1963 atmospheric test ban treaty and the non-proliferation treaty.

WHAT FOR?

To what does all of this amount? The activities to which we loosely refer as the U.S. technical collection system were never planned according to any single purpose, nor are they administered by a single organization. Rather, the "system" consists of over a hundred semisovereign multimillion-dollar programs pursued by the military services (some through the National Security Agency), by the Pentagon's National Reconnaissance Office, and by the Central Intelligence Agency. The Intelligence Community Staff contains committees to coordinate the various agencies' plans with regard to technical collection, and the Congressional intelligence committees also sometimes prod the system toward coherence. Yet coherence is elusive, because coordination is *ex post facto* to budgetary planning. Each program is driven by distinct purposes, and each has its own constituencies.

The most fundamental distinction amongst the programs is expressed in the way their budgets are grouped for presentation to Congress. On one side most (though not all) satellites, with their ground-based processing systems, are grouped under the category National Foreign Intelligence Plan (NFIP). On the other side, most land-, air-, and sea-based collectors are grouped under the category Tactical Intelligence and Related Activities (TIARA). The NFIP category consumes about $18 billion, of which $7 billion goes to the National Reconaissance Office.*

Note first that the fundamental distinction is between "tactical" and "national" intelligence. This reflects in part the basic bureaucratic compromise made at the "founding" in 1947 between "departmental" intelligence (the things that the military services, the State Department, the Treasury, and the Department of Justice would be allowed to do for themselves) and "national" intelligence (the "services of common concern" that were to be provided by the CIA).† But now ask: What could be the contemporary meaning of "national" as opposed to "tactical"? In practice, national emphatically *does not mean* that whereas the military services retain primary responsibility for making sure that their tactical operations are well supplied by technical intelligence collection, the President of the United States reserves and sets apart a category of intelligence machines peculiarly suited to national strategic *operations*. In practice, "national" intelligence has meant intelligence useful exclusively for *policymaking in a peacetime that is assumed to be endless*, and particularly useful for the arms-control process.

The most practical public evidence for this is the existence of a program called Tactical Exploitation of National CAPabilities (TENCAP). It was instituted in the late 1970s at the behest of senior military officers and Congressional intelligence staffers. They realized that the products of technical collection could be somewhat useful to the military for wartime targeting of enemy units, as well as for avoiding the enemy's best blows. But they also realized that, as a result of a long series of decisions, operational military commanders had not even been cleared for national intelligence. Either they did not know the satellites existed, or they did not know how the satellites could help them—much less could they get the information on a timely basis. TENCAP gave operational commanders

---

*This is a good time to sketch the remainder of the U.S. intelligence budget. Published sources agree that the CIA budget is roughly $3.5 billion, NSA roughly $4 billion, and TIARA about $13 billion. The General Defense Intelligence Program (GDIP) gets about $2 billion, while the other members of the community, including the FBI, get very little. *Washington Post*, 4 October 1990, p. 4.

†Of course, in the years after 1947 the CIA did not possess either high-altitude cameras or sophisticated antennas. In 1956 the CIA developed, and for several years operated, the U-2 reconnaissance aircraft. But as the space age dawned, the CIA decided not to try to establish a bureaucracy to design, launch, and operate a fleet of satellites. So the Director of Central Intelligence, as the chief coordinator of all U.S. intelligence activities, set up organizational means to exercise influence over those elements of the armed services (chiefly the Air Force) which did these things. This influence—and this is our point—has in fact been enough to give to these NFIP programs a focus. Following the CIA, most cognizant U.S. officials refer to this focus as "national."

the clearances, and made a few physical arrangements for delivering national intelligence products to them. But TENCAP was an afterthought, an effort to use national intelligence for actually fighting if need be, whereas that intelligence had been optimized to observe the Soviet Union with a view to striking deals with it. TENCAP was used in the Gulf War of 1991.

Technical collection (and processing), which has consumed perhaps 80 percent of the U.S. intelligence budget, has produced much more film and tape than the U.S. has been able to analyze. But despite the expenditure of scores of billions, technical collection has not magically lifted the curtain of secrecy that surrounds the Soviet Union, either for the purpose of fighting wars or of striking deals. The gap between what top government officials expect of technical collection and what it can actually deliver has grown.

THE WIDENING MISMATCH

As the years have passed, U.S. collection has gone from technical wonders to technical near-miracles. Images have become sharper and antennas more sensitive. Nevertheless, even as the quantity and quality of images has increased, as the number of signals intercepted has multiplied exponentially, and as better processing techniques have heightened the usefulness of every scrap of data, the U.S. has learned less and less about the military (and political) matters that are the *raison d'être* of technical collection. The reason is that the interaction between the technology being observed and the technology used to do the observation has increasingly worked against the observer. There is every reason to believe that this mismatch will widen in the future. This growing gap compounds the inevitable role of assumptions in the processing of technical collection. As a result, more "facts" about a narrowing base of subjects have produced what is arguably more relative ignorance than ever.

In the early 1960s, as satellites began to deliver sharp pictures of Soviet missile pads, airfields, and tank parks, analysts became able to write "hard" numbers of military equipment into their estimates. They became able to regularly associate electronic signals with photos of the equipment emitting them, to describe events observed, and to cite where and when they had occurred. This convinced analysts who had known next to nothing about the Soviet Union that they now knew next to everything. At the new CIA headquarters outside Langley, Virginia, wallpaper appeared in the inner lobby, showing a close-up of downtown Moscow in which each house is several inches wide. No one seriously argued for the wallpaper's implication—that U.S. intelligence now knew the Soviet Union inside and out. Nevertheless, the CIA projected the impression that the revolution in technical intelligence had produced omniscience, and many of its officials acted as if they believed that. At the very least, many U.S.

intelligence officials came to believe in the absolute integrity of the technical data they were using. Not only did they not entertain questions about the extent to which the other side might be managing its exposure to technical collection. They also did not question the comprehensiveness of their take. They accepted practically what none would accept theoretically: that technical data speaks for itself (a picture is a picture), and that what it says is all that need be said—i.e., that the object to be observed is defined by our capacity to observe it.

But the data that technical collection produces speaks only through the assumptions that govern its processing. Hence, U.S. intelligence has reported what it has seen and heard through small keyholes, and has extrapolated it to stand for the much larger reality beyond the keyholes. *The assumptions that govern the extrapolations have proved perhaps more important than the technical characteristics of the cameras and antennas.* To see this most clearly let us examine how the assumptions of the arms-control process have intertwined with those of technical intelligence to limit the value of sophisticated collection devices.

Assumptions, Arms Control, and Imaging Satellites

Nowhere did these factors so clearly combine to produce knowledge of the trees and ignorance of the forest as in the SALT I treaties of 1972. In 1967 the U.S. government noted that the Soviets were building large SS-9 missiles, each of which carried a 25-megaton warhead. Thus, despite relative inaccuracy, each SS-9 threatened to destroy an American "hard" target, such as a missile silo. The U.S. government feared that if the number of SS-9s were to approach that of U.S. strategic targets—roughly 2,000—the U.S. would be vulnerable to a disarming first strike. The greatest, the most central, of our strategic objectives was to prevent this from happening. The U.S. government had pictures of SS-9s, and formulated its public statements, negotiating positions, *and* intelligence requirements in terms of the SS-9.

The actual grounds for the U.S. government's fears, however, were generic: We really wanted to avoid *high numbers of Soviet warheads with the combination of nuclear yield and accuracy required for strategic warfare (counterforce)*, regardless of whether they were carried by the SS-9 or by anything else. But because the U.S. government identified the counterforce threat with the SS-9, the U.S. proposed a treaty designed narrowly to forbid the construction of any more SS-9s. Those U.S. officials who suggested that the treaty ban any and all warheads that could do the job of an SS-9 were dismissed with the (true) observation that such a treaty would be unverifiable by our satellites. Only a treaty focusing narrowly on the SS-9 arguably could be verified. But this line of logic drove even further. Because U.S. satellites could not see into Soviet factories, the U.S. had no idea of how many SS-9s were being produced. So we really could not verify limitations on the production of the SS-9, either. Yet these satellites could count and measure the holes in the ground into which the SS-9s were deployed. So the principal provision of the SALT I interim agreement on offensive weapons of 1972 limited the Soviet Union to 308 holes in the ground of a certain size, and the U.S. government loudly pronounced itself satisfied that it had forever exorcised the threat of counterforce weapons.* That was a fateful double-leap.

In fact, the satellites proved to be perfectly able to inspect the deployment areas often enough to observe construction or major modification of these holes in the ground. Their resolution proved to be plenty good enough to measure the diameter of silos within 5 percent. Since 1972, the satellites' periodic inspection of Soviet ballistic-missile fields have shown conclusively that *absolutely* no new SS-9-size holes have been dug. Nor have *any* smaller missile silos been enlarged to SS-9 size. So the architects of the SALT I treaty truly crafted a perfect fit between the treaty and the capacity of U.S. intelligence to verify it. And there were no violations of SALT I at all. The satellites verified that, period. Yet, the satellites aided and abetted a strategic reversal. Starting immediately after the signing of SALT I in 1972, the satellites learned, in ways unrelated to the criteria of the SALT I treaty, that the number of Soviet counterforce warheads rose from some 300 to over 6,000!† The United States' worst strategic nightmares of the 1960s became reality right under the watchful eyes of U.S. intelligence. What went wrong?

In narrow terms this was not an intelligence failure at all. The imaging satellites performed precisely as advertised. But the assumptions according to which they were used turned out to be very wrong. Note that the satellites themselves did not *cause* U.S. officials to adopt these assumptions. Nevertheless, U.S. policy-makers put on a particular set of blinders in part because a particular set of satellites was available. Who knows what would have happened without these satellites, or given satellites with different capacities? There is no limit to the human capacity to "see" what one wants to see. We only know that this is but one of countless examples of a growing disproportion between the things that satellites *actually* observe and what analysts, high officials, and the press *assume* that the things observed mean.

---

*The statement by Henry Kissinger to the U.S. Senate was typical: "When you think of the concerns that we have had for the past 25 years about first strike and counterforce, it seems to me [that SALT I] is of first importance, politically, psychologically and militarily." Testimony before the Armed Services Committee June 28, 1972; *Military Implications of the Treaty on Limitations of Antiballistic Missile Systems and the Interim Agreement on Limitations of Strategic Offensive Arms Hearing*; 92nd Congress, 2nd session (Washington, DC: GPO, 1972).
†See below, Ch. 5.

Telemetry and Missiles

A similar phenomenon occurred regarding the telemetry from the SS-9 missile. It affected SALT I, and kindred phenomena affected subsequent treaties as well. As missiles are tested they carry instruments to monitor temperatures, pressures, and the performance of subsystems. The readings are then broadcast via perhaps 100 channels to engineers on the ground—and to any foreign intelligence agency that can manage to listen in. But the intelligence service that intercepts the telemetry, unlike the engineers who designed it, does not know, and so must postulate, which channel of the signal relates to which instrument. It must also postulate the *scale* on which each channel is to be read. The answers we get about a missile's performance depend far more on choices about how the telemetry is to be processed than on the sensitivity of the antennas that gather it. While the tools for collecting telemetry have improved, those who process it have had to make harder and harder choices. The following is an example of the *easy* choices we once faced and flubbed.

As the SS-9 was being tested in the late 1960s, perhaps the biggest question in the minds of U.S. officials was: Is it accurate enough to destroy U.S. missile silos? The instrument most crucial for accuracy is the accelerometer within the inertial unit of the guidance system. But the SS-9 apparently transmitted three different readings from three different accelerometers. Were all of the accelerometers on the same scale? Were some reporting with systematic bias? Did the Soviets intend to take one or two of the readings, or did they mean to average all three of them? Only the Soviets knew the answers to these questions. We had to guess. Since the Soviets had known since 1957 (when a U.S. transport plane from Turkey crashed on Soviet territory with tapes of U.S. telemetry intercepts) that the U.S. was reading their telemetry, they might well have chosen to bias this telemetry to deceive the U.S. Or perhaps they did not so choose.

The very ambiguity of the accelerometer data gave American analysts the liberty to interpret it as they wished. And they wished to believe that Soviet missile-makers were either unwilling or unable to make silo-killing missiles. The American analysts chose the interpretation that would support their wish. Unfortunately, that interpretation turned out to be mistaken. By the late 1970s it was undeniable that the Soviets had developed a counterforce missile force, and one of the reasons why the U.S. did not is that it had mistaken what the Soviets were doing. Again, this was not the fault of the machines. Yet the mistake is incomprehensible except in terms of the machines' characteristics.

In the late 1970s and 1980s the mismatch between our telemetry collection and Soviet missilery grew. The Soviets began to encrypt telemetry, reducing U.S. collectors to monitoring the "externals" of the transmissions—that is, at what point in the missile's flight particular channels turn on and off. In the

1980s, the Soviets also occasionally transmitted powerful beams of "noise" at U.S. telemetry collectors, masking even the externals.

The advent of other, albeit spectacular, intelligence technologies has not made up for the decline of telemetry. Radars on land (the Cobra Dane on Shemya Island in the Aleutians) and at sea aboard the USS *Observation Island* (the Cobra Judy ship) are accurate enough not just to count the warheads that come from Eurasia into the Pacific test range, but also to accurately gauge their shape and reaction to atmospheric resistance—in effect weighing them. This, together with rough information on the missile's acceleration gained from geosynchronous DSP satellites, is enough for a rough calculation of the missile's lifting capacity ("throw weight" or maximum military potential). But of course such knowledge, however useful for inferences, should not be confused with knowledge of the missile's actual capacity: how many warheads it carries, of what yield, with what accuracy, with what reliability, and with what flexibility in targeting. Whereas once upon a time telemetry could disclose how many warhead stations existed on a missile, now the entire panoply of U.S. intelligence can't. The best that the best-placed radars can do by themselves is to tell how many "release maneuvers" a missile's postboost vehicle makes. Thus today, and in the future, intelligence cannot support treaty provisions such as those of SALT II and START that attempted to limit the number of warheads that any given kind of missile might carry. Indeed, technical intelligence cannot go beyond a guesstimate about whether two missiles are of the same *kind* or not. And the worth of that guesstimate is qualified by the arbitrariness of the categories that are the basis for distinction. Under the INF treaty of 1988, and the START treaty of 1991, just as under the SALT II treaty of 1979, a missile might be wholly new and yet "old" for treaty purposes—or vice versa. As we will see below (Chapter 4), attempts to address such problems by more closely defining what treaties allow and prohibit have proven counterproductive.

This is terribly significant from the standpoint of arms control, but not so significant from that of strategic policy or military operations. After all, the basic strategic question of the 1960s and 1970s (Will the Soviets build a war-fighting countermilitary force?) has long since been answered. That force is there, in sufficient quantity and quality, and whoever inherits it will not lack the technology to make the warheads ever smaller and more accurate. Nor is there any doubt that the latest-model Soviet missiles are mobile.

So the questions that U.S. technical collection must answer for the 1990s are of an operational nature: Where at any given time are the missiles? Under what conditions will they launch? How can we stop them if they do? But, as we have mentioned, U.S. intelligence was never meant to address such questions. Nor, until quite recently, was it meant to provide information on the characteristics of the exhaust plume of each missile, on the thermal and physical characteristics of decoys and warheads in all phases of flight, or on the physical resistance of missile skins to various kinds of lasers. This sort of information is quite useless for arms control, but is essential for antimissile defense. Yet in the face of diminishing returns and a new and pressing set of questions, much of U.S. technical intelligence remains equipped to seek out answers to only traditional arms-control questions.

Comint

Perhaps the best example of diminishing returns is the vacuum-cleaner approach to communications intelligence. Perhaps 90 percent of the dollars spent for Comint pay for satellites and other systems that rather openly intercept and filter mass communications: the vacuum cleaner. Perhaps 10 percent goes to the so-called "clandestine" signals intelligence, i.e., surreptitious placement of (or walking, driving, floating, or flying) a recorder close by the source of an interesting signal. Yet these few clandestine sources provide about half the results that the U.S. government finds useful. That percentage is rising, primarily because the vacuum cleaner is running against three trends: encryption that is ever better, ever cheaper, and ever more widespread; the shift of sensitive communications to non-air media, such as fiber-optic cables; and the explosion in the amount of uninteresting communications.

The ultimate purpose of communications intelligence with regard to arms control is to provide solid evidence about the other side's intentions. Yet no one inside or outside of the U.S. government claims that the U.S. has ever intercepted a conversation or message in which Soviet leaders discussed what they wanted to achieve through the arms-control process.

As regards the rest of the world, the late 1970s and 1980s saw the beginning of the end of easy pickings for American Comint. Whereas once upon a time most of the world's governments used codes and code machines that were playthings for American codebreaking computers, the age of the microprocessor and of the Data Encryption Standard, a complex mathematical algorithm developed by private cryptographers, have made it possible for private companies (never mind banana republics) to buy unbreakable codes. Not everyone has bought at the same time. But, for example, when in 1987 President Reagan publicly quoted a communication between the Libyan government and its consulate in Berlin in order to accuse the Libyan government of complicity in a terrorist act against U.S. servicemen in Berlin, the Libyan government modernized its code systems. Thus Libya joined the growing number of countries whose communications are readable only when code operators make mistakes like failing to turn the machine from "off" to "on" or when spies provide the keys to the codes.

124

Of course, vacuum-cleaner Comint can't be expected to produce information on people who do not use official communications links. If the Libyan terrormasters had communicated with their agents in Berlin by making a regular phone call from a phone booth in Rome or Cairo, for example, they would not have needed any codes at all. The chances of their call being picked out of the air would have been less than that of a courier to Berlin dying on the Autobahn.

By an analogous token our Comint has been of little use with regard to most of the political decisions that have shaped our world. When Mexico's President Lopez Portillo nationalized his country's banks in 1982 and started the great "Third World debt crisis" of the 1980s, the U.S. government was caught by surprise because he did not lay the groundwork by teletype or official calls. In a similar vein, the U.S. cannot expect that the Russian government will put "on the air" a decision about its objectives for dealing with the Ukraine, or that the leaders of Russian factions will put their message into media which the Soviet government—never mind ours—monitors.

Indeed, as Barton Whaley and others have shown,[23] the widespread use of electronic communications and the interception thereof have not made politico-military surprise less prevalent in the modern world than before. Quite the contrary: The U.S. has been surprised by every major world event since 1960—the Tet offensive that proved to be the turning point in the Vietnam War; the Soviet invasion of Czechoslovakia; the Yom Kippur War in 1973 and the ensuing Arab oil embargo; the Soviet invasion of Afghanistan; and the rise of the Polish Solidarity trade union in 1980, and the manner in which it was crushed in 1981, to name just a few. *The revolution that swept Eastern Europe in 1989, an event that ranks in importance with World War I, was wholly unheralded by technical intelligence. Antennas sensitive to millionths of amps, and orbiting cameras that could detect mice on the earth's surface, did not see hundreds of millions of people ready to overthrow the communist world.*

The bottom line must be this: Technical collection has produced a lot of data that commands attention. But since for the most part this data has not spoken for itself, it has given American intelligence analysts a latitude for interpretation which they have not used well. Some technical data has spoken for itself, but too late. For example, in 1978 U.S. satellites clearly photographed tanks around the Presidential Palace in Kabul on the morning after the Soviet-supported coup of Hafizullah Amin against Mohammed Daoud; and in 1973 they gave an accurate update of the fighting in the Sinai after the surprise of Yom Kippur. And of course, as we have already noted, by the late 1970s U.S. satellites had given solid proof that the gamble of SALT I had not worked. This all inspired a 1979 cartoon by McNelly in *The Richmond News-Leader* that sums up the proposition that technical data trails events. It shows a pair of Soviet missiles on the White House lawn as a presidential aide cries out that U.S. intelligence confirmed the Soviets' violation of SALT XXIII's prohibition against Soviet missiles south of the New Jersey Turnpike. The point is valid regardless of the enemy, and more valid for the weapons of the 1990s than for those of the 1970s.

WHY U.S. TECHNICAL COLLECTION WON'T DO IN THE 1990S

While U.S. technical collection has grown by straight-line extrapolation of old approaches, weapons have changed fundamentally. Missiles, the principal targets of U.S. intelligence during the past generation, are rather simple devices. All of a missile's functions relate to going from point A to point B. Hence it is possible to make some sense of pictures and intercepts about missiles by relating them to the fundamental function of missiles. Size, distance traveled, load carried, maneuvers made, and the rest are both meaningful and externally observable characteristics. In other words, missiles are extraordinarily easy intelligence targets, and peculiarly susceptible to U.S. technical collection. But most modern weapons depend on technologies whose operations are *not* externally observable. Consider the case of what may be the prototypical weapon by the turn of the century, the space-based laser.

Even many high-quality, close-up pictures of a laser weapon will not tell us anything significant about its effectiveness. Not even a trained observer standing next to it as it operates would know how much power it has, how flat the wavefront of its beam is, how accurately it aims, or how many times it can fire. Nor would telemetry from tests in space do much good. Even if telemetry could be read, it would not mean much because it would refer to actual performance only indirectly. To see why, compare the usefulness of telemetry for lasers and for, say, cruise missiles. Whereas telemetry from the test of a laser and of a cruise missile may both refer to the percentage of power at which they are being run, the figure for the cruise missile is meaningful because it can be related to its observable speed and altitude, but the figure for the laser's power is useless because it lacks meaningful reference. What would X percent power input mean? The same would be true for other parameters as well.

Now consider a mainstay of modern and future weaponry: phased-array radars. How efficiently do they sort their data, and how accurate are the instructions they pass to antimissile interceptors? These very questions may also be asked of the newer infrared satellites at geosynchronous orbit that are providing ever better tracking data on missiles, and of yet newer ones on the drawing boards that will do so for warheads. The answers depend on factors that simply do not yield to external observation—namely, the quality of the detectors (in the case of infrared instruments), and also the quality of the data processing. For that matter, how well set up are individual missile-interceptor stations (or, for that matter, antimissile laser weapons) to receive information from primary missile-tracking stations? That depends almost entirely on the quality of their computer software, which of course cannot be observed externally.

Then there is a host of questions about how well shielded these systems' circuits are against kinetic, nuclear, or electromagnetic effects. Their designers will discuss these matters in their offices. But they won't put them "on the air" for the American vacuum cleaner to pick up, and no amount of passive physical observation will yield any data at all on them.

Now consider the changing relationship between missiles and intelligence. In the 1980s U.S. intelligence—especially those officers most wedded to arms control—felt cheated when the Soviet Union began producing long-range missiles small enough to move about easily on trucks or rails, because they could be manufactured, stored, or fired if not quite anywhere, at least far more widely than could old-style, fixed behemoths. This spawned a host of proposals for "cooperative measures" of verification, the best-known of which are associated with the INF treaty. These proposals are attempts to square the circle: Whether in Russia, Iraq, China, or any place at all, a missile cannot be hidden for purposes of safety and operational effectiveness while at the same time be shown for the purpose of being counted. And if a piece of military equipment is inherently nondistinctive in appearance, why would its owner make it or station it distinctively unless he were militarily unserious? But if he were that, why would he have the equipment in the first place? And if he were serious and used all the means of concealment and deception at his disposal, what would be the chances of picking them out by using devices that cannot look within the crowd? Rather, through "cooperative technical verification," anyone building a covert force could funnel to its adversary masses of data that, by agreed definitions, signaled compliance with agreements even as he was producing the prohibited armaments.

This problem will be especially acute in an age in which antimissile defenses are a significant factor because antimissile equipment has always been nondistinctive. The distinction between antiaircraft radars and interceptors and antimissile radars and interceptors, once difficult to draw, is now well-nigh impossible to make. Here too the arms-control process has helped to push U.S. technical collection into irrelevance. In 1985 the U.S. government judged the Soviet radar at Krasnoyarsk to be a violation of the ABM treaty. But it was only one of nine identical installations around the USSR, eight of which do not violate the treaty but all of which are equally useful for antimissile defense. Because of the treaty, the pictures and intercepts of those eight have proved irrelevant to U.S. antimissile defense planning.

The newest antimissile equipment, based on infrared detectors, small and powerful computers, and laser weapons or hit-to-kill vehicles, requires manufac-

127

turing operations not so different from those for television sets or communications satellites. This line of development is analogous to that of chemical weapons: They can be produced by the same equipment that produces pharmaceuticals or fertilizers. *In sum, because modern technology is a versatile servant of the human will, the superficial glances at such technology that U.S. technical intelligence is capable of providing will raise more questions than they answer, and invite intelligence officers to answer them with their own assumptions.*

The mismatch between the weapons of the 1990s and the technical means of collecting information about them means that U.S. intelligence will be ill-equipped both for monitoring arms-control agreements *and* for carrying out military operations. Imagine a ban on antimissile, space-based lasers. How would they be defined? Certainly the treaty would specify impermissible levels of power, beam quality, accuracy, etc. But since these would be impossible to verify by mere observation, the treaty would probably provide for some sort of "on site," or even "hands on" inspection of lasers nominally intended for antisatellite work, or even for planetary spectrography (à la the 1988 Phobos probe). But the relationship between the models superficially observed in space and the ones "intrusively" visited on the ground would remain a matter of faith.

Indeed, in case of major war the United States may not get much benefit at all from U.S. intelligence satellites, because they were designed and built on the assumption that outer space would remain a privileged sanctuary, and that no one would dare destroy U.S. intelligence assets. Alas the Soviets chose to build the antisatellite equipment that the U.S. chose *not* to build. The people who inherited that equipment could decide to destroy U.S. satellites not just as part of an attack on the U.S. but also perhaps to carry on a civil war with some privacy.

The U.S. government's choices about intelligence technology will also result in missed opportunities. The same developments that have made missiles small, cheap, plentiful, and mobile (though not in the U.S.) make it technically possible to make satellites so cheap as to be ubiquitous. The same developments that make encryption ubiquitous make it possible to make signals collectors well-nigh invisible. In short, the only reason why American technical-collection equipment in the 1990s will be large, expensive, few in number, obvious, vulnerable, and ineffective rather than small, cheap, plentiful, stealthy, hard to hit, and effective, will be because in the 1970s and 1980s the U.S. government made the wrong choices.

Unprotected Collection

Intelligence collection, both technical and human, must not be judged on its own terms alone, as one would judge an investigation of nature. Intelligence concerns human activities, and human beings, unlike God, go to great lengths to disguise their work. So perhaps the most serious charge that can be made against the fruits of U.S. collection concerns not the collectors but another set of people: the counterintelligence officers who should have guarded the integrity of the collectors' work. How and why they failed to do so is the subject of the next chapter.

4

Fragmented Counterspying

We have uncovered Boyce and Lee, Kampiles, Truong, and
Barnett rather quickly after they became traitors, and that is a
reasonable indication that our counterintelligence is working well.
                    – *Stansfield Turner*
                              Director of Central Intelligence

The foreign counterintelligence threat, in terms of our program, is
as follows. . . .
                    – *William Webster*
                              Director, Federal Bureau of Investigation

Some companies regard quality control
as an opportunity to glory in the integrity of their product. Others think about
quality control as little as possible, or even view it as a hindrance and a potential
source of embarrassment. The U.S. intelligence system's approach to counterintelligence is of the latter kind. As a result, the U.S. intelligence product, and thus
a substantial part of American statecraft, have received only fitful protection.

To a greater extent than intelligence collection, American counterintelligence
(CI) "just growed" from disparate roots. The various federal agencies that "do"
some CI have never viewed their activities as part of a comprehensive system.
The military runs ships, tanks, and planes. The CIA runs spies and produces

estimates. The FBI catches crooks. In the process, they all "do" counterintelligence. Hence the U.S. has not one CI, but many, and the various pieces of American CI do not form a coherent whole. The major federal agencies regulate their intercourse with regard to CI through "memoranda of understanding"— the bureaucratic equivalent of treaties among sovereign nations. Hence American CI is the geometric resultant of countless decisions by top officials for whom CI is at best a peripheral concern, at worst just a bother.

Our discussion of American CI begins with its pieces: military CI, the Federal Bureau of Investigation, and the CIA. Once we have come to know the players, we discuss how they go about their business. Having done that we are then able to examine the mismatch between what American CI does, the job American CI has set for itself, and the tasks that our political and strategic situations require of it.

Military Counterintelligence

U.S. military forces, like all others, have always tried to penetrate their enemies' intelligence while protecting their own secrets. One of the perennial fields of military CI is signals. Thus during the Civil War, as telegraphy was becoming a principal means of communication, the Union Army established the Signal Corps to transmit coded telegrams, guard the Union's codes, as well as intercept and decode Confederate telegraphic traffic. It did so at the suggestion of Gen. Alfred Meyer, a telegrapher who had decoded smoke signals from the Comanche scouts who were watching the U.S. Cavalry in New Mexico. Like smoke signals, intercepted and decoded Confederate telegrams told how well the enemy was observing the movements of U.S. troops. In our time, the Army uses electronic penetrations of enemy battlefield intelligence to target long-range artillery and battlefield missiles almost automatically. "Signals counterintelligence" has meant counterpunching. American military forces in action, like all others, have also routinely guarded against spies and saboteurs by finding or planting informants among people who could be (or become) spies or saboteurs. During the campaign against Philippine insurgents in 1901, the Army set out to protect its commander, Gen. Arthur MacArthur, by gathering intelligence on, and hence capturing, the rebel Aguinaldo, who had planned to kill MacArthur.

Peacetime American military CI evolved very slowly from the establishment of the Office of Naval Intelligence in 1882, and of the War Department's (Army) Military Information Division in 1885. At the very beginning the handful of individuals assigned to peacetime Army and Navy intelligence paid next to no attention to security—never mind CI. For example, only after the turn of the century did military intelligence promulgate even the most rudimentary security rules regarding civilian access to military installations.

From the beginning there has been a big difference between Army and Navy

CI. The Navy, traditionally having only ships and yards to protect, has chosen to combine investigations of enemy espionage and sabotage with investigations of the garden-variety sabotage committed by sailors who want to stay in port, and with investigations of criminal activity. When the air arm that became the U.S. Air Force separated from the Army in 1947, its Office of Special Investigations (OSI) was modeled after the Navy's Office of Naval Intelligence (ONI) rather than after the Army, where criminal matters are handled by a Criminal Investigation Division (CID), and where counterintelligence deals solely with threats to the Army and the nation. According to an early account, the Army's "Military Information Division has much more complex duties . . . in keeping track of enemy activities within our own borders and foiling them."[1] Hence, since Army CI has not bothered with thefts, drug trafficking, etc., it has been less involved with the daily lives of military units than with the outside world.

By World War I the Military Intelligence Division's counterintelligence work in the field included investigations of personnel, and listening in on our own communications to determine their vulnerability. It also routinely injected false information into vulnerable U.S. communications links so that if indeed they were intercepted, the enemy might not make good use of them. But because U.S. forces in France did not have to worry about threats from the local population, Army CI did not run informants into the French population.

The Army did not have much to worry about on the home front, either. But worry it did. The American public's perception of danger from German agents (surely fed by nativist sentiments and by dislike of foreign-born political radicals) fueled an expansion of military CI within the U.S. far beyond the Congress' willingness to fund it. Hence the Army commissioned thousands of volunteer intelligence officers across the country who took their commissions as a warrant for vigilantism. Since then, the extent to which the military should protect itself against potential espionage or subversion of its troops or disruption of its supply lines has been the subject of much controversy.

During and after World War II the number of regular military CI officers and civilian CI specialists grew into the thousands; they were stationed with every major command, both at home and abroad. They worked either alone or with the FBI to discover or manipulate foreign espionage in the armed forces. Before the mid-1970s the services routinely considered persons and groups who had access to servicemen and who could use that access for espionage, sabotage, or subversion as fair targets for infiltration. Military CI officers would recruit spies to report on potentially threatening persons, and keep files on them.

During the Vietnam war, when many Americans openly worked to defeat the U.S. by causing disaffection and sabotage on military bases, military surveillance of American civilians grew apace. In the 1970s this practice was denounced as an infringement of civil rights. Consequently, the Defense Department promulgated a series of guidelines called the Defense Investigative Program, which, under the supervision of the Defense Investigations Review Council, restricts the service components to investigating only those American citizens subject to the Uniform Code of Military Justice, plus foreigners. Today, when cases inevitably lead the military services' CI components into contact with U.S. civilians, the components must present the case to the FBI, which must decide either to assume or direct the case, to authorize the military component to pursue it, or to order that it be dropped. Similarly, the components are limited in the files they may keep. These guidelines have fixed American military CI into a wholly reactive posture. Today, Army CI has about 1,400 officers and enlisted men. The Naval Investigative Service employs 366 civilian special agents (and almost as many support personnel), and the OSI employs a total of 600.

Each of the military services also tailors special counterintelligence operations to protect the usefulness of especially secret devices for the collection of military intelligence. As we shall see later, this involves an assessment of the various ways in which hostile intelligence services can learn about the devices, and sophisticated ways of rendering this information useless. The Army has taken the lead in this regard.

Finally, the military is still the leading element in American codebreaking. At the beginning of the U.S. involvement in World War I, the War Department formed, over and above the Army Signal Corps, the Code and Cypher Section—MI-8, headed by a conveniently commissioned civilian, Herbert O. Yardley. This began the practice, now multiplied many thousandfold in the National Security Agency, of civilian mathematicians employed as a central cryptographic pool for the military. After the war a civilianized MI-8, partially financed by the War Department and partially by the State Department, set up shop in New York. Known as the "black chamber," it furnished the State and War Departments with solutions to foreign governments' codes. After Herbert Hoover's Secretary of State, Henry Stimson, withdrew support with the epithet "Gentlemen don't read other gentlemen's mail," the group went out of business. The Army's share of its support went to the Signal Corps, which continued the tradition of hiring civilian codebreakers. In 1937 an Army civilian, William Friedman, broke the Japanese diplomatic "Purple" code which was the basis for the cryptologic successes that played such a major role in World War II's Pacific Theater.* This tradition of civilian–military cooperation in cryptology received a big boost during World War II.

---

*In 1940 the US team built an analogue of the Japanese cipher machine that had produced messages in "Purple" code. This was an intellectual achievement far superior to that of the British cryptologists who figured out later models of Enigma from the early-model Enigma in their possession. In 1942 the U.S. team broke the Japanese naval code.

Today the National Security Agency (NSA), led by Army, Navy, and Air Force general officers (on rotation) is a huge pool of military and civilian cryptoanalytic manpower on whom the rest of the U.S. government relies for breaking the communications of (among others) hostile intelligence services and terrorists. The NSA is not primarily a counterintelligence agency. But without the NSA's capacity to intercept and decode communications, U.S. counterintelligence would barely exist. Communications intelligence (Comint) and other signals intelligence (Sigint) can be useful in checking out information. For example, in 1964, when Soviet defector Yuri Nosenko told the CIA that he had defected when he did because his office had received a telegram telling him to return to the Soviet Union, the NSA was able to report, definitively, that no such telegram had been on the airwaves at that time.[2] In addition, NSA lends its technical expertise to CIA's and FBI's efforts at "bugging." But while the NSA is very keen on security about everything it does, it does not *do* any CI with regard to its own collection operations, because its management heretofore has not seen any need or use for it.

The FBI

The Federal Bureau of Investigation has the lion's share of the funds and personnel in American CI. For the most part, the FBI *is* American CI. Founded in 1908, the Bureau was really launched by the hysteria over spies and subversives that accompanied and followed World War I. There was indeed a wave of radical violence in America at that time. Members of the Industrial Workers of the World (IWW), together with left-wing socialists and anarchists— many foreign-born—were staging violent strikes and spreading the specter of revolution. These "Reds" were not in league with the Kaiser, and were not about to overthrow the Government. But they scared enough Americans to bring on themselves massive repression by local, state, and federal authorities, in addition to private vigilantism. In 1919, under Attorney General Alexander Mitchell Palmer, the Bureau of Investigation became the federal government's chief weapon against radicalism. The biggest part of the Bureau, the General Intelligence Division, headed by young J. Edgar Hoover, did not so much investigate as it disrupted and arrested these domestic enemies. The obvious excesses in this repression led the subsequent Attorney General to confine the entire Bureau, now under J. Edgar Hoover's leadership, to investigating violations of law. Although the decade 1924–34 saw the FBI busy enforcing Prohibition (with the help of Army and Coast Guard codebreaking) and fighting other organized crime, the FBI never abandoned its anti-espionage, antisubversion mission.

As World War II approached, the FBI recruited informants among American Nazis and communists—the presumably disloyal. Indeed, the FBI kept track of all who fit the category of "enemies, foreign and domestic"—including the Ku Klux Klan. In the absence of a civilian intelligence agency specifically assigned to operate abroad, the FBI even developed networks of informants in northern Latin America. Throughout this time the FBI's efforts to protect the vast majority of the population against its fringe elements gained the affection of the American people. Few Americans saw the FBI as a threat. So far had the FBI come from the days of the "Red scare" that J. Edgar Hoover opposed the wartime internment of Japanese Americans on the ground that no evidence existed of their disloyalty.

The period 1945–55 was the FBI's finest hour. During the war there had been precious few Nazi and Japanese spies in the U.S., while the US–Soviet alliance effectively curtailed the attention that the Bureau gave to Soviet espionage.* But by the fall of 1945, the FBI had turned sharply toward the Soviet threat. The defection in Canada of Soviet code clerk Igor Gouzenko brought massive evidence of Soviet espionage in North America, including on the MANHATTAN Project. And the defection in Washington of Elizabeth Bentley (a communist who served as the KGB's contact with spies in the U.S. government) put the FBI face-to-face with a classic detective problem: Gather evidence to prosecute known spies and uncover unknown ones. By the mid–1950s the FBI, through cryptology, surveillance, and detective work, had "cleaned up" the vast wartime Soviet espionage network.

In the postwar period the FBI continued to fight foreign spies and subversives according to the crime-fighting model that had brought it so much acclaim: Identify the troublesome individuals, gather evidence against them that would stand up in court, and then arrest them, so that they could be jailed or expelled. The FBI was not averse to leaving informants in radical organizations for long periods of time, or to using them to disrupt or guide the organization. Indeed, during the late 1950s humor in American leftist circles had it that the Communist Party U.S.A. consisted primarily of FBI informants. FBI Special Agents "on the beat" knew very well that to arrest a known spy was usually to exchange a known problem for an unknown one, because the hostile intelligence service would most likely just recruit another one. Nevertheless, for the FBI, intelligence was only a means. The FBI were and remain, first and foremost, cops.

Part of the FBI's police–CI function was surveillance of hostile foreign

---

*One FBI Special Agent describes assignments to the "Soviet beat" of the FBI during the war as "Siberia time." Note that, in the FBI's lingo, Special Agents are full-time, career employees of the FBI. They are the Bureau's equivalent of the Navy's Line Officers. Special Agents, like detectives, have any number of paid and unpaid informants, who are sometimes called "agents" but never confused with Special Agents.

diplomats and their premises. In this regard, J. Edgar Hoover much resented that the newly established CIA (like the wartime OSS) also had an interest in representatives of hostile governments—not to mention in Latin America. Part of the resentment had to do with the presumption that the CIA might be more willing than the FBI to tolerate known spies for the sake of intelligence. Hence the establishment of the CIA entailed a series of bureaucratic compromises about which agency could do what, and where.

The stakes in these struggles were simply pieces of bureaucratic turf. The FBI, however, portrayed its demand for exclusive counterintelligence jurisdiction within the U.S. as an attempt to protect the American people from the CIA, an organization presumably accustomed to fighting the nation's enemies with the strongest possible weapons in an arena without ground rules. In reality, and contrary to conventional wisdom, the CIA has *no* weapons with which to threaten civil liberties. The FBI, not the CIA, has the power of arrest. The FBI, not the CIA, can work with federal and state prosecutors. Nevertheless, the myth that the division of responsibility for CI has something to do with safeguarding civil liberties is an enduring one.

At any rate, the FBI also has the unique responsibility of carrying out, or supervising, all CI investigations in the U.S. The military services, the Treasury's customs service, the CIA, the State Department, indeed all government agencies, are obliged to call on the FBI to manage whatever contact anyone associated with them might be having with hostile intelligence services. No other intelligence agency may hold files which relate to CI matters on any U.S. person not their employee. Nor has the FBI wholly given up its foreign portfolio. Since law enforcement is an international problem, the FBI maintains liaison with the internal security services of major West European and South American countries. Through its "legal attachés" abroad, the FBI can follow up, to some extent, on the foreign ramifications of its American CI cases. However, the FBI must coordinate its Foreign Counterintelligence (FCI) activities in any foreign country with the CIA's station chief in that country. The rule is: If Americans are to be investigated anywhere, the FBI will do it if at all possible. Within the U.S., *only* the FBI can conduct CI operations, period.

The FBI's primary FCI activity is the identification, surveillance, and neutralization of resident officials from "criteria countries"—that is, from countries hostile to the U.S. whose intelligence services are judged to be active in collection and covert action against the U.S. Of course, the FBI also attempts to recruit double agents, runs them as "FCI sources," and reports the positive intelligence gained from them to the CIA. While most Americans believe that the CIA protects them from the KGB's wiles, in reality such protection as they have comes primarily from the FBI.

The FBI's activities against terrorists both foreign and domestic are run out of the Criminal Division. The ostensible reason for keeping terrorism out of the FCI division, which works with the CIA, is to safeguard the civil liberties of Americans. The disadvantage of cutting antiterrorism off from FCI is that the Criminal Division does not have even the very limited liaison with the rest of the intelligence community which FBI/FCI has. Counterterrorist coordination is in the form of interagency working groups and (more frequently) the personal relationships between FBI Special Agents and their counterparts in other agencies.

The FBI, like the CIA and the several parts of the Defense Department, regularly gathers information on terrorism. But there are no common U.S. files, nor any common plans, except for a network of "memoranda of understanding" between the agencies. These define the workings of the "lead agency concept," which is to say the circumstances in which one agency will "take the lead" in responding to a terrorist attack, while others follow. For example, if terrorists were to hijack an American aircraft, the Federal Aviation Administration would be the lead agency *so long as the plane's doors were closed.* Once they opened, the FBI would become the lead agency, unless of course this occurred outside the U.S.—in which case, according to the memoranda of understanding, the State Department would become the lead agency.

The American civil strife of the 1970s significantly shaped the FBI's role in CI. The U.S. fought a war in Vietnam without declaring war. Because the U.S. did not legally have an enemy, nothing that any American did could possibly have fulfilled the constitutional meaning of treason, namely to "give aid and comfort to the enemy." The FBI, however, investigated those Americans who were trying to defeat the U.S. cause in Vietnam just as it had investigated communists and Nazis. This time, however, because the country was not legally at war, and because the Bureau's "targets" were far better connected with the U.S. government than communists and Nazis had been, they successfully argued within the government that not they but the FBI had stepped outside the law.* The result was a series of executive orders (President Carter's 12036 [1978] and Reagan's 12333 [1981]), as well as internal guidelines, that have restricted the FBI's FCI ever more strictly to investigations of violations of law. If

---

*Similarly, during the mid-1980s the U.S. government was effectively at war with the government of Nicaragua. But there was no declaration of war because the President wanted to keep his options open. This, however, gave many Americans the option of working with the Nicaraguan government to defeat the U.S. U.S. counterintelligence was again in a difficult position. NSA monitored the foreign telephone conversations of Nicaraguan officials and often recorded them discussing common strategy with American members of Congress. The U.S. government helped them keep their secret.

a given matter has no "criminal nexus," the FBI cannot even clip newspapers about it. In 1978 this chain of events and reasoning led to the Foreign Intelligence Surveillance Act (FISA), which requires permission of a special court even to intercept the communications of foreign embassies and extends to foreign corporations in the U.S. all the immunities of U.S. citizens.

The details of what is and is not allowed are far less significant than the fact that, for the FBI, counterintelligence has become largely a matter of adhering to procedures. The guidelines, the FISA, the executive orders in their various forms and in the several permutations of circumstances and authorizations they treat, assume (1) that any CI activity or concern begins with an allegation or a bit of evidence suggesting that someone is or may be working for a foreign power *in a way that implies a breach of U.S. law*, and (2) that CI's attempt to check out the allegation or evidence should be more or less vigorous, more or less "intrusive," according to whether the evidence is strong or weak and, above all, whether the subject of the investigation is or is not a "U.S. person." According to the situation, authorization for the activity will have to be sought at a higher or lower level, and the fruits of the investigation may be disseminated to other intelligence agencies more or less freely. The paramountcy of procedure determines the character of today's FBI/FCI far more than the actual content of the standards.

The CIA

The CIA was meant to pull together all the nation's intelligence resources for purposes of analysis, collection, and covert action. But not for purposes of counterintelligence. Primarily because the FBI's powerful chief, J. Edgar Hoover, was able to guard his bureaucratic turf, the CIA was not to be allowed even to have copies of everything the FBI collected, ostensibly to safeguard civil liberties but surely to prevent outsiders from criticizing the quality of the Bureau's work. Naturally, in the course of pursuing cases (which nearly always have both domestic and foreign ramifications), the FBI has been quite willing to share such data with the CIA. But *this has always happened on a case-by-case basis.*

The most important feature of CIA counterintelligence is of an entirely different nature, namely a deeply ingrained resistance to independent quality control of espionage and covert action. The founders of the CIA brought that resistance with them from the OSS. The founder of OSS, Gen. William Donovan, did not have CI in mind when he started. He did not get around to instituting a counterintelligence section, called X-2, until July 15, 1943. During the previous year he had tried to stimulate his intelligence and operations sections (SI and SO) to pay more attention to whether their contacts were penetrated by the Germans, as well as to build a central registry against which their contacts might be checked. Indeed, sporadic efforts at quality control (e.g., Joseph Curtiss' meticulous analysis of agent reports at the Istanbul OSS station, which showed the entire amateurish operation to be controlled by the Germans) were proving the need for CI. They were also proving that the espionage and operations sections were unwilling or unable to cover their own activities.[3]

None of the people who ran X-2 had ever done CI before. They learned on the job. Their guidance was twofold: British practices, and the nature of the job itself. The Washington headquarters of X-2 compiled a central registry of contacts and agents from the various stations' contributions, and argued with the headquarters of SI about the *bona fides* of agents. In perhaps its most clamorous case, X-2 embarrassed SI by proving correct in its doubts about a supposed source within the Vatican on whose credibility SI had staked its reputation.[4]

In the London OSS station, which proved to be the training ground for a whole generation of American counterspies, X-2 handled the liaison regarding both the Ultra decrypted intercepts and the Double Cross committee that managed German double agents. Through Double Cross, X-2 saw up close that the German services were operating with agents whom they trusted but who were under hostile control. Hence X-2 personnel could imagine how American agents might be manipulated. In sum, whereas SI was looking at espionage from one side only, X-2 learned to look at it from both sides. Ultra taught X-2 to check human sources against the results of signals intelligence. When the name of a prospective agent showed up in German communications, X-2 would have to tell SI that sources which could not be discussed showed that the agent should not be used. The most thorough performance came from the Rome station of X-2, which James Angleton headed at the end of the war. Not only was it most able in its use of registries and of Ultra. It also produced useful profiles of German intelligence units, and showed how intelligence about enemy intelligence could be used to predict troop movements as well.

The rest of OSS never allowed X-2 to follow trails of foreign intrigue into OSS itself. Each part of the organization handled its own security apart from counterintelligence, and generally did a terrible job of it. The story of Soviet penetration of OSS is an old one. In 1945 Elizabeth Bentley told the FBI that seven members of William Donovan's staff were Soviet agents, including Donovan's legal adviser, Duncan C. Lee. Subsequent accounts based on decrypted Soviet traffic have claimed that the total was much higher.[5] In sum, because of the penetrations, the existence of OSS was a boon for the KGB.[6] The leaders of OSS were anything but ignorant of the pro-Soviet propensities in the ranks. Their reluctance to allow X-2 or any semi-independent body to meddle in their security may have reflected the view that gentlemen can best deal with differences amongst themselves in private. At any rate, the rest of OSS resented

X-2 for its secretiveness, methodical suspicion, adversarial attitude, and habitual obstructionism more than it appreciated X-2's contributions.

The founding fathers of the CIA had come from the SI and SO branches of OSS. They were not about to reestablish X-2. They immediately established an office of security, because they accepted the abstract proposition that the Soviet KGB and its satellite intelligence services, as well as other services, would try to penetrate the CIA and disrupt its operations. But even though hostile intelligence officers were always high on the list of the CIA's preferred targets for recruitment, the early CIA did not assign to specific individuals the task of "going after" hostile intelligence services, and of looking at the CIA's own espionage and covert action operations from the standpoint of hostile intelligence. In practice, for the fledgling CIA, counterintelligence meant case officers were to produce recruitments and run agents while paying due attention to the possibility that they might be fabricators or be working for the other side. The CIA's covert actioneers, who were trying to build "resistance" networks in Eastern Europe, or free trade unions in the West, were supposed to get the job done with similar due caution. The CIA's analysts kept a registry of names; the office of security had the job of worrying about penetration. But neither had any responsibility for CI.

By 1953 events had shown that this was not enough. From the very first, most of the agents that the CIA had sent to build resistance networks in Eastern Europe had either disappeared or obviously fallen under hostile control. In 1953 the Polish government revealed that the biggest of these resistance-building operations, the WiN (Polish initials for Freedom and Independence), had been under the control of Polish intelligence from the very outset. Two years earlier, all doubt had vanished at the CIA that Kim Philby, the man designated by Britain's MI-6 to be liaison with the CIA, was in fact a Soviet agent and had compromised much of what the CIA had done. In addition, in 1953 Allen Dulles, newly frocked as Director of Central Intelligence, may have learned that James Kronthal, his successor as chief of station in Berne and a man he wanted on "his team" at CIA, had been recruited as a Soviet spy.* Hence necessity led Dulles, somewhat like Donovan before him, to establish a separate counterintel-

---

*Joseph Corson, Susan Trento, and Edward Trento, *Widows*. The evidence with regard to Kronthal is highly suggestive. A pederast, Kronthal had been recruited by the Gestapo in the 1930s. He had served successfully in the OSS and had become Allen Dulles' friend. Dulles tried to recruit him for a high position in the CIA. Kronthal committed suicide within hours of his meeting with Dulles, under circumstances suggesting that he wished to spare his friends embarrassment. Corson *et al.* make a strong case that he was being blackmailed by the KGB. Some former CI officials who are familiar with the case suggest that "It's not that simple," but concede that the facts are too embarrassing to too many people to be made public.

ligence group. To head it he chose James Angleton, the man who had argued most strenuously against WiN and had become America's "Mr. CI." The staff featured Raymond Rocca, Angleton's former deputy in Rome; Newton Miler; and William Harvey, a tough former FBI man who had kindled doubts about Philby. This CI staff functioned for 21 years, until dissolved by William Colby in December 1974.

The CI staff was a far less potent thing than X-2 had been. Whereas X-2 had been coequal with the espionage and action branches, the CI staff was a very subordinate part of the Directorate of Plans, which was dominated by those branches. In effect, Dulles had made the smallest possible concession to the necessity for an independent CI. Whereas X-2 had been able to argue its case against SI to Donovan himself, theoretically on an equal level, the CI staff would have to argue its case against the Directorate of Plans (which later took the name Directorate of Operations, or DDO) to the chief of that very directorate. This basic fact was less telling than it otherwise would have been because of James Angleton's personal status. Because Angleton had the privilege of walking into the DCI's office unannounced, officers of the DDP complained that they feared the CI staff.[7]

At the height of its powers the CI staff numbered some 180 people[8] (as against perhaps 7,000 in the Directorate of Operations). But the CI staff did not even have the right to send its people abroad to check on operations, never mind to run their own. Some now blame the CI staff for never having penetrated the KGB, or run an operation. But recruiting agents and running operations is precisely what the CI staff was never allowed to do. Indeed, when the CIA found itself with a double-agent case on its hands—or, more often, when there was doubt about whether an agent or a potential recruit was or was not a double-agent—the CI staff would have to cajole an *ad hoc* involvement in the case. Angleton never did gain the right to station CI people permanently abroad. Nor did the CI staff ever gain the right to examine any and all information available to the CIA for its possible relevance to counterintelligence. It could only analyze agency data on a case-by-case basis, and make suggestions.

The heart of the CI staff's activity consisted of "keeping the serials," i.e., an index of facts and pieces of case files that might (or might not) be put together as pieces of a puzzle to indicate the true nature of a Soviet operation, or the true results of an American operation. Another group on the staff examined the methods of communist intelligence services in order to draw conclusions about where and how they might act next. Another group investigated leads to possible penetrations of the CIA. Angleton's CI staff had a comprehensive mentality and a proactive attitude. But the CI staff's files were nowhere near as big or as comprehensive as those of the Registry at Britain's central counterintelligence agency, MI-5. Moreover, when CI analysts made a hypothesis, they did not have the authority to check it out. And of course the CI staff had only the faintest acquaintance with the new world of satellite intelligence.

The staff, like Angleton, deeply believed that penetration of hostile intelligence services is the most effective form of CI, and that analysis is the second most effective. But, in practice, since it was not in a position to recruit agents, "penetrations" consisted largely of defectors who raised more questions than they answered. CI analysts were often kept busy making the staff's "case" on cases initiated by other parts of the CIA—or by the arrival of new defectors.

Thus the bureaucratic precariousness of the CI staff, combined with the uncertainties inherent in the CI business, reduced the final product of the CI staff to the insertion of uncertainty into the CIA's human collection and analysis. This periodic cold shower was as necessary as it was resented. Its usefulness, however, depended on the willingness of top CIA management to arbitrate the details. Since that willingness was often absent, pointless quarrels ensued. This also tended to degrade the value of human intelligence against that of technical intelligence. The latter was just as much in need of questioning, from the standpoint of CI. But it never got it.

AMERICAN COUNTERINTELLIGENCE OPERATIONS

FBI Operations

The FBI maintains operating units in every major city in the United States called "field offices." Four of these (New York, Washington, Chicago, and San Francisco) have more special agents than the rest of the offices combined. The FBI has "legal attaché" offices at most U.S. embassies abroad. Out of a total of some 9,500 Special Agents, the FBI assigns some 2,500 to Foreign Counterintelligence (FCI). A handful of FBI Special Agents at headquarters are assigned to FCI analysis.[9]

The FBI means to protect the U.S. against spies and terrorists, much as it protects against the Mafia: Keep the bad guys away from the vitals of society by warning government employees, university researchers, defense industrialists, and others that they may be approached; identify the bad guys, keep track of them, and identify their specific targets; warn the targets and arrest those who are caught in flagrante with the bad guys; infiltrate the bad guys to find out what they are going to do next. Then assess the full extent of the damage the bad guys have done, and the identities of all whom they have co-opted; perhaps disrupt some of them; investigate leads that indicate that this or that individual may be working for the bad guys.

The FBI's tools for FCI are no different from the tools it uses against the Mafia—but it uses those tools differently. Perhaps the foremost FBI tool is surveillance. The FBI concentrates on the people and things they find to be *prima facie* interesting: diplomats and other employees of Soviet embassies, trade missions and the like, as well as the buildings where these people work and live. To make the job more manageable, the U.S. government restricts Soviet and Chinese diplomats to a 25-mile radius of their embassies, except for special travel permits.* Each of these persons is a "case," with its own file. The FBI labels them with an A if the person has been positively identified as an intelligence officer, and a B if there is concrete evidence to suggest that he *may* be. All other cases are labeled C. Out of a hypothetical 100 employees of a Soviet or Cuban embassy, a dozen will have been identified as intelligence officers by their activities in previous posts. These are A cases. Since a total of perhaps 40 out of 100 may be presumed to be intelligence officers, the FBI must stick a tentative label B on perhaps 30 other embassy employees, to distinguish them from perhaps twice that many others who are presumed to be nonintelligence personnel, who are labeled C. Much of the daily work consists of trying to winnow out the category Bs into As and Cs.

The FBI spends a big percentage of its effort "physically surveilling" (following) the A cases. Surveillance picks them up when they leave their homes in the morning and tries to stick with them until it "puts them to bed" at night. B cases get random surveillance, and C cases get none unless there is a specific reason to give it to them. The surveillants look for evidence of clandestine communication as well as overt contacts. They file reports on behavior.

The first indication that the subject of surveillance is an intelligence officer, or that a known intelligence officer is about to do something interesting, will be the precautions he takes against being surveilled, in order to make sure he knows whether he is being followed: taking circuitous routes on his way to anywhere; often doubling back; driving down one-way streets; taking buses to the end of the line and back. In 1985 when FBI teams, tailing Soviet diplomats during the presence in the Washington, DC area of suspected spy John Walker, noticed the diplomats driving around suburban Maryland in a "dry cleaning" pattern, they knew that the chances were high that some kind of clandestine communication would occur. Surveillance was tightened, and the Soviets were indeed observed "dead dropping" instructions in a tree. Of course, embassies that harbor spies know that they are being surveilled. So, at a random moment on any given day, a high percentage of its officers tend to leave the embassy, scatter to the four

---

*This, plus the even more restrictive procedure instituted in 1986, was an act of retaliation for the draconian controls that the Soviet Union and communist-ruled countries had long practiced on all foreigners. In 1990, when the Polish government became fiercely anticommunist, Polish diplomats ceased to be under the restrictions. But Romanian diplomats continued to be affected, as did Cuban ones.

winds, overload the surveillance system, and help several of their numbers to melt into the great anonymous flow of American life.

Standard techniques of surveillance are labor-intensive. The FBI is acutely aware that, far from having the dozen or so Special Agents to surveil each A case with any degree of assurance, it has at best a one-to-one ratio with the As, and a tenuous one with the rest. So surveillance of foreign officials just has not played the same role for the FBI in the U.S. as it played for the KGB in the Soviet Union.

The FBI also takes pictures of everyone going in or out of the Soviet embassies, legations, etc. This has proved useful for following up leads, and for prosecutions. In 1985, when KGB defector Vitaly Yurchenko told the CIA that in 1982 an employee of NSA had given the Soviet Embassy information about the U.S. Navy's tapping of a Soviet cable in the Sea of Okhotsk, the FBI was able to run a check of the pictures of people entering the embassy against the picture file of employees of NSA.* Thus the FBI easily identified Ronald Pelton, who was later convicted of espionage. NSA records the embassies' coded message traffic, and works with the FBI to plant "bugs" in and around the embassies and to catch transmissions to and from agents. It also conducts some state-of-the-art audio surveillance—e.g., bouncing laser beams off window panes, or radio waves off inside walls, and stripping off the conversation that may be part of the return.

FBI surveillance gets to first base when it catches a hostile intelligence officer in contact with an American who is a potential source of information or influence. But then the FBI must decide whether the American is a mere target for recruitment, a witting agent, or someone who is being exploited unwittingly. Here the FBI relies primarily on the Special Agent's number one skill: the interview. Often an interview with someone being courted by a KGB officer culminates what the Bureau calls a "preliminary investigation." Suppose a Soviet cultural attaché who has previously been identified as an intelligence officer meets openly with an American professor of mathematics who has written on cryptology. A preliminary CI investigation would seek to determine the nature of the relationship between the two. But the preliminary to the preliminary must be to determine how the professor would react to a visit by FBI officers asking him, directly, what the contact was about. If the Bureau judged the professor to

---

*Note however that the FBI could have done this back in 1980 when Pelton called the Soviet Embassy on the telephone (monitored by the FBI), identified himself as a U.S. intelligence officer, and said he would be coming in. The FBI limited itself to asking whether anyone at NSA recognized the voice on the telephone. The lesson: Bureaucracies seldom do all that they are theoretically capable of doing.

be directly approachable, the interview would at least warn him about what the Soviet is trying to do. If the professor were friendly, the interview would yield information about previous contacts, and reports of future ones. If the professor were very friendly, the FBI might wish to use him as a "double agent," feeding him material to give to the Soviets, while learning more about the Soviets' operating methods, the personalities involved, and so on. If the mathematician were not judged amenable to direct questioning, however, CI officers would want to surveil him in order to form their own conclusions.

The FBI's use of double agents is not usually so ambitious. Its minimum goal is to gather enough evidence of espionage to arrest and jail the Soviet officer, or expel him as *persona non grata*. Something like this happened in 1978 to Vladik Enger and Rudolf Chernayev, Soviet citizens employed by the UN, and Vladimir Zimyanin, a Soviet attaché to the UN. The FBI, working with the Office of Naval Investigation, had asked a Naval officer to volunteer to sell secrets to the Soviets. The officer was dangled, and the three aforementioned Soviets took the bait. They met the Lieutenant Commander on the New Jersey Turnpike. As soon as money and documents changed hands, the FBI arrested them. Zimyanin had diplomatic immunity and left the country. The others were sentenced to 50 years in the federal pen, and were later exchanged for five Soviet dissidents in a Soviet prison. The principal gain to the U.S. was that the KGB's fear of an FBI dangle was somewhat reinforced. The KGB gained the U.S. government's tacit assent to its equation of dissidents with spies.

Perhaps the FBI's greatest success in a double-agent operation that it initiated was also in cooperation with military intelligence. In 1966, Army CI and the FBI together chose Sgt. Ralph Sigler to be dangled before the Soviets in Mexico. The Soviets bit, and over the next decade Sigler became so important to the Soviets that they used him to contact one of their deepest-cover agents, Rudolph Herrmann, an "illegal." Herrmann established two "dead drop" sites near El Paso, Texas. Maps of the two sites were found in Ralph Sigler's belongings after his death. Evidently the KGB had asked him to fill them or empty them for Herrmann. Since Sigler was working for the FBI, this may have led to Herrmann's identification and capture.[10]

Catching illegals—foreign spies sent to infiltrate American society posing as legitimate citizens—is surely an awesome task in this society of immigrants. The FBI has never been able to even make a meaningful estimate of how many illegal spies are in the U.S.—never mind a coherent plan for identifying them. Its plan has been to penetrate as deeply as possible into the Soviet spy network in the U.S. (as for example with Sigler) in the hope that sooner or later an American agent will be asked to help contact an illegal. But the way the FBI caught the first and biggest Soviet illegal of the postwar era, KGB Col. Rudolph Abel (who was living in New York under the name Emil Goldfus) is also the primary way it has made most of its catches: Another KGB officer (in Abel's case this was a frightened incompetent named Reino Hayhanen) defects and gives him away.

The FBI's dream is to identify a Soviet intelligence officer, catch him in some embarrassing situation, talk him into becoming an "agent in place," and use him as a penetration into Soviet intelligence. Alas, this dream has often turned into a nightmarish mirror-image of itself. In 1962 two Soviet intelligence officers under cover of the Soviet UN mission in New York approached the FBI and offered to spy for the U.S., if the U.S. would provide them with a shopping list of secrets they had been ordered to steal. J. Edgar Hoover code-named the two "Fedora" and "Top Hat," gave them what they wanted, and took what they provided directly to Presidents Kennedy, Nixon, and Johnson of the United States. Unfortunately, the FBI later had reason to believe that these two had been working for the Soviets.* The penetrators were penetrated.

The FBI has earned a reputation for sending agents undercover to infiltrate organized crime. In the 1950s this reputation expanded into the field of counterintelligence when J. Edgar Hoover announced that FBI Special Agents had assumed fake identities and joined the Communist party, as well as other subversive organizations. This afforded the FBI significant access to Soviet spy networks in the U.S. This facet of the FBI was publicized by Herbert Philbrick's book *I Led Three Lives,* and by the TV series of the same name.

The FBI's clandestine tradition runs much deeper than the CIA's and is very real in domestic cases. For example, in 1982 an FBI Special Agent joined a terrorist group in Los Angeles and foiled their plans for murder by teaching them to fire pistols by jerking with the second bend of the index finger (guaranteed to

---

*As regards Fedora, see below, pp. 153, 154, 169. The story of Top Hat is more complex. His real name is Maj. Gen. Dimitri F. Polyakov, of the GRU. His partisans in the FBI claim that he identified four "moles" in the U.S. military in 1960s: Sgt. Jack Dunlop, Lt. Col. William Whalen, Yeoman Nelson Drummond, and Sgt. Herbert W. Boekenkaupt. But all of these people had either lost access or fallen under suspicion before Top Hat identified them. He continued to report for 20 years despite the fact that, as many in the FBI believed, Soviet Security was all over him. They noted his nonchalant ways—including his acceptance of a pair of fancy shotguns in payment. The most bizarre episode concerning Top Hat was the BBC's inquiry into his fate, in the course of preparing a documentary and a book intended to impugn Americans skeptical of Soviet sources. The Soviet authorities' position, uncritically reported, was that a 1978 article in *New York* magazine had led to Top Hat's arrest in 1982, conviction in 1985, and execution in 1988. On January 14, 1990, *Pravda* even published an announcement of the execution—which, however, did not mention Top Hat's Russian name. See Tom Mangold, *Cold Warrior,* Ch. 15. The most reasonable explanation for the Soviet position, including announcing an execution two years later in a way that is meaningful only to a specialized foreign audience, is that the KGB wanted to add wind to the BBC's sails.

cause a miss). But when it comes to foreign counterintelligence the Bureau infiltrates not with Special Agents but, like the CIA, through informants or agents who are sometimes recruited, but who often offer their services.* Also, much of the FBI's work consists of sharing cases with the CIA. A case in point: In 1966, when KGB officer Igor Kozlov contacted the CIA and offered to spy for the U.S. if the U.S. would allow him to recruit Nicholas Shadrin (A.K.A. Soviet Navy Capt. Nikolas Artamonov, who had defected to the U.S. in 1959), the FBI had to be the "lead agency" in the case because Shadrin had become a U.S. citizen, and the initial contacts would take place in the U.S. In later years, when Shadrin's meetings shifted abroad, operational control shifted to the CIA.[11] In this and in many other instances, notably the Army–FBI case of Ralph Sigler, which agency is in charge determines how the case is handled and how it comes out.

Procedures dominate the FBI's FCI work also because the FBI is a law-enforcement organization with the power of arrest. Over the years the Bureau, the courts, and the Congress have increasingly assumed that when the FBI investigates or simply collects newspaper clippings about someone, it creates a burden—or a potential burden—for that person. Hence the FBI may investigate only when there is "probable cause" to believe that the subject of the investigation may have committed, or may be about to commit, a violation of law. This is called the "criminal standard."

Much of the FBI's CI workload consists of quasi-police investigations of leads about violations of the espionage laws, or leaks. Thus the FBI is involved in "cleaning up" or damage-controlling the security lapses, CI defeats, and bad luck of the rest of the government, and every CI case involving an American ultimately becomes an FBI case. For this reason, although John Walker and Jerry Whitworth had stolen code books for the Soviets from the U.S. Navy, it was the FBI that "broke the ring" because Walker's wife turned him in to the FBI, and because when Whitworth tried to anonymously strike a deal for his own

---

*Aversion to undercover work seems to have grown throughout the U.S. government, regardless of the objective and regardless of popular support. The limit case is the Justice Department's Drug Enforcement Agency. Its work obviously requires its employees to act like drug dealers and mingle with them at high risk to themselves. There is every reason to believe that popular support for these activities is very high. Hence one would expect that those DEA agents who go undercover would get the best that their agency has to offer in terms of pay and honors. But the reverse is true. As has always been the case at the CIA, and has become the case at the FBI, the undercover people at DEA have been regarded as socially inferior to those who keep regular hours and whose upbringing makes it impossible for them to appear as anything but U.S. civil servants. See particularly the saga of Michael Levine, New York Times, 21 November 1988, sec. B, p. 1. See also Mr. Levine's book Deep Cover. The same discrimination occurs in the CIA, where nonofficial cover officers suffer substantial financial and career disadvantages (see Ch. 3).

surrender, he contacted the FBI. The Bureau's principal task in the Walker case was to make sure that the evidence would stand up in court. In the Walker case surveillance did the job. But in a host of others, especially leak cases, the Bureau forms a picture of the situation from great numbers of interviews, supplemented by the polygraph.

"The interview," which we have already touched on, is an art form at the Bureau, and every Special Agent must be first of all a good interviewer. The Agent is supposed to know what he is looking for, what the person he is talking to is supposed to know, and the reasons why that person might or might not want to talk. The Agent then gets "the subject" talking, perhaps by making him feel important, and steers the conversation by any number of psychological ploys. No matter if the story is one-sided or mendacious, the Special Agent encourages it so long as it contains the basis for sharp questioning later on, or leads to others who may shed light on the subject. Then the Bureau may come back with more information and ask the subject to dig himself out of a hole he had previously dug. In the hands of a trained Special Agent, simple liars simply dig their holes deeper, increasing the pressure on themselves to give valuable information.

The interview, multiplied many times and contained in a "case file" which also contains records of surveillance and wiretaps, etc., is the basis of the FBI's *modus operandi*. The special agent in charge of the case builds the file by deciding who should be interviewed next and what he should be asked. Of course "the case" is seldom self-contained. The skillful Special Agent will look at other case files for connections, and may ask subjects in one case questions relevant to another. He may even ask for information from CIA, or ask NSA to look over old intercept tapes. *In short, the principal investigator in any case is both the chief collector and the chief analyst.* Like a city detective, he builds the case from widely scattered sources. But "the case" is the intellectual principle on which the FBI organizes its work. Now and again the Bureau decides to put more emphasis on one or another area. Rarely does this mean that all case files in the area are analyzed together for basic directions. More often it means more people are sent to follow possible leads coming out of individual cases. "Going after tech transfer" (the illicit transfer of U.S. technology to foreign powers) means getting more cases in the field.

The more sources, and the more different kinds of sources, that point in the same direction, the more solid does the FBI's case become. Thus the case against convicted atom spy Julius Rosenberg was solid, despite the latter's refusal to be interviewed. He had been identified as the case officer for his cousin David Greenglass, who had been laboriously identified as the occupant of a house in New Mexico which had been the conduit of information stolen from Los Alamos.[12] The chain of evidence stretched from decrypted Soviet telegrams to confessions of convicted spies through physical identification of individuals.

By contrast, the FBI seldom builds a solid case against high government officials who leak information. Such investigations occur all the time. There is seldom a shortage of people willing to point the finger at one or more possible culprits. But, when interviewed, the targets of the investigation almost always flatly deny involvement, and point their fingers elsewhere. The FBI then lets the matter drop, because it can seldom resolve the contradictions through other kinds of evidence—unless someone is foolish enough to try to prove his innocence by submitting to the polygraph.

Finally, let us consider the polygraph, the tool that has become first among equals in the FBI's kit. "The subject" is attached to devices that monitor his blood pressure, pulse, and other physical reactions as he responds to questions. The theory is that his body will react differently when he says things about which he is not worried (e.g., today is Friday, June 23) than when he says things about which he is worried (e.g., "I've never met John Doe,"), and that he will be more worried about telling lies than about telling the truth. Theoretically, the polygraph is very useful in resolving the conflicts that usually arise between different accounts by people with contrasting motives. It sometimes works well to strap someone onto the machine (which the subject does not know is not plugged in) and just talk. However, polygraph examinations are inadmissible as evidence in court—a fact that the Bureau often cites when it invites people to prove their point by submitting to a polygraph. Nevertheless, it is very difficult for a bureaucracy to believe that someone is lying who has passed the polygraph, or that he is telling the truth when the squiggles on the paper tape seem to say he is not. The polygraph is attractive above all because it relieves the person evaluating the interview of the responsibility for making and defending judgments. Somewhat like the CIA's search for a "truth serum" that led to the drug experiments, the polygraph represents the search for a technical solution to quintessentially human problems: Can I trust this man? Is he telling the truth? Where do his allegiances lie?

The toughest part of the CI job is to make and justify judgments that involve preferring certain character traits or allegiances over others. But with the polygraph it would not matter if the subject were a Catholic, a communist, or a vegetarian, celibate or promiscuous. If he passed he would be "in"; if he didn't he would be "out." Of course, "everyone knows" that the polygraph can be "beaten" by people trained to do it; that people who are more scrupulous are more vulnerable to looking like liars than those who are not; that the questions asked make the difference between a polygraph that is difficult to fail and one that is difficult to pass; and that a reaction which is deceptive to one operator is quite all right to another.

The bizarre case of Richard J. Miller, an FBI Special Agent arrested and tried for passing information to the Soviet Union, shows a reasonably full panoply of the FBI's counterintelligence operations. It is atypical only in that the first trial ended with a jury unable to convict Miller on charges of espionage. The Bureau's own employees noted anomalies in Miller's behavior following the failure of his career to thrive. A preliminary investigation yielded probable cause for a full investigation, including surveillance. A romance with a Soviet woman intelligence officer was observed. Arrest followed. But Miller claimed to have been initiating a dangle operation on his own. Interviews and polygraphs led the Bureau and the U.S. attorney to believe the *prima facie* evidence that he was a spy. Then, in court, Miller successfully argued that a good Mormon boy like himself might be simply incompetent, but not a spy.*

CIA Operations

Counterintelligence operations at the CIA mean primarily two tasks: keeping the agency free from Soviet penetration (or moles), and trying to turn members of hostile intelligence services abroad into American moles. The Office of Security, whose principal (indeed, almost its sole) tool is the polygraph, screens people before they become CIA employees. It asks whether the individuals have been agents of foreign intelligence services, whether they have habits that would make them vulnerable to recruiting (drugs, homosexuality, fraud), and whether they are truthful in their answers to the U.S. government.

The policy of this office (honored in the breach) is to reinvestigate CIA employees every five years, whether they need it or not, as well as when questions arise about an individual's behavior. Everyone acknowledges that this sort of passive security is essential, but that it is inherently penetrable. The Office of Security does not concern itself with what is generally acknowledged to be the primary means by which the CIA can expect to catch hostile moles within its own ranks—namely the recruitment and management of CIA moles within the ranks of hostile services—or, more commonly, of defectors from those services. The business of defectors is much less straightforward, and everyone at the CIA seems to get in on it.

The fact that a majority of Soviet-bloc defectors have been employees of the KGB or satellite services, and indeed that a significant minority of walk-ins from the free world have been involved with communist intelligence services, has been a double-edged sword for the CIA. On the one hand, these people have had the "access" to tell the CIA about precisely the thing it wants most to know: Have *they* managed to acquire moles among *us?* On the other hand, these intelligence walk-ins are precisely the people best equipped to carry out operations of deception and disruption against U.S. intelligence. In fact, though

---

*The second trial resulted in a conviction, and a life sentence that was later overturned. The third trial resulted in a 20-year prison sentence.

they have brought much information, they have never fingered a "mole" still on active duty within the CIA. This is either good news, or it is very bad news. *No wonder then that the day-to-day business of CI at Langley has been to determine the* bona fides *of defectors bearing different tales while following up their leads. No wonder also that the handling of intelligence defectors has been disruptive.* Another font of disruption is that the loss of a source has inevitably led to inconclusive studies about how the loss might have happened.

The defectors of the early postwar period posed no problems for the CI staff. Igor Gouzenko, a GRU code clerk who defected in Canada, carried with him telegrams that began to unravel the tangled chain that took American atomic secrets to the Soviet Union. British scientist Alan Nunn May, who had handed over American secrets in Canada, was named directly, and directly arrested. Gouzenko's telegrams were of only limited use in unraveling the more important network that led from David Greenglass at Los Alamos to Henry Gold in Philadelphia, Julius Rosenberg in New York, and Klaus Fuchs in London. The evidence that allowed the FBI and the CIA to stop the operation, and eventually led to the trial and execution of Julius and Ethel Rosenberg, came primarily through the decoding of messages sent by the Soviet Embassy in Washington in 1944. Gouzenko's telegrams helped a bit. An old Soviet codebook helped some more, and ingenuity did the rest. But this was not the CIA's doing. Rather it was that of the FBI, following up the work of Army civilian codebreakers.[13]

The same cryptologic breakthrough showed that the Soviets knew of secrets that the CIA had passed to British intelligence. When the CIA confronted the British with the proposition that some of their intelligence people in Washington must be working for the Soviets, they readily admitted that Donald MacLean, a British diplomat who had served in Washington, had long been suspected of being a Soviet agent. In 1951, after much pressure from the CIA, the British agreed to take MacLean into custody. But he was warned, and fled to Moscow together with his partner in sodomy, Guy Burgess, also of British intelligence. The FBI's William Harvey, supported by the CIA's James Angleton, then forced the British to come to terms with the fact that the relationship between Burgess, MacLean, and Kim Philby (the outstanding young man of British intelligence), as well as a host of other circumstances, pointed to Philby as the greatest of moles. Philby left British intelligence in 1951, fled to Moscow in 1963, received the Order of Lenin, and wrote a book about his espionage.*

The GRU's Colonel Popov, who "walked in" to the CIA station in Vienna in 1952, did not pretend to give the U.S. any moles. Nor did another GRU colonel,

---

*Harold (Kim) Philby, *My Silent War*. In 1990 the Soviet Union issued a postage stamp with Philby's picture on it.

Oleg Penkovsky, nine years later. Both of these defectors gave information that was unique. There was no question of not accepting them. CI played no role while their cases were "live," other than to protect the secrets they were giving and to watch for anything that might uncover them. After Popov's arrest in 1959 there were fruitless arguments over whether he had been lost to a mole or to mere errors in tradecraft. The CI review of Penkovsky's arrest in 1962 caused no stir, because it focused on tradecraft. Thereafter, questions arose about the length of time that Penkovsky had been under Soviet control before his arrest was announced. The process yielded little that was positive.

But KGB Maj. Anatoli Golitsyn, who defected in Helsinki in 1962, started a CI process whose results were on balance negative. Golitsyn brought with him information even more interesting than the others had. He had remembered seeing copies of documents of the French and British intelligence services, the SDECE and MI-5, and he remembered imprecise indications about CIA agents or employees who were working for the KGB. This set off a multinational, multiyear scramble that caught perhaps a dozen spies but thoroughly disrupted French, British, American, and Canadian CI. Many have blamed Golitsyn himself for this, and indeed Golitsyn himself sought to transcend the role of source and become an adviser and analyst of Western CI files. Unfortunately the U.S., British, French, and Canadian services are to blame for allowing Golitsyn to become a catalyst for intra-Western strife. These services were working with so little hard information about Soviet intelligence, and could not discipline themselves to make proper use of the fragmentary facts Golitsyn brought.

Golitsyn had remembered reasonably specific things about high-level documents from the French government and from NATO in France. French investigators were able to focus on a few possible sources at NATO headquarters in Paris, and soon caught Georges Pacques *in flagrante.** Meanwhile, investigations of the leaks from within the French government caused so much hate and discontent that the conduit of Golitsyn's material (France's liaison with the CIA, Philippe de Vosjoli) feared for his life, resigned from the service, and went underground. President de Gaulle reshuffled his intelligence chiefs and broke contact with the CIA. In Britain, Golitsyn's recollections led to the arrest of a low-level spy in the Admiralty, John Vassall. But they also set off counterproductive suspicion that the head of CI was a Soviet mole. In Canada, Golitsyn's material pointed to a high-level officer, James Bennett. With the CIA's help the Canadians planted information on Bennett alone that the CIA would be meeting a Soviet agent at a particular time and place in Ottawa. If Soviet

---

*Pacques had not been employed by NATO when Golitsyn had seen the documents. So the identification of Pacques had been a side-benefit of Golitsyn. The man who stole the NATO documents Golitsyn had seen remained undetected.

intelligence officers tried to observe the nonexistent meeting it could only be because Bennett had warned them. A Soviet officer showed up, despite a snowstorm. The Canadians arrested Bennett, but never found corroborating evidence. The Norwegians, for their part, followed Golitsyn's leads to a Norwegian secretary in Moscow who had given her body to a KGB officer. She admitted the relationship but denied betraying secrets. Years later another defector, Oleg Gordievsky, pointed out the correct Norwegian secretary.[14] Golitsyn's information, while imperfect, was better than the use that Western services made of it.

At CIA Golitsyn's memory, and his subsequent analysis of files, led to a molehunt. The method was to check personnel files of the 14 people who more-or-less fit one of Golitsyn's descriptions (e.g., an officer who served in Berlin whose name began with K and ended with y) and, where doubts persisted, to investigate the individual. The chief suspect was Peter Karlow. Theoretically, every intelligence service should be able to function while entertaining doubts about penetrations. But the very fact that CIA officers were investigated (but none was charged) struck many as monstrous. These officers later received financial compensation for their hampered careers. Yet in the world of CI there is seldom clear guilt or clear exoneration. Interestingly enough those at CIA who most strongly supported the innocence of the suspects among their own rank, were most willing to cast suspicion on a Soviet émigré named Igor Orlov in Alexandria, Virginia, who was much harassed but never charged.[15]

At any rate, our larger point is that hunting down the implications of the recollections of rare-as-hens'-teeth defectors is a bad caricature of CI.

As regards the CIA, it was clear by the mid–1960s that CI had become so unpopular—because of molehunts but above all because of its constant questioning of the value of sources—that a revolt against it would be set off by the next spark. That spark was provided by KGB Maj. Yuri Nosenko, who hurriedly defected in January 1964, and claimed to have reviewed the KGB file on President Kennedy's assassin, Lee Harvey Oswald. As we have mentioned, signals intelligence surely established that Nosenko had lied about the immediate cause of his defection, a nonexistent telegram. Every report on the several interrogations of Nosenko mentions his copious lies. But his story that there were no "moles" in the CIA, and that Soviet intelligence had never had a relationship with Oswald before, during, or after Oswald's residence in the Soviet Union, offered both the CIA and the FBI the chance to close the door on "the Soviet connection" to the Kennedy assassination. It also offered the CIA the chance to end the molehunt started by Golitsyn.[16]

The struggle over Nosenko's *bona fides* split the CIA into warring camps— and not only the CIA. The FBI's top source, a Soviet UN employee code-named Fedora, backed Nosenko's story about the (nonexistent) telegram.[17]

J. Edgar Hoover, who had brought Fedora's reports directly to President Johnson, backed Fedora. Hoover went so far in his anger at the anti-Nosenko party at CIA (which by implication denigrated his best sources) that he cut off the FBI's cooperation with the CI staff. Clearly the great Nosenko affair was the antithesis of the quiet, long-term, methodical skepticism that was supposed to underlie the CIA's approach to CI. By 1968 the case had long since ceased to be about Nosenko and had become about which factions in the CIA would win, and which would lose. In the end the affair was settled without regard to intellectual niceties, strictly by bureaucratic *force majeure*. Indeed, because the CI staff was on the losing side in the Nosenko case, that case marked the beginning of the end of its influence.

Among the interesting reflections that the Nosenko case cast on the methodology of CIA counterintelligence is that the agency wound up officially approving him even though he had failed the polygraph. This shows that, in a way, the CIA is correct in its claims that the polygraph is not the final word in its judgments. In the Nosenko case, however, no one suggested that, despite the polygraph, Nosenko was really telling the truth.* Instead, the pro-Nosenko faction found *reasons* for the lies—personal pathology, desire for self-aggrandizement, etc. The anti-Nosenko party did not base its argument on the polygraph, either, but rather on a whole issue of lies and contradictions to which Nosenko had admitted or which had become otherwise obvious. The truth or falsity of Nosenko's words, however, like the guilt or innocence of Capt. Alfred Dreyfus in turn-of-the-century France, had ceased to be the main issue of "the affair."

After the demise of the CI staff in 1974, and the reassignment of responsibility for CI to case officers and station chiefs, *the machine* became more important to the CIA's CI than ever. In 1979 the CIA's Director, Adm. Stansfield Turner, told the Senate Select Committee on Intelligence that he could not imagine the CIA being penetrated.[18] At the same time he pronounced himself confident that the information that the CIA had received from hostile intelligence officers who had walked in to the CIA must be correct. Turner cited the polygraph as the basis of his confidence. However, interestingly enough, Turner was among those who enthusiastically endorsed giving Nosenko his *bona fides*, despite his having failed the polygraph. In August 1985, CIA Director William Casey expressed a similar sentiment: Largely because of the polygraph, the CIA was winning the "spy war" with the KGB, having given up very little and gotten a lot.[19] The working

---

*Once the pro-Nosenko party was given charge of the case in 1968, it administered a new polygraph test to Nosenko which it characterized as the only "fair" one he had ever received, which he supposedly passed with flying colors, and which totally satisfied the new team. Nevertheless the new team did not deny that he had lied.

assumption of those who direct the CIA's human collection system is that because the Soviets thoroughly feared the polygraph (even though they do not use it themselves), they did not even try to send false defectors.

Nevertheless, the years 1979–88 were ones of intellectual ferment for CIA CI—albeit at the margins. The stimulus for this came (as we shall see) from a variety of embarrassing instances that gave the public the impression that the CIA was incompetent about CI. The substance of the ferment were the suggestions of congressional committees, the National Security Council, and private academics that counterintelligence should consist substantially of analysis.[20] In 1983, pursuant to these suggestions, the CIA had formed a Foreign Intelligence Capabilities unit—a handful of analysts within the Directorate of Intelligence whose sole job was to look for attempts of foreign intelligence services to manage the perceptions of U.S. intelligence. During the same year William Casey, in his capacity as director of the entire intelligence community, established another group of analysts from throughout the community to bring to bear upon counterintelligence facts and ideas from espionage, signals intelligence, imagery, the FBI, and so on. In 1985 Casey also established a training course for analysts held at Camp Perry, Virginia, to "sensitize" them to the possibility of deception. By the late 1980s, as the idea of central analysis of counterintelligence topics gained currency throughout the community, the FBI began to argue at interagency meetings that *it* is the agency most naturally fit to perform that function. This was the context in which, in 1988, the CIA consolidated its various CI activities with the CI staff, the foreign intelligence capabilities group, and others, into a Counterintelligence Center.

The CI Center is composed of a score of people from both the analytical and the operational sides of the CIA. It is supposed to be a place where analysts look both at U.S. agents (their *bona fides*, how they are handled) *and* at what hostile intelligence services may be doing to influence, control, or deceive U.S. intelligence operations. The center is supposed to allow direct communication between analysts and operators on individual cases. It is supposed to make it easy to formulate hypotheses about what may be going on, and to check them out. The CI Center did not represent a new CI methodology at CIA—only the possibility that the subject might once again be taken somewhat seriously.

By 1990, however, the advocates for CI having moved on, bureaucratic priorities reasserted themselves. The staffing of the CI center was cut, and so were funds for teaching analysts about deception.

THE WIDENING MISMATCH

Because effectiveness in CI (or lack thereof) seldom is an event but is among the most disputable causes of events, the bottom line of counterintelligence is always open to interpretation. As the archives of formerly communist countries open, it will be possible to make definitive judgments on who duped whom during the Cold War. At this point in time, working with partial knowledge, we must content ourselves with noting opportunities that the American CI system gave to hostile services, and the way it grasped opportunities that offered themselves. What emerges is an impression, no less firm for being undefinable, that American CI at its best has had a tenuous grip on its job, and that over the years specific shortcomings have merged into a way of life. The first of these shortcomings is the primacy of social and bureaucratic considerations. We do not mean to argue that this is a peculiarly American affliction, but that it hurt American CI badly.

Social Inhibitions

Even as British CI refused to make the connection between the extraordinary successes achieved by Kim Philby in exposing German agents in Spain, his passionate connection with the Spanish Republican cause, his marriage to a communist, his uncanny success as head of MI-6 counterintelligence against the Soviet Union at spotting Soviet double agents, and even his friendship with suspected Soviet agent Donald MacLean, the young CIA never considered that James Kronthal—alumnus of OSS, one of the CIA's founding fathers, the man who filled Allen Dulles' shoes as Station Chief in Bern—might have been recruited as a KGB agent. Surely Kronthal's pederasty, which had got him entrapped by the Gestapo a dozen years before the Soviets might have gotten to him in 1948, should have drawn attention. But whereas the United States' enemies looked for weaknesses, those in charge of securing the young CIA, like their British mentors, implicitly trusted members of their class.[21]

As the founding generation of U.S. intelligence slowly passed, solidarity based on social class was replaced by cultural and political solidarity in the face of conservatives, the military, and McCarthyites, whom the Brahmins of U.S. intelligence lumped together into a lesser caste. The CIA, and to a lesser extent the FBI, have considered themselves havens for enlightened political liberals. Hence they have been far more protective of leftist than of conservative opinion within themselves. In this regard, consider the FBI's "background investigation" in the late 1970s of a man we shall call Mr. X, one of the 20 or so Americans who had access to any and all intelligence secrets he desired. What the FBI did not find remarkable about Mr. X speaks volumes. Right before gaining his access, Mr. X had cochaired an international action project alongside a former minister of a communist government. He had been a U.S. official in Iran in the early 1970s, but had been sent home for having crossed the line between reporting on the anti-Shah movement and joining it. Yet the FBI report on which his clearance was based mentions none of these things. The FBI of the 1950s, whose tone had been set by graduates of Fordham, a blue-collar Catholic university in the Bronx, would have pointed out these political facts. The FBI of the 1970s, however, would only "flag" *personal* indiscretions. X's indiscretions were political, not personal.

The CIA welcomes not only politics such as those of Mr. X, but "advanced" lifestyles as well—especially for more senior officers. Take the case of John Paisley, a high-ranking CIA official in the 1970s last seen on his sailboat on Chesapeake Bay in September 1978, and whose presumed body was found nearby a week later too badly decomposed for positive identification. His lifestyle would have raised the eyebrows of the average American, but did not raise those of the CIA office of security. When Paisley had joined the CIA in 1951, he wrote on his job application that he had never been to a communist country, and he passed the polygraph. However, he let it be known to colleagues that he *had* been to the Soviet Union, *and* that he continued to favor the radical politics of his youth. By the early 1970s he was one of the organizers of sex parties for fellow CIA officers in the Washington suburbs, orgies reportedly involving, among others, Karel and Hanna Koecher and *The Washington Post's* Carl Bernstein.[22] Koecher, a Czech defector, had passed the polygraph and had become a contract employee of the CIA, translating reports from agents in the Soviet Union. This alone gave him next-to-direct access to the agents' identities. But the Koechers' physical intimacy with CIA officers added even more.

It is more than a little remarkable that defectors should be given such access under any circumstances, and even more remarkable that the circumstances in which these defectors got it should raise no eyebrows. In retrospect, the importance of the Koechers' physical access is unmistakable. In 1984 Karel Koecher was indicted as a Czech spy, and in 1986 the Soviet Union accepted the Koechers in exchange for jailed human-rights activist Anatoli Shcharansky.

But let us return to the man responsible for that access. Weeks before Paisley's disappearance, he had been officially accused of being a mole. Be that as it may, he had surely been living in a building also occupied by KGB officers from the Soviet Embassy, including one Vitaly Yurchenko—indeed, on the same floor. He had also had unexplained special access to *The Washington Post's* building nearby. Yet there was no CI interest in Paisley at the CIA. On the contrary. To the end, Paisley was regarded highly enough to be assigned to monitor a presidential panel that was questioning the CIA's dovish conclusions about the Soviet Strategic buildup of the 1970s. In 1978 the CIA called Paisley's disappearance a suicide without CI implications, despite lack of evidence (and a body three inches shorter than Paisley's personnel records say that he was). The CIA also discouraged the Senate Intelligence Committee's investigators from digging deeper, out of expressed concern for Paisley's reputation. Presumably for the same reason, the Paisley case was not reopened when the arrest of the Koechers in 1984, and the defection and redefection of Vitaly Yurchenko in

1985, raised new questions about Paisley. It is difficult to avoid the conclusion that the CIA was more concerned for the professional reputation of living officers than for the personal reputation of one it presumed dead.

By contrast, when the slightest irregularity attaches itself to someone outside the orbit of the CIA's sociopolitical preferences, the CIA's reaction is swift, loud public condemnation and, if possible, punishment. In 1978 the CIA forced the resignation of David Sullivan, a midlevel CIA analyst (who, entirely incidentally, had worked under Paisley) for having shown to Richard Perle, then of the U.S. Senate staff, a document that Sullivan had written critical of the quality of the CIA's analysis. The threat of failing a polygraph was effective in eliciting from Sullivan (a U.S. Marine Reserve officer) all other instances in which he had criticized the agency's performance out of channels. Although Perle and others were fully cleared to read documents that Sullivan had shown them, the dastardly nature of Sullivan's actions was standard fare for congressional testimony by CIA Director Stansfield Turner and, into the 1980s, by Deputy Director Bobby Ray Inman. The CIA wanted to make sure everyone understood that the agency would thoroughly root out this sort of thing and this sort of person. By contrast, there was plenty of room in the CIA not just for the likes of John Paisley, but for good memories of him as well.

The intelligence community shares this socially selective tolerance with the U.S. government Establishment at large. Consider the case of Richard Burt, in 1979 a reporter for *The New York Times*. As we will soon see, Burt published details about the United States' principal source of communications intelligence. There is a law—Section 798, 18 U.S. Code—that makes any unauthorized use of any classified data about U.S. communications intelligence a crime. In legalese, Section 798 (known as "the Comint statute") creates a "straight liability" crime: You commit the act, you are guilty. If the Comint statute meant anything, it meant that Burt had committed a felony. Yet not only did the Carter Administration's Directors of the CIA and the FBI, and its Attorney General, make no move against Burt: The Reagan Administration appointed Burt to positions of prestige and power, finally including U.S. Ambassador to Germany, and overcame opposition to his confirmation from the Senate. By the same token, when in 1987 *The Washington Post's* Bob Woodward, in his book *Veil*, published the details of the government's plans for a revolutionary new means of gathering communications intelligence, not only did the government not invoke Section 798 against Woodward—highly unofficial growls from the Director of the NSA notwithstanding—no high official even turned the matter over to the Justice Department. The U.S. government did not even conduct a serious inquiry into who might have given Woodward the information. Woodward's book named and thanked several high intelligence officials for their cooperation in preparing the book. A serious investigation would have had to begin with those officials—and that is precisely why none was begun. Society is "thicker" than security.

As we have noted, the biggest complaint against counterintelligence is that it consists of questioning the good judgment, and sometimes the loyalty, of people on one's own side. Of course the complaint is justified, but so is counterintelligence. After all, to the extent that hostile intelligence services are not impotent, all their efforts at penetration and deception must have resulted in at least *some* U.S. intelligence officers who were fooled into accepting agents that they should not have accepted, or in reaching *some* conclusions they should not have reached. But, in a nutshell, U.S. intelligence has been as reluctant as British intelligence ever was to entertain self-criticism—indeed, it has been increasingly effective at rooting out suggestions of its own insufficiency. In the intelligence community, as in certain schools, everyone is presumed to be above average.

Technical Coverage
The second, and perhaps the most important, of the widening fissures in American CI is that the growth of technical collection has not been matched by the expansion of CI into technical fields. Well into the 1980s, fewer than a handful of CIA CI officers, and no FBI FCI agents at all, were cleared to know how U.S. intelligence satellites work. Most had no idea of the peculiarities of performance that allow the satellites to see some things and not others, and be subject to some countermeasures but not others. Moreover, these officers saw no reason to inquire, and when asked why they did not, retorted "What does all that high-tech stuff have to do with CI, anyhow?" In an age when most information came through technical means, American CI was still focused exclusively on people.

For their part, the managers of satellite collection programs are mostly ex-engineers who see their job strictly as meeting technical challenges: higher resolution, greater sensitivity of antennae, reduction of weight, increases in reliability and mission life, better on-board processing, etc. Technical program managers, including Adm. Bobby Ray Inman, once Director of NSA, assumed that the take from such systems is inherently "pure."[23] For some this conclusion was axiomatic: After all, because a picture shows what it shows, the information it contains is by definition real. In 1990 the CIA's Office of Imagery Analysis produced a large pinkish button advertising itself, featuring the motto "Seeing Is Believing." (By the same token, a radar signal with certain characteristics does in fact have those characteristics.) Others thought that the take was pure because they believed the Soviets could not imagine that the U.S. would have the capacity to see or intercept as much as it did. But, in reality, over the years the take became increasingly *im*pure, increasingly subject to the will of the KGB and of the Soviet General Staff's deception directorate.[24] As the Soviet Union, and other countries too, gained more and more knowledge about how U.S. technical systems work, they increased their capacity to manage their exposure to those systems. In fact, since 1962 the Soviet "satellite warning program" has issued time tables to various parts of the Soviet military–industrial complex describing which U.S. intelligence satellites will be "in view" of them when, and what to do or not to do during those periods.*

As a result new satellites, or satellites with new capabilities, or satellites that are in new and unexpected orbits, have seen or intercepted things very different from those that are picked up by satellites that are where the Soviets expected them to be. In its first days in 1977, the KH-11 saw a *wholly mobile* firing unit of the SS-11 missile, apparently on maneuvers in woods far away from any known missile-deployment area. This observation was downright revolutionary. Since 1962, when satellites began photographing Soviet missiles on their pads, the United States had based its entire strategic policy on the supposition that the Soviets had no mobile missiles at all, that they had only one missile per launcher.[25] This supposition had been solidly based on observation. Until 1977 no missile (except the experimental SS-16) had ever been seen in a mobile configuration. *Mobile* SS-11s had not been seen before (and have not been seen since). But then again, no U.S. satellite had been unknown to the Soviet satellite warning program before.

American imaging satellites were not designed to hide. They have followed sun-synchronous orbits that maximize time over the Soviet Union during daylight hours, even though that has advertised their function. Some American intelligence officers used to argue that the Soviets could never be *certain* of how much or how well each satellite could see. Although the area within the KH-11's line of sight is easily calculated, how much of that area the satellite can photograph at any given time depends on its design, including (foremost) the power supply, its on-board processing capacity, and the maximum angle from nadir at which it can look.

Alas, the Soviets have learned many such details. One source has been the arms-control process. For example, in 1977, soon after the KH-11 was launched, the Soviets used the SALT I treaty's provision against interference with "national technical means" of verification to elicit information about its "look angle." They stretched a canvas high over one of their missile silos. The U.S. did not protest, since the satellite could look under the canvas from the side. Then the Soviets lowered the canvas. Since the U.S. could still see, it did not protest. Yet another lowering of the canvas and the U.S. protested its treaty rights. The Soviets quickly removed the canvas. They had learned what they wanted.

*In 1991, as KGB nuclear custody units evacuated Germany, they left behind copies of satellite warning notices.

What the Soviets did not learn about the KH-11 through the arms-control process they learned in 1978 when a young CIA officer, William Kampiles, sold the entire operating manual of the KH-11 to the Soviet Union for $3,000.[26] Since then the basic KH-11 has been modified several times, and, according to a variety of public sources, now has an infrared feature that allows it to take pictures (of sorts) at night. But the new features do not invalidate the knowledge the Soviets have gained. As we have mentioned, in 1988 the U.S. augmented its stock of imaging satellites with a radar-imaging satellite named Lacrosse.[27] We noted that the targets of its radar beams know that they are being observed, and very precisely what kind of image Lacrosse is delivering to the U.S.*

American signals-intelligence satellites were able to operate with a certain amount of secrecy until the early 1970s simply because of technical wizardry. It was easy enough for the Soviets to imagine that low-orbiting American satellites would carry antennas, and easy enough to order military units, communications stations, and the like to turn off electronic equipment during the brief, predictable minutes every day when these satellites would be passing overhead. But it was much more difficult for the Soviets to imagine how the U.S. might build an antenna big enough to pick up signals from geostationary orbit (22,300 miles away) and make it light enough to be placed there. Living under a permanently "staring" antenna would pose no insoluble problems. But the Soviets were not willing to start tackling those problems until they knew they had to. Thus, in 1973 Soviet space-track radars picked up another American satellite at geosynchronous orbit. It was Rhyolite—a giant umbrella of hair-thin wires designed to intercept telemetry from Soviet test missiles. But because the Soviets had never tried to build such a thing, they might well not have thought this was it. They could have hypothesized "telemetry collection" as the mission of the radar blob they saw. But mere hypothesis would not have been sufficient warrant for expensive countermeasures. Yet between 1974 and 1976 hypothesis became fact when the Soviets received the most intimate details about Rhyolite from Christopher Boyce, who was employed at Rhyolite's manufacturer, TRW, and his friend Andrew Lee.[28] Since then the satellite's name has changed three times, and it has undergone several major improvements. But this pales in significance with the fact that the Soviets know that their telemetry is being picked up by an American satellite.

In 1976, Soviet radars picked up another American satellite at geosynchronous orbit. Without further information, Soviet CI analysts might have thought

---

*The converse, however, is not true. Radar images of any object are quite unlike what the human eye sees when it looks at that object. Sharp corners reflect more of the radar beam, and other shapes less. Radar imagery does not "see a tank." Rather, it sees something that compares reasonably well with records of the "radar signatures" of tanks from various angles. Infrared imagery is closer to visual imagery. But what one is looking at is often far from obvious.

that it was another Rhyolite, and limited their proposed countermeasures to missile tests. But there *was* further information—from Geoffrey Prime, an agent of theirs in Britain's codebreaking agency, GCHQ (Government Communications Headquarters.) He reported that he had been assigned to translate certain telephone conversations between Soviet officials as part of a project in cooperation with the American NSA. The Soviets naturally had to notice that the West possessed *only one half of* the conversations, that all the conversations had taken place over long-distance microwave circuits, and that the half that Prime was translating had originated in the northwestern part of the USSR. Since no American or British antennae lay in line between the northwestern and southeastern ends of the conversations, they probably drew the line beyond the eastern end, out into space. When that line hit geosynchronous orbit, it also hit the figure-eight orbit of the new U.S. satellite. Of course this did not prove that the blob on the radar screen was intercepting the conversations. However, proof positive would come soon. On July 16, 1979 Richard Burt, then a reporter for *The New York Times*, wrote a story about an American geosynchronous satellite named *Chalet* which had the capacity to intercept Soviet telemetry (i.e., it was a huge, sensitive antenna), although, said Burt, it was primarily intended for another purpose. To experienced intelligence officers this was equivalent to spelling out that the satellite's primary purpose was communications intelligence. None of the improvements or name changes which *Chalet* has undergone since 1979 could possibly have caused Soviet intelligence officers to forget that microwave telephone transmissions along lines-of-sight that strike U.S. satellites are likely to be intercepted.

The U.S. intelligence community has never formally asked itself how the Soviet Union has used these and other items of knowledge about how it is being observed. U.S. intelligence has taken note of the satellite warning program. The informal consensus is that the program simply tries to hide as much—across the board—as is consistent with the operational efficiency of the Soviet military. But this makes no sense. There is no evidence at all that the Soviets were so mindless as to cut their exposure without considering the effect of each cut, and considerable evidence that by showing certain activities and not others (that is, by exposing themselves thoughtfully to cameras they know well), the Soviets were endeavoring to give the U.S. certain impressions. The relevant *counterintelligence* question, however, is "How, given what we know they know, can we conduct our imagery reconnaissance to minimize the possibility of their interference?" But those in charge of American CI usually consider this question in bad taste.

By the same token, although they note that most of the "interesting" traffic has been shifted away from electronic means of communication that the Soviets know are intercepted, U.S. intelligence managers refuse to consider how the

Soviets might manage their electronic exposure. They note sadly that after the mid–1970s the Soviets encrypted more and more of the telemetry from their missile tests until, by 1990, only a tiny percentage of telemetry was "in the clear." But they ignore the obvious question: On what basis do the Soviets choose *which* telemetry channels to protect, and which few to broadcast for the Americans to read? U.S. intelligence managers, glad to get whatever information they can, treat the "clear" telemetry information as if the Soviet choice had been random—even though chances are slim that it is so.

U.S. intelligence managers are sorry that less and less interesting information travels in the clear over Soviet microwave telephone and teletype links, and that Soviet authorities routed more and more interesting communications onto either land lines or encrypted circuits. They know that all the trends in computer science and communications equipment are making encryption better, cheaper, and ever more pervasive. They rightly regard these trends as obstacles to U.S. technical collection. But they do not squarely ask why the Soviets would knowingly leave in the clear and deliberately transmit some "interesting" material over a few of the communications channels that the U.S. is obviously monitoring. The standard answer at NSA and CIA is that since the Soviets cannot be precisely sure about the mathematical models by which the U.S. chooses among the channels it could theoretically record, the Soviets would be leery of using any of these channels for disinformation, lest the message not get through at all or get through too heavy-handedly. But this makes little sense. The Soviets know which of their communications are interesting to the U.S., and they know that the U.S. mathematical models, if they are any good, maximize access to interesting transmissions. They too can build mathematical models. Hence, to have a reasonable chance of getting their messages through, Soviet counterintelligence need only play the same mathematical games played at NSA, with the advantage of already knowing their own key variable.

Even the most brilliant and daring efforts of U.S. technical collection, which yielded rich harvests until the early 1980s, have since come to naught. In the 1970s, U.S. Navy submarines located a communication cable running under the Sea of Okhotsk. The cable connected the Soviet Navy's Pacific Fleet with headquarters. Since the Soviets judged the cable to be secure, they did not bother encrypting the information they transmitted over it. The U.S. Navy, however, managed to tap that cable, and installed a huge bank of recorders next to it. Every year a U.S. submarine would sneak into the area, install fresh tapes, and return the ones loaded with Soviet communications. This information was not timely, but it was plentiful, and above all pure. So valuable was it that by the early 1980s the U.S. government had begun a multibillion-dollar project to make the flow simple and instantaneous. It involved tapping a Soviet undersea cable near the northwestern city of Murmansk with an American cable, buried under the sands of the Arctic Ocean's floor, and reaching all the way to Greenland. This intrusion into Soviet communications would have provided foolproof, timely warning of any Soviet decision to go to war. In case of war, it would have served a function analogous to that of Ultra in World War II. In peacetime it would have provided an invaluable "ground truth" against which to measure other intelligence on the Soviet military. But Ronald Pelton, an employee of NSA, told the Soviets about the cable tap in the Sea of Okhotsk.[29] Following this act of espionage, a Soviet submarine retrieved the U.S. recorders. Subsequently, journalist Bob Woodward, in his book *Veil*, revealed—and thus killed—the plan for the on-line Arctic cable tap. The latter was a classic bureaucratic *coup de grâce*. Powerful factions within both CIA and NSA had opposed the direct-cable tap because it would have been expensive and would have taken money from current programs. After the revelation of Pelton's espionage the direct-cable tap program was hanging by a thread. In such circumstances it is not unusual for high officials to leak a program to a favorite reporter.*

Thus, on the threshold of the 1990s, U.S. technical collection had become so well-known, so predictable to the Soviet Union, that it was difficult to even think of how counterintelligence might help it. Indeed, because of arms control, U.S. technical collection was actually evolving away from the normal understanding of secret intelligence and in the direction of *cooperating with* the Soviet Union to gather technical data about Soviet weapons. In other words, far from making sure that the U.S. received data untainted by the other side's knowledge, the arms-control process has increased the proportion of data that U.S. technical systems pick up at times, in places, and in ways agreed upon with Soviet authorities. However valuable such information might be, it is misleading to think of it as intelligence.

An extreme case illustrates the point: In April 1985, as part of the controversy over the Soviet Union's construction of a large radar at Krasnoyarsk in violation of the ABM treaty, Paul Nitze, the President's chief negotiator on arms control, having said "unequivocally" that it is "an early warning radar," (i.e., not a violation) proposed, as "a Reagan administration official," that the Soviets agree to turn on the radar while the appropriate U.S. satellite (in this case, the Jumpseat Elint satellite) was in the appropriate place. The U.S. could then

---

*The careful reader will note which senior intelligence managers Bob Woodward singled out as having been especially helpful in the preparation of *Veil*. The fact that these individuals had opposed the on-line cable tap project for years does not prove that they killed it by leaking it. But one could imagine worse bases for an investigation. Still, the practice of killing a project by leaking it has become so much a part of high bureaucratic culture in Washington that no investigation occurred.

declare that the signal from the radar was not optimal for antimissile defense, and that hence the radar was not an important problem with regard to the ABM treaty.[30] This stillborn proposal for a "mutually palatable solution" was a classic case of the very opposite of counterintelligence thinking with regard to technical collection: The Krasnoyarsk radar, like other computer-driven, phased-array radars, could put out a variety of signals, and use the returns variously, according to the software employed at the time. Moreover, the appropriateness of any given radar wave form for ballistic-missile defense is a matter of opinion. Hence, the proposal was virtually an invitation for the Soviets to convey certain data, which certain officials in the U.S. would use for their own intramural purposes.*

By the same token, the U.S.–Soviet treaty on Intermediate Nuclear Forces signed in December 1987 carried with it a cooperative scheme of verification: The U.S. could station observers outside the portals of one missile assembly plant (at Votkhinsk) and measure the size of containers leaving those portals. Since the text of the treaty defines precisely what the U.S. may and may not look at, it allows the Soviets (should they wish) to formally satisfy the U.S. while doing precisely what they wish. Other schemes have been proposed to monitor nuclear testing by locating seismic sensors on Soviet soil. The Soviets would provide data on the size of their tests, and the sensors would confirm such. But of course those in charge of the sensors would not have a chance to independently determine a scale of reference, or to get a look at preparations for individual tests to check for seismic dampening measures. In connection with the negotiations for a treaty reducing strategic armaments, U.S. officials proposed a variety of "cooperative measures according to which the Soviet Union would allow U.S. intelligence to place sensors at key points in specific factories." They accepted "portal monitoring" of missile *assembly* plants. The Pentagon had proposed stationing observers at the places where solid rocket motors (i.e., the giant tubes of fast burning rubbery compounds that power the missiles) are poured. Since these are indispensable to a missile, hard knowledge of how many are produced would be a firm point of reference for other intelligence. But the Soviets objected. So U.S. officials agreed to consider the number of rocket motors coming into the designated assembly plants to be the total rocket motors produced by the Soviet Union. As in the case of SALT I, U.S. officials were willing to equate knowledge of ephemeral facts from a source known to the other side (in this case, contractually controlled by the other side) with essential facts unknown to us and that the other side openly worked to conceal. This may or may not be good policy. But it is bad epistemology. These trends tend to turn

---

*Note by the way that in October 1989 Soviet Foreign Minister Eduard Shevardnadze officially declared that the Krasnoyarsk radar had always been intended to be a violation of the ABM treaty. *New York Times*, 24 October 1989.

U.S. means of technical collection into tautological channels to which the term "intelligence" is hardly applicable.

Human Coverage

The CI coverage of human collection has gone from marginal to almost nonexistent. After the firing of James Angleton in 1974, the CI staff became a group of temporary detailees from the geographic branches of the DDO. Their personal and institutional interest is to approve, rather than to find fault with, the recruitment and running of agents. The rule of the new CI staff is clear: The Soviet Union is security-crazy and does not willingly part with any classified information whatever, for any reason. Hence, by the CIA's definition, there can be no such thing as a Soviet double agent who buys his way "in" with real classified information. Hence all Soviet classified information the CIA receives is *ipso facto* reliable. With the principal preoccupation of CI so neatly taken care of, what's left?

The CI staff's principal occupation since 1974 has been to do "CI surveys" of CIA stations abroad. Theoretically every station should be surveyed every five years. But since the job does not have high priority, its accomplishment has lagged. As one might expect, these surveys are heavily quantitative, and do not involve substantive judgments on cases. They note how frequently the station has changed its safe houses and its relationship with the local CI service. In other words, they deal with operating *conditions*. The *substance* of operations is assumed to be good, and beyond the scope of modern CIA counterintelligence.

But even well before the downgrading of the CI staff in 1974, U.S. espionage had been badly covered. For example, in 1988 the CIA was shocked when Maj. Florentino Aspillaga, who had defected to the U.S. from Cuba's intelligence service, the DGI, recited to his debriefers the names of Cubans whom the CIA thought were secretly spying for the U.S. but who (obviously) were known to, and controlled by, the DGI. Worse yet, Aspillaga's list included *all* those whom the CIA had thought of as agents in the previous 20 years. The surprise should not have been total. In 1978, five Cubans had testified at the eleventh World Festival of Youth in Havana that they had offered their services to the CIA, had been accepted, and for ten years had served as double agents, fooling the CIA on behalf of Cuban intelligence. One of them, Nicolas Sigaldo Ros, said that he had passed three of the CIA's polygraphs, and served between 1966 and 1976.[31] Like so many communist infiltrators into U.S. intelligence, he laid out the embarrassing record of how he had fooled the CIA. For the CIA such a record—having literally *all* of its human sources in a fairly important country controlled by the hostile service—cannot be explained by bad luck or occasional lapses. There was obviously a pattern of incompetence, even under James Angleton.

Perhaps penultimate confirmation of the pattern came in 1991. CIA officers were allowed to examine the files of the East German Staatssicherheitsdienst (Stasi) after they came under control of the unified German government in 1990. According to a CIA report that found its way to the press, "Most East Germans recruited by the CIA as spies since at least the early 1950s were double agents secretly loyal to the Stasi . . . scores of agents recruited by the agency were working for the other side."[32] To have most of one's agents working for the other side is not evidence of normal human imperfection. That kind of performance makes intelligence a net liability for one's side.

Is there reason to believe that the CIA performed any better against the KGB than against the DGI and the Stasi? On the contrary, the available evidence is that it followed the same pattern. The origin of that pattern is excessive eagerness for controlled sources, combined with seemingly invincible arrogance about foreigners. For example, in 1975, soon after the downgrading of the CI staff, the CIA authorized the recruitment in Moscow of Sanya Lipavsky, a young Jewish physician who had had some contact with Soviet nuclear submarines but who now shared a room with one of the major Soviet human-rights activists, Anatoli Shcharansky. Prior to 1975 the CIA had not accepted overtures from potential agents in Moscow, judging them too likely to be KGB dangles. But now, perhaps eager to show what it could do without Angleton's encumbrance, the CIA accepted Lipavsky and provided him with equipment for secret communications. In March 1977, however, Izvestia published Lipavsky's true account of his collaboration with the CIA, along with false allegations that Shcharansky and other dissidents were also working for the CIA. By biting on Lipavsky's bait the CIA had given plausibility to the Soviet practice of jailing dissidents as spies.[33]

A different side of the same coin may be seen in the case of Alexander Ogorodnik, a Soviet diplomat whom the CIA had apparently recruited in Colombia in 1973 by noticing his love of money. He was code-named Trigon. By the mid–1970s, the CIA had become so self-confident that it was actually handling its Soviet recruits in Moscow, despite the blanket of surveillance that the KGB had spread over the city. Time had dulled whatever lesson the CIA had learned by handling (and losing) Oleg Penkovsky in Moscow in 1962 (possibly) through "casual" contact with the wife of a British diplomat. At any rate, on July 15, 1977 the KGB arrested CIA officer Martha Peterson as she was turning over a hollowed-out rock in a Moscow park. She was servicing Trigon's dead-drop with gold coins and espionage equipment.[34] Because Peterson was obviously set up for the arrest, Trigon had just as obviously been "blown" sometime before. The only sure thing is that he was under KGB control for an undetermined time before Peterson's arrest, and hence that the material he passed during that undetermined period was deceptive. But for how long? Perhaps he had never been "for real" in the first place, or perhaps he was for real but Karel Koecher, a

Soviet agent working in the CIA's AE Screen unit, which processed Trigon's material, gave him away very soon after his recruitment. Or perhaps he was "blown" by the KGB's surveillance of his contact, or perhaps by a technical penetration of the U.S. Embassy, or thanks to the Walker spy ring's cryptologic assistance, or perhaps by the decoding of messages between the CIA headquarters and the Moscow station. *The point is that Trigon could have slipped through any or all of these holes in the sieve of American CI.**

The most clamorous instances of the inadequacy of human CI concerns defectors. Of these, perhaps the most instructive cases were those of KGB Maj. Yuri Nosenko, beginning in 1964, and of high KGB official Vitaly Yurchenko in 1985. Not having access to the KGB's records, it is impossible to know "for a fact" whether either defector was real or fake. However, knowledge of what happened to both in the U.S. makes it clear that in both cases bureaucratic considerations led the CIA to officially accept stories of the kind that a reasonable person would hardly accept if his own private interests were in the balance.

When Yuri Nosenko had first contacted the CIA in Switzerland in 1962, the CIA had judged he was a KGB dangle, and had decided to have nothing to do with him. Then in January 1964 he showed up again, told the CIA he had to defect immediately, and immediately set about answering the United States' most burning questions about Lee Harvey Oswald. In 1964 the U.S. government wanted very much to believe that the Soviet Union had had nothing to do with the assassination of John F. Kennedy, and that his assassin, Lee Harvey Oswald, had been just a nut. The problem was that Oswald was a very peculiar nut—a loudly self-proclaimed communist who had probably spied for the Soviets as an enlisted man in the Marine Corps guarding a U-2 base, and who had then gone to live in the USSR. There he had been given unusually plush arrangements in Minsk, and had been allowed to marry the "niece" of a GRU officer.† These facts were troublesome to the U.S. government, and presumably worrisome to the Soviet government. Nosenko's story—the KGB had never had anything to do with Oswald—was at once too pleasant and too unlikely to be

---

*The loss of Trigon, too, set off a series of recriminations in Washington. Officious voices from the new CI staff pointed in the direction of David Aaron, the Deputy National Security Adviser in the Carter Administration, alleging loose talk with a Soviet diplomat. As under Angleton, the real culprit for the internecine strife was an excess of possible explanations and a dearth of hard facts.

†Marina Oswald's relationship with Soviet intelligence may or may not be familial. Soviet women who "work" Westerners usually introduce their controllers to the man they are "working" as "my uncle." At any rate, permission for Western men to marry and emigrate with Soviet women was anything but routine, even under Gorbachev. In the early 1960s it was most unusual.

true, and most of its checkable parts turned out to be certifiable lies. Moreover, as the years passed, the Soviet agent who had confirmed Nosenko's story, the FBI's Fedora, returned to the USSR under conditions that suggest he had been on the Soviet side all along. So the *prima faciae* picture was of an elaborate deception.[35] This is not to say that the KGB told Oswald to shoot Kennedy. On the contrary, it suggests that the KGB was horrified when one of its people had, and tried to cover up the connection.

On the other side of the ledger, Nosenko had provided a few leads. But the people Nosenko identified as Soviet assets in the West were mostly no longer useful to the Soviets. Nosenko's biggest present, Army Sgt. Robert Lee Johnson, had already drawn suspicion on himself and was no longer producing. Other leads were even more dubious. Instead of new facts, he gave bromidic explanations of old CIA failures: Soviet CI sprinkled the shoes of Americans with "spy dust" so they could be tracked throughout Moscow. Popov had been caught by surveillance of a mailbox. Former DCI Stansfield Turner was particularly impressed that Nosenko told the CIA about 52 microphones in the U.S. Embassy in Moscow.[36] True. Alas, Nosenko had also assured the CIA that the *new wing* of the U.S. Embassy was unbugged. But later the U.S. found 130 microphones there, the effectiveness of which had been enhanced by the false sense of security Nosenko had given.

How could this sort of thing counterbalance the fact that Nosenko was not who he claimed to be, that he had not defected for the reason he claimed, and that clearly false details of his story were confirmed by people who gave the strongest reasons to believe they were on the Soviet side? Intellectually it could not. However, some nonintellectual arguments weighed heavily on Nosenko's side: In brief, to draw the conclusion that Nosenko was a dispatched Soviet double agent would have forced the U.S. government to entertain the troubling proposition that President Kennedy had been killed by a Soviet agent (whether or not on orders of the Soviet government). The CIA would also have had to indict itself, both because it (and the FBI) had been taken for a ride by other Soviet double agents as well, and because both had failed to pay attention to a Lee Harvey Oswald, who deserved it. It proved easier to contradict every reasonable norm of CI than to reach a conclusion potentially damaging both to U.S./Soviet relations *and* to the corporate self-interest of the intelligence community.

At least as important, as we have previously mentioned, the question of Nosenko's *bona fides* became identical to that of whether the collectors would prevail over CI, *and* identical to whether liberals would prevail over conservatives at CIA. Hence the pro-Nosenko case quickly dispenses with the merits. It does not deny Nosenko's lies, but attributes them to a conscious desire to build up his image with the Americans, or to a subconscious one to match his famous father, or to a "muddled" personality, or to the nastiness of the interrogation. Nor does the case vigorously assert the worth of Nosenko's information. Rather, the pro-Nosenko case rests on the alleged incompetence and character flaws of Peter Bagley, then Deputy Chief of the Soviet Division, *and* of James Angleton, *and* on how nastily they treated Nosenko. The definitive pro-Nosenko book mentions that DCI Richard Helms decided to grant Nosenko's *bona fides* not because he believed Nosenko, but because it had become inconvenient not to. Only then did he appoint new people to write new reports on the case. Were they better informed or more objective? The book claims that the new team "had no motive other than a growing concern for the civil rights of a man", and that all Nosenko's lies "were all found to have logical explanations" and were "fully accepted." This has all the flavor of a winners' version of history.*

A generation later a similar affair occurred when Vitaly Yurchenko defected from the KGB in August 1985, describing himself as Deputy Chief of the First Chief Directorate's Department for North America. The CIA quickly described his defection as the greatest of coups. Here was the man who could shed light on the reasons why the CIA had lost valuable agents in the past, and who could unmask Soviet operations in the present. And indeed there was a crying need for explanations. In 1985, long-standing U.S. agent Igor Gheja in India, Sergei Bokhan in Greece, and British MI-6 agent Oleg Gordievsky defected in fear of their lives. Gordievsky had to escape from the Soviet Union itself. Another U.S. agent, A. G. Tolkachev, was arrested in Moscow that same year. There was also a long string of earlier defeats, among these the disappearance of U.S. double agent Nicholas Shadrin in 1975, and the old but still divisive controversy over Nosenko.[37] As for present KGB operations in the U.S., the Deputy Chief of the First Chief Directorate's Department for North America should have had them all (or at least the biggest) on the tip of his tongue.

However, despite offers of multimillion-dollar bonuses, Yurchenko did not deliver significant information about the Soviet espionage network in North America—nothing about locations of dead drops or names of agents. Although some agency officials affected appreciation at Yurchenko's mention of a list of Western journalists whom the KGB considers "reliable" (information already suspected but totally unusable by the U.S. government), the CIA was unable to

---

*Tom Mangold, *Cold Warrior*, pp. 206, 212, 213. The book also presents the opinion of Oleg Gordievsky that a man of Nosenko's rank could not have "defected as a false defector" as "formal" confirmation of Nosenko's *bona fides* (p. 220). Note, however, that Gordievsky does not claim specific knowledge. Rather, his inference of a specific CI fact from his general knowledge of the Soviet system is precisely what Anatoli Golitsyn made his living from, and the practice that Mangold and his pro-Nosenko sources so appropriately decry.

deliver to the White House any impressive take whatever from Yurchenko, leading President Reagan to label it "not anything new or sensational."[38]

Yet, the CIA judged Yurchenko so important for its own intramural purposes that during September and October 1985 it touted him to the news media and authorized production of a book about him, and thereafter defended his importance and *bona fides* throughout official Washington. The CIA's behavior is understandable because Yurchenko gave the CIA something it wanted more than it wanted the names of Soviet operatives in New York, San Francisco, or even Peoria. Namely, Yurchenko reassured the CIA that the KGB had never managed to recruit *any* of the CIA's personnel, and had *never* sent false defectors or dangles who had bought their way in with classified information. Thus the CIA could rest easy with its dearest assumptions confirmed: It never had been penetrated, and it never had been deceived because the KGB was so stiff about releasing "feed" information as to be incapable of deception. There would be no need for self-examination or recriminations. Everyone had done a good job. Yurchenko had saved reputations.

Yurchenko also gave the CIA specific relief from the ghosts of the past. Like Nosenko two decades before, he claimed that the KGB had gotten on the trail of the CIA's agents not through any insufficiency on the CIA's part, but through "spy dust"—fine, slightly radioactive dust sprayed on all U.S. Embassy personnel. But whereas Nosenko had claimed that the dust was used for physical surveillance, Yurchenko now claimed the dust rubbed off on mail handled by Americans, and that Moscow post offices thus identified the CIA's addressees. In addition, Yurchenko gave the CIA obvious clues to the collaboration of Edward Lee Howard, a former CIA officer whom the CIA already knew had contacted the Soviets, and suggested that Howard had helped identify Tolkachev. He also gave clues leading to a retired (and already suspected) spy in Canadian CI. All of this was useless from the standpoint of counterintelligence, as was Yurchenko's pointing to the trail of Ronald Pelton, who had already left the NSA and whose damage to the Navy's cable tap operation the U.S. had known about ever since a U.S. submarine had visited the cable tap site almost three years earlier and found the equipment gone. For the KGB Pelton was expendable. But for the CIA it was all catnip.

However, like most stories too good to be true, this one clashed with reality. It turned out that Howard, at most, was responsible for divulging operational techniques (as if the KGB had not known them before), but that he could not have blown Tolkachev because Tolkachev had been recruited *after* Howard had left the CIA. As for spy dust, CIA technical experts found it technically unsuited to the use Yurchenko suggested. More directly disturbing, although Yurchenko denied that the KGB had recruited any U.S. government employees recently, the CIA knew very well that during Yurchenko's tenure the KGB had indeed accepted several such American dangles. Yet *Yurchenko refused to name some of them, even when the CIA debriefers steered the conversation in their direction.* Just as glaring, if the U.S. government is correct that the Soviets had enjoyed a relationship with senior U.S. Diplomat Felix Bloch since 1972, a man in Yurchenko's position would have known about him if he knew anything at all. *Yet Yurchenko gave no hints about Bloch.* In other words, everything Yurchenko had to say was either something that the KGB realized the agency already knew, or it was of marginal significance. Moreover, by September, Yurchenko had already clammed up. He had spoken his piece and would not go further. It was absurd that the Deputy Chief of the North America Department of the First Chief Directorate had so little to say.

By mid-October 1985 the CIA had an embarrassment on its hands. To try to resolve Yurchenko's contradictions through hostile interrogation would not only have risked a recurrence of the internecine war over Nosenko's *bona fides.* It also would have discredited the very top officials who had declared Yurchenko living proof of the supremacy of the CIA over the KGB.* So, apparently, someone in the U.S. intelligence community decided to give Yurchenko every opportunity to return quietly to the Soviet Embassy. On November 2, 1985 the CIA gave him new clothes, and the telephone number of the Soviet Embassy, which he called. Of course the FBI was listening in. But it sounded no alarm bells. Then a lone CIA officer took him to lunch near the Embassy. Yurchenko told him that he was leaving, and the officer watched as he left.

But Yurchenko did not go quietly. Within 48 hours, gleeful Soviet Embassy officials were rounding up American reporters for a press conference, where a buoyant Yurchenko told of being drugged by the CIA and transported across international borders. The words of this blatant lie were almost precisely the ones he had used to tell the CIA of what the KGB had done to Nicholas Shadrin ten years earlier in Vienna. The Soviets then delivered Yurchenko, all alone, to the State Department, where he convinced both U.S. officers and medical personnel that he knew exactly what he was doing by returning to the USSR.

---

*On 31 October, 1985 CIA Deputy Director John McMahon sat in the office of Sen. Malcolm Wallop (R-WY) and assured him "I would bet my career" on Yurchenko's authenticity. Forty-eight hours later, Yurchenko had redefected. (Personal interview with Sen. Wallop, 4 November 1985.) The CIA's circle of admirers was no less committed to the proposition that Yurchenko had shown the superiority of Western intelligence. Christopher Andrew of Cambridge stated (before the "redefection") that Yurchenko was more valuable than "20,000 seduced West German secretaries." *Newsweek,* 4 November 1985. After Yurchenko's redefection, and after Klaus Kuron, chief of double-agent operations for the BND confessed to having been a Stasi agent, one wonders how many Yurchenkos Mr. Andrew thought Mr. Kuron was worth.

Giving no sign of any Hamlet-like attitude, he left the Department waving two-finger victory signs. In staging the conference and returning him to the State Department, the KGB showed that it did not consider Yurchenko either a traitor the full extent of whose treason must be determined, or an impulsive fellow who had changed his allegiances twice and might easily change them a third time. The Soviets obviously felt they had sound reasons for this brazen confidence, and looked like people who were having fun. The CIA's line—that Yurchenko was a confused fellow who sincerely defected and then sincerely redefected—inspires much less confidence.

In February 1986 the CIA tried to mitigate the embarrassment by spreading the word to the major network news programs that the KGB had executed Yurchenko and charged his family for the bullet. National Public Radio carried the story. Within weeks, as if to belie the CIA again, Yurchenko held another press conference in Moscow, at which he promised to write a book about the CIA.[39]

Now consider the rhetorical question that CIA officers ask in hushed tones: If Yurchenko was a fake, what good did the operation do for the KGB? For the sake of what would it have gone through all that trouble? We suggest three answers. First, he administered to the Americans a dose of tranquilizers with regard to past operations and any penetrations that were ongoing—e.g., Felix Bloch. Second, Yurchenko was able to answer perhaps the most important CI question troubling the KGB in 1985. Since 1968, John Walker had been giving the Soviet Union a powerful set of keys to U.S. communications. This all-time greatest of sources had just been arrested, and the Soviets were loath to believe press accounts that his wife had turned him in. Given the importance of the Walker case, it would make sense for the KGB to go through a lot to make sure that the U.S. had not caught Walker through a penetration or through other methods that might allow the U.S. to detect and manipulate a future Walker. Yurchenko often turned his debriefers' conversation to Walker, and was able to confirm that the public version of the story was indeed correct. Third, no one should underestimate the value that the KGB put on rubbing in its victories in CI.

All of this notwithstanding, the CIA maintains the contradictory propositions that Yurchenko told real, valuable information, *and* that the KGB never tolerates the release of real information *and* that the KGB tolerated Yurchenko's release of real information. The CIA's official position remains that Yurchenko was a real defector, and that everything he said to the CIA in August, September, and October 1985 was credible, but that everything he has said since is a lie. We for our part contend that the CIA's handling of Yurchenko shows that the CIA is far more concerned with protecting the *reputation* of its human collection than with protecting its integrity.

A much simpler case than Yurchenko's perhaps even more clearly shows the same will to believe stories that serve institutional ends. In 1982 a 19-year-old Nicaraguan soldier named Orlando Jose Tardencilla Espinosa was captured (or let himself be captured) in El Salvador. He told the CIA and the State Department that he had been trained by Soviets in Ethiopia as part of an international communist effort to overthrow the government of El Salvador. In March of 1982 the U.S. government, which had been trying to make that point in public, placed the young man before a press conference—where he promptly denied the whole story and, *à la* Yurchenko, accused the U.S. of kidnapping, drugging, and torture. He got a hero's welcome back in Nicaragua: He had earned his pay and taught the U.S. a lesson.[40] Those paid to guard the integrity of U.S. human collection had merely noted that his story sounded true and that its details checked out. They had not questioned the teenager's motives, much less had they taken the elementary precaution of staging a "dry run" before a fake audience. A 19-year-old armed with the fundamentals will outdo a whole government that forgets them, every time.

Covering Covert Action

There is no distinct line between guarding human collection and guarding the integrity of U.S. actions abroad. Both require correct judgment about the people with whom one is dealing: who they are, what is their access and power, what they want, who else knows about them, what they are doing with that knowledge. This leads us to our fourth point. U.S. officials had been "had" over the years by the Polish WiN in 1947–53, in the Iranian arms-for-hostages scandal of 1984–86, and by the Panamanian soldier–despot Manuel Noriega in 1975–89, as well as in a host of other situations, because U.S. covert action neglected basic principles. We leave these for later discussion, and focus here only on the subissue of counterintelligence protection of CA—and of some overt policies as well.

Consider first the case of Manuel Noriega, who rose from chief of the Panamanian National Guard's intelligence service in the 1970s to despot of Panama in the 1980s. Lack of facts about Noriega was never a problem for the U.S. The CIA and Army intelligence began to pay Noriega in 1955 as a young thug who was building a personal following by distributing the profits of drug-running and protection rackets. They knew him as a murderer. They knew him as the boss of the "Hunting and Fishing Club of Panama," which was a conduit of arms from Cuba to be used for extortion, drug running, etc. They knew him as a man with a warm relationship with Cuba's Fidel Castro and later Nicaragua's Daniel Ortega. They knew him as the power behind the charismatic throne of Gen. Omar Torrijos. But they also knew him as a man who reported to U.S. intelligence on his conversations with the aforementioned communist leaders. Noriega assured the U.S. that he knew of, and countered, any attempt on the part of foreign communists to infiltrate Panama. Just as important, he promised orderly cooperation in the implementation of the 1978 treaties turning over U.S. control of the Panama Canal to Panama. U.S. intelligence did not doubt that Noriega was also reporting to the communist powers, to some extent. But for some reason they figured that Noriega was somehow "our man" and that he could be manipulated to suit U.S. purposes. So, between 1955 and 1986 the Army paid Noriega a total of $162,168, and the CIA paid him $160,058.[41] But U.S. intelligence gave him more than money. It gave him trust.

Because of this basic CI misjudgment (with whom we can work and with whom we can't), Noriega again and again surprised and embarrassed U.S. intelligence officials. In 1976 they were much surprised to learn that Noriega had recruited spies among U.S. Army personnel at a U.S. communications intercept station in Panama. In 1979 they were surprised when he took absolute power after Torrijos died in a mysterious airplane crash. All through the early and mid-1980s they were surprised when he expanded Panama's role in drug-running into the U.S., when he crushed and mocked the results of free elections, and when he led Presidents Reagan and Bush on a merry chase for two years as he privately negotiated his own departure but publicly consolidated his power with the help of Cuba and Nicaragua. There was no reason for U.S. intelligence to be surprised—except that Noriega's counterintelligence had beaten U.S. counterintelligence again and again and again.

The line between counterintelligence and just plain judgment of character is a thin one. As we shall see, the CIA provides "intelligence support" to a variety of Third World governments in a double attempt to both support and gain influence on them. The feasibility of such operations depends on an accurate assessment of the malleability of the target regime's leading personalities. Facts are seldom lacking. Take Iraq's Saddam Hussein, recipient of "intelligence support" during the 1980s. His ruthlessness was legendary. Yet the CIA—and the rest of the U.S. government—apparently concluded that a man who all his days had risked his life and taken others' could be led along by American bureaucrats who had never lived a day as demanding as Saddam's was on average.[42] The U.S. government apparently wanted influence over Iraq badly enough not to consider that Iraq's dictator might be taking advantage of the U.S. to build up his power for purposes that the U.S. would find threatening.

By the same token, the Iranian arms-for-hostages scandal occurred because the U.S. government was so eager for access to a "moderate faction" within the hostile Iranian regime with which it could cooperate that it was unable to resist the lure of counterfeit "moderates" therein. During the Iran–Iraq war of 1981–88, Iran was eager for spare parts for its U.S.-equipped military. Every year any number of Iranians unsuccessfully contacted the CIA, offering to sell intelligence in exchange for arms.[43] As early as 1980, Washington had been awash with contacts on behalf of the "moderate" Ayatollah Montazeri. But these moderates too wanted arms—not the kind that might be used to kill the Ayatollah, but the kind obviously useful to fight Iraq. They claimed they wanted these to "bolster their credit." In the case of Iran, just as in the case of the Polish WiN, the U.S. knew about this "moderate faction" (its existence, power, and purposes) only what the faction itself provided. There was no "quality control" on the information. Any CI officer worth his salt would have said something like "And you are going into a major operation strictly on the basis of what they've told you? Are you kidding?" But no CI officers at all were assigned to the operation.

All around the world, the label "moderate faction" has been a nearly foolproof lure for the CIA, as for the U.S. government in general. But (as we will see in Chapter 6) the label has covered a variety of actual plans and actual characters that have ill-served the U.S. We do not mean to imply that good CI research into these people's motives and plans would have changed policy. As the case of Noriega shows, even plentiful information does not necessarily overcome incompetent policy-making. Sometimes, facts on the people the U.S. supports are unwelcome precisely because they call into question the wisdom of choices already made. The purpose of CI is not to tell policy-makers what to do, but to paste a "Surgeon General's Warning" on what appears to have been the perennially favorite "moderate" brew of U.S. policy-makers.

In sum, American policy-makers take CI all too lightly. The most obvious results are the dead bodies of foreigners who get in the way. Thus, in 1990 the U.S. government received warning from the Jordanian intelligence service that its agents inside Palestinian terrorist groups in Syria had detected a plot against a U.S. diplomat. Secretary of State James Baker, over the objections of the CIA, used the specific information to remonstrate with the Syrian government. His assumption was that the terrorists were something other than agents of the Syrian government. But the terrorists quickly got the information, and tracked down and killed the agents in their ranks.[44] Our point here is that CI is useful only to serious statecraft.

Analysis from the CI Standpoint
This brings us to our fifth point: the insufficient role of analysis in American CI. How inadequate the analytical practices of American CI have proved to be may be seen by a glance at the most significant espionage ring since that of the "atom spies" in the 1940s, that of John Walker.

From 1968 until 1984—16 years—Walker, his brother, his son, and his associate Jerry Whitworth, sold to the Soviet Union the operating manuals of the U.S. Navy's best code machines, together with volumes of daily settings. Thus not only were the Soviets able to read U.S. Navy communications as easily as the

U.S. Navy. Their cryptologists also may have been able to program their computers to break other American encoded communications that would otherwise have been far beyond reach. Through Walker the Soviet Union understood the capacity of key U.S. weapons systems and learned of U.S. strategic directions long before they were implemented. Because of Walker, had there been a war, the Soviets would have had a tactical advantage comparable to that which the Allies possessed over Nazi Germany through knowledge of Ultra. Walker might well have made the difference between a Soviet victory and an American one. Yet for 16 years U.S. counterintelligence had not a hint of this potentially mortal hemorrhage. Had Walker's wife, Barbara, not called the FBI (and persisted after being shunted aside), the Walkers would have continued to operate.

Prior to Barbara Walker's telephone call, there was no "Walker Case." Nothing triggered the attention of the U.S. counterintelligence system. Note well: A CI system more heavily based on analysis than our own would have taken note of numerous warning signs. But, given our own system's lack of analysis, its lack of attention to the warning signs was absolutely normal.

Consider the "barking dogs" that went unheeded in the Walker case. During the latter years of the Vietnam War, the Soviet-directed air defense network of North Vietnam always had advance warning of the specific targets that U.S. naval bombers would strike—even when the planes were diverted in midair. Elsewhere, by 1970, it had become part of the U.S. Navy's folkways that Soviet naval ships and intelligence-gathering vessels could be expected to show up precisely on schedule and at the right place to cover U.S. naval exercises.* When an intelligence satellite would blast off from Cape Canaveral, somehow the Soviets were always there. Obviously they were doing something other than guessing. As one admiral put it, "It is as if they had a copy of the Op Plans. Something is wrong."[45] Also, during the 1970s Soviet submarines around the world began to evade American surveillance just as if they knew precisely where and how that surveillance was to take place. Just as bad, Soviet antisubmarine aircraft would fly directly to the areas where U.S. submarines were patrolling. "They're finding our boomers" was the "dirty secret" of U.S. naval intelligence in the early 1980s. John Barron reports that in 1980 President Carter secretly prepared to launch a 5,000-man rescue operation into Iran, but called it off when the Soviets gradually built up 22 full divisions on the Iranian border. Each of these (and a host of other) events individually suggested, and *together* fairly shouted: The Soviets are reading our communications! *But there was no person*

---

*This author, as a Lieutenant (jg) on the intelligence staff of the U.S. Second Fleet during that year, heard that refrain any number of times, and joined other officers in gallows humor about the Soviet intelligence ships that were always at the right place at the right time.

177

or office in the U.S. government with the responsibility to look at all of these events together and to follow their implications. The disturbed admiral, the sailor shaking his head at yet another timely appearance of an antenna-loaded Soviet trawler, and the frustrated submariner had no place to take their concerns.

If there had been analysis, surely it would have connected many specific Soviet actions to messages transmitted over certain cipher machines, either the KWR-37, the KG-13, the KL-11, or the KL-47. Then a list of perhaps 100 custodians of those machines at any given time could have been quickly winnowed by checks of foreign travel and unexplained affluence. Surveillance would have done the rest. But alas, *the logic of U.S. CI runs from people to events, not the other way around.* In the U.S. CI system "the case" consists of evidence concerning *individuals* rather than of evidence concerning *subjects*, analysis of which might reveal the hand of hostile intelligence. U.S. counterintelligence works "bass ackwards."

By the same token, consider the United States' belated recognition circa 1977 that the Soviet Union probably tried to deceive the U.S. with regard to the accuracy of its missiles. The analytical process that led to the recognition was not abstruse. The U.S. government could have accomplished it in 1970 quite as well as in 1977. But no U.S. agency designated the subject of missile accuracy as worthy of counterintelligence attention. So the subject remained unanalyzed until a private analyst under contract to the government chose to take an interest in it.[46] Any properly cleared analyst who questioned the statistical chances that the chief indicators of inaccuracy—the multiple accelerometer readings obtained through telemetry—exhibited random differences would have had to conclude that these chances were low. If at the same time that analyst had been able to evaluate the credibility of Fedora and Top Hat, the agents who confirmed the presumed inaccuracy, he might well have concluded that a statistical improbability buttressed by agents who had previously confirmed known falsehoods indicated deception. The U.S. analysts who looked at the multidisciplinary data about Soviet missile accuracy for seven years without asking such questions were not stupid. They did the "positive intelligence" job they were paid for, and did not notice the existence of a CI case because they had not been asked to. Had they looked at the subject from the standpoint of CI they might well have seen both the case and its resolution.

Legal Confusion
Our sixth point is that the tradition that equates CI with law enforcement has increasingly made for bad CI *and* bad law enforcement. As we have mentioned, evidence of possible criminal activity has become just about the sole standard by which American officials decide whether someone (and only by coincidence a

subject) is worthy of being looked at from the standpoint of CI. This has led U.S. officials to confuse protection of the public with prosecution of individuals. This equation does not always hold for mere crimes, and seldom holds with regard to CI.

Perhaps the most outstanding example of how the criminal standard has failed not just with regard to CI but also in the fight against organized crime is the case of the People's Temple. During the 1970s a self-styled Reverend, James Jones, gathered a cult around himself in the San Francisco Bay area. His religion had nothing to do with God, the creator of Heaven and Earth, or with Jesus Christ, Mohammed, or the Buddha. It was a secular cult whose ideology consisted mostly of resentment against American society and whose practice consisted primarily of unquestioning obedience to Jones as "the Father," or "Dad." Jones and his followers were political leftists loosely associated with the California Democratic party.* They were also disposed to cooperate with foreign enemies of the U.S. as best they could. The FBI was aware of contacts between Jones and the Soviet Embassy. It had received reports of massive amounts of weapons trafficking by Temple officials and of involuntary membership in the Temple. Here then were armed weirdos who might well be holding people against their will (they surely were holding children, whose consent was inherently questionable) and trying to cooperate with the Soviet Union. It would not have taken heroic effort to interpret the Temple's behavior as an indication that its members "may have violated or may be about to violate" any number of laws, thus justifying a full investigation under the "criminal" standard. But the FBI was not about to plant informants in a group that claimed to be religious and was politically well-connected. Nor (and for the same reasons) was the CIA so inclined after the group established a commune in Guyana in 1976. As a result, in 1978, when the People's Temple murdered visiting U.S. Congressman Leo Ryan, and then committed mass suicide and murder (246 of the 911 dead were minors and presumably did not fully consent to their own deaths), the U.S. intelligence community was surprised.

Asked by the Senate Intelligence Committee why the U.S. had failed to protect the lives and liberties of 246 American children, Judge William Webster, then Director of the FBI, replied that if the FBI had felt itself free to infiltrate the People's Temple it might well have infiltrated the Catholic Church—a statement of remarkable intellectual self-abnegation. To that he added a classic bureaucratic copout: "While the group was in the U.S., its activities did not

---

*Washington Post, 6 May 1980, p. A2. Documents found at Jonestown as well as a probe by the California Department of Social Services mention connections with former Lt. Gov. Mervyn M. Dymally, Los Angeles Mayor Tom Bradley, and State Assembly Speaker Willie Brown.

reach the FBI's criminal threshold; while when it went abroad and its activities did reach that threshold, it was out of the FBI's jurisdiction."*

Perhaps the FBI had also been influenced by the fact that, about a year before the mass murder–suicide, a recently retired FBI Special Agent, M. Wesley Swearingen, had delivered a copy of the Bureau's tiny file on the People's Temple to the Justice Department, which immediately opened an investigation —not into the People's Temple but into the FBI's possible harassment of an extremist political group! The burden of Swearingen's charges seemed to be that the Bureau was keeping the file while planning no arrests, hence violating the "criminal standard."[47] But if the Bureau's leaders had not confused CI with criminal law, they could have explained to the Justice Department that the Temple was engaged in activities inherently dangerous to the civil liberties of its members *and* to the interests of the U.S., and that the FBI's intelligence-gathering burdened no one, while providing the opportunity to safeguard many. But this sort of thinking while technically allowed under the criminal standard is foreign to its spirit.

One reason why the criminal standard drives intelligence officers to go out of their way to stay out of trouble with extremist groups is its susceptibility to *ex post facto* interpretation. The standard began in earnest in 1972 with the Supreme Court's *Keith* decision, which prohibited wiretapping of Americans without a court order for national security purposes unless the Americans had "significant" ties with foreign powers.[48] In fact, the FBI had long since applied the test of foreign ties to its own judgments on the matter. But what kind of foreign ties constitutes sufficient warrant for a wiretap?

In 1969 the FBI had begun an investigation of the Weather Underground, an offshoot of the student radical organizations of the 1960s which had intimate ties with the Cuban government, and which conducted a campaign of bombings around the U.S. throughout the early 1970s. In the course of this investigation the FBI wiretapped a William Price, who was close to members of the Underground and had traveled to Cuba with the Venceremos Brigade, a group of procommunist Americans. On April 10, 1978 a Federal Grand Jury convened by the Justice Department indicted the former Acting Director of the FBI, Mark Felt, and his then Chief of Counterintelligence, Edward Miller, who had approved the wiretap on Mr. Price. The essence of the argument against the two—which ultimately prevailed in court—was that while the Underground was a legitimate target for wiretapping under the "standard," Mr. Price himself had not committed specific acts that would designate him as a "member" (whatever that meant) of the Weather Underground *or* as a legitimate target in

---

*Webster was not speaking for the CIA, which has responsibility for espionage abroad but has no charter to protect Americans abroad. This author heard the statement.

his own right. The same FBI officials were defendants in a civil suit for the same action. Ironically, in that suit the plaintiff was represented by the law firm of the father of Bernardine Dohrn, a founder of the Weather Underground.

What happened to the *Keith* standard between 1972 and 1978? *Quite simply, power to evaluate what it meant had changed hands.* Given a different evaluation of the standard, the procedures that counterintelligence men had established for their own protection became instruments for their prosecution, and even persecution.

This and similar instances drove the FBI to ask for court orders for just about all of its investigative decisions. The Foreign Intelligence Surveillance Act of 1978, which establishes a special secret court to approve requests for electronic surveillance, regularized this practice with regard to wiretapping.* Since 1978 the FBI has lobbied to expand the Act's coverage to other investigative techniques as well. The Bureau would prefer to be "covered" every time it hires an informant to report on any group, including Americans. Interestingly enough, the American Civil Liberties Union and such anti-U.S. intelligence groups as Morton Halperin's Center for National Security Studies and the Institute for Policy Studies have supported both FISA and its expansion. Why?

The explanation may be found in the legislative history of FISA, which guides the law's application by both the executive branch and the courts. Groups like the ACLU, through able congressional staffers, have been able to write much of this history. The key committee report describes what cannot be done under FISA by specifically referring to groups (some of which the staffers themselves had belonged to) which had worked against the U.S. during the Vietnam War.† Thus, the other side of the coin that authorizes electronic surveillance in certain circumstances establishes certain kinds of labels, words, and deeds as legal *guarantees* that there will be no surveillance. Obviously anyone who wishes to conduct espionage and the like with guarantees against interference from the FBI need only follow the guidelines laid out in the legislative history of FISA.

The criminal standard has had yet another effect along these lines. Over the

---

*The Special Court is an anomaly in the legal systems of democratic countries. The court meets in secret, and its decisions are secret. All proceedings are *ex parte*, i.e., without the presence of the interested party. The government presents its request to the court, and there is no counterargument. In principle, this is no boon to civil liberties. Whereas the object of a wiretap might subsequently have argued that it had been improper to surveil him, under the Act he is faced with the fact that a court has already been presented with the facts and found against him—all without his knowledge. U.S. Senate Select Committee on Intelligence, *Report on the Foreign Intelligence Surveillance Act*, U.S. Gov. Printing Office, 1978, especially the separate views of Sen. Malcolm Wallop.

†See U.S. Senate Select Committee on the Judiciary, *Report on the Foreign Intelligence Surveillance Act*, U.S. Govt. Printing Office, 1978.

years the FBI, as well as Army and Navy intelligence, have settled civil suits brought by radical organizations by agreeing to consent decrees that prohibit them from investigating these groups in the future. Prototypical is a suit filed against the Army's infiltration of the Berlin Democratic Club in Germany in 1974.[49] The Army had argued that it has the duty, especially abroad, to keep track of groups that are out specifically to subvert the morale of soldiers and perhaps commit espionage. But it agreed to a consent decree that it would not do so again without an order from a regular federal court. In a similar way, in subsequent years the FBI has agreed to court decrees restricting its surveillance of other organizations. Thus, anyone wishing to prepare espionage or terrorism need only note which organizations are exempt from surveillance by consent decree, and what activities they must avoid to be certain of not being investigated under the criminal standard.

Evidence of "probable cause" to satisfy the criminal standard might come, as it would have in the case of John Walker, as the result of analysis and the narrowing of possibilities. But analysis is among the scarcest of commodities in American CI.

Seriousness

In sum, lack of analysis, manpower, coordination and (above all) seriousness have opened the door to the success of what the Soviet Union viewed as its most important intelligence-gathering campaign: to obtain Western technology. The Soviet Union is gone, but the door remains open for whoever wants to walk through it. There is no doubt that in the 1970s and 1980s more officers of the KGB and GRU, as well as of the intelligence services of Eastern Europe, were engaged in buying or stealing American technology than in any other task. According to reports of the KGB's Department T obtained in the West, the various Soviet ministries methodically targeted individual American companies for specific items of hardware, in effect placing orders, and declared themselves quite satisfied with the deliveries.[50] The U.S. Defense Department agrees that the Soviets got what they were after. In a September 1985 report prepared jointly with the CIA, the Pentagon states that in the 1980s some 5,000 Soviet military projects benefited from Western hardware.[51] The report lists virtually every major Soviet weapons system and its Western (usually American) components. Not all of the technology was acquired by outright espionage. Perhaps the majority was purchased through complex diversionary schemes that took it through series of dummy purchases. Some items, like the ball-bearing grinding machines that played such a large part in the SS-18 guidance systems, are purchased legally after specific lobbying campaigns result in U.S. export licenses. But Soviet intelligence has played an indispensable role in all modes of acquisition: identifying who has the item and how it might be shaken loose,

182

identifying the objectives of espionage, setting up the diversionary schemes, and supporting the lobbying campaigns.

The Soviet effort is a model: The 1,000 officers in Department T are scientifically qualified and up-to-the-minute in Western technical trade journals. They know precisely what they want and where to get it, and work through multiple covers. American counterintelligence, quite simply, has been overwhelmed—the very definition of a mismatch. It is unreasonable to expect FBI Special Agents, who are unspecialized cops outnumbered by specialized robbers, to blunt such a thrust, especially since their lack of analytical support and their case-by-case approach limits them to a purely reactive posture.

CI IN THE 1990S: MISSION IMPOSSIBLE?

The current system wouldn't begin to meet the United States' needs for CI in the 1990s. First, the U.S. entered the 1990s with its intelligence system— sources *and* methods—largely known to hostile services. American CI also carried into the 1990s a heritage of unsound practices, bad habits, and lack of CI data base difficult to overcome. Second, the 1990s are sure to prove full of regimes that are neither fish nor fowl, with elements whose relationship to the U.S. will be ambiguous. American CI does not do well with ambiguity. Third, both technological and social trends continue to diminish the effectiveness of the methods on which American CI has relied most heavily. On the other side of the ledger, the destruction of communism in Eastern Europe, and in the Soviet Union, combined with factional strife, *potentially* provide American CI with innumerable avenues for penetration. But to take advantage of them U.S. CI will have to change completely. Hence the U.S. faces a stark choice: Rethink and rebuild the CI structure from first principles and from the bottom up, or concede the United States—at least its military forces, industrial technology, and intelligence system—as a field where hostile intelligence services may play at will.

Starting in the Hole

Counterintelligence is not magic. Only magic could erase from the minds and ledgers of the world's intelligence services the well-known identities of nearly all CIA case officers. Only magic could prevent new CIA case officers recruited, trained, and posted like today's, from becoming just as prominent "sore thumbs" abroad as are today's. So long as the Soviet armed forces survive, they will retain substantial knowledge about U.S. technical collection systems. So long as the successors to the KH-11, Rhyolite, Chalet, and Jumpseat work on the same principles as their predecessors, mere CI arrangements, for example, shifting the orbits of current satellites, can have only marginal effects. To achieve results both more serious and long-lasting, CI arrangements would have to deal with systems not yet compromised. Similarly, the fragmentation of jurisdiction among the various components of American CI, the jurisdictional seams and hence the blind spots that result therefrom, are too well known even to terrorist and drug traffickers to be papered over lightly. Syria and Iraq will continue to have no trouble with American CI. The U.S. can count on hostile services running operatives against the CIA within the U.S., and against the FBI abroad—i.e., where those American services are least ready to cope. The U.S. telecommunications systems, a marvel designed for every purpose *but* security, cannot be easily changed. The way that Americans do business with foreigners is even less subject to being protected by the current police methods. In fact, the trend is toward looser security practices in commerce and communications, combined with tighter restrictions on when a person may become the subject of an investigation.

The present CI system carries into the 1990s a set of practices and habits that have failed the test. The first of these is the attempt to perceive and understand individual CI cases without analyzing the "CI problem" in any given field of endeavor. Under James Angleton, the data available for CI scrutiny was but a small fraction of all the multidisciplinary data available to U.S. intelligence on any given subject (including any country). Since 1975, while there has been talk of going beyond the case method, the *responsibility* for CI analysis is nowhere to be found in the vast U.S. intelligence bureaucracy. In the 1990s the various bureaucracies' hold on their information appeared greater than ever.

Another unhealthy habit carried into the 1990s is that of intelligence collectors who assume that *their* particular bailiwick is inherently immune to hostile penetration, deception, or manipulation. Over the years this habit has led to the perversion of one of the pillars of counterintelligence, the "damage assessment" that normally follows any realization of hostile services' successes. Like any acknowledgment of one's own errors, damage assessments require large doses of humility, honesty, and commitment to change one's ways. But over the years, whenever the arrest of a spy or the compromise of a satellite has occurred, the foremost concern of senior U.S. intelligence officials has been to make sure that the satellite or human operation involved does not lose its share of the budget. The resulting damage assessments are slow, haughty, no more honest than they have to be, and classified so that virtually no one may read them.

This was certainly the fate of the assessment of the damage done by Geoffrey Prime's and Richard Burt's disclosure of the Chalet satellite between 1977 and 1979. Geoffrey Prime walked in to the Soviets in Berlin in 1968. The Prime case finally broke in 1982. Not until a year later, and then only at the direct, repeated urging of virtually the entire U.S. Senate Intelligence Committee, did the CIA commission a comprehensive damage assessment. It took a year. The results bearing on the degradation of the worth of Chalet were restricted to perhaps a dozen persons on an "eyes only" basis. It is difficult to avoid the conclusion that the chief concern of those who did the report was to protect the budget for Chalet. Regardless of what the Soviets had learned about Chalet, the intelligence community wanted to continue operating it as if they had learned nothing.

In 1985, after the redefection of Vitaly Yurchenko, the CIA's "damage assessment" about this KGB officer who had spent two months discussing the interaction of the KGB and CIA with the CIA's highest officials seemed to be nothing but an effort to convince the public, the Congress, and the President that CIA had made no major errors, and indeed had come out ahead on the deal. As Edward Epstein has argued,[52] the temptation to self-justification, once accepted, turns CI on its head and makes it an active (though mindless) accomplice of hostile intelligence. Furthermore, *the habit of self-justification is progressive.* As instance follows instance, and the chain of covered-up questionable judgments grows, the incentive for calling attention to the next failure decreases.

AMBIGUOUS REGIMES

The revolution of 1989–91 left behind confusion that may take decades to resolve. Whereas by the end of 1945 it was obvious that no one need worry about Nazi intrigue ever again, the end of 1990 left a host of communist agents throughout the world in ambiguous positions. Even the clearest of cases, that of Germany, was not all that clear. Even before East Germany officially ceased to exist on October 3, 1990, it had disestablished the KGB's local affiliate, the Staatssicherheitsdienst (Stasi), and the German people were not so united on any other question as they were on the obliteration of the Stasi. And yet getting rid of the Stasi was not so simple. Its tentacles reached deep into the governments of East and West. German government investigators are reluctant to dig too deeply, lest too many high-ranking people be embarrassed. There is also great pressure to integrate as many former East German officials into the Federal Republic's bureaucracy and armed forces as possible. Hence the virtual certainty that the U.S. will be dealing with some German officials who are Soviet agents.

As regards the other countries of the former Soviet empire, the certainty is more obvious: Their bureaucracies were touched by the revolution only at the top. Thousands of agents have been turned over to direct control by the KGB, which can discipline them more than ever with the threat of throwing them to the wolves. And yet in the 1990s these agents have freer access to the West than ever, as representatives or citizens of friendly governments. The U.S. CI system had a difficult enough time dealing with hostile Poles or Czechs when they were clearly labeled as enemies. It has not begun to consider how to handle them as they come mixed with friends, and perhaps wielding some covert influence on people in their countries who really want to be friends of the U.S. The same is now true of the former Soviet Union.

After August 1991 the West was awash in Soviet citizens trying to establish all kinds of contacts, and universally portraying themselves as part of the movement for renewal in that country. It seems there were never any communists in the Soviet Union. It is sometimes easy enough to check on the past of these newly minted liberal democrats and find that they used to work for the KGB. But, the relevant question: "What is this man's real agenda, what are his real roots today?" is more difficult to answer.

The biggest Soviet campaign of 1991 was economic aid, ostensibly to help "privatize" the country. The sums delivered (never mind asked for) were denominated in billions of dollars. But the Westerners who heard the requests knew remarkably little about the political affiliations—or even the intentions— of those doing the asking. They had no knowledge of the channels through which such people would distribute the resources, whom the resources would strengthen, and to what end. These Soviet suitors came as economists, and Western governments sent economists to deal with them.

The U.S. government is not equipped to keep track of the various approaches made by various Soviets to various parts of American society, to apply knowledge to these approaches, to warn the targets of what they might be getting into, and to follow up as the contacts take their course. The result amounts to a license to operate among people so eager for "new Soviet men" that they will take anyone uncritically. The implications for the transfer of technology and resources, and for the covert exercise of influence, are obvious.

5

Getting It Wrong

For a quarter century the CIA has been repeatedly wrong about
the major political and economic questions entrusted to its analysts.
— *Senator Daniel P. Moynihan*

We may not always be right. But we're never wrong.
— *A popular saying at CIA*

Facts have meant less to American
statesmen and commanders than the bureaucracies that have blended secret data
with library materials and their own sociopolitical prejudices. Overall, bureaucrat
analysts have rendered unto their readers less enlightenment than was inherent
in the raw data.

Let us see what these bureaucracies have been about, the intellectual
tendencies they have shared, the methods they have used, the products they have
produced, and the lessons we may draw from them. We will begin by describing
who they are.

Who They Are

General William Donovan used to say that intelligence is no more mysterious
than McGuffey's *Second Reader* and just about as sinister. He meant that the

world's libraries are filled with interesting information, and that scholarly research alone can produce much good intelligence. If scholars also have access to the data provided by espionage and reconnaissance, little of importance can be hid from them. Thus, thought Donovan, the primary tool of intelligence is the index card. Hence, in the fall of 1941, before the formal establishment of the OSS itself, Donovan used his mandate from President Roosevelt to create Research and Analysis (R&A), the first unit of OSS, which began to turn out intelligence reports long before any of the OSS's spies were in the field. Throughout the war, most of the OSS reports delivered to high-ranking personages in Washington came from R&A, and relied little, if at all, on clandestine sources. By 1945, R&A had some 2,000 employees, and certainly the highest density of Ph.Ds of any government agency.

Research and Analysis was part of a brand-new chapter in the history of intelligence. Until the twentieth century, analysis of intelligence had been the exclusive prerogative of chief executives and generals (or, as in the case of medieval Venice, ambassadors). But modern international conflict came to involve more variables than ever before. The Imperial Powers, on whose assets and liabilities the sun never set, had been the first to recognize the need to pull together information from a wide variety of sources. Thus in 1901 Britain established the Committee on Imperial Defense. But it employed only a handful of archivists–researchers. Only when World War I drew on all the moral and material resources of societies around the globe did the major powers decide they needed massive amounts of information about the industries, transportation systems, and societies of enemies, allies, and faraway suppliers. Foreign offices, universities, and libraries were the obvious sources, and legions of bureaucrats were needed to do the sorting.

During the interwar period the world's major foreign offices established research staffs, and armed forces' intelligence services retained peacetime analysts who focused on the next war. These staffs were small by today's standards, but large indeed compared to their pre–World War I size. The U.S. Office of Naval Intelligence (including all functions) was cut to under a hundred employees in the 1920s—as opposed to 22 in 1914. In each nation common sense dictated that all sources of information be channeled into a single agency where, if not one mind, then at least one set of minds could make the most of it all.

In the 1920s, Britain was alone among the democracies in trying to follow this common sense. But even there, by 1925, the jealousy of the several departments of government prevailed. The Foreign Office prized its Research Department as an element of its own function: To speak authoritatively on foreign policy.

To understand foreign armies was obviously essential to the preparations for beating them, and the British Army wanted to make that entire complex of decisions for itself. The Admiralty thought similarly about foreign navies. In the 1930s, however, as the British bureaucracy slowly confronted the coming conflict, necessity gradually moved it toward *de facto* integration. By 1931 a separate Industrial Intelligence Center (IIC) was created. In 1936 the Royal Air Force found that it could not build target folders (descriptions of potential bombing targets) without the IIC, and established *ad hoc* committees with it. As other agencies joined, these grew into the Joint Intelligence Committee, formally established in the summer of 1939. The JIC served as the central repository of information for the British government throughout the war.

In Germany, where the government was much more oriented toward conflict, the integration of intelligence had proceeded much faster (though in the heat of war the Nazi regime's feudal tendencies wrecked that, too). By 1939, Germany had produced handbooks on the countries where German forces might be operating that explained everything from roads and bridges to nutrition.

In interwar America the armed forces, the codebreakers, and the State Department had been slowly building their capacity for collection. Since America was psychologically farthest from war, the several parts of U.S. intelligence saw even less reason than their British counterparts to think of integration. William Donovan, however, had followed the growing integration of intelligence in Europe, and made himself the spokesman for an idea whose time had come. His pitch to President Roosevelt in 1941 on behalf of stepped-up U.S. intelligence activities concentrated not so much on the need for new sources of information as on the need for coordination of information from existing sources.[1] In July 1941 Roosevelt gave him the title of Coordinator of Information (COI). His first act was to set up the analytical branch. The OSS would have a brain (and a tongue) before it had eyes and ears.

Research and Analysis in World War II

One may not put R&A's contribution to the war either on the level of Britain's Ultra or on that of the U.S. codebreakers' unraveling of the Japanese naval codes that so aided the U.S. Navy's victory at Midway. R&A's first major act was to prepare, on two weeks' notice, complete area handbooks for the U.S. forces that invaded North Africa at the end of 1942. Economists attached to R&A also did a creditable job of calculating German production of tanks and other vehicles from the serial numbers of vehicles lost on the battlefield—despite the Germans' attempt to make the serial numbers useless by leaving large portions of each series unfilled. All in all, R&A's was a solid performance which yielded its intangible fruits on the staff level.

Research and Analysis' work consisted primarily of quick studies from open sources. Setting a pattern for the future, much of R&A's work was done by people who knew nothing about the subject they were writing on—not even the language of the country. All they knew they learned from the masses of information that the "collectors" (in R&A's jargon that meant the library researchers) had lain before them.*

One of R&A's undoubted contributions was that it allowed a certain sector of the American professoriate to take part in the war. Robin Winks' *Cloak and Gown*, a sociology of American intelligence, points out that the "coaches" and "quarterbacks," the handsome and adventuresome on America's elite campuses, had gone off into espionage and counterespionage (SI and X-2), while the muscular athletes had gone into Special Operations (SO). Had it not been for R&A, argues Winks, the "weenies and wimps" of American academe would have had nowhere to go.[2] Instead they came to Washington, were inspired by the aura of a great, good, victorious America, and stayed on to set the tone for the postwar period.

Intellectually and politically that tone was overwhelmingly liberal. The R&A professors were remarkably monochrome in their social preferences. It is impossible to read their memoirs and interviews without being struck by their distaste for their fellow Americans whom they regarded as provincial, unsophisticated, reactionary, religious, and lacking in good taste about the finer things in life. Their ideal was the urbane, progressive, secular British aristocrat, or the equally urbane and progressive professor. Such attitudes were far more pervasive among them than was any sympathy for communism. Senator Joseph McCarthy and others simply misinterpreted as a pro-Soviet orientation the visceral anti-anticommunism and other social attitudes that colored the work of R&A and, later, of CIA. It is impossible to understand the R&A and the CIA without realizing that many of their officers considered themselves the underappreciated "best and brightest" of the earth, or at least of the United States. They were the people to whom the powerful just *had* to listen.

R&A bequeathed to CIA a cadre with definite views on intelligence analysis.

---

*See, for example, a firsthand account by Russel Jack Smith, who later rose to the post of Deputy Director for Intelligence (DDI) at the CIA. Smith, a professor of English literature, tells of his embarrassment at showing his papers on Japan to a State Department that still considered language and experience to be prerequisites for analysis. He also tells of misgivings at writing what would become the official U.S. government view of Thailand without ever having laid eyes on a Thai. Russel Jack Smith, *The Unknown CIA*, pp. 25, 27–28, 77.

The real task of intelligence, they believed, was to weave "a matrix that carried conviction" and was "firm enough to support an official government statement." The facts were secondary. On a given day the amount and quality of facts available would vary. But every day the government would have to act, and would need some basis for acting. Somebody, they believed, had to take the responsibility for giving decision-makers officially authoritative reasons for what they were doing, and it might as well be them. They thought it both ironic and inappropriate that the clandestine services should receive so much publicity for work done best in secret, and analysts so little for "thoughtful, dispassionate judgments on world affairs" that can be done as well in the light of day as in the dark. Their daily preoccupation was to create the bureaucratic conditions under which they could command information from throughout the U.S. government and, above all, have the unchallenged right to say what it meant.[3]

A generation later, in 1978, this view became bureaucratic reality when people with this outlook on intelligence took control of the White House and the CIA, and renamed CIA's Directorate of Intelligence "The National Foreign Assessment Center" (NFAC)—as if no one else in the country had the right authoritatively to assess foreign matters. Given the pluralistic nature of the U.S. government, the NFAC was never more than a bureaucratic pretense, and the name itself was done away with three years later. It is important now only as a paradigm of what has animated the CIA's intelligence analysis from the beginning.

The Central Intelligence Agency

From the beginning, CIA analysts have defined themselves in contrast to collectors (especially the spymasters within the CIA itself), in contrast to analysts from other agencies, and as the rightful partners of policy-makers.

Donovan's recommendation to President Roosevelt of September 1944 for postwar U.S. intelligence made clear that the principal job of Central Intelligence would be to analyze information collected *from other U.S. government agencies*. Nevertheless, Central Intelligence could employ some collectors of its own to fill gaps in the information provided by the armed forces, the State Department, and so on. Thus, when after three years of intense bureaucratic maneuvering the National Security Act of 1947 established the CIA very much along these lines, the "saving remnant" of R&A came out of the diaspora they had endured in the State Department, and into their promised agency, where they supposed they would be masters of the house. When in the 1950s they found out that analysis would continue to be overshadowed by espionage and operations, just as in OSS, their bitterness was bolstered by the daily experience of having to write reports with nary a bit of help from clandestine reporting. By the late 1960s, which Russel Jack Smith describes as the "golden age" achieved by laborious improvement in the clandestine service, clandestine reporting was contributing to only *one-third* of the CIA's reports.

It is easy to understand (if not necessarily to sympathize with) the *cri de coeur* of the CIA analysts that E. Drexel Godfrey expressed in *Foreign Affairs* in 1978: Those who recruit spies make ethical messes and cause international complications far out of proportion to any good they do. The average clandestine report, say CIA analysts out of bitter experience, is far less useful than one on the same subject from the Foreign Service. By lowering the prestige of the CIA as a whole, clandestine collectors make it less likely that the good judgment of hard-working analysts will get its due in the White House, the State Department, and the academic community. Besides, clandestine collectors have partisan mentalities and are full of anticommunist prejudices. In short, they barely deserve the company of civilized, productive, progressive people like the analysts; much less do they deserve the primacy which is theirs in CIA.[4]

The CIA analysts started off at a distinct disadvantage with regard to the State Department. For the first decade or so, until the U-2 aircraft and the satellites started yielding their bounty, CIA reports were mainly rehashes of British liaison reports and State Department cable traffic. Moreover, CIA analysts have no sociopolitical quarrels with Foreign Service officers, whom they see as being (almost) as intelligent as themselves, as well as sharing the same progressive, urbane ideals. (Foreign Service Officers do not quite reciprocate.) Nevertheless, CIA analysts argue that their views of the world are worthier than State's because only CIA is privy to *all* sources. In interagency meetings, not even State has been spared the standard CIA put-down: "Your judgment on situation X is reasonable, given the information available to you. However, we have a source—that we cannot discuss—which, in the context of all available information, shows convincingly that *our* judgment, not yours, is correct." Besides, say CIA analysts, State is not immune to viewing intelligence from the perspective of its parochial duties, however important these might be. Only CIA analysts, who have no operating responsibilities, can have the intellectual detachment essential for definitive foreign assessment.[5]

With regard to the military, the attitude of CIA analysts is devoid of ambiguity: Military intelligence is to intelligence as military music is to music. Those polyester-clad Pentagon civilians, no less than uniformed officers, are nothing but advocates of military special interests. They are the subordinates of tank drivers, pilots, carrier admirals, etc. At best they wear blinders and are prisoners of a narrow point of view. They did not go to the right schools, they are not broadly educated, and they see life in terms of simple conflicts. At worst they are dangerous—the purveyors of inflated threats, the engine of the dreaded action–reaction principle that in 1914 drove Europe into "the war that nobody wanted" and that might yet drive the world into nuclear extinction. Throughout the Third World, say CIA analysts, the military sees enemies instead of "root causes" of instability. If the military's simple-minded views were followed, the U.S. would long ago have wasted itself on the wrong side of no-win wars. To be agents of peace, intelligence analysts should be cool, detached observers rather than partisans of struggle. Day to day, CIA analysts see no higher calling than to moderate, or even to submerge, the voice of military priorities in the executive branch, the Congress, and the press.

The CIA's attitude toward policy-makers is most problematic. Former CIA analyst Thomas Hughes, in *The Fate of Facts in a World of Men*, describes another tenet fairly common at the CIA: Intelligence analysis "comprises all the major evaluative and predictive functions" in foreign affairs, and "leaves the policy-maker little or nothing in the decision-making process except the ceremonial finale."[6]

It is amusing to read Russel Jack Smith's account of his storming into the office of Director of Central Intelligence Richard Helms to protest a decision that President Lyndon Johnson had made about Vietnam after having received a CIA analysis: "How could he have made that decision after what we wrote!"[7] Helms had to explain that the President is after all a free man with his own mind and his own understanding of responsibilities that he, not the CIA, bears to the American people. On reflection, no one at CIA questions the policy-makers' bureaucratic and political right to make policy, or denies that intelligence is but one element of policy making. And yet it is impossible to be around CIA for long without realizing that in their heart of hearts the analysts think they are more expert at policy than the policy-makers, and that they believe their profoundest obligation is not so much to draw pictures of the outside world as it truly is, but rather by drawing pictures of the outside world to help bring about good policy in Washington.

Sherman Kent, an ex–Yale professor who took over the CIA's Board of National Estimates in 1952 and set the tone for CIA analysis until our time, best expressed the ambiguity of the CIA's relationship to policy-makers in his book *Strategic Intelligence*.[8] The formula given to analyst trainees is not too gross an oversimplification of Kent's book: "Get into bed with the policy-makers, but remain pure." Kent says that like any other professional, the intelligence analyst can serve his client only if he knows the client's needs. Authoritative policy guidance enables the analyst to be relevant. On the other hand, the analyst must not be swept up by enthusiasm for any policy. He must retain the intellectual independence that can identify the problems that policy will face in the real world. But Kent also notes, correctly, that policy-makers are not very generous with guidance. Instances of clearly articulated foreign policy have been the exception, not the rule, in the U.S. since 1945. Yet Kent's counsel explicitly bars analysts from dealing with ambiguous policy guidance by examining the potential threats, opportunities, and consequences inherent in each of the alternative courses that U.S. policy might follow. The result of Kent's approach, combined with the disposition of CIA analysts to be policy activists who "know better," and given the tendency of Presidents, Secretaries of State, and the like not to set policy but rather to have it emerge as the result of innumerable clashes between bureaucrats over day-to-day affairs, has been to turn CIA analysts into just another set of "players" in the policy process. At once their greatest asset and liability has been the pretense that they are not players at all.

Defense Analysis and Production

In 1961 Defense Secretary Robert McNamara established the Defense Intelligence Agency (DIA) principally to create a single voice for the intelligence branches of the military services, each of which was touting its own version of "the threat" on Capitol Hill in support of its parent service's budget requests. Under the Joint Chiefs of Staff, the DIA was to be the place where the services fought out their differences over the threat and came up with a single (and cumulatively lower) estimate. When CIA was preparing a "national" estimate for top policy-makers, it would have to deal with only one (not three) military points of view. In addition, why should three staffs produce three largely overlapping daily intelligence summaries for U.S. military units? The DIA would produce *one*. Why should the U.S. Army, Navy, and Air Force produce separate books on the army, navy, and air force of, say, Iran, each of which would have to contain the same data about Iran's radars? The DIA would produce a *single* book on the "electronic Order of Battle" for Iran and neighboring countries. To these ends the DIA would consist of officers and enlisted men "detailed" by the three services for a few years, and of a cadre of permanent civilian experts. The DIA would be strictly an analysis and production shop. It would have no collectors of its own, except that it would train, supervise, and be the first recipient of reports from the 500-odd U.S. Army, Navy, and Air Force attachés in U.S. embassies around the world. A general or admiral would be in command, and ensure the agency's fidelity to the Joint Chiefs.

Over the years the DIA did indeed do away with some of the services' duplicative analysis and production. But it by no means eliminated their intelligence components as players in the Washington policy arena. Every time that any service cared about an issue, it made sure that its point of view was argued in the highest intelligence councils, appended to national intelligence estimates, and covered in the press. One of the better-known instances of this was the controversy between 1977 and 1981 over whether the Soviet "Backfire" bomber did or did not have intercontinental range. The Assistant Chief of Staff for Intelligence, U.S. Air Force, and not the Director of the DIA, made the point in the national Estimates, before Congress and in the press, that the real experts on airplanes in the U.S. government believed that the Backfire bomber is intercontinental. In other words, the existence of the DIA did not eliminate three players, but rather added one. When the services agreed, the Director of the DIA became the representative of a united defense establishment against the CIA. This happened most significantly in the 1970s with regard to the size, scope, and purpose of the Soviet strategic buildup that had begun in the mid–1960s.

Inevitably, the DIA must be understood in contrast to the CIA's Deputy Directorate of Intelligence. The first impression one receives after taking the George Washington Parkway from the CIA's wooded domain overlooking the Potomac to the new DIA building on the tidal flats of Anacostia is that one has come down in class. Everything about the people seems lower, from rank and pay to pretenses. Clothing changes from wool or cotton to synthetics. When occasionally a DIA civilian, or a retiring military officer, is offered a job at CIA he is regarded as having made a major step up. DIA employees cherish good relations with the folks "up the river" because the latter control who gets to sit on which interagency committee, and may even grant a DIA employee the privilege of chairing one. Besides, a trip up the river, if not adversarial, can result in meeting interesting people and breathing a tonier air. Indeed, until 1985 even senior employees of DIA could not aspire to the pay and status of Senior Executive Service. It took an act of Congress to give them that chance. Yet by 1990 the proportion of DIA employees enjoying that status was less than half of the CIA's. Just as important for self-image is the institutional myth that while CIA analysts are true intellectuals who work for the President, the folks at DIA are journeymen who serve the Generals.

Yet some at DIA argue differently: The CIA's vaunted intellectual independence, they say, is actually indulgence in its own pet prejudices. What the CIA calls the parochialism of military intelligence, they argue, reflects the fact that DIA must wrestle with real-world military problems conscious that its judgments may be tested in battle. "Departmental" intelligence, they say, is real, responsible intelligence that produces reams of data on which people will stake their lives, whereas the CIA turns out political puffery.

The State Department

When the alumni of OSS Research and Analysis left for the new CIA in 1947, the State Department renamed its own R&A unit the Bureau of Intelligence and Research (INR). This bureau consists of a cadre of permanent analysts, filled out by rotating levies of Foreign Service Officers. Since at State FSOs are the ruling class, the permanent analysts have enjoyed significant influence only when the FSOs assigned to INR have been very junior.

Through INR, State keeps a foot in the door of the intelligence community. Through INR, State is theoretically entitled to receive "all-source" intelligence, which proves useful in writing the Secretary of State's daily briefing, which consists mostly of reports from U.S. embassies. Second, the existence of INR and the papers it produces allow State to claim that its positions with regard to the great questions facing the U.S., no less than anyone else's positions, are supported by all-source analysis. In other words INR helps State guard its own turf. Third, through INR State gets to participate in the intelligence community's most important products, the National Estimates, and to influence matters far from its turf. Readers of "the Estimates" often marvel at instances when the Director, Bureau of Intelligence and Research, Department of State takes a position with regard to abstruse matters of weapons technology about which State has no sources and which State officials are obviously unequipped to judge.

What is INR doing? Obviously it is engaging not in intelligence but in policy-making. For instance, the INR may not have known enough to judge evidence about the accuracy of Soviet missiles, but it knew enough to realize that Estimates concluding that Soviet missiles are relatively accurate tend to support arguments for more vigorous U.S. military programs. Since State's reflexive position is that greater U.S. military power works against its perennial goal of U.S.–Soviet *entente* in general, and arms control in particular, State routinely does what it can to shape intelligence estimates to give as little support as possible to American militarism. When Estimates have to do with possible Soviet violations of treaties, the delegation from the INR acts as defense attorney for the Soviet position. Similarly, because it is also axiomatic at State that the U.S. ought to support "progressive" movements around the world, and that such support becomes unlikely to the extent that these movements are perceived to be communist, State routinely works to water down conclusions regarding these movements' ties to the Soviet Union or to the men who actually pull terrorist triggers. INR always sees communist governments, and indeed leftist movements, as enjoying substantial public support. But State does not like right-wing regimes or movements. So the INR usually tries to push the Estimate to indicate that, say, Guatemala is collapsing and that the black anticommunist guerrilla movements in Africa are servants of South African apartheid. It is all terribly predictable.

The National Security Agency

The National Security Agency is in a peculiar position. It is not supposed to have opinions on broad topics. Its products are supposed merely to report on signals intelligence. Nevertheless, Sigint is such a powerful source in and of itself, and as we have seen inherently requires so much analysis to yield any results at all, that NSA slowly has been drawn into the circle of the CIA, the DIA, and INR.

Some of the NSA's best studies examine the "take" from a particular set of Sigint sources over a period of time. In 1979 a routine NSA study of its "take" from Soviet military units in Cuba for the previous ten years concluded that one of these units fit the SIGINT profile of a motorized rifle brigade—a combat unit. This caused a major political controversy that hurt the Carter Administration's reputation. Another study of the signals of a Soviet military exercise in 1982 allowed NSA to reconstruct it well enough to permit Secretary of State Alexander Haig to publicly charge that the Soviet Union was practicing a first strike against the U.S. Thus NSA, whose representatives once attended interagency meetings only as source persons, has become a more-or-less regular participant in discussions on the substance of intelligence products. In the 1980s NSA "took" footnotes in Estimates to stake out its own position. Unlike the other analytical agencies, however, the positions of the NSA are not predictable.

The NSA has its own personality. Since it is part of the defense establishment, it shares in the polyester culture of the Pentagon. But the Sigint business is detached enough and prestigious enough so that NSA does not suffer from an inferiority complex. Few employees of NSA dream of going over to CIA. The analysts especially give the impression of people who are happy to be working with the results of state-of-the-art equipment. They believe that while others may produce opinions, they turn out "hard stuff." Their view of the world may well be too narrow, but it is for real.

Identity and Intelligence

We do not mean to unduly single out INR for predictability. In fact, before walking into an interagency meeting on any given issue one can lay successful bets on what the representatives of the CIA, DIA, and the military services, as well as INR, will say. Nor do we break new ground in pointing this out. After all, part of the CIA's brief for its own existence has always been that intelligence analysis should not be left to anyone connected to any operating department, because the inevitably partial outlook of the department will bias the analysis.[9] We simply note that detachment from departmental responsibility has not prevented the analysts at the CIA from being every bit as predictable as those from the DIA and the INR. It is not too gross an exaggeration that when considering any given threat DIA will overestimate, CIA will underestimate, and INR will blame the U.S. for it.

Each U.S. intelligence product, from the National Estimates to the Order of Battle books, to the highly classified intelligence newspaper for top officials, the *National Intelligence Daily*, is produced by a method peculiar to it alone.

Nevertheless, the analysts who produce all the United States' intelligence products have propensities that more or less, willy-nilly, affect all of them. So, before examining each of the kinds of intelligence products that the United States has turned out, let us glance briefly at the tendencies they all share.

Intellectual Tendencies

Distinguishing Fact from Opinion

U.S. intelligence products tend to bridge the inevitable gaps in data with the analyst's own judgment, without clearly distinguishing for the "consumer" which is which.

To be fair about it, one must understand the analyst's predicament. After World War II the United States became history's quintessential *status quo* power. Its overarching goal: stability in the face of a worldwide challenge from the Soviet Union, communist China, and communist movements presumably allied with them. The United States had chosen to leave to others the choice of the times, places, and manners in which individual battles would be fought. But in order to prepare to fight anywhere, anytime, one must know about everything, always—never mind insufficiencies of information.

In 1948, when the Secretary of State was surprised by the outbreak of "La Violencia" in Bogota, Colombia, he and the President were displeased, and demanded a full report—which the "intelligence" analysts at the CIA and State Department had to cook up with the few facts that lay at hand. In the same year, when the Soviet Army blocked access to Berlin, the U.S. government wanted to know why. The analysts didn't know—but, since they had to answer, they gave their opinions based on distant impressions of Stalin. In 1950 the U.S. government yearned to know who was responsible for the attack on South Korea. United States intelligence could only speculate on the shape of the triangle of Stalin, Mao, and Kim Il Sung.

The memoirs of the early analysts are clearer than their original reports about how very little evidence they had about the burning questions of the day. But the policy-makers who read the intelligence community's reports on those events did not want to agonize over tidbits of evidence. This dovetailed with the intelligence officers' embarrassment at having written on the basis of so little. So the policy-makers got the basis for action that they wanted, and the intelligence analysts got to play the role *they* wanted. All sides acted as if their judgments were based on secret sources that in fact did not exist.

Over the years, this tendency has manifested itself more in the National Estimates than in less "finished" products. "We believe" is probably the most common sentence starter in the National Estimates. Beginning in the 1950s, under the influence of Abbott Smith (whose style was adopted by his more senior colleagues), the Board of National Estimates increasingly left out not just sources, but also facts, on the supposition that people at the highest level neither wanted them nor needed them, and that the Estimates' provenance was authority enough. Since then the typical Estimate has consisted of "file facts" followed by abstract judgments, and then by global conclusions. For example (in the usual order): the fact that the Cuban Army sent 60,000 men to Angola; followed by a "We believe" about the sentiments of returning veterans; and then a global conclusion about the chance of revolt in the ranks of the Cuban Army during the next five years. Thus in 1970 Russel Jack Smith's tongue was only half-in-cheek when he told Sherman Kent, "There hasn't been a fact in a National Intelligence Estimate in five years."[10] The second most common phrase in the Estimates is "We have no evidence" or (its variant) "We have no confirmed evidence." That is longhand for "no." But since the Estimates often have very little evidence for *any* proposition, the difference between "We believe" and "We have no evidence" is subjective.

At the other extreme, Order of Battle books will list the known characteristics of, say, a foreign radar, but will leave blank the space after, say, "power source," if the fact is unknown. In the middle, most American intelligence products are a matrix of fact, assumption, and judgment that is difficult to disentangle. For example, as we will see, the estimates of Soviet military spending depend on a complex methodology, which is far more responsible for the result than any of the individual facts that go into it. But the tendency in U.S. intelligence is to discuss neither the assumptions nor the facts that go into a product. Hence the paradox: The more important the product, the higher the level of decision-making that it is supposed to support, the less opportunity it provides the reader to reach his own judgment on the matter, and indeed, the greater the proportion of speculation to fact that it is likely to contain.

Empiricism

The second intellectual tendency of the intelligence community is to take into account things only as formally defined, and (often) only things that one can count. Whatever one does not define—for whatever reason—or cannot be counted is then treated as nonexistent for practical purposes. This is empiricism: not simply a stress on facts, but rather the assumption that the facts that the analyst is considering are all there is to consider. Empiricism is the dominant intellectual fashion of the twentieth century. We have described its manifestations in the collection of technical intelligence. But how does it apply to the analysis of intelligence topics? In the 1960s, Secretary of Defense Robert McNamara ruled the Pentagon through his Program Analysis and Evaluation

Office (PA&E), the very institutionalization of empiricism. Perhaps the proto-typical judgment of PA&E was that in 1964 the United States possessed neither too many nor too few, nor even about the right number, of mortars it would need to fight a major war—but *precisely* 270 percent of the right number of mortars. Since the 1960s the Pentagon has evaluated everything from components of weapons systems, to procedures, to entire wars, through computer programs.

The essence of the approach may be seen in Quincy Wright's massive A *Study of War*, which gathers a host of quantitative facts about past wars, reduces unquantifiable ones (such as "hostility" and "interest") to quantities, and tries to predict future wars through a formula that is supposed to express the relationships between and among the various quantities. The empiricism of intelligence analysts is not usually so mechanistic. Nevertheless, it is quite normal for intelligence analysts both to see reality through their own intellectual constructs, and *not* to see the distinction between the constructs and reality.

A good example among many is the controversy over the number of enemy troops that were in South Vietnam, which stretched between roughly 1965 and the 1985 trial of a libel suit brought by the former U.S. commander in Vietnam, Gen. William Westmoreland. The heart of the controversy was a system for counting enemy troops developed by CIA analyst Sam Adams, which differed substantially from the system used by the U.S. Army. The Army counted regular combat units both of the North Vietnamese army and of the Vietcong guerrillas, and multiplied their number by the number of soldiers in each kind of unit. Sam Adams also counted irregulars. But of course Adams could count actual guerrillas even less accurately than the Army could count soldiers. Since Adams could not put his finger on each and every guerrilla in turn, and since the essence of irregular fighters is that they hide the fact that they are fighters, he was reduced to estimating their number by extrapolating reports from some districts to all districts. The base estimates, in turn, had been made by combining interviews of villagers with reports of clashes with irregulars.

The Army objected on two grounds: The count of "irregulars" was "soft," and besides, an irregular fighter is seldom the combat equivalent of a regular soldier. On this methodological basis, charges of politicized dishonesty flew in both directions. The clash had political significance because a lower count portended hope of an early, successful conclusion to the war, and a higher count portended the opposite. For our purposes it is important only to realize that the methodological niceties escaped nearly everyone. At bottom, neither side's numbers were written in the stars. There was no "ground truth" to which either set of numbers could be compared. The entire controversy, which had a significant impact on careers and reputations, as well as on bureaucratic and public opinion, took place on the level of empiricist ephemera.

When intentions are to be analyzed, the effect of empiricism is even more marked. There is no reasonable way to quantify the indices of human motivation; all attempts to do so lead to conflict with reality. The most popular method, only a bit oversimplified, is to keep track, on the one side, of all the harsh statements, rejections of negotiations, etc., and on the other of all the mild words, proposals of negotiations, etc. Thus, for example, in the West a few statements by the Palestine Liberation Organization in which blood lust is relatively scarce is taken as evidence of the PLO's moderation, and any increase in relatively bloodless statements speaks loudly enough to analysts to drown out the PLO's bombs in buses and marketplaces. In this case the empiricist's practice of treating all facts as equal led the CIA in 1980 to publish the opinion that "One man's terrorist is another man's freedom fighter."[11] Empiricism provides the intellectual means for substituting comfortable concepts for uncomfortable ones under the guise of methodology, and for safeguarding fond illusions from intellectual challenge.

Analysts who subscribe to empiricism also tend not to take seriously, not to understand, that other people are moved by love, hate, devotion to God, lust for vengeance, the cruel joy of conquest, or political ideology. Such analysts have difficulty understanding a world that is full of these motives. When all facts are equal, it is also impossible to distinguish between better and worse motives, better and worse causes. One consequence of this approach is to construct *ersatz* categories such as "moderates" and "extremists," and stuff one's favorites or *bêtes noires* in them. If practiced in a thoroughgoing way, empiricism can even blur the distinction between friend and foe, a distinction vital to the survival of any organism.

Mirror-Imaging

The third intellectual propensity of U.S. intelligence analysts is also a means of dealing with uncertainty. In a nutshell, it consists of using knowledge of one's own side to make up for what one does not know about the other side—in effect, mirror-imaging. This succeeds when the other side just happens to be like one's self, and fails when reality just happens to be different. Trouble is, mirror-imaging often is confused with intelligence.

The Soviets "must know," they "probably realize," they "cannot possibly believe". . . . Such words characterize all National Intelligence Estimates. One egregious example is the NIE of September 1962, bearing the signature of Sherman Kent himself, that refuted reports from agents in, and refugees from, Cuba about the presence of Soviet ballistic missiles on the island. Quite simply, reports of eye witnesses were overcome by beliefs about what the Soviets would and would not do, based exclusively on what the CIA analysts knew they themselves would or would not do. But intelligence officers are paid to look outward, not inward. In this case they were watching something happen and saying "This can't be happening, because I wouldn't do it." CIA Director John McCone, on his honeymoon in the south of France at the time, cabled President Kennedy to contradict his analysts.[12] Yes, the Soviets could, and might very well have, put missiles in Cuba. McCone had no more information than the analysts did. In fact, being otherwise occupied at the time, he had less. But he was not looking inward. CIA analysts have since defended their mirror-imaging in the September 1962 Estimate. Sherman Kent told anyone who would listen that his judgment on what the Soviets *should have done* was better than Khrushchev's, and that events proved it. As late as 1980 Ray Cline, the DDI in 1962, was quoting him approvingly on this point.[13] But, *pace* Kent and Cline, the name of the game was not to second-guess Khrushchev, but to figure out what he was doing. The analysts simply played the wrong game.

Mirror-imaging is most common in scientific and technical matters, especially when hard data is scarce. A common train of thought runs as follows: "So they are building widgets, eh? Well, since we too have been working on widgets, and since there is only one way to build a modern widget, we can readily make sense of any data on their widget program." But is there really only one way to build a widget? The initial decision to understand the data on "their" program through the optic of ours precludes serious consideration of what might be the most important conclusion that could be drawn from the evidence—i.e., that their program is different.

Thus in 1967–69 U.S. intelligence analysts, influenced by Defense Secretary Robert McNamara, interpreted the huge yield of the Soviet SS-9's warhead (25 megatons) as evidence of an inefficient attempt at preparing to blow up American cities. McNamara, widely supposed to be the world's leading authority on nuclear matters, *was* preparing to blow up Soviet cities, and had taken the more efficient path of loading up to 14 bomblets of 40 kilotons each aboard each U.S. Poseidon missile. Because the overpressure generated by a nuclear explosion is inversely proportional to the cube of the distance from the center of the explosion, the scattergun-style Poseidon could more effectively devastate a wide urban area than could the SS-9's single big bang, and could do so with a total yield of only 3 percent of that of the SS-9s. Hence the U.S. intelligence community's early scorn—and its blindness. In fact, the huge yield on the SS-9 was meant to compensate for the missile's relative inaccuracy, and the combination of yield and accuracy was reasonably designed to yield a 90 percent chance of destroying a U.S. missile launch-control center with one shot. Worthy of contempt when looked at through the U.S. mirror, the SS-9 was worthy of admiration when looked at from the very different perspective of those who made it.[14] By the same token, in 1990 analysts underestimated Iraq's ability to separate out enough uranium-238 for nuclear weapons because the Iraqis did not have enough centrifuges. But the Iraqis were doing the job very well (albeit inefficiently) with electromagnetic devices of 1930s vintage.

Cultural mirror-imaging is also pervasive. The U.S. educational system just does not turn out many people who understand other cultures.* The unspoken assumption of intelligence analysts is that the rest of the world is more or less like themselves (only perhaps a bit less competent). We have already mentioned the analysts' inability to comprehend religion. There is also a tendency to disregard noneconomic motives, with the exception of "nationalism." But, for example, tribalism, which is far more common in the world than nationalism, might as well not exist for U.S. intelligence. As regards the Middle East, newspaper cartoons and popular jokes are clear about the tendency for one group to willingly suffer just so another will, too—in other words, cut off one's nose to spite someone else's face, or pursue revenge unto self-destruction. But U.S. intelligence nevertheless applies the model of the rational actor maximizing his material advantages.

Sometimes when data is very scarce, conscious mirror-imaging is the only way to try to make sense of little pieces of information. But when an analyst follows this practice unconsciously, he is likely to conclude again and again that the country he is watching is doing purposeless, inefficient, even incomprehensibly stupid things. Such a chain of judgments should be a dead giveaway that the analyst is working from a frame of reference foreign to the phenomena he is observing. Long ago, Machiavelli cautioned analysts to be on guard when an intelligent enemy makes what appears to be a stupid mistake.[15] Few analysts have read Machiavelli.

The Demand for Certainty

The intellectual propensities of U.S. analysts may well be due substantially to those of the policy-makers they serve. The nature of the supply may be due to that of the demand. There is a demand for certainty, not for answers like "Damned if *we* know," or "Here are three alternative explanations; *you* choose," or "There are a few fragments of data, and what they mean, if anything, is *anyone's* guess." The consumer wants to be told what "it" means. He gets what he wants. Finally, the consumer really cares much less about what

---

*Here we must mention that this problem has worsened in recent years. The "multiculturalist" orthodoxy on American college campuses has nothing to do with learning Arabic or reading Confucius. Rather, it is an ideology incomprehensible beyond American campuses. The study of languages is at an all time low in America, and declining.

is going on in the outside world than he cares for how *the image* of what is going on in the outside world will affect his own and his friends' struggles in Washington, DC.

How else can one explain what happens (and does not happen) as a paper goes from the analyst who first writes it to the President of the United States—and often also to the newspaper headlines? As the paper rises bureaucratically, each successive layer of editors usually knows less about the subject than the previous layer, yet has more power over what the paper will say.* The scrutiny gets chronologically longer as the paper rises. The paper may have been drafted in three days. But the branch will spend a week on it, and the division two weeks. It will take six weeks to get through the interagency groups, which may meet four times, ten days apart. So it takes well over two months to "prepare" a paper that actually took only three days to write.

What sort of knowledge did the people who had the paper most of the time apply to it? Did they simply check out every fact and name in the encyclopedia? Considering the paucity of facts in U.S. intelligence papers, and the kinds of mistakes that often appear in them, this cannot be. For example, one report on Soviet scientific developments referred to that great Russian chemist who conceived the periodic table of elements as Mendelevsky. A report on Nicaragua spelled the first name of the Sandinista official Jaime Wheelock "Hymie." An NIE on the Middle East contained a map in which Syria was labeled Iraq, and vice versa. Surely there was *someone* paid out of the $30-odd billion that finances U.S. intelligence who had heard of Mendeleev and Jaime, and who knew Iraq from Syria. Our point is that the process did not put such people in charge of these intelligence products. How then does one resist the conclusion that U.S. intelligence managers care less about accuracy than they do about how a paper will affect U.S. policy? As Sovietologist Richard Pipes has noted, in most U.S. government discussions about the Soviet Union that country might as well not exist.[16] The real subject is the day's struggle in Washington.

How U.S. Intelligence Produces Its Products

Let us now look at each of the United States' intelligence community's "product lines," mindful that each "product's" strengths and weaknesses are the result of bureaucratic history, of form, and of struggles over substance.

*Very occasionally a senior analyst—e.g., the Defense Intelligence Agency's John J. Dziak, author of various books on the Soviet Union—will be an active scholar in his own right, even as Sherman Kent had been a historian of France. But since the 1960s this has been even rarer than before.

The Estimates

The flagships of the U.S. intelligence fleet are the Estimates: The National Intelligence Estimates (NIEs) by which the intelligence community regularly covers the world for top decision-makers; the special NIEs that are ordered up to provide background for a breaking crisis; and the interagency intelligence memoranda (IIMs) by which the various parts of the community get their act together. The community prizes the Estimates most highly, and many consider them the principal *raison d'être* of the U.S. intelligence system. Just as William Donovan built the OSS around R&A, the real founders of the CIA—Allen Dulles, William Jackson, and Mathias Correa—wanted to build the CIA around the process by which the CIA would produce the estimates.

For the founders, the essence of the CIA was its centrality. By this they meant that U.S. intelligence should speak with one voice (the CIA's) on "national" matters. The chief complaint of the January 1, 1949 Dulles–Jackson–Correa report was that the establishment of the CIA had not succeeded in subsuming the competition for the policy-makers' attention:

> Where the Office of Reports and Estimates [of the CIA] produces estimates, it usually does so on the basis of its own research and analysis and offers its products as competitive with the similar products of other agencies, rather than as the coordinated result of the best intelligence product which each of the interested agencies is able to contribute.[17]

The report noted that CIA estimates were circulated to the "State, Army, Navy and Air Force, which appended their views." The report did not even allude to the quality of the product. Its objection to the current situation was that "None of the agencies regards itself as a full participant contributing to a truly national estimate and *accepting a share of the responsibility in it*" (emphasis added). The report's remedy was to establish at the CIA an Estimates Division which would command the other agencies' information and participation. "The finished estimate should be clearly established as the product of all of the contributing agencies in which all share and for which all take responsibility. It should be recognized as the most authoritative estimate available to policymakers."[18] In other words the founders' principal concern was to get out of a "competitive" situation.

Once competition was done away with, the estimates might not always be correct, but they would always be bureaucratically unchallengeable. The CIA might not always be right. But it would never be wrong.

This Estimates Division was indeed established under DCI Walter Bedell Smith in 1950. Since that time both its name and its organizational scheme have changed several times,[19] but its function has remained remarkably constant. It has always consisted of people whom the CIA considered to have "national" character. Each of these individuals, having primary responsibility for drafting Estimates in a particular field, would gather the relevant information from the community, then either draft it or assign someone else to do so.* Then the originating party would convene representatives of the various agencies to "coordinate" the draft. Presentation to a body of either hand-picked "outside" wise men, or heads of intelligence agencies, or both, would follow. Finally, the Director of Central Intelligence would review and sign the Estimate, and then present it to the policy-making community—the bureaucracy of the President and the Congress—and to friends in the press.† In the early days the system turned out about 25 Estimates per year. In the Reagan years the number rose to a yearly rate of about 80.

What is in any given estimate? Quite simply, enough to bring a policy-maker who has never heard of the subject "up to speed" on the basics of the situation, to project further developments in the area, and to guide the policy-maker in the choices that are on the agenda. Special NIEs written during crises—e.g., the September 19, 1962 Estimate on Cuba—neglect the basics and concentrate on the foreign adversaries' choices of the moment. By contrast, the 1983 Estimate on Mexico, done after the shock of Mexico's financial and political turmoil of August 1982, was a virtual primer on Mexican politics.

Ex post facto complaints notwithstanding, the estimators love to project and predict. But they are anything but clear about the nature of the intellectual

---

*The chief difference between an official of the Board of National Estimates (BNE) of the 1950s and a National Intelligence officer of the 1980s is that whereas the former typically would ask a member of the BNE staff to do the initial draft, the latter would have the choice (and the burden) of asking someone in the intelligence community to do the job. See Harold Ford, "Estimative Intelligence," p. 91.

†This is as good a time as any to reiterate that the CIA is neither virginal nor shy about the press. Agency officials make a public show of secrecy. But in fact, as any frequent visitor to Langley can observe, there is a steady traffic of favorite reporters in and out of CIA headquarters. Nor are the reporters always there of their own initiative. They get calls: "I think we have something that might interest you." And they come. Previews of estimates are no more common than other matters. Thomas Powers' portrayal of Frank Wisner, the first Director of the Deputy Directorate for Plans, might as easily apply to a majority of the officials of similar rank who have served in the agency: "Incoming papers might be a foot deep on his desk in L Building in the morning, but Wisner would neglect it all if he noticed a wrong-headed column by Scotty Reston in the morning's *Times*. Nothing took precedence over getting Reston straightened out." Thomas Powers, *The Man Who Kept the Secrets*, p. 73. Note also that no one at the CIA disputed Bob Woodward's claim in *Veil* that he had had dozens of very private sessions with DCI William Casey in Casey's office. The records of journalists' private visits to Langley are voluminous, but the Privacy Act shields them from the Freedom of Information Act. Informal contacts at the top are legion. After all, the point is to play in the policy process.

judgments they make. Thus the various Vietnam estimates after 1966 correctly predicted that the U.S. bombing would not shake the will of North Vietnam's leadership to pursue the war. The prediction was based on the observation that the bombing had merely made it necessary for North Vietnamese leaders to put more men and materiel into the "pipeline" in order to maintain a constant supply to their fighting forces, and on the supposition that they would be willing to do the same in the future. However, the prediction was accurate only because the government was seeking to answer an artificially narrow question: Should we stop *the* bombing (i.e., of a particular kind), keep it up, or step it up? The estimates did not question the paradigm of the bombing, i.e., whether the will of the North Vietnamese leadership would be shaken by a *qualitatively* different bombing program. So, while correct in strict terms, these estimates were misleading because they contributed to hiding the nature of the choices available to U.S. policy-makers.

Whether or not the estimates shed light on the choices before U.S. policy-makers, they are surely written to influence those choices. This tendency is present even in the most encyclopedic of all NIEs, known as number 11-3-8 (which stands for the Soviet Union, strategic forces, and intentions respectively.[20] It is the banner of the flagship line. This annual product usually consists of an inch-thick summary and three 3"-thick appendices. Ever since the 1950s, the U.S. government and public opinion have recognized Soviet strategic forces as the foremost element of the "Soviet threat." Rightly or wrongly, they have also taken the ongoing development of those forces as the best index of Soviet military policy as well as of the world military balance, and also as the foremost piece of evidence in the debate over the future of U.S. military policy.

The chief question of the mid–1950s was "How many bombers should the U.S. build?" In the late 1950s the question was how fast should we be pushing our development of ballistic missiles. In the mid–1960s, as the U.S. was designing the successors to the land-based Minuteman and sea-based Polaris missiles, the question became "What job should they be optimized to do? Should they be city killers or missile-silo killers?" Virtually everyone agreed that the new missiles should have multiple warheads, but weren't sure of what kind. This latter question lasted until the mid–1980s, when it was replaced by the question of whether U.S. missiles should be mobile. In the late 1960s a major intragovernmental debate opened on whether the U.S. government should build antimissile defenses that carried into the 1990s. Each year, as the U.S. national security bureaucracy, Congressional staff, and the major media wrestled with a particular aspect of these questions, the authors of NIE 11-3-8 pitched their product to the debate. One may question the accuracy of 11-3-8. But no one can deny that year after year it stuck very close to the terms of the U.S. debate. It surely served U.S. policy-makers. How well is another question.

Competition

From time to time, charges that 11-3-8 and other estimates have injected unchallenged error into policy debates have prompted the President's Foreign Intelligence Advisory Board, the Congressional oversight committees, and independent observers to prescribe that the estimates be written by different groups in competition with one another. In 1976 President Gerald Ford had created a special team of outside experts (which became known as the B-team) to examine the data on which that year's 11-3-8 was based. The B-team argued within the executive branch, to the relevant congressional committees, and to public opinion, in unclassified form, that 11-3-8 had been wrong for a decade. And it did so convincingly, in part because the CIA was unable to dismiss it for not being privy to "all" the information. So, for the following decade, 11-3-8 followed the intellectual precepts of the B-team. The CIA's performance improved, but the agency much resented the experience.

Evidently the B-team episode convinced the entire CIA establishment that *absolutely* nothing was more important than making *absolutely* sure that no group of outsiders would *ever* have the right to pronounce itself on the topic of an estimate on the basis of all the information that had gone into the estimate. No one would ever be given the *standing* to prove CIA wrong again. On January 19, 1977, in his last appearance as DCI, before the Senate Foreign Relations Committee, George Bush three times turned aside point-blank questions by Sen. Hubert Humphrey (D-MN) about why 11-3-8 had been so wrong for so long. After the Republican party won the presidential election of 1980 on a platform which included a promise of competitive intelligence analysis, Director of Central Intelligence William Casey, and his deputies Bobby Ray Inman (in 1981) and John McMahon (in 1982), lauded the concept of competitive analysis at their confirmation hearings. But they invariably contended that competition meant pitting the agencies against one another to produce a single product. In short, they upheld the system that produces NIEs and refused to expose the Estimates' judgments to criticism based on equal access to data. Hence, if an NIE got a bad reception, the CIA could always reply "Too bad. The critics don't have the full information and cannot challenge the joint judgment of all the experts." Thus in 1984, and again in 1986, the U.S. Congress wrote into law, via the Annual Intelligence Authorization Act, specific requirements that the CIA submit itself to B-teams on specific topics.[21]

The CIA simply ignored the plain intent of the law. Why? Interest in influencing policy a certain way, fear for reputations, and desire to protect the edifice built "at the Creation" certainly are factors. But there is another. The items on which the Congress had demanded competitive analysis represented very substantial interests within the U.S. government.

Take one out of many similar bones of contention: The possibility of nonacoustic (in this case radar) detection of submerged submarines. No one in the West (or perhaps in the world) knows whether it is possible to scan the ocean surface with radar and interpret the returns in ways that notice changes in the size or shape of ocean waves due to the pressure waves generated by submerged submarines. In the early 1980s the U.S. Navy ran a small pilot project on the subject, and concluded that this was impossible. In an Interagency Intelligence Memorandum the CIA did not support the Navy, while NSA opposed it. The Navy has a vested interest in maintaining that submarines are inherently undetectable by nonacoustic means, and its pilot project had examined only part of the possibilities. So a broad left–right coalition of Congressional staff pushed for a competitive analysis, the result of which would have been to sharpen the issues for further research. The Navy then "called in its chips" with the CIA. Unless the CIA supported the Navy on something it considered vital, the Navy would support competitive analysis on things that the CIA considered its own alone. So in the next Interagency Intelligence memorandum the CIA joined the Navy. Congress notwithstanding, there would be no competition.

In sum, the estimates process, originally intended to overcome departmental interests, simply created a new one, the CIA, and has encouraged all these interests—however much they compete amongst themselves—to unite to protect their oligopoly.

The Data Base

Nobody looks at an Estimate or an Interagency Intelligence Memorandum in order to better plan or execute a military or political operation. For that, people need facts, not carefully hedged judgments. In the crunch, intelligence has been valuable insofar as it has been able to respond to the question "What have you got on [so-and-so]?" That is why, insofar as military or political operations are concerned, the most significant task an analyst can perform is to organize the data base into a usable form. However, regardless of the importance of "index cards," managing them has been a thoroughly unrewarding job compared to writing the estimates, to current intelligence, or even to basic studies.

The first attempt at managing the U.S. intelligence data base was a direct extension of R&A's work during the war. Just like R&A, but with more time and forethought, the new CIA set about compiling a "book" on every country in the world. Want to know where you can land in Ruritania? Look at the Ruritanian volume under A for airports or B for beaches. You would find maps; data on wind direction, weather, tides, and sand and soil conditions; and roads, bridges, and the capacity of the population to maintain them. Under other headings you would find historical reasons why the locals might or might not like America; who's who; how the locals' religion and family customs predispose them for or against a host of things; military and political secrets; status, location, and leadership of military forces—and more. And, in fact, by the early 1960s every U.S. military post had, if not the whole world-spanning library, then at least part of the National Intelligence Survey (NIS). But by the late 1960s the NIS had been abandoned completely. Why?

The principal reason lay in the intellectual discipline that the NIS imposed on the analysts. Since the series was written in narrative form, the writer had to decide which fact fit where, if at all, and how it would relate to the other facts mentioned in that sentence, paragraph, page, and chapter. Then, as facts changed, the entire matter would have to be rethought. And the NIS imposed a moral discipline as well. The master principle by which every fact was fit with every other one was conflict. After all, these were not handbooks for bird watchers, but for Americans who might be fighting, coercing, subverting, shoring up, or resisting, in each country. Nor were the potential opponents just anyone. They were communists. So every time an analyst handled any fact, however small, about any country, his mind would have to take on the perspective of a warrior against communism. These disciplines proved to be too burdensome, both intellectually and morally.

One reason why these burdens proved insupportable is that the founders of U.S. intelligence seem not to have imagined they existed. In his 1949 critique of Sherman Kent's *Strategic Intelligence*, Willmoore Kendall* had noted that the central analytical apparatus of U.S. intelligence rested on an implicit agreement about the anticommunist focus of U.S. foreign policy.[22] But what if there were controversy over basic policy? What if it were not clear who the enemy is, or to what end we should fight him? Then surely one would organize the data differently. Hence, argued Kendall, U.S. intelligence analysts ought explicitly to take U.S. objectives into account. So long as they did not, disagreements or simple uncertainty over policy would undermine the integrity of their product. And this is precisely what happened. By the late 1960s uncertainty over goals, the analysts' slow-down strike against the intellectually laborious revisions of the NIS, and the lure of more exciting work in other analytical fields combined to doom the NIS.

Analysts sought refuge in computers.† It is indeed much more efficient to store facts in a computer than to integrate them into the text of a book. But computer storage is so easy precisely because it does not require the analyst to think very hard about how he is doing the filing. How important is a given fact? How does it relate to other facts? When does it become obsolete? Computer storage tends to postpone the crucial analytical questions about the data base.

*Yale professor and OSS alumnus.
†Computers were eliminating the mechanical difficulties of updating the NIS. But the problems of the NIS were not mechanical.

Thus all too often computer data bases have become huge and not-so-useful dumps.

The principal exceptions are the Order of Battle books. The task of filing and updating the names, numbers, locations, and equipment descriptions of military forces is intellectually straightforward, and made-to-order for computers. Hence certain kinds of military analysis are easier than ever. For example, suppose that a particular artillery unit is moved to point A. What volume of fire could it pour into area B? Just punch in the question and the computer will project the number of artillery tubes and the weight of their salvos on B. What if, instead of the artillery unit, a squadron of a particular model of fighter–bombers were called for? Given its bomb load, historic frequency of sorties, range, and fuel consumption, how much ordnance could it drop onto zone B? This sort of information is now available at the push of a button. By the same token, it is now child's play to update the movements of thousands of ships on the world's oceans, keep track of entire naval fleets and, given knowledge of ships' characteristics and history of resupply, to instantly project the power they could or could not theoretically exercise on any point of the globe at any given time. Order-of-battle intelligence has become so much like playing computer chess that U.S. analysts sometimes forget they are also dealing with inherently unpredictable human entities.

Political data bases, by contrast, are computer-unfriendly. Sure enough, biographic data can be filed and cross-checked. Indeed, U.S. analysts have not yet begun to exhaust the capacity of computers in this regard. But how does one reduce intentions, allegiances, and steadfastness to computer-format? Who belongs to whom, and for what purpose? Who is whose friend, and how far does the friendship go? Analysts rarely handled such questions well, even when the NIS format forced them to the fore. Since the demise of NIS, political data gets filed as collected, and the criteria by which it is collected are less analytical than ever—meaning that the hard but politically meaningful questions get glossed over. So when a policy-maker wants to know what Mr. X is good for, the computer is likely to spit out his résumé at best.

It is deeply ironic that the CIA's Directorate of Intelligence, which until 1981 had been organized along functional lines (economic, military, and political affairs), reorganized itself along geographic lines just as the floods of unorganized data made it most difficult to retrieve meaningful data on a geographic basis.* Once upon a time the data might have been organized to highlight a man's relationship to a party or an industry. Now one takes one's chances. Suffice it to

---

*In this author's view the argument between organizing analysts geographically or functionally is of tertiary importance.

say that every President and most National Security Advisers since Kennedy have expressed displeasure with the quality of the political data they have received from U.S. intelligence.

Since the late 1970s, partly as a result of easy computer sorting, a whole set of data bases has emerged that are organized by subject—e.g., terrorism, drugs, the U.S.-Mexican border, foreign intelligence capabilities. In addition, of course, informal data bases have been established by the offices that carry out substantive studies. As in a major university library, the materials are most useful when they happen to be swept into the acutely focused "collections" on the desks of individual researchers who have defined their topic.

Current Intelligence

Current intelligence is journalism—with two differences: It is classified, and the target audiences seldom receive competing products.

The President's Daily Brief (PDB) heads the category. There are no obvious criteria by which to either include or exclude an item from the PDB. The CIA wants to give the President what he needs to do his job, it wants to please him, and it wants to influence him. It does not want to argue with him. So the dominant question quickly becomes "What does he *want?*" Jimmy Carter wanted details. Lyndon Johnson wanted juicy tidbits. Richard Nixon wanted the deepest secrets. Ronald Reagan liked to go "Wow!" The managers of the PDB gave each his wish.

As regards substance, the agency tries to give the President deep intelligence background both on the day's news and on issues that are "up" for his decision that day. Often, however, the choice of items is dictated by what little "hot" stuff is available. Once upon a time a satellite picture was enough to impress a President and justify an item in the PDB. As satellite pictures became common, they often served as visual background for a text all too full of "We believe". The logical conclusion of this development occurred under President Ronald Reagan. Reagan wanted a show, so the CIA would prepare briefings consisting of file photographs of (for example) Soviet or Cuban footage, taped from television broadcasts, which served as background for the agency's message. One of Reagan's favorite briefing videos about Soviet space weapons was actually an animated cartoon, complete with a "bang" from an explosion in space that was as loud as it was incongruous. This mode of presentation blurred any distinction between fact and judgment, fact and fiction, intelligence and advertising, reality and artist's conception.

In short, although the PDB does contain some precious secrets, it is not the King's jewel box. One former senior intelligence official who read it every day for six years said of it: "If you were accustomed to getting your daily news from some newspaper in Iowa you might be impressed by the PDB. Otherwise, it is not anything to write home about."[23] From time to time, especially after crises, presidents have expressed similar thoughts. In October 1989, in the wake of a botched coup against Panama's dictator, Manuel Noriega, President George Bush complained that he had not been given enough intelligence, while in December 1989, as the U.S. invasion of Panama was unfolding, Bush's Chief of Staff, John Sununu, told the press that CNN Television news had proved more valuable than the daily intelligence briefing.

Such remarks do indeed reflect poor intelligence collection and analysis. But when high officials ejaculate "Bad intelligence!" they are as often as not diverting attention from their own responsibilities. There is never enough intelligence to guarantee instant success at no cost and never enough to overcome entrenched prejudice. Presidents must act on the information they have at any given time. For example, it is difficult to blame the CIA for the United States' mindless tilt toward Iraq in the 1981–90 decade. In the 1980s, Iran was the devil itself for the entire U.S. government. Had the CIA broken ranks and hoisted warning flags at raising up Beelzebub against Satan, would anyone have listened?

The CIA is unique among the world's intelligence agencies in that, during any given week in the mid-1980s, it was delivering as many briefings to the legislative branch as it was to the executive branch. Not only did the intelligence committees of the U.S. Senate and House of Representatives receive the briefings, but also the two armed services committees, the appropriations committees, the committees on foreign affairs, and occasionally the finance committees. The Congressional committees are an easier audience than the White House in that the members who call for the briefings often just want the CIA to confirm their prejudices. The staff who arrange the briefings treat CIA just like anybody else who is to appear before Congress. They want to know which line the witnesses will take on this or that to make sure that the appearance will serve the interests of the people doing the arranging.* When interests converge, the audience can be counted on to applaud. The most obvious

---

*This is a good time to point out how mistaken is the conventional wisdom that in the 1970s congressional committees dragged unwilling leaders of the CIA over the proverbial coals to force them to reveal the "family jewels." In fact, ever since the mid-1960s a civil war had been raging within the CIA. In the mid-1970s one faction in this war simply hooked up with its allies in Congress and staged hearings that embarrassed and destroyed its internal rivals. As a result, between 1975 and 1980, fully 90 percent of the CIA's "supergrade" employees (GS-16 through GS-18) turned over. In 1980 the CIA awarded a medal to the Chief of Staff of the Church committee, who had led this supposed assault. It had been no assault at all, but just another of the inside-outside operations that are the stuff of daily life in Washington, D.C.

example is that of the appearance of the CIA study group on Soviet military spending before Sen. William Proxmire's (D-WI) Joint Economic Committee. Both participants were out to publicize one message: Soviet military spending isn't so worrisome.

But Congressional committees can be tough audiences because they are uncontrollable. Sometimes a senator will walk into a briefing, be struck by what he hears, and relentlessly pursue a line of profoundly embarrassing questions. The CIA used to fear Sen. Henry "Scoop" Jackson (D-WA) in particular because, after characterizing himself as just a "country lawyer from Everett, Washington," he would give the "current intelligence" briefers lessons in history and geography. In the last years of his life he sometimes reminded his briefers that in the 1950s, as Soviet crews were digging the Salang tunnel in Afghanistan, he (not the CIA) had predicted that someday it would be the route of a Soviet invasion. Another hazard of congressional briefings is the presence of staffers whose daily bread comes from showing that a witness does not know what he is talking about. Hence a regular feature of DCI Stansfield Turner's Congressional current intelligence briefings was the request that staffers be put out of the room.

Congressional briefings are most often done by "current intelligence" people because the members are likely to call either for background on something that is happening—a Third World coup, or the East European Revolution of 1989—or for background on current legislative controversies, which themselves turn largely on current events. Often the current intelligence people (who are basically desk-bound journalists) bring along "the experts" from the study groups. Thus in 1981, when Israeli airplanes destroyed Iraq's nuclear reprocessing plant, the Osirak reactor, the CIA brought along an "expert" whose expertise consisted of following the news and putting the approved spin on it. (The "spin" happened to be that the Israelis had committed an outrage.) Alas, the fellow could not manage to explain the difference between the kind of reactor fuel reprocessing that produces significant amounts of weapons-grade plutonium and the kind that does not. He also had a hard time pronouncing the word "neutron." So the committee focused not on his spin, but on the CIA's incompetence. Sometimes, however, the background experts, who may have no knowledge whatever of current events, dazzle the audience and give the CIA's reputation a mighty boost just by teaching the basics of their subjects.

The biggest and best-known of the current intelligence products in the U.S. is the *National Intelligence Daily*, the *NID*, a newspaper of some 20 pages classified with most of the U.S. government's major codewords, some 400 copies printed each night for about 1,000 "top" people in Washington and carried throughout officialdom every business day by the CIA's "paper boys." Any given story in the *NID* is sourced to however many intelligence agencies agree with it.

So, writing the *NID* is not entirely unlike the writing of National Estimates: A CIA editor asks an office for an item, or receives it unsolicited. If the editor decides to run it, he asks for opinions on it from around the community, and then works them into the text. Items run from one to five paragraphs. They report on current events, e.g., on elections, as well as on intelligence scoops. They also give background for continuing stories.

How useful is it? If 100 people familiar with both the *NID* and *The New York Times* had to choose one of the two as their only source of information, well over 90 would choose the *Times*. But *NID* does provide satellite pictures and occasional direct references to secret communications, and sometimes gives the reader a few days' edge on which issues will appear in the press. Generally it is not a waste of time. But since the *NID* is a "community" product, seldom does any item that is either controversial or from a highly valued source appear in it.

Below the *NID* are a host of daily summaries prepared by the CIA, the State and Defense Departments (for embassies, naval ships, and military commands), and interagency working groups dealing with such varied subjects as foreign aid, arms-control negotiations, and drug interdiction. In a sense, this is where the wheel of intelligence meets the road of policy. Yet this also is where current intelligence has most seriously fallen down on the job. Why? First, the "consumers" are not doing the sorting, and those who do the sorting know little (and care less) for the needs of lower-ranking consumers. So, a ship in the southwestern Pacific may receive speculation on arms-control agreements rather than the latest on tests of antiship missiles. Second, the detailed stuff, such as data on tests of antiship missiles, also sometimes tends to be the most highly compartmented. So the sensitivity of the source puts the data in the category of "national" intelligence. This sort of thing comes to a head during crises, when, if everything works right, current intelligence and study groups on a particular subject are brought together with the policy-makers, and units in the field are especially targeted to receive what they will need. As good an example as any is the fact that the U.S. Embassy in London was kept fully abreast of U.S. satellite information on the deployment of Argentine forces *during* the Falklands War in 1982. This helped the British to defeat the Argentines. However, *prior* to the outbreak of war, when the U.S. Embassy in London might well have used such facts to help the British avert the Argentines' miscalculations, it would have been out of character to add U.S. Embassy London to the distribution list of incoming stuff on Argentina.

So the needs of military commanders for current intelligence have been filled not by the "current intelligence" shops at CIA and DIA, but rather by TENCAP, a program we earlier described which brings the results of some "national" means of collection (e.g., ELINT satellites) directly to users. Beyond that, local commanders, embassies, etc., are their own best collectors *and* analysts of current intelligence because they have both the incentive and the insight (if not the tools) for doing it right.

The Widening Mismatch

Aggressive Ignorance

Upon first coming into contact with "national" level U.S. intelligence products, the proverbial man from Mars would first be struck by their ignorance—not bias, not bad judgment, but ignorance of basic facts, compounded by an aggressive lack of curiosity. He would wonder whether somewhere in the bowels of the U.S. government there was not some agency keeping the U.S. government well-informed while the store-front intelligence community deceptively paraded its ignorance. Examples are all too easy to find. And it will not do to dismiss them, as former Deputy Director of the CIA Ray Cline does, by saying "Intelligence is always wrong" because it must hazard guesses in highly uncertain situations which can resolve themselves in unpredictable ways. If this were so, it would be manifestly better to have no intelligence at all. On the contrary, countries hire analysts hoping that their knowledge of the present and past will correlate well with good judgment about the future. By the same token, misjudgment of the future is often rooted in ordinary ignorance of the past and present. Let us leave aside for a moment the why, and look just at the ignorance and the wilfulness.

In 1976, CIA Director George Bush before a Joint Committee countered the statement "There is a great deal of malnutrition in China." "This statement," said Bush, "comes as a surprise to me."[24] Citing his own experience as Ambassador to China, Bush supported "their own [the communist Chinese government's] theses that there is a basic level of nutrition for the entire population," and he called on the CIA experts he had brought to the hearing for enlightenment. The record shows that none of the experts offered any caveat. And yet several million human beings had starved to death in China during Mr. Bush's time in China and at the CIA. During the great Chinese "thaw" of the mid-1980s, Western visitors were routinely regaled with horror stories of the starvation which, said the Chinese, had been common knowledge. Yet the CIA "knew" that it didn't exist. Oh, there had been reports in the press about it, which is why the Committee had asked Bush the questions in the first place. But Bush and his CIA knew better than to give these reports any credence—they were sure enough not to bother targeting space-based Comint collectors to check on the matter.

In 1984 the CIA's chief analyst on Afghanistan was asked by another committee about reports from the Afghan Mujahedeen (reports confirmed by

Olivier Roy, *Le Monde's* on-the-scene correspondent) that Soviet troops were methodically destroying irrigation systems throughout that arid country, so as to end agriculture and empty the countryside of potential supporters of the resistance. Not so, said the analyst, although the agency had noticed that here and there, as a byproduct of military operations, Soviet troops had indeed destroyed a few irrigation systems. But, asked the committee, had the agency followed up the thousands of reports of such things among the four million Afghan refugees? It had not. The committee pressed: Considering that the Soviet Army had successfully followed such a policy of destroying the hydrological basis for agriculture during its wars against the Basmachi rebels of Central Asia in the 1920s, why did the agency not look into reports that the Soviets were following that strategy in Afghanistan? Basmachi rebels? The analyst was "not familiar" with them. After all, he complained, he was the analyst of Afghanistan in 1984, not of events in other times and places. Did he not feel obliged to look into similar events elsewhere, whence he might learn to better focus his research on Afghanistan? No.

Harry Rositzke, in his standard, authoritative work on U.S. intelligence, written after 25 years near the top of the agency, including major responsibility for the U.S.S.R., wrote in 1977 that the Soviet record in public health is outstanding.[25] But in fact the Soviet Union has always had an abysmal record in the field. Prior to communism, life expectancy had always been lower in the lands which became the Soviet Union than in Western Europe. But since the communist revolution of 1917 the gap has consistently widened, not narrowed. To be sure, Soviet propaganda had always claimed that communism had brought better public health. But there was never any shortage of reports to the contrary. Novels and émigré reports were full of the truth: unsterilized needles, medicines left out to bake or freeze, horrid sanitation, campaigns to reduce public health among target populations. But it was part of the mythology of the Soviet Union (and of socialist countries in general) that they had a solid public health system. Only in 1987, when the Soviet government itself admitted that its health standards were abysmal did the CIA abandon its adherence to the official mythology. But Rositzke and an entire generation of "experts" had simply preferred to believe the Soviet government rather than those who had an axe to grind against it.

In 1958, as the possibility arose that Fidel Castro might take power in Cuba, so did a debate about whether or not he was a communist. There was no shortage of reports to the effect that he had joined the Party while a student at the University of Havana. Because access to people who had known him in those years posed no problem, neither did checking out the reports. But the CIA, apparently *without* checking out the reports, concluded that Castro was not a communist. After January 1, 1959, Castro instituted the façade of a liberal–

democratic government during the crucial year while he seized absolute power by joining the most faithful nucleus of his armed forces to the Communist party. Nevertheless, not just during the period of the façade, but also throughout the 1960s and 1970s, even as other parts of the CIA were talking about bizarre plots to kill him, there was a vigorous debate among CIA analysts over how much the U.S. government had *pushed* Castro into communism by not helping him build socialism. This debate continued until 1977, when Castro told journalist Barbara Walters and the television cameras that, yes, he had joined the Party at the university and had been a faithful Communist ever since. Then, in 1986, journalist Tad Szulc published the story of how Castro had taken power under false pretenses.[26] But we are not aware of any soul-searching among the CIA's analysts about why they discounted reports of Castro's communism and of his shadow government.

Finally, whenever an unanticipated change in government occurs in the Third World, or the CIA proves wrong on an assessment (e.g., the prediction in *NID* on February 15, 1989 that the Soviet puppet government of Najibullah in Afghanistan would fall within six months), the CIA defends itself before Congress by saying "We had only [one or two] analysts on that country." The implication is that if the agency had been given more money it would not have been so ignorant or mistaken. Leave aside the fundamental problem: More people do not guarantee better analysis, especially if the facts are lacking. For the sake of argument, grant instead that quantity equals quality. But surely, with several *thousand* analytical personnel at the CIA, even the tiniest of the world's 160 countries can rate a half-dozen analysts without making a big dent in the total manpower pool. Why then are there never enough analysts where the action is? What are they doing? By the CIA's own definition, they are looking the wrong way.

Let us now turn to the major fields in which National Intelligence has spoken.

STATICS

In the 1950s few paid any attention to the ten or so studies per year that CIA's economic analysts produced. By the late 1970s CIA economists were producing 80 or so studies a year, and annually fielding thousands of questions from Congress and the bureaucracy. Their 1977 paper on the Soviet Union's production of petroleum was front-page news. By the 1980s their annual paper on Soviet military spending was eagerly awaited by all sides in the battle over the U.S. military budget, and was the stuff of national controversy. Alas, as they grew in importance these studies became more certifiably wrong than ever.

The 1977 study on Soviet oil came while it was fashionable to think that the world was fast running out of nonrenewable resources. According to conventional wisdom, at the time, only some 15 years' worth of proven oil reserves remained for the free world, and the world economy would shut down by the late 1980s. But what about the world's largest oil-producing country, the Soviet Union? The CIA said that it too was running out; that by 1979 it would cease to be a net exporter of oil and gas, and soon thereafter its otherwise expanding economy would be competing for the dwindling supply of Mid-East oil just as its supply of hard currency—about half of which had been gained by selling oil—would be drying up. So the Soviet Union would be tempted to compete for Mid-East oil in noneconomic ways. This analysis fit well with the Carter Administration's Malthusian, "shrinking-resource base" view of the world, and fed the "Carter Doctrine"—a commitment to use American troops to keep the Soviet Union out of the Persian Gulf.

But the Soviet oil study was wrong in every possible way. First, Soviet domestic production in oil and gas kept climbing at a steady rate. Within two years the biggest controversy on the United States government's plate was a long-term contract between the Soviets and Western European countries that would have made the latter dependent on Siberian natural gas. Second, the Soviet economy—never up to world standards—had already begun a historic, catastrophic decline.* The Soviet Union experienced energy troubles, all right, but of a kind directly opposite to what the CIA had forecast. Instead of an energy shortage, the world of the 1980s experienced an oil *glut*. Between 1979 and 1984, world oil prices *fell* by more than two-thirds in real terms. This, of course, dramatically reduced the hard currency that the Soviet Union reaped from its still-abundant oil sales. The Soviet Union did indeed commit aggression against a country to the south, Afghanistan. But the motives had nothing to do with the intellectual fashion in Washington (shortages of material resources), but rather with old-fashioned *hubris*.

The CIA's performance with regard to the Soviet economy in general is just as bad. By the late 1980s the news media were carrying almost daily accounts of Soviet economists and government officials describing the horrid state of the Soviet economy. By every possible standard, the Soviet civilian economy was an unmitigated disaster at every level: 4.5 times as many tractors produced only one-third the food as in the U.S., while twice as many machine tools produced only one-fifth the goods. But virtually none of the Soviet outputs were qualitatively competitive. So the inefficiencies were greater. In distribution, huge percentages of the products were lost or spoiled. Soviet citizens traveling to the Third World would gasp at its prosperity, and even African students would experience a drop in their standard of living when they were sent to Moscow.

*By 1992 the former Soviet Union risked becoming a net importer of petroleum products. But this had nothing to do with depletion of oil fields. A near collapse of the industrial infrastructure was responsible.

Statistics were meaningless—or, worse, outright deception. Real growth, albeit modest, had existed in the past only insofar as the numbers of people in the labor force, and the gross amount of natural resources applied to the economy, had increased. There had been no increase in per capita productivity in decades. The burden of military spending on the economy was literally incalculable because prices, and indeed money itself, were meaningless in the Soviet Union. Political and bureaucratic pull were the Soviet Union's currency, not the ruble. The military sector took up on the order of a third of the economy. But at least the military's resources were being used efficiently. So mere demilitarization would not help much. One would think that a disaster of this magnitude, lasting so long, would have been self-evident.

But not to readers of the CIA's studies of the Soviet economy. For the CIA, the Soviet economy was humming along at rates of growth comparable to those of the West, or even higher. According to the CIA, between 1961 and 1985 the Soviet economy grew at a robust 3.9 percent per year.[27] To be sure, said the CIA, this was a big comedown from double-digit rates in the postwar years. But the economy continued to provide steady improvement in people's lives. A ponderous bureaucracy and low-quality products notwithstanding, the system provided a solid and equitable—if spartan—living. And military spending (more on this below) was comparable to that in the West.

Where did the CIA get this view? From the same place it got the inspiration to write in its 1987 *World Factbook* that the *per capita* GNP of East Germany was higher than that of West Germany. Few in the polite academic company favored by CIA analysts would have contested these views. After all, in 1987 John Kenneth Galbraith, eminent Harvard economist and the very standard of acceptability at CIA, wrote that simply walking Soviet streets was enough to convince one that there was solid well-being. The CIA preferred Galbraith's blinders to the evidence.

The CIA's circuitous expression of its economic judgments leads one to question whether its faults result from ill-chosen methodology, or whether it chose the methodology precisely to produce the results. The CIA agrees that "We very likely overestimated the size of Soviet GNP relative to U.S. GNP" and attributes its mistakes to "the complexity of international economic comparisons that plagues not only us but other organizations as well."[28] But it defends its numbers as "more informative than the contradictory statements that continue to emanate from the Soviet government"—hardly an affirmation of objective truth. The agency also defended itself against the critics of its performance in this field by citing qualifying remarks in its earlier papers. Yet the very worst case these remarks depicted was a growth rate of 2–2½ percent in the 1980s—not the outright collapse that actually occurred. Couple this with the CIA's

220

continued defense of its complex analytical models, and it is difficult to avoid the conclusion that CIA wilfully believed in the Soviet Union as a stable communist superpower.

This is clearest with regard to the CIA's performance on Soviet military spending. Because the amount a nation *spends* on its military matters is far less important than what it *gets*, there was no good reason for the CIA to spend much energy on this subject. But the amount the Soviets spent was significant as currency in intramural American debates. In the 1970s the United States spent about 6 percent of its GNP on defense. The Soviets claimed to be spending only some 3 percent of a GNP that was itself less than half of the United States'.[29] Very few Westerners thought that the Soviet claim was entirely accurate, or the Soviet Union quite so pacifically inclined. Everyone conceded the Soviets' penchant for exaggerated self-justification. But to have said that the Soviets were deliberately lying by a huge factor would have given aid and comfort to the proposition that the Soviets were on their way to a significant military advantage and that the United States ought to spend more. And surely the consensus of polite opinion has been that the U.S. ought to spend less on military things. So, somehow, right-minded people at CIA had to find a middle position.

The CIA's complex methodology boiled down to this: The CIA took note of the entire Soviet Order of Battle (tanks, planes, missiles, soldiers, rifles, etc.), including its level of technical sophistication, and even the standard of living of personnel. Then it figured out how many dollars it would cost to purchase all these goods and services *in the United States*. Because the U.S. is set up to provide goods and services very different from those in the Soviet Union, and because the cost of doing business in the U.S. is different as well, the result was an essentially artificial figure. Some of the numbers are in fact truly startling. For example, Soviet ballistic missiles, if manufactured in the U.S., would cost up to five times less than U.S. missiles. This despite the fact that the differences in sophistication are small. This, then, is one "finagle factor." Then, in order to compare this artificially dollar-denominated set of goods and services with the whole ruble-denominated Soviet economy, the CIA had to translate the dollar figure into rubles. But the ruble–dollar rate of exchange set by the Soviet government ($1.61 per ruble) obviously was unrealistic, and the actual free-market rate (always pennies per ruble) is meaningful only for purposes of international exchange, not for the internal worth of goods. So the CIA created its own ruble–dollar ratio every year for the purpose of arriving at a (CIA-generated) ruble total for military spending that could then be divided by the total Soviet GNP—denominated in rubles according to Soviet statistics. The ruble–dollar ratio is a second finagle factor.

After all this abstract labor the CIA (until 1976, at least) figured that the

Soviet Union spent about 6 percent of its GNP on defense. Considering that the CIA figured Soviet GNP to be about half that of the U.S. (in fact it turns out to have been less than one-fifth), and that the percentage spent was about the same, the CIA's figures meant that the Soviet Union was spending only about half of what the U.S. was.

How could the Soviets, on about half the money spent by the U.S., maintain five times as many tanks as the U.S., 2.5 times the manpower, twice as many submarines and aircraft, an antimissile defense, and an air defense system with 10,000 radars, 12,000 surface-to-air missile launchers, etc., while the U.S. had no antimissile system and only vestiges of air defense? Were the Soviets magically efficient? This conundrum fazed the CIA not at all. But the second was tougher. In 1976, Soviet Party Chief Leonid Brezhnev mentioned in a speech (not meant for Western consumption but which émigrés brought to the West) that the military sector may have been taking up as much as 15 percent of Soviet GNP.[30] The CIA reacted by trying to discredit the source by an "improperly administered" polygraph test.[31] Later that year, however, when a group of outsiders (the B-team) challenged its estimates, the CIA doubled its figure to 12 percent. But—and this provided the fuel for continuing disputes— the CIA did not change its method.

So after 1976, while the Soviet military—the tanks, the planes, the missiles—continued to grow at obviously substantial rates (perhaps 4 percent per year), and while technical improvements might reasonably be supposed to have added another 4 percent to the costs, the CIA assumed that the growth had been about 3 percent overall. *In other words, the Soviet Union paid nothing at all for technical improvement, and very little for expansion.* Thus, year after year reality and the CIA diverged ever farther. By the 1980s the CIA's yearly appearance before Sen. Proxmire's Joint Economic Committee was the occasion for charges that President Reagan's requests for increases of 5 to 8 percent in the United States military budget were overkill. By 1988, however, Soviet economists traveling to the West had given currency to the view that Soviet military spending accounted for at least 18 percent of GNP, and perhaps much more. The 1989 CIA estimate—again without revision of the method—reflected this change while keeping the methodology.

No sooner was that done, however, than the Soviet Union shifted the ground of this debate within the U.S. Mikhail Gorbachev announced that the military budget was 84.2 billion rubles (including military space), a figure that U.S. analysts unanimously considered unrealistically low, but that he would be cutting that spending by 1.5 percent in 1989 and perhaps by 7 percent in 1990. By November 14, 1989, *The Washington Post* was reporting that CIA analysts had confirmed the 1.5 percent cut, and that two leading Democratic politicians, Sen.

Sam Nunn (D-GA) and Rep. Les Aspin (D-WI), had cited this as support for the proposition that the U.S. military budget should be cut.

One is led to ask by what secret wonders the CIA analysts could pick out events so small as to positively confirm a 1.5 percent cut. And a cut in what? Surely not in the fictitious figure of 84.2 billion rubles. But then in what? What new information underlay the new estimate? How secure was that information? What role did the abovementioned finagle factors play? These were not secrets. There *were* no answers. In April 1990, Mikhail Gorbachev said that military spending amounted to 19 percent of GNP, which would have put it at 120 billion rubles. So much for the relevance of the controversy over the 1.5 percent cut. Alas, such intelligence questions were eclipsed by naked policy disputes. By March 1990, CIA Director William Webster was telling the Congress that the Soviet Union had basically ceased to be a military threat, even while the Secretary of Defense, backed by the DIA, was saying the opposite.[32] There was no debate at all about the factual grounds for these diametrically different claims.

In April 1990, Soviet economists attending a conference at the American Enterprise Institute in Washington, DC, stated that Soviet military spending was at least 200 billion rubles.[33] This figure was in line with those produced over the years by DIA analyst William T. Lee, by the simple method of subtracting figures for civilian activities from Soviet aggregate economic figures—the so-called residual method. In sum, American taxpayers financed intelligence estimates of Soviet military spending that obscured reality. This was a tempest in a teapot. Other failures had serious consequences.

DYNAMICS

Perhaps the most important of the national intelligence products have been the NIE 11-3-8 series. After all, if intelligence is to do anything at all, it is supposed to warn of the rise of forces that can defeat the country in war. Surely no failure of American intelligence compares in seriousness to this NIE's misprision of the size, scope, and purpose of Soviet strategic forces between 1965 and 1979. In a nutshell: Over 1965–69, the NIEs said that the Soviets were not even going to try to build as many missiles as the U.S. In 1969, when Soviet missiles approached the U.S. number, the NIEs said that they would not exceed it substantially. In 1970, 1971, and 1972, when the number (and throw weight) of Soviet missiles exceeded that of the United States' substantially, the NIEs went overboard predicting further quantitative increases, but said that the Soviets would not try to convert these advantages into the capacity to deliver at least one silo-killing warhead on each U.S. missile silo. Between 1973 and 1976, when it became undeniable that the Soviet Union was building the capacity to deliver at least three silo-killing warheads on every American missile silo (plus every other

American strategic target) while using only about half of its missile force, the NIEs argued that the Soviets were not really preparing to fight, survive, and win a war; that even if they were, they would not soon succeed; and that if they did succeed, it would not matter.[34]

The quantitative misestimates of 1965–69 literally jump out from the accompanying illustration (see Figure 5–1). On the right-hand side of each graph is a vertical dotted line indicating the NIEs' predictions of Soviet ICBM deployments by 1970–71. Except for the estimate made in 1969, the range is very broad—250 launchers. Yet every year the new low estimate is about as high as, or higher than, the previous year's high estimate. Clearly this was a galloping situation, and the estimators were lagging 'way behind. Now note the line on the left side of each graph, which represents the number of new silos the Soviets started. It is identical, except for a two-year lag, with the middle line, which represents the number of silos the Soviets completed. There is nothing arcane about this. The fact that someone begins work on a missile silo, which takes about two years to complete, is very substantial evidence that two years later there will be a completed silo. Silo construction began in 1963. By 1966 at the latest, the rate of completions matched the rate of starts. Yet the 1966 estimate for the future (vertical dotted line) is consistent with a rate of completions which was as yet uninfluenced by the rate of starts. In other words, it manages to be as low as it is only by being wilfully blind to the rate of silo starts. Throughout the 1965–69 period, the CIA *never* used the rate of starts as a basis for projections.

But what about after 1966, when the two parallel lines were streaking upward? The NIEs' projections are consistent chiefly with one judgment: *The last silo we observed being started was about the last that would ever be started.** Like Sherman Kent, who in 1962 saw no reason why Khrushchev should do what he in fact did in Cuba, the authors of 11-3-8 simply saw no reason why the Soviets should do what they were obviously doing in the field of strategic weaponry. So they expected them to stop. In 1979, Secretary of Defense Harold Brown complained of Soviet strategic programs: "When we build, they build. When we stop, they build"—as if by some law the Soviets should have followed American patterns. But the whole point of intelligence is to discover *foreign* ways.

Then in 1970, just as Soviet silo starts leveled off, the intelligence community started projecting Soviet missile construction as if the building boom would continue in full swing. To be sure, the NIEs never went so far as the

---

*This is the tautological basis of John Prados' defense of the NIEs: There never were more missiles at any given time than the NIE said there were. In that sense, of course, the NIEs were correct. But they were incorrect in discounting the continuation of the trend. See John Prados, *The Soviet Estimate*, pp. 183–199.

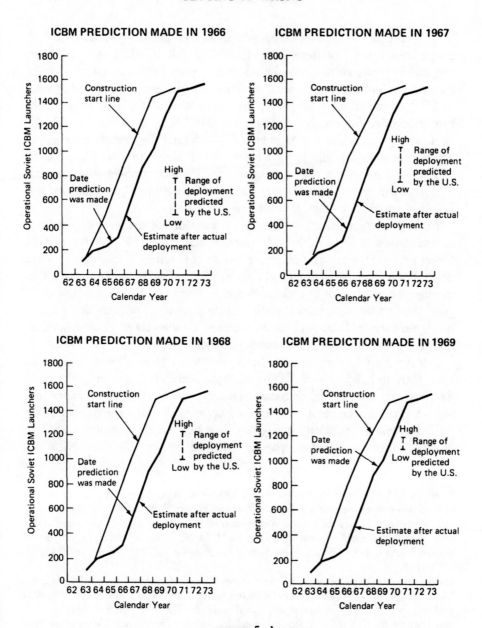

FIGURE 5–1

Nixon-Kissinger White House, which projected 2400 Soviet ICBM silos. Nevertheless they did project some 2000. Actual construction stopped at 1400 silos. Again, the evidence was overpowering. Yet again something superseded the evidence. Once again this something was not in the Soviet Union, but rather in the minds of American intelligence and executive officials.

225

This time the top item on the agenda of the right-thinking people in the U.S. government was the Strategic Arms Limitation Talks (SALT). A SALT treaty was widely perceived to be the key to dealing with the Soviet threat. A broad spectrum of 'enlightened' opinion, as we have seen, defined that threat in terms of SS-9 missile silos.* Conversely, the importance of SALT came from the supposition that the number of SS-9s was threatening to rise, and that SALT could stop it. Of course the number of SS-9s did not rise, and there never was any evidence that it would.† Nor was there any evidence that the SALT I treaty of 1972 had anything to do with stopping the number of SS-9s. It appears that U.S. policy-makers and intelligence analysts simply defined "the problem" in a way that would allow them to "solve" it.

Reality, however, overflowed the boundaries of the definitions. Beginning *immediately* after SALT I, the U.S. received incontrovertible evidence that the Soviet strategic threat was multiplying—but not in terms of numbers of silos or SS-9s. Rather, it grew far faster and more efficiently than it could ever have done through the building of one silo after another, or one missile after another. It grew through the introduction of the fourth generation of accurate, miniaturized, multiwarhead counterforce missiles, i.e., *through the qualitative exploitation of the quantitative base of missiles and silos laid down in 1963–72.*[35]

Nor is it possible to attribute the Soviet shift to the treaty, or to U.S. decisions circa 1969 to build non–silo-killing multiple warheads. Since the new Soviet developments were of a highly technical nature, and thus had to be planned over at least a half-decade before they showed up in hardware, it is obvious that *the NIEs had simply mistaken an ongoing, long-planned, long-term shift from a quantitative to a qualitative program.* Much as in the 1960s the NIEs had

---

*Thus James Schlessinger said: "At the time of SALT I we thought that if we could get control of the SS-9 or its replacement, we would have a handle on the throw-weight problem. What we were unprepared for was the enormous expansion of Soviet throw weight represented by the SSX-19 as the potential replacement for the SS-11." U.S. Congress, Senate, Committee on Foreign Relations, U.S.–USSR Strategic Policies (Washington, DC: U.S. Govt. Printing Office, 1974), p. 5.

†Note that Harold Ford, presumably reflecting the views of some of his former colleagues at the CIA, cites the CIA's refusal to agree to the Nixon Administration's alarmist views of the SS-9 as evidence of the CIA's intellectual and moral rectitude. But Ford does not mention that, quantitatively, the CIA still went too far beyond the evidence. Ford's qualitative argument (that the CIA was correct in its estimate that the Soviets would not put MIRVs onto the SS-9) depends on the genealogical distinction between the SS-9 and the SS-18. The Soviets *did* put MIRVs on the SS-9, together with other improvements, that made it the SS-18. CIA said there would be no counterforce threat. In fact, the threat of the "heavy" MIRVed Soviet missile came true on a scope greater than the Nixon Administration, never mind the CIA, had imagined. See Harold Ford, "Estimative Intelligence," pp. 73 and 96–100.

refused to see the quantitative problem, in the 1970s they simply missed the qualitative problem. That is because they focused on old weapons rather than on the will to build new ones with qualitatively different capacities.

Indeed, the NIEs projected that the replacement for the SS-9 would be a single-warhead big missile—a bigger and better SS-9. So all we had to do was limit the number of these big missiles and we would be okay. Wrong. The NIEs also projected that the replacement for the SS-11 would be a "new small ICBM" which would not have silo-killing capability. So all we had to do was to prohibit converting small ICBMs into large ones. Wrong. The NIEs dovetailed perfectly with U.S. strategy at SALT. But not with reality. Instead, the fourth-generation ICBMs wound up being loaded (*in toto*) with more than 6,000 silo-killing warheads.* *Thus the NIEs supported the U.S. in solving a nonexistent problem through arms control, while the real one grew to menacing proportions.* How come? Why?

The intellectual mechanism is evident enough. The estimators simply assumed that the Soviets could not possibly be after the capability to wage nuclear war. Because the NIEs evaluated Soviet forces using indices derived from the U.S. policy of mutual assured destruction, the Soviets' quantitative buildup of single-warhead behemoths just *had to be* driven by mistaken estimates of what it would take to do the MAD job. "Right-thinking" Americans could bring the Soviets to their point of view through calm instruction and generous concessions in the SALT negotiations. Brezhnev's evident desire for a "peace dividend" would take care of the rest. The NIEs of 1972–74 flatly agreed with Henry Kissinger that the Soviets just would not risk the concrete benefits of the network of relationships of *détente* by building a missile force designed for war. Never did the NIEs ask: What could a military commander bent on victory *do* with the 1,400 ICBM launchers that the Soviets were allotted under SALT I? What if the Soviets were to put silo-killing MIRVs on over half of these 1,400 missiles? Why would the Soviets *not* want 6,000-plus counterforce warheads? Such a high number makes perfect sense to someone who wants to allot three to each of the United States' roughly 2,000 missile silos, aircraft parking areas,

---

*It is commonly assumed that the SS-18 is loaded with ten warheads. Electronic data indicates that it carries 14 warhead stations. There is no reason to believe that it cannot carry more. Indeed, the throw weight of an SS-18 is such that it can carry at least 30 warheads. If one designs a postboost vehicle to perform up to 30 release maneuvers, and everything works fine in the labs, operationally testing seven, eight, nine, or ten warhead stations per flight, and rotating the stations tested on each flight, will yield high confidence that all will work as designed. The benefits of limited operational testing permitted by arms-control agreements should be obvious. The U.S. government assumes that the 308 SS-18 missiles (now replaced by the even bigger, more accurate SS-26) carry 3,080 warheads, 350 SS-19s carry 2,100 warheads, and 150 SS-17s carry 600. But reality could be very different.

submarine pens, and command and control sites. But the U.S. analysts proved unable to comprehend such terms, and hence were unable to see the evidence before their eyes.

There is another set of reasons as well. By the 1970s, U.S. intelligence had become overtly politicized—both intelligence professionals and policy-makers had come to regard it principally as a means of bolstering or undercutting arguments for this or that policy. In the specific case of NIE 11-3-8 the CIA, at Henry Kissinger's orders, "withheld" or "embargoed" from the estimators an NSA intercept of a telephone conversation between Leonid Brezhnev and a weapons designer in which the two made sure that the replacement for the SS-11, the new SS-19 missile, would fit within the terms of the SALT I treaty that Brezhnev was negotiating, *and* which made clear that the missile was going to be much bigger than the SS-11, *and* that it would carry multiple warheads.[36]

How much difference would this information have made? Given the analysts' and policy-makers' single-minded commitment to a SALT treaty, the feeling that to stand in the way of the treaty was socially unacceptable and in bad taste, perhaps the information would have made very little difference. Kissinger, Defense Secretary Laird, and the entire administration made clear that they had a policy, and that those who trafficked in intelligence which tended to undercut that policy would be treated like traitors. In addition to that, and surely more significant, it happened that the Kissinger–Nixon policy of détente, of which SALT I was the centerpiece, was very much in accord with what the CIA's dominant mindset *wanted to believe* about nuclear war and the Soviet Union.

And so U.S. intelligence analysts managed to make a national "surprise" out of a 15-year, reasonably well-documented movement of millions of men and machines. These analysts prospered so much that only outsiders—the B-team again—could gainsay them. Nevertheless the bureaucrats maintained their monopoly.

In the upper reaches of the U.S. government, Political Correctness demands opposition to anti-missile defenses. CIA analysts as late as 1989 strongly backed one of the standard arguments against the U.S. building an antimissile defense—that the Soviet Union would and could do *anything and everything* required to overcome it. The Soviets would replace their entire stock of long-range missiles with new, as-yet-undeveloped fast-burn models to cut down their exposure to American defenses. The new Soviet missiles would also be built of yet-undeveloped materials able to withstand as much radiant energy as exists on the surface of the sun.[37] The Soviets would make spinning missiles, warheads complete with three-dimensional sensors and foolproof decoys, and so on, *ad nauseum*. Never mind that the cost of all this, had it been possible, would have dwarfed the cost of the Brezhnevian military buildup. The Soviets would surely do it. How did the CIA know? Just as it knew that the Soviets would do *anything* to win in Vietnam and Afghanistan.

LOOKING INWARD

The disparagement of facts neither began nor ended in the Nixon Administration. Was there ever a time when producers and consumers of intelligence were more concerned with doing something with or to the outside world than they were with intramural play? Those who have experienced the interaction of intelligence and policy after the 1960s have known Washington, DC as a policy-making jungle where, for most, the outside world is only a backboard against which to bounce balls meant to strike other Americans. Day in, day out, few in intelligence or policy-making fear foreign trends adverse to their country more than they fear what their domestic enemies can wreak upon their individual careers, nor do they see national opportunities more appealing than those of personal success.

In December 1979, former Chief of Naval Operations Adm. Elmo Zumwalt gave what may be the most concise account ever of this matter: "I have never had more wheat and less chaff more freely volunteered than in the four or five years since I relinquished my official responsibilities."[38] As an assistant to Secretary of the Navy Paul Nitze in the mid–1960s, Zumwalt first experienced the manipulation of the flow of intelligence designed not to clarify the enemy picture but to shade it for policy-making purposes. In sum he found that, over his career, the higher he had climbed, the more difficult he had found it to receive intelligence keyed to the outside world, and the more he found that people were giving intelligence to him, or withholding it, in order to influence not the outside world, but him in his intramural capacity. The lesson is paradigmatic: The more important the subject, the more intellectual bias and political distortion filters the intelligence on it so that, the greater the policy-maker's responsibility, the less useful the intelligence product he gets is likely to be.

THREATS AND OPPORTUNITIES

Let us now look more specifically at how national-level intelligence has handled threats and opportunities, both in the Third World and *vis-à-vis* the Soviet Union.

Consider Vietnam. None of the Vietnam estimates ever told any president anything like the following: "Having examined the enemy's strengths and weaknesses, we hereby identify his jugular. Cut it here, and you will win. You may or may not want to bear the costs. This is your decision. But we, as experts on the enemy, have identified what it will take." Nor did any estimate say: "Having looked for the enemy's weaknesses, we must tell you there aren't any.

He has all the cards, and has armored himself against any possible move that you might make. What you do is up to you, but as best we can figure, staying will be a lot tougher than leaving." From 1953, when the U.S. began to try to prevent Ho Chi Minh from driving the French from Indochina, until 1975, when the U.S. definitively left the region to the communists, the thrust of the dozens of NIEs on the region was twofold: Possible U.S. clients are too this or too that to be helped, and this or that stratagem won't work. Instead of clarifying the president's options, the estimates helped to foreclose them one by one. Instead of telling presidents what decisive things they *could* do, they dropped hints about what they couldn't do. Thus, less by argument than by bureaucratic influence, the analysts helped drive the policy-makers into half measures that proved disastrous. The fact that the policy-makers were inclined in this direction anyway does not relieve analysts of the responsibility to pose clear alternatives.

Sherman Kent had wanted intelligence to take no account of U.S. policy. Intelligence was to talk about the enemy while refraining from analyzing threats or opportunities to specific policies, and above all without considering alternative ways of winning. But the Vietnam experience showed that policy concerns explicitly shoved out the door implicitly climb back in through the window, and that both intelligence and policy suffer thereby.

In 1953 the CIA told President Eisenhower that if present trends continued, "The French political and military position may deteriorate very rapidly."[39] The implicit thrust of the agency's position (but of course it did not argue this overtly) was that further financial aid to the French was futile. In 1954 things did get worse. Eisenhower's close associates—the Secretary of State, the Secretary of Defense, the Chairman of the Joint Chiefs of Staff—favored using nuclear weapons in support of France, or at least threatening to use them, since this had worked nicely to end China's aggression in Korea. Eisenhower asked the CIA for a report on how such use would be viewed in Asia. The CIA, without discussing any polling techniques, reported that Asia would find it intolerable, and that "The Chinese would take whatever military action they thought required to prevent destruction of the Viet Minh."[40] Of course the CIA's report was based on no knowledge whatsoever.

Again and again throughout the Vietnam War the CIA raised the specter that China, or the Soviet Union, or North Vietnam, would do *anything* to win. *Anything?* In 1954 would the Chinese government, hardly in power, with Stalin just dead and a power struggle atop the Soviet hierarchy, have judged it better to suffer as many nuclear bombs as the U.S. government cared to deliver, without possibility of retaliation, for the sake of solidarity with a vaporized Viet Minh? Perhaps. But the CIA gave no evidence that China had so resolved—nor of course that such a course would avail the Chinese anything. In 1968, after the Soviet invasion of Czechoslovakia, with Soviet divisions arriving on the

Manchurian border and China's primary preoccupation being to avoid a Soviet invasion, would China have done *anything* for North Vietnam? As for the Soviet Union, what might doing "whatever is required" have meant? Would it have meant, as the CIA implied, that the Soviet Union would have risked war to make sure its supply ships reached Haiphong? In 1972, when President Nixon, briefly casting aside CIA's advice, mined the port of Haiphong to keep Soviet supply ships from reaching Vietnam, the Soviet Union did not go beyond a mild diplomatic protest.

Nixon knew that the CIA was wrong, and often cursed it. But he did not attack it intellectually. Perhaps he was too busy with more important things. Be that as it may, the presidents who read the CIA's sloppy reasoning and did not castigate it intellectually did not contribute to CIA's integrity or to the integrity of their own war effort.

In 1954 the CIA identified Ngo Dinh Diem as the sole South Vietnamese nationalist with a chance to pull the country together as an alternative to the Viet Minh. But the agency analysts' understanding of what Diem had to do to be viable was directly contradictory to what Diem himself thought was needed. Essentially the agency, following its analysts, wanted Diem to become a Liberal Democratic Socialist reformer who would redistribute land to friends and enemies alike, be religiously neutral, and allow opposition that he considered disloyal.* William Colby, the CIA's Chief of Station in Saigon, realized how unrealistic and counterproductive these standards were.[41] But the U.S. government listened to the analysts. It fomented a coup that killed Diem and left Vietnam with American puppets as leaders, until the U.S. cut the strings on them in 1975.

As regards the war itself, we have already mentioned the issue of enemy troop strength. The other major intelligence issue concerned the bombing. The CIA argued endlessly that, despite the bombing, North Vietnam would persevere. The hidden message: We might as well stop it. More to the point, the analysts seemed never to have considered reexamining the very complex compromises that had made the bombing policy what it was, and how those compromises might be changed *with a view to winning the war.* Because they themselves implicitly defined good policy as anything that limited U.S. involvement, and deemed any serious threat to the North Vietnamese regime to be *ipso facto* bad policy, they were willing to examine ways of losing, while it seems never to have crossed their minds to look for ways of winning.

Consider the nature of the bombing. By the end of 1971 the U.S. had

---

*Note well that liberals in America, when in charge of government at any level, of university faculties, or of CIA directorates, take care to hire and award contracts to likeminded folk and to exclude others.

dropped 6 million tons of bombs on Indochina, three times the tonnage dropped by the air forces in all theaters of World War II. Some 3 million of these tons were dropped on South Vietnam. Tiny, nonindustrial North Vietnam alone absorbed more bombs than all of Germany and Japan, plus the Normandy beaches and the Ploesti oil fields and Guadalcanal—and *including* the two 20,000-ton-equivalent nukes that scorched Hiroshima and Nagasaki. Why so many bombs were having so little impact on North Vietnam is a genuinely interesting question in the context of intelligence analysis.

The answer must begin with where, how, and why they were dropped. The U.S. government set up elaborate criteria for permitted and forbidden targets. The President himself made the final decision on whether an individual target met the criteria. Ninety percent of all bombs dropped on North Vietnam were devoted to this computerized target list. The other 10 percent were dropped on targets of opportunity by "armed reconnaissance" aircraft. Not surprisingly, most of the damage was done by this smaller category. The places on the target list, which soon became obvious to the North Vietnamese, became bomb sinks, while military trucks parked undisturbed in the shadows of Buddhist pagodas—which the atheist regime had long since turned to profane use. Neither CIA nor DIA addressed the question of the nature of the targeting, confining itself to abstract comments on the "will" of the North Vietnamese.

The analysts were not responsible for the bombing policy; they just failed to raise the right questions about it. But they were partly responsible for the *manner* in which the bombing was administered: gradually, notch by notch. In 1965 the CIA had reported that the North Vietnamese leadership would not be able to tolerate the destruction of the works of socialist construction. Hence it made sense for the U.S. government to raise the level of violence slowly. So the American squadrons would fly in, knock out the antiaircraft sites on their way to the targets, and lose a few pilots, then they would wait as the antiaircraft sites were rebuilt, fly in after some more targets, and lose some more pilots. This notion of what the bombing could achieve made sense only in terms of a view of the North Vietnamese leadership that was wholly divorced from reality. But even as reality proved their political judgments wrong (when the North Vietnamese showed that they had learned to deal effectively with the bombing), the CIA analysts did not return to military common sense. Instead they grasped another image—that of the irrational, fanatical North Vietnamese, utterly fearless, who would stop at nothing.

The best refutation of this image comes from the American prisoners of war, who had an all-too-intimate acquaintance with the North Vietnamese military. They say that the heavier the bombing got, the more the North Vietnamese worried that America might be about to use its power to defeat them. Hence while the U.S. bombed, the Vietnamese were relatively nice to their captives.

However, during the periodic "bombing pauses," when it appeared that America's power would not matter, they gleefully tortured American prisoners. When President Nixon unleashed the "Christmas bombing" of 1972, a campaign very different from the previous ones, which took out whole sections of Hanoi's industrial belt, and marched inward toward Party headquarters, terrified North Vietnamese guards became positively servile to their American prisoners.[42]

The CIA's picture of the irrational North Vietnamese, following the picture of the North Vietnamese who would cringe at the material destruction of the works of socialist construction, was not based on any fact, secret or otherwise. It was not even mirror-imaging. It was fiction that fit a changing rhetorical need.

Now consider the CIA analysts' similar but much simpler performance with regard to Nicaragua in 1982–84. As with regard to Vietnam, they were considering whether the U.S.-backed force could win a war against a communist opponent. As before, the agency's views were important in the intragovernmental debate, in Congress, and in public opinion. After all, it is one thing to back a force that stands a chance of victory, and quite another to throw money, lives, and prestige into a course that will leave one's enemies in place and angrier than ever. As in Vietnam, the CIA's operations people were in the field helping the anticommunists fight, but, also as in Vietnam, the U.S. government had decided to join the fight without the objective of victory and with means that would render victory unlikely. Once again the analysts opposed the U.S. role in the war, and once again the CIA delivered a National Intelligence Estimate that examined the situation in narrow terms and said (correctly, given the limitations of the wrong terms) that the U.S. venture would not work. And of course no sooner was the estimate done than its conclusions appeared in *The Washington Post*.[43] The dominant argument among reporters and in the halls of Congress after news of the NIE appeared was that if even the CIA's own analysts thought it foolish to support the anticommunist Contras, clearly President Reagan's policies must have been based on bad judgment. The NIE certainly lent itself to that argument.

But—just as in the case of Vietnam—the CIA's product was bad analysis. If the analysts judged the Contras, as then constituted (some 15,000 men with rifles, machine guns, and grenades), insufficient to bring down Nicaragua's communist government (with 75,000 troops armed with tanks, helicopters, and artillery), the analysts should have specified what numbers and kinds of weapons would have sufficed. The NIE did not even discuss whether the Nicaraguan government might have an Achilles' heel, and where. When asked why they did not address such questions, analysts replied (Sherman Kent–like) that to have done so would have soiled their hands with policy matters. Yet by writing as they did they had certainly pushed policy in the direction they preferred, and had done so without giving the U.S. government a full picture of the threats and opportunities it faced in Nicaragua.

In 1989 and 1990 the CIA analysts ended their performance with regard to Nicaragua by predicting that the Sandinistas would win the elections scheduled for February 25, 1990 by at least 15 points. Secret CIA data confirmed public opinion polls. Not incidentally, a Sandinista electoral victory would have vindicated the CIA analysts' policy preference that supporting the Contras had never been a good idea. But on February 25, 1990 the Sandinistas *lost* by 15 points. Alas, no "agonizing reappraisal" of CIA's analytical methods followed.

Finally, let us turn to the biggest bundle of threats and opportunities of all, the dègringolade of the communist world beginning in 1989. In less than two years the governments of Eastern Europe, and of the Soviet Union were overthrown. Their societies utterly rejected communism. Environments that had been hermetically sealed became penetrable by journalists, businessmen, and just plain gawkers. One fact was obvious to anyone who looked: For better or worse, the peoples of Eurasia had taken their fates into their own hands. Whose agendas would predominate was anyone's guess. Yet until August 1991, the CIA's analysts (very much in tune with the U.S. government) looked at the entire scene through one assumption—that Mikhail Gorbachev was the key to it all—and with only one U.S. policy in mind: to work with Gorbachev not to dismantle the Warsaw Pact, never mind Soviet power, but to turn them into partners for "global stability." To this they added the assumption (disguised as knowledge) that perhaps the major brake in the revolution was the desire of the peoples of the empire to retain the benefits of socialism even as they rid themselves of its oppressive features. They were wrong on all counts.

Until the East German elections of March 1990 removed all doubt, the U.S. government's collective mind did not see the reunification of Germany as the inevitable consequence of the revolution in East Germany. Why? For the same reason that it did not see that revolution coming: Analysts thoroughly misjudged the people's feelings both toward their government and toward socialism itself. The CIA line on East Germany had not deviated far from East German propaganda: The citizens were proud of their collective accomplishments, and jealous of their social security under socialism. They would gladly take some more freedom, but would never want to be submerged into West German society, which they regarded as inferior in many ways! This indeed was the mindset of the "progressive" (and privileged) classes with whom the U.S. community had contact, and whose progressive social views it shared.

As Lewis Gann has written: "Every truck driver, every cleaning lady knew that the GDR rested on nothing but brute force, that it would disintegrate once there was no army to defend it. Why did not the poets know this, or the novelists, or the historians, or the political scientists?" The answer is that a rosy view of socialism has been a requirement for admission to the best academic company in the West. Thus Sir Ralf Dahrendorf, a preeminent expert on German affairs, wrote that "The GDR is the first modern society on German soil."[44] With U.S. agents in that country controlled by the Stasi, CIA was in no position to challenge conventional wisdom. On this basis it was logical for the U.S. in the winter of 1989–90 to position itself against immediate German reunification. Indeed, on the eve of the March 18, 1990 elections which saw conservative parties overwhelm socialists of every kind, the CIA assured the U.S. government that the socialists would win big.

In 1989 and spring of 1990 the CIA's line on other East European countries was similar, and for similar reasons. On the basis of CIA estimates, which again agreed with those of the State Department (a reform communist should lead Hungary, anyone but Lech Walesa should lead Poland), it was logical for the U.S. government to look at the future in terms of better relations with a socialist Eastern Europe, which would retain its membership in the Warsaw Pact. The future would be a better version of the present. Hence the U.S. government negotiated an arms control agreement guaranteeing a Soviet military presence in Eastern Europe even as new political parties in the region vied with one another to put as much distance as possible between themselves and socialism, and as newly elected governments in the region were demanding that the Soviets withdraw altogether. U.S. intelligence analysis did not *determine* such policy. Rather, both intelligence and policy followed from the same dull preference for the status quo over a new reality filled with promise and peril.

Nowhere is this clearer than in the case of the Soviet Union itself. Gorbachev was indeed the man who, beginning in 1987, encouraged Soviet citizens to speak up about the evils around them, and who, willy-nilly, demobilized the Party. But by 1989, Gorbachev had obviously lost control of the events he had set in motion. By 1990, thousands of newly empowered individuals throughout the Soviet empire, not Gorbachev, became the proper focus of U.S. intelligence attention. Instead, the primary focus of CIA's estimates was: "Will Gorbachev succeed?" The question was ill-conceived.

First, since the U.S. never had independent knowledge of what Gorbachev's objectives were, the question "Will he succeed?" was mere speculation based on hypotheses. The consequent question "How can we help him succeed?" was three times removed from knowledge. Second, since by 1989 the world's press was carrying reasonably good accounts of the objectives, propensities, and capabilities of dozens of newly powerful groups and movements in the Soviet empire, failure to focus analysis on them was an especially egregious choice of the insubstantial and less important over the substantial and more important. As a result the U.S. government's collective mind trailed far behind events.

The list of the topics that CIA analysts did not cover is identical to the list of the most important developments of 1989–90. Why and how did the Soviet Communist party and its "Sword and Shield," the Second Chief, and Fifth, and Sixth Directorates of the KGB, so suddenly lose the internal coherence by which they had killed or imprisoned those who threatened their privileges? How did the KGB Third Directorate's control of the armed forces, which had neutralized them politically for 70 years, break down? Which officers of the armed forces and KGB came to think of themselves as Russians rather than Soviets? How did National Fronts in the non-Russian republics manage to organize themselves so well that they not only shut local Communist parties out of politics, but began to deal with one another as sovereign governments?

So it was that on Aug. 1, 1991, even as a consensus that the Soviet empire must die had spread from its subjects to its uniformed defenders, the President of the United States, fully briefed by U.S. intelligence, stood before the people of Kiev, Ukraine, and, having called his predecessors' anti-Sovietism "bluff and bravado," told his audience that the United States supported the Center and its leader. His only reference to the national aspirations of the Ukrainian people were the words "local despotism."* How well informed was this? Nineteen days later, the Soviet Central government having collapsed of its own weight, President Bush, having received the best U.S. intelligence had to offer, told the world's cameras that the U.S. supported its full restoration, and confused Gorbachev's position at the head of an unelected, universally hated government, with legitimacy. He made the equally great factual error of judging that the KGB–military coup of the previous day had been directed against Gorbachev. In fact, the coup's junta had swept Gorbachev aside on the way to crushing the real threat to the old system: Russia's elected government. Bush, briefed by our best analysts, failed to see that the real dividing line ran not between the junta and Gorbachev, but rather between Gorbachev and all those who wanted the end of the Soviet Union. Moreover, since those who were rallying against the junta were doing so around Boris Yeltsin and the idea of Russia, it was obvious except to official Washington that, should Gorbachev return, he would have no constituency and no power.

As we have mentioned, presidents sometimes have minds of their own. But as regards George Bush's commitment to Gorbachev, one will scan the press in vain for evidence of contemporaneous dissent by CIA analysts. The President's futile attempts to reconstruct the Soviet Union did not end there. The U.S. was the 39th country to recognize the independence of the Baltic states, and in the fall of 1991 was making the existence of a central government in Moscow something of a prerequisite for humanitarian aid.

*This speech may be remembered by the label William Safire gave it: "Chicken Kiev." *The New York Times*, 16 September 1991.

Our point is not that these were silly policies. Even less is it that George Bush was more prone than his predecessors to believe in the current Soviet dictator.* Rather, our point is that Gorbomania and similar phenomena have been based on intellectual misprisions too gross to be called error. It is as if the analysts were in another world, or at least out of the ball park.

Why the Analytical System Won't Do in the 1990s

Time has either resolved or obviated the intellectual controversies of the postwar period. For 40 years analysts defined themselves as moderates or liberals by reference to a system of socialism that no longer haunts the world of the 1990s. Analysts have looked at foreign politicians from Tibet to Timbuktu as moderates or hard-liners, as if they defined themselves by greater or lesser commitment to the U.S. or to the Soviet Union. But most have always defined themselves by belonging to one side or another of quarrels important to them, or simply by personal allegiances. For a generation analysts have extolled (and occasionally analyzed) the benefits of arms control. Yet in the 1990s it appears more clearly than ever that the extent to which a foreign nation's armed forces pose or do not pose a threat depends on that nation's internal character rather than on international commitments. In other words, the issues of the 1990s may be more pleasant to deal with, or they may be more terrible. But they will surely be different from those by which U.S. intelligence analysts have defined themselves.

In January 1982 Robert Gates, then the CIA's newly appointed Deputy Director for Intelligence, crammed the bulk of the agency's senior analysts into its main auditorium and told them in effect to pay less attention to the preoccupations of their offices, their tribal quarrels, and to pay more attention to the real world. He told them to learn languages, and to become substantive experts. But his biggest bombshell was that thenceforth the agency would keep files of what each analyst had written, and that at promotion time senior management would look at how each analyst's record compared with reality. Almost a decade later, Gates claimed that he had made *some* progress in transcending old battles, in gaining expert analysts, and in teaching them (as DCI James Schlessinger used to say) "that they work for the U.S. government and ought to produce useful information." But he gave the distinct impression that he had barely scratched the surface.[45] In 1991, Gates became Director of Central Intelligence (over the strenuous objections of many CIA analysts) and inherited an analytical system badly in need of reform.

---

*Richard Nixon and Jimmy Carter believed that Leonid Brezhnev shared their purposes. Carter even kissed Brezhnev in public in 1979. Gerald Ford, having received the best briefings, told the world in 1975 that Poland was "free."

There is no reason to be complacent even with regard to the simplest of all problems, the Order of Battle. It seems that in 1989 the intelligence community *for the very first time in history* compared its rather solid estimates of Soviet production of major military items—tanks, aircraft, missile launchers, etc.— with its count of these very same items stationed with operational military units, and found that the count of operational weapons was only about half the count of weapons produced. Even after subtracting the weapons that the Soviet Union exported (all rather well catalogued), the analysts were left with a huge discrepancy. Where did the weapons go? Why had the United States not seen them? Why had it not thought to look?

In February and March 1990 there came related shocks. First the newly freed East German government found 24 Soviet SS-23 missiles hidden on its territory,[46] then the newly freed Czech government found 23 SS-23s hidden on *its* territory. Under the INF Treaty the Soviet Union was supposed to have withdrawn *all* such missiles, *and the CIA had certified that the Soviet Union had done so*. But the Soviet Union had not. On September 18, 1991, the U.S. government revealed that CIA officers who examined former East German military documents noticed that the Soviet Union had equipped all these SS-23s with nuclear warheads. During the treaty negotiations the Soviets had claimed that their SS-23s in Europe were not nuclear-equipped, *and the CIA had certified that they were not.* U.S. intelligence rubber-stamped a quantitative and a qualitative deception. This raised a host of uncomfortable questions: Why had the CIA put faith in procedures that had not worked? What else had it missed? What is the nature of the CIA's misestimate of the Soviet armed forces? The analysts had not asked the right questions because they were not interested in the answers. The answers were not comforting. True, the predictability of U.S. technical collection makes hiding easier than finding. But U.S. analysts had not thought to look for nondeployed weapons—in part because, until the verification provisions of the INF, START, and CFE treaties, they had not even considered the problem of "nondeployed weapons" as significant.* The United States thought of war as a spasm in which reserves would play little part, and was reluctant to take into account things it did not see. Also, to have suggested that U.S. collectors could not monitor compliance with arms control agreements

---

*The first two of these treaties, breaking the tradition of the 1972 SALT I treaty, explicitly took account of the total number of missiles produced on either side. That naturally led to the question "Where do they go once they are produced?" The CFE treaty sought to distinguish between Soviet forces in Eastern Europe and similar Soviet forces in the Soviet heartland. This raised the question of counting and keeping track of the entire inventory. When CIA and DIA analysts attempted this in the summer and fall of 1989 they found that their figures did not match up. See Bill Gertz, "US Fails to Count Half of Soviet Arms," *Washington Times*, 5 February, 1990, p. A-5.

would have been the most antisocial of acts for an American analyst. Such failures to ask questions, and such an uncritical adoption of assumptions, reflect the primacy of intramural over external considerations.

With regard to more complex matters, the outlook for performance in the 1990s is grimmer. The world of the 1990s seemed increasingly diverse. Despite superficial signs of a uniform world culture (cassette recorders, jeans, soda pop, burgers, rock groups), Africans are becoming more African, Asians more Asian, Russians more Russian, etc. The often astonishingly good English spoken by young people from Moscow to Mecca—never mind the Indian subcontinent, where it is the *lingua franca*—has led many U.S. analysts to the disastrous conclusion that foreigners can be understood in terms of what they say in English. On the contrary, their English words are *our* symbols, to which *they* do not necessarily attach the same meaning or convictions *we* attach. Listening to foreigners speaking English does not allow analysts half a chance to understand them in their own terms, to see where they are coming from.

It is true that in the mid–1980s there was some revival of language skills among U.S. intelligence analysts. But few if any of the new arrivals are the sort of scholars who dedicate their lives to penetrating a culture. The CIA's best Arabists or China hands are people who may have the capacity to read an Arabic or Chinese newspaper and who follow the fortunes of the Saudi royal family or the Chinese Politburo. But they are not the kind who can feel the pain, shame, pride, or rage in a polite Chinese or Arabic expression, understand a historic or literary allusion—or usually even laugh at a joke. How then can one expect the intelligence community to provide insights into the possible long-term relationship between factions in Cambodia, Angola, Afghanistan, or even Nicaragua, much less Russia? The roots of peace, war, revolution, and allegiance run deep. But our analysts are shallow.

Just as important is the fact that the current analytical system won't do in the 1990s because it will continue to encourage habits of intellectual irresponsibility in the consumers of intelligence. The primary reason why the current system has thrived for 40 years even though policy-makers have regularly expressed disdain for its products is that it has provided them some freedom from responsibility for judgment, something "authoritative" to lean on when making tough decisions, and a likely scapegoat when policy turns sour. Perhaps American policy-makers have not regretted the absence of intelligence analysts who scout out threats and opportunities because they themselves have preferred to let events set their agenda. If American policy-makers want to choose their agenda, they must hire different analysts.

6

Sorcerers' Apprentices

He was more alarmed . . . by the possibility of noisy success than by the prospect of a quiet failure, failing to see that failure itself is the noisiest thing of all.

– Thomas Powers

At its height in the 1950s, covert action took up half the CIA's budget. By 1990 it was taking only about 1 percent. Nevertheless, most books and journalism about the CIA deal chiefly with covert action (CA). In Congress, hearings on penny ante covert action pack hearing rooms, while few members or staff show up to deal with multibillion-dollar satellites. Why does CA draw so much attention? Because arguments about covert action really are arguments about American foreign policy. Controversies over intelligence estimates, or over whether or not to believe a certain defector, excite people because they *indirectly* validate or indict Americans' judgments. But the questions that covert action raises—Whose side are we on in the world? Whom shall we help, whom shall we oppose? How?—are "hot" because they are the flip side of the core *domestic* questions: Who, and whose agenda, shall rule in Washington? Who among us is right, and who is wrong?

Precisely because so many have fought over it, the state of CA at any given time has been a reliable barometer of U.S. intelligence. The CIA had changed substantially between the 1950s and the 1980s. During the intervening years those who wanted to win the Cold War lost out to those who wanted to manage a perpetual competitive–cooperative relationship with the USSR. Those who wished to influence the heart of international problems were replaced by people who defined success in terms of the achievement of operational objectives such as secretly passing money or arms. Nevertheless, through all these changes the CIA has maintained a constant image of itself as the indispensable option "between doing nothing and sending the Marines," and as the most progressive part of the U.S. foreign-policy apparatus.

The standard left-wing and right-wing myths about the CIA are complementary with the CIA's self-understanding and with one another: For evil or for good, American covert action has been perhaps the most important influence in the world since 1945. *Our* view, by contrast, is that American CA has made little difference in the world. There is no evidence that, absent American covert action, the important conflicts of the 1940s and early 1950s, never mind those of subsequent years, would have turned out differently. The most evident consequences of American covert actions have concerned the people, ranging from Lithuanians to Kurds to Meos to Nicaraguans, who have responded to the CIA's call, have exposed themselves to their enemies—and have been decimated. Also, covert action unintentionally fostered the growth of political parties and elites, from Rome to Santiago to New York, who do not wish America well. Within U.S. politics it fostered the substitution of the question "Are you for or against covert action?" for substantive discussion of foreign policy. Indeed, covert action has been more important *within* the U.S. government than in the outside world. Most important, it has been the faithful expression of the mentality of the American foreign policy class—of their values and of their changing standards of workmanship.

The Founding

General William Donovan was *acting* on President Franklin Roosevelt's behalf well before his appointment as Coordinator of Information. In December 1940, Donovan traveled from Iraq to Portugal and all around the Mediterranean picking up information and, wherever he could, bolstering anti-German sentiments. He could not promise anyone that the U.S. would go to war with Hitler, nor could he commit the U.S. to aid anyone. But it so happened that, after meeting with Donovan, Yugoslavia's General Simovic unleashed a long-planned coup against the Regent, Prince Paul, who was negotiating an alliance with Germany. Donovan encouraged the coup, but did not cause it. Neither did he cause Hitler's subsequent invasion of Yugoslavia that delayed the start of Operation BARBAROSSA for a crucial six weeks. But the correlation between Donovan's visit and German troops caught by winter at the gates of Moscow helped fuel enthusiasm for a postwar American covert-action service.

So did the wartime bravery of OSS Special Operations people (SO). Together with their British counterparts, SO delivered supplies to anti-German forces throughout Europe, coordinated them with advancing Allied forces, and arranged escape networks for downed Allied pilots. Thus, as U.S. forces landed in French North Africa, American agents armed some friendly native groups there. But Special Operations did not make the difference between a friendly and a hostile reception in French North Africa. That was made by diplomacy, and above all by the fact that the U.S. was fighting France's ancestral enemy. Special Operations surely helped the French resistance hamper German movements during the Normandy landings. But a case can be made that the help that OSS gave to anti-German partisans in Europe caused more trouble for the U.S. in the long run than it was worth in the short run. That is because the OSS's arms distributions did not discriminate against the communists, and because the communists used American arms to stake claims to political power in the postwar world. In 1948, the CIA had to fight these very communists.

At the end of World War II, General Donovan could not convince the U.S. government to maintain a peacetime agency for spying—much less one for Special Operations. The reigning orthodoxy at the time had it that a new world order of U.S.–Soviet cooperation had dawned. What use would there be for psychological operations and commandos? When OSS was disbanded, SO was transferred to the War Department.

Saving Western Europe
During 1946 and 1947 conventional wisdom shifted: Now the Soviet Union was trying to take over the world, and fast. Since Europe was prostrate and America was rich, just about every European with an American connection was asking for American money, and anticommunism became a potent calling card. Transnational organizations, like labor unions and churches, got money from their American counterparts. Well before the U.S. government had formulated policies to stop communism, individuals were trying to do the job by giving money to likeminded Europeans. Secretary of the Navy James Forrestal privately collected money for French trade unionists. By June 1947, the U.S. government's strategy was set: Secretary of State Marshall outlined a plan to channel billions of dollars into Europe through people and institutions that were reliably anticommunist. It was a political as well as a military plan, and it began to have an effect the moment it was announced. By the summer of 1947, all sectors of Western European opinion *including, albeit reluctantly, the powerful French*

and Italian Communist parties, had accepted the Marshall Plan.* So, until the fall of 1947 there was no talk within the U.S. government of using Special Operations to save Europe from communism.

In October, however, the French and Italian Communist parties declared political war on the Marshall Plan. Washington pushed the panic button, especially over the prospect that a Communist–Socialist coalition might win the Italian elections of April 1948. Conventional wisdom became dogma. Labor leaders and left-of-center European politicians included the warning that their countries might "go communist" in their pleas for aid. On November 14, 1947, President Truman signed NSC Directive 1, and followed it up with numbers 2 and 3 in February and March of 1948. These documents threw the entire weight of the United States against the Italian Communists. That included the newly established Central Intelligence Agency. Declaration after declaration told the Italian people that U.S. aid would stop if the Communists were elected. Meanwhile, the flow of American food to Italy increased. So did the flow of military hardware to the Italian armed forces. The U.S. government also organized a letter-writing campaign from Italian–Americans to their relatives in the old country. On top of all this, the fledgling CIA flooded Italy's noncommunist parties with money for campaign activities and for "organizational support." A lot of people suddenly became wealthy, and dispensers of wealth. To Giuseppe Saragat, a Socialist leader who disliked his party's tight alliance with the Communists, the CIA provided the money and incentive to start the Social Democratic Party. Against the advice of James Angleton, its foremost expert on Italy, the CIA even gave money to left-wing Socialists in hopes of weaning them from the Communists. On April 18, 1948, the Italian people gave the Communist–Socialist coalition just 34 percent of the vote, while the Christian Democratic Party got 48 percent and a majority of the seats in parliament. Washington rejoiced and took credit for having saved Italy. The CIA used the Italian campaign as its badge of usefulness, and as a model for future activities.

Today we have a better perspective. Until September, 1947 the Italian Communist Party (PCI) had tried to shade its revolutionary, pro-Soviet, anti-American image because it knew that it ensured electoral defeat. It also

---

*Both Parties had already been forced out of their governments' cabinets. They had grumbled, but accepted the expulsions because the alternative was to start civil wars that would surely have destroyed them. Now they accepted the Marshall Plan for similar reasons. Although the Plan was clearly aimed at cutting down their influence, they knew that most of their countrymen looked on it as economic salvation. In the summer of 1947 the Communist parties judged that it would be best not to stand in their peoples' way.

judged that its own armed units would stand no chance of reversing the verdict of the electorate against the Italian armed forces. That is why the PCI preferred a strategy of alliances. The PCI brought this judgment to the founding meeting of the Cominform at Sklarska Poreba, Poland, on September 30, 1947. Jacques Duclos brought an identical one for the French Communist Party. There, Stalin's man, Andrei Zhdanov, harshly vetoed the French and Italians' plans and ordered them to lead the "masses" in a violent antibourgeois and anti-American campaign.* Zhdanov gave no plans by which the French and Italians could win, and they themselves developed none. As befitted Stalin's good soldiers, they asked no questions. They saluted, and led a campaign of strikes, riots, and electoral confrontation that *they knew* was suicidal. The Communists knew that the very word "America" had become the equivalent of "good" in Italy, and had no illusions about how the Italian people would react when they painted the elections as a choice between "Washington and Moscow."[1]

How did Washington, then, come to the judgment that the Italian people might "go communist"? American officials accepted the judgment of the noncommunist leftist Italian politicians with whom they sympathized. These, once having been somewhat sympathetic to communism, may well have projected their own uncertainties onto the masses. By contrast, conservative Italian politicians—e.g., Mario Scelba—did not have such uncertainty or such fears. Why did Washington choose to channel so much of its involvement covertly? Again the explanation lies in a special relationship with the non-communist left. All noncommunist parties wanted American money. But while conservative politicians were eager to be publicly identified with the U.S., leftist ones wanted their American connections to be under the table.

In the end, no one argues that without U.S. covert action the Communists would have won, although some[2] argue that the margin would have been smaller. This author's view is that the margin of the Communists' defeat was determined by the frontal nature of the Communists' assault.

Over the 25 years during which it ran, the "Italy covert action" did have some undeniable effects. It financed and "made" some of Italy's most prominent politicians, among them Giulio Andreotti (who first handled the American financing as Prime Minister de Gasperi's private secretary) and Amintore

---

*We can only deduce what Stalin thought he was accomplishing by using his French and Italian troops as political cannon fodder. While nobody in the Cominform ever hinted at plans for conquering Western Europe, the concrete plans for completing the conquest of Poland, Hungary, etc. were the order of the day. Stalin seemed to consider that conquest as anything but a foregone conclusion. Thus the combination of loud, purposeless action in the West with quiet, purposeful action in the East suggests that Stalin was causing turmoil in Western Europe to tie down the Americans' attention there—to give them a bellyful of victories in sham battles while Stalin was winning uncontested the only battles he was interested in fighting.

Fanfani—men of historic personal corruption. Later, it also made happen the pet scheme of the Italian noncommunist left that we will discuss below.

The results of the Italian election made covert action very popular in Washington, and spawned imitations. Anyone over age 50 at the CIA knows by heart the story of how the French dock workers, organized by the communist trade union confederation CGT, were threatening not to unload ships bringing Marshall Plan aid to France. Had they succeeded, so goes the story, the Marshall plan would have failed and Europe would have gone communist. The French government is supposed to have been too frightened of the communists to take control of its own docks. Had the government tried to clear the docks, there would have been civil war. Instead, the CIA gave money to the AFL's Irving Brown, who passed it to French friends who organized the free labor confederation, Force Ouvriere, plus squads of countertoughs under the scarfaced organizer–poet Pierre Ferri-Pisani, who made clear to the communist labor bosses that if they tried strongarm tactics on the docks, they themselves would have their *"gueules cassées."*

To accept the CIA's version of how Western Europe was saved from immediate danger one has to accept that the French government, the French Army, and Charles de Gaulle would have rolled over and played dead, or would have been overrun by the communist mobs, and yet that these mobs were artfully disarmed by the CIA's judicious distribution of cash and encouragement. The French government and disinterested Western observers were of a different opinion.[3] By the same version of history, as we will describe below, covert action helped nail down Europe's long-term democratic future by building up noncommunist leftist politicians and cultural figures.

Delusion in the East

Saving Western Europe was fun—meetings with toney progressive politicians and intellectuals in excellent restaurants, and the positive reinforcements of success. Quiet (and not so quiet) defectors from the local Communist parties confirmed the obvious: Western European communism was retreating into a political ghetto. There was credit aplenty to be claimed, and there were careers to be made. The CIA put as much effort into Eastern Europe. But this was dirty, ultimately heartbreaking work with hard-line displaced persons, in the face of repeated defeats. And it showed some of the flaws that would undermine all subsequent American covert action.

The root of the problem—more fundamental than communist security, Kim Philby's treason, and the CIA's amateurishness—was that covert action was an uncoordinated facet of a policy that the U.S. government could not bring itself to think through. The U.S. government was acting out President Roosevelt's inherently ambiguous commitment at the Yalta conference of February 1945.

On the one hand the U.S. was content to let the Soviet Union enjoy predominant "influence" in Eastern Europe. On the other hand, the U.S. government felt that Yalta justified the self-determination of Eastern Europe's peoples. The Cold War too was ambiguous. Whereas the U.S. government wanted peace, it believed that Stalin was poised for aggression, that war was likely, and that even if it were not, the U.S. ought to prepare to defeat the Soviet Union. Underlying all this were divisions in American politics. "Progressives" wanted to get along with the Soviet Union at the cost of accepting its conquests, but conservatives wanted to "roll back" communism. The compromise doctrine of the U.S. government, "containment," was open to both interpretations. In this context, the U.S. tried and failed to extrapolate the Special Operations of World War II.

Consider the most technically successful of these operations. Between 1948 and 1952 the CIA air-dropped trained Ukrainians with radios, gold, weapons, and ammunition to join anti-Soviet Ukrainian nationalist fighters in the Carpathian Mountains. These men were reliable, and they joined a movement that was probably more secure (if only because it was under more military pressure) than the French partisans to whom the OSS had sent similar things. The Ukrainians held out for four years—as long as the French partisans had, and under far tougher circumstances. In the end the resistance was confined to mountain caves, but continued to transmit until it was wiped out to the last man. Whereas in France, as time passed, regular U.S. forces had brought more and more pressure to bear on the National Socialist occupiers, and the partisans' ability to maneuver and recruit grew, time brought to the Ukraine a Soviet army less and less constrained by external events.

Other operations were technically flawed. Albania's security services would have known about the CIA's training and landing of guerrillas in Albania beginning in 1949 without the help of Kim Philby because the CIA recruited guerrillas among Albanian expatriates without CI checks on the recruits. Thus the guerrilla bands were so thoroughly infiltrated that the Albanian services had specific information about who would land where. The Albanian services' lack of subtlety—they met and arrested, or killed, or scattered every landing party— should have alerted the CIA's Frank Lindsay and his deputy John Bross that something was deeply wrong. But they dragged on the operation for four years, at the cost of dozens of lives.

No one who has talked with the CIA veterans of these missions can fail to note that, like spymaster Harry Rositzke (See Chapter 3), they were detached from the fate of the men they sent in harm's way. A rare written account of these Ivy-league handlers rings true: They did not have it in them to have "a last shot of booze with a couple of rock-faced ethnic types before they got into their black jump suits for a flight into eternity."[5] These religious, unglamorous people were not the kind one might have met at dinner at John Bross' stone mansion overlooking the Potomac—not real people.

Operational shortcomings were not, however, the worst fault of the operations. We have already noted that the CIA's covert-action contact in Poland, a creation of the Polish security service, named WiN, embarrassed CIA and cost the lives of a few Polish émigrés. Suppose, however, that WiN had been for real. How would the CIA have handled a movement that actually was challenging the Soviet Union's control of an East European country? Alas, experience suggests that if the CIA had faced that choice the result would have been hundreds—perhaps thousands—of dead, betrayed Poles.

The proof came in Berlin in 1953 and Budapest in 1956. There is no truth to the charge that the CIA's radios (Radio Liberty and Radio Free Europe, as well as the Voice of America) had been inciting the peoples of Eastern Europe to riot by promising American help. However, that incitement and perhaps that promise were implicit in perhaps every public word from the mouths of American officials after 1947: America believed that freedom in the world is indivisible, and that its own freedom depended on undoing the unjust, illegal Soviet occupation of Eastern Europe. The radios reflected the U.S. government's public position. But the U.S. government had two other positions, not so well advertised: the latent Rooseveltian view that the U.S. ought to cooperate with the Soviet government; and the doctrine of "containment," according to which the U.S. would deal with the Soviet empire primarily by letting it stew in its own juices. What would the U.S. do when those "juices" finally ate through the communist pot? In 1953 and 1956 the CIA, like the rest of the government, resolved its internal differences over that question in a way that meant death for anticommunists. In 1992, long after the peoples of the East had broken the Soviet empire, the U.S. government was still nursing wishes for good relations with that empire.

In 1953, workers in Berlin's Soviet zone were pushed into revolt by raises in their work quotas, and pulled by hope that the death of Stalin might have weakened the Soviets' will to repression. The CIA's Berlin station chief, an idealistic German immigrant named Heinrich Hecksher, wanted to arm the rioters. He asked for permission from headquarters. The request arrived in Washington on a weekend, and got no higher than John Bross, the deputy chief of the Soviet–East European Division, who turned it down. Hecksher reportedly wept as the Soviets, having realized that the West would not support the workers, crushed them with tanks. CIA Director Allen Dulles learned of Bross' decision later and was reported unhappy about it. The U.S. government, the CIA included, had decided by high-level indecision. In 1956 the U.S. government (President Eisenhower, on the advice of Secretary of State John Foster Dulles) officially decided not to help the Hungarian people during the month it took for Soviet tanks to crush their rebellion. The CIA's Frank Wisner, who had rushed to the Austro–Hungarian border to coordinate the help he so much wanted to give to the Hungarians, was so struck by the sight of battered refugees that he suffered a nervous breakdown from which he never really recovered. Others at CIA greeted this event, which ended covert action against the Soviet empire, with a sigh of relief. At least the CIA had not *caused* these disasters, and it could now concentrate on more pleasant things.

The Golden Age

Like water, bureaucracies flow in the direction of least resistance. Since the free world of the early 1950s eagerly welcomed American influence, it provided the Golden Age of American covert action. By 1952, after bitter struggles with the State Department for exclusive control of covert action,* the CIA had 2,800 officers in 47 countries, and a budget of $82 million per year assigned to covert action. What did all these resources accomplish? The CIA made new governments in the Philippines, Iran, and Guatemala. In addition, the Chief of the Directorate of Plans felt that from his office he could "play" world public opinion like a "mighty Wurlitzer [organ]." As we shall see, however, the CIA's political influence was due not to expertise in its trade but to the United States' overall prominence in the world. The effortless making and unmaking of governments did not go beyond 1954, while the successful support of foreign politicians and propaganda lasted only until the mid-1960s.

In August 1953 Mohammed Mossadegh, Prime Minister of Iran, resigned in what amounted to a *coup d'état* by the (then) young Shah of Iran, Mohammed Reza Pahlavi. The CIA's Kermit Roosevelt got the National Security Medal for engineering the affair. The reason was straightforward: Mossadegh, an old man whose political convictions loomed small next to his quirky penchant for tweaking Westerners, had nationalized the Anglo–Iranian Oil Company. A month-long round of negotiations during which Mossadegh had toyed with Averell Harriman while lying on his bed led the U.S. government to the conclusion that Mossadegh was irrational and ripe for exploitation by the communists.[5] The Shah, King in name only, had every incentive to lay claim to

---

*The histories and memoirs of the CIA from the period 1948–1952, as well as conversations with "old boys," show a preoccupation with this struggle—including a famous incident in Bangkok in which officers from the CIA's OSO exchanged shots with officers from the OPC, an agency controlled by the State Department but administered by the CIA—so intense that one wonders how much energy the people involved had left for the outside world. On the shooting incident see the Church Committee's Final Report, Vol. IV, p. 37. Note that one of the sorest points in the controversy between OSO and OPC was a widespread disparity in salaries. This was as intramural a fight as there is. Also see Lyman Kirkpatrick, *The U.S. Intelligence Community: Foreign Policy and Domestic Activities.*

the power of his throne, and had been looking for ways to rally support against Mossadegh. The CIA helped him to rally that support by distributing a lot of money to a lot of Iranian generals and a few politicians.[6] *But—and this is crucial—the money was important chiefly as a sign that the U.S. government (and the British) truly backed the Shah, truly wanted Mossadegh out, and would stop at nothing to get their way.*

The Iranians who got the money were safe enough to join the most powerful country in the world. There was nothing clandestine about the operation. The budding coup was the talk of Teheran for weeks, and Mossadegh tried to rally support. Indeed the coup's success depended entirely on the people involved knowing that mighty America was committed to it. *If the CIA had hired, say, Swiss bankers to pass around the money anonymously, the operation would have failed.* The operation's success was not due to the skill with which it was carried out, much less to the keeping of secrets. Rather it was due to the presentation of a resolute (or what appeared to be a resolute) U.S. policy, and the reputation for success that the U.S. openly enjoyed in Iran. What, then, was the point of the pretense?

During the spring of 1954 the CIA overthrew the Guatemalan government of Col. Jacobo Arbenz in an operation that, although very different, also succeeded because it showed (rather than hid) the United States' hand. Arbenz was a "progressive" soldier who hated the U.S., had expropriated lands belonging to the United Fruit Company, and legalized the Communist party. In an earlier age the U.S. Marines would have deposed him outright. But in 1954 the CIA armed a rival Colonel named Castillo Armas and several hundred men in Honduras. The little force's preparations were advertised and magnified by a rebel radio run by the CIA, which prominently featured anti-Arbenz statements by top U.S. officials. Thus every Guatemalan was told that the U.S. wanted Arbenz out, that Castillo Armas was fronting for something much bigger, and that when all was said and done, Arbenz would surely be out. On June 18 the rebel army crossed the border. But the fighting consisted chiefly of a few old World War II P-47 and B-26 aircraft that dropped leaflets and made noise over Guatemala City. Meanwhile, CIA agents in various parts of Guatemala radioed each other (on Guatemalan Army frequencies, to be sure of being heard) as if they were commanders of rebel units converging on the capital. On June 27 a panicked Arbenz resigned and, soon thereafter, fled. Had he stuck to his guns he probably would have won. He lost because he let himself be stampeded by the image of an unstoppable United States.

In retrospect, this approach to overthrowing a government *lowered* the United States' prestige. Potential targets—certainly Fidel Castro—learned that perhaps the U.S. was unwilling to send the Marines, and that if they just did not panic and defeat themselves, they could defeat the phantom "rebels" and the U.S.

would not actually intervene. In other words, the Guatemala operation is the sort of thing that works only once. Finally, especially since the Eisenhower Administration took credit for the event, witness *Time* magazine (July 26) and *The Saturday Evening Post* (November 6),[7] one has to ask "What *was* the point of the pretense?" It is difficult to avoid the conclusion that these were old-school-tie boys playing games made possible by an extraordinarily favorable situation.

Now consider the CIA's triumph in the Philippines. In 1952 the country that the U.S. had liberated in 1945 was troubled by the communist Hukbalahap insurgency and, even more, by lack of good leadership. The U.S. government—the State Department and the CIA working closely together—found a good leader, installed him in the presidency, and gave him lots of help in defeating the Huks. The American hero was Edward Lansdale, perhaps the CIA's quintessential CA man, the subject for Graham Green's *The Quiet American*. Lansdale showed good judgment in picking Ramon Magsaysay as the candidate to back in the Philippine presidential elections.[8] But no one made any effort to conceal the fact that Magsaysay was America's man. Nor should they have. In the Philippines of the 1950s, the image of America was that of heaven itself, and pictures of General MacArthur adorned humble homes next to crucifixes. Just about every politician was trying to show himself as the man who would bring the best relations with the U.S. So both Lansdale and the U.S. Ambassador campaigned with Magsaysay. They remained his close advisers and financiers until his premature death in 1957. This was a success by any standard. But the only reason to attribute any covertness to it is that it was run by the CIA—which is to think backward about such matters. In sum, and as described in *The Quiet American*, the covert actioneers of the Golden Age bestrode the Third World as the dispensers of health, wealth, and wisdom about any and all topics.

In Washington, covert action was acquiring the reputation of a magic bullet, an art form that offered inexpensive solutions to difficult situations. The covert actioneers received daily confirmations of their significance through clippings of the articles that agents inserted in the world's press. Through the "mighty Wurlitzer" of its propaganda network the center presumed to "play" world public opinion like an instrument. And indeed, every time the center gave an order some stories *did* show throughout the world. But this did not mean that there was such a thing as world public opinion or that CIA had changed it. The bulk of the covert actioneers acted as couriers between headquarters, which provided the stories, and agents who would merely make money by publishing them. Seldom would the agent and his case officer tailor the story to local needs. Usually headquarters would strike a theme (or "note") and simply translate it into the world's languages. The idea was to serve U.S. foreign policy in general rather than to take sides in the myriad of the world's parochial concerns. But of course since people everywhere are interested in their own parochial concerns, American propaganda was often incomprehensible.

Another reason for the irrelevance of America's opinion-molding is that the people at headquarters were speaking to the concerns of liberal intellectuals like themselves. At CIA, just as at the State Department, "world opinion" meant the editorials of London's *The Times*, Bombay's *Times of India*, *Le Monde* of Paris, and perhaps Tokyo's *Asahi Shimbun*. It was the opinion of the "noncommunist left"—politicians, academics, musicians, literati: the sort of people one might find on the lecture circuit of American universities. Now, it is entirely normal for people who have not traveled and who also are not trying to influence foreign nations to notice chiefly those foreigners who speak one's own language, think in one's own terms, and fit one's image of what they should be. But here were the would-be manipulators of the world speaking gibberish to most of the world's peoples.

While words from Washington did little good *and* little harm, the *money* that the CIA gave to the noncommunist left, both in the U.S. and abroad, produced "successes" with unfortunate consequences.

Two examples will suffice: Italy and Chile. In Italy, after the Christian Democrats (DC) won a majority of the seats in the 1948 elections, the CIA put its money and advice behind two causes: making sure that the DC would not govern alone, but rather in conjunction with the Social Democrats; and strengthening the hand of the left wing inside the DC. The idea was that the Social Democrats would work with the left DCs to move the entire government closer to the positions of the left-wing Socialists, who would then see their way clear to abandoning their alliance with the Communists. On the level of policy this meant a fuzzing of the differences that had been the basis for the Italian people's decision at the polls in 1948. On the organizational level it meant feeding the patronage machines of Fanfani, Saragat, lesser "moderate" godfathers, and even of the left-wing Socialists. This policy continued even though the elections of 1953 and 1958 produced decreases in the strength of the coalition and the steady rise of the Communists–Socialists.* Nevertheless, between 1958 and 1963, the CIA financed its Italian clients in an effort (fraught with some violence, and threats of more) to force the majority in the DC to accept the left-wing Socialists as coalition partners—the "opening to the left." The expectation was that upon entering the government the left-wing Socialists would detach themselves from the Communists. For reasons explained elsewhere (Chapter 4), they did not. Instead, they joined up with some DC leftists

---

*By the time the CIA had finished administering its anticommunist medicine, the Communists were receiving nearly 34 percent of the vote (what they and the Socialists had received together in 1948) all by themselves.

and a growing band of intimidated DC centrists, demanding the entry of the Communist party into the governing coalition. They also wanted to purge Fascists (i.e., anticommunists) from the ranks of the other parties in the governing coalition. If the purpose of the covert action had been to save Italy from communism, the action had to be judged counterproductive. By the time CIA covert involvement in Italian politics ended in 1974, Italy was in turmoil. Anticommunist politicians and authors were being shot on the streets in a kind of "open season." Edgardo Sogno, the former chief of the Liberal party's anti-Fascist partisans, was jailed on charges of mounting a Fascist plot; and the Communist party was becoming an unofficial member of the government.[9] Between 1978 and 1982 however Italy saved itself without the CIA's help.

In Chile a somewhat similar tale had a harsher ending. In the 1950s, when the CIA began funneling money into the country, there was no danger of a Socialist–Communist takeover. Nevertheless, the dogma that the noncommunist left (and the farther left the better) was the surest barrier to communism led the CIA to build up the Christian Democrats, and especially their left wing. The CIA's aid did not stop the growth of the Socialists and Communists. However, it did slowly reduce the influence of the Conservative party among noncommunist voters, and it moved the Christian Democratic Party to the left. In 1965, a year after the CIA's main triumph (the 1964 election of Christian Democrat Eduardo Frei as President),[10] this author attended a conference of Christian Democratic parties at the University of Notre Dame at which the Chilean delegation wrestled inconclusively with the questions "How do we distinguish our ends from those of communism?" and "Why should we try?" In sum, the CIA not only had split the anticommunist camp, but also had undermined part of it.

By the election of 1970, Chile's Christian Democratic party was in the hands of Radomiro Tomic, who may have been as eager for cooperation with the Communists as was his Socialist opponent, Salvador Allende. While Tomic's campaign decreased the DC's credibility as an antisocialist force, it did not entirely erase its capacity to split the anticommunist vote. By this time the CIA had realized that Tomic's DCs were just too hostile to America to be supported. But, in part as a result of the State Department's intervention, the U.S. government just could not bring itself to support the Conservative candidate, Jorge Alessandri. So the CIA tried to beat Allende literally with nobody, paying for some meaningless anti-Allende propaganda. Allende won 36 percent of the vote, Alessandri 34 percent, and Tomic, the residual beneficiary of so much CIA covert action, 27 percent. There having been no winner by majority, the Chilean congress decided the election. The Christian Democrats showed how perceptive the CIA had been in fostering their careers by siding with Allende, despite a last-minute CIA effort to dissuade them. The result of Allende's election was a period of chaos and privation for Chile, leading up to an army coup in 1973, followed by repression. Not until 1990 did Chile recover from the CIA's successes of the 1950s and 1960s.

How could bright people make such misjudgments? By unreflectively following the CIA's American Liberal culture. Sometimes even Liberals (e.g., William Colby's advocacy of South Vietnam's Ngo Dihn Diem) would back a non-leftist leader somewhere in the world because he was the most capable anticommunist on the spot. But even in such cases, other liberals would argue that the foreign leader either must be made into a liberal, or must be cut off. Some of the leading covert actioneers have been eloquent witness to this in writing and in person. *Facing Reality,* by a former chief of the Covert Action staff, Cord Meyer, describes the stars of the liberal firmament not as guides of the mind to be followed when right and discarded when wrong, but as *family.* The theologian Reinhold Niebuhr even presided at one of Meyer's weddings. In Meyer's mind non-liberals hardly exist. The same goes for the well-known article "I'm Glad the CIA Is Immoral,"[11] by Meyer's predecessor, Tom Braden. Their disdain for American conservatives is not cerebral but visceral, the kind that Brahmins have for lower castes. Not dispassionate judgment about foreigners, but rather domestic class consciousness drove the CIA's political action during the Golden Age.

The relative secrecy in which they worked made it possible for CIA covert actioneers to run an undercurrent of foreign policy that the liberal Americans for Democratic Action (ADA) characterized as "positive advances over the declared foreign policy of the United States."* A common saying at CIA in those days was "We are the real revolutionaries." Thus for example in the Algeria of the 1950s the CIA befriended the National Liberation Front (FLN) that was fighting to drive out the United States' ally, France. What the CIA did in Algeria did not help the FLN much, but it told a lot about where the CIA's heart lay. In 1961 the CIA secretly arranged a trip to the U.S. for medical treatment for Frantz Fanon, the Algerian rebel and author of *The Wretched of the Earth.* The Third World cult of which Fanon is perhaps the principal guru does not often

---

*Quoted in Cord Meyer, *Facing Reality,* p. 90. One particularly embarrassing instance of the CIA's "progressive" foreign policy was the hasty visit in 1956 of a CIA official in Cairo to General Nasser, who was about to receive a special envoy of the State Department (George Allen) with a stiffly worded reproach of Nasser's purchase of arms from communist Czechoslovakia. The CIA man told Nasser to disregard the note "because we [CIA] shall be able to remove its effect." This action at cross purposes is all the more poignant because the Secretary of State, John Foster Dulles, was the brother of the DCI, Allen Dulles. But Nasser appropriately ridiculed the whole U.S. government by making the incident public. *Washington Post,* 24 September 1956. CIA "old boys" claim that the purpose of the visit was to soften the blow, not to undercut the State Department. But the subtlety was lost on Nasser.

reflect on the fact that he died in the arms of the CIA.* The agency was proud of its support for decolonization everywhere, even though it would soon find itself at odds with the tyrannies it spawned—including Algeria's.

The most prominent instance, in terms of money spent and emotional capital invested, in which the CIA "got out ahead" of overt government policy was the funding of "international organizations"—namely (and with the exception of labor unions) groups of writers, artists, professors, and students, in the United States and around the world. The program supported magazines, conferences, and (above all) people. Needless to say, the people who got the money were very much like the people who gave it: noncommunist leftists. The rationale for the program was that after the war the communists had set up popular front organizations in the various intellectual fields and were dominating international conferences in those fields. These fronts bothered the kinds of people who had been caught up in them, and those who looked upon people like Norman Mailer as authority figures. Intellectuals who were totally *outside* the communist orbit dismissed the fronts for what they were, and the general public took no notice. In other words, it was not self-evident that the U.S. government had an interest in paying some leftist intellectuals to quarrel with others of their kind. Nevertheless, in 1950 the CIA began to give money to people to fight within the fronts and to set up counterfronts.

The chief instrument was the Congress for Cultural Freedom (CCF).[12] Its chief organizer, administrator, and conduit for CIA money was Michael Josselson, a former Army officer who had worked on de-Nazification. The CCF, headquartered in Paris, financed cultural warriors organized in national committees around the world. It sought to "make an impact" for freedom and against communism through declarations, articles, conferences, and what not. There was even a European tour by the Boston symphony, organized by Nicholas Nabokov (cousin of Vladimir), during which the musicians performed Nabokov's symphony.† The event in the congress' life that most reveals its character was the running battle between headquarters (and Josselson) and the American committee. The Americans objected to the stream of anti-American accusations coming out of the congress' activities (basically equating the U.S.

---

*See Peter Geismar, *Fanon*. The CIA was not alone in the quiet support of "progressives." In *The Game of Nations*, State Department officer Miles Copeland describes how he and like-minded friends "found" and fostered a young Egyptian officer named Gamal Abdul Nasser—to the point that John Foster Dulles referred to Nasser as "your Colonel." In *The Fourth Floor*, former U.S. Ambassador to Cuba Earl E. T. Smith similarly describes the help that both State and CIA idealists gave to a young man named Fidel Castro, who, they thought, was a soulmate.
†This performance, at U.S. taxpayer expense, may have been the only one the work ever got. What it did for human freedom is unfathomable.

with Nazi Germany.) Meanwhile, Josselson was pressuring the Americans to move farther and farther leftward, to accept and engage in more anti-Americanism. Josselson believed that the more anti-American the congress sounded the more credible its anticommunism would be. But to whom? And at what price? At one point Josselson, the CIA man, pressured the American committee to join in denouncing the death sentence of Ethel and Julius Rosenberg. Whom would that have accredited and discredited? The Americans finally left the CCF in 1957. The most typical of the CCF's activities, however, was not any nation's accreditation but the financing, and the feeding of individuals in excellent restaurants.* Whether the general public was uplifted by the CCF's activities no one can say. But surely hundreds of liberal intellectuals had their careers, bank accounts, and gastronomies uplifted at taxpayer expense.

The story of the CIA's funding of the National Students Association (NSA) has been told many times since it appeared in *Ramparts* in March 1967. The following account of this author's experience with the NSA—surely a worm's-eye view—points to the heart of the matter.

In 1963–64, as a junior at Rutgers University, I took part in a referendum campaign to withdraw from the NSA because I did not like its politics. We won. The following year, the NSA brought paid organizers to Rutgers, spent more money than seemed possible for a student organization, and reversed the result. In 1965, I was the token pro–U.S. person invited to speak about the Vietnam War at the national convention of the NSA in Madison, Wisconsin. There I rubbed shoulders with people my age who talked easily about all the places in the world where they had been or were about to go—places like Lagos, Djakarta, Santiago, and Paris. Since for me and my friends a phone call to Philadelphia was a memorable expense, I marveled: *Some*body was giving these people *un*believable amounts of money. As I moved about, I noticed that the NSA and the New Left Students for a Democratic Society, and the emerging black racist groups, were practically indistinguishable. At my panel on the Vietnam War, the only subject of interest to anybody (but me) was how to help North Vietnam defeat the United States. My thoughts turned to the money so abundantly coursing through the veins of this organization: Some enemy of the United States must be doing this. The CIA ought to look into it! A year and a half later, in *Ramparts*, I found out that the CIA had known about the NSA's funding all too well.

Despite the fact that the NSA and the Congress for Cultural Freedom had taken to opposing not just a policy of the United States, but to hating the United States itself and everything it stood for, those in charge at CIA sincerely regretted having to stop funding the organizations. The CIA's covert actioneers hated

*Arnold Beichman, an original participant in the American committee, recalls that the first topic of discussion in any meeting were the restaurants at the next meeting site.

255

losing members of their class with whom they sincerely sympathized and whose loss entailed a diminution of their own self-respect. Never again would CIA covert actioneers so believe in their work. After 1967, CIA covert action ceased to be an inner-directed driving force. It also ceased to be militantly liberal. In the 1970s it became half-hearted, technical, cynical. But that is getting ahead of our story.

1960s Failures

For the CIA's top-of-the-line covert action the 1960s started two years early, in Indonesia. In the fall of 1956 the Dulles brothers, flush with easy success, decided to "teach a lesson" to that country's neutralist dictator, Sukarno, by mounting an army rebellion against him on the island of Sumatra.[13] The objectives of the operation were never clear. The Dulles brothers did not want to overthrow Sukarno. They did not mount the operation to defeat him, nor even to incapacitate him. They wanted to cause him enough trouble so that he would have to come to the U.S. Ambassador, hat in hand, and ask for relief, which would surely be granted *if* Sukarno would stop fostering the growth of the Communist party, reverse his entente with communist China, and stop being so anti-American. Presumably, if he refused, *then* the U.S. would think about a serious move against him. But U.S. policymakers—and the CIA—apparently never asked why Sukarno should have heeded a bluff that the U.S. government had advertised as such. Since the government had not made the case to the American public that Sukarno was an enemy, and hence could take no public action, covert action carried substantial risks for the U.S. President. What would the American people think of a President with a secret agenda? But U.S. policy-makers did not think things through.

So, in 1957 the U.S. recruited the rebels, who were happy to be part of something they thought was fully backed by the U.S. The CIA sent arms, as well as paramilitary experts to run the rebels' command and communications. Other CIA officers flew the "rebel air force" consisting of old B-26s. In February 1958 the rebels declared Sumatra independent. But Sukarno's far superior armed forces moved in without nonsense. Then in May a CIA pilot was shot down after accidentally bombing a church. Now Sukarno had it in his power to embarrass the U.S. government before the American people. The Dulles brothers instantly pulled the rug out from under the rebels, whose leaders, together with their CIA handlers, had to sneak to the coast to be rescued by the U.S. Navy. The U.S. government ate humble pie before Sukarno for years thereafter. The CIA's revenge, filming Sukarno's kinky sex life, was insignificant in comparison with the U.S. denial of landing rights to Dutch aircraft when the Netherlands tried to stop Sukarno from seizing western New Guinea. This was a prototype for subsequent operations whose participants would not be so lucky.

In 1960 the Eisenhower Administration recognized that its backing of Fidel Castro's takeover of Cuba had been a mistake, and set about reversing it. The plan, an invasion by a CIA-organized army of Cuban exiles, was not entirely a bluff of the kind that had toppled Arbenz, and it was certainly more purposeful than the failed Indonesian operation. For one thing, by 1960 the U.S. government had already publicly identified Castro as an enemy. Nor did the plan rely primarily—as some have charged—on the expectation that the Cuban people would rise up and overthrow Castro upon hearing of the invasion. Nevertheless, in the most important sense, this was the weakest plan yet: Although the U.S. government was not able to hide its sponsorship of the rebel army (stories and interviews on the preparations had appeared in *Life* magazine), it was unwilling to tell the world, as it had in Guatemala in 1954, that at the end of the affair its enemy would be out. Never did the U.S. seriously consider recognizing the rebels as the legitimate government of Cuba. Also, the plan had no way of forcing the "end game." The military plan was not wholly without integrity, and did stand a chance of "success," namely of establishing 1,400 rebel soldiers inside Cuba. What would happen *after* operational success? The U.S. government never considered that. Nor did it address the questions "Why should Castro and his 200,000-man army panic after the rebels' 'success'?" and "Why should the Cuban people risk their lives in revolt if the U.S. government thinks it best to play Hamlet?"

Upon taking power in 1961, the Kennedy Administration neither canceled the plan nor acted to increase its chances of success. Instead, it repeatedly cut into its already marginal military integrity. First it moved the landing site away from a populated area (where popular sentiment might have been engaged directly) to the remote mangrove swamps of the Bay of Pigs. Then it reduced the number of air strikes that the "rebel air force" (old B-26s flying from Central America) could make on Castro's airfields from 45 to 16 to 8. Why? The principal mover behind these changes, UN Ambassador Adlai Stevenson (who had been and continued to be involved in CA in Italy) had a soft spot in his heart for Castro, and a softer one for the Third Worlders at the UN who would oppose the operation. His argument, which President Kennedy accepted, was that these moves were necessary to reduce the operation's visibility. And indeed they did. But, as Kennedy found out too late, they also guaranteed the survival of parts of the Cuban air force, which used the natural advantage of proximity to the battle* to quickly establish air superiority over the trap into which the exiles

---

*The number of aircraft on either side is less important than the number in the battle at any given time. Flying from Central America, the rebel air force *totaled* only about one and a half airplane-hours per day in the battle. Flying from minutes away, the Cuban planes were always there. That is why destroying them had been the key to the plan.

had landed. The United States' failure at the Bay of Pigs became one of the most visible—and most embarrassing—events of the time.

Why did the CIA go along with a foredoomed plan? In part because the man running it, Richard Bissell, hoped that once it was underway the President would not dare let it fail. And why did Arthur Schlesinger push upon the President conditions that guaranteed failure? Apparently in the hope that Kennedy would cancel the plan. *Both sides seem to have looked upon the operation primarily as a lever on U.S. policy-making rather than as something with a life of its own.* As for Kennedy, like other presidents he was willing enough to compromise between those who wanted to do something right and those who did not want to do it at all, by deciding to do it but not to do it right. The operation's nominal covertness may have eased the decision by holding out the hope that any failure would be quiet. Nothing was farther from the truth.

The report of the CIA's Inspector-General, Lyman Kirkpatrick, on the Bay of Pigs took everyone involved to task for having failed to ask elementary questions about the relationship of ends and means. But the agency's reaction made clear that it had learned the wrong lessons. Allen Dulles, who was about to be replaced, felt that the President had let the agency down, even though no one at the CIA had fulfilled the first duty of a staffer toward the boss: Warn him when he is about to blunder, and offer your resignation. The senior ranks too retreated behind hurt feelings. According to one account, John Bross rallied them behind the proposition that, despite the failure, "Kirkpatrick might have been more *understanding.*"[14] In other words, gentlemen should not be given grades below "C." At CIA, class ties outweight competence as well as security.

After Indonesia and the Bay of Pigs, covert actioneers lost much of the self-confidence of the Golden Age. They scaled down the projects they proposed while presidents, as well as Secretaries of State and Defense in turn, became more skeptical of covert action. Yet the most fundamental characteristic of covert action did not change: Neither presidents nor anyone else took responsibility for integrating into the rest of U.S. policy those projects that were approved, to make sure that the entire complex of actions pursuant to policy actually paid off. On the contrary, the 1960s saw a further decentralization of foreign policy-making. More than ever each agency, and parts of agencies as well, had its own foreign policy. Soon committees and *sub*committees of the Congress, and finally individual legislators, joined in. Foreign policy came to mean the geometric resultant of actions that various parts of the U.S. government took for their own reasons. This resultant could only be determined retrospectively. Thus, for presidents and Congress, covert action became one element of a complex equivocation—not a policy tool but a policy hedge.[15]

The primary purpose of secrecy (initially, keeping information from the

258

foreign governments against which operations were being run) became keeping it from Americans in or out of government who might object to the policy implications of the activity. The main thing that covertness concealed was failure to make clear-cut, success-oriented decisions on policy. For the CIA itself, each covert action became a self-contained "job," the success of which was measured in terms of tasks performed rather than results achieved. For the rest of the government, covert action became strictly the CIA's business. Nowhere was this clash of purposes clearer than in the quintessential struggle of the 1960s, Vietnam.

The Vietnam Debacle

Like other agencies, the CIA brought to Vietnam discordant ideas and programs. Each was implemented largely on its own terms, although sometimes they clashed. A faithful account must be arranged by kinds of programs. But of course the programs overlapped.

The first program might be described as close support, or intelligence support, for a client at the head of an underdeveloped country. Thus when William Colby transferred from Rome to Saigon in 1958, his job was to build a guiding relationship with Ngo Dinh Nhu, chief of South Vietnamese intelligence and brother of President Ngo Dinh Diem. Colby, and many others at the CIA, judged that the Ngo brothers were leaders of their country in their own right, and that no one else on the scene would be as effective at holding the country together. Hence they worked to give Diem what he needed to strengthen his own political base while fighting the communists. The second program was "nation building." Arrogant as it might sound in the 1990s, the American academic and government establishment of the 1960s thought it knew how to build nations. Students of political science studied "scientific" tomes on the subject,[16] and the man who served as National Security Adviser to President Johnson actually wrote one.[17] Their common formula combined political freedom, the breakdown of "traditional structures," nationalism, economic *dirigisme*, "land reform," and U.S. foreign aid for "infrastructure." Before such revolutions, neither communism nor any other bad "ism" would stand a chance. The Liberal "nation builders" did not like Diem because his priority was not "nation building" but rather building his regime by rewarding friends and despoiling enemies.

The period 1958–63 saw a continuous quarrel between the partisans of these two approaches within the U.S. government. Colby, first as the CIA Chief of Station in Saigon and later as the chief of the East Asia Division, tried to keep some balance between the two. But the nation builders won out, and the CIA station was instructed to arrange the *coup d'état* that killed the Ngo brothers. Ho

Chi Minh called the coup a "gift from heaven,"[18] and launched a full-scale war. Deprived of self-rooted leadership, South Vietnam became a playing field for American programs, overt and covert.

Later, under the pressure of war, the U.S. government urged Diem's successors to do what it had overthrown Diem for doing—run programs that might well be characterized as "land and arms to friends, death to enemies." Part of this was the PHOENIX program: All available intelligence would be focused on identifying Vietcong officials in the villages, who would then be "turned," captured, or killed. PHOENIX killed some 25,000 people. Because of mistakes and abuses, the real number of cadres killed is surely much lower. Thousands of cadres died in the Tet offensive of 1968. Nevertheless, after about 1970 the Vietcong were never again a force in South Vietnam, and William Colby was able to take an unescorted holiday trip across the Mekong Delta. PHOENIX was strongly attacked as immoral within the CIA, as well as outside.

Interestingly enough, programs that resulted in the death of friends were *not* labeled as immoral. In 1967–68 the CIA infiltrated five-man teams into North Vietnam to harass the enemy's rear. When President Johnson ordered a halt to the bombing of North Vietnam in October 1968, the CIA stopped flying supply missions for the teams. At least 45 men were left to die. The CIA had trained thousands of Montagnard tribesmen in the highlands of South Vietnam. They too were left to die. Many more allies died in Laos: There the CIA had begun arming H'mong tribesmen in 1962 to help them protect themselves against the communist Pathet Lao. Under the leadership of Ted Shackley, and with an initial investment of only a dozen CIA paramilitary supply specialists, the H'mong tribesmen—some 250,000 overall—eventually fielded an army of over 30,000 men, ably commanded by Gen. Vang Pao. They held the northwest corner of Indochina and tied down substantial North Vietnamese forces. But in 1975 the U.S. cut off their supplies, and the North Vietnamese virtually annihilated the tribes, using even Soviet toxin weapons against them. Only some 10,000 survived.[19] The CIA suffered no pangs of conscience about causing the death of friends.

Just about all of the CIA's actions in Vietnam were well-known to the enemy. What purpose, then, was served by keeping them secret within the U.S. government and from the American people? The general answer is that neither the CIA nor the rest of the U.S. government was willing to decide what they were doing in Vietnam, and why. Hence they were unwilling to defend it before one another and the American people. In short, secrecy was an attempt to evade both intellectual and political responsibility. Let us see specifically why.

The United States' support of clients in Laos was the consequence of yet another failed attempt to work out "spheres of influence" with the Soviet Union. Bargaining over Laos had begun in the mid–1950s, and the U.S. thought several times that it had an agreement for the neutralization of Laos under a "troika" government led by Prince Souvanna Phouma. But, time after time, the Soviets violated the agreement, and by April 1961 the communist Pathet Lao, beneficiaries of a thousand-plane Soviet airlift,[20] nearly ruled the country. The U.S. government could have accepted that. Or it could have told the world—but, above all, the American people—what it was going to do to reverse the situation, and where the effort would end. It could then have used Shackley's program, or the U.S. Army's.[21] But the U.S. government was afraid to admit that it had been had in Laos, and also was afraid both to confront the Soviet Union and to confront internal opponents of confronting the Soviet Union. However, the U.S. government was *also* afraid of letting the Soviets have Laos. So Shackley's operation, which could have been an object of pride, was treated as something to be ashamed of. Just how counterproductive this was can be seen in the conduct of Sen. Stuart Symington (D-MO), who not only had praised Shackley's program when he was briefed on it, but who actually had stayed at Shackley's house in Vientiane, Laos. In 1972 Symington expressed "shock" at learning about the "secret war".*

As regards PHOENIX, the U.S. government never confronted the questions "Why are we killing *anybody* in Vietnam? Whom should we be killing in order to secure the independence of South Vietnam most quickly and with the least expenditure of lives?" Had it done that, it would have had to conclude that the most justifiable and cost-effective targets were the highest-ranking people with the most responsibility among the enemy. In that case, the U.S. government would not have trumpeted "body counts" of peasant fighters but would have gone after Ho Chi Minh and his Politburo. However, the U.S. government's objective always was to make a deal with Ho, not to kill or defeat him. So why kill anybody? Political confusion is the reason why PHOENIX was covert.

Moral confusion is the reason behind the failure of the CIA's highly publicized "assassination plots." None ever killed anyone. The most famous, Operation MONGOOSE,† directed against Fidel Castro, stands well for the others. The CIA talked with gangster Sam Giancana, and (separately) experimented with exploding cigars, exotic poisons, and the like. But no one was ever sent to kill. The reason is that while two presidents broadly hinted that they wanted an assassination, neither ordered it, and while any number of CIA

---

*Thomas Powers, *The Man Who Kept the Secrets*, pp. 178–79. One is reminded of the actor Claude Rains in the movie *Casablanca*, who receives the proceeds of a casino even as he proclaims that he is "shocked, shocked" at its existence. Similarly, in April 1984 Sen. Daniel P. Moynihan (D-NY) denounced the CIA's mining of Nicaraguan harbors *and* the fact that it had been kept secret from him, about a week after he had been briefed on it and had raised no objection. This author was present at the briefing, a few feet from Mr. Moynihan.

†Mongooses kill snakes.

officials talked around the subject, none would stand in front of another, take responsibility for doing the job, and explain why. And so the plot, like others, spilled only ink.

The final covert action with regard to Vietnam was perhaps the most revealing: Beginning in 1969, Henry Kissinger held a series of negotiations with the North Vietnamese in Paris. The U.S. government went to great pains, including an emergency loan of French President Georges Pompidou's aircraft, Henry Kissinger wearing disguises, and staying at the apartment of the U.S. defense attaché, all to keep secret the fact that negotiations were taking place. Why the secrecy? Because during those years the Nixon Administration was trying to give the American people the impression that it was committed to prevailing in Vietnam, even as it was negotiating a pullout behind the American people's backs.

Thus we see that in Vietnam covert action was much less a matter of secret operations and trickery to undermine the enemy's position than it was a means for keeping the American public and the rank-and-file of the U.S. government "on board" for a voyage whose reasons, and destination, top leaders refused to think about rigorously. As regards allies, covert action recruited cannon fodder for unserious campaigns.

The Cruel 1970s

Covert policy usually is policy to which insufficient thought has been given. Moreover, a policy that requires a democratic government to hide its ends from its people almost always results in a breach between that government and its people. Hence covert policy is usually counterproductive both at home and abroad. But by the 1970s the U.S. government had developed a veritable phobia against discussing the ends and means of foreign policy. For such a government, covert action had the fatal attraction of a cop-out.

In 1975, as Southeast Asian allies both overt and covert had their fingers smashed off the skids of rescue helicopters with rifle butts, or were herded into death camps, or were sprayed with toxins, the U.S. was sending another set of covertly recruited allies to their deaths: the Kurds of Iraq. An ancient people of the mountains south of the eastern Black Sea, today's Kurds are divided by the borders of Turkey, the former Soviet Georgia, Iran, and Iraq. In 1972 the Shah of Iran asked Henry Kissinger to cause trouble for Iraq. That country's Ba'athist dictator, Hassan al Bakr (and the power behind him, Saddam Hussein) had given the exiled Shi'ite Ayatollah Khomeini a base from which to destabilize Iran, and was claiming Iranian territory. The Shah feared that Iraq was using Khomeini to help prepare a war to annex Iran's oil fields to Iraq's Shi'ite Southern provinces. (Ironically, Iraq made that attempt nine years later, when Khomeini was already in power in Teheran.) The Shah wanted him to stop. Kissinger gave the job to the CIA, which settled on giving arms and encouragement to Iraq's always restive Kurds, now led by the able Mustafa Barzani. A Kurdish rebellion in the north would take Baghdad's attention off the southeast.

Here is how the House Select Committee on Intelligence Activities described this covert action: "The President, Dr. Kissinger, and the foreign heads of state hoped that our clients would not prevail. They preferred instead that the insurgents simply continue a level of hostilities sufficient to sap the resources of our ally's neighboring country. *This policy was not imparted to our clients, who were encouraged to continue fighting*" (emphasis added).[22] The CIA spent $16 million to play this card.

Then in 1975 the Shah and the United States snapped at the offer by Iraq to trade the renunciation of territorial claims and the expulsion of Khomeini for the cessation of help to the Kurds. Iraq instantly launched a murderous offensive against the Kurdish people. They were shot, starved, and gassed. The Barzani clan was broken. An activity such as that against Iraq (or perhaps against the Kurds) in 1972–75 could only have been carried out covertly—that is to say, in the absence of discussion. Any airing of the consequences would have drawn objections on grounds both moral (What good could possibly counterbalance such deadly betrayal?) and practical (Who will deal with us after this? Will moving Khomeini to Paris do the Shah any good? Why pay to remove from Iraq a Khomeini who was at least as dangerous to the Iraqi empire as to the Shah?)

When the subject of the Kurds comes up, CIA officials jut the jaw and cite the need for harsh measures to survive in a cruel world. But this retail Machiavellism masks wholesale naîveté. Acts of betrayal that are part of a purposeful pattern of success differ from those which the improvident commit willy-nilly. The former do not engender the massive, deadly rejection and contempt which this sort of covert action has brought on the United States.

The United States' policy in Angola is another example of the use of covert action in a vain attempt to avoid responsibility both for action and for inaction. In 1974 Congress had passed the Hughes–Ryan amendment to the Foreign Assistance Act of 1961. This required the President to report any "special activity," i.e., covert action, "in a timely fashion" to the committees on Intelligence, Foreign Relations, Armed Services, and Appropriations of both the House and Senate, and that he certify "finding" each activity to be "important to the national security of the United States." Hughes–Ryan literally prohibited nothing. However, it challenged the President to put his prestige behind any covert activity. To a President so inclined, Hughes–Ryan would have been a welcome invitation to frame issues and force his congressional detractors to vote on them. But Hughes–Ryan had an intimidating effect on timid presidents, and up and down the bureaucracy as well, because it made policy-makers accountable. So, when in 1980 the Congress passed a law dramatically reducing the

263

reporting requirements of Hughes–Ryan but retaining the key requirements for formal sign-offs, it made little difference. By and large the Hughes–Ryan system for allowing covert action—consisting less of regulations than of a play on attitudes—is in force today. This system got its test-drive in Angola.

When a group of young Portuguese officers infiltrated by communists took over the Portuguese government in April 1974, they quickly granted independence to their African colonies. Before these officers managed to purge the communists from their midst 18 months later, these communists—in conjunction with the Soviet Union and Cuba—had well-nigh managed to put their African clients into power in Angola and Mozambique. By the end of 1974 the communist MPLA* had received the bulk of Portuguese army stocks and was in a dominant position in the capital city, Luanda.

On January 22, 1975 President Ford approved a secret finding that it was important to the U.S. to right the balance in the struggle for power in Angola, and that therefore $300,000 should be given to Holden Roberto, a sometime client of the CIA since the 1960s. The money was not to be spent on arms. Then what was it for? Some suggested that it was meant to send "a signal" about U.S. involvement. If so, then that signal signaled the opposite of resolve.[23] Meanwhile, the Soviets were sending significant shipments of weapons to the MPLA and the Cubans were sending hundreds of advisers. On July 9, 1975, MPLA forces drove those belonging to Roberto and to Jonas Savimbi, leader of UNITA,† out of Luanda. Immediately thereafter, President Ford signed a new "finding," directing the CIA to support Savimbi and Roberto with $32 million worth of arms, food, and other supplies. But in August, Cuba and the Soviet Union coordinated, respectively, the arrival of 15,000 Cuban soldiers accompanied by modern equipment. This proved decisive. By December 1975, when the Congress passed an amendment by Sen. Dick Clark (D-IA) prohibiting expenditure of covert funds in Angola, and the President signed it, the battle was already over in Angola.

The U.S. covert aid obviously was too little and too late to compete with an overt, muscular Cuban–Soviet invasion, on top of the advantages that the MPLA already enjoyed. But that is not our point. Rather, it is to ask what President Ford (or anyone else) could possibly have thought he was accomplishing by sending covert aid, and why he signed the Clark amendment.

The options, as the U.S. government saw them, were to "make a big deal out of Angola," to do nothing, or to engage in covert action. Making a big deal meant asking the Soviet Union to stop what it was doing, or the U.S. would

*Popular Movement for the Liberation of Angola.
†National Union for the Total Independence of Angola.

abrogate the SALT I treaties, suspend grain sales, and curtail trade. If this did not stop the Soviets, then the U.S. could have recognized Savimbi and Roberto as the provisional government of Angola, and shipped them arms directly. There was justification enough for this. The SALT I treaties, grain sales, and trade were part of a package that also called for cooperation in the world. Obviously Soviet actions in Angola were the opposite of cooperation. But to do any of this the President would have had to explain why his *détente* with the Soviet Union had been a mistake, and to outline a different approach to U.S.–Soviet relations. The President was not willing to do that. Neither was he willing to do nothing and let Angola "go down the drain." That would have given bad signals to the United States' friends in the region, principally Zairean President Mobutu. Note well: There were no practical reasons why any U.S. aid to anti-Soviet forces in Angola should have been any more covert than the aid that the Soviets and Cubans were sending to their clients. The advantages of covert as opposed to overt action were presumed to lie not in Africa but in Washington. And what advantages were these? *Vis-à-vis* whom? The President wanted to spare himself the trouble of explaining a difficult choice to the public. So, unwilling to pay the price for successful intervention, and unwilling to pay the price for no intervention at all, the President choose to intervene *pro forma* without giving serious thought to the prospects for success. He did not realize that this would be the most expensive course of all. Part of the price was to make policy-making in Washington more irresponsible than ever.

Senators Clark, Cranston (D-CA), and Tunney (D-CA) offered their amendment to prohibit U.S. *covert* action in Angola—nothing else. They had the luxury of fighting for the outcome they wished (victory by the communist MPLA) without ever having to take responsibility for advocating it. Indeed, they could claim credibly that their amendment had nothing to do with the substance of the struggle in Angola. Their amendment did not even "tie the President's hands." If the President truly felt that America's interests were at stake, he could always come to Congress with a regular request for funds. Senators Clark *et al.* argued that they were only trying to spare the American people another commitment, like Vietnam, the terms of which were not well thought out. In fact, however, Clark, Cranston, and Tunney were making substantive policy by betting that the President would not rise to their challenge, would not explain the issues to the American people, and would not force votes on them. President Ford played into their hands. He refused to force a substantive showdown, and instead forced a vote on whether he should have the prerogative to make commitments the extent of which he could not discuss publicly. The Congress voted (really rather sensibly) against covert policy-making.

The sequel to this affair took place in 1985. In the intervening decade, CIA officials and conservatives in the executive branch blamed the Congress for the United States' decline in the world, and cited the Clark amendment as one of the principal manacles on the President. Also during those years Jonas Savimbi became so popular in Washington that a majority of both houses was ready to vote aid to him. In 1985, liberal Rep. Claude Pepper (D-FL) introduced a bill to repeal the Clark amendment. The Reagan administration's State Department worked quietly against the repeal. After the repeal, an event occurred which shed more light on covert action than anything before or since. Secretary of State George Shultz wrote a confidential letter to House Republican leader Robert Michel, asking him to use his "influence to discourage" legislation by Reps. Pepper and Jack Kemp (R-NY) to provide overt aid to Savimbi.[24] Michel refused, Shultz's letter was leaked, and an embarrassed Secretary of State* rushed to tell the Congress that the CIA would provide Savimbi $50 million a year, in covert aid. Why the resistance to repealing Clark? Because the Administration was no more eager in 1986 than a decade earlier to explain, above all to itself, what it expected to accomplish. If, in 1986, there had been a full-scale debate on the question "What do you think you are accomplishing by sending Savimbi $50 million?" the Administration would have been stuck for an answer.

FARCES IN THE 1980S

During the 1940s, covert action had been an adjunct to policy in Western Europe and a half-hearted policy in the East. During the 1950s it had been a "magic bullet" as well as the secret, "progressive" vanguard of policy. In the 1960s it became one of many tools thrown helter-skelter at a given problem. In the 1970s it was a substitute for policy. By the 1980s major covert action had become the explicit denial of policy. Let us look first at the cases of Nicaragua and Afghanistan. These were public issues from the very first. Putting them into the category of covert action hid nothing at all from any enemy of the U.S. It only impeded the formulation of policy and warped the public debate.

Consider the "findings" under which the U.S. aided the Nicaraguan resistance to the Sandinistas.[25] Within weeks of the Sandinistas' 1979 takeover of Managua, President Carter's Director of Central Intelligence presented to the Congress a "finding" that the U.S. could not abide a totalitarian regime allied with Moscow in Central America, and authorized support to democratic

---

*Rep. Claude Pepper, a Democrat, wrote Shultz a "shocked" letter (October 25, 1985) comparing Shultz's confidential actions with his President's public words, and former UN Ambassador Jeanne Kirkpatrick wrote a column in *The Washington Post* that boiled down to the word "shame!" (October 26, 1985).

elements in that country. The Carter finding spelled out the purpose: to "change the emerging totalitarian nature" of the regime.[26] This, while not an explicit authorization to arm the Nicaraguan resistance, provided for covert funds to the Contras (as the Sandinistas had already labeled all their opponents, some of whom were already buying and using guns). The intention to change the regime was clear to the members of the Congressional committees that heard the Carter finding. Many members asked whether the Administration was serious about its intention, and a few asked about the connection between the diagnosis of the ill and the prescription for the cure, but literally none chose to stand in the way. For the subsequent two years, as the Contra rebellion gathered steam and became more and more military, U.S. covert funds continued to flow to them under the Carter finding, unchallenged in Congress.

In the fall of 1981 the Reagan Administration submitted its first finding on Nicaragua. It was even more eloquent than the Carter Administration's had been in its description of the dangers of a communist beachhead on the North American continent. The Reagan finding called for specifically authorizing covert support of the Contras' paramilitary actions against the Sandinistas.[27] But why? To accomplish what? Here, the Reagan Administration was even more vague than its predecessor. It talked about weakening the Sandinistas' capacity to spread revolution, and about promoting democracy. The Administration hid its indecision behind the label "covert action," even though all the facts of the matter were very public.

The perception of possible lack of unity and resolve within the Administration led to the first Congressional attacks. These were mere probes at first. In December 1982, Sen. Ted Kennedy and Rep. Tom Harkin offered amendments to the pending Defense Appropriations Bill for fiscal year 1983. These amendments would have prohibited the CIA from using any allocated funds "for the purpose of assisting [any] group or individual in carrying out military activities in or against Nicaragua."[28] These amendments were voted down overwhelmingly.

Nevertheless, despite lack of serious pressure, the Administration worked out a deal with Rep. Edward Boland (D-Mass), Chairman of the House Permanent Select Committee on Intelligence, to support an amendment prohibiting CIA from spending "for *the purpose of overthrowing* the government of Nicaragua" [emphasis added]. Thus a precarious line was drawn between assisting a group of insurgents, which was allowed, and actually working toward the overthrow of the government, which was prohibited. The Administration's strategists knew that its intelligence finding did not explicitly envisage overthrowing, and saw the Boland amendment as a clever way of getting (albeit backhanded) Congressional endorsement of its program. Instead, the Boland amendment set off a massive campaign in the Congress and the press to show that the Administration was violating "the intent of the law" by supporting Nicaraguans *whose intent* was to overthrow the Sandinistas.*

So throughout 1983 and 1984 the Administration strove mightily by word and deed to prove that it was not trying to overthrow the Sandinistas and that its aid was designed to be insufficient for that purpose. Statements to this effect by CIA Director William Casey were broadcast again and again by Radio Managua, to the consternation of the Sandanistas' enemies. And indeed the U.S. government pointed out that it still recognized the Sandinista regime as the legitimate government of Nicaragua. But then what was the U.S. doing? Congressman Dave McCurdy (D-OK), reasonably objected that it was unreasonable to do one's enemies only *a little* harm. The Administration tried to find other rationales for the program, inventing the objective of "interdicting supplies to El Salvador" out of whole cloth. Meanwhile, DCI Casey, and his chief of Latin America operations, Duane Claridge, believed that as the momentum among the Sandinista resistance elements mounted, a tide would sweep the Sandinistas from power. But they would hardly whisper their thoughts, except among friends. This ingenuity succeeded only, in the bitter words of Undersecretary of Defense Fred Iklé, in the Administration's policy being "ratcheted down." In each succeeding year, new versions of the Boland amendment got tighter and tighter, and the Administration's public arguments became weaker and less self-confident.

So far down did President Reagan go that in June 1984 he decided not to contest in the Congress the latest, most restrictive version of the Boland amendment (which now took the formula of the original Kennedy–Harkin amendment and denied CIA funds to Contras). He decided not make Nicaragua an issue in the 1984 election. But, having decided to give up trying to win, he did not want to pay the price of losing. He decided to continue to finance the Contras, but to get the money not from the U.S. Treasury, but from foreign governments and private individuals. *While signing into law the appropriations bill containing a revised Boland amendment prohibiting any U.S. government funds for "supporting, directly or indirectly, military or paramilitary operations in Nicaragua by any nation, group, organization, movement or individual," the chief executive of the U.S. government decided to*

---

*As the Congressional report notes: "The Administration took a more constricted view: As long as the United States itself was not seeking to overthrow the Sandinista government, the objectives of the Contras to replace the Nicaraguan government were irrelevant." U.S. Congress, *Iran–Contra Report*, p. 396. *The Washington Post*'s cartoonist, Herblock, effectively mocked the strategy by showing CIA director William Casey with a paper bag over his head giving bags of money to men with guns boarding a plane for Nicaragua.

use his position to provide such funds. * This was not a covert decision. "Everyone" in Washington knew about it. Throughout 1985, liberals in Congress gnashed their teeth at the "private" Contra supply operation run out of the White House—but did not attack it in public.

Then, briefly, in early 1986 the President posed the issue somewhat as follows: "There is a war in Nicaragua. I am requesting $100 million for those who fight for freedom. By your vote you will show whose side you are on." Congressional opponents decried his "divisive" tactics, but voted for the money in droves. The Nicaraguan operation had long since ceased to be covert. But the Administration still refused to discuss its objectives. Soon, however, the "covert" aspects of the operation returned in force to wreck it.

In the fall of 1986, agents of Iranian factions in Lebanon made public dealings between the White House and Iran to exchange American arms for U.S. citizens held in Lebanon, funds from which dealings were flowing to the Contras. Thus the controversial program of Contra aid was mixed in the public mind with the universally unpopular Iranian regime. Only then did many of those who opposed aid to the Contras feel politically safe enough to accuse President Reagan and his team of having violated the law. Hence the vehicle for the Iran–Contra scandal of 1986 to 1990 was not the substantive issue of who should win the Nicaraguan civil war. Rather, it was the "safe" (for the opponents) procedural issue of whether the President had lawfully or unlawfully circumvented part of a bill he had signed. The fuel for the scandal—the American people's distaste for Iran—had absolutely nothing to do with the Congressional "fact-finding" hearings, the purpose of which was to discredit any and all anti-Sandinista efforts. This Byzantine way of doing business was the fruit of covert action, 1980s style.

The President, for his part, chose to fight on the weakest ground. Only after the Iran–Contra affair became public did the Administration assert that Congress lacked the authority to restrict the President's options in Nicaragua. The *Congressional Report* correctly reads: "At no time prior to the public disclosure of alleged violations of the Boland Amendments did the Administration come forward to challenge their constitutionality. On the contrary, Congress and the American people were routinely being assured that the statues were being observed, "in letter and in spirit."[29] But the Administration preferred to thrash in this tangled web of its own weaving rather than to connect the ends and means of policy. Hence the Contra aid program died. However, it was not widespread knowledge that killed it. The program was destroyed by the

---

*U.S. Congress, *Iran–Contra Report*, p. 41. The legality of obtaining third-party funds for U.S. policy in Nicaragua was also doubtful, and James Baker even expressed the opinion that solicitation and control of third-country funding for the Contra program was an "impeachable offense." *Ibid.*, p. 403.

publicizing of the contradictions between the several "tracks" that the President was following, and by the fact that, when faced with the need to reconcile those contradictions in an unfavorable atmosphere, the President did not demand an up-and-down vote. He agreed to be defeated.

The history of covert support to the Contras shows that the decline of covert action in the U.S. government is due neither to an excess of information in the public domain (leaks) nor to any fault in technique. It is due to a lack of capacity on the part of presidents to formulate policies and to force opponents to oppose them on the merits. Presidents have themselves chosen covert action as half-measures when they have been unwilling to force the issue.

In the case of Afghanistan, presidents used covert action to run away from an issue, even though it enjoyed near-unanimous support from the American people and Congress. The Soviet invasion of Afghanistan had barely begun when, in January 1980, Sen. Birch Bayh (D-IN) told a television audience that the Carter Administration had directed the CIA to supply arms to the Afghan resistance, the Mujahedeen. The American people's—and the Congress'—support for the Afghan resistance was broad and solid from the beginning. It never wavered. Nor was there ever any doubt in anyone's mind about where the Mujahedeen's support was coming from, or that it was getting there through Pakistan. The most justifiable use for covertness is to protect an operation against the enemy. Much less justifiable is to hide an operation from one's own people. But three administrations of both parties kept aid to the Afghans in the category of covert action for the worst purpose of all: to put off having to make critical choices about policy. In pursuit of this lofty goal the U.S. government raised the cost of the operation, lied to the Congress and the American people, sacrificed lives in the field, and left Afghanistan in the hands of Soviet surrogates even after the Soviet Union itself collapsed.

When the CIA, in consultation with the State Department, began to send arms to the resistance, no one specified what the program should accomplish. But by sending only small arms, the CIA implicitly decided that U.S. policy would be to exact a cost on the Soviet occupiers, at the price of Afghan lives. The CIA purchased old Soviet military equipment from Egypt and China, some of it in terrible condition, paying more for junk than it would have for good Western equipment, in order to maintain "cover." The agency explained to Congress that Islamic governments would be affronted by a large Western role. Moreover, in the words of CIA Deputy Director John McMahon, the Pakistanis absolutely refused to allow "even Everready brand flashlight batteries" to reach the Afghans, much less sophisticated American arms. But the Mujahedeen themselves soon sent a steady stream of envoys to Congress and the media, where they found receptive audiences for the following proposition: We are being armed just enough to fight and die, but not enough to liberate our country. If you Americans give us what we need, primarily air defense missiles and long-range mortars, we can defeat the Soviets. If you give us these things no Islamic country, including Pakistan, will object. The history of the Afghan "covert action" is mostly that of the clash between the Mujahedeen's vision and that of the CIA–State Department.

A necessary preface to the story is that the CIA and State actually had a vision: The U.S. and the Soviets should manage their perpetual struggle without trying to inflict major defeats on one another. The Soviets would not allow themselves to be defeated in Afghanistan, and would do "whatever it takes" to win. If the U.S. pushed too hard, the Soviets might even invade Pakistan. Then would the bipartisan congressional hawks be willing to defend Pakistan? If not, the U.S. would lose much. If so then we would risk World War III. Thus, by assuming that the nation is unwilling to face the consequences of purposeful policy, cloistered bureaucrats relieved themselves of the responsibility to present meaningful choices. Hence the preference for covert action.

Every year between 1980 and 1988 the Congress appropriated roughly double the amount of money the executive branch requested for the Afghanistan effort. But when the Congress also tried to specify that the money be spent to give the Afghans shoulder-fired antiaircraft missiles, the CIA said no. The CIA claimed to be "all for" giving air defense to the Afghans but regretted that the Pakistanis would not allow American missiles in. Moreover, said the CIA, it was already providing the Afghans with Soviet-made SA-7 antiaircraft missiles (purchased in Eastern Europe). If the Congress *really* insisted, the CIA would be willing to pressure the Pakistanis to let in a few Swiss-made Oerlikon transportable antiaircraft guns. Besides, said CIA, would Congress want to be responsible in case the Afghans sold American missiles to Muslim terrorists somewhere?

The CIA's protestations of willingness to provide anti-air protection was insincere. The SA-7 missiles were proving ineffective (having been subtly sabotaged in Poland). CIA argued that the SA-7s would shoot down airplanes only if the "Muj" were willing to crawl under Soviet runway flight paths and shoot at point-blank range. But the Muj were not interested in raising the body count of Soviet aircraft. Since the Soviet strategy of depopulating the Afghan countryside depended on the easy, low-level strafing of villages, the Muj wanted to force Soviet aircraft to abandon these missions by spreading defensive missiles around. The CIA's proposal to supply Oerlikon guns did not deal with that key need. Any serious AA gun requires a big supply of ammunition. To use any Oerlikon, the Muj would have had to divert scarce mule trains to stock and prepare a site. But they did not need air defense for a few prepared sites. They needed it on the spur of the moment, in lots of places. The CIA was stalling.

Its suggestion that the Pakistanis might accept the Oerlikon, however, had whet Congressional curiosity. Might the Pakistanis accept U.S.-made Stinger missiles as well? Deputy Director McMahon swore again and again, all over Capitol Hill, that they would not. But in 1984 and 1985 four separate delegations of congressmen (Charles Wilson (D-TX)), congressional staff, senators (Orrin Hatch (R-UT)), and Department of Defense civilians returned from Islamabad with the same tale: Pakistani President Mohammed Zia ul Haq, his Director of Intelligence, General Akhtar, and the director of the Afghan program, Brigadier Yussef, all were eager to see the Mujahedeen get Stingers. The delegations, which were accompanied by CIA officials, also reported that these officials attempted to keep the question of Stingers from being raised, and were angry when it was. By early 1986 it was clear to those inside the government who had been working on the Afghan issue that John McMahon and the CIA bureaucracy had lied. Not only were Stingers soon on the way to Afghanistan (the warning about diversion to terrorists had been a throwaway line), but McMahon also resigned. Stingers started arriving in substantial numbers by late 1986, and during 1987 they changed the character of the war. The Soviet military strategy in Afghanistan was defeated.

During 1988, however, the Soviets moved the conflict onto more congenial ground—they struck at the U.S. government's imprecisely (in part because covertly) formulated objectives. The new Soviet strategy was to trade retreat of Soviet forces for the United States' abandonment of the Muj. State and the CIA, which had never wanted victory, promptly declared that victory would be achieved the day the last Soviet combat soldier left (February 15, 1989). They judged that, by withdrawing, the Soviets had washed their hands of Afghanistan, and predicted that the Afghan puppet government would fall quickly. But the Soviet Union saw the withdrawal as anything but a washing of the hands. It refused to evacuate its Afghan clients, and instead helped them to fortify and retreat into the fertile major valleys of Afghanistan, leaving the Muj only subsistence villages. It continued to pour in a superabundance of military supplies, and even food, using massive air power to keep the convoy routes open. The Soviet strategy counted on the agreement with the U.S. to prevent the U.S. from giving the Muj the equipment they would need to break into the fortress valleys—namely, tanks and artillery. The Soviets proved to be correct. After February 15, 1989, their clients remained in firm possession of the "useful Afghanistan." In September 1991 the Bush Administration agreed with the first post-Soviet government that both sides in the Afghan civil war would have their supplies cut off on December 31. This settlement left Afghanistan's communist tribe in possession of more material assets of all kinds than the Muj. Why should anyone have regarded the settlement as good? The answer was covert.

Let us now turn to the two typical small covert actions of the 1980s, Chad and Yemen—one a success, the other a failure. First Chad. In 1981 the new Reagan Administration chose Libya's Muammar al-Qaddafi as a suitable first target in a campaign to restore U.S. prestige in the world. Qaddafi had an indefensible image in the U.S., and could not really hit back very hard. U.S. allies in Africa—Egypt's President Sadat and Sudan's President Jaffar Nimeiri—who were targets of Qaddafi's assassination attempts, wanted something done about him. The U.S. government decided to "quietly bleed" Qaddafi by supporting the anti-Libyan forces of Hissène Habré in Chad. In fact the U.S. operation "piggybacked" on, and helped to finance, a larger French operation.[30] The U.S. involvement probably did no harm. The immediate disclosure to *Newsweek* that the U.S. was "going after" Quaddafi[31] had no effect, and neither did the CIA's insistence that Habré promise not to use U.S.-financed weapons against his political enemies! At any rate, by 1984 Habré had taken the capital of Chad, N'djamena, and gradually extended his control over the entire country. In these terms, the action was a success. Note however that in 1990 Habré was overthrown by Libyan agent Idriss Deby. More important, if the purpose of the action was to "do something" about Qaddafi so as to at least safeguard Sadat and Nimeiri, we must note that Sadat was assassinated in 1981 by people who, if not run by Qaddafi, were of his stripe; while Nimeiri was overthrown while visiting the U.S. in 1985. Qaddafi went on to commit outrages against the U.S. greater than any he had committed before, and was persuaded to pause only by a very overt raid in 1987 by some 20 American FB-111 bombers that almost killed him. The raid killed some 100 soldiers and, allegedly, a baby girl. However, over the years the U.S. has turned down the chance to support anti-Qaddafi plots on the ground that they might lead to his death. Nevertheless, the CIA recruited some 600 Libyan soldiers captured in Chad as an anti-Qaddafi army. These men soon had cause to regret switching loyalties. When Qaddafi's proxy recaptured Chad, the CIA began a search for a place to resettle them as refugees. Whether it is worse to kill the likes of Qaddafi or to treat one's friends this way is a question that deserves open, not covert, consideration.[32]

The operation against Soviet-dominated South Yemen resulted in a dozen hanged Yemenis. What else might have been expected of it? In 1981, pursuant to a desire to "make things uncomfortable" for the South Yemeni government, which was making a serious attempt to take over Saudi-allied North Yemen, the CIA worked with Saudi intelligence to train and dispatch small teams into the South to scrawl antigovernment slogans onto walls, and carry out petty sabotage. The idea was to lead the government to worry about its home base and forget its foreign ambitions. There were technical flaws. The CIA, for the sake of deniability, neither approached the team members nor did counterintelligence investigations on them. Besides, a bunch of non–Arabic-speaking Americans asking questions about Yemeni laborers in Saudi Arabia would have positively advertised their recruitment. So the operation may have been infiltrated from the first. Then too, all the team members knew one another, so that the arrest of one almost invariably would lead to the arrest of all. Finally, the teams would not go without assurance that they were working for the mighty CIA—which, they supposed, would pull them out of trouble if they were captured. But the fundamental flaw was conceptual and moral: What good would scrawls on walls do that would justify risks of lives? The covert actioneers seem not to have asked.[33]

No Focus in the 1990s

As we have seen, in the 1990s the world promised to be in greater flux than during the essentially static post–World War II decades of US–Soviet bipolarity. As we will see (Chapter 9), many of the decisions that affect great events are susceptible to being influenced by agents of influence. The leadership of any number of Parties, movements, and even countries can be changed through influence from abroad. The U.S. might well profit from doing this sort of thing. But the U.S. will not have the option of doing it so long as the CIA and the rest of the government continue to view covert action as they have.

In 1991 the U.S. Senate Intelligence Committee debated a new law to regulate U.S. intelligence. As regards covert action, the debate concerned the constitutional propriety and the prudence of demanding that the President submit to Congress all proposed covert actions before undertaking them, or at least within a number of hours after they are undertaken. This debate was based on the premise that a covert action may be legally defined. Moreover, it missed the paramount point: Are executive branch officials willing to deal with policy in terms of clear objectives, and of means reasonably calculated to achieve those objectives? Are senators and congressmen willing to help them do it? Law can affect this point only tangentially—not by setting forth timetables for submission of projects but rather by setting forth objectives that the projects must serve. Similarly, law can barely touch the second key point: Only rarely will a covert action stand a chance of doing any good by itself. Most of the time, covert action will be only one part of a larger plan. Law can, at best, require Secretaries of State and Defense to "sign off" on covert-action plans. As James Madison long ago pointed out, laws can give officials an interest in doing their jobs well.[34] But only history can teach the difference between a job done in statesmanlike fashion and one done badly.

As we have seen, the problem with U.S. covert action is that its practitioners view it as a means of dodging their responsibilities as policy-makers. The foregoing, however, shows that covert action offers only the illusion of escape from accountability. In fact, when covert action fails, the sinister image of cover-up adds to the onus of failure, while the focus on concealment rather than on substance deprives those involved in the controversy of the opportunity to learn from it.

7

Intelligence and the Gulf War

There were so many disclaimers that . . . no matter what
happened they would have been right. And that's not helpful to
the guy in the field.

— General H. Norman Schwarzkopf

The proof of the pudding is in the eating.

— Old proverb

Evaluations of peacetime intelligence,
like those of peacetime military forces, can only be theoretical. Only war itself
allows definitive judgments. The Gulf War of 1990–91 was hardly representative of every possible war the U.S. might fight. Nevertheless, it posed many of the
intelligence problems that any war poses—albeit in ways specific to its time and
place. In the previous four chapters we have made a number of judgments about
the fitness of U.S. intelligence. The performance of U.S. intelligence in and
around the Gulf War confirms them.

U.S. intelligence performed pretty much as one might have expected: The closer its relationship to the act of shooting weapons, the better the performance; the farther away, the worse. Tactical intelligence was generally excellent, while "national" or strategic intelligence was quite unsatisfactory. The CIA, though formally in charge of coordinating the intelligence effort, was practically useless. Technical intelligence was good (with certain glaring exceptions), while human intelligence was almost nonexistent. Let us look more closely, dividing the subject into its components as before.

COLLECTION

For the first time in the history of warfare no military unit (on the American side) had to interpret intelligence about the enemy on the basis of less than certainty about its *own* location. Through little electronic boxes that triangulated signals from Global Positioning System (GPS) satellites, every American unit always knew precisely where it was. And this information, though not about the enemy, made a big difference.

When we discuss technical information useful for firing upon the enemy, we touch lines of distinction between intelligence and "fire control" that advances in technology have all but blurred. Clearer than ever, however, is the usefulness of the devices that provide it. Consider, by way of example, the Airborne Warning and Control System (AWACS). This airplane-mounted radar and computer system, flown to the rear of friendly air forces, detects both friendly and hostile aircraft. Its computers figure out which friendly aircraft are best positioned to deal with which hostile ones, which course and speed each should take to do it, when each intercept should occur, and which weapons system is most likely to be effective in each case. Regardless of whether one calls AWACS' product "intelligence," air forces guided by AWACS have an enormous advantage over ones that are not. While allied planes shot down some 40 Iraqi planes in air-to-air combat, not one allied plane was lost therein. By the same token, J-STARS, another airplane-mounted radar and computer system, flies to the rear of friendly *ground* forces and detects both friendly and hostile tanks, trucks, artillery, etc. It then figures out who can best hit whom, and passes along the information. U.S. forces "killed" more than 3,000 tanks while losing only three! This result is obviously due to more than J-STARS. But J-STARS' information was part and parcel of the U.S. Army's and Air Force's approach to AirLand battles.

Electronic eyes replaced human eyes very well. Whereas even in the Vietnam War naval gunfire had been directed from the fringe of a target area by brave junior officers scurrying around toting binoculars and radios, by means of which they would adjust the ships' aim (according to their estimates of number of yards off-target) with words like "up 200—right 50," now the battleships received precise information from a new generation of fearless "spotters"—the TV-equipped, pilotless aircraft that circled the targets. Most observant of all, and closest to the action, were the dauntless TV cameras in the nose cones of munitions that gave a kamikaze-eye view of targets, allowing pilots or computers to guide them in, right up to impact.

Battlefield reconnaissance was total and multispectral. At the low end of the electromagnetic spectrum, long-wavelength radars probed the desert sands to map minefields. Shorter-wavelength, airplane-mounted, side-looking radars kept up surveillance of the enemy's immediate rear, even during periods of bad weather. When photoreconnaissance aircraft were ineffective, American antennas located on the ground, and also those on aircraft, intercepted higher radio frequencies coming from throughout Iraq, and localized and recorded them. Consequently, U.S. forces had located every Iraqi command-post radio and every radar-guided gun on the battlefield long before the shooting started. Higher up the spectrum, TR-1 photographic aircraft delivered imagery coverage. Their only limitation was that they could not be everywhere at once. In other words, in Kuwait and southern Iraq, no major units, and few minor ones, existed or moved without being constantly seen, heard, or felt by U.S. tactical intelligence.

This was entirely to be expected. The enemy's lack of movement and his unwillingness to even challenge the movement of U.S. technical collectors allowed these collectors to perform optimally. But the very quality of their performance under these ideal circumstances raised questions about what it would be like against an enemy that was shooting down reconnaissance aircraft and maneuvering rapidly over vast areas.

The *strategic* performance of U.S. technical collectors was more mixed. In sum, insofar as the targets were fixed and did not attempt to hide or dissimulate, collection did an excellent job. But against mobile, camouflaged, or deceptive targets it did badly. In Chapter 3 we mentioned that "national" technical collectors (the satellites and such) had been optimized for peacetime use and that, only as an afterthought, a program called TENCAP had been devised to make them at least somewhat useful to military commanders. In the Gulf War the commanders complained that they could not get a photograph out of "national" channels that was less than a day old.[1] True, the photoreconnaissance airplanes under military control were technologically far inferior to the satellites. But they had the advantage of not being part of a system geared to peacetime purposes.

The greatest strategic failure of reconnaissance also was predictable. Although U.S. imaging satellites had almost daily coverage of Iraqi troop movements in the months before and after the invasion, they could not supply enough facts to overcome the analytical prejudices that led to mistaken evaluations of Iraqi intentions. In July 1990, as satellite imagery showed Iraqi troops massing in battle formation on the Kuwaiti border, all but one U.S. analyst judged that they were *not* going to invade. But that is why they were there. During August, as satellite imagery showed the Iraqis digging into the Kuwaiti sands, U.S. analysts unanimously judged that they would attack Saudi Arabia, which seems never to have crossed Saddam Hussein's mind. None of this is the satellites' fault. But once again it makes our point: Imagery cannot be counted on to dispel prejudice.

On the positive side, when the reconnaissance that worked on the battlefield was applied to the Iraqi military–industrial complex as a whole, it yielded a good inventory, particularly of the electronic command and control system. As bombing raids eliminated broadcast and beamed communications, and as orders obviously continued to flow, long-wavelength radar reconnaissance even found a trench for a fiber-optic cable heading south from Baghdad. An air raid soon cut it. The rest of the Iraqi infrastructure was so well catalogued that tens of thousands of air raids simply disarticulated it.

On the negative side (again), despite total coverage of the electromagnetic spectrum, communications intelligence never provided the slightest hint of Iraq's strategic intentions, either before, during, or after the war. Nor did Comint supply anything about Iraq's dealings with Iran or the Soviet Union, which were of overriding importance. (More on this later.) Also to its discredit, the massive concentration of U.S. reconnaissance assets on the problem of mobile missile-launchers in a small, largely flat, desert country—ideal circumstances—failed to yield even a total number of missiles and launchers available. Much less did it allow the U.S. to strike the missiles before they were fired. Finally, the Iraqis' Soviet-supplied techniques for camouflage, concealment, and deception effectively hid a large part of Iraq's nuclear weapons program. After the war, some six months of on-site inspections by 40-man teams backed by the world's military forces, and the fortuitous help of defectors, were required for the U.S. to gain a general picture of that program.

Again, this was totally predictable from the nature of the U.S. technical collection system, and quite ominous. As we have pointed out, the U.S. strategic reconnaissance system was premised on revisiting the known locations of static missiles in order to take good pictures of them for arms-control purposes. It was not built to find mobile missiles in unknown locations that the enemy was trying to hide. It was based on the assumption that leaders would put communications "on the air" in ciphers that the U.S. could break, rather than send them by land lines or in unbreakable codes. It was based on the assumption that the enemy would use the same on-the-air communications network that he used in peace. Finally, it was based on the assumption that our chief adversary would not deceive us. But the Gulf War showed that the combination of U.S. imagery and signals satellites does not stand a chance of finding mobile missiles in a vast country during war, or even of counting them during peacetime.

U.S. technical collectors' marginally acceptable job of identifying Iraq's few facilities related to chemical and nuclear weapons suggests that its performance with regard to the vast, spread-out Soviet system (regardless of who controls it) is probably much worse. Given that after the war the U.S. judged that it had destroyed Iraq's nuclear reagents only to be told by a defector that significant quantities had been hidden successfully, it is safe to bet that the U.S. technical collection system stood even less chance of getting substantial information on secret Soviet weapons laboratories and stockpiles, and hence that U.S.–Soviet treaties that limit sophisticated weaponry had been imprudent.

The U.S. human-collection system, predictably, was almost completely absent from the fray. The exception was the Army's and Marine Corps' battlefield human intelligence. American soldiers effectively took polls of the Iraqi army by helicopter-borne raids that captured representative groups of prisoners. Well-handled interrogations yielded just about anything one might have wanted to know about the enemy forces' morale, training, supply, and tactical leadership. Just before U.S. ground forces struck, small groups of special forces moved into position to physically observe the enemy's main forces. Battlefield human intelligence was indeed "all that it could be."

By contrast, the U.S. fought the entire war without the slightest insight from human sources about the workings of the Iraqi regime, its strategic intentions, or its alliances. Many Americans speculated about those intentions and alliances. Some argued—correctly—that the Soviet Union was really on Iraq's side and that, at a crucial point, Mikhail Gorbachev would extend his covering wing over Saddam Hussein's regime, and offer it a safe exit from the war with its military power intact and its prestige raised to the skies. And in fact on February 16, 1991 this is exactly what happened. But nobody *knew* that this would happen. For the same reasons no one knew why Saddam Hussein rejected an offer that virtually guaranteed him victory. This ignorance was a totally predictable result of the CIA having virtually no one under "nonofficial cover," and precisely *twenty* (and no more) employees who spoke Arabic. None of these, however, had any aptitude for undercover work in the Arab world.

In the Gulf War against an opponent who did not know how to grasp victory when it was offered to him, lack of human intelligence caused no disasters. But it is never a good idea to fight an able opponent without knowing what he is after.

COUNTERINTELLIGENCE

In a defensive sense, as regards technical collection, American CI was totally successful: Because no Iraqi aircraft ever overflew U.S. forces, Iraq never got any photographic intelligence. Because U.S. forces observed electronic emissions control discipline (EMCON) while changing position, Iraq was never able to tell by its "ears" what its "eyes" could not see. Of course the U.S. had the luxury of total control of the air and of moving on its own schedule and in total safety—hardly normal conditions in war.

In the technical offensive sense (seeing through enemy deception), American CI did quite badly. U.S. analysts were frequently taken in by Soviet-supplied techniques of camouflage and deception, causing Allied pilots to waste bombs on what looked like missile launchers. It is also entirely possible that intentionally flawed camouflage on a civilian bomb shelter was responsible for leading U.S. analysts to conclude that it was a command post, and hence to having it bombed. In this case Iraq gained a propaganda victory. More importantly, Soviet military officers who examined the performance of their equipment and techniques in Iraq apparently concluded that the performance of their deception techniques against the Americans was their only cause for cheer.

Human defensive CI worked well near the battlefield because the desert environment allowed the U.S. near-total control over access to the area. The news media, eager to avoid charges of helping the enemy (as in Vietnam), lent themselves to reporting essentially what they were given.* On the other hand, the allied war machine leaked at the top. President Bush cleared all his moves—including the timing of offensives, and above all his objectives—with Mikhail Gorbachev, who promptly informed Saddam Hussein.[2] Hence, for reasons entirely extraneous to intelligence, there was a gross disparity in the *strategic* information available to the U.S. and Iraq.

ANALYSIS

Tactical–technical analysis was competent. U.S. analysts figured out how to deliver thousands of disarticulating cuts to the Iraqi military machine. It helped that the machine stood still and never tried to fight.

Strategic analysis was very different. U.S. analysts never explored the paramount strategic question: How do we defeat Saddam Hussein's strategy? The lesser reason is of course that the U.S. did not have hard information on Iraq's strategy. But analysts could hardly even theorize about Iraqi strategy because the President of the United States had preempted the entire matter of U.S. and Iraqi objectives. Prior to August 2, 1990 it was an axiom of U.S. policy that Iraq was, if not an ally, at least on the way to becoming one. After August 2, the President declared that "the problem" was Iraq's occupation of Kuwait, and that the United States' objective was to liberate Kuwait.

Thus U.S. policy impaired analysis of Iraq. Briefly, since 1980 the State

---

*In the aftermath of the war the U.S. press questioned its own docility, while the armed forces seemed to rejoice in having used the press to convey some disinformation to the enemy. See *New York Times,* 5 May 1991.

Department and the CIA had deemed Saddam Hussein the new pillar of U.S. policy in the region. Despite congressional opposition, the U.S. government removed his regime from the list of those sponsoring terrorism. And the U.S. favored Iraq during its war with Iran. After the end of that war, as Iraq stepped up its pressure on its neighbors, U.S. policy was to conciliate Hussein, and even to favor the takeover of the Kuwaiti part of a border oilfield as part of a "settlement." The U.S. government apologized for a Voice of America broadcast that had been critical of the Iraqi government's brutality. So, in July 1990, when Iraqi troops moved toward Kuwait, not only was U.S. government policy not to think about the possibility that Iraq might invade, but also not to think of what Iraq's long-term objectives in the region might be. When Saddam did invade Kuwait, this thoughtlessness led naturally to concentrating on Kuwait, to the exclusion of more important questions. Did Saddam Hussein plan eventually to invade Saudi Arabia, or just to overawe it into paying him subsidies? How would he pursue his ambition to become the new Saladin?

Such questions were most important because they bore directly on how the U.S. should fight Saddam. The U.S. could have chosen any of several objectives: to decapitate the regime by killing Saddam and as few others as possible, to destroy the regime by attacking the Ba'ath party and the secret police, to dismember Iraq by helping its non-Sunni–Arab majority to go their separate ways, and so forth. The U.S. armed forces could have pursued any of several operational objectives: destruction of Iraqi forces stationed in the Kuwait area, or ignoring those forces (which had no capacity to move) while destroying Iraqi forces protecting the regime near Baghdad. Or, U.S. forces could have cut off both the Baghdad and Kuwaiti garrisons while concentrating on the marginal forces holding down the Kurdish people in the north and the Shi'ites in the south. Each of these objectives had its own set of advantages and disadvantages. Intelligence could usefully have explored what stood in the way of each objective and how the enemy might have regarded them. But by making it U.S. policy that the problem was Kuwait and only Kuwait, the President focused analysis on how to liberate Kuwait.

It was not the fault of U.S. intelligence that it was forced to scout the path to an objective which, if won on its own terms, would have allowed Saddam Hussein to gain all of his objectives, including dominance over Kuwait, and would have left the U.S. the humiliated loser. It was not the fault of U.S. analysts that, thus constrained, they spent their time during the war speculating on such patently silly questions as whether Iraq planned to bring the 150-odd aircraft it had sent to safety in Iran back into the war. Saddam was obviously counting on those airplanes for *after* the war. But for U.S. analysts to have focused on the postwar world would have raised questions that George Bush did not want to face.

281

For the same reason, U.S. analysis of the Soviet role in the war was crabbed. The President's policy was that the Soviet Union was an ally of the U.S., and that the war was actually the first test-drive of a "new world order." Hence U.S. intelligence was genuinely surprised when Mikhail Gorbachev tried to extend his covering wing over Saddam.

All of this highlights the effects of Sherman Kent's policy of excluding explicit consideration of U.S. policy from intelligence analysis. Had the recommendations of Kent's rival, Willmoore Kendall, prevailed, U.S. analysts might well have compared the possibility that Saddam was playing for long-term postwar advantage with the U.S. policy of simply driving him out of Kuwait. The reader of such a report, perhaps the President, might well have noticed the mismatch and interpreted intelligence accordingly. As it was, U.S. analysts tacitly (i.e., unreflectively) left the President to make decisions about the war as if the survival of Saddam Hussein had been a secondary issue rather than the primary one.

In March 1991, after the end of hostilities, the CIA judged that Saddam Hussein's regime was "diseased" and would be overthrown in 6–12 months. But by April, after Saddam's remaining troops made a bloody show of putting down the Kurdish and Shi'ite rebellions, the CIA changed its estimate. This further illustrates three points we have made about CIA analysis. First, it is too often ready to support U.S. policies with which it agrees, even though it has no factual basis for doing so. Second, it is ignorant not just of dynamic facts but of the statics of which it writes. Meaningfully to have judged Saddam's regime as diseased, one would have to have understood what makes it healthy. (In the short run, Saddam's capacity to kill and reward his own, and in the long run the tendency of Iraq's Sunni Arabs to support whoever will oppress Kurds and Shi'ites.) The moment that it was clear that the U.S. would not interfere with Saddam's repression, it should have been clear that his regime stood on solid ground. Third, CIA analysis is willing to follow and rationalize the newspaper headlines. But who needs that?

COVERT ACTION

Here too performance was typical. Covert action was used as a quiet countercurrent to the mainstream of U.S. policy. Its consequences were not well thought out. It ended as tragedy for the foreigners involved and as an embarrassment for all Americans.

The core policy question was: Shall we remove Saddam from office (or kill him, which in Iraq amounts to the same thing) or not? President Bush, in his taped broadcast to the Iraqi people in September 1990, had disavowed any intention of interfering in the internal affairs of Iraq. He had promised the same thing to Mikhail Gorbachev and to the United Nations. However, he also signed a secret "finding" granting broad authority to the CIA clandestinely to undermine Saddam's rule and to support opposition forces within Iraq.[3] As in so many other cases, the U.S. government had not really decided which alternative to choose, and so it chose both—one secretly.

Some of the effects of CIA covert action were simply silly. When the war began on January 17, the world's news media were filled with accounts of Iraqi tanks and helicopters defecting to the allies. Within hours, however, journalists seeking confirmation from the Egyptian and Saudi newspapers that had originated the stories found that they had been fabrications. The CIA's intention in planting the stories had been to start an avalanche of defections. The intention was fine. But why would anyone have thought that the ploy might succeed? After all, the incentive to defection that it provided was nothing compared to the disincentives that Saddam provided: death to defectors and their families. And, after all, President Bush was telling the Iraqi people that, as far as he was concerned, Saddam was *their* problem, and that, come what may, the U.S. would not stand between Saddam and the Iraqi people. Why should Iraqi troops have committed suicide by deserting? And so this ploy did neither good nor harm.

Because President Bush's overt policy had been so clearly not to challenge Saddam internally, the CIA's contacts—indirect, to be sure—among the independence-minded peoples of extreme northern and southern Iraq (Kurds and Shi'ites respectively) moved no one to revolt. At first, that is. Then, during February, President Bush openly called for Saddam's overthrow. And Kurdish radios in Saudi Arabia, at the instigation of Saudi intelligence and the CIA, chimed in. This, combined with the rout of the Iraqi army from Kuwait, and the statements by U.S. commanders on CNN that they had "slammed the door shut" on Iraq's best units and would shoot down any airplanes or helicopters that took to the air, convinced Iraqi Kurds and Shi'ites that it was safe to revolt.

But the fact of their revolt finally forced President Bush to ask himself whether he really wanted it to succeed. He had put off thinking seriously about it until he had to. The fact that one of his two policy tracks was covert had helped him to do it. When he finally did confront the core policy question, he decided that he really prefered an Iraq governed by Saddam Hussein to an Iraq that had lost its non–Sunni Arab subjects, perhaps to Iran, and whose Kurdish subjects would be stirring up trouble in Turkey. And so Bush quietly ordered his commanders not to interfere with Iraqi helicopters. Iraq quickly found out, and unleashed carnage on the Kurds and Shi'ites.

In the end, Bush incited millions of people to lay their lives on the line, and then watched as hundreds of thousands were slaughtered. He also watched as Saddam thus regained at least some of the prospects for long-term success that he had lost through his other misjudgments. Thus did Bush's failure to confront alternatives—abetted by covert action—tarnish even military victory.

Our point here is that in the Gulf War intelligence followed policy, and George Bush set policy incompetently. He initially failed to recognize Saddam as a serious threat, and he did not dissuade him. Hence the brutal invasion of Kuwait. Bush failed to recognize that Saddam himself was the problem, and therefore U.S. forces killed thousands of Iraqi soldiers—poor devils who wanted to be elsewhere—and spared Saddam. George Bush worshiped stability, so he condemned hundreds of thousands of innocent Kurds and Shi'ites to death. Even perfect intelligence could not make up for a policy so incompetent.

TIME FOR A CHANGE

In the aftermath of the Gulf War, President Bush quietly let Director of Central Intelligence William Webster know that he wanted his resignation. Webster, who had served since 1987, had embarrassed no one. The President removed him because the Gulf War convinced him that he should not simply oppose the growing sentiment in Congress to make major changes in U.S. intelligence but that his Administration should have its own views about improving intelligence. Neither Webster nor the bureaucracy had any. Hence Bush's appointment of Robert Gates.

The Gulf War added one more set of arguments to a debate about intelligence reform that had been going on for many years. Whether any arguments prove decisive, however, we will shortly consider.

8

Reform

When thou goest to [intelligence agencies] take a whip.
— *Friedrich Nietzche (sanitized)*

Had logic ruled, presidents of the United States would have conceived the U.S. intelligence agencies to fit reasoned lists of requirements, and would have reformed the agencies periodically as their needs changed. As we have seen, however, U.S. intelligence grew from bureaucratic imperatives. Presidents, although they have often expressed dissatisfaction with intelligence, have never taken the trouble to study its problems and mandate solutions.[1] U.S. intelligence has always seethed with proposals for reorganization and reform. The books produced by the founding generation are full of organizational controversies: Should analysts or collectors run the CIA? What should be the relationship between the CIA's counterintelligence staff and the geographic divisions of the Deputy Directorate for Operations? What about relations between the FBI and the CIA? Who should be responsible for initiating proposals for covert action? Who should approve them? Who should be notified? When? Who should submit budget requests to whom? Some of these proposals from within the bureaucracy have been driven by differing appreciations of what the job requires. (Note, for example, the 1949 debate between Sherman Kent and Willmoore Kendall on the focus of intelligence analysis.) Most of these controversies, however, have been driven by social antagonisms and have consisted of bureaucratic power plays. Robin Winks has even compared the centerpiece of U.S. intelligence to a university campus. And indeed the debate over reform thus far has resembled nothing so much as the squabbles amongst university professors and administrators. As Henry Kissinger has often noted, such squabbles tend to be particularly venomous because the stakes are so small—careers and reputations. The end of the Cold War however produced a consensus, as broad as it is inchoate, that U.S. intelligence should be reformed fundamentally. Let us now see the logic of the positions in the great reform debate of the 1990s—a debate the roots of which are in the 1970s.

THE CHURCH COMMITTEE

In the 1970s some intelligence officers allied with like-minded liberal staffers in the Congress—e.g., William Miller for Sen. Frank Church (D-ID) and David Aaron for Sen. Walter Mondale (D-MN)—and produced a set of comprehensive proposals for reform. The result was a set of hearings by Select Committees of the Senate and House of Representatives in 1975 and 1976.* They publicized the real and imagined wrongdoings of some in the intelligence community, and fostered the careers of others. The Congress itself legislated no changes, but did give political backing to a set of insiders who implemented their agenda and thoroughly purged their opponents whom they labeled enemies of civil liberties. By 1980 over three-fourths of the CIA's roughly 400 officers at rank GS-16 through -18 had not held that rank four years before, and virtually no one who had been in senior positions prior to 1975 remained in place—except for the winners in the internecine battles. The hearings also covered a major internal realignment of functions and personnel. Counterintelligence, covert action, and human collection were deemphasized, while technical collection and analysis took bigger shares of the budget. The CIA rose in importance relative to other components of the community.

All of this happened because of discrete pressures, alliances of convenience, and broad ideological kinship, not because of any master plan with regard to intelligence. The changes, however, amounted to new priorities because those who won the battles of the 1970s shared something of a coherent attitude toward politics and intelligence. The argument that underlay the Church Committee hearings was that the U.S. had more to fear from a surfeit of intelligence than

---

*The records and publications of these Select Committees, popularly known as the "Church" (Senate) and "Pike" (House) Committees, are among the richest unclassified sources of information on U.S. intelligence.

from external threats. The legislative prescription was a bill (S-2525) to "charter" U.S. intelligence. It was a codification of the changes in U.S. intelligence that the revolution of the 1970s had brought about. It would have "authorized" all of the United States' intelligence activities while specifying the conditions under which they could have been conducted. The point of the bill was to draw bureaucratic boundaries. It was supported by a coalition of left-wing politicians in Congress and of the intelligence officials who had won the battles of the 1970s. Both the agencies' new orientations and the bill that would have codified them were essentially oriented inward. Neither was meant primarily to deal with a fast-changing world.

THE PERFORMANCE LOBBY

By the late 1970s, however, challenges to the argument that had underlain the Church Committee had doomed the reform bill. The nature of the new debate may be seen in a pair of articles in *The Wall Street Journal* of February 23, 1979 by two members of the Senate Intelligence Committee, Walter Huddleston (D-KY) and Malcolm Wallop (R-WY). Huddleston was leading a last-ditch effort to pass a version of S-2525. Wallop opposed it, claiming that the American people were threatened not by the agencies' excess capacities but by their incompetence. He cited their misestimation of Soviet missilery and of the Iranian revolution, and argued that there is no relationship between the quality of intelligence work and the level of intrusion into civil liberties. The bill, said Wallop, set forth no mission, and no standards of performance. Any reform should be designed to strengthen the agencies' capacity to do their jobs. Huddleston admitted that U.S. intelligence had not performed well. He insisted that the charter bill was meant not to restrict, but to authorize, intelligence. This shift of position meant that advocates of the bill were trying to justify it on grounds opposite to those on which it had been conceived. This proved impossible to do. Wallop and his associates had shifted the terms of the debate. No longer would the debate be about how to protect civil liberties against the rogue elephant of U.S. intelligence. Now it would be about how to energize a standard bureaucratic animal into doing its job.

On July 1, 1980, Wallop and Paul Laxalt (R-NV) introduced S-2928 and S-2929. The substance of these bills was reflected in the Republican Presidential platform for 1980. The bills provided detailed statements of the missions of U.S. intelligence, intended to be used as standards for gauging performance. They also would have separated the office of Director of Central Intelligence—the President's chief adviser on the subject—from that of Director of the CIA, who would have served one term of ten years. This was designed to remove the CIA from politics and to end the leading role of one part of the intelligence

287

community over the whole. The bills provided for at least two competing sets of estimates on important questions, for shifting to a smaller but better-covered corps of human collectors, and for central analysis of counterintelligence data.

THE "OLD BOYS"

The Wallop forces were unable to parlay their victory on the agenda into many actual reforms of the agencies because another factor entered the debate. The intelligence officials who had lost out in the revolution of the 1970s, allied with old conservatives led by Barry Goldwater (R-AZ), advanced the proposition that the main fault with U.S. intelligence was quite simply that, in the 1970s, it had been "restricted." They posited that the decades prior to the mid–1970s—their time—had been a kind of Golden Age in which U.S. intelligence had functioned just right. They claimed that the Hughes–Ryan Amendment had made covert action well-nigh impossible, that the Freedom of Information Act (which requires all U.S. government agencies to respond to requests for information) had undermined foreign governments' and prospective collaborators' confidence in U.S. intelligence, and that the practice of such as the magazine *Counterspy* of identifying CIA officers abroad destroyed their effectiveness. Fix these items and, perhaps above all, publicly honor "the professionals," and all would be well. The "old boys" expressed bitterness not so much at their colleagues who had purged them and now ran the agencies, as at the politicians who had covered them. Their position seemed to be a paraphrase of Stephen Decatur: "My agency, may it always be right. But, right or wrong, my agency."

Thus by 1980 there were three agendas for reform: one aimed at further specification of the conditions and procedures under which U.S. intelligence would act; another generally opposed "restrictions" but really was concerned most about the agencies' prestige; and the third focused on performance.

THE REAGAN SYNTHESIS

The Reagan Administration advanced all of the abovementioned agendas slightly, but not in ways that seriously threatened the bureaucratic *status quo*. Above all, only three outsiders were appointed to positions of responsibility for intelligence.[2] The 1970s revolution in personnel was neither reversed nor continued in a different direction. Reagan put U.S. intelligence on autopilot.

The performance agenda received primarily lip service. A few counterintelligence analysis programs bore a few fruits in the early 1980s, but were largely eliminated by late in that decade. Analysis was streamlined for policy relevance during the Robert Gates years. But there was never a hint of competition. Collection, both human and technical, continued to roll on rails that had been laid down decades earlier.

The "old boys'" agenda got legislative action. Already in 1980 (S-2284)* the Congress had reduced the Hughes–Ryan Amendment's requirement for reporting covert action from eight congressional committees to the two Intelligence Committees, which operate largely in secret. In 1982 the Congress passed, and the President signed, the Intelligence Identities Protection Act, which punishes whoever discloses the identity of any undercover employee of American intelligence in the course of a "pattern of activities" which "impairs or impedes" the intelligence activities of the U.S.† In 1985 the Congress passed an amendment to the Freedom of Information Act that makes clear what the original act had also made clear: Intelligence agencies don't have to release material they don't think they should. And of course from 1981 to 1985 the President's words about the intelligence "professionals" were full of praise. Nevertheless, the "old boys" never saw the return of the Golden Age—nor did they get invited back to headquarters.

The Church Committee agenda, too, made some gains, largely by taking advantage of the Administration's missteps. In 1981 the Reagan Administration replaced its predecessor's executive order on intelligence (E.O. 12036) with its own (E.O. 12333). The differences were almost entirely a matter of rhetorical tone. But 12333 increased somewhat the CIA's authority to investigate the domestic end of foreign cases (e.g., at UN headquarters in New York). This specter of "CIA espionage on innocent Americans" fueled discussions and demands for assurances about procedures. The Iran–Contra affair, which President Reagan ran from the NSC rather than the CIA, rekindled efforts to define the NSC as an intelligence agency, as well as ongoing efforts to define when a President must report covert action, without running afoul of the constitutional separation of powers.

In sum, during the Reagan Administration intelligence changed very little. As the end of his presidency approached, Ronald Reagan, true to the pattern of other presidents, criticized the support he was getting from intelligence.

Congress by Default

By 1985–86—the so-called year of the spy—there was much to complain about. The defection and redefection of Vitaly Yurchenko looked bad. So did the revelations of the damage done by John Walker and Ronald Pelton, the escape of

---

*S-2284 was originally called the "National Intelligence Act of 1980." It was 178 pages long, and was, in effect, a Church committee bill. The Intelligence Committee totally rejected the "Church" agenda and retained only the bill's *number*. The new content, named "Intelligence Oversight Act of 1980," was three pages long.

†In other words, the Act does not cover the general public for casual disclosures, nor journalists or scholars whose disclosure of an identity is incidental to their legitimate jobs. It punishes only wilful campaigns to wreck U.S. intelligence.

Edward Lee Howard, the several scandals at the U.S. Embassy in Moscow. As the 1980s ended, it became clear that U.S. intelligence had missed not only the cataclysms in faraway Eastern Europe but had been mistaken about the sentiments of the electorate in nearby Nicaragua. Having entered into a treaty on missiles in Europe that the intelligence community claimed it could monitor, the government found that U.S. intelligence had missed *dozens* of missiles. Finally, while the collapse of communism in Eastern Europe prompted most bureaucracies in Washington to draft plans to reshape themselves for a new world, the U.S. intelligence community seemed to want very much to stand still. So what if both the key intelligence questions and the environment in which they would have to be sought were new? No one might disagree with Mr. Ted Shackley's observation that "Ninety percent of the existing intelligence requirements for Eastern Europe are obsolete."[3] But the agencies' typical response to changes in the world is not to hire new people to do new things but to put new names on old doors. President Bush, for reasons we have already alluded to, was not disposed to second-guess the community. But Congress was.

Congress is not well-positioned to shape intelligence. Even the most activist of legislators readily admit that intelligence is properly an executive activity. In general, Congress lacks the required expertise. True, legislators and their staffs are better positioned for access to all parts of the community than all but a handful of executive officials. Yet few make use of their prerogatives to become experts. The rule that members of the Senate Intelligence Committee may serve no more than eight years, and members of the House Intelligence Committee no more than six, helps to hold down expertise. The habit of "professionals" who testify on "the Hill" constantly, to repeat elementary lessons and to avoid serious discussions unless pressured, lowers the level of discussion and above all wastes precious time. Moreover, when the small number of expert committee members try to educate their fellows they must bring to the witness table genuine authorities. But, Catch 22, one can hardly seem authoritative unless one is on the inside, and the pressures on insiders to stick to their agency's interests when testifying before Congress is enormous. Thus the process of expert consultation often grinds down even the sharpest intentions to reform. Add to this that most of Congress has a bad conscience over what the Church Committee did, and it is easy to see why Congress' mighty powers of purse and statute usually produce only tiny changes.

In addition, even when Congress includes a specific directive in the annual Intelligence Authorization Act that the agencies dislike, the bureaucrats tend to observe it only to the extent that they believe the sponsor of the directive will be willing and able to punish the disobedient party in following year's budget cycle—assuming that the responsible party can be found, and that the member and his expert staffer are still on the committee. Thus the agencies barely complied with the various reform provisions of the Authorization Acts of 1982–85, and only as long as their sponsors were on the Committee. They never paid any attention to the reform provisions of the Fiscal 1987 Act because the sponsor was not on the committee. Nevertheless, at the threshold of the 1990s, Congress (rather than the agencies themselves, or the President, or any of his appointees) took the lead in intelligence reform. In 1989 the Senate Intelligence Committee appointed an expert panel on counterintelligence, and its chairman, David Boren (D-OK) let it be known that he was considering a broad agenda for reform.

The public debate began in the summer of 1990 on the *The New York Times'* op-ed page. On June 14 Roger Morris, a former NSC staffer, laid out the position (herein paraphrased) of those who supported the Church Committee: "U.S. intelligence is inherently dangerous. This is a good time for pulling whatever capacity it has for intruding. Let us reduce it to the role of gatherer of pictures from the sky in ways coordinated with the Soviet Union." Rep. Ron Dellums (D-CA), a member of the House Intelligence Committee, argued that *all* of U.S. intelligence ought to be dismantled "nail by nail, brick by brick."[4] On January 21, 1991, Senator Moynihan introduced the "End of the Cold War Act," which, among other things, calls for dismantling the CIA—though not the functions of intelligence; and on May 19, 1991, Moynihan published his own op-ed in *The New York Times* to that effect.

On August 10, 1990, representing the "performance" school, I wrote in the same *Times* (as I have argued at length herein) that to deal with the dangers of the post–Cold War world U.S. intelligence would have to get back to basics—with human collectors who can mix with a wide variety of people, technical collectors that can track mobile targets, counterintelligence that controls quality, and a leaner corps of analysts who give choices to policy-makers. I concluded that "It takes less money to do intelligence well than to do it badly—providing one knows how." The action, however, rested with Senator Boren and his counterpart in the House, Rep. Dave McCurdy (D-OK).

Boren, McCurdy, and Gates

Senator Boren's op-ed of June 17, 1990 prefigured the bill he previewed on February 6, 1991. Boren summarily rejected the Church Committee's premises: "Intelligence excesses" he wrote, "are largely behind us." His argument consisted almost entirely of a list of tasks to be done (some old, some new) which, in his view, U.S. intelligence is not well-enough equipped to do. He mentioned the need to deal with the old agenda of Soviet strategic rocket forces, the intentions of Soviet (and presumably post–Soviet) leaders, and their KGB, as well as with a new agenda of terrorists, drug traffickers, Third World biological weapons, and industrial espionage. "We must," he wrote, "do all of this with less money than the agencies had been accustomed to."

The Boren bill's aims are ambitious and, on the surface, hardly distinguishable from those of the Wallop/Laxalt "performance" bills of a decade before. As regards collection, both seek to foster "classic human source intelligence." Like Wallop and Laxalt, Boren and McCurdy are aghast at the low number of foreign-language speakers within U.S. intelligence, and at the agencies' incapacity to penetrate. Boren wants technical means to handle "new and complicated arms-control agreements." If taken seriously, that has to mean tackling the problem of mobile missiles that the Gulf War so dramatized. Whether anyone likes it or not, successfully "verifying" such missiles also allows shooting at them. Like Wallop/Laxalt, and indeed like General Schwarzkopf, Boren and McCurdy are exasperated with the huge number of analysts who spend more time, it seems, arriving at interagency agreements than at ascertaining facts and sharpening issues. They would like to foster responsibility for judgments and, perhaps, competition. Perhaps most of all, Boren and McCurdy seemed to be concerned with improving counterintelligence.

What this will amount to remains to be seen: It is not clear how well Boren and McCurdy understand what they are about. The finest example of this regards counterintelligence. In May of 1990 Senator Boren received 13 recommendations from the blue-ribbon panel he had appointed to study the subject.[5] Five of these proposed instituting or raising penalties for engaging in or abetting espionage. Four dealt with rules under which CI investigators work, and four advocated toughening personnel security standards. If this is all Senator Boren has had in mind, he might achieve at best a small gain in security after a huge debate on the (largely nonexistent) trade-off between CI and civil liberties. Concern for counterintelligence can be negated by innocent acceptance of a definition of CI that is mistaken and serves bureaucrats' narrow agendas. To improve CI, one must tackle the agencies' phobia about CI analysis—a phobia rooted in a reluctance to have their own judgments questioned. One also must deal with other matters which mean nothing to the average American but which raise the hackles of intelligence bureaucrats (such as independence for CI people within the agencies, and mandates to CI people not just to identify hostile espionage but to turn it back upon itself). In the course of developing their bills, Boren and McCurdy faced innumerable temptations to adopt "expert opinion" from within the agencies as the fulfillment of their own sensible requirements. *What their agenda comes to depends first of all on how far beyond the agencies' their own understanding reaches.*

It also depends on Robert Gates, who became Director of Central Intelligence in November 1991. Gates' own understanding surely reaches beyond that of the agencies. He was one of the rare career CIA analysts who learned the language of the country in which he specialized—Russian. He also earned a Ph.D. Over the years he built a record of caring whether his (and others') analyses actually matched what happened in the real world. His tours on the staff of the National Security Council (1977–79 and 1989–91) also strengthened in him the realization that intelligence exists for the sake of statecraft. His "outside tours" and his rapid rise allowed him to avoid becoming part of the agency's culture and factions. In addition to that, he developed—most unusually for an analyst—a sense of the importance of counterintelligence.

As regards collection, Gates had a user's understanding of the difference between what is needed and what the collection system supplies—and little sense of commitment to the perpetuation of that system. He had none of the traits that inhibited his predecessors from reforming the agency. There was nothing in Gates resembling William Casey's nostalgic love for the agency, or George Bush's undue respect for its professionals. Unlike Stansfield Turner, who was willing to discomfit professionals but concentrated on intramural enemies, Gates was more likely to hire and fire with an eye to its effect on intelligence about the outside world. Unlike Richard Helms, he was not likely to approach the job like a captain who would maneuver but not restructure a basically sound ship. Unlike William Colby he was not likely to settle factional scores, and unlike Allen Dulles he had no romantic notions about the intelligence business and no prejudices in favor of the CIA's ruling class. He was more likely to resemble John McCone—except that he was a generation younger when he took the job, and that, while reform had not been on the agenda in the 1960s, by the 1990s reform *was* the agenda.

Whose Agenda?

The principal reason why in 1991 "everyone" agreed that U.S. intelligence must be reformed is that its principal focus, the communist world, had collapsed. Yet that collapse does not dictate the shape of reforms. It is surely as mistaken to suggest, as do some supporters of Senator Moynihan, that the postcommunist world requires that the CIA's functions be split between the State and Defense Departments,[6] as it is to suggest that because the future will bring troubles of its own we must respect the U.S. intelligence community's internal borders. *It is more important to define what any particular job, e.g., espionage, is to accomplish, how it is to be accomplished, and to hire the right kinds of people to do it, than it is to decide for which bureaucracy these people will work.*

It would be tragic if reform came to mean mere retrenchment. As we have mentioned, the second Russian Revolution of our century has barely begun, and may yet yield noxious fruits. More important, even if the old set of dangers had passed entirely, simply to reduce our vigilance would guarantee that the next set of dangers would catch us unprepared. Nor should one think that budget cuts of X percent by themselves would result merely in a corresponding reduction in warning capacity. Bureaucracies normally cut "muscle" to preserve fat. Hence mere retrenchment would leave us with intelligence agencies incapable of helping the country abroad, but well heeled enough to remain players in Washington.

The very worst would be to use the feeling of safety engendered by the collapse of communism as an opportunity for indulging in the vain quarrels of the past. The very nomination of Robert Gates was almost undone by the desire of many Senators to dramatize the Iran–Contra scandal of 1987 so as to cast aspersions on President Bush while posturing as defenders of propriety. Some—reflecting sentiment at CIA—preferred not to wrestle with the demanding agenda of reform that Gates would bring and instead preferred to take a vacation from policy by accusing Gates of having been insufficiently zealous in rooting out the scandal. Under the guise of making sure that no scandal could reoccur, some wanted to settle bureaucratic scores,[7] and others wanted to reinvigorate the Church Committee's agenda of substituting procedure for substance.

But true reform does not consist of procedures, budgets, or of drawing bureaucratic "wiring diagrams," much less of bureaucratic vendettas. It consists of figuring out how the needs of the future differ from what present bureaucracies can deliver, and then acting dispassionately. In non-threatening times governments can reform armies and intelligence services safely and at leisure. But when the discipline of danger and haste is lacking, what can ward off temptations to pursue trashy agendas under the guise of reform? Only an unusual capacity on the part of high officials to see their objectives and to keep their eyes on them.

REFORM AND COUNTERREFORM

What the President—and the Congress—will accept by way of intelligence reform will depend on what sort of case the reformers make to the public and how they handle the inevitable counterattacks from the bureaucracy. Congressman McCurdy has said that the reforms will take place whether or not the intelligence agencies go along. That is easier said than done, especially since the agency bureaucracies know and are committed to what they want, while the reformers have to figure out what they want, muster their own will, and make their case. Any would-be reformer must begin by explaining what is wrong, and how the proposed reforms will fix it.

But how will the reformers (Gates, Boren, and McCurdy) decide what they want, and what sort of case they want to make for it? Standard Washington practice calls for holding congressional hearings and appointing executive commissions. Abstractly, there is nothing wrong with that. In practice, how one structures a hearing or a commission well-nigh predetermines its result. Who will speak? What will be asked? Most often, in most fields, hearings and commissions are dominated by the bureaucracy's agendas and quarrels. In intelligence this has been especially so.

McCurdy has promised to swear in witnesses, so that the threat of prosecution for perjury will obviate his having to "read between the lines" of intelligence officials' testimony. In the long run, that will do little good. Unless he himself and his staff have a clear idea of what they want to achieve, they cannot call the witnesses who will enlighten them about it. If the congressional intelligence committees, or Robert Gates for that matter, accept the intelligence bureaucracy as the fountain of wisdom on their subject, they could produce a reform in name only. Witnesses can lead the committees down the garden path without coming close to exposing themselves to charges of perjury. By honestly being the narrow-minded people they are, bureaucrats can simply help Boren and McCurdy reinterpret their thoughts, and call old things by new names. They can obfuscate and water down, confident that at least a year must pass before the committees find out they have been sidetracked and another before they muster anger, by which time either the legislators or the bureaucrats will be gone from their posts. No. Reforming bureaucracies means first of all adopting intellectual points of departure outside the bureaucracies themselves.

So, in the end, reforming intelligence is not so much a matter of whipping bureaucracies, of breaking old careers and making new ones, (although that too is needed) as it is of understanding the art—what each of the functions of intelligence is about, what is good performance, what is bad. Congressional hearings won't teach that, because congressional committees can't call the kinds of people who could really teach them the subject: the Kautilyas, the Machiavellis, the Thucydides of this world—the historians of success and failure. Yet such people are available to anyone who will study them. The point here is that a reform can be no better than the models to which it aspires.

A serious study of intelligence, just like the serious study of any other practical discipline, will not yield recipes for success. It will yield *a way of thinking about the subject* akin to that of those who have been successful. The following chapters try to distill the wisdom of the ages about intelligence—or, as in the case of technical collection, to apply that wisdom. The historical record of exemplary successes and failures will not tell Messrs. Boren, Gates, and McCurdy (or any reader) what to do. But, having shared a thought with the real Machiavelli, one is less likely to be led astray by imitators.

PART *III*

Principles and Precepts

9

Access to Secrets

Seek and ye shall find.

– Jesus, Sermon on the Mount

Problems and Methods

Intelligence collection, much like politics itself, is the art of the possible. Any target of our curiosity offers the collector several avenues of access. The art consists of rejecting preconceived notions of how the information *ought to be* gathered, and of using the available avenues for all they are worth. Here we concentrate on the methods of collection—the ramifications of the fundamental principle of collection, i.e., *access*, both human and technical, or, how not to spy in vain. On the human side we show the importance of matching the collector to the target. Then we argue that thought about espionage ought to run from the nature of the source to that of the collector. Hence we explain that engineering the collector's cover, far from being an adjunct of the operation, is its very core. Finally we show how human intelligence should be gathered in a variety of circumstances. Our technical argument is similar. We argue that technical collectors are less the result of blind technical developments than of human choice. The nature and cost of each machine, we contend, should be determined primarily by the end use to which the information it produces should be put. Then, after discussing the various factors that affect the performance of technical collectors, we list the sort of collectors we believe make sense in this turn-of-the-century environment. We end by cautioning that technical collection is best fit to provide information about means rather than ends.

Methods of collection have evolved along with what is to be collected. Yet even the newest methods correspond to those used in ancient times. Gatherers of intelligence have always been asked to produce images, to record and interpret signals, to evaluate the characteristics of weapons, to report on the wealth of nations, and of course to conduct espionage. Governments have always wanted images of foreign cities, armies, equipment. Human beings with good memories and sketchpads sitting on mountaintops or in treetops, or floating down rivers or galloping by on horseback, were replaced by balloonists with cameras; then by aircraft; then by satellites with cameras and even more exotic devices. As long as armies have had signals, opposing armies have tried to read them. Just as signalmen manned the first radios, signalmen performed the first radio intercepts. The tools, both mathematical and physical, for *decoding* have been quite similar to those for *encoding*. The codes which were invented with paper and pencil were solved on paper. Those devised by computers can only be attacked using computers. As weapons have become more complex, more and more specialized knowledge is required to understand them. But the principle is an old one and applies both to men and to machines: Armorers have been the most successful in seeking out intelligence about armor.

Over the centuries, spies have had to adapt their techniques to the information to be sought and to the security measures deployed against them. In our times, minicameras and tape recorders have done away with the need for spies to memorize reports, just as satellite-linked burst transmitters have done away with the need for weeks of walking to deliver reports. But today, as ever, the human intelligence officer must know at whom he is looking, and pay attention to what he is supposed to be looking for.* Today, as always, he must be creative about how he presents himself to his source and about how he hides what he is doing. The constant principle of human intelligence-gathering is: Find out where the information is, or who has it, and put someone close enough to the person or place to get it.

The sources change, operating conditions change, the men and machines appropriate to gaining access change. But the task of collectors remains the same:

*Thus reportedly in 1989 the CIA officers who were assigned to observe the meeting between U.S. State Department officer Felix Bloch and KGB officer Reino Gikman in a Brussels restaurant failed to notice whether Bloch entered the restaurant with a handbag or left without one. The purpose of the observation was to determine what, if anything, Bloch was giving to the Soviets. *The New York Times Magazine*, 13 May 1990.

to engineer access. Let us now explain the principles of human and technical access to intelligence information.

Human Access

The Collector

The characteristics of the person sent to gather information often make the difference between information that is useful and information that is worse than useless.

When the children of Israel first approached the Promised Land, Moses chose 12 spies, one from each of the tribes. According to the book of *Numbers*, the Lord himself had specified that each be "a ruler among" the people, and Moses dutifully picked spies who were "heads of the children of Israel."* Note that while the spies were somehow representative of Israel, they were *not* picked because of any particular aptitude for the job, (and that their lack of aptitude proved decisive.) Always a details man, Moses told the spies to notice whether the inhabitants were "strong or weak, few or many," and "what cities they be that they dwell in, where in tents or in strongholds." He also asked about the condition of the land. But when the 12 returned, it was clear that nine of them had gone with the wrong mindset. The nine came back with details about grapes, figs, milk, and honey. Instead of useful details about the inhabitants they brought back nonsense about giants. They had no interest in fighting, and wanted to go back to Egypt. Their inadequately focused minds—representative of their tribes—cost Israel 40 years in the wilderness.

By contrast, the Ulysses of *The Iliad* dressed himself as a beggar and entered Troy, where he made good mental notes of the Trojans' strengths and weaknesses. Others would have made a likelier beggar, and others yet were higher in command. Ulysses went because he was best able to get in *and* to notice what needed to be noticed. By the same token, Julius Caesar himself reconnoitered Britain before invading it, and also insisted on leading the reconnaissance operations in both the eastern and western theaters of the Roman Civil War. Like Ulysses, he went himself because he wanted to make sure that the things he wanted noticed would indeed be noticed, and evidently did not

---

*Book of *Numbers*, Ch. 13, 14. Giving the Israelites intelligence about the Amalechites was obviously not the Lord's first concern. Had it been, He presumably would have demanded that the spies be representative of the best-qualified rather than of the average of the princes of Israel. Rather, this divine preference for social representativeness over mission-specific skills was obviously intended as a trial. As such it succeeded in proving to the Israelites how unworthy they were of the Land of the Covenant. Be that as it may, the espionage mission proved counterproductive to its earthly purpose.

trust anyone else to have the requisite powers of observation. For that reason too Rome's General Sertorius went so far as to learn the Celtic language, put on a sheepskin, and wander among the barbarians.

But if the commander cannot be his own spy, how can he increase the chance that particular aspects of reality will be noticed? During World War I, Sir Godfrey Huggins, then Prime Minister of Southern Rhodesia, sent two spies, each with known and different biases, to scout the Portuguese Army in Mozambique.* He was refining a practice taught by the fourth-century B.C. Greek military writer Eneas Tacticus, whose remedy for ignorant reports was to put three scouts, all experienced in war, in each place.[1] The commander could then "triangulate" what he wanted to know.

If, however, the success of a particular espionage job depends on the spy noticing certain things, why not simply find (or perhaps train) spies for whom noticing such things is second nature? This simple insight was the basis of perhaps the most rational system of espionage ever devised—that of Kautilya's *Arthasastra*.[2] Each kind of spy would have its own specialized beat and peculiar assignment. Kautilya's spies were: the "fraudulent disciple," the "recluse," the "householder," the "merchant," the "ascetic," the "classmate or colleague," the "fire-brand," the "poisoner," and the "mendicant woman." For example, the recluse "shall carry on agriculture, cattle rearing, and trade on the lands allotted to him for the purpose. Out of the produce and profits thus acquired, he shall provide all ascetics with subsistence, clothing and lodging, and send on espionage such among those under his protection as are desirous to earn a livelihood, *ordering each to detect a particular kind of crime* committed in connection with the King's wealth. . . ." (emphasis ours) The householder spy, for his part, "shall carry on the cultivation of lands allotted to him," while the merchant spy "shall carry on the manufacture of merchandise . . . ," and so on. So every part of society would be sown with spies apt to pick up particular kinds of information from certain kinds of people. Following the principle that "Purity of character shall be ascertained through persons of similar professions," reports would be believed when received from three independent sources.

In times and places far away from Kautilya's India one will surely think of different categories of spies (e.g., the "bartender"). One will figure out how he should live, with whom he will come into contact, and what he is to look for. But Kautilya's principle is the basis of common sense about espionage everywhere. No one profession, one nationality, one state of life, one *curriculum vitae*, allows one kind of person to understand all others and solicit all others. Hence any

---

*The officer spy reported that the Portuguese soldiers were rabble who would flee at the first shot. The sergeant spy reported that the Portuguese were sturdy peasant lads who would give a good account of themselves if led well.

302

person or any given set of human arrangements that reports well about one set of sources in a given set of circumstances will almost never perform as well against other sources or in different circumstances. Because it is worse than a waste of time to press people who habitually talk to farmers to talk to scholars, and vice versa, the notion of an all-purpose human intelligence collector is silly.

This means that most contemporary writing on espionage is very wrong. To state that "cover" for human intelligence collectors is either "official" or "nonofficial" is like saying that food is divided into steak and nonsteak—true, but misleading. Similarly, to think in terms of a rigid distinction between case officers and agents, and then to divide the latter into recruited and walk-ins, defectors-in-place and defectors, is to leave out a myriad of ways in which human beings can gather secrets—it is like saying that food is something that comes from supermarkets or is brought by waiters. Again, partially true but mentally crippling. Just as food is anything that nourishes, espionage is whatever human arrangement procures information. A system of espionage works best when the characteristics of the source match those of the collector.

Back Engineering

When one wires an electric circuit, one works from the load to the source. To engineer human access one must work from the characteristics of the source to those of the collector.

Code clerks like John Walker or private secretaries like German Prime Minister Willi Brandt's Günther Guillaume, or supermoles like Kim Philby, are the dreams of the world's spymasters. Leaving aside volunteers, how does one go about getting such agents? The answer, as regards both the great ones and the not-so-great, seems to lie in targeting the peculiarities of certain groups of people. In the 1930s, Soviet agents knew Western intellectuals well enough to realize that a straightforward "Will you work for peace; will you work with us?" would be sufficient, as often as not. This is how Hede Massing and Harry Dexter White recruited people like themselves among left-leaning U.S. government officials. In the 1970s the East Germans effectively targeted (among others) the dedicated, not-so-young, not-so-attractive women whom senior West German government officials often hired as their secretaries, through Prince Charmings who seduced them into giving not only themselves but the contents of their bosses' drawers, too. They also attracted high-ranking, fashionably leftist officials who liked to think of themselves as being in the vanguard of "good relations" with the socialist regime in the East that was very popular in progressive sectors of West German society from the 1960s all the way to 1989. This illustrates an old truth: When a particular social group takes its special friendship with a foreign power as a badge of superiority over its domestic rivals, that group is a fertile recruiting ground for spies. As for low-level military personnel (who sometimes have very important jobs), the techniques are ages-old too: If one cannot run bars or brothels near military bases, haunt such places with recruiters who can mingle with soldiers as easily as can bartenders or whores. And of course one must be ready to receive walk-ins. Let us explore several basic approaches.

Suppose one wished to recruit a harbor master in Havana or just to talk to him about the kind of cargo that has been coming into his port. With whom might the harbormaster speak more or less freely? Certainly not with anyone who had no business in the harbor. But suppose that the Mexican oil company PeMex was proposing to replace the oil-offloading equipment in Havana harbor. An official of that company would naturally be talking with the harbormaster and, over the course of some weeks, might well find out all he needs about other cargoes without the harbormaster ever realizing that someone had collected intelligence from him. If in the course of conversation the harbormaster appeared to be amenable to an offer to consciously report intelligence, the Mexican petroleum official would be in the best position to make it.

Who would be most likely to get a Muslim Sudanese colonel to talk sincerely about who in his army was truly willing to make peace with Christian rebels in the south of that country? Perhaps if the colonel dealt repeatedly with a famine-relief official who himself was a Muslim with a military background, the colonel might talk. An Egyptian or a Saudi military attaché might have some luck, too, because the Sudanese colonel might reasonably see either as channels of assistance. And again, these very people would be most likely to judge whether the colonel might be willing to betray some of his comrades, or all of them.

Who can get to a German chemical-company executive about his and his collegues' sales in Russia or Iraq? Several approaches might work, depending on the individual's propensities. If he were of one sort, a high-quality courtesane could become his confidante. If he were of another sort, perhaps an official of the Italian chemicals giant Montedison might offer assistance on good terms to expand the operations, and thereby at least get into a conversation on the subject, which the German executive could not rudely break without also hurting an important business connection.

Likewise, scientists the world over, even if they are working on highly classified projects, have a hard time cutting off discussions with fellow scientists. The standard rationalization by which the scientist treads upon classified ground is "I won't talk about the project at all. I'll stick to the basic scientific principles involved." However, to a fellow scientist who has been thinking precisely about how to apply the principles of his field to a particular military problem, this sort of talk is transparent. Moreover, since the boundary between what is "basic" and what is project-related is a matter of opinion; it is enough that the intelligence-seeking scientist be professionally attractive and subtle in directing the conversation. But if, in addition, he can offer professional rewards (recognition, travel, access to famous facilities and people), both scientists together might toy with the hazy boundaries, without having to surmount crises of conscience. But if such a crisis should be required, who better to manage it than someone who is already professionally respected?

Whom should one send to elicit information from nationalist groups anywhere? The question really is: How can one gain a nationalist's confidence? The obvious answer is to send a kindred soul who has a good ostensible reason for being there, *and* perhaps something to offer. Former Soviet Azerbaijanis are kin of Iranian Azerbaijanis. An Iranian Azeri who has business in Baku could easily project the sympathy and bring the material gifts that would open both hearts and channels of communication. Azeri nationalists in Baku would speak to such a man without fear of being noticed, and without skewing their words for effect. At his discretion, this businessman might confide in a few locals that he is really representing a foreign government friendly to their cause, and task them with providing specific information. Of course he would then have to come up with substantial material tokens of the foreign power's sympathy.

A less intrusive approach is to send scholars, or even journalists, who know how to be sympathetic and who can offer only the satisfaction of "telling the world" or "setting the record straight." That alone, as shown by the stories filed by *The New York Times'* Bill Keller from Baku in January 1990, provides valuable insight into the roles which the various factions of the nationalist movement played vis-à-vis Moscow. Keller investigated reports that Azeri nationalists had begun a genocidal campaign against Armenians in Baku, prompting a Soviet invasion in January 1990 aimed at restoring "civility." After a long round of interviews, Keller found that the KGB had promoted this image by putting on television anti-Armenian Azeri extremists, who may have been KGB employees, while denying media access to mainstream Azeri nationalists, who were agitating not against the Armenians but against the Communist party. These nationalists had succeeded in making the Party irrelevant. Keller's firsthand human collection was powerful evidence that the Soviet government fomented strife through its agents as a pretext for military intervention aimed not at restoring civility but at ensuring the survival of the Communist party.[3] Keller's collection was overt. But one can imagine how easily such able journalists might set up networks of sources at various depths within the nationalist movement.

In short, espionage does not have to involve transfers of loyalties. Indeed, in an ideally designed operation the recruitment uses no "flag" at all, neither a false one nor a true one, because the source is not conscious of betraying anybody. In ideally designed operations, both the source and the intelligence officer are "doing what comes naturally"—but in a milieu artificially crafted by the collector.

Real operations will fall short of the ideal. In practice, what one might call "observation reporting" will often fall short of the reports from sources who have made a decision to spy. But a collection operation is likely to be productive to the extent that it identifies who has the required information, and what kind of persons normally associate with the source, and then either find a collector on one's staff who fits the profile, or go out and hire one—thereby putting close to the source someone who is personally equipped to develop that source to the maximum possible extent, and who is intellectually equipped to understand the substance of the milieu in which he will find himself.

Cover

Because the essence of the operational art is to match the qualities of the source and the collector, it is no exaggeration to say, along with Kautilya, that *there are as many kinds of intelligence collectors as there are kinds of cover.* Indeed the cover of any operation largely determines the quality of that operation, and largely predetermines its success or failure. The suppositions, all too common in intelligence services, that all the time and expense devoted to giving intelligence officers new labels or altogether new identities is a kind of overhead cost that must be paid to do the job of espionage, and that time spent "living one's cover" is time lost to intelligence work, is true only to the extent that the cover has been badly designed. True enough, a fellow whose cover job is, say, making contacts in a local trade ministry will naturally come into contact primarily with people in that bureaucracy. If his "real" job is to recruit and run people from other categories, he is in trouble. But to the extent that the cover has been tailored to the mission, the intelligence officer will find no better avenue of contact with the target group than living his cover. Let us see what that means.

For the source, the best cover is no cover at all. Say that an official in the government of country X decides to tell his secrets to someone from country Y. He need only not *un*cover his intentions. To do that he must cover his contacts with country Y, i.e. make sure that they do not draw the attention of hostile CI. But the best way of doing that is to make no changes at all in the way he lives and works, above all no changes in the kinds of contacts with country Y that he had had over the years. The operation will be most secure if the collector covers his own insertion into the source's uncovered contacts with country Y. Obviously the quality of the operation will depend on how good the contacts were before the operation started.

The collector's task, to collect while not appearing to be collecting, requires him to enter into a role that naturally puts him very close to his source. This means that ideally the contact, or at least the channel between source and collector, has to be regular and should predate the instance when collection takes place. Ideally, the collector (e.g., an Iranian oil tool-buyer in Baku or an American retiree in Guatemala) is in place for many years and has had regular contact with the source well before being called upon for the intelligence mission.

The KGB calls its chiefs of station Rezident. This term evokes a role far different from the one that he and his contemporary American counterparts play, a role more akin to that described by Kautilya. It evokes the idea that in the world's important places there live people on whom an outside power can count for information. These persons, who are very much part of the scenery, will keep their eyes and ears open to how local events may affect the interests of the country of their allegiance, and they will build their own networks of friends and informants. Such "residents," unlike full-time collectors who must produce reports to maintain their place in their bureaucracy, report only when there is something to report. Their primary function is to be there when someone in the faraway capital asks "Who is our man in eastern Ruritania?" or "Who is our man in the Ruritanian business community?" The ancient Greek cities employed Proxenoi, prominent local citizens who took care of the affairs of the foreign city that designated them (Alcibiades was Sparta's Proxenos in Athens), much as "honorary consuls" do in the modern world. The Roman Republic, and later the Empire, developed vast networks of resident friends in neighboring lands. In the early part of the twentieth century, British diplomats had a similar network of unofficial residents throughout the world on whom they could count for information. Likewise, after World War II, France's economic and cultural presence in its former colonies maintained good informal networks. Indeed, in the 1960s, when the U.S. flooded Indochina with professional intelligence officers, France often managed superior intelligence through the use of a network of sympathizers that had long since become part of the scenery.

Hence the most effective human intelligence system would consist of seeding as many foreign places and professions as possible with residents. It is far easier to do that by recruiting people who are already in place, who are successfully making their lives in a given environment and enjoying it, than to somehow hire outsiders, train them to be something they are not, and then ask them to live lives of burdensome duty. The advantages of one intelligence service having permanent collaborators, among African farm-equipment dealers, the Saudi travel agents who organize the Hadj, and the very different travel agents who organize the aristocracy's constant pleasurable wanderings abroad or among say French journalists who frequent the Arab world's francophone aristocracy speak for themselves. But there are also difficulties. Such collaborators cannot be

307

employees, and must be managed as allies. At any point, they will serve according to their own motivation and judgment. Then there must be constant worries about the reliability of people who live lives apart from the bureaucracy. Finally, the more a collaborator collaborates, the thinner his cover must wear.

One may ameliorate these difficulties to some extent by recruiting collaborators as one needs them, even as armies recruit "stay-behinds" when they fear being pushed back. But that defeats part of the purpose, which is giving the collaborator the chance to build his network of informants unobtrusively as part of his daily professional activities. Moreover, hastily recruited foreigners also leave doubts about their motivation and security. On the other side of the ledger, we must note that no nation on earth is inherently better set up than the U.S. to recruit foreign collaborators. The French have an attractive universalist high culture. The Soviets had an ideology. But America is both a set of principles *and* a multiethnic reality. Anyone can aspire to both. What, after all, distinguishes an American from any other human being anywhere else in the world? Only an act of will.

To achieve cover both deep and widespread with one's own nationals is yet more difficult. One may find among one's people those who may pass for Trinidadian refinery executives or Brazilian professors. But then one must persuade the Trinidadians or Brazilians to let them use the cover—with all the risks to security that this implies. The alternative is laborious: to build "illegal" identities for one's own officers in countries where that is relatively easy to do, like Mexico, in order to be able to use the cover in countries where it is very difficult to build them.

Descending another rung, one may build the sort of nonofficial cover that was once common in the CIA: placing professional intelligence collectors in ones' own country's businesses, the professions, journalism. People thus covered can go almost anywhere, except where their nationality would put people on guard—that is, where they are needed most. A British oil engineer could circulate in Iran during the 1980s, whereas an American could not. On the other hand, nothing prevents such nonofficial cover officers—or diplomats either, for that matter—from passing themselves off as locals or as citizens of third countries for a little while, if they are at all able. One may imagine an American intelligence officer accredited to Hong Kong as a diplomat, or under cover as a businessman (providing he is of Chinese origin and speaks perfect Chinese), crossing the Chinese border, changing into Chinese clothes and, U.S. passport in his pocket like a reserve parachute, traveling the length and breadth of that country enjoying most of the advantages of legality as well as some of those of real cover.

We must not forget, however, that the purpose of cover is to get the right collector in contact with the right source under the most propitious circumstances.

Planning and Executing Espionage

Running "controlled" agents is a mechanical function easily performed and easily taught. Its essence is to exchange information. The collector gives questions and receives answers. The source receives moral and material support plus advice about security, and gives his views about what he will have to do in the future. The collector exercises some judgment about the application of security procedures, and a little regarding the source's motives. But he neither develops the questions nor understands the answers. However, as every journalist knows and every intelligence officer should know, managing all other kinds of sources is a far more complex matter.

First there is the crucial act of picking and approaching the target. Nothing determines the "catch" of espionage operations like the design of the net and the choice of fishing grounds. Espionage networks take many years to build. They are what they are and cannot be substantially adapted. If one's collectors in Mexico are divided into the sort of people who are accustomed to approaching people in the drug trade, and the sort who hobnob at top bureaucrats' cocktail parties, and then a desperate need arises for in-depth information on grass-roots Mexican labor organizers or junior military officers, no amount of trying will shorten the time required to find and hire people capable of good relations with the new target groups, and then the time required to actually build these new human relations. In the absence of the right tools, one may try the wrong ones—and expect lousy results. In espionage there is good long-term planning and bad long-term planning. But there can be no good short-term planning.

The picking of targets and engineering of approaches is an intellectual art. Anybody who thinks about it in the right way can do it. Here is an example worthy of emulation. In the 1930s the German Abwehr wanted information on France's high-technology aircraft industry. So in 1938 a Polish–French agent of the Abwehr, a loudly anti-Nazi financier named Oplinsky, bought the magazine *Aero*, which was to the French aircraft industry in the 1930s what *Aviation Week and Space Technology* is to the U.S. aerospace industry in our own time.[4] The magazine's reporters were loyal Frenchmen. But one can imagine how the Abwehr manipulated them by setting their agenda: If it wanted more coverage on engines, the new owner would assign the reporters to engines. More important, like all other reporters, those working for Oplinsky learned more than they wrote. Aircraft engineers often divulge secrets in order to explain nonsecret material to reporters, but pledge the reporters to secrecy. The loyal reporters may have promised to keep the secrets, and put their notes in the magazine's safe, to which only the editor had access. So for years the Abwehr simply tapped into a high-level human channel of French communication. Once the Abwehr had successfully bought the magazine under cover, it had effectively conquered a listening post. There was no need to recruit and run sources. The information flowed naturally. Imagine what a hostile intelligence service could do to the U.S. aerospace industry if it controlled the established, natural access of *Aviation Week?* The art would consist of covering the purchase. Imagine the returns that a foreign power—or even a foreign aerospace company—might enjoy were it to recruit even one well-connected *Aviation Week* reporter to act as its secret agent. The principle is simple: When one looks for information about any subject anywhere, it is good practice to begin by asking who normally gets it, and then to figure out how to tap into that channel covertly. Recruiting foreign reporters, businessmen, and such who already have access is obviously more cost-effective than building cover from scratch.

The art of recruitment and management of sources, of actually carrying out espionage plans, is less intellectual and more instinctive. Few are cut out for it. Whereas all successful journalists have to recruit their own sources, only a small minority of intelligence officers do that. This is due both to differences between the personal attributes of journalists and run-of-the-mill intelligence officers, and to the differences between the kinds of recruitments they practice. Obviously it is more difficult to ask someone to betray his government at the risk of being shot, as recruiters of controlled sources do, than it is to ask a source to betray his boss at the risk of being fired, or simply to give information to make a splash without getting wet. That is why intelligence officers find it easier to make recruitments under pretense of working for private businesses or friendly governments, or to ask only for information about "the bad guys," than to force flat-out choices between opposing loyalties. It is why they find it easiest of all to recruit sources who feel that there is a common interest between the collector's country and their own, and that the cooperation does not involve betrayal. This was certainly the relationship that existed between Jonathan Pollard and his Israeli recruiters.

But, as journalists know, a relationship without means of pressure requires subtlety and, above all, a realistic appraisal of what can and cannot be expected from the source. Thus, whereas an intelligence officer managing a "controlled source" tends to squeeze the source to the limits of what he can deliver and, *faute de mieux*, accept what the source has to say on matters beyond that source's reach, someone who is managing a cooperative source and finds that source inadequate will simply recruit another one. Our point is that the journalist's more flexible approach may more consistently produce both recruitments of sources and efficient management of them. All this said, it is true that some individuals, regardless of their titles, can elicit cooperation better than others. Only success itself identifies them.

Inaccessible People, Denied Areas, and Wartime

How does an espionage system penetrate groups of people—a terrorist cell or a Politburo—who trust only those they have grown up with, or who have shared "the trenches" with them? How does it penetrate countries that war or warlike regimes have rendered impenetrable? The general recipe is straightforward: Surround the target with your networks as best you can, and take whatever opportunities may come. And come they will, by virtue of the group's or the country's efforts to accomplish things in the world, or because of internal conflicts, and perhaps, because of defeats. The espionage system must make the best of the access it has, and not waste its resources reaching for the unreachable.

The network is most important. Closed terrorist cells in the Middle East are part of the semiopen entourages of terrorist chieftains who are part of overt Palestinian politics in which Arab governments take major parts. A good network would include bureaucrats in Arab foreign and interior ministries, and personages in Palestinian politics, recruited exclusively to report what they hear about the violent ones. It would also include professors at Arab universities, or reporters at Arab newspapers where the terrorists have followers to whom they advertise and explain their actions, and of course teachers at schools within Palestinian refugee camps. It should also include some Saudi moneymen. These ears surrounding the violent ones would listen for discord among them. Then agents would place the discordant factions in contact with people who would finance them, while listening sympathetically to reports about their evil enemies.

As regards the Soviet Politburo, even before the revolution of 1989 its members talked to hundreds of people. We must understand that the priorities of top bureaucrats have to be the very opposite of secrets. On any given day since October 1917, Moscow has been awash in underlings hurrying to be seen fulfilling the priority *du jour* of their superiors. Like bureaucrats everywhere they would open their sentences with "The boss wants. . . ." Had there been a well-constructed foreign intelligence network in Moscow, it would have taken the pulse of "what the boss wants" in every possible field.

Newspapers and specialized magazines are valuable sources for such networks. What they report about the priorities of leaders and agencies can be used as bases for questions posed by diplomats, newspaper people, professors, and visitors of every sort. Even in its most introverted period, the Soviet government eagerly sought out foreign visitors for every sector of Soviet society—youth, journalism, labor, industry, agriculture. Of course Soviet authorities preferred foreigners who were well-disposed to the regime. Nothing but lack of enterprise, though, ever prevented Western intelligence services from infiltrating collectors into these delegations of "useful idiots", or from recruiting some of their members as intelligence officers. Executives of major Western businesses offered a more consistent opportunity for high-level access—provided they could be persuaded to follow the agenda of intelligence collectors. The general point with "denied" people is to take every opening "the system" will give, not waste resources on what it won't, and to learn to make decisions on the basis of what information is available.

Wartime means tighter controls. But even in wartime no nation closes itself completely, except of course to its enemy. That is why there is only one absolute rule about espionage against a wartime enemy: The collectors must be, or must look like they are, either natives of the target country or from third countries. Enemy aliens can be effective collectors when they pass themselves off as traitors to their country, and then act as double agents. Much of the human collection in wartime must take place in third countries. Even there, however, citizens of the belligerent powers are likely to be under extra scrutiny, and official representatives may be expelled, interned, or hunted down, much as in the 1980s Americans were hunted down in Lebanon. So, in wartime, human collection (insofar as it does not consist merely of receiving defectors) is especially dependent on good cover. Those intelligence systems that failed to invest in good cover during peacetime and find their shallow-cover operations swept away by war are forced to build new undercover networks from scratch under the worst of circumstances. Not the least of the problems is that the new networks might be built using remnants of the old ones, and, since those might have been compromised, the new networks might be under enemy control from the first. The moral of the story is that there is no substitute for making cover good on the first try.

In wartime, straightforward "illegal" operations are especially difficult, unless the target country's security system has been broken by invasion, massive flows of refugees, or bombing. More likely to be fruitful are operations using channels—commercial, diplomatic, or humanitarian—which the enemy government keeps open with third countries. But even if one manages to recruit able people who already work in such channels, or to place one's own people there, such collectors are likely to do little good (and possibly much harm to themselves) by trying to recruit "controlled sources." However, it is easy enough for clandestine services to penetrate even war-mobilized societies deeply enough to discover the point of view, the mood, of various sectors. Thus agents recruited among or posing as third-country visitors might answer such important questions as: Do they really think they can do that? Up to what point will they put up with this policy? Who really supports Mr. X?

In sum, successful human collection depends on sending the right person for the right job. That means being willing to constantly reshape and restaff the clandestine service to match changes in the target. Just as in business the whole idea is to get to the customer and then to satisfy him, the whole point of espionage is to get to, and then to satisfy, the source of information.

Technical Access

Choices

Just as there is no one kind of person who can pick up all the signals that may emanate from the world's varied interesting people, there is no one kind of machine that can capture the signals reflected by or emanating from all the machines that are interesting to intelligence. Just as there is no one guise by which human collectors may enhance their access, every particular way of deploying intelligence machines affects *their* access to information; what they will be able to gather, and what they will miss. What technical collection systems produce depends not so much on the level of technology as it does on choices about how to use it.

Let us see what technical collection may contribute to strategic and battlefield intelligence in the remainder of the 1990s. We begin by describing why the *end use* of information must govern the conception of the device that collects it. Then we explain the various decisions that must be made regarding the system's electromagnetic and spatial cover, as well as about its physical survivability. Our main point follows: How modern technology lends itself less to learning the enemy's intentions than to gathering information to target the enemy, to preempt him, and to prepare countermeasures.* We end with some observations on how to plan for technical collection, and how to use its products.

The Primacy of End-Use

Everything on earth (and beyond it, too) either generates some kind of energy or reflects it. A battle tank, for example, reflects the sun's visible light, as well as the sun's infrared energy—heat. It also radiates the heat of its engine. Its 30 tons of ferrous metal detectably disturb the earth's magnetic field. Its engine's electrical system emits electromagnetic energy. The tank's body reflects radar waves. The tank's radio may broadcast on several frequencies. The tank may carry air defense systems that employ radar directors, while the rangefinder for the main gun emits laser radiation. If the tank carries nuclear munitions, some nuclear radiation will escape from them. Ships and big missile-launchers— almost any large piece of military equipment—also emit or reflect all these kinds of energy. Put into the right place a video camera, an infrared camera, a radar imager, a radar detector, a laser detector, a radio receiver, and an ampmeter (maybe even an X-ray machine and a radioactive-ion counter) and, without eyeballing the tank, you will know where it is—day, night, fog, camouflage,

---

*Given the sensitive nature of the subject, this unclassified treatment sticks close to first principles. We do not discuss any systems that the U.S. has or may acquire. We only discuss how, given modern technology, such systems (whether or not they exist) might perform.

whatever. You will also know whether it carries nuclear munitions, where it is pointing its weapons, where it is going, and possibly why—in all, more than one would normally care to know about it.

But why would anyone want to have all that data? Moreover, even if one tried to deploy all those sensors around a tank, the tank's owners could prevent it, just as the FBI would prevent a foreign government from parking a van across from the White House with acoustic, electronic, and laser listening devices aimed at the Oval Office. Add the fact that sensors vary widely in expense, and that technology limits their effective ranges, and, in order to limit rationally one's efforts at collecting data, one is driven to asking *why* one wants it. Does one want to know where the tank is going or, regardless of that, what it is doing? Does one want to study the tank, or does one want to kill it?

Answering different questions requires different sensors. To know precisely where the tank is so that it can be hit or avoided, the sensors need to identify and locate it precisely. To tell whether or when the tank is moving toward battle, so that the battle may be prepared or preempted, sensors must generally locate the tank in a bigger environment. This second set of sensors must be different from the first. To tell how the tank is put together, so that one may devise countermeasures, yet a third set of sensors must look at one model, closely, for a long time. Given the different jobs they must perform, each kind of sensor has its own optimal mode of deployment.

So, whether a sensor reacts to light or to magnetism, or to microwaves or to VHF, whether it is located in low earth orbit or at geosynchronous orbit, in the air or on the ground, whether the sensor is fine or gross, expensive or cheap, should depend on a clear understanding of the mission. *To the extent that thought processes run in the other direction, from a particular kind of sensor or a particular kind of operational concept and back to the mission, only dumb luck will prevent the technology from being used inefficiently.*

The Issues

How much area do we wish to cover, and with what? A radar on the ground is limited to its line of sight,* by its power, and, if it is pulse radar, by its Pulse Repetition Rate (PRR.)† That means it can see a low-flying airplane 10 miles

---

*The exception is OTH-B: Over-the-Horizon, Backscatter. This new technique, embodied in a radar that became operational in Maine in 1990, and will be in others that are to become operational in California and Florida in the 1990s, causes the ionization of air molecules in the upper atmosphere, which then "scatter" electromagnetic waves in the general direction of the radar's transmission. When these waves strike objects they return and, bouncing off the ionized layer, wind up at the receiving station. The system's enhanced range is compensated for by low accuracy.

†For the latter the range is equal to the distance that light can travel in one second, divided by the

away, seconds before it arrives; a high-flying airplane 200 miles away, 15 minutes before arrival; and intercontinental missile warheads only when they reach the highest point in their trajectory—15 minutes from impact. What if it were based in space? Greater altitude will give longer lines of sight. But longer lines of sight are useful only if adequate power and PRR are available. Fine images a thousand or more miles away require enormous amounts of power, and facilities the size of big buildings. If the radar is looking at the ground, it also needs a computer to sort out targets from "ground clutter." This means that while space-based radar has plenty of potential intelligence uses, pinpoint location and imaging at very long ranges is not one of them.* So the answer to the question "How much space do we wish to cover?" depends on the answer to the *prior* question "For what purpose?" Only by answering the "purpose" question can one move to the question "with what?" and then work on a useful technical solution to the problem of "coverage."

As we have said lower orbits trade proximity to the target for briefer glances and narrower fields of view. What good, then, are radars for orbital reconnaissance? It is technically impossible to keep constant track of tank-size or missile-launcher-size mobile things on the ground by radar imaging from geosynchronous altitude. Doing it from low orbital altitudes would require hundreds of state-of-the-art devices that cost in the billion-dollar range apiece. So if reconnaissance is the objective, one must turn away from radar to visible and infrared light.

What coverage can we get with cameras? Here too there are trade-offs between distance, space covered, time between glimpses, and the size of things noticed. Relatively cheap electro-optical cameras at high altitudes deliver excellent images in both the visible and infrared spectrum of areas hundreds, even thousands, of miles across. But all one can notice is large topographic features. Expensive satellites orbiting at altitudes of 100 miles can pick out a duck on a pond, but can (on average) visit a given spot on the earth not quite once a day. To see tank-size objects, a not-too-sophisticated satellite should be no more than 500 miles up. To provide the possibility of constant surveillance of any spot from that altitude (remember limitations on power supplies and processing capacity) would require some three dozen platforms. Do we want one, or a few, or dozens of satellites at altitudes high, medium, or low? Do we want them to

---

number of pulses per second, divided by two (because the pulse must make the return trip from the target).

*Hence the project, which figured prominently in the early SDI budgets under the category of Surveillance, Acquisition, Tracking, Kill Assessment (SATKa) involving precise radar imaging and mensuration of thousands of missile warheads and decoys at ranges of thousands of miles, was a classic example of a collection plan conceived from the wrong end.

deliver high-quality, medium-quality, or low-quality images? To make sense of these choices one must ask: For what purpose do we want to see these objects? What *about* them do we want to see? If we wanted to kill the objects rather than study them, it would not be worth our while to pay for technology to deliver sharp images. Recognition and targeting might not require images at all.

Consider cloudy weather and camouflage: Radar and magnetic anomaly detection can pierce them. But we have seen that imaging radar is impractical for wide-area surveillance. Magnetic detectors can't produce images at all, no matter how close the sensor gets. Yet *one can conceive of radar and magnetic sensors of tolerable sophistication and cost that, although not delivering images of objects, nevertheless note recognizable variations in the background.* By studying the patterns of such variations one might well arrive at correlations between any given pattern and the presence of tanks, or mobile missiles, or trucks.

Consider now the physical safety of the technical collectors. The modern battlefield, whether in the Falklands, Central Europe, or the Mid-East, is photographed and radared from land, sea, air, and space. Its communications are similarly intercepted, and its electronic emissions recorded. Sensors are sown throughout it to note the passage of men and equipment, etc. But every one of these mechanical spies is as vulnerable to a bullet as was Mata Hari, as vulnerable as the "expendable" second lieutenant who normally serves as a forward artillery observer. Moreover, each is liable to being blinded or deafened or jammed or deceived. Most important, the information from any given source seldom gets used until it is processed through at least one "processing center" or combat information center. There sit the linguists with earphones—the men watching the radar scopes, looking at the electronic countermeasure screens for indications that a particular signal has been picked up in a particular location. There stand the officers evaluating the situation and reporting to commanders, or assigning weapons directly. Destroy one of these centers, and the sensors that feed it are rendered useless.

So battlefield technical collection must protect the sensors and the processing center alike. The options for doing this are sixfold: deception, defense, stealth, mobility, "hardness," and sheer multiplicity.

For sensors, multiplicity makes much sense. If the enemy destroys a satellite or a battlefield communications intercept receiver, the effect depends on whether the unit destroyed was one of two or one of 20. It also depends on how many sensors of that kind one has safely stored away. Thus consider a typical peacetime trade-off from the perspective of wartime: X dollars would buy satellite A in a configuration that would give one year's lifetime in orbit. For only 2X dollars, the satellite can be made to last five years. Hence the more expensive version is a peacetime bargain. But in war, one would consider it a bargain at many times the cost to have five of the cheaper versions of the satellite, either in orbit or ready to launch. One may not wish to engage sensors in contests of attrition any more than one engages in such contests with second lieutenants. But one should avoid having unique sensors for the same reasons that one tries to avoid subjecting commanders-in-chief to enemy fire.

It also makes sense to build sensors as "hard" as possible. Thus radar and communications receivers—even optical focal planes—can be equipped with fuse-like devices that shut off the inflow of energy the instant it threatens to damage the sensor. This sort of thing can protect an imaging satellite from being blinded by a low-power laser, or a communications satellite from being deafened by a beam of noise. Similarly, a frequency-hopping feature on a radar transmitter allows it to sidestep jamming. Too, by insulating circuits one can go a long way toward negating the effects of the electromagnetic pulses generated by nuclear explosions. And indeed the state of the art of physical hardening of the surface of a satellite might well allow it to withstand the onrush of the X-rays from a 1-megaton detonation as close as 10 miles. As for processing centers on the ground, there is every reason to insulate circuits and to bulldoze piles of dirt around them. All such measures are as important as requiring artillery observers to wear helmets, ear protectors, and flak jackets, and to dig foxholes. But nothing will protect either human or technical sensors against a direct hit by a powerful weapon.

Absolute protection comes from the enemy's inability to locate the sensor. Artillery observers have learned to keep low profiles. Although the usefulness of "stealth" aircraft as weapons is open to argument, their usefulness as bearers of sensors is not. Nor is there any reason to believe that the techniques for reducing radar cross-section and absorbing radar energy (by which some enterprising aerospace engineers have reduced their sports cars' vulnerability to police radars) cannot be applied to satellites. A lesser but still substantial degree of safety comes from unpredictable mobility. Given enough fuel, satellites can change orbits— perhaps right before the initiation of hostilities. By the same token, the more that ground-based listening posts are moved, the less the chance of a ballistic missile or an artillery shell finding them.

Still, if one wishes to protect things that are difficult to move, disguise, and harden, and which are impossible to multiply (like processing centers), there is no alternative to defending them. Antiaircraft and antimissile batteries belong next to such centers just as they do next to command posts. As for satellites, they can be furnished with modest "shoot back" packages to intercept interceptors, just as scouts and soldiers who service battlefield sensors are issued self-defense weapons.

Disguising sensors is perhaps the most effective defensive measure of all. Aircraft, whether they carry cameras or bombs, protect themselves against heat-seeking missiles by dropping flares that, to the missile guidance system, look more like the plane than does the plane itself. Planes also confuse radar-guided missiles by radiating electronic signals that create electronic false targets. By the same token, intelligence satellites under attack might release foil balloons. On the battlefield, electronic listening devices can be emplaced in buildings or in burned-out trucks.

Beyond physical safety, deception can give technical devices the capacity to collect unexpected intelligence. While nothing can do that for a radar imaging satellite (which does not so much *look* at things as it *touches* them), deception can enhance the capacity of other imaging satellites, and even of some nonimaging radars. Were there to be a satellite for the radar detection of moving, submerged submarines (by the analysis of anomalies in surface waves), its effectiveness would depend substantially on the submarines' not knowing the satellite's orbital schedule. After all, if the submarine is not moving when the satellite is passing over, it can hardly generate disturbances of the ocean's surface. The only way of keeping secret the location of such a satellite—other than stealthing the satellite—would be to build good decoys of it and occasionally to scramble them. Of course the satellite would have to be careful not to irradiate stretches of ocean patrolled by ships that might thereby identify it. With satellites that collect passively (imaging and communications intercept satellites, for example), decoy and stealth strategies are much simpler propositions. The payoff for this deception is the ability to see through efforts at deception that the observed side might mount.[5] Comparison between the "take" from "covered" and overt satellites should always be interesting.

Consider also clandestine signals intelligence. Obviously the take from any operation depends on the physical access that the operation's cover provides. If a hostile intelligence service were to persuade a computer repairman, plumber, or policeman working in the White House to carry a briefcase or toolbox equipped with antennas and recording devices, it could collect the President's telephone conversations. Most of the world's decision-makers are theoretically much easier to target through this method. Once upon a time one needed an embassy, or a safe-house, next door to the target in order to eavesdrop on it. Later, technology shrank the "package" necessary for that sort of thing to van-size. Today, a briefcase will do, and soon a cigarette pack might. As the size of the package has shrunk, the possibilities for giving it cover, and thereby access, have increased.

What Makes Sense?

Let us now see what sort of technical collection might best support military or political combat, or strategic decisions, or long-range preparations.

For combat, only the most specific collection will do: A missile of type X is rising from point A and heading for point B. A regiment of tanks (or of mobile missiles) is at grid coordinate Y. A fire-control radar for weapons system Z has just been turned on in location C. President (or Commander) G has just given the following order. . . . To gather information on each of these kinds of targets requires particular kinds of sensors. Some examples follow.

Suppose one wanted to keep track of mobile missiles, tank regiments, and so on. First, the satellites would have to keep a very wide area in constant view. To do that (given the earth's rotation), at least three dozen satellites at altitudes of 500 miles would be needed. Since the missiles, tanks, etc. would have to be kept in view regardless of night or cloudy weather, the satellites could not rely on photography alone. They would have to carry multispectral sensors—visual, infrared, magnetic, and possibly radar. These satellites would also carry receivers tuned to the fire-control equipment and communications links of the military units being observed.

Anyone familiar with the cost of the finest modern sensors would quickly realize that a satellite that carried the best of the abovementioned devices fit for maximum performance at such distances would cost many billions of dollars per copy. Perhaps someday the cost of such sensors will be much lower. But for our time one must realize that the mission of tracking and targeting large military objects does not require excellent images of any kind. It requires just enough recognition of the difference between an environment where military item A is present and one where it is missing—that is, a complex of "signatures"—to be able to report that device A is at location X at time Z. Thus a satellite equipped with suboptimal cameras, magnetic detectors, radars, and antennas could probably be made for a price under a hundred million dollars, low enough for a large fleet to make sense.

Such satellites would have to be ubiquitous. Hence, though the location of any given satellite at any given time might be hidden in a variety of ways, the existence of the complex of satellites would have to be overt. The secret of the satellites' effectiveness would be what "signatures," precisely, the satellites would accept as evidence of what.

This approach to this intelligence problem beats sending stealth airplanes to roam the enemy country until the pilot's eyes rest on the missiles or tanks. Multispectral sensors in orbit are likelier to see the target than is the human eye at 20,000 feet altitude, they would be cheaper, and easier to defend. Since they would be obvious wartime targets, their protection—other than by their quantity—would have to consist of decoys that they would release when attacked.

Locating and tracking missiles and warheads in flight so that space-based antimissile weapons can recognize them and hit them is an entirely different problem. Dealing with that problem requires high-quality infrared equipment. To identify a missile during the initial or boost phase of its flight, one needs an accurate spectral breakdown of the missile exhaust. To get that, the sensor needs a spectral range broad enough (and sufficiently divided). Since the "signal" (the heat coming from the boosting missile) is intense, the sensor need not be super-cooled. The satellite could then instantly compare what it sees with a memory bank of exhaust characteristics, and make an infallible identification. Given the great distances that the missile travels, and the ballistic nature of its path, accurate tracking is very easy.

Tracking and identifying warheads and decoys during the midcourse and terminal phases of flight so that ground-based antimissile weapons can hit them is a substantially different problem because during these phases warheads and decoys are relatively cool and difficult to distinguish from the background of space and from one another. Telling them apart requires precise measuring of thermal differences, speeds, and even fine imaging. That in turn requires the very best infrared sensors, cryogenically cooled to near-absolute zero to make them supersensitive, backed by computers that evaluate the minute differences in the objects they see. Such equipment can be carried on high-flying aircraft.

Technical collection in peacetime is especially useful for preparing technical collection in war. Since combat collection must increasingly depend on instruments that recognize specialized "signatures," banks of such signatures must be gathered. Since weapons will increasingly depend on the functioning of complex technologies, the design of countermeasures must depend on understanding those technologies.

The instruments that gather signature banks differ from those that use them primarily in their deployment and in the way they process their data. Thus in the 1970s the U.S. Air Force built a device called Space Infra Red Experiment (which died buried in a warehouse) that was supposed to orbit the earth with supercooled infrared detectors, each specialized for a different mission, taking readings of everything from other satellites to missile boosters, to reentry vehicles. Many of the same missions were later performed at far greater expense under the SDI program. One of these involved setting a focal plane atop sounding rockets to be fired from Alaska into the path of Soviet missile warheads heading for impact on the Pacific test range. As the focal plane followed its own ballistic path, it would get a good look at the thermal characteristics of the warheads and decoys as they all descended. The data from these collection shots was used to calibrate similar sensors in the Airborne Optical Adjunct (AOA), an infrared package atop a high-flying Boeing 767. This is a battlefield sensor whose job is to distinguish and locate reentering missile warheads very precisely so that they may be intercepted. In fact, the development of instruments that gather signature banks often is an indispensable step in the development of modern battlefield sensors. After all, the basic technical question involved is what, precisely, a given sensor should look for.

This is the heart of vital research on the nonacoustic detectability of submarines: What submarine-generated disturbances, if any, can computer analysis of radar returns from sea surfaces detect? Various combinations of frequencies, power levels, and analytical parameters must be winnowed out by trial and error. Somewhat more directly approachable are the research tasks concerning the capacity of blue-green laser beams to penetrate ocean depths and return reflections of submarines. Whenever a new weapon, or a new sensor, or a new way of examining sensor data comes along, so must the necessity to understand "how *this* looks to *that*."

We have already discussed (Chapter 3) the limitations of technical collection in understanding the weapons of the 1990s. Given how little information the external observation of a laser weapon or an optical sensor may yield, it may make far more sense to save the money that might be spent trying to understand the weapon, and devote it to locating and destroying it. Any and all intelligence about enemy weapons may also be less valuable than building more and better ones for one's self.

The exception to this rule of thumb regards the ways in which modern weapons receive information and transmit it. Here are potentially great vulnerabilities. If a tank or a space-based laser uses a low-powered laser-radar to lock-on its pointing-and-tracking system, perhaps the beam can be deflected, or the receiver can be overloaded by a more powerful laser. If the pointer–tracker uses radar, that may be jammed. How do mobile missile batteries communicate with headquarters? If, by studying the character of the signals, one can gain insight into the design of the equipment, it may be possible to disrupt that equipment at crucial times. *All this implies shifting the focus of collection programs away from the weapons' gross performance characteristics (which one cannot do anything to influence) and toward the precise parameters of the weapons' links to the outside world (which one may well be able to disrupt).*

To locate fire-control radars or other electronic emitters requires only the simplest of receivers. The problem is making sure that the coverage remains adequate under wartime conditions. That is a matter of sheer quantity. That is why there is a legitimate presumption against anything that complicates and increases the cost of such sensors. Making sure that the information is quickly passed to the military commanders who need it is a technical problem akin to that which "electronic mail" companies of Silicon Valley solve with the greatest of ease. Modern technology also has provided a variety of sensors which, when attached to satellites, airplanes, ships, or tanks tell the simple but vital tale "You are being irradiated by frequency X, which is a fire-control device for weapon Y, which may be on its way to you now."

Communications intelligence that is useful for combat can be collected anywhere. Nevertheless, such is less likely to come from general sweeps of telephone and teletype traffic (which produce mountains of tapes that take years to analyze) than it is from highly targeted operations against people and places known to be relevant. Military forces routinely lay miles and miles of telephone lines connecting command posts with forward units. It is entirely possible for aircraft—the stealthier the better—to drop packages of intercept equipment near enough to these lines to pick up the information emanating from the wires. These miniature packages could record the information, and routinely burst-transmit their take to passing satellites, which in turn would relay them to the ground. When military forces are heavily using regular microwave telephone links, it would also make sense to drop such packages within line of sight of the most remote telephone relay towers one could find. Since no source of military communications intelligence (other than access to cryptographic keys) beats Officers Club bars, it would also make sense to focus clandestine communications-intelligence missions against places where enemy officials gather. Thus, for example, even in peacetime a serious intelligence service, or a serious entrepreneur who wished to sell his wares to intelligence services, would have every hotel bar in the city of Geneva wired for sound whenever a "peace" conference was in session.

Finally, the collection of basic communications intelligence (conversations that reveal the nature of human beings and their relationships) is far easier than the collection of communications intelligence about what people are going to do. Few people live and work entirely in guarded compounds. We have already discussed the relative ease with which "access agents" can be run at individuals. It is even easier to run technical access agents at places that target individuals frequent, especially for nonbusiness purposes. Modern techniques for bugging rooms, cars, airplanes, even restaurant tables, make it easy to record people's unguarded interactions. But this sort of communications intelligence is much less a technical enterprise than it is a human one.

Technical Collection, Means, and Ends

When the end-use of technical collection is strategic decision-making, the foremost thing to remember is that, with rare exception technical collection delivers facts that bear only indirectly on the enemy's intentions. That is because, by its very nature, technical intelligence is intelligence about *things*. An army is pausing in its withdrawal from a region—or has decided to stay. A regime has lost the will to live, or is merely acting indecisively. A military force is really counting on this missile, this operational approach, this submarine, or it is a vestige of another era. In such situations, technical collection delivers facts that bespeak intentions, but they do so ambiguously. Technical means can only tell "what they are doing," not why. To realize this is not to denigrate technical collection, but rather the starting point for making the best possible use of it.

An army withdraws from a country wherein it had bolstered a native ally.

322

Imaging satellites can watch the ships leave, and communications-intelligence satellites follow the chatter of regimental radios as they cross borders. But does the departure really mean that "they" have really "washed their hands" of the situation? Medium-resolution imaging coverage every week or so, and regular monitoring of communications nets, are quite enough to tell whether "they" are in fact continuing to provide logistical assistance to their local clients. Imaging surveys usually are enough to indicate what sort of deployment and strategy their clients' army is following. But who can tell if the logistical lines will speed up or dry up in a crisis, and how the clients' residual army will react? Technical coverage of South Vietnam in 1973–74 and of Afghanistan in 1989–90 would have yielded similar (though not identical) results: Outside supporter departs, leaving logistic lines intact; locals take up defensive positions that have proved solid in the past. Nothing visible or audible from the air or space would have foretold that the American logistic stream in Vietnam would dry up while the Soviet logistic stream flowed, and no technical information could have foretold the success of the North Vietnamese attack on Ban Me Thuot in 1975, or the failure of the Mujahedeen attack on Jalalabad in 1989.

During 1991 a controversy arose between the U.S. and the USSR regarding the Soviet Union's compliance with a treaty that would have required it to destroy all tanks, armored personnel carriers, and artillery pieces east of the Ural Mountains in excess of the numbers of similar equipment allotted to the North Atlantic alliance in Western Europe. Satellite photography showed clearly that the Soviet Union moved some 70,000 such items from the western to the eastern side of the Urals, and that it failed to destroy another three divisions' worth of such equipment remaining on the western side above the limit. But U.S. negotiators agreed with the Soviets that the undestroyed equipment remaining in the West had been properly reclassified as belonging to the Navy, while 75 percent of that which had been moved to the East should be reclassified as protection for missile bases. Obviously, data about numbers of tanks (and similar figures) say nothing about how such tanks will be used in a crisis, and whether U.S. negotiators were wise or foolish.

During the summer of 1990, clashes between Russians and Lithuanians, Latvians and Estonians, and among Russians, raised the question of whether the Soviet regime had, or had lost, the will to live. Boris Yeltsin, newly installed President of the Russian Republic, even set about constituting some police into a Russian—as opposed to Soviet—KGB.[6] This clearly was the sort of development followed better by news reporters on the scene than by cameras peering from space. While straightforward signals-intelligence monitoring of the location of military units added to the news reporting important facts about KGB troops being positioned for attempts to maintain control, they made no greater contribution than they had to the understanding (or rather to the misunderstanding) of the Polish crisis of 1980–81. Nor are there technical solutions to this sort of problem.

Missiles, as we have said, are ideal targets for technical intelligence. Even so, technical collection can only shed light on the role that a missile force of a certain quantity and quality *might* play in foreign military strategies. We have already examined the inconclusive American debate in the 1960s and 1970s over the function of the Soviet ICBM force. In the 1990s the ballistic missile—whether manufactured in Argentina (the Condor) or modified in Iraq (the Super SCUD, renamed Stone)—has become common throughout the world. The State-of-the-art of missile guidance and the miniaturization of nuclear warheads are hardly intelligence questions anymore. In the 1990s one has to assume that a missile will hit its target. Nor is the lethality of ballistic missiles loaded with chemical weapons in question. But the technical frontier that missile manufacturers faced early in the 1990s—on-line retargeting—does not seem to be amenable to technical collection. Certainly the actual load of any given missile is not. So in the 1990s, more than ever before, technical collection could only provide the wherewithal for strategic speculation on the role that even this most transparent of all weapons might play in a foreign strategy. The *hard* facts from technical collection will fall into two categories: what the weapons are roughly capable of, and where they are at any given time. Such facts will be useful for two purposes only: a general perception of danger, and specific acts of preemption.

Technical collection is inherently tied to action. Hence it is more useful for gathering the basic parameters of an enemy, and for actually fighting that enemy, than for discerning if he really is an enemy, or how he is going to proceed. Pictures and intercepts are hard data, all right, but they are very finite, and never speak for themselves. Moreover, technical collection is most useful when one realizes what any particular source can give, and what it cannot. The beginning of wisdom about technical collection is to realize what there is about a particular problem (say foreign missilery) that is accessible to technical collection, and what is not. Finally, the instruments of technical collection, like the military hardware they are most fit to spy on, take a long time to build. Which targets are covered by technical sensors at any given time, and how they are covered, is the result of years of planning and mountains of money—almost as much time, and many times more money, as are required to build human spy networks. The fundamental requirement is for a government to decide what sort of information it wants about any given subject, well before it needs it.

10

Quality Control

Be generous with counterintelligence.

– Sun Tzu

We have already seen that counterintelligence often makes the difference between collecting facts and picking up the enemy's "chicken feed," between seeing through the complexities and ruses in the enemy's activities and either missing the point or seeing the wrong one, between covert activities that have a chance of bearing fruit and those that are foredoomed. CI, the quality-control of intelligence, is the key to the struggle between states and armies for a favorable disparity of knowledge. We have also seen how the U.S. intelligence system, because of the primacy of bureaucratic considerations, has practiced a fragmented, crabbed version of CI. Our task here is to show what constitutes competent CI: Why certain CI practices work while others do not. In short, how to think about CI.

We will explain what heretofore our illustrations have only suggested— namely, that CI concerns all other aspects of intelligence; that it must use all of the elements of intelligence as part of itself, while at the same time CI as a whole must be part of the analysis, collection, and covert action practiced by intelligence services. In its inward-looking perspective, CI is a double-check on one's own intelligence operations.* In its outward-looking perspective, it is the sharpest weapon in the intelligence arsenal.

Analysis as Part of CI

Those who think of CI as consisting primarily of investigations could not be more mistaken. Properly conceived, CI consists primarily of analysis. That is because CI is concerned with that part of the enemy (its intelligence service) most apt to hide or disguise what it does. By far the hardest part of any CI case is to realize that the case exists—that some person, some thing, has the enemy's hidden hand in it. Just as a shopper improves his efficiency if he figures out what he wants, and telephones stores before trudging to the mall, so the CI man who looks for spies will waste less shoeleather to the extent that his mind has roamed the field and focused his investigative efforts. Successful hunters also know the difference between analyzing habitat, weather, and the like before going to the right places to look for tracks, and just tromping around the woods. Those who confine CI to investigations, like those who roam the malls or tromp the woods, will sometimes stumble across what they are looking for. But those who do best are constantly refining the maps by which they will navigate the forest—the hypotheses they will test against reality.

When it is done well, CI analysis consists of looking at the fields of activity—say, one's own defense industries, the policy of country X toward subject A, or a particular intelligence operation—using evidence and hunches *to make hypotheses about how hostile intelligence might be involved in the field, and testing those hypotheses.* Step by step, the analyst traces the effect back to the cause. And, here and there, the analyst may ask for an investigation.

To Catch a Thief

One may begin by considering what the service may be after, and how it might proceed. This is the old principle: To catch a thief, think like a thief. If you regard some of your own secrets, some of your own operations, as particularly important or vulnerable, so might the enemy. This can lead to paranoia. Thus it was that in 1990 the Soviet government charged that Western computers shipped to its country contained in their packing cartons devices that transmit to satellites information about where they are delivered, and devices within the computers that store and transmit data to "portable spying equipment."[1] Had the Soviet government investigated these charges it would have concluded that the scheme is impractical because most of the computers would have been in areas

*The term of the trade for the inward orientation of counterintelligence is "Operational Security" or OPSEC.

not accessible to so-called portable spying equipment. In general, however, such mild paranoia is useful because it leads one to examine facets of reality one might have neglected. When paranoia directs attention away from reality, though, it becomes counterproductive. The Soviet government blamed "computer viruses" introduced by the Germans for the troubles at a Soviet shoe-making factory. Yet Soviet factories have been known to snafu in grand style all by themselves. Our point is that a somewhat hyperactive imagination on the part of analysts about what the enemy might do can lead them to focus on moves that the enemy might well already have made. The price for this will be a certain number of false alarms. By contrast, a hypoactive imagination will give enemy intelligence a free ride.

The most obvious contrast in our time concerns the United States' and the Soviet Union's attitudes toward the construction of their own embassies in the other's capital in the 1970s and 1980s. The Soviets, because they assumed that the Americans would try to implant listening devices in the new Soviet Embassy in Washington, and because they anticipated various techniques that the U.S. might employ, insisted that every bit of concrete be poured on the construction site. They also imported a significant percentage of the labor force, and assigned security people to follow American construction workers around. Nothing could be brought onto the site which the Soviets had not inspected. By contrast, the U.S. Embassy in Moscow was built of large concrete slabs that had been prefabricated in the Soviet Union. The building was designed by a Soviet émigré living in the U.S., who later returned to the Soviet Union. The labor force was Soviet, and had token U.S. supervision. There should have been no surprise, then, that when construction was nearly completed, a congressionally mandated security survey found that the *entire building* acted as a microphone. Not coincidentally, while the Soviet building had been placed on the highest point in Washington, DC, giving it the greatest opportunity to eavesdrop on communications in the area, the American building had been placed next to the Moscow River (just about the lowest spot in the city), with the attendant disadvantages for communications intelligence. The U.S. first decided to demolish its nearly completed building in Moscow, then to build a secure superstructure onto it, and finally to rent it to American businesses. One side had thought the matter through and *expected* its embassy to be a target. The other had not.

To analyze a situation is to see opportunities, both for the hostiles and for one's own side. Targets certain to act as magnets for hostile services can be useful grounds for observing hostile officers at work, placing dangles before them, and perhaps penetrating the would-be penetrators.

How does one know at any given time what the enemy considers a target? Often the enemy publishes or broadcasts his interest. Thus a variety of nations have made no secret of their interest in Western businesses that deal in high technology and have multiple subscriptions to most high-tech trade publications. Hence it might be fruitful to hypothesize that companies whose achievements have been talked up, say in *Aviation Week and Space Technology*, would be targeted by some intelligence service. But whose? And what precisely would they be after? The first step would be to find out to whom any given technology would be particularly useful. Only after this analytical step would it make sense to make particular inquiries and lay specific traps.

Suppose that a survey of *Aviation Week* for the previous year showed an emphasis on the development of mirrors for the optical trains of high-energy laser devices by the TRW Corporation of Redondo Beach, California, and on the manufacture of new kinds of corporate aircraft by the Beech Aircraft Company in Wichita, Kansas. Some analysts might hypothesize that Russian leaders were so interested in retooling their aircraft industry to compete in the corporate aircraft market that they would try to steal Beech's work. Other analysts might conclude that since the Soviet antimissile defense program is deficient in optical trains for high-energy lasers, Soviet espionage would target the TRW facility. It would be easy enough to test both hypotheses by following up on requests for information and proposals for sales, interviewing employees about proposals they have received for consulting arrangements, checking on travel to the area by suspected agents, etc. Beyond information on specific operations, such investigations would yield insights into a more important question: Is the Russian government more interested in laser weapons or in business technology? Note: The root of such insights is the analysis of trade magazines from the hypothetical viewpoint of hostile intelligence.

Similarly, since covert influence operations are usually part of broad-gauged campaigns most of which are conducted aboveground, these campaigns are reliable guides to starting-points for investigations. Thus in the late 1980s agents of Iraqi dictator Saddam Hussein were organizing Jordanians while Saddam (himself an atheist) was proclaiming himself the liberator of Jerusalem. So, Jordanian King Hussein's counterintelligence rightly started its search for Iraqi agents by looking under the Islamic fundamentalist label. Consequently, when the open pronouncements of Jordanian Islamic fundamentalists suggested that it was important to sanctify the army, the King's analysts could fruitfully deploy investigators to root out Iraqi agents in the army. After all, intelligence is an instrument of policy, and policy must be pursued largely by open means.

Patterns and Imagination

Now consider analysis of the hostile service's patterns of behavior. On the most trivial level this means helping to discern intelligence officers from diplomats, trade representatives, and whatnot. Intelligence officers will often spend more money, take more security precautions, and seek out connections

328

that go beyond what one might expect. Thus when a "professor" travels to a foreign country and tells his hosts that he can "deliver" the attention of high-ranking personages of his government, one may hypothesize that he is more (or less) than a professor. Similarly, when one notices that an ambassador is fearful of his driver, one may hypothesize that the driver is more than a chauffeur. Thus also, when trying to determine the veracity of a high-level defector, it makes sense to ask him to describe the unusual successes that allowed him to rise unusually high. This sort of reasoning takes only common sense. Yet it will uncover most human schemes—except those hidden under complex patterns of events.

To analyze complex patterns, however, one must examine data from widespread sources and constantly ask whether any given item fits a pattern, as if one were looking at potential pieces of a jigsaw puzzle. Even to be able to ask whether an enemy's actions are partially due to his penetration of one's own intelligence one must see enough of a pattern to say "They can't be *that* smart, or *that* lucky." Witness that in 1964 Syrian intelligence noted that Israeli news was broadcasting decisions of the Syrian cabinet. The Syrian military had noted that Israeli guns were hitting Syrian artillery positions before they had been overflown by Israeli aircraft. This led the Syrians to try to pinpoint an illegal radio signal that had been originating from somewhere inside their country for years. It helped that the signal was broadcast each day at 8:30 A.M. It also helped that the signal was not on the air at all during the time that one of the few people privy to all the secrets was out of the country. Looked at separately, the facts meant nothing. Together they led Syrian intelligence to the apartment of Kamal Amin Taabet (really an Israeli named Eli Cohen), who had worked his way into the top ranks of Syria's ruling Ba'ath party.[2] They hanged him.

The most common type of CI analysis is the damage assessment. After one discovers a spy or loses a source or, the enemy identifies a piece of intelligence hardware, or the enemy scores a series of successes, it is only reasonable to reconstruct analytically how the damage occurred, and how it might continue. If this is done well, the losses might not be quite in vain. The most common form of damage assessment consists of damage control—cutting off tainted operations —and of attempts to fix responsibility by checking who on one's side might have been in a position to betray the information. But access lists are usually too long to be useful, and cutting off tainted operations, like amputations to fight gangrene, is so painful that it is sometimes not done thoroughly. Moreover, both of these procedures look inward, at one's own faults. A damage assessment that focuses on what the hostile service has demonstrated about itself, however, can be a powerful offensive tool.

The point is straightforward: Any intelligence operation will be evident to whoever assembles enough data and asks the right questions. The intellectual search for the right elements is the essence of CI. Pattern analysis can help. But if the hostiles know the pattern on which you focus, it becomes a powerful tool in their hands. Moreover, lest pattern analysis numb the mind, it must be the servant of imagination.

Sometimes it is not enough to sit back and watch for signs of enemy activity. One must hypothesize what the signs would be like if they were there, and then check to see if they are or not. Peter Wright, a scientist recruited into Britain's MI-5, tells a prototypical story of a fruitful train of investigations driven by an analytical insight. His superior, who lacked technical training, had been trying to explain how Soviet intelligence in London had been able to evade surveillance. MI-5 had investigated the surveillants and found them loyal. Now MI-5 was stuck. Wright suggested that the Soviets *might* be doing electronic direction-finding on the surveillants' car radio transmitters, correlating the results with the known movements of their own agents and thus finding the holes in the British net. In principle there was a way to check whether or not this was happening. Radio receivers capable of receiving more than one frequency use local oscillators to tune in the desired frequency and block out the others. As they do this, they emit harmonics to the frequency to which they are tuned. Theoretically, a nearby receiver could pick up these harmonics. But could British CI get an appropriate receiver near enough to the Soviet receivers? MI-5 put such a receiver into a van with radio-transparent walls and parked it near the Soviet consulate. A British surveillant's car drove by, and the Soviet receiver physically proved to the MI-5 receiver that it was listening to the surveillants' frequency. Once MI-5 had proved the principle, it was able to use it to localize the illegal agents in London who were receiving coded signals sent from Moscow.[3] Analysis of the traffic going to illegal agents also made it possible to identify the role that each agent played in the network, and hence made it easier to follow up leads about them.

Analysis, however, often raises more questions than it answers. Thus Peter Wright's examination of the Soviet Embassy's behavior during the arrest of illegal agent Gordon Lonsdale suggested that it knew that British CI was closing in on Lonsdale's address, but did not warn him. Why? Perhaps the people in charge of monitoring the movements of British CI were not allowed to know about Lonsdale, or perhaps, as Wright believed, the Soviets stood by to safeguard a mole in British CI. We are however less concerned with Wright's conclusions than with his method. Since high-frequency radio is no longer an important means for communicating with agents, Wright's techniques are now useful only as a reminder of the basic principle: All action, whether human or physical, disturbs the environment in some way. Find that disturbance and you have a key to the action.

There is no substitute for imagination in CI because there is no end to new devices, and no limit to the ways in which they may be used in the struggles between intelligence services. Take radar. It can penetrate clouds and see faraway objects. But because radar is gullible, radar camouflage and deception are an old story to military operators. Indeed, as we shall see below, the entire field of machine-gathered intelligence is even more rife with possibilities for mutual manipulation than is that gathered by humans.

Central Control

For analysis to play its proper CI role it must be able to survey all of the intelligence data available to one's own government, and it must be able to somehow direct the rest of CI. That is because by itself, analysis can produce only hypotheses, which become valuable only if they are tested. To test them requires setting up experiments, gathering data, setting up surveillance, making or modifying equipment. Moreover, it will not do to analyze any given case apart from all other cases, and indeed apart from any data that might possibly be relevant to these cases. Indeed the very core of CI is the judgment that certain facts ought to be looked at from a certain perspective, and that it may be possible to manipulate someone's perception in a certain way by releasing some secrets and guarding others while distorting information about yet others. This role can only be played by one organ in any one government.

This function requires very special people. To either craft or detect deceptive schemes that involve various kinds of spies and technical sensors, one must understand both the world of espionage and that of technology. The hypothesis about radio receivers that occurred instantly to Peter Wright could have occurred only to someone with a technical education. Those without such an education, no matter how worthy in every other way, would never have thought of it. The best case in point is that of Isser Harel, the legendary chief of Israeli intelligence in the 1950s and 1960s. In the early 1960s Harel, the very paragon of skepticism, fooled himself into thinking that Dr. Otto Joklik, an Austrian who was working on Egypt's rocket programs, was being useful to Israel, first as a spy and then as a secret envoy to German scientists who were being asked to work in Egypt. But Joklik was not anybody's agent. He was a purveyor of pseudotechnical mumbo-jumbo to Egyptians and Israelis alike.[4] If Harel had understood technical matters, his fabled "nose for a spy" (or for a fake) would have had a chance to come into play and avoid the embarrassment that he and his country suffered from their involvement with Joklik.

One must understand the subject matter of the deception. No knowledge of CI technique, not even the most highly developed instinct for CI work, can make up for ignorance of the issues of policy that the deception is trying to affect. One may easily enough judge that a stream of reports depicting an opposition leader in country B as corrupt and inept is coming, at least in part, through agents of the government of country B. But to understand precisely why this is happening requires a thorough knowledge of what country B's government might be after.

Then of course one must have the power within one's own government to shape investigations and to do the things necessary to take advantage of a deception effected or discovered. Since renaissance men will not always be at hand, prudent governments (e.g., the British in World War II) may constitute committees of specialists in various intelligence disciplines, leavened by people brought in precisely for their lively minds. But only proximity to the chiefs of intelligence and of government as a whole can move CI analysis from being correct to being effective. In sum, serious CI analysis must be central in three ways: It must work from a central repository of facts; it must be done by people who are expert in the various disciplines of intelligence and government; and it must be done by people who can command at least some investigations.

CI as Part of Analysis

Good analysis means asking the right questions. Yet what sort of questions analysts ask or do not ask is most often not an intellectual decision but a bureaucratic one. The right bureaucratic arrangement, often by itself stacks the odds in favor of success. I can think of no better illustration of this than the story of how the U.S. discovered the Soviet leadership's arrangements for riding out a nuclear war.

In 1983 each of the U.S. intelligence agencies reluctantly* established small units especially tasked to look for the possibility that the Soviet Union had somehow deceived the U.S. through U.S. technical collection systems. To these groups the agencies assigned their least-prized people and facilities. Then the agencies gave them data that had long since been squeezed dry of reportable facts. But the new groups, poor in every other way, had a unique intellectual focus, and that made all the difference.

A Different Perspective

An Air Force sergeant looking at an old roll of film on a peeling Formica table in a run-down World War II Quonset hut made a startling discovery: What had long been identified as a wind tunnel to test aircraft near the Moscow suburb of Sharapova could not possibly be that. The sergeant realized that, given the building's alignment, a wind tunnel in it would have blown down nearby

---

*The Congress, in its Fiscal Year 1983 Intelligence Authorization Act, had strongly encouraged the agencies to do this, as had a National Security Decision Memorandum signed by the President.

structures. The discovery of this lie made it a straightforward matter to learn the truth it had been intended to hide. The unit ordered up film dating to the "wind tunnel's" construction. It showed that, for years, trains had arrived at the site empty, and had left full of dirt. When the analysts added up the volume of the dirt, they realized that the Soviets had hollowed out a small city very deep underground. A search of old film from surrounding areas showed that similar excavation had gone unremarked. And why not? Why should analysts who had been tasked to report military activity or to identify new buildings have paid any attention to whether railroad cars sitting on sidings were empty or full? Looked at in a new light, however, evidence fairly leaped out at the analyst—evidence of devices to supply filtered air to the underground complex, of years-long projects to furnish it with everything needed to ride out a nuclear war, and of rapid subway lines that connected the complex to downtown Moscow and to the nearby Vnukova Airfield.[5]

Again: The difference between being blinded and being enlightened by the enemy's deceptive ploy lies first in approaching the data with a CI mentality ("Now, let's see, what kind of tricks might they be playing?"), and second in having access to enough data to check out one's own hypotheses. But above all it requires a certain perspective. Analysts are normally hard-pressed to draw conclusions from sketchy, uncertain data. For the analyst to dwell on the possibility that the data might also be deceptive is to condemn himself seldom to deliver clear answers. So while it makes sense that one set of analysts look at a field of data and ask the straightforward question "What does it say?" it also makes sense for another set of analysts to look at the same field and ask "Is the enemy trying to shape our perceptions here?" Decision-makers worthy of their titles should demand that the analyses they receive include answers to both sets of questions.

Cases vs. Subjects

It follows from everything we have seen that CI analysis, properly understood, is entirely *a priori* of cases. Instead it *looks for cases* by treating every analytical question as if it *might be* a CI question. Because one simply cannot know where or when evidence of deception will turn up (who ever would have thought of focusing on the possibility of fake wind tunnels in the Moscow suburbs?), the search for deception must be routine. Deception, the hand of hostile intelligence, might or might not have shaped *this* picture, *this* agent report, *this* intercept. But chances are we will never know by looking at the picture, report, or intercept alone. More likely, evidence of the hand of hostile intelligence could manifest itself as the connection (or lack thereof) between two facts—for example, a report from a trusted agent, or a diplomatic note that confirms a series of intercepted communications, followed by the discovery that the enemy had reason to know that his communications were being intercepted. That is why those who do CI analysis are likelier to see the evidence to the extent that they have all the elements of the matter before them. Hence, whenever one gathers "all the elements" of any matter concerning conflict, in order to pass judgment on them for any reason, one also ought to take the opportunity to pass judgment on them from the standpoint of counterintelligence.

Analysis should concentrate on subjects rather than persons also because the very best spies' lives will give no indication whatsoever of espionage. This is what British Prime Minister Harold Macmillan (correctly) argued after the conviction of Soviet spy George Blake in 1961.[6] Blake, who had spied for nine years, had been an ideological convert to communism who had kept his conversion secret. He was not paid. Hence no analysis of lifestyle nor any other facts pertaining to him alone could have caught him. But Macmillan's contention that there is no defense against the Blakes of this world is mistaken. If the spy's patron makes *any* use at all of the take, perceptive analysis can begin to trace the source of the loss.

The analysis itself should go beyond noting anomalies (a wind tunnel that would blow down buildings; or, as in the case of Iraq in 1991, a willingness to go to war, coupled with reluctance to fight battles). It should mirror the steps by which the deception—if it is there at all—might have been mounted. First, consider what the foreign government might be after. Do "they" really want us to develop this weapon, or not? To go to war in this occasion, or not? Do "they" want that regime to survive, or not? What do "they" want us to believe about their aims? Of only one thing can we be sure: Whatever direction "they" are pushing us in is calculated to serve their interest, not ours. As Aesop's fables teach, "Beware of the counsel of enemies." Once one has an hypothesis as to what the deception might be, one should check it against the information being received regarding the matter at hand. The crucial part, then, is to review the operational security of the sources and methods by which one has gained each item of information. Has the enemy let us steal something he wanted us to know? At this point it might be useful to order up more data to resolve any questions raised.

None of the above is to suggest that lack of proper CI analysis is the biggest factor in the success of deception. No, the biggest factor is the desire of leaders to believe in their pet theories, and the willingness of enemies to play to those beliefs. Virtually never is deception a brute-force effort to replace reality with fabrication. Virtually never does the deceiver try to shut evidence of the truth out from his target's mind. Rather, the nuts and bolts of deception consist of creating enough intellectual room for the target's own prejudices to come into play. The essence of deception is to give the target an excuse to believe what he wants to believe. All the evidence in the world will not convince a man of what he does

334

not want to believe, while the merest hint may lead him to move mountains of evidence that stand in the way of his favorite conclusions. Recall that in 1944 the Allies had been on the Normandy beaches for two weeks before Hitler abandoned his belief that the Normandy landings had been a diversion. The Allies' deception had helped lead Hitler to mistake the place of the landings. But the landings themselves, more powerfully than any CI analysis, destroyed any intellectual basis for Hitler's belief. By then, however, Hitler had so long defended the proposition that the attack would come at Calais that abandoning it was embarrassing. The deception had sunk its roots below the intellect and into the stratum of human self-regard. CI analysis is strictly a tool of the mind. But the mind does not always determine action.

Collection as Part of CI

Any information about the enemy obtained without his knowledge is potentially useful for counterintelligence. Without knowing what you know, the enemy cannot confidently lie to you. The wider the base of solid positive intelligence, the easier it is to do CI. Conversely, to the extent that the enemy has confidence in his appraisal of the extent of your knowledge, he is free to operate beyond that knowledge, there to prepare whatever surprises he wishes.

Knowledge of Knowing

In this regard it is useful to note the explicit distinction of Nikolai Brusnitsin, writing presumably for an American audience on behalf of the USSR Ministry of Defense, between "intelligence" and "control." Brusnitsin defines control as "obtaining by an agreed procedure, authorized data, stipulated by agreements, on the subject of the treaty. . . ." He then says, "All we have to do is agree on the composition of the national verification facilities, the procedure of the verification, the way we are going to use technical equipment, the degree to which obtained data should be detailed, and the procedure of [sic] exchanging them."[7] He presents a table showing the photographic resolution required to detect certain elements of military forces (e.g., aircraft, submarines, missiles, radars) to determine their purpose, and to detect detailed changes in them. He asserts that U.S. intelligence satellites (and, tacitly, Soviet ones also) "meet all verification requirements." If the U.S. were interested in peace and cooperation, he says, the U.S. should be content with information received through these satellites and as provided for in the data exchanges specified by arms control treaties. Brusnitsin argues that because the U.S. wants intelligence, "unauthorized data on the facilities and actions of the other side, not stipulated by mutual agreement, and data not covered by the treaty or obtained not in the agreed manner," it must be interested in something other than peace. The clarity of Brusnitsin's demand—that the U.S. limit its knowledge of an adversary's military to channels wholly known and predictable to that adversary—highlights the difference between information obtained through sources known to the target or through sources unknown to the target.

The first goal of any CI system is to restrict the capacity of hostile intelligence to collect, or at least to be aware of the limits of hostile collection. To limit one's own knowledge about any other government to what that government wants known about itself is to grant that government a basic CI victory. The alternative is to struggle to make sure that the data one receives is *not* "stipulated by mutual agreement," and *not at all* obtained in an "agreed manner," indeed that it is obtained in an *unexpected, secret* manner. As we have seen (Chapters 3 and 4), and as I have argued at length elsewhere,[8] greater predictability of U.S. intelligence is one of the benefits that the Soviet Union received from the arms-control process. This is one of the many means by which Soviet CI struggled for a greater measure of control over channels of information about itself. Brusnitsin's argument was itself an act, albeit minor, in that struggle.

Let us now look at the standard methods of collecting on the enemy's sources and methods, while keeping in mind that, in CI, it is often difficult to distinguish between two valuable but sometimes incompatible goals: to collect information and to control the channels through which information flows. First consider human sources.

Human Penetration

The ideal penetration of a hostile service comes from "seeding." One establishes clandestine relationships with bright young people in the enemy's country who are deeply committed to one's own side, urging them to hide their commitment and to get hired by the hostile intelligence service. Then one watches these "seeds" grow and bear fruit. Since the prime requirement for seeding is long-term loyalty, it can only be tried on the basis of religious, racial, or ideological affinity. Thus during the Wars of the Reformation the Catholic Church trained young Englishmen in French seminaries who, it hoped, would infiltrate the Protestant Establishment. Thus also religious solidarity has made Sihks efficient infiltrators of governments on the Indian subcontinent for hundreds of years. A combination of racial and ideological solidarity helped keep Larry Wu Tai Chin, hired as a U.S. Army translator in 1943, faithful to communist China until his capture a generation later. And of course ideology was the bond that kept Cambridge University's "Magnificent Five" faithful to the Soviet Union through their careers in British intelligence. Yet the very qualities that make good candidates for seeding make them obvious targets for security. Hence seeding works only in very permissive environments. Whereas the Magnificent Five's Marxist faith and (for three out of five) homosexual lifestyle drew no unfavorable attention as they rose through the ranks in the 1930s and 1940s, by the 1950s these very qualities might have led security officers to their doors.

In the 1950s and 1960s, when the Iraqi and Egyptian police captured rings of local Jewish spies for Israel, the Mossad learned the painful lesson that the usefulness of local Jews as Israeli seeds was as obvious to Arab services as it was to Israel.

If one cannot seed, then one may transplant: One sends a likely-looking fellow to a third country, where he builds a solid identity before moving to the target country. This in fact is the way most illegal agents get into desired positions. If one pays attention to detail, the technique works well. Thus Egypt sent Kaburak Yacovian, an Egyptian Armenian, to Rio de Janeiro to assume a Jewish identity, and then transplanted him into Israel. But his unfamiliarity with Jewish customs raised questions. A glance at his fake birth certificate answered them: It certified that he had been born in 1938 in Salonika, Turkey. The Egyptians had designed the operation using maps from before the Greek–Turkish War of 1912, in which Greece incorporated Salonika.[9] Thus also Israel sent Eli Cohen, an Egyptian Jew, to establish himself as a Syrian in South America, whence he could move into Syria. Cohen was caught because of the way he operated, not because of the way he was transplanted. The transplant technique works best against societies where immigration is well accepted, or that keep good relations with overseas communities of their nationals. In its pure form it would not work against, say, Japan.

If one cannot plant or transplant, one must try to pick the fruits already on the trees. Recruiting anybody to be a spy is an act of seduction. Recruiting hostile intelligence officers amounts to seducing seducers—an art in itself. Approaches that rely on deception (such as false-flag recruitments) will work only with the most naïve. In May 1983, Sharon Scranage, a black CIA employee at the U.S. Embassy in Accra, Ghana, was recruited by her Ghanaian lover, Michael Agboutui Soussoudis, ostensibly to work for the intelligence service of that Black African country. But the requests for information were framed by the very Red service of East Germany that was "advising" the Ghanaians.[10] Most intelligence officers, however, are sharp enough to understand who or what lies behind ploys. This highlights the fact that seduction does not rely primarily on deception. No one was ever seduced without knowing what was happening. Intelligence officers know all about switching sides. The trick is to find the officer's particular vulnerability—a need for money, love, revenge, etc. Then the most effective pitch is the most direct: "We both know what we are doing here. . . ." Thus in

1938, the German Abwehr recruited René Besson, the chief of French counterespionage in the Luxembourg border area, simply by noticing his love of money and pitching him cold.[11]

Nor was anyone ever seduced against his will. If an intelligence officer who knows all the tricks allows himself to be played along, it is either because he has already chosen to defect or because he is playing along with the knowledge, and is in fact under the control, of his service. So, when dealing with people who know what they are doing, it is better to dispense with the foreplay and, should they accept the pitch, put one's efforts into checking their *bona fides* and getting the better of the exchange.

There is less to worry about when trying to recruit people who are close to, but do not belong to, the hostile service. These people include employees of foreign embassies or of companies whose products the hostile services buy, or members of political or social groups used by the hostile service. Such people can identify hostile officers and report on conversations with them. The relationship of services with their favorite people is a double-edged sword: It facilitates access to the outside world, but also provides an avenue by which outsiders may seduce those close to it.

The most common means of recruiting CI sources, however, is more akin to rape than to seduction. The source is given a choice between cooperating and suffering harm—or seeing his family harmed. This is what happens to enemy agents who are identified, and what usually happens to people over whom the CI service has power. Aleksei Myagkov writes that when he joined his KGB unit inside the Soviet Army in East Germany, his superior told him to forget the lectures he had heard about fancy recruiting techniques, pick out the people he wanted as agents, and give them a choice between cooperating and having their lives ruined. Because brutal regimes work this way, they excel in the quantity of CI sources they have. Quality is another matter. Agents recruited by force have every incentive to fabricate information. One of the incentives is that services that recruit by rape are typically less interested in finding out what is actually happening than in presenting large numbers of reports to their political masters.[12] The success of the operation, then, depends on the capacity of the CI service to keep pressure on the recruit, usually by threatening to "burn him" by revealing his collaboration to the other side.

Recruiting agents by force is easier than keeping them faithful. The KGB set up a special office to recruit dozens of agents among Soviet Jews who were emigrating to Israel and the U.S. But, considering the large number of arriving immigrants who, as soon as they were out of the KGB's clutches, were eager to tell Israeli and American CI about their recruitment, the KGB was for the most part wasting its time, and possibly setting itself up for defeats. A substantial percentage of the people caught in sex traps also turn themselves in. Often,

when someone reports falling into such a trap, the punishment is not severe.*
Forceful recruitment, however, works if the agent can be made to commit acts
that make him a criminal in the eyes of those against whom he is operating.
Thus, even after reversals of fortune, the KGB might be able to count on some
of the thousands of agents it forcibly recruited solely because they would prefer
not to have to explain to their fellow citizens why they chose to ruin other
people's lives rather than seeing their own ruined. Also, someone like John
Walker, who has committed serious crimes, or any source inside a terrorist
organization that has a reputation for killing informants, is at the mercy of the
people who run him. In the end, whether forceful techniques "work" depends
on the objectives of the recruiters. These may be simple. For example, between
1987 and 1989 British CI apparently ran Paddy Flood, a forcibly recruited agent
inside the Irish Republican Army. The British appear to have used Flood's
information to make arrests, with little thought for the consequences the agent
would bear.[13] How much is an agent worth? Cynics would say he is worth no
more than it would take to replace him, and no more than the use value of the
information he can bring tomorrow.

Sometimes the objectives are complex. In 1941 the Abwehr's Oberstleutnant
Reile arrested Roman Czerniawsky, a former Polish officer who was running a
resistance network in France. He offered to arrange Czerniawsky's escape, and to
guarantee the safety of his jailed subordinates if Czerniawsky would agree to go
to Britain and report to the Abwehr. Reile did this fully expecting that
Czerniawsky would report to British intelligence. But he figured that he could
gather valuable information by reading through the lines of the lies that
Czerniawsky would send.[14] Maybe he could, maybe not.

The most common means of actually getting a source inside another service is
as we have previously discussed, the dangle. This, the intelligence version of the
common police "sting," is a high and dangerous art because it plays directly to
every intelligence service's main vulnerability, eagerness for information, and
because it raises explicitly the key issue implicit in all CI collection: *Who has the
greater control of any given channel of information?*

The critical part of any dangle is the presentation. The least subtle kind is the
defector (e.g., Igor Kozlov in the Shadrin case) who brazenly walks in, identifies
himself as a hostile officer, says he wants to defect-in-place, to become a double,
and asks for information to give his parent service so he can improve his status
there. Those who receive him cannot but have doubts about giving "feed

---

*Maurice Dejean, France's Ambassador to the USSR in 1960, was simply dismissed from the
diplomatic service. His worst punishment may have been his interview with President Charles de
Gaulle, who is reported to have said "Eh bien, Dejean, on couche. . . ." (Well, Dejean, one has
sex. . . .").

material" to such a person, especially if he has brought nothing of substance. If he has brought a stack of codes, that is another matter. Virtually always the self-proclaimed defector-in-place brings some information, and sometimes he asks for information in return. Thus the service that receives him cannot simply decide whether he is a hostile dangle or not. It also must decide about the value of the information exchange that is taking place. At the same time, the receiving service must weigh the possible relative value of the mutual penetration that may be taking place. This most unsubtle approach usually forces the kind of calculation that should take place with regard to any contact with a hostile service: *What do we think we can get out of this?*

This question is as valid for those who send the dangle as for those who receive him. After all, those who send must always wonder just how firmly the other side has bit, and just how the other side chose or "doctored" the material it gave the dangle to pass on. The receiving side must ask the same questions about all the information it gets from any volunteer. So, if both sides play any given dangle case as it should be played, the case will be less a clearcut victory for one and defeat for the other than a contest of strategies resulting in gains and losses for both.

Now consider how to evaluate the worth of the gains. Both sides have the opportunity to feed the other deceptive material. But deception only makes sense for a government that has a political or military objective that could be served by it, and that is internally organized to take advantage of it. If a government is not "in it" to deceive the other, then its objective must be control of the channel in the long run. In that case, it must be prepared to give the dangle what he says he has been asked for in order to keep the operation going until such time as it wants to make use of the channel for deception. Such an operation then becomes a contest to see who can give away fewer real facts while getting the most—a contest of analysts. If however the objective is to push the penetration deeper, then the contest requires big bets: first that the double is really "ours," and then that the long-term benefits of giving him material that will truly impress the other side will outweigh the short-term loss inherent in giving up such material. The losses are going to be real and in the present. So, for the bet to make any sense at all, one had better have a good idea of the benefits that one expects in the future. "Having our man in there" is not in itself sufficient justification for feeding real secrets to a hostile service.

The primary subtlety in dangle operations also concerns the presentation. Under the best of circumstances the receiving service will think that it has discovered one of the hostiles' more vulnerable members, and that, through hard work and skill, it has made a secure, clandestine recruitment. The sending service may believe that the recruiters believe just that. Thus in 1952 the CIA hired David Atlee Philips and set him up as a struggling businessman in

Santiago, Chile. After his cover was well established, the CIA let it slip to a man suspected of being a Soviet double agent, precisely to expose Philips to recruitment as an American double agent. When the Soviet offer came, the operation became a success—in technical terms. But it is an open question whether the results were worth the trouble of setting up the cover and then blowing it. The game *must* be worth the candle.

Technical Penetration

Now consider how one service gets inside another's technical sources. The principle is the same as that of the dangle. On one end a CI service, in cooperation with its country's military forces, generates an electronic signal that a hostile service may intercept. Or it allows some of its code keys to be stolen. Or it generates some military exercise to be photographed and listened to from the sky. In each case the service wants to train the hostiles to listen and look in certain places and ways. The purpose is either to convey a message, or to set up the hostiles to receive a message later, or to tie up the hostiles' resources so that they won't look or listen so hard elsewhere. On the other end, a service may allow its hostile counterpart to learn some things (true or false) about changes in the ways that its instruments are watching or listening. Thus it invites the hostiles to take advantage of opportunities to feed these sensors their favorite messages, while paying close attention to what messages the hostiles are so keen on getting across.

Just as with human sources, what a service will learn from a technical dangle depends less on the subtlety of the approach than on the sense of purpose and balance of skills that each side brings to the operation. Even the most inauspicious approach of all can yield results. Suppose that, through a spy, the hostiles have learned of the existence or the capabilities of a satellite—regardless of what kind. From the standpoint of security, this is a loss. It is also a CI opportunity. If the service can bridle its vengeful instincts for a while and give no hint of having discovered the spy, it may turn the loss into a gain. Once the service discovers the date when the hostiles learned about the satellite, it should determine the subtle ways in which the hostiles have changed their exposure to it. Even if (as is unlikely) the hostiles merely cut down their exposure, they surely did not do so uniformly. Then the service should formulate hypotheses as to what larger purposes lay behind the nature of the hostiles' changed exposure. Then, to test these hypotheses, the service should gently feed to the spy information about further changes in the technical collection system, and see how the hostiles react. Ideally, the feed information should lead the hostiles to make themselves more vulnerable to collection. If they believe our message that the next model of satellite X will no longer have capability A because it is being shifted to satellite Y, the hostiles might conduct operations in view of satellite X that they had previously hidden. If they believe that the satellite is about to add capability B, they may institute security measures that will be a bother to them and give us hints about what they are hiding.

If the espionage concerns codes and has been going on a long time, the reverse penetration can be particularly deep. Narrow the spy's access a bit, but keep on giving him codes for certain code machines. Then send out messages over those machines that give false information about changes in the service's own security, and see how the hostiles react. The hostiles, hearing that (for example) the service would no longer do physical surveillance in a certain city, might well switch agent meetings to that city, and right into a well-disguised spotlight. Each message could be an invitation to the hostiles to show themselves in a particular way. Each reaction would reveal something about the hostiles' intelligence plans and assets. Only when the channel has become useless should one arrest the spy. The point is: *Take any opportunity to let the hostiles show off before a hidden sensor (or a sensor with a hidden agenda). And if there are no such opportunities for real, create fraudulent ones.*

On the other side of the equation, one should create as many opportunities as possible to let the hostiles show off *their* sensors. To do this, conduct activities that the hostiles will want to observe, craft those activities to elicit reactions, and alert analysts to watch for those reactions. Suppose one wishes to learn about the sensors that the other side is using to track one's ships at sea. To check whether a particular satellite is doing passive electronic tracking or not, have the fleet make major changes in its announced destination while it is using its electronic equipment and the satellite is "in view," and see whether enemy submarines and surface observers move to intersect the fleet's new path. One can virtually calibrate the sensors of hostile satellites by ordering one's ships, during important exercises, to operate only one kind of electronic equipment at a time, while watching for signs that the ships are being tracked.

Whenever two governments are engaged in negotiations about the movement or composition of military forces, both possess channels through which to calibrate the other's sensors. The same goes for data-exchange forums billed as "confidence-building measures." Either government has the option of moving (or not moving) troops or equipment, lying about it, and seeing whether the other side objects to their lie. The art here consists of choosing the people or objects to be lied about, their quantity and location, and the timing, so as to isolate a particular hostile sensor as much as possible. The same ploy can use false claims about the characteristics of military equipment. False claims about size can be used to calibrate visual sensors. False claims about, say, warhead weight can calibrate radar sensors. Finally, claims about what did or did not happen during a given night can help to establish whether the hostiles have infrared sensors, and how well they work; claims about events under cloud cover can measure the effectiveness of radar sensors; and claims about movements of forces that restricted their use of electronic equipment can gauge the effectiveness of electronic intercepts. In wartime, probing attacks are the surest (albeit the most expensive) way of forcing hostile intelligence to use, and thereby to risk revealing, the capacity of its sensors.

CI as Part of Collection

Deception *in* collection is the best way of guarding against deception *through* collection. To do the former, one must have good ideas about the keyholes through which the enemy can observe one's own collection, plus a plan to distort what the enemy sees. This applies equally to human and to technical means.

Human Operational Security

Some espionage operations are more visible to the enemy than others. Diplomat–spies, as we have seen, are always a short step away from being identified. Hence whoever runs an "official cover" operation must act on the assumption that the hostile service has his people under surveillance. He can make good use of that. In the simplest instance, if he knows that the surveillance ends when the lights go out in his officers' bedrooms, he can assure his officers that, by first feigning going to bed, they can go and meet their agents without fear that their contact might be identified and perhaps "doubled." A diplomat–spy who knows that surveillance "puts him to bed" can free himself for awhile by spreading stories that he is bedridden with the flu. By the same token, anyone who wants to recruit sources in a certain milieu must consider how to outwit the CI measures specific to that milieu. If the target people are required to report their contacts with peoples of countries X and Y, an approach by someone who is or appears to be of nationality Z will be less likely to produce a contaminated contact. The principle is straightforward: Learn what hostile CI is looking with and looking for, and deceive it.

This over-the-shoulder perspective on the art of collection begins by asking what the hostile service is likely to know about one's own operations. Consider a diplomat–spy. Even if he is not specifically identified as an intelligence collector, the hostiles surely know that he is in the business of gathering information on the government's behalf, and hence will keep track of his contacts. Therefore, operational security for diplomat–spies must consist of making meetings either clandestine or plausibly innocent. But anti-surveillance maneuvers, or "dry cleaning," evade surveillance at the price of confirming that the diplomat is a spy, and that he acted as such at a given time. The most direct method for a diplomat–spy to beat surveillance is disguise: The officer walks into an airport, ducks into a bathroom, and emerges looking like somebody else. If then

343

someone were waiting in the bathroom disguised as the officer, the surveillants would follow the decoy, certain that they had control of the situation, while the real officer went about his business unsuspected. But this sort of thing cannot work often. Hence, for a diplomat–spy, the main counter-CI effort must be to make his moves appear inoffensive. A Soviet ambassador anywhere in the world who spent time with members of the local Communist party would surely have drawn the local CI service's surveillance. If, however, the ambassador spent his time with businessmen or others of conservative reputation, he could have expected his contacts to escape surveillance. The most useful ploy, however, is for the diplomat–spy to do his cover job during his every waking moment. If then the cover job is well designed to put him in contact with his intelligence targets, CI will have a difficult time with him.

The whole point of avoiding surveillance of the spymaster is to avoid surveillance of the agent. The primordial question of human operational security is what the hostiles might know about the agent, and what they might be doing with that knowledge. The answer consists of a review of the whole operation: How secure was the officer to whose attention the agent first came? What circumstances suggest that the agent might have been a dangle? How well have we screened our subsequent contacts with our agent from electronic and physical surveillance? How well have we checked up on him to see whether the hostiles are on to him at all? From our knowledge of the agent's environment and of the hostiles' habits, what problems might arise? How well have we tested him by asking questions to which we already know the answers? Is there anything in the material we have received from the agent that might indicate he is under hostile control? If so, what might they be trying to do to us?

This is not to say that a service ought not to accept agent reports unless these questions are answered. Often an attempt to send other agents to check up on the first agent either is impossible or would do more harm than good. These questions, however, ought to be ever present, so that one will not fail to follow up any item of information that suggests the enemy's hand is in the operation, and also so that one's analysts will refrain from excessive confidence in the source's reports.

There are ways, however, not so much to cut down the chances of having an intelligence officer (or an agent) detected as of finding out about suspicion perhaps early enough to protect him. Sometimes, when agents are about to meet their case officers, their service will run surveillance on the surveillants. More rarely the service will run some analyses to see whether any available information indicates that the hostiles might be on to the agent. Ideally, but seldom in practice, for every operation that puts an agent in harm's way there should be another, separate penetration, to "check his back track." Once in a while a collector manages to build a warning system into his own operation: During

World War II, for instance, Soviet spy Richard Sorge, who was posing as a German journalist in Tokyo, was able to secure at least that half of his spying that took place in the German community. He had a deep affair with the German ambassador's wife. Had she heard any hint that Sorge was under suspicion, presumably she would have told him. When the suspicions came, however, they did so from the side of the Japanese authorities. If Sorge had managed to sleep with the wife of the Tokyo police chief as well, he might never have been caught.

Another way is to run the equivalent of an operation against one's own operation. In 1940, U.S. Army Maj. Ivan D. Yeaton, military attaché at the U.S. Embassy in Moscow, privately called for a secret FBI investigation of the security of the Embassy's codes. The FBI sent a man disguised as a courier who quickly noticed that Soviet intelligence (and indeed anybody else who wanted it) had access to the code room. The point is that because operational security often is mistakenly seen as unproductive activity, chances are that it will be neglected unless someone takes particular interest in it.[15]

Technical Operational Security
The operational security questions with regard to technical means of collection are similar. The answers, however, can be less speculative.

Consider a typical intelligence satellite: What can one expect its targets know about it simply because it exists? Even though the workers who build it say nothing, the fact that specialized people (say electronics, but not optics people) are working on a highly secure project will give some hints. The location of the satellite (say in geosynchronous orbit) will confirm that it has nothing to do with cameras, and will send intelligence analysts to cross check their files on the people who worked on this project with files on people who previously worked on state-of-the-art antennas for long-range interception. Perhaps the overlap is substantial. Basic radar mensuration of the satellite can be expected to yield the antenna's gross size. From all that, plus the satellite's geosynchronous location, analysts can make informed guesses about what the satellite is intercepting. Now, *the people who own the satellite should take as a point of departure that the people on whom the satellite is targeted know at least these facts, and that they are likely to have gained some more through espionage. That is, they are likely to know quite a bit.* This much is straightforward. Then comes a speculative step: How well does the target understand the guidelines by which the owners interpret the satellite's data? In other words, do *they* understand how *we* translate pictures or wiggles on pieces of paper into answers to our questions? Do they understand what alterations in the pictures or wiggles would mean to us?

If the satellite's owners know how the target understands their satellites' vulnerability, they can attempt to foul up that understanding by planting a variety of false stories about the satellite for the targets to pick up, or by employing some of the stratagems we discuss below. If they don't, they leave to the target the option of using the satellite as a channel of disinformation.

As discussed above (Chapters 3 and 4), technical collection systems are narrow keyholes through which one tries to take glimpses of big phenomena. The narrower the keyhole, the less chance of checking the image one sees with the broader world. The target country's CI service may well manage its armed forces' exposure to technical systems, in order to lead the observers' analysts to their favorite conclusions and to keep them in comfortable mental ruts so long that their favorite prejudices harden into cherished axioms. If, however, the owners of the cameras and antennas deceive their targets about where these technical means are at any given time, or about their capacities, or even about their existence, they will gather facts that the target's CI service does not expect to be gathered. Hence the target's CI service will be unable to choose the facts to shape the observers' perceptions.

How then can the observers deceive the targets?[16] Surely removal of imaging satellites from sun-synchronous orbits would make them quantitatively less efficient collectors. But it would be a first step in improving the products' quality. Of course the target's radars sooner or later would find the old satellites in their new orbits. That is why another essential step would be to simultaneously place into new random-access orbits a sizable number of decoy imaging satellites. Perhaps some of the decoys could emit some housekeeping signals while the real ones communicated strictly through relays. In much the same vein, new satellites could be more easily protected by constructing classified cover stories for them, and perhaps leaking or allowing that "information" to be stolen. Such deception would work to discredit any true data that might be gathered about them. At any time, reshuffling and redecoying the satellites could restart the contest.

In fact, confusing an enemy about the identity of any given object in space is not terribly difficult compared with confusing him about the identity of a person. When Sputnik I was launched in 1957 the whole world could follow it, not only because it broadcast its location but also because, though tiny, it was the only thing then orbiting the earth, other than the moon. And when America's somewhat larger satellites were launched, they too were easy to identify. Even untrained radar operators couldn't miss them, since they were the only objects of their kind. By the late 1960s, however, enough satellites and junk were in orbit that identification of any given object in space had become something of a problem. Information on each new object—including its radar and electronic signatures, as well as its orbit—had to be entered into a central computer registry at time of launch, and the registry had to be regularly updated. As early as the early 1960s it became impossible even to guess intelligently at all that each satellite might be doing. Eventually the satellites at geosynchronous orbit were kept track of the most rigorously, because of the relative scarcity of slots at that orbit. But even they have not necessarily been well identified by function.

This precarious recordkeeping can be fouled up by clandestine launches. The space shuttle would be excellent for this purpose, since it could dispense any number of satellites, unannounced, while out of sight of the target's space-track radars. If it launched its clandestine satellites into an orbit occupied by spent satellites or pieces of debris while recovering such junk, the deception would be very difficult to detect. If the shuttle did not deceive by substituting a live satellite for recovered junk, it could cover its clandestine launch by releasing large numbers of cheap decoys. Clandestine satellites can also come from deep space. They could be launched and stored too far away for earth-based radars to see, and brought back quietly to the southern side of near-earth orbit. Perhaps several decoys could come first, to test the targets' reactions. The real satellites' actual orbits could be decided upon by watching those reactions. At any rate, the introduction of uncertainty about the location of satellites would be most valuable during periods when the target country might be considering shooting at them. Eventually the target country might solve the puzzles that decoys, substitutions, and clandestine launches presented to them. However, if the puzzles were set before them in a crisis, they surely could not solve them in time to carry out their original plans.

Let us now briefly discuss camouflaging in space, in relation to the three kinds of means by which objects in space may be detected: radar, optical, and passive electronic instruments. Anyone who has ever worked with radar knows how the shape of the object being looked at can drastically affect the return, even from short-wavelength radars, depending on the angle at which the object is viewed. Especially if the object has sharp corners, a slight variation in angle can give a return that is either bigger or smaller, but that will certainly be different from what it otherwise would be. Aircraft designers have developed the art of enhancing and reducing radar signatures so that small things can be made to look big, and big things can be made to look small. The implications for decoys are obvious: Instead of building them as simple foil balloons in the precise shape of the satellite they are to simulate, one could build them in ways that would enhance the features peculiar to the target satellite—while providing the target satellite with pop-out foil bulges to mute those very features at crucial times. Thus even if radar can see a satellite, it can be misled about what that satellite is. Radar-tailored decoys of tanks and aircraft are commercially available. Radar-tailored decoys of space objects are equally feasible.

The surest way to see a satellite is through fine space-based, electro-optical instruments operating in the infrared spectrum—especially after the satellite has been identified as an object of interest. Since satellites are relatively "cold"

347

bodies, radiating very little energy other than what they reflect from the sun, any optical instrument that seeks to identify them from a distance must have a focal plane supersensitized by cooling to near-absolute zero. The products of such instruments are not fine images, but infrared signatures. These can be quite distinctive. But they also can be easily altered, or even duplicated. To alter the infrared characteristics of the satellites one may add insulation in some places and perhaps some sources of heat in others. It is conceivable, too, that infrared signatures may simply be reduced to very low levels. But the prerequisite for any sort of masking or alteration of any satellite's infrared characteristics is a detailed analysis of those characteristics. Such analysis would also allow the design of cheaper objects that would yield signatures close to those of the real satellites.

It is easy enough to deal with an antenna that tracks your satellite by picking up its transmissions: simply route your satellite's downlinks through relay satellites. You can spoof such antennas either by placing downlinks on decoys or by appearing to beam commands to decoys. Such deception cannot be successful from every angle. But whoever would discover it can be forced to surveil every possible target from a variety of angles. Thus for practical purposes live satellites can appear dead, and dead ones alive. In other words, if the owner takes some initiative, anyone wishing to identify his satellite can be faced, at a minimum, with tremendous uncertainty.

Making a satellite difficult to identify also contributes to its physical safety, especially in wartime. No other protective measure can be as effective. If an enemy knows the precise location of a satellite, the passive defense of that satellite is very difficult. The use of exterior armor, hardening of electronic components, shielding of optical components, and/or antijam programming of transmitters and receivers, can radically increase a satellite's resistance to laser radiation, electromagnetic pulse, and other nuclear effects. Bigger engines, and generous supplies of fuel for those engines, can help a satellite to evade simple co-orbital interceptors or to get out of the way of preprogrammed "dumb" mines—if there is enough warning. But no satellite can be expected to survive a direct hit from a kinetic kill vehicle or a guided nuclear weapon, or a space-based laser or particle beam. Active defense of satellites against such threats, though certainly feasible, is costly. The greatest protection for a satellite is ignorance (or doubt in the enemy's mind) about where the satellite is located.

Covert Action as Part of CI

CI not only helps provide the disparity of knowledge by which one government's armies and diplomats may take advantage of another's. It is itself a weapon, because it can lead the enemy to harm himself. It can do so by giving him information that he thinks comes from elsewhere, by confusing him about information he has, and by the actions of double agents. Action against the enemy *through the enemy's own intelligence* is the very consummation of CI.

Feeding Destruction

Feeding the enemy self-destructive information is the oldest of arts. In 1268 a certain Babyars, Sultan of Egypt, worried about the strength of the Christian community in Mesopotamia, and about the good order of the Mongol empire there. Both worries rested on the good relations between the Mongols and the Christian Patriarch of Baghdad. Babyars fixed that. He wrote a letter to the Patriarch thanking him for the information he had sent (he had not sent any) on the Mongols' army. He sent the letter by courier. Then he paid a band of thieves to kill the courier and sell his letter to the Mongols—who promptly killed the Patriarch for treason, and began to oppress the Christians. Mongols and Christians suffered; Muslims rejoiced. The plan went to the heart of the matter. But it would have counted for nothing if Babyars had not had a good relationship with the thieves, and if the thieves had not had the skill to sell their wares. The Mongols left themselves open to the scheme by their practice of taking intelligence where they found it without asking too many questions.

The easy part is to figure out a message which, if accepted by the enemy, would lead him to mistake friend and foe or to take counterproductive actions. The hard part is matching the message to the means available to deliver it convincingly. The recipient must believe that the information is the result of his hard work, that it is the payoff from what he supposes is his victory in the battle of CI.

A successful "feed" of destructive information is indeed the winner's reward, the payoff for the sacrifice it takes to establish control of a channel of communication. In the case of Babyars, imagine the cultivation of bands of thieves over the years, imagine providing them with goods by which to establish friendly relations with Mongol officials. We have already mentioned how George Washington saved Newport, Rhode Island from the British by a scheme similar to Babyars'—except that Washington used a "Tory" farmer instead of a band of thieves. One can only imagine what that farmer had to do and to endure over the years to earn the confidence of British authorities. Had not the occasion arisen to use his access and trust, all that work would have been wasted. A *successful feed should not be considered an operation in and of itself, but rather the fruit of a long fight for control over a channel of information.* Therein lies the art.

Once one has infiltrated the enemy's covert-action apparatus, even a little effort can go a long way. According to recently released British archives of World War II, James Klugman, a communist stationed at the Cairo headquarters of the Special Operations Executive, together with leftist sympathizers, falsified reports from Yugoslavia to suggest that Draza Mihailovic, who headed the Yugoslav Army of the Homeland, was collaborating with the Nazis. Mihailovic's communist rival, Josip Broz, alias Tito, was openly charging precisely that. Britain's Prime Minister, Winston Churchill, was hardly disposed to believe a communist over a Christian royalist. But given the evidence from his own SOE, Churchill cut off Mihailovic and shipped 18,000 tons of arms to Tito, who used them in substantial part to kill his rivals and impose upon Yugoslavia a bloody communist system that took half a century to shake off.[17] Because the basic decisions were made according to data in intelligence channels, they were shielded from skeptical eyes for nearly that long, adding insult to the injuries that Mihailovic and his partisans suffered.

Sometimes the loser is easier to identify than the winner. Sometimes it is clear only that an organization lost control of an important channel of information, that through the channel it learned something it thought terribly important, and that it acted on that information with disastrous results. Who controlled the channel remains a bone of contention. Thus on September 30, 1965, the Indonesian Communist party attempted to behead the Indonesian armed forces, murdering six generals and their families. Others barely escaped. The surviving generals organized a countercampaign of anticommunist terror that probably killed more than a half-million people and ruled Indonesia for a generation. What happened? There had been a long-simmering feud between the armed forces, who were conservative Muslims, and the communists, who had grown in influence under the protection of President Sukarno. By 1965, with Sukarno ill, there was open speculation about a violent struggle for succession. The Communist party apparently got (certainly false) information that Sukarno was dying, and unleashed the long-planned coup on short notice. There is widespread agreement that the communists were fatally deceived. But by whom? Former CIA officer Ralph McGhee, strongly supported by the left-wing press, charges that the CIA was responsible for the deception.[18] Others charge that right-wing elements of the Indonesian Army were responsible for "inducing or at a minimum helping to induce" the coup.[19] Be that as it may, somebody who didn't like the Communist party had control of a communist agent, and used that control to devastating effect.

Causing Confusion

Even without control of enemy channels of information, merely by being aware of how they flow, where the dangers are, one may cause confusion in the target's intelligence services, and thus make possible maneuvers that would not otherwise be. This is most obvious with regard to the transfer of technology and the breaking of embargoes. The standard tech-transfer operation consists of a chain of companies. The chain purposely avoids what hostile CI considers significant. In 1968, for example, a company registered in Germany by German speaking people with German names bought 200 tons of uranium oxide from a Belgian company. The material was to be used by a subsidiary in Genova, Italy. The barrels were loaded in Antwerp onto a Liberian-registered freighter declared for Genova. But the uranium ended up in Haifa, Israel, because all the companies, and the ship, were owned by the Israeli government.[20] The point here is that, knowing which documents the seller and the port authorities would require to let go of the uranium, the Israelis provided them. Throughout the 1970s and 1980s, Soviet tech-transfer operations typically involved the following steps: A company registered in the country where the technology was produced would buy the technology, ostensibly for domestic use. Once that hurdle was cleared, it would sell the technology to another domestic company, which however would have a subsidiary in a NATO country. Shipping to the subsidiary without a sale raises fewer questions. Once the hardware was abroad, the subsidiary would change the label and sell the hardware to another company in a neutral country. Thence the technology would be either bought openly by the Soviet Union, or nominally shipped to yet another country but then diverted to the Soviet Union. At every point the authorities would get the documents they expected. And the Soviets would get what they wanted.

Confusion of hostile intelligence, however, is also an end worthy of being sought for its own sake. We have mentioned that between 1920 and 1927, British and French intelligence accepted agents of Soviet intelligence as their channel of communication with putative anticommunist conspiracies. The KGB earned a solid result: It sowed doubt in the minds of Western intelligence about the viability of any but government forces in the Soviet Union. However, there is little doubt also that the Soviet Chekists were having fun. The agent they sent to start the Sindikat (later, Trust) operation in 1920 called himself Opperput. Now, there is no such name in Russian. However, the letters "oper" and "put" are the beginnings of the Russian words for "operation" and "deception."[21] The Chekists were being cheeky. CI is grim. A little indulgence in the pleasures of victory—like a football player's dancing in the end zone—keeps it from being unbearably so. Also, one must not undervalue the professional attractiveness of an operation that puts an agent in contact with the highest levels of enemy intelligence, lets him trade some hard information for bunkum, and ends with a laugh in the enemy's face. Stalin himself announced that the Trust had been a Cheka operation all along.

In a similar way, on December 23, 1957, Egypt's Gamal Abdul Nasser pinned a medal on his Chief of Air Force Intelligence, Gen. Mahmoud Khalil, and publicly brought to an end a series of meetings dating back to August 1956, in which Khalil had received money and instructions from British intelligence to foment a coup against Nasser. The Egyptians took their pretentious former colonial masters for an enjoyable ride.[22]

Now consider how control of a double agent can serve more than just morale. Throughout the 1950s Egyptian intelligence ran Fedayeen against Israel. Israel knew that one of its Egyptian agents, a Bedouin named Talaka, was actually working for the Egyptians. On July 11, 1956 they told him to carry a package, ostensibly containing codes, to the chief of the Gaza police, who, they falsely told the agent, was also an Israeli agent. As the Israelis expected, Talaka took the story and the package to Egyptian intelligence HQ in Gaza instead, where it was opened at a high-level meeting. It was a bomb, and it destroyed the leadership of the Fedayeen attacks.[23]

CI as Part of Covert Action

We can glimpse the meaning of operational security in covert action by asking how British intelligence might have avoided defeat at the hands of Nasser in 1956–57 and Stalin in 1920–27. Before attempting to recruit General Khalil as the leader of the plot, the British might well have recruited his secretary, perhaps under the false flag of another Egyptian special service—not to take part in any plot, but simply to report on Khalil. Also, unbeknownst to the General, they might have placed observers on some of the figures whom the General was supposed to recruit for the plot. This would not have guaranteed success. But it would have insured the British against a counterplot as simple as the one that the Egyptians actually ran.

By the same token, the Soviet Sindikat–Trust scheme in 1920–27 was fragile. It worked only because the British (and the French, and the Russian émigrés) did no independent checking whatsoever. Had any of the parties recruited a Russian or a foreign communist, or even a Western businessman, to travel where the Trust's agents had reported strikes and battles, to look and listen for these events, they would quickly have found reason to doubt. Whether or not the British officers who dealt with the Trust ever heard of the principle that only *independent* sources can confirm one another, they surely violated it. The point here is that to secure a covert action, one must run a separate espionage operation against it.

The KGB has done a variation of this with regard to all its "popular front" operations. In its very prototype, Willi Munzenberg was spied on by his number two man, Otto Katz.[24] Throughout the Spanish Civil War the Republican side was riddled with special agents of the KGB, and with very special ones checking on the plainer specials. Every Communist party has had Moscow's *hommes de confiance* to keep an eye on the rest. Yet while multiple lines of liaison with a group ensures that one will be able to control it (often at great cost to its efficiency, as evidenced by the murderous chaos within the Spanish Republican forces), they do little to warn the group about the extent to which hostile intelligence knows about it. To do that, one must run a separate collection operation against the hostiles.

Ironically, the most prominent excuse for excluding CI from covert action is security. The argument goes like this: We had a hard enough time recruiting the agents we have without drawing attention to our project. As our agents set to work they risk drawing attention to themselves anyhow. And you want to disturb the situation further by recruiting, or sending more people into it to snoop around? A related argument may add: We are trying to run this operation strictly through third parties. We have told them to be careful whom they recruit, and so forth. But if we try to do CI for the operation ourselves we are going to have our fingerprints all over it.

These arguments point to real burdens and dangers. But the size and intrusiveness of the separate CI operation are things that one can control. On the other hand, to do without CI to avoid this set of dangers means to make a blind bet on a single set of people over whom one has no control. So one must choose between dangers one can control and those one cannot.

Another set of CI principles pertains to the very structure of a covert action: Actions that involve fewer people will less likely be infiltrated than those that involve more; actions in which the period between conception and consummation is shorter will be more secure than those in which it is longer; and actions in which participants have no choice between success and death will be more secure than those from which there are many exit doors. Machiavelli tells of Ellanicus, who recruited a conspiracy against Aristotimus, tyrant of Ellea, by asking the recruits to his house, explaining the plan, and then, once his servants had effectively taken the guests prisoner, saying "Either you swear to go now and do this thing, or I will turn all of you over to Aristotimus." The principle here is straightforward: Tell people only as much as they need to know, only at the last possible moment, and share the purpose of the conspiracy with only one other person "of whom one has the longest possible experience, and who be moved by the same reasons as you."[25] In this regard Machiavelli tells the story of Emperor Commodius, who had written an order for the murder of Marzia, one of his better concubines, and two of his close friends, among others. Commodius put it under his pillow. Marzia saw it, and safely entered into a conspiracy with the two friends. There was no need for Marzia to check up on the motivation of her two accomplices. They poisoned Commodius and, when he vomited, they stabbed him.[26] This episode illustrates yet another principle: The less committed to paper, the better.

Good operational security is an obvious side benefit of a well-crafted conspiracy. By the same token a collection operation or analysis that otherwise proceeds according to sound principle will tend to be more resistant to hostile intelligence than one not so well-crafted. In sum, operational security consists of looking at the basic principles of intelligence from the point of view of hostile services.

FRICTION

As we have seen, the essence of CI is the capacity to look at things from a variety of perspectives, figuratively to have eyes in the back of one's head. It is also obvious that if one strictly applied the principles described herein, one might become so preoccupied with operational security, with testing hypotheses about what the hostiles know and don't know, as to paralyze most of those government activities that depend on intelligence. The occupational hazard of CI is the temptation to suspend judgment, to dally indefinitely in a beguiling "wilderness of mirrors." It is truer of CI than of any other part of the craft of intelligence that no one has the resources, no one has the time, to really do it right.

In practice, there is always a contest for resources and attention between those who want to get the job done and those who want to make sure it's done right; between those who want to take things on appearance and those who seek hidden meanings. There is no *a priori* way of resolving such conflicts. The only sure principle is that the issues should not be decided by either side. Intertwined as CI is with the rest of intelligence, it functions well only to the extent that it is independent of it. Like all quality-control shops, it is necessarily somewhat adversarial to the rest of the enterprise. That is why, while it must work *with* every department, it must work only *for* the chief executive officer.

How much CI is "good enough for government work" depends on how the government wants to spend its resources. The argument here is that to pay due attention to the principles of CI may be the most economical thing a government engaged in conflict can do. Hence Sun Tzu's advice: "Be generous with counterintelligence."

11

Subversion and Policy

The covertness of any action is incidental equally to its
effectiveness and its morality.

– Sen. Malcolm Wallop

There are no wholly open or wholly
secret acts. Governments often act openly, but for unavowed reasons. Thus
during the Persian Gulf War of 1991 the Soviet government officially supported
the U.S.-led coalition's goal of forcing Iraq to withdraw from Kuwait—but its
acts were calculated to safeguard the Iraqi regime.* Neither international law nor
political theory treats a government's threats, blandishments, support, or
opposition any differently when they are done with greater or lesser degrees of

---

*In August–December 1990 the Soviet government demanded, as the price for its support of
U.S. demands on Iraq, that the U.S. government limit its objective to securing Iraq's withdrawal
from Kuwait, and that the U.S. eschew overthrowing the Iraqi regime. In January and February
1991 the Soviet government offered Iraq the chance to withdraw from Kuwait under its
guarantee that the Iraqi regime would not be threatened and would suffer no reprisals. If Iraq
had accepted, it would have retained the power to dominate the Middle East immediately after
the end of hostilities. The Soviet enterprise was conducted almost exclusively by open means.
But it was treacherous nonetheless.

secrecy. Nor are overt acts of interference (embargoes, tariffs, threats) any less intrusive than covert ones. Acknowledgment of the source of an act does not justify an unjust one, and hiding a just one does not condemn it. Few would argue that Syria's murderous control of the Lebanese government through military force is in any way preferable to the discreet influence of France's agents in the Ivory Coast, one of Africa's few oases of peace and prosperity. A politician who acts at the behest of foreigners does so regardless of how many people notice—or care. Common sense and philosophy are more concerned with the results of actions and the motives of the actors than with whether all the relationships involved in the action have been avowed. Neither the efficacy nor the moral worth of any action depends on how well the press covers it—or why.

Interference in the internal affairs of other governments, increasing the influence of one's friends and decreasing that of one's enemies within them, is the very purpose of foreign policy. However, *whereas overt acts speak to the other side's body politic, as it were, from the outside, covert ones are meant to exercise influence from within—to exercise prerogatives which that body politic normally reserves for its own members*. Thus interference from within is properly understood as subversion: turning from below. But, as we have seen, secrecy is not the only means by which one can gain a seat within a foreign government's councils. One may as well cover one's agents in foreign councils by open threats and promises, and by deception.

Our subject here is that tool of statecraft called subversion—what it can do, and how to do it successfully. This is neither a handbook of subversion nor a brief for it, but rather a set of insights into its basic principles. We begin with a discussion of what serious subversion requires, followed by an examination of the major techniques of subversion and what they can accomplish. Then, since any given technique produces different results when applied to different regimes and circumstances, we examine the peculiar vulnerabilities and resistances to subversion of the world's regimes, including our own. Finally, we describe the art of matching the results one desires, the opportunities offered by the target regime, and the subversive techniques available.

Agents

Agents of influence in foreign countries are merely the indispensable *tools* for subversion. Nor is subversion the mere use of these tools. The spreading of information, the fostering of events, provocations, assassinations, and guerrillas are the *means* of subversion. Just as war itself consists neither in building weapons nor in shooting them, nor in killing, but rather in doing these things according to a reasonable plan for victory, subversion does not consist of acquiring agents or running covert actions—even technically perfect ones.

Rather, subversion is the "turning from below" of foreigners from neutrals or obstacles in the way of policy into instruments of victory. First let us look at the tools and how one acquires them.

Agents of Influence

Any and all acts of subversion require agents of influence. These people may or may not be part of the target's body politic. Their usefulness depends on their access to influence within the target country, on their personal aptitudes for leadership, and on the will they bring to their task as agents. It also depends on their cover. As one seeks out and works with agents of influence, one must always keep in the forefront of one's mind what one is trying to accomplish. The reason for this is that there is no such thing as the ideal, all-purpose agent. The only rule for success with agents of influence is to match the kinds of agents available to the jobs one wants to get done, and to balance the grasp of one's influence operations with the reach of the agents one actually has.

Whoever the agent, he is useful only to the extent that he is well-matched to the people he is seeking to influence. This is the very same calculation that intelligence services make when recruiting for espionage, and indeed the one that governments make (or ought to make) when choosing ambassadors. In 1991 the South African government, eager to get its point of view across to Americans who had ostracized it because of its former policy of racial separation, appointed as Ambassador to the U.S. a Mr. Harry Schwartz, who had made something of a career of opposing that policy. Similarly, before World Wars I and II the British sent to Washington William Wiseman and William Stephenson,[1] respectively, whose polished manners fit perfectly into the anglophile American foreign-policy establishment. These semiofficial envoys "worked" U.S. officials to come to Britian's aid. By the same token, the Soviet Union showed good judgment in sending to the U.S. the "journalist" Vladimir Pozner, whose looks and language are those of the American liberals he was trying to influence.

Consider people who have obvious capacity as leaders, as well as influence in their country, but whom the fortunes of war and politics have driven to seek help abroad. What sort of relationship, if any, one should have with such people depends on what one is trying to do. There is no better example of a thoughtless approach than that of the Chinese communist government toward Angolan leader Jonas Savimbi in the 1960s. Impressed by Savimbi's personality and his position in the Ovimbundu tribe, Angola's largest, the Chinese eagerly financed him. They discounted the fact that neither Marxism nor anything else attached him to China. And so Savimbi took China's money, giving nothing in return. If China had recognized that Savimbi did not have it in him to be anybody's long-term agent, it might simply have exchanged financial support for what Savimbi could have done for it at some point: attack the Angolan representatives of China's long-term Soviet adversaries. But because the Chinese had their eye on a recruitment rather than on specific gains, they wound up making no gains at all.

By contrast, shortly after the death of Mohammed in A.D. 632, the Christian Emperor of Byzantium had an opportunity to break up Islam by supporting Musaylamah, an attractive, unscrupulous challenger to the Prophet's successor, Abu Bakr. There seems to have been no thought of a long-term relationship, much less of Musaylamah converting to Christianity. The idea was to bring about a battle. It worked, although Musaylamah lost it. The Caesars of Constantinople never did manage to subvert Islam, but they staved it off for almost a thousand years by finding a succession of secret short-term allies in the various Muslim camps. Many short-term deals added up to a rather long-term success.

Ordinary people too may be useful in influence operations, providing one is realistic about what they can accomplish. A government or a political movement invites a professor, a journalist, or a bureaucrat for a series of visits and treats him well. If all goes well the guest will become well disposed toward his hosts, will be regarded in his own circles as an expert, and will spread his hosts' views. By the same token any country can easily identify those foreign officials, who for their own reasons favor it. The most natural thing in the world is to cement a relationship and take it as far as it will go.

In some cases, ordinary people will even become paid agents. Consider: In 1979 the French government convicted journalist Pierre Charles Pathé of having served as a paid agent of influence for the Soviet Union within French journalism for two decades.[2] During the last decade of Pathé's service, the French press had become predominantly anti-Soviet, while until the early 1970s it had been rather pro-Soviet. But surely neither orientation had been due to Pierre Charles Pathé. His arrest caused more éclat than anything Pathé had ever written. Not the likes of Pathé, but rather, dominant intellectual figures (e.g., Jean Paul Sartre) had influenced the proud editors of Le Monde to echo Soviet themes and exclude contrary ones. The real subversion of the Western press consisted of the formation of the attitudes of reporters and editors, and of the ability—on the part of Soviet and Third World regimes—to play to those attitudes. More significantly subversive than any Pathé were the innumerable boosts that the Soviet government gave to the egos of Western intellectuals by assuring them of their brilliant contributions to peace and progress.

The Pathés of this world are useful in the short term primarily as claques: to applaud or boo vigorously at the right time in the hope of leading a stampede. In the long run one can hope that by their sheer numbers they will create a subculture that will dominate their professional milieu. But of course it is beyond any country's capacity simply to buy and handle an entire sector of another's society.

It is no use for a would-be subverter to complain that the people who seem willing to be recruited have too little influence, or even access to power, while the influential ones seem beyond his reach. Let him rather consider, concretely, how useful any of his contacts may be. No one should dream of using friends who run an auto-body shop to try to influence foreign policy. But perhaps if one is thinking of infiltrating and exfiltrating people to and from the country, the body-shop's owner could be quite useful. In 1980 precisely such low-level contacts made possible the United States' attempt to rescue hostages from Teheran. Moreover, low-level contacts are often indispensable way stations to high-level ones. Often the most fruitful approach to a politician is through people who are socially acceptable to him. With money for entertainment, and with the possibility for spreading money around, virtually anyone can become a magnet for influential people. Finally, one may well invest time in the recruitment of young people who may someday be influential. Virtually every embassy, every intelligence service, does this—some better, some worse.

All of this is worthwhile if one has plans in mind, and a waste of time if one does not. The most comprehensive discussion of this subject, Kautilya's *Arthasastra*, assumes that any government will want to employ every manner of agent: "fiery spies" (agents provocateurs), beggars, harlots, seers (today one would say "academics"), mechanics, and on and on. And indeed if one thinks in terms of a permanent state of war—as did Kautilya, or if one happens to be engaged in war—one will grasp at whatever handle is available, and regret not having prepared others.

Let us now turn from potential to actual usefulness. An influential friend in the enemy camp is harder to find than a good spy. A spy is nothing but a set of eyes and ears. His job is passive and his pretense of loyalty depends on secrecy alone. But an agent of influence must maintain his position as a valued member of the enemy's inner circles while giving counsel that leads the enemy astray. This balancing act requires such skill at pretense that often it cannot be carried on the basis of cynicism. Often the high-level agent of influence is so driven by motives so complex that his mind actually reconciles the contradictory roles he plays. He often sees himself as loyal to both the causes he serves.

Harry Hopkins, the most powerful adviser to Franklin D. Roosevelt, the most powerful President of the United States, was also a devoté of Stalin. He honestly believed that Stalin meant to do well by the U.S. and the world, and that the best thing that he, Hopkins, could do for the U.S. and the world was to do what Stalin wanted.[3] Hopkins effectively removed from positions of responsibility for dealing with the USSR any and all Americans the Soviets told him were barriers to good relations. No wonder that the Soviet Union considered Hopkins an agent of influence. It assigned him a KGB controller, Ishak Abdulovich Akhmerov, who would convey Stalin's "personal" requests and thanks.[4] For Akhmerov and the KGB the fact that Hopkins was not a conscious traitor improved his worth as an agent. No need to tell him to "act naturally." Hopkins was not acting. The KGB showed good judgment in neither trying to interfere with Hopkins' view of himself, nor attempting to push him beyond the role he had chosen for himself, but rather in making it easier for Hopkins to be all he wanted to be.

Hopkins was not the only Soviet agent around Roosevelt. Alger Hiss, a high-ranking State Department official who was both a spy and an agent of influence, accompanied Roosevelt and Stalin to the February 1945 conference at the Crimean resort of Yalta where the postwar division of Europe was decided. Neither Hopkins nor Hiss knew of the other's relationship with the KGB, which steered each man according to his peculiar motivation. Together the two agents insulated Roosevelt enough from anti-Stalinist views so that his own will to believe in Stalin predominated.

The lesson here is that the most valuable agents, whether conscious traitors or not, are people who have achieved positions of influence through their own abilities—important people who, for their own reasons, decide to become allies. The process of making a potential ally into an actual one is one of discovering what moves him, and agreeing with him on it. It amounts to hopping aboard a train and fueling it judiciously, but not trying to steer it lest it derail.

Given exceptional commitment and ability on the part of the agent, it is possible to help him acquire access. There is no better example than Armand Hammer (1901–1991). A red-diaper baby, Armand Hammer learned from his father (an abortionist) to make money by circumventing the U.S. embargo on trade with the new Bolshevik regime. Lenin described Hammer to Stalin as "a small path leading to the American business world." Over the next 70 years a succession of Soviet dictators helped make Hammer a very rich man, confidant of presidents (especially Republicans), and the conduit of billions of dollars of aid to the Soviet economy. The Soviets made Hammer a sales agent for some of their oil (and for lots of Libyan oil), and they paid him commissions on business that he brought to the East.* At the time of his death in 1991 Hammer's company, Occidental Petroleum, was valued at almost $4 billion. But it turns out that, unbeknownst to the stockholders, some 60 percent of the company's value

---

*In fact nearly all American businesses that have invested in the Soviet Union (other than on the basis of taxpayer-guaranteed credits) have lost money and effectively made net contributions to the Soviet economy. Joseph Finder, *Red Carpet*.

either had gone into "investments" in the Soviet Union (i.e., gifts) or had been siphoned off to Hammer's influence-buying in Washington.[5] Among other things, Hammer simply paid "retainers" to ex-members of the White House staff, and gave concessionary loans to members of President and Mrs. Reagan's staffs. In 1984, at Hammer's suggestion, Reagan even used him as a private channel to Mikhail Gorbachev on the subject of arms control.[6] Hammer had contributed heavily (indeed illegally) to Richard Nixon's campaign. After Hammer's conviction, President George Bush pardoned him.[7]

Armand Hammer is something of a limit case of the power of money as regards influence. Politically he was poles apart from the Republicans he was influencing, but he did not approach them politically. Money was both his sword and his shield. Over the years, any number of people pointed out to high-ranking Republicans that it ill suited any president—especially a Republican—to have a relationship with Hammer. For the most part they got answers like the one this author got in 1981 when he raised the point with Michael Deaver, Ronald and Nancy Reagan's right-hand man: "He's got a lot of money, you know." Small amounts passed in secret to the likes of Mr. Deaver would be called bribes. Large amounts to the same people, spread politically, are called munificence, or even philanthropy. Money (provided that it is dispensed with what the target regards as "style") is powerful cover, indeed.

A much grosser and less significant instance underlines the point. In 1979 a former reporter-turned-business-consultant named Craig Spence arrived in Washington, DC and started throwing parties. His contacts, his business, and the luxury of his parties spiraled upward together. Soon the parties became a magnet for the stars of the Washington news media, senators, and even cabinet officers. Spence also provided some of his guests with male prostitutes, for whom they paid. Spence recycled the money into the business. The essence of the business was pyramiding contacts and money. But in the process Spence got more than money. He got access—even to the west wing of the White House after hours.[8] Had Spence's motives been political, the technique could have given professional manipulators or recruiters for espionage the opportunity to work U.S. officials under favorable circumstances.

Agents need not be entirely friendly. Anyone who has ever built a task-oriented political coalition knows that a man's disposition with regard to the task at hand is far more important than how he views everything else in the world. Again, the essence of the art of agents of influence is to figure out who is disposed to do what. The acme of the art is to find someone who loathes all your objectives except one, and to so present yourself to him as to lead him to ignore the disagreements while stimulating him to act in the area of converging interest. This often requires approaching the prospective agent under a false flag. But to think of it as recruiting obscures what is actually happening: Another temporary, partial ally is being brought into the field.

It is important whenever possible to rely on the agent's own motives. Machiavelli teaches, and experience confirms, that people's willingness to promise service to others is inversely proportional to the probability that they will be called on to deliver.[9] The sort of loyalty that produces self-sacrifice is to be treasured. But often one must rely on the more common loyalties that do not appear to involve sacrifice at all. In other words, in most cases the agent of influence will be in business for himself.

Finally let us consider agents who are pressured into the service of others. This is as uncommon in influence operations as it is common in espionage. Sometimes, however, a government will favor the career of a foreigner whom it can blackmail. This is what the Soviet Union apparently did with Kurt Waldheim, who rose to the post of Secretary General of the UN with strong Soviet support. The Soviets had possession of his record in the German Army, which showed that he had been a Nazi and involved in massacring civilians in Yugoslavia.[10] During his years as Secretary General, Waldheim was very responsive to Soviet concerns, and the Soviets kept his embarrassing secret.

More often, a government will install a client in a high position within a foreign government or group by economic or military power. Such people are called puppets. History teaches that managing puppets is seldom very profitable, and that being one almost never is. Making puppets is straightforward: Find people who are willing to make a Faustian bargain of their independence in exchange for the money, and the political or military support they need to stay on top of domestic challengers. Much of Machiavelli's The Prince[11] is a historical argument that people who think of themselves as influential because they are conduits of foreign power are kidding themselves.

Hence real leaders who accept substantial foreign aid are at pains to diversify it and to prove to their domestic constituencies how independent they are. This is what Machiavelli's Cesare Borgia (who began as a puppet of his father the Pope, and of the King of France) did[12] and what Charles de Gaulle did during his wartime exile in 1940–43 when his nearly total material dependence on Great Britain led some Frenchmen to think of him as a British puppet.* Moreover, to

---

*An exasperated Winston Churchill once asked Charles de Gaulle why he, who commanded so little power at the time, insisted so intransigently on France's every interest and point of honor, no matter how minor. De Gaulle replied that Churchill could afford to overlook minor affronts to Britain because he was the securely recognized chief of a mighty empire while he, de Gaulle, could not afford not to be jealous of any of France's prerogatives precisely because total support for France's rights was his principal claim to authority. See Charles de Gaulle, Memoires de Guerre, Vol. 1 L'Appel, pp. 262–263.

the extent that people consider one of their countrymen a puppet, they tend to look beyond him, to his foreign manager. Thus it is questionable whether the Germans gained or lost by administering the territories they occupied during World War II through obvious traitors rather than through Gauleiters.

This poses a straightforward problem for whoever manages foreign agents either by compulsion or simply by providing total support. Except in rare cases (such as that of Kurt Waldheim) where the relationship is covered by secrecy, the handler must strike a balance between letting the agent get "out of control" and making him contemptible. Add to this the fact that people who live by others' means tend to fit themselves into clients' roles. Often they do not even try to sink political roots into their own soil, and live in the political equivalent of the Cargo Cult. The U.S. government found out, after the murder of Vietnam's Ngo Dinh Diem, that this independent agent, while prickly, offered more than the placid puppets who followed him. Alas, the role that true puppets play best is that of pawns who are sacrificed somewhere along the way.

One of the most imitable masters of puppetry was Louis XIV, France's Sun King. In the 1670s England's Charles II, a King whose appetite for armed forces and opulence exceeded his ability to get money from his own parliament, became addicted to French subsidies. The terms of the two Kings' secret alliance called for Charles to return England to Catholicism. But Louis often cautioned Charles to put the big project on the back burner. Louis really wanted most what Charles could give most easily—the total subordination of England's foreign policy in the Low Countries to France's interest. Charles was happy to oblige on both counts. Louis was also financing some of England's leading opposition figures. His able ambassador, Barillon, played one side against the other, and England ceased to be a factor in world affairs. When Charles' brother, James II, ascended the throne he felt obliged to apologize to the King of France for convening the English parliament without having asked Louis' permission, and James's chief minister asked Louis for more money by pointing out "how important it is that the King of England should be dependent not on his own people but on the friendship of France alone."[13] Despite this high degree of power, Louis XIV never tried to manage the internal affairs of England in a positive way, knowing full well that if France had caused the total victory of any English faction over another on a domestic matter, especially religion, the entire English body politic would quickly have turned on France. So he kept to his wise policy of accepting only foreign policy concessions in exchange for his secret gifts. It was not Louis' fault that James II wrecked the subtle arrangement by trying to ram Catholicism down English throats, and thus brought on the Glorious Revolution of 1688.

Occasionally there are agents who combine forced dependence and initiative.

The finest example in our time is Cuba's Fidel Castro, a fiercely independent man whose lifetime choice of communist dictatorship made him materially dependent on the Soviet Union. Through economic levers, Moscow reined in some of his initiatives (such as guerrilla warfare in the Caribbean in the late 1960s) and multiplied the size of others (witness the deployment of circa 80,000 troops in Africa in the late 1970s). None of this broke Castro's spirit, which survived the fall of the Soviet Union itself.

Groups

Most polities and all empires have contained groups that were disgruntled or could be persuaded to be. The bases of dissension are as diverse as mankind. In Thucydides' Greece there were oligarchs and democrats, subject populations, tribal minorities, natives, and colonists. Every other action in the Peloponnesian War, it seems, turned on rallying or excluding some faction. Wherever the Roman legions went, the long-term issue was decided by the strategy *divide et impera*. This was the daily practice of the British, French and Soviet empires. The wars of the European Middle Ages involved pursuading the other side's vassals to defect or limit their participation. The Wars of Religion, of the French Revolution, and the struggles of our own time, have involved contests for the allegiance of every imaginable kind of group behind the enemy lines—"fifth columns" to use the term that Gen. Francisco Franco coined during the Spanish Civil War of 1936–39.*

Groups often make a greater impact than individual agents but are more likely to follow their own internal imperatives than direction from outsiders. One must take them or leave them for what they are. As with individuals, one must begin by looking for a handle: "What do they want? What interest could they possibly have in getting involved?" This handle often has more to do with the circumstance in which the group finds itself than with the group's fundamental purpose. Hutus might hate Tutsis, Shi'ites might groan under Sunni rule, Georgians might live for independence from Moscow. But whoever would move them must point to reasons why, given the circumstances, they ought to move *now* and in *this* particular way. Hence, while one must be conscious of whether the group's basis is religious, economic, or ethnic, one must pay even more attention to what the group fears or wants here and now. Hence recruiting groups as agents of influence is primarily a matter of offering specific outlets for

---

*Franco once explained to reporters that he was going to attack a city with five columns of troops. The reporters, seeing only four, asked "Where is the fifth column?" Franco replied that it was already inside the city. This got the reporters' attention, and set the city's defenders on a destructive search for the "fifth columnists."

their hopes and fears. Money is most useful for helping the group to do its job. However, as a means of motivation money makes even less sense for groups than for individuals. In short, groups, like nations, are best thought of as political allies rather than controlled agents.

Anyone can be an ally. Because Marxist–Leninist ideology relegates military forces to the role of enemies of the "working class," the Soviet Union did not seek allies among foreign military forces until the 1960s. When officers such as Egypt's Nasser and Guatemala's Arbenz took power in their countries and exercised it in favor of Soviet foreign policy, the Soviets distrusted them. When the Soviet Union overcame this prejudice, it was able to build excellent relations with Third World military leaders, some of whom (e.g., Ethiopia's Col. Mengistu) took power and made their countries Soviet satellites. If Marxism teaches anything, it is the enmity between "capitalists" and "proletarians." Yet from the very first V. I. Lenin believed that, because the profit motive is inherently apolitical, businessmen could be led to "sell the rope" with which they would later be hanged. Similarly, anti-Semitism did not stop Germany's National Socialists from making use of Jewish businessmen. In 1990, Iraq's Saddam Hussein, an inveterate atheist who, during an eight-year war with Iran had presented himself as the slayer of Shi'ite fundamentalism, drew cheers from Muslim fundamentalists (including Shi'ites) all over the world during his confrontation with the U.S. by presenting himself as their champion. These groups did not question his credentials because he offered them the emotional release they sought.

Alliances with groups within a target country can yield benefits according to their kind. Militaries yield coups, businessmen yield money, labor unions yield strikes, religious groups yield moral suasion, and journalists are megaphones, while violence-prone people yield intimidation and provocation. All yield access to the target's body politic.

Working with a group is a more subtle matter than working with individuals. Only a few of the group's members may know how deeply their leaders are involved with a foreign power. And of those who are involved, the foreign power may choose to pose special trust in even fewer. Even under the most favorable circumstances, control of foreign groups is imperfect. The Soviet Communist party's International Department employed genuine long-term experts to control nonruling Communist parties and movements. The leaders of these groups were so devoted that they spent their vacations in the USSR and went there for medical treatment. In addition Moscow's special *hommes de confiance* (like Jacques Duclos in France and Armando Cossutta in Italy) sought above all to keep the Party faithful. Nevertheless, in the 1980s, when the Italian party's wider leadership saw their own political survival at stake, they distanced themselves from Moscow, and Soviet control mechanisms among Italian Communists altogether ceased to matter. The French remained faithful to no purpose.

Many of the groups used for subversive purposes are hardly controlled at all. It is enough that they be "objective allies," which is to say that they do useful things regardless of motive. The point is to help them do it. But objective allies can as easily ruin a plan as help it along. The finest example of this is the role of the Red Brigade terrorists in the rise and plunge of the Italian Communist party's fortunes in the 1970s. The Red Brigade's roots were in the Party's wartime organization of the same name. After the war it first changed its name ("Red Flying Squad"), then went underground, and then moved to Czechoslovakia. In 1970 a few radical communists unconnected with the Party traveled to Czechoslovakia to bring back the spark of an organization that would terrorize those who stood in the way of a communist victory. That spark ignited young, middle-class, ultracommunists. Up to 1976–77, as the new Red Brigade's terrorism struck exclusively those who resisted the Communist party's demands, the Party enjoyed the best of all worlds: It warned recalcitrants against incurring "the ire of the people," while disassociating itself from violence. Moreover, no one could help but notice that while others lived in fear, Communists and those of whom they approved were physically safe. During this period the Communists denounced the police as Fascists, and stood against all attempts to fight terrorism. But in 1977–78, just as the Communist party was reaping the rewards of the situation and taking over more and more state powers, the terrorists, following their own logic, began to strike Communists and communist collaborators along with everybody else. They became a nuisance to the Party. In 1978, when the terrorists killed the former Prime Minister, Aldo Moro, the man who was brokering the Party's entry into power, they became a deadly liability to the Communist party, which bitterly regretted every wink and nod it had given them.

So, if it is dangerous simply to encourage uncontrolled groups to enter the fray on one's side, and if the best attempts at control can fail, how can one use groups most subversively? First, there is no substitute for understanding what the group wants or is capable of wanting. A clear mutual understanding of purposes and priorities is worth more than any control mechanism. Nor is there any substitute for realizing *in good time* if and when the group is about to become counterproductive. Second, the best (though not infallible) assurance that allied groups will not go astray is the rapid, evident fulfillment of the operation's goals. Alliances, like all other organizations, live on their own momentum and make sense only in relation to their goals.

Finally, consider the peculiar kind of group that Willi Munzenberg labeled "innocents' clubs" and that have since become known as "front groups." Their essence is the division between the few who know the organization's purpose and the many who do not, plus a pyramidal structure in which the lower levels have many "innocents," and few who are "in on the secret," while at the higher levels the proportions are reversed. Here the task is threefold: to manage the leadership class, to keep the innocents content, and to promote the group's credibility with the target. The key to the first two tasks is to recognize that one is dealing with two sets of people who are "in it" for very different reasons. The easiest way to wreck a front group is to demand of its rank-and-file things that set them apart from their neighbors. To some extent, exposure is the natural result of use. The history of communist front groups has been precisely one of social sectors that have been used and disillusioned, and whose cadres have been left exposed. In the 1940s and 1950s communists used up their welcome in labor unions. By the 1960s and 1970s, whenever an advertisement appeared in a Western newspaper for a pro-Soviet political cause, it did not take much experience to guess which intellectual luminaries had signed it. So by the 1980s hard-core pro-Soviets had worn out their welcome, even among intellectuals. Thus also, in the long run, the problem of maintaining credibility can only be solved by finding new social sectors whose innocence is unspoiled and whose credibility has not been blown. In this regard, the communists' embrace of environmentalism in the late 1980s is noteworthy.

Infrastructure

Plans for subversion make sense to the extent that they are based on existing individuals and groups who are willing and able to play subversive roles. It is clear from the foregoing that the search for allies is a subtle and time-consuming job most difficult to do well under the pressure of circumstances. And so any government that wants to have a choice about engaging in subversion later must get acquainted with its targets now. The first step is to put into the field people who are "at home" in the target's language and culture, who understand where each part of the target's body politic is "coming from" and where it wants to go, *and above all who can imagine how each part might be useful in the future.* To do their jobs well these scouts must think subversively—even though no policy of subversion may exist. Second, someone must build relationships with the individuals and groups who might later be useful. The differences between sympathetic contacts, patronage, and alliance lie in purpose. It is usually good policy to sow no confusion among potential allies about the kind of relationship that one is trying to create.

Building material infrastructures (the capacity to transfer money and arms) involves the establishment of bank accounts, dummy businesses, and secret warehouses. This requires far less time and subtlety than building human infrastructures. They key items in any subversive infrastructure, however, are the minds of the planners who can fit the available human and material tools to the needs and circumstances of the moment, and come up with a reasonable plan. Let us now see what these tools can accomplish.

Means and Ends

Propaganda

Usually, people are moved less by what another person says than by the authority of the speaker. In our time, mass communication has led some to think that words can move people all by themselves. In fact, however, the effect of any message depends at least as much on what people think of the source as it does on the content. It is useful to think of the various means by which one affects the source's image as "cover." Consider the role of fear in enhancing the effect of messages. Edward Mead Earle has written: "Something approaching naked fear . . . of aerial bombing played a large part in causing people [in Britain in the 1930s] to make the worse appear the better reason and to misjudge the true character of their interests. This is not to say that the people of France and Britain were craven; it is merely to suggest that because of the threat from the air it was easier to persuade them than it otherwise would have been that there was merit to Hitler's claims, and that discretion was the better part of valor."[14] Nazi propaganda was a model of the "good cop/bad cop" ploy: One aspect emphasized the destructiveness of war, while the other argued that the Nazi regime really wanted peace, and that those who doubted the Nazis were the real warmongers. Fear covered the message's flaws and escorted it past the defenses of the mind.

Fear is not the only cover for propaganda. *Any* powerful emotion (hate, desire, etc.) can be a vehicle. Intense emotion eases or even suspends the audience's judgment regarding the prescription. The strongest emotions of all combine fear of impending catastrophe with loathing of the kinds of people—different from *us*—who are the putative causes of the catastrophe. This is the reason for the success of apocalyptic propaganda by the Anabaptist sects of the Renaissance that indicted bishops and Jews for the coming "end of the world,"[15] and in our time for the success of environmentalist propaganda that indicts "environmental criminals" who do not belong to the social class of their accusers.

The basic point of propaganda is to tell people the sorts of things that result in their saying "I knew it all the time! Why, those. . . ." In other words, it is to play to people's prejudices—to use what the audience knows, or *thinks* it knows, to legitimize the message. The part of the message that wins the audience's attention and establishes the source's credibility (a purely subjective concept) is akin to deposits into a bank account, while the exploitation, however subtle, is akin to withdrawals. To the extent the message is well-crafted, the audience will look less closely at the credentials of the source. Indeed, almost regardless of the source's identity, whenever it speaks it must establish that it is on the audience's side. Propaganda that is hostile to the audience is something of an oxymoron. This was certainly the case with Allied propaganda to Germany during World War II. It accused the entire German people of criminal responsibility for the war, and then called for unconditional surrender. Instead of separating Nazis and Germans, the propaganda pushed them together. Propaganda must be "audience friendly."

The exceptions confirm the rule. In the early 1990s whenever the Soviet government accused anyone of being an enemy of communism, it invariably convinced the audience that the accused was on the people's side. Hence it is fair to say that the Soviet government's propaganda against people like Boris Yeltsin and Oleg Kalugin (and indeed against antiregime activists, whether their bases were ethnic, religious, or otherwise) gave these people credibility that they could not easily have earned for themselves.

Disguising the source of propaganda is not an end in itself, but rather a means to increasing the chances that the audience will regard the message as coming from an acceptable source. Pretending that one's message comes from any given source may be useful, given the prestige of that source with the intended audience. Thus while it is worth much effort to recruit an agent of influence within the information ministry of a government that is credible to its population, it is probably counterproductive to speak to that population through the voice of a government that is hated by the population, even if one can easily do so. By a similar token, consider under what conditions one's agents within the target's body politic might make effective subversive propaganda. Only if the target's government is credible to the population is there an advantage to tailoring the message within the bounds of acceptable discourse. If the government is not credible, agents must make it openly revolutionary rather than subversive. Target governments react to revolutionary propaganda by putting it "beyond the pale"—thus wasting the effort it took to get the message expressed "from the inside." The point here is that since there is a difference between subverting a government and fomenting a frontal attack on it, there also is a difference in the propaganda that serves the two ends. *Subversion by disguised sources of propaganda is possible only to the extent that the body politic being subverted enjoys credibility* and *is foolish enough to accept the propaganda as legitimate criticism*. On the other hand, to subvert a government or an establishment that does not enjoy credibility, one can simply speak the truth about it from the outside. No need to disguise the source.

This is why, although it is technically possible to produce and disseminate accurate fakes and forgeries concerning national or religious leaders (e.g., broadcasting a dictator's resignation), such propaganda can be effective only in the very short run—until it is denied. It is most useful if the faked publication or broadcast is close enough to the truth so that the denial will be unconvincing (for example, giving a false account of a meeting that actually took place) and yet far enough from the truth to cause the desired effect. This kind of propaganda is also effective to induce misunderstandings, to set people against one another—what the Nazis called *Zersetzung*, a kind of scrambling of expectations and allegiances. Of all the techniques of subversion it is the one that most clearly raises the question: "To what end?"

By itself, propaganda seldom achieves major results. It does little good to tell people that they are oppressed. Chances are they already know it all too well. They are more likely to appreciate encouraging thoughts about what they might do about it, and even more to appreciate news that they are not alone in their struggle. This of course was the principal point in Charles de Gaulle's magisterial broadcast to France on June 18, 1940. He told the French people that they had lost a battle, but not the war, because France, he said, "is not alone, is not alone, is not alone." In subsequent broadcasts he struggled mightily to give evidence that this was so. Had it not been so, all his eloquence would have been in vain.

Our principal point is that strong policies that give evidence of their own success are by far the most effective propaganda. People are interested above all in what any given situation portends for them. They want to know who intends what with regard to things they care about; they want to know who will win, and what that means for *them*. People are only too willing to believe that which is convenient. The art of propaganda consists primarily of substance and presentation. Only a small part of the art involves pretense about sources.

Pressure on Governments

On Sunday, November 4, 1978, President Jimmy Carter walked out of church and saw a group of people holding placards which, in religious terms, chastized the "Enhanced Radiation Warheads" that the U.S. government was about to deploy with its forces in Europe. President Carter decided to cancel the deployment. The Soviet Union had sought this result by mobilizing thousands of protesters around the world. According to the U.S. government, the KGB spent some $100 million on the campaign.[16] But most of this broad-gauged effort was actually counterproductive. In Europe, the rallying of leftists forces around "hard" anti-American positions forced moderate politicians such as Germany's Helmut Schmidt to rely on conservative forces which were themselves energized by the sight of their enemies. In the aftermath of the affair European leftists were more isolated than ever. In America, too, the sight of a united, pro-Soviet left energized conservative forces.

The Soviet victory on the neutron bomb came not from the huge scattergun blast of agents and groups, but from a couple of pellets that happened to hit the target that mattered in the right way. Jimmy Carter, the only man who had the power to make the decision the Soviets wanted, is a pious man who responded to the language of piety spoken by people who seemed to be more motivated by religious than by political concerns. The Soviets might have saved themselves work, money, and collateral losses had they used only their agents under religious cover. In 1983–84 the Soviets tried essentially the same broad-based, overt-covert campaign to prevent the deployment of intermediate-range missiles in Europe. Not only did the new U.S. President, Ronald Reagan, not cave in, but conservative forces throughout Europe rode the issue of Soviet interference in the Western alliance to electoral victories. The Soviets lost the entire campaign because their overt activities raised opposition from voters. They might have done better if they had targeted their pressure more precisely on the elites who were more susceptible to it, while involving voters as little as possible. Which is to say if they had been more covert.

The point here is one that lobbyists know well: Pressure on governments is a matter of knowing who actually gets to make a given decision, finding out what it takes to "get to" him, and then doing *only* that. The success of the operation depends almost exclusively on discovering what will move the decision-maker, and on being able to approach him with that motive and no other. Mere access to the decision-maker won't do. The person with the access—unless he is an alter ego, as Harry Hopkins was to Roosevelt—must be credible from the appropriate angle. Moreover, as every lobbyist knows, you must exercise influence while letting as few people know about it as possible. People who know about "the play" but are not playing a role on your side can only complicate matters.

Thus, after 1984, the Soviet Union's drive to remove U.S. missiles from Europe focused on the only man who could do it: Ronald Reagan. The Soviets approached him not through leftist preachers, who would have repelled him, but through his natural friends, businessmen—including Armand Hammer—who flattered him with the prospect of achieving through the force of his personal vision the millennialist goal of eliminating nuclear weaponry. So efficient was the Soviets' playing of Reagan's chords that at the October 1986 summit meeting at Reykjavik, Iceland, Reagan eagerly agreed to withdraw the U.S. missiles from Europe, and almost committed the U.S. to total nuclear disarmament. Afterward, the entire U.S. government national security bureaucracy, backed even by such liberal organs as *The New York Times* editorial page, worked feverishly to reverse Reagan's hasty personal decision.[17]

This is not to say that every decision-maker can be subverted on every decision if one looks long enough for the key to his motivation. On the contrary, instances of governments quietly reaching inside other governments to fine-tune their decisions are relatively rare. But when they happen, they do because sensitive biographic intelligence has revealed the opportunity, and someone happened to be in a position to "help" the target do what he so passionately wanted to do.

In 1985–86 the government of Iran performed the remarkable feat of reaching inside both the Israeli *and* the U.S. governments. Its initial insertion was very gentle: Iranian arms purchases offered Israel the sort of deal it could not pass up—sell some obsolete weapons for cash. This seemed to be an old-time Persian–Israeli deal. The only losers would be Arabs. Then, once the ship was loaded, the Iranian agents began to set the hook: Teheran would not pay for *this* cargo; it wanted somewhat more modern antitank missiles. The Israelis wanted to sell, but needed permission from the U.S. Having suckered the Israelis with money, the Iranian agents were able to count on Israeli help in contacting the Americans. By making their approach along with the Israelis, the Iranians benefited from Israel's reputation for making good deals. However, the Iranians offered the Americans something that they wanted as much as Israel wanted money, namely the prospect of political influence *and* the politically precious release of Americans held in Lebanon. At this crucial point, the Iranians could count on the Israelis' financial interest in helping to sell the Americans on the scheme. But once the Americans were sold, they threw caution to the wind. The Iranians ended up with the antitank missiles, plus antiaircraft missiles, because they understood by which handles their targets could be manipulated.[18]

Governments can sometimes build the influence of groups within foreign societies. But *normally, political pressure exercised by groups is a blunt instrument.* The outstanding examples in our time are the bureaucracies and state-owned businesses that virtually monopolize public life in Third World countries. These were financed largely by foreign aid from the governments of the U.S., Japan, Britain, and France, of which only the latter has tenuously tied its aid to their staffing and hence gained a bit of control over them. In general, however, the "Iron Law of bureaucracy" has taken over: The groups financed by foreign aid follow their immediate, domestic self-interest and are quite unresponsive to the people who created them.

The limit case is surely the attitude of the Palestine Liberation Organization and of lesser Palestinian organizations toward their chief financier, Saudi Arabia. After 1948, Palestinians settled—albeit precariously—throughout the Arab world. Generally capable and hard-working by Arab standards, they became important in Egypt, Syria, and Lebanon, and occasionally indispensable (e.g., in the Persian Gulf states.) In Jordan they became the majority. None had any doubt that the Saudi royal family had financed their organizations. And yet, in the Gulf crisis of 1990–91, the Palestinian organizations strongly backed Iraq in its threats against Saudi Arabia, and the Palestinian masses bayed for the blood of the Saudi royal family. Saddam had effectively seduced them with something they valued more than the money they had received in the past—namely, hopes for the future.

The beginning of wisdom regarding groups in foreign societies is that with rare exceptions they will be driven by their own agendas. Bargaining with a group's leaders about adjusting their agendas to conform with that of a helpful foreign power is an illusion that lasts only in the absence of pressing domestic factors. Hence it makes sense to foster a foreign group only to the extent that one's country would benefit by the advancement of that group's "natural" agenda.

Sometimes foreign help can provide critical support to groups that end up playing a major role. In the 1980s—despite U.S. government opposition—American labor helped Poland's labor movement with money and communications equipment. Poland's *Solidarnosc*, an expression of Polish civil society rising up under the cracking communist pavement, might have cracked the pavement without American labor's aid. Nevertheless, that aid was heartening, practically helpful, and may well have been catalytic. In the end, each such act is a gamble. As we will see below, however, the only way to improve one's chances of a good return is for a government to help foreign groups only as part of a larger, well-orchestrated policy.

Provocations

"Let a hundred flowers bloom," said Mao Tse-tung to the Chinese people in 1957, much as a child cheating at hide-and-seek might yell to his playmates "Come out, come out, wherever you are!" Many Chinese who held views that diverged from Mao's accepted the invitation to speak up. No sooner had they done him the favor of identifying themselves, than Mao had them arrested or purged.

To provoke is to incite people to do what they are inclined to do, but had forborn doing. By acting, they blow their cover. A secondary meaning of provocation is to somehow incite animosities within the target group. Yet another is to stage an incident, allegedly involving a foreign power, which one then takes as an excuse for doing what one always wanted to do. Provocation may be the most common of all subversive techniques.

When the Gestapo and the Soviet KGB met at Zakopane, Poland, in December 1939, they joined in a program to infiltrate the Polish underground.

The Soviet/Nazi agents would join the underground after giving evidence of their interest in fighting the occupation. Once in, they would provide occasions in which both occupying forces could catch large numbers of the underground. But these operations pale before the biggest provocation of all: In 1944 the Soviets informed the Polish underground of the date when the Red Army would enter Warsaw. But they lied. When the Polish underground rose, the Soviets stopped their advance, giving the German Army all the leisure it needed to kill the Poles. So, provocation did much to clear the way for the imposition of communism on Poland.

Since Near Eastern statecraft seldom regularized the process of succession to power, its history is full of *coups d'état*. The permutations are infinite, but a typical passage in the Persian *Book of Kings* may involve one contender inciting another (through false information) to make his bid for power, while informing yet a third that the second was going to move. The first would then be in position to vanquish the weakened rivals. Another time-tested provocation is to "frame" the enemy's most effective adviser, and then watch the enemy weaken himself.[19] Before World War II the German Abwehr had a plan to allow Stalin's KGB to steal "information" to suggest that the Soviet Union's ablest general, Tukachevsky, might have had clandestine contacts with the Germans. But Stalin was 'way ahead of the Abwehr. He fabricated the information himself to give himself an excuse to purge not only Tukachevky, but the vast majority of Soviet military officers as well. In our time the Israelis have found it easy to provoke deadly struggles within the Palestinian groups because the level of distrust in those organizations is so high. However, one should not confuse successful provocations in such cases with successful manipulation. No one can tell where such processes end.

Provocation yields its most reliable results when one has substantial control of the situation. Thus, at the Nuremberg trials the Abwehr's Gen. Erwin von Lahausen testified that in the summer of 1939 he had provided Heinrich Himmler's Sicherheitsdienst with Polish uniforms, which it used in an "attack" on the German border point of Hohenlinde, while other agents "attacked" the radio station at Gleiwitz. Hitler used the incidents to justify his long-planned invasion of Poland. He need hardly have bothered. No one was convinced. On the other hand, Stalin's provocations convinced millions. The biggest was the 1934 murder of Leningrad Party boss Sergei Kirov, which the local KGB commander had done at Stalin's orders. Stalin's long-planned great purge began the moment he stepped off the train in Leningrad with that very KGB agent as the first victim. Stalin succeeded not only in thoroughly purging the Communist party, but in getting even such unlikely people as Winston Churchill to say that the purge trials were genuine.[20] Credulity was surely aided by the lack of surviving witnesses to the contrary.

374

Paramilitary

Among the most effective forms of propaganda is the propaganda of the deed—the sight of a corpse, and the feeling that one may be next. Nothing so cements a movement for the long run as martyrs, nor changes a government so definitively as killing its members or supporters.

The most basic paramilitary action is assassination—the killing of specific enemy leaders. Contrary to conventional wisdom, assassination is the most morally justifiable of all acts of war: If it is just to kill anyone in pursuit of a political goal, it is more just to kill an officer in the enemy army than a draftee, and *most* just to kill those who are orchestrating the contrary effort, namely the commanders-in-chief. The problems with assassination are practical: What will the killing of *this* individual in *these* circumstances accomplish? Just as St. Thomas Aquinas argued that regicide is permissible only in the act of establishing a better government, the killing of a foreign leader makes sense only as part of a well-thought-out plan to achieve the ends of the war. But a war waged against underlings will be as ineffective as it is immoral.

Unless one uses *force majeure* (for example, the Soviet assault on the Afghan Presidential Palace of December 1979, or puts a cruise missile into the target's bedroom window), the art of assassination lies in securing an individual killer's access to the target. Once that is done, the job is as simple as driving a pickaxe into Leon Trotsky's skull, or pulling a trigger. Access can be achieved either through recruitment or through penetration. It is difficult to imagine how the target's security could be so remiss as to leave in the entourage anyone who might be highly motivated to kill the boss—someone, say, whose family the boss had outraged. And yet, historically, the fatal mistake of tyrants is precisely allowing access to themselves by people who have reason to kill them.[21]

The difficulties in recruiting as assassins people who already have access to the target are well known. The would-be assassin's motivation must be strong, since the risk of being killed is high. Moreover, whoever is recruiting the prospective killer must ask why, if he is so motivated, has he not already done the job himself without prompting. Finally, if one is recruiting someone who had been mistreated by his boss, "pitching" him gives him the wherewithal to become his boss's darling, simply by reporting the pitch. These difficulties may be overcome by a kind of anonymous recruiting: promising to pay a reward to whoever kills the target, or to his next of kin.

Infiltration is certainly possible, given dedicated people. The textbook infiltrator was Ramon Mercader, the young Spanish–Soviet agent who contacted Leon Trotsky's entourage in 1939 by getting a mistress within it. He then spent a year gently working his way up in the entourage and into position for the assassination. Then, in a Mexican prison, he hid his Stalinist connection for 13 years.[22]

375

When the target is not a chief of state, infiltration into the right position is easy—especially since the infiltrator does not necessarily have to do the killing. He can simply note the target's habits and schedule, and either plant a bomb or indicate a travel route. Just how possible it is to pierce security may be seen in the 1980 murder of Italy's Gen. Carlo Alberto Dalla Chiesa, who had defeated the Red Brigades but whose total security cocoon did not last a month when he took the job of chief Mafia hunter and Prefect of the Mafia stronghold of Palermo, Sicily. A car bomb killed him, his wife, and their daughter.

The greater the number of people one thinks of killing, whether overtly or covertly, the more pressing does the question "Then what?" become. The euphemism "paramilitary operations" should not obscure the fact that when a government takes a hand in killing people it is committing an act of war, initiating great changes at the cost of great suffering. To make war effectively (and justly) one must have a clearly defined set of ends which, if achieved, would end the quarrel and leave the situation substantially better than it was (enough at least to counterbalance the evils of the war.) One also must have a plan that puts the means employed at the service of the ends sought. There must be a good chance that if all is done according to plan, victory will result. To do otherwise is irresponsible both materially and morally. Thus covert war cannot be the mere indiscriminate supply of arms to people who want to fight. In covert as well as in overt military operations, supply is naturally subordinate to operations, and that in turn is naturally subordinate to strategy.

The Duke of Wellington's Peninsular Campaign against Napoleon's forces in Spain in 1808, which gave currency to the word "guerrilla" (little war) is the exemplar. Britain's involvement in Spain was not a secret, but rather was "covered" by the Spanish people's hatred of the invaders. The Duke not only delivered supplies, but also a strategy borrowed from Hannibal: Use speedy maneuver to turn overall strategic inferiority into tactical superiority. True, the Peninsular Campaign was a diversionary action. But it had its own integrity. The Duke was not fighting to the last Spaniard, but rather to defeat such forces as Napoleon could spare for Spain. Finally, because the casualties of covert wars are just as dead as those of overt wars, covert war demands just as passionately that the ends be worthy of the means.

The Target

Because each kind of regime has its own peculiar strengths and weaknesses, each will offer peculiar opportunities for, and resistance to, subversion.[23] To be effective, subversion should aim to affect the ruling part of the target regime. If a regime featured a figurehead presidency and an army powerful both politically and militarily, it would be wasteful to try to influence that president's counselors or to sponsor a *coup d'état*. The army would be a more logical focus. Similarly, the world is full of regimes whose ruling parties have armored themselves against direct influence from the rest of society, and, *a fortiori*, from foreigners. While retail subversion by manipulating factions within these disciplined regimes makes no sense, it is possible to subvert them wholesale by helping the rest of society to mobilize itself. Let us now look at how several types of regimes may be subverted.

Democracies

At first glance, one may deem democracies vulnerable to every kind of subversion and immune to none. Every astute observer has noted the propensity of democracies to faction.[24] Buying and selling access and influence is legitimate business. It is difficult to distinguish legitimate from illegitimate transactions. Agents of influence abound. It is relatively easy to sow illegals, and not impossible to implant moles. But consider how the structure of democracies guards them against subversion. The powers of government are distributed, and the competence of each branch is limited by constitutions, laws, and the jealousy of other organs. No official may transgress the bounds of his authority. Democracies enjoy a kind of compartmentalization: Each compartment may be easy to breach—but there are so many! So while an agent of influence may alter this or that policy, even a large number cannot hope to affect the polity. Moreover, as de Tocqueville pointed out, because democracies are ruled by public opinion, and public opinion follows fashion, aroused democracies can enforce conformity more strictly than any dictatorship. Hence any foreigner's subversive success against a democracy is always liable to be wiped away by outraged public opinion.

The logical foci of subversion in democracies (in ascending order of importance) are: governing elites, parties, and public opinion. Ambition is a powerful subversive. Democracies tend not to satisfy their elites' taste for obsequies. Thus Alcibiades betrayed Athens, Coriolanus betrayed Rome, and in our time the most numerous secessions from democracies have been *"trahisons des clercs"*—by intellectuals and would-be aristos who despised their societies for giving them insufficient recognition. American university campuses have long been dominated by a subculture for which deep hostility to the rest of the society is axiomatic, and whose members are positively eager for chances to stop what they regard as the worst blight on the planet, the United States of America. This counterculture often is effective in bureaucratic decision-making. But *trahisons des clercs* have self-limiting effects: When people from this pool try to act in the public arena, their very dissonance with society often promotes the opposite of their causes.

In democracies, countercultures are most important simply as constituents of

377

the body politic. At any given time some citizens will be raising claims against others, on the basis of class, ethnicity, religion, or fancy. Foreign governments may support those claims morally or materially. In the end, parts of the polity may do as the Romans of the first century B.C. did all by themselves—"Treat each other as foreigners."[25] In our time, Lebanon is the paradigm of a polity whose different religious and social communities had worked together reasonably well until its neighbors encouraged each of the communities to assert themselves. This subversion turned the communities into tribes divided by warring gods and by endless lists of avengeable injuries.

Since public opinion holds democracies together and determines their character, and since the substance of public opinion is always "up for grabs," the most effective subversion that any democracy can suffer is foreign aid and comfort to antidemocratic elements in its domestic opinion. The Nazis sought to weaken their democratic enemies by introducing anti-Semitic tracts and agitators within them, judging this so much "poison."* They were more correct than they knew about the corrosive effect on democracy of wrangling over group rights and wrongs. Abraham Lincoln identified the question Who shall live off whom? as the "serpent," the original sin of politics, and particularly fatal to democracies.[26] There are always people who are more than ready to hear how their group has been or is about to be disadvantaged by another, and about how it ought to "get back its own." The basis for such resentment can be social as well as economic. This is the principal weak spot of democracies, and thus the major inroad for subversion.

The Communist Model

Machiavelli counters the conventional wisdom of the ages according to which tyrannical regimes are solid. Rather, he explains, they are brittle.[27] Until recently there was little dissent from the proposition that modern tyrannies, whose ruling parties are larger than those of their ancient counterparts, and whose technical means of controlling the population are so superior, were well-nigh immune to subversion.† But the collapse of communist regimes in Eastern Europe and the Soviet Union has shown modern tyrannies to be as brittle as ancient ones, and in

---

*In this regard they followed both Gaetano Mosca and, significantly, Karl Marx: "Gift infiltrieren wo immer ist nur ratsam." See Paul Blackstock, *The Strategy of Subversion*, p. 51.
†Among the rare dissents were those of this author and of Abram Shulsky in Roy Godson, ed., *Intelligence Requirements for the 1980s: Covert Action*, pp. 100–104 and 127–130. Note also Richard Pipes, *Survival Is Not Enough*. Pipes argued that the USSR had feet of clay and that U.S. foreign policy should aim to collapse the USSR. This is also the argument that Richard Pipes and Angelo Codevilla incorporated in the report of the 1980 Presidential transition team for the State Department.

some ways even more vulnerable to subversion. This insight is applicable to the feudal remains of communist organizations in the former Soviet Empire as well as to the provincial regimes in China, North Korea, Vietnam, Cuba, Serbia, et al.

The armor of communist regimes against subversion is obvious: Their secret police have several overlapping blankets of surveillance over anyone with responsibility, and substantial surveillance over ordinary citizens. Their vulnerability to subversion was self-evident only to such as Alexandr Solzhenitsyn. Unlike Western officials, he knew that the communists' claims of identity between the Party and "the people" (i.e., civil society) were the exact reverse of the truth. He pointed out that for communist regimes to function, millions of people must tell each other things that both the speaker and the listener know are false, and that people could secede from the regimes simply by telling the truth to one another.[28] Hence, counseled Solzhenitsyn, the most subversive of acts against communist regimes is to spread true facts so widely as to undercut inhibition against speaking them. American propaganda, wrote Solzhenitsyn, should not have been telling the Russian people about America, and "silly things" at that. Rather, it should have been telling them the truths about Russia that the Soviet regime was trying to keep out of circulation, and things that would allow them to build a civil society independent of the regime.[29]

The anticommunist revolution that began in 1989 has left the surviving regimes (or remnants thereof) more fragile, more vulnerable than ever. The prerequisite for using the strong medicine of subversion against these revolution-prone regimes, however, is a commitment to their demise, even if that demise be catastrophic. Five approaches, singly or in combination, would take advantage of these regimes' peculiar vulnerabilities.

The first approach is to strike at the gap between reality and public life, to force officials to confront their own hypocrisy and make their exercise of power unbearable. Because that gap is wider in a communist regime than in any other kind, anyone and everyone in authority is forced to be a hypocrite. Oligarchies are an old story in the world. But the oligarchs who administer "socialist" countries must try to justify themselves on the basis of egalitarianism. These officials try to keep their privileged lifestyles secret. Intelligence can gather facts about officials' homes and meals, about their vacations, their children's privileges. Then radios can broadcast them, and handbooks on the lifestyles of the leadership for a given area can be spread about that area. Something like *glasnost*, with all its subversive effects, can be forced onto the organization. *Knowledge that the knowledge is widespread* makes it easy for citizens to look each other in the eye and tell each other the truth. It shames the exposed officials and makes them ineffective and vulnerable to their colleagues. This is especially useful in the atmosphere of the 1990s, where many communist officials have shed their label and are struggling to present themselves as "reformers" while nevertheless retaining their powers and privileges.

The second approach relies on the fact that communist oligarchies are organized along feudal lines: overlapping personal constituencies. This has always ensured violent internecine conflict. Until the anticommunist revolution of our time, however, outside powers lacked the knowledge and the "trade goods" to manipulate the feudal factions within these oligarchies in a positive sense. But, especially after August 1991, the masses of "former communist" (or soon-to-be "former communist") officials in contact with the West were positively soliciting special relationships with Western governments in order to gain advantages in their intramural struggles. Simply by dealing with some and not others, Western governments can strongly influence who prevails.

The third approach is to provide (again by way of radios and written material and, where possible, through personal contacts) some of the means by which civil society can reconstitute itself—or, to put it another way, to give citizens ways of dealing with one another as if the regime did not exist, the means of seceding from the regime in their daily lives. This involves providing reliable news about their own country—and above all news that they can use. Ideally one could provide information on which goods were available from what sources, and who was in particular need of this or that. Radio courses could be given on how individuals or localities can set up businesses and how they can receive technical assistance in their field. Last but not least, radios can provide religious services, and broadcast guides to which religious bodies are and are not infiltrated by the regime.

Fourth, one can subvert communist regimes by spreading to independent-minded individuals and localities the most potent material tools of subversion and secession: telephones and fax machines, desktop publishing equipment, broadcasting equipment, and, yes, hard-currency cash.

The example of Poland in the 1980s and of the Soviet Union in 1990–1991 suggests that in communist countries Gresham's Law works in reverse: Real money drives out, or at least sets the standard for, fake money. In Poland the dollars in the hands of the few Polish–American retirees, and the deutschmarks in the hands of Poles who had traveled to West Berlin, allowed a rudimentary private economy to lay solid foundations. In the Soviet Union, holders of foreign currency gained god-like powers[30] as the ruble ceased to be the principal means of exchange. Since there was not enough *valuta* (hard currency) in circulation, however, barter became the principal means of exchange. This deprived ministries of much economic power, but left quite a bit in the hands of factory managers, i.e., of the communist Nomenklatura. That power could easily be subverted were large numbers of people to possess even small amounts of hard cash in small bills. Economic aid to communist (or ex-communist) countries (or trade, for that matter) that puts cash in private hands subverts the old order. Contacts funneled through that order bolster it.

In Cuba, and to a lesser extent Vietnam, a few green dollars from relatives abroad have allowed some families to bribe some local officials and purchase some independence. In China, hard currency is eroding the regime at the local level. After 1991 few communist officials anywhere could be expected to turn down offers of hard cash. It remained for Western governments to demand worthy services in return.

Finally, the most subversive act of all against any regime is to treat it as illegitimate. Some regimes are so internally secure that they don't care about how they are regarded in the world—but communist regimes never felt secure at home, and have always worked hard to convince their people that the rest of the world thinks well of them. The intended messages are: "If *they* accept us, you should too," and "Do not hope that foreigners will ever stand on your side against us." So it is easy to subvert communists in power by witholding smiles and by suggesting with every word that one is dealing with jailers only out of pity for the prisoners and not a moment longer than necessary, while giving maximum possible moral support to the enemies of the regime. Outsiders can affect battles within communist regimes by letting all sides know that there is succor for freedom fighters and defectors, but none for communists who kill.

The Third World

Most Third World dictatorships, even if they are one-party states (e.g., Zimbabwe) do not have capillary ruling parties legitimized by ideology. Whether the dictatorships are based on cliques or tribes, the power to make government decisions rests on few people. This means the number of possible agents of influence *within the government* is also small. Yet because neither royal families nor dictators control their entourages, much less society in general, as do totalitarian regimes, most who might be candidates for this role usually are easy to approach. In most Third World dictatorships (even in old royal families grown too large—Saudi princelings number some 5,000), loyalty to fellow members of the ruling class is low. Hence it is easy to find persons or factions ready to accept help in building their own influence. Similarly, in such environments little may be required to cause one faction to increase its suspicion of another. *Coups d'état* are frequent.

In much of the Third World (outside Latin America) society is not strong enough to buffer conflicts within the ruling group. On the contrary, tribal and religious divisions within society may be bases for such conflicts. These divisions may easily be inflamed, and themselves become more important than anything the government does. As for agents of influence within society, they are easy to approach and recruit. As for public opinion, it usually does not exist on most questions of public policy. In most instances, it does not even exist on questions of how the country should be governed. However, it can be very powerful on religious or ethnic questions, almost always against the government or a major constituent of society.

All of this is to say that subversion is a straightforward matter. The people involved often do not look terribly far into the future, nor do they ask too many questions. Nothing shows this so well as the political–ideological syncretism of many Third World tumults. Anyone who watched the Iranian revolution of 1978 unfold on television screens could not help but notice incongruities of which the crowds seemed unaware: Muslim mullahs led crowds brandishing Soviet-made AK-47 rifles and shouting un-Islamic slogans that sounded as if they had been written in Moscow, together with quotes from the Koran. Palestinian Arabs (Sunni Muslims) formed the spearheads of Persian Shi'ite groups. Bazaar merchants, known to argue over pennies and quite unknown for disinterestedness, threw millions of dollars' worth of food and other goods to fuel the crowds. The point here is that almost anyone's money and cadres, judiciously used, can undermine a Third World government and society.

The easy operational conditions often lead to the mistaken conclusion that it is easy to accomplish one's goals in the Third World through subversion. That is not true even in the medium term. Since everyone can operate easily, gains can quickly turn to losses. It is a grave error to count on any subversive tool or move, or agent, or group, except in the context of particular operations preferably backed by military force. Thus, just as the Saudi royal family made a bad bet between 1967 and 1990 when it financed various Palestinian organizations in the hope that they would be faithful tools in time of need, in 1991 it made a worse one when it decided to support Saddam Hussein against Kurdish and Shi'a rebels in the hope that, after Saddam had crushed them militarily, he would be overthrown by Sunni Arabs in his entourage. Even in the Third World, subversion is not that reliable a tool.

In the Third World as elsewhere, subversion is but one tool among others—meaning that its usefulness depends on seizing the right occasion with the right *combination* of tools. That is to say it depends on policy.

Strategy and Subversion

The art of policy consists of matching the results one seeks with the opportunities that the target is offering, as well as with the personnel available. The immediate product of policy is a strategy. To think in terms of a "strategy of subversion" is to miss the whole point. The point is victory. Subversion may be a greater of lesser part of the plan that leads to it.

Only in one sense is this not quite true. All actions in the service of strategy, from bombast to bombing, are intended to undermine the will of opponents. As Sun Tzu sees it, subversion is what conflict itself is about. And indeed the sixteenth-century unifier of Japan, Hideyoshi (one of Sun Tzu's most devoted readers), won his biggest battle by demonstrating to his rival, Yoshihisa, that he had been able to penetrate his entourage and his domain in ways that Yoshihisa had never thought possible. Confronted by a powerful foe who seemed to be several steps ahead of him and who offered magnanimous terms, Yoshihisa simply gave up, his will to fight thoroughly subverted.[31] But of course killing the opponent may even more surely remove his will to fight.

Neither Myth nor Magic

Strategy, of which subversion is a tool, is the very opposite of abstract thinking. It is not to be confused either with declarations, no matter how eloquent, or with any measure or attitude pursuant to them, no matter how strong or clever. Rather, strategy is the articulation of interests; the choice of objectives which, if achieved, would satisfy those interests; the commitment to achieve those objectives; the judgment that certain measures will actually achieve those objectives; and, lastly, the actual employment of those measures. In brief, strategy is the thoughtful thread that connects and balances the things that governments want with the things they do. It implies a coherent (though not necessarily correct) analysis of the situation, a choice of objectives, a choice of plans reasonably calculated to achieve them, and the ability to carry the intended measures to completion. This last is crucial. A policy is a plan for dealing with reality. If preferred measures cannot be carried out, the objectives should be redefined accordingly. Charles de Gaulle argued that France's Third Republic had wasted the nation's substance and prepared its collapse because it could not muster "that complex of interrelated plans, of decisions matured, of measures brought to term. . . ."[32] When considering subversion it is essential to keep both feet on the ground, because the subject seems to encourage disastrous flights of fancy.

Those who engage in subversion are even more likely than other human beings to mythologize their past successes into caricatures of what actually happened, and then to apply these artificial models in vastly different situations. Thus Ernesto (Ché) Guevara, one of Fidel Castro's lieutenants in the takeover of Cuba (1956–58), casting aside the fact that the dictator Fulgencio Batista had left the country chiefly because of growing resistance from the middle class and strong pressures from the U.S. government, spread the myth that a small band of revolutionaries in the Sierra Maestra mountains had grown by attracting more and more peasants into its ranks, and had defeated larger and larger government military units until it had overwhelmed the capital. After several years of preaching this propaganda, Guevara came to believe it, and tried to act it out in Bolivia. He was quickly killed.

Plans for subversion, like other plans, must stand up to such questions as: "How do we win?" "What do we do if the enemy responds thus-and-so?" "Why should these people play the role we assigned them?" "What do we do if X or Y changes his mind?" There must always be a Plan B. The point here is that, like anything else in the real world, subversion does not work by magic or mystique. If and when it becomes impossible to execute part of the plan, one will have to choose between making up the difference, or somehow liquidating the operation. Since subversive forces, like regular forces, may be cut off in enemy territory at any time, one will surely face the choice of either trying to rescue them through open means or letting them perish. The modern Anglo–Saxon tradition that looks on secret agents as expendable might profit from the Japanese tradition that regards the agent as worthier than other men.[33] It seems reasonable to consider whether one wants to commit covert assets where one is unwilling to commit overt ones.

From a larger perspective, we have already indicated that because it almost never makes sense to base a strategy on one kind of force alone, subversion should seldom if ever be employed except as one among many instruments of conflict. Seldom if ever is subversion an option in and of itself, something to be chosen instead of something else. On the contrary, it should seldom if ever be employed except as part of success-oriented strategies the main burdens of which are carried by diplomacy, economics, or arms. By the same token, actual responsibility for, and command of, subversion should rest precisely where rest responsibility and command for the entire strategy.

Light Cavalry

If subversion cannot deliver victory on the cheap, what is it good for? It is useful to think of subversive forces somewhat as classic military thought regards light cavalry: a means for harassing the enemy's rear, generally fouling up his communications, provoking effort that saps his strength, and contributing to specific battles. Just as light cavalry seldom wins big battles but often contributes mightily to winning wars, so subversion can contribute to strategic successes if its role in a given strategy is well understood.

The key is analysis of the situation to figure out whether and how subversion can make a difference. A model of such analysis is Machiavelli's demolition of the old Florentine prejudice that the city of Pistoia was to be managed through its factions. Machiavelli showed that this approach worked only so long as Florence was the only power to which the factions could turn. When other powers intervened, Florence had to chose between breaking Pistoia's factions by brute force or risk losing its position there.[34] Elsewhere he makes the same point from another direction. Why, he asks, did both Hannibal and Scipio have such good reputations for inducing cities to come over to their side despite the fact that their approaches were diametrically different? He concluded that neither Hannibal's reputation for cruelty nor Scipio's for mildness was responsible. Rather, both succeeded when they had very powerful armies.[35] Hannibal's roars proved not so frightening, and Scipio's blandishments were not so alluring, when they were unaccompanied by armies that had the odor of victory about them. Yet again, Machiavelli shows that while money can buy allies in the enemy camp, only the near prospect of victory can make them stay bought.[36] The teaching is clear: Subversion works as an adjunct of power. But it can never be a substitute for it and, like light cavalry, tends to irrelevance when the big guns are brought to bear on the quarrel.

Subversion is useful both to the weak and to the strong. But it is not a long-term cure for weakness, and indeed, if misused, is a way of both wasting strength and getting into trouble one cannot get out of.

Uncovering

Pretense should cover subversion only long enough for subversion to succeed. It is neither necessary nor possible to maintain secrecy, or pretense, about subversive activities, after the operational phase has passed. Often it is wise to abandon the ruse prior to that stage. One way or another, sooner or later, the truth of who tried to do what to whom must come out. And when it does it may magnify the effects of the operation, as happened when Stalin revealed the details of the Trust deception; or it may cause such a negative reaction against those who carried it out as to outweigh any benefit they had ever got from it (this certainly was the case with President Reagan's diversion of money from the sale of arms to Iran to Nicaragua's Contras). Our point here is that planning for any subversive operation must include how and when to make the operation public. We suggest two guidelines for such plans: First, the focus should be on the substance of the operation, not on the pretense. Second, the entire operation should be consistent with the standards of the regime sponsoring it.

Obviously, any operation that involves pretense with regard to foreigners requires either pretense or secrecy with regard also to some parts of one's own government, and perhaps even to the general population. This naturally comports the possibility that those not privy to the secret will be moved by personal resentment once they learn it, and use the matter as grist for scandal—especially if they disagree with its purposes. There is no way of avoiding the personal affronts. But there *is* a way of mitigating their effect. But that is so only if, as we have stipulated, the subversion is part of a larger operation, that the government has made sure is well-supported. The bigger the secret, the more support should the government try to build for the "open" parts of the operation. The principle is straightforward: He who wills an end also wills the means necessary and proper to it. This is yet one more incentive for the government to do what it should do anyway—namely, make sure that the subversion is in fact necessary and proper to the enterprise. If the government has done that, it can treat any disclosure of the secret as one more opportunity to build support for the overall policy.

Governments should do secretly abroad only such things as they could profitably defend at home. What kinds of activities are practically defensible depends on the nature of the regime that does them. Any given regime will cringe at the sight of some events and be strengthened by others. Prudent governments refrain from doing things that are, as it were, anticonstitutional. Thus in 1990 the Soviet leaders who had helped to topple Romania's communist dictator, Nicolae Ceauçescu, heard the Moscow crowd shout "shoot them, like Ceauçescu." Even if the Soviet leaders had had nothing to do with Ceauçescu's downfall, the sight of it fanned anticommunist fires at home. In 1984 the government of Iran sent agents disguised as pilgrims to occupy the holiest mosque in Mecca. It hoped that the affair would tarnish the reputation of the Saudi royal family as guardian of the holy places. But the revelation that the Iranian government had in fact desecrated the mosque hurt its own reputation within Iran itself as well as in the other Islamic countries. By the same token, American public opinion strongly disapproved of the U.S. government for having tried to prevent Chile's Salvador Allende from being chosen president by that country's parliament even though he had received a plurality of the vote. The U.S. government violated abroad the very principle by which it lives: He who gets the most votes wins.

By contrast, acts of subversion that are consonant with the nature of the regime that does them wind up strengthening it. Between 1949 and 1989 honest Germans cheered West Germany's rescue of East Germans even though bribery was the means. In 1991, truth-loving Americans cheered when they learned that their government had put out false stories about its intent to force an amphibious landing in Kuwait in order to keep Iraqi troops away from the main areas of U.S. military operations in the Gulf War. We may suggest that in 1990 Soviet apparatchiks cheered Mikhail Gorbachev's decision to exfiltrate their old East German ally, Erich Honecker, out of the reaches of the judicial system of a united Germany to live out his days in communism. Little did they know that they themselves would not.

Any government, then, may profit by subverting others—so long as, in the process, it is careful not to subvert itself.

12

Getting It Right

I am wiser to this small extent, that I do not think that I know
what I do not know.

— Plato, The Apology of Socrates

Information does not become intelligence until someone recognizes its importance. This may happen in a moment of recognition, or it may be the end of long analysis. In either case, producing intelligence out of raw information affords perhaps more opportunities for "getting it right" and "getting it wrong" than do collection and CI. Herein we discuss how to make good intelligence—how to "get it right." We argue that people see as they do because they are who they are, and we provide thoughts by which to match analysts to various intelligence subjects. We argue that substantive knowledge is the intellectual key to good analysis, and explain the cardinal points of politics, military affairs, and economics that analysts should be familiar with. We end with a case study that integrates political, military, and economic matters: Palestinian terrorists operating in Syria.

Who Can Turn on the Lights?

Those who ask the right question, focus on the right subject, distinguish between the essential and the ephemeral, do not necessarily get the right answer. But they are usually "in the ball park." Moreover what they come up with is sure to be valuable in and of itself.

In 1973 the authors of Israel's annual Estimate, a compendium of political and military information bearing on whether the Arab world would wage war on Israel, had no doubts about who the Arab decision-makers were, what their political interest and military capabilities were, and which options the Arabs were considering. The Israeli estimators had good information about inter-Arab debates and Egyptian–Syrian troop movements. The estimators did not know the actual decision to attack (which was held to a group of eight men, until two days prior to the war). On the morning of Yom Kippur, 1973, just as Egyptian units were preparing to attack the Bar-Lev line on the Suez Canal, the estimators realized that their judgment that the Arabs would not attack had been mistaken because they had viewed the evidence through the optic of what they called a "concept." According to this concept, the Arabs would not start a war they knew they could not win.

The estimators put Israel in mortal danger because they shut out of their calculations the possibility that Egypt's President Sadat was not out to win, but only to make a good showing. *Otherwise, they did a good job*—better than most intelligence analysts ever do, and *good enough to serve as a model of good analysis*.

YOU SEE AS YOU ARE

By way of contrast consider that, in the 1960s–1980s, the CIA's concept of the irrationality of nuclear war simply put beyond the pale of polite discussion the Soviet Union's evident preparations for nuclear war. Consider also that the performance of British intelligence with regard to the Nazi military buildup of the 1930s amounted to: The evidence suggests a military buildup so disorderly as to be unacceptable even to Englishmen, never mind to order-loving Germans. Hence, there must be something wrong with the evidence. By the same token, before World War I, French military intelligence, in full possession of the facts concerning the firing rate of German repeating rifles and machine guns, still looked at German divisions in terms of numbers of men, rather than in terms of the amount of fire they could deliver. For French intelligence, war was about men and horses and courage, not firepower. Unlike the Israelis these people did not just make mistakes. They were 'way out of the ball park. They failed to see the reality in front of their noses *because they were who they were*.

It is a commonplace in Washington that where you stand depends on where you sit. According to this crude determinism, a man's views are determined by the interests of his job. Marx, of course, had posited that thought is the mere "superstructure" of any human being's relationship to the means of production. But one does not have to be any kind of determinist to notice that some people are so absorbed by an environment, or an idea, that they can see only within its bounds—or that some people are not educated to see certain aspects of reality, or that they are educated *not* to see them. The sources of human obsession and disinterest, of "educated incapacity,"* or of intellectual incapacity, are legion.

The question before us is: What sort of arrangement can maximize the chances that those charged with analyzing intelligence will see the threats and opportunities facing their country as they are, from the perspective of foreigners? While nothing can guarantee good performance, we argue that the answer lies in a combination of *responsibility* for the success of the operations, knowledge of the *substance* with which the information deals, and familiarity with the *operations* on which the information bears.

Responsibility

When Robert Gates warned CIA analysts in 1982 that the accuracy of their judgments would be taken into account at promotion time, they reacted as do professors whose academic freedom is threatened. But intelligence is not an academic exercise. The analyst contributes to decisions that make the difference between his country's victory and defeat. He shares responsibility for the outcome of operations. Anything that lightens the weight of that responsibility on the analyst's shoulders reduces his incentive to scout paths to victory. The analyst who sees himself as neutral will tend to order data according to his own intellectual priorities (or those of his social class, or of his bureau.) This will be so especially if his government is not clear about its own priorities.

But an intelligence analyst cannot be a neutral technician, a hired hand who (at best) gives his dispassionate judgment or (in the worst case) grinds his own axe. Judgment of the enemy and judgment of one's own course of action really are two sides of the indivisible function of command. Hence intelligence analysts, like military or foreign service officers, must be selected from among those intellectually qualified people who want to join the fray on their country's behalf. This does not mean that one will hire cheerleaders, but rather that commitment to the ends of one's country truly frees the analyst to search for the means.

Mere accountability does not ensure correct judgment. After all, responsibility

---

*Herman Kahn used this term to denote the incapacity of specialists to see things that are obvious to anyone who is not trained to ignore them.

did not prevent the absolute monarchs of old from making dreadful analytical misjudgments. Indeed, the power that goes with responsibility often is an incentive to lack of intellectual rigor. Thus in August 1912 the Tzar of Russia failed to question his ministers' made-up figures about the speed of Austrian mobilization, and hence ordered Russian cavalry reinforcements to the borders of the Austro–Hungarian Empire, which in turn spurred Austria to increase its anti-Russian preparations.[1] No one would question the Tzar, and he did not question himself.

But responsibility, like the prospect of being hanged, generally does tend to concentrate the mind, and while concentrated minds can make mistakes too, they are seldom out of the ball park. The Israeli analysts of 1973 made a big mistake. But they had no more than one blind spot. Acute consciousness that their own lives depended on their work kept them focused on the essentials of the situation. They assembled excellent data on the Egyptian and Syrian armed forces and identified their vulnerabilities. They had no doubt about who was the enemy, or that they had to figure out how the enemy might best use his forces. So, once the war started, their products proved useful.

How can governments that do not share Israel's unenviable sobering relationship to danger choose intelligence analysts who will focus on the essentials at least as well as did the Israelis of 1973?

Substantive Knowledge

The analysts need knowledge of their field *from the standpoint of those who operate in it*. To put himself in the shoes of a Lebanese or Russian tank commander an analyst needs more than academic skills. He needs sympathetic knowledge of Maronite, or Shi'ite, or Russian Orthodox culture as it applies to armed forces. Such immersion in history may be gained by specialized study and travel. But a feel for what it is like in the armed forces, and specifically in tanks, can come only from experience. By the same token, an analyst of a patronage-based political party such as Mexico's PRI has to know what it feels like to be on the giving and receiving end of political plums. By the same token, some political words (e.g., "subversion"), like words referring to sexual activity, have meaning only to those who have "done it."

This is why the Soviet Union hired as analysts in the Defense Council's Information Center senior figures—distinguished military commanders, political operators from the Central Committee's International Department with long experience in the management of political skullduggery, managers of industries, and the like. In Israel's military intelligence, too, the analysts are soldiers who have proven themselves in their fields. The proper model for intelligence analysts may well be the staff of the U.S. National Security Council: senior figures chosen for substantive expertise, for operational inclination, and for their desire to accomplish what the President wants to get done. But of course the NSC does not use its staff to analyze intelligence.

Again, experience and motivation do not guarantee openmindedness, nor do they ensure against mirror-imaging. They only increase the chances that the analysts will be in the ball park.

Seers and Doers

A proper relationship between analysts and policy-makers can further lengthen the odds in favor of good analysis. First, intelligence analysts must stick to facts gained through special sources and methods. Intelligence should not purvey views on fertility in Bangladesh. Nor should analysts exert gratuitous pressures on policy-making. It would be artificial to bar a bright officer from communicating an insight gained from a newspaper just because his job title read: Intelligence. But it is common sense to maintain the distinction between intelligence and other kinds of information, lest the category itself dissolve in the broad flow of what goes into decisions. In fact, intelligence is but one distinct part of this flow. *How it fits with all other parts is not properly an intelligence judgment, but an executive judgment.*

Thus U.S. presidents have often paid less attention to the *President's Daily Brief* than to a daily situation summary prepared by the staff of the White House Situation Room, which includes relevant intelligence but is written from the standpoint of the president's agenda. The intelligence in this summary may not be profound, but it *is* in the ball park.

The producer of intelligence, then, is naturally subordinate to the person responsible for action. This does not mean that the producer abdicates his intellectual integrity. Quite the contrary: His job is to present his special knowledge, including its incompleteness and ambiguities. His job also is to draw for the action officer the several logical consequences of the facts for the decisions that the action officer must take. In short, the intelligence producer's job is to eschew manipulation, and to put the proverbial monkey of responsibility for deciding about ambiguities and relevance clearly where it belongs: on the action officer. Both the intelligence officer, who chooses and analyzes the facts, *and* the action officer, who decides what to do, have their own separate specialty. But for each to perform his own well, both must become intellectual partners.

A fair illustration of this was the analysis by British intelligence prior to World War II of the German economy's ability to support war. Intelligence officers made clear to policy-makers that the various figures on German manpower consisted largely of British assumptions and hence could not be relied on. As regards the hard data on German production of and trade in food, fuel, and minerals, the intelligence officers tried to figure out how key imports might be cut off, and conferred with policy-makers regarding the things that Britain would have to do to cut them off. Since policy-makers saw no way of putting pressure on key neutrals like Sweden and Turkey to cut off trade with Germany, the overall assessment of the British government was that the German economy would not be a limiting factor in a short war.[2] Everyone agreed that the German economy could not sustain a long war. Unlike Hitler, none of the British had factored Germany's conquest of most of Europe into their long-range economic calculations. But no arrangement can guarantee intellectual boldness.

If the producer of intelligence is to be the intellectual partner of the action officer, he must be his peer. He can neither be a kid hired out of college nor a professional "intelligence manager" who is a third-hand masseur of papers generated by junior analysts. The British signals-intelligence analysts at Bletchley Park at the beginning of World War II could not understand the wealth of material they were receiving because they did not know military matters. So the British brought in new analysts: military officers senior enough to put themselves into the shoes of the German commanders who had written the messages, and who therefore could figure out their relevance to British interests. Nor can the action officer afford to keep the analysts in the dark about the alternatives that *he* is considering.

One thousand years before Sherman Kent, the Indian statesman Kautilya had noted that attempts to separate analysis and policy-making would work to the disadvantage of both. When matters concern "the perception of what is not or cannot be seen, the clearance of doubts as to whatever is susceptible of two opinions, and the inference of the whole when only a part is seen," wrote Kautilya, it will not do to seek advice on the basis of hypothetical plans. Those whose advice is sought abstractly will neither understand the question nor care about the answers they give: "Ministers, when called for their opinions regarding a distant undertaking . . . either approach the subject with indifference or give their opinions half-heartedly. This is a serious defect."[3] In sum, the analysis of intelligence is inherently tied to the purpose for which the intelligence is needed. Action officers and analysts have responsibilities peculiar to their own jobs. But for each to do his job, his mind must reach deeply and sympathetically into the other's.

A natural corollary of this is that, at any level of government, analysts must be few in number. There is no logical limit to the number of researchers and assistants that an analyst might employ. But the analysts who actually impose order on data, who make "the inference of the whole when only a part is seen," and do so responsibly by virtue of their contact with action officers, cannot reasonably outnumber such officers. And indeed, it is unrealistic to think any government can find analysts by the thousands but executives only by the hundreds. The intellectual experiences needed for good analysis are as rare as the qualities needed for command. In short, the analyst must be the commander's peer. Moreover, the analyst has to have the personal status to tell the commander "I don't know," and get away with it.

Centrality

If analysts are to be closely tied to specific government functions, what happens to the principle of centrality? The CIA's dismal record does not invalidate the principle that in order to make sense of any piece of data one must lay it next to every other piece of data available; that the more comprehensive, the more *central* the data base, the more likely is one to see through ruses and to focus further collection well.

In the 1940s those in America and elsewhere who sought to provide central intelligence analysis had no choice but to think in terms of a single repository of data and a single analytical service. Would this service be attached to the Army, or the Navy, or the Air Force? Or to the diplomats? It clearly made the most sense to attach it to none of these, but rather to their common boss, the President. This arrangement led to the inconveniences we have described at length above. Today, however, given the capacity to store vast amounts of data in computers, and to transfer whole databases in encrypted form to any office in the world in a matter of seconds, there is no *physical* reason why *every* repository of intelligence data anywhere cannot be as comprehensive, as *central*, as any other repository. Today there is no reason why anyone who sits at a computer terminal to analyze intelligence on behalf of any part of a modern government should have to work on any basis other than "all source information."

Indeed, in recent years in the U.S., as well as in other advanced countries, analysts from various departments have done their best to turn their individual projects into all-source projects. *But while technology is fostering the evolution from one to many equally central analyses, bureaucracy pulls in the opposite direction.* The departments that collect the information want a near-monopoly of judgment about the value of their programs. Those who exercise a monopoly on central analysis want to maintain that monopoly. Their pretext is that the more people who have their hands on information, the greater the chance that it will leak. But if one truly values minimizing the number of people with access to secret information, one ought to be inclined to our view that analysis is best done by few highly qualified, highly focused people in the operating departments of government, rather than by armies of people who work for one central analytical agency.

There is also the misconception that because the chief executive of the nation is the funnel of authority, he should be the funnel for information as well. This crabbed view of command has used modern communications and data-processing equipment to stultify not only the intelligence functions of bureaus, embassies, and military units, but their *operations* as well.[4] But analysis is inherently a function of decision-making at every level where decisions are made. To the extent that a chief executive's office does not wish to substitute its own judgment for that of the operating parts of government, it must grant them the right to form their own views of the intelligence relevant to their missions. To the extent that the several parts of the government are not responsible for their own analyses, they will spend energy interfering with the analyses of the chief executive and of other departments as well, so that in the end no one will be responsible for any judgment.

The chief executive's needs for analysis flow from its function: directing and supervising all operations of government. Of course, the chief executive's depository of intelligence data *should* be central. But the purpose of its centrality is peculiar. The chief executive's analysis shop has better things to do than to gin up details on Ruritania, or being one of the battlegrounds where departmental representatives fight to influence national policy. Rather, its proper function is to develop its own perspectives based on the products of the analytical units belonging to each of the major departments of government. Moreover, by so doing, the chief executive's analysts could improve the quality of intelligence judgments in the departments.

By the same token, the existence of "central" analysis in the major departments would put healthy pressures on the chief executive's own analysts. A chief executive who was presented with the differences between several sets of analysts, each having equally central access to information, might not enjoy having to think through the controversy. But, having done so, he might well make more responsible decisions. In sum, by a proper combination of organization and technology it may be easier than ever for analysts throughout a government to improve each other's performance through competition. For executives, such competition would mean responsibility. Some would think this wonderful. Others would want nothing to do with it.

How

To turn reports into evaluated intelligence is to take into account the epistemology of the data, and the data's relevance to policy. The analyst must question the assumptions of the program that produced the report: If the report is from an agent within a group of Russian nationalists, the analyst must ask such general questions as how representative of the amorphous category of "Russian nationalists" the agent's group is. He must also ask about the access that the agent has had, and about the agent's judgment: If the report comes from an imaging satellite and is about the movement of a nucelar-armed military unit, general questions would deal with the relationship between what was observed and what may not have been observed—e.g., the commander's allegiance, or the relationship between the unit's officers and the outsiders who control their nuclear weapons. Specific questions would concern whether or not the unit's ostentatious movement was part of a deception plan. The analyst must also take into consideration any evidence or argument that counterintelligence experts have about the report *or about the programs that produced it*. After that, the analyst has to figure out the relationship of the report, if any, to opportunities and threats facing his country. Only if such a relationship exists should he prepare the report for presentation. The following are the principal norms for such preparation.

Truth in Labeling

Nothing so affects the quality of an intelligence product as does the degree to which it exposes the nature of the evidence and the train of logic leading to its conclusions. This holds for raw reports just as much as it does for estimates. German spy schools would teach students to report observations as follows: "What is that?" the instructor would ask. "A sheep," the students would say. "What?" he would ask more sharply. "A white sheep," they would say, catching on. "No," the instructor would say. "What you must say is that at 1643 hours on 28 September 1944 on the right side of the road from Vienna to Breitenbrunn you saw a sheep that was white on the side that faced you."[5] Those intelligence products that clearly separate facts from interpretations inspire confidence. Those that do not create discord.

Consider the reports that reached Syracuse in 415 A.D. about the approach of a huge Athenian expeditionary force. Hermocrates, the leader of the oligarchic party, presented the intelligence much as an American director of the Defense Intelligence Agency might. He spoke briefly of "a great fleet and army" and dwelt at some length on the Athenians' apparent strategy: to capture Syracuse by surprise, and then the rest of Sicily by default. Hermocrates said that if the Syracusans took appropriate precautions, the Athenians were bound to fail. The leader of the democratic party, Athenagoras, much like a CIA analyst, accused Hermocrates of presenting rumors that could not possibly be true because the Athenians just had to know that an expedition against Sicily could not possibly succeed. He accused Hermocrates of making up pretexts for military preparations that would benefit the oligarchs. The ensuing debate in Syracuse fed domestic strife and lost time because it was not over facts and logic, but rather over the motives of internal factions. The 1990 clash between the U.S. Secretary of Defense and the Director of Central Intelligence over their agencies' differing estimates of "the Soviet threat" was unenlightening for the same reason.[6]

Intelligence data, by nature fragmentary, requires human synthesis. But since there usually is more than one way of synthesizing information, a report may contain less information about the real world outside than it does of the insights and inclinations of the analyst. Since Descartes, modern philosophers have debated epistemology *ad nauseam*. But in the end, because every individual is responsible for his own decisions, the extent to which any individual's perceptions are subjective or objective is moot. An intelligence analyst, however, is but part of the collective mind of his government, and is not fully responsible for the actions of that government. So, it matters greatly that he transmit an *objective* picture of the data. In most cases where facts are thin, objectivity can only consist of making clear just how thin they are.

But epistemological honesty is difficult for intelligence organizations to achieve, especially when they themselves are composed of multiple organizations. On July 5, 1940, as invasion fever was running high in Britain, the Joint Intelligence Committee (JIC) issued an "appreciation" that a full-scale invasion might soon be expected. This caused quite a stir, until the operational authorities found that the only hard data in the report consisted of German preparations for increased air operations against England, plus a few long-range guns installed opposite the Dover coast. There was no evidence of an invasion fleet anywhere. The chain of reasoning consisted of hypothesizing motorboats (which had not been observed) carrying tanks. In sum, the JIC reflected the converging predilections of the Navy for keeping destroyers close to home, and of the Army for coastal deployment.[7] In this case the JIC did little harm except to cause busy officials to lose time and energy uncovering its epistemology.*

This must be our main point. Whether the sources be agents or multibillion-dollar satellites, the worst thing that analysts can do is to extrapolate or imagine an item into relevance. Among the worst thing a decision-maker can do is to fail

---

*A less-than-direct connection between evidence and conclusion is potentially troublesome, not just (as we have seen) because it invites prejudice and rightly diminishes the value of the information to the user. It also inspires a cynicism about information on the outside world and corrupts the decision-making process. Thus Machiavelli counts as clever and effective the way in which some Roman commanders coerced the Augurs to convey the impression that the gods had given a good omen about upcoming battles (Machiavelli, *Discourses* XIII and XIV). The commanders did not think there was much connection between the eagerness of the sacred chickens to pick, and success in battle. So Appius Pulcrus, confronted with nonhungry chickens, had them thrown into the sea, saying "Let's see if they're thirsty," and then fought the battle, while Spurius Papirius had the sacred chicken-handlers put into the front line and saw to it that they were "accidentally" killed. But in the long run this sort of thing was anything but clever because, Machiavelli reports, it soon became fashionable for Romans to interpret customs and oaths in their own interest, as if neither the gods nor the enemy mattered, but only intra-Roman jockeying for advantage. It would have been far better for the commanders to openly challenge the relevance of chicken-picking to battles.

to confront openly that his intelligence isn't giving him much to go on. Honesty on both sides about where knowledge ends and judgment begins is the *sine qua non* for both analysts and commanders to do their jobs well.

On Its Own Terms

A corollary to this point is that analysis of military topics must be in military terms, analysis of political topics in political terms, and so on. Contrast, for example, Quincy Wright's approach to the analysis of war, which is prototypical of the training that many of today's intelligence analysts in Western countries have received in college. Wright compiled an impressive number of statistics about every quantifiable aspect of the belligerents in the major wars of the nineteenth and early twentieth centuries, and tried to develop theories about the causes of wars in terms of these quantities.[8] But Wright could not account for the basic cause of any war—a "cause" on behalf of which people are willing to kill and be killed. Such a "cause" may or may not animate leaders, who may or may not succeed in pulling followers along.

This is not to say that situations are to be understood in terms of a single dimension. For example, Paul Kennedy explains the success or failure of major wars in terms of economic capacity,[9] succumbing to the historian's temptation to believe that what happened *had* to happen, and neglecting the actual decisions, the presence or demise of individual leaders, that actually made for victory or defeat. Kennedy argues that because Germany was no match economically for its enemies, it never stood a chance in World War II. In fact, Germany had won World War II by June 1940 despite economic inferiority. Hitler offered Britain magnanimous terms. Had Churchill not been Prime Minister, might not Britain have accepted them? What if Hitler had not attacked the Soviet Union? What if he had not delayed the attack two months? What if, in the course of the attack, he had behaved like a liberator rather than a murderer toward captured Belorussians, Ukrainians, and Russians?

The principal thesis of Kennedy's book was that the worldwide military responsibilities that the United States had undertaken after World War II had become an unsustainable drain. The U.S. was suffering from "imperial overstretch." Leave aside the figures—in the 1980s the U.S. was devoting only 6 percent of GNP to defense compared to the Soviet Union's 25–35 percent. If "overstretch" means anything, it must be relative. And indeed the Soviet political system, *not* the American, collapsed in 1989–91. Was *it* "overstretched?" The crowds that surged throughout the Soviet empire seemed to have nothing of the sort on their minds. These crowds were after far more than material goods. They hated foreign and domestic communism for reasons so many and complex as to show the utter irrelevance of the concept of "imperial overstretch."

Our point is that intelligence analysis must stick close to the terms in which foreigners are actually conducting their quarrels, and not let its own methodology seduce it into solipsism.

Mirror-Imaging

Understanding other people, other enterprises, on their own terms is the very opposite of putting one's self into other people's shoes. To put foreign people into foreign shoes the analyst must begin by being very clear about where *he* is coming from—by making the potential mirror-image explicit, so that its features can be rejected one by one. The whole purpose of the process is for the analyst to keep his feet firmly on the ground of the evidence, no matter how unsatisfactory the evidence might be.

The analyst knows what *he* would do about the Ukraine if he were in Boris Yeltsin's shoes. He can imagine Yeltsin's goals and the pressures upon him. But when a report comes in from a source that purports to give insights into a plan of Yeltsin's, the analyst must ask what he actually *knows* about Yeltsin's hierarchy of values and mode of reasoning. Speculation and hearsay will not do. In the absence of hard knowledge the analyst must limit himself to evaluating the source, and must accompany the information with the *caveat* that it might be interpreted differently according to different views of Yeltsin.

The technical analyst knows how his office or his government has evaluated antimissile devices in the past. But he must also know that those criteria are arbitrary. In the U.S., the Fletcher Panel, which laid out the SDI program, stipulated that an antimissile laser has to deliver on the order of $100,000$ J/cm^2 on a missile at a distance of $5,000$ km. How should an American analyst treat a hypothetical report of plans for a Russian laser that can deliver $5,000$ J/cm^2 at $3,000$ km? The analyst must ask himself whether there is a way in which such performance, although obviously not up to his government's official conception of how to do antimissile work, could actually do such work according to *another* conception. His report should state that although the prospective weapon does not qualify for the antimissile role according to one set of criteria, it does according to another set.

The most common antidote to mirror-imaging is stereotyping. It is also the most dangerous. Stereotypes are part of life, come from experience, and are generally partially correct. But intelligence is about specific instances, not general propositions. It is generally true that Russian society works on a lower technological level than Western society. But any analyst who used that stereotype to evaluate reports about the Russian armed forces would be making a serious mistake.

How, for example, should one analyze figures concerning the accuracy of Soviet submarine-launched missiles? Telemetry data yields an estimate of how the missiles' guidance system performs. But perhaps the biggest component in the accuracy of an SLBM is the mechanism that determines the submarine's position at the time of launch and feeds it into the guidance system. Since there is no data on this mechanism in Soviet submarines, the analyst is tempted to assume that because of overall technical inferiority, the Soviet mechanism must be only X percent as good as Western ones. And so it may be. But even if it were, the analyst must not let this "fact" determine his conclusion about the relative accuracy of Soviet SLBMs. After all, there are operational ways of obviating technical disadvantages. The submarines *could* fire from presurveyed points on the ocean floor. This is diametrically opposed to the operational doctrine of U.S. submarines. But if it were Soviet doctrine to use SLBMs this way, the inferiority of position-determining mechanisms would be irrelevant. A good analytical product would note the unknowns.

Technical stereotypes are dangerous because the development of technology is always uneven. Again the Soviet Union is a good example: A society where only about half the hospitals had hot running water in 1990 also has the world's finest armored personnel carriers, and air and space defense equipment.* Recall that in 1957 the Soviet Union was first into space, and in World War II it had the world's finest tanks. Remember too that Argentina surprised Britain in 1982 by sinking the destroyer H.M.S. *Sheffield* with a high-tech French air-to-surface missile. A country's general technological level is seldom relevant to the only significant question: What is it going to bring to bear here and now?

Social stereotypes are almost as dangerous. Athenians and Spartans saw one another through strong stereotypes. It is not surprising then that the Spartan who had the greatest success against the Athenians was Brasidas, who acted more according to Athenian than to Spartan stereotypes, while the Athenian general who had the greatest success against Spartans was Nicias, who surprised the Spartans by acting like one of *them*. Russian generals over the centuries have earned a certain reputation for stolidity and lack of imagination. But the German intelligence analysts who tried to figure out the main axes of Russian offensives in 1943–44 were usually baffled by the sophistication of the Russians' deceptive maneuvers.

Our point is that however generally valid social stereotypes may be, there is

---

*For example, the Soviet SA-12 surface-to-air missile is bigger, faster, and has a more powerful radar than the closest U.S. cognate, the Patriot. The Soviet Union has the world's only ballistic missile defenses, while the U.S. is spending money to *learn* whether we might someday be able to develop one. The Soviets have two operational antisatellite systems; the U.S. none. The Soviet An-225 cargo aircraft can carry twice the payload of the U.S. C-5B Galaxy. The Soviet Blackjack is the world's largest supersonic bomber. The Soviet Union has more than twice as many armored personnel carriers as all NATO countries combined. See Department of Defense, *Soviet Military Power*, and the yearbooks published in London by Jane's.

always a chance—especially when one is dealing with a diverse people—that the particular decision-maker who is the subject of analysis will defy them. In *this* instance will "they" be like us? Or the opposite of ourselves? Or somewhere in the middle? Only hard data should be part of the answer. As should be this caveat: Just because "they" share a given characteristic with us does not mean they share another which, as far as *we* are concerned, is related to the first. Thus a fiercely anticommunist Russian nationalist may be committed either to divesting the Russian people of their imperial burden, or to extending the Russian empire. There is no substitute for knowing the facts.

Or is there? Machiavelli argues that it really is not necessary to know the characteristics of all foreign things as long as one knows the general principles of conflict and one's own objectives, and hastens to do what is necessary to win.[10] Given those conditions, all enemies and all circumstances are transparent alike. An army is an army and a hill is a hill. It is better to occupy the hill than to bother trying to understand the enemy, or even reconnoitering the ground. Machiavelli's point seems to be the opposite of Jomini's maxim: "How can any man say what he should do himself if he is ignorant of what his adversary is about?" But Machiavelli is no more preaching solipsism than Jomini is advocating being driven by the enemy. Both point to elements of the proper analytical attitude: Be aware of the otherness of the enemy, but don't let it obscure the fundamentals of the situation.

Opportunity Analysis

There is no doubt, however, that understanding the asymmetries between one's own side and the opponent is the greatest of advantages. That is why perhaps the primary job of intelligence analysts is to spot such discrepancies. The intelligence analyst, *as a professional fighter*, should constantly be looking for "openings."

When Allied intelligence examined the German army that had launched the Ardennes offensive on the Western front in 1944 they noticed, beyond its lack of air cover, its short supply of fuel. Here was an obvious key to the specific direction of the German spearhead (Allied forward fuel dumps), and an equally obvious guide to Allied tactics, namely to run the Germans out of gas. World War II also provides plenty of instances of analysts who failed to see strategic opportunities and threats before their very eyes. Thus one gets no sense from the deliberations of Mussolini's government in the spring of 1940 that it considered its decision to enter into the war on Germany's side a difficult one. After the first few days of the German attack on France, was there even much of a war left to enter? This fact obscured the huge potential liabilities. By joining the German side, Italy would make tiny territorial gains at the expense of France. But the long-term enjoyment of even these was dependent on a shrewd analysis of the Nazi regime. Would the Nazis stop after conquering France? Italy had no interest whatever in buying into a larger war. But Italian analysts, including Mussolini, did not adequately understand the chaotic, undisciplined nature of the Nazi regime and of Hitler's mind, nor its long-term designs on the East, nor the self-defeating ways in which such a regime would pursue these designs.

On the other side of the ledger were Britain's peace offerings: Churchill's letter to Mussolini in May 1940 granted Italy all she had ever wanted from Britain in Africa.[11] But was Britain in a position to grant anything or was she, as Hitler would say the following month, a chicken about to have its neck wrung? The Italian analysts' failure to see the perfect match between a vindicated Churchill and an embattled island people who had not yet lost the habits of greatness is an example not of miscalculation but of carelessness. They hardly made an effort to see a major opportunity and a major threat.

Sometimes not even all the facts cogently argued can stem the decision-makers' recklessness. One of history's prime instances of this was the Athenian assembly's decision to launch the Sicilian expedition. Nicias explained how very difficult was the task, how illusory were the opportunities, and how real were the threats not just to the expeditionary force but to Athens' own strategic position. Nevertheless, he was calmly voted down. But Nicias' method stands as a guide to sober analysts. First, he asked, what is our objective, and how does this enterprise affect it? In the fifth century B.C., Athens' prime objective was prevailing in the Peloponnesian War against Sparta. Had the Assembly understood that Sicily was incidental to that objective, it might have better appreciated the fact that taking Syracuse and Sicily was as big an enterprise as taking Sparta and the Peloponnese. And what if the Athenians took Sicily? How would they run it? Then Nicias questioned the reliability of reports from Sicily that financial and military support for Athens would be forthcoming. He judged it unlikely (and indeed it turned out to be untrue) that the small cities which had asked for Athens' intervention would be as wealthy as they claimed, and he judged it a mere presumption that the larger cities would join Athens just because they were ethnically related. Finally, he pointed to the troubles that the expeditionary force would be leaving behind. By taking on such a faraway commitment, Athens would upset the balance of power nearby. "Stumble," he said, and "your enemies will be upon you in a moment."[12] And so they were. In sum, Nicias was on the lookout for all the concrete ways that Athens could both win *and* lose.

What is an opportunity? What is a threat? These questions do not pertain to any special analytical discipline, but to statecraft itself. Power is an opportunity or a threat depending on who holds it. A power vacuum too may be an opportunity or a threat, as may be either stability or instability. The entire art of threat/

401

opportunity analysis consists of imaginatively matching one's own situation against those of others. It involves one's own purposefulness and the evaluation of others', the evaluation of one's possibilities and of the possibilities of others.

Consider the West's analysis of Stalin at the beginning of the Cold War. In 1945 it had been in bad taste in Washington to speak of Stalin as anything but "Uncle Joe," the all-powerful, benevolent partner in the United Nations. Accordingly, the West even delivered to Stalin millions of displaced persons marked for death. But by 1947, official tastes had shifted diametrically. Stalin was the devil incarnate, with a timetable for the conquest of the planet. From an attitude of utter complaisance in his regard, American officials switched to acting as if Washington itself were under siege. Just as earlier they had seen boundless benevolence, now they did not soberly examine what opportunities Stalin's concrete weaknesses might offer. If they had, they would have noticed that Hitler, not Stalin, had provided the glue for the Soviet empire during the war, and that it would have been impossible for Stalin to motivate that empire to fight against America, or indeed even to crush nationalist uprisings in Eastern Europe supported by the West. In the late 1940s Stalin was primarily preoccupied trying to reassert the totalitarian communist grip he had relaxed during the war, was fighting major insurgencies in the Baltics and the Ukraine, had major questions about the reliability of the Army, was by no means confident that he could seize Eastern Europe (much less lands occupied by Western armies), and was playing a weak hand internationally.

But Western intelligence saw only one threat to Stalin—a shadowy group of "hard-liners" in the Secretariat who were supposedly pushing Stalin for war against the West.[13] Hence it saw something of a community of interests between the West and Stalin. So the West would resist Stalin's encroachments on Western Europe, but would make no efforts to roll back Soviet power in the East, lest such efforts play into the hands of the "hard-liners." President Truman would refer to "Poor Joe" and go out of his way not to make life harder for him. But rumors of hard-liners standing in the wings was Stalin's well-crafted ploy to justify internal repression and to soften up softheaded foreigners.

By contrast, consider the analytical performance of John Churchill, Duke of Marlborough, in England's struggle against the empire of Louis XIV in the closing years of the seventeenth century. England had spent its resources on the Continent strengthening the United Provinces of the Netherlands, and fighting siege campaigns against formidable French fortresses in Flanders. The area most accessible to English military power was also the most difficult one in which to achieve results. By contrast, the south German hinterland of the French Empire was much less solid.

Bavaria and Austria were not fortified, but only loosely garrisoned. A victory over French and allied arms there would revive the political independence of the area and could not be easily undone, an effect far greater than the fall of any fortress in Flanders.[14] Here was a golden opportunity—on two conditions: First, an English army would have to march 400 miles to the area, and second, it would have to win a major victory. Fulfilling the first condition would be made easier because long, fast marches were unusual in those days, and hence would be unexpected. But still, in order to take advantage of the opportunity, Marlborough had to devise a complex, Roman-like organizational scheme for supplying his army and moving it quickly. He would not even have noticed the opportunity had he not had the desire and the confidence to try something unusual.

By the same token, consider the British Army's "Plan 1919," which the Allies would have used to end World War I had the offensive of 1918 failed.[15] This was essentially a plan for Blitzkrieg. Throughout the war, first the British Admiralty under Winston Churchill, and then all the combatants, had developed tanks for crossing the "no man's land" between opposing trenches. All sides had fruitlessly dreamt of breaking through the other side's trench lines and making vast flanking movements through soft supply lines. But whenever breakthroughs had occurred, forces could not get through fast enough, far enough, with enough artillery support. The opportunity for a decisive breakthrough would be there only if an army equipped itself with enough tanks which possessed enough speed and range, and if it supported those tanks with the equivalent of unlimited-range artillery, namely airplanes. By the end of World War I, Western analysts had finally seen both sides of the equation. So "Plan 1919" was *a typical act of opportunity analysis—part cognition and part commitment to do one's part.* Like a rockclimber who considers a few outcroppings of rock to be a route, an analyst sees opportunities to the extent that he is eager to take on tasks. It is essential for analysts to keep in mind, however, that opportunities do not come gift-wrapped with guarantees of effortless success.

Perhaps the opportunities that are easiest to exploit are the hardest to perceive—namely, the ones that appear upon uncovering an enemy's deception. Just imagine how easily Hitler could have defeated the Normandy landings if he had seen through the Allies' deception. He could have given the impression that most of his troops in France were preparing to move to the Pas de Calais, while in fact they were getting a running start on a massive concentration in Normandy. After all, deception is used most often to turn a weakness into strength. To see through deception is to get a private look at the enemy's weakness, and to redouble it. This is why analysis meant to uncover deception is perhaps the most remunerative of all opportunity-oriented analyses. As we have seen above (Chapter 8), one goes about uncovering deception in part by formulating and testing hypotheses about the circumstances in which it might be practiced. Speculation about enemy plans, weaknesses, and possible ruses is one of the bases for such hypotheses.

Having examined the general principles of all analysis, let us now look at the principles that govern specific kinds of analysis.

What

The principles that govern the analysis of any topic flow from the substance of that topic. Once one understands the importance of facts in a given context, one may ask of the data whatever questions one wishes. Political analysis, for example, may produce a political estimate, a political database, or any number of other products. That is why *it makes no sense to talk about how to do Estimates, or Indications and Warning, or Current Intelligence, or data bases. Rather, we will discuss how to analyze politics, military affairs, political economy, and specialized interdisciplinary subjects such as terrorism.*

POLITICS

Political analysis must combine the statics of comparative government with the dynamics of events. As we have said, statics are the background of intelligence, available to anyone who wishes to study them. By far the bulk of mistakes in political analysis come from faulty understanding of the basics. More to the point, even analysts who boast long acquaintance with a country make basic mistakes, because they had looked at the country while asking unenlightening questions. We cannot here give a full account of things political. Rather, we provide a basis for distinguishing the more important from the less important questions about the bases of politics. After we have done that, we will glance at how one may fit reports of specific political events into basic knowledge.

Politics is the clash of human purposes, interests, and visions of goodness. The sum of the formal and informal circumstances in which such clashes occur we call a *regime*. Thus the first step in analyzing foreign political matters is to understand any given regime. The wrong way to go about understanding a regime is to look at the label—words like "democratic," "authoritarian," "totalitarian," "capitalist," and "socialist." The same adjectives can describe utterly different systems, and the common characteristic is rarely the most important from the point of view of intelligence.

Democratic elections can produce regimes of diametrically different character. The First French Republic fostered a way of life as nasty as that of America was pleasant.[16] Today, life in democratic Switzerland is much more like that in authoritarian Singapore—that is, productive, orderly, free from arbitrary force—

than it is in democratic India or even Colombia. For that matter, in the late 1970s, military-ruled Chile exhibited more of the characteristics usually associated with democracies than Chile had before a bloody coup ousted an elected government. Indeed that government, headed by Marxist Salvador Allende and run by communists, had been elected by the same peculiar version of democratic mechanism that had chosen Hitler's Nazi government in 1933. But that mechanism does not always produce totalitarians. It also produces the Israeli, Italian, and Greek governments of our time. Before 1958 that democratic mechanism functioned in France. DeGaulle scrapped it for another, equally democratic one, that produced different results. Then of course there is Mexico, where fake elections make for yet another brew.

Now consider the label "authoritarian," denoting unelected regimes that do not try to radically reform society. Hafez Assad of Syria, for example, once launched an attack on dissidents in Hama, the country's third-largest city, that killed tens of thousands of people. Uganda's Idi Amin was no reformer either, but a cannibal whose unruly personal and tribal appetites consumed perhaps one-tenth of the country's population.[17] On the other hand, other authoritarians, such as Taiwan's Chiang Kai-shek and Korea's Chun Doo Hwan, gave their countries peace and prosperity. Authoritarian Francisco Franco of Spain gave his country both of these, and a smooth transition to democracy, too. Some authoritarians rule alone, or as head of a nominal party (as does Iraq's Saddam Hussein), while others have ruled as head of a real party, such as Paraguay's Alfredo Stroessner. Then there are some, like Libya's Muammar Qaddafi, who violently try to change society but only scramble the top layers. At what point do such people become totalitarian?

Communism is the modern limit-case of totalitarianism. Fidel Castro imposed communism through "block committees" that even tried to regulate each Cuban family's caloric intake. But if "communism" is understood by way of opposition to "capitalism" it does not tell us much about life in any country. In Poland the farms remained in private hands, and communist oppression drove the Church's roots even deeper. But in Cambodia, communist social engineering razed not just institutions, but perhaps one-third of the population. Peru, along with most of the rest of Latin America, certainly qualifies as "capitalist." Anyone may hold property or enrich himself, yet the right to participate in major business is reserved for friends of the regime. Hernando De Soto called it "crony capitalism."[18] Indeed, economic life throughout the "capitalist" world is more or less restricted by regulations instituted at the behest of interest groups that use government power to disadvantage competitors. Among these are safety and environmental regulations. These, and any number of "social" regulations, can make all the political difference in the world.

Sweden is a "socialist" country where fully 94 percent of GNP is generated by the *private* sector. But national government tax rates are 57 percent of GNP—the highest in the world, and the government acts as head of a nationwide family. Also, Sweden has, in the words of former U.S. Ambassador Rodney Kennedy-Minott, "a law for everything, from walking dogs to raising children," and people who volunteer information on each other's breaches of regulations. Thus it was the subject of a book entitled *The New Totalitarians*.[19]

In sum, an analyst who seeks the meaning of a political report will find little help in knowing that it concerns a "nationalist" in an "authoritarian" country with a "capitalist" system. What then should the analyst know about the country?

Culture

First he should know about the culture. Although it does not explain everything, culture answers some interesting questions. Why, for example, should an analyst believe reports of peasant uprisings in China but not in India? Such events are common in the history of China because Confucian tradition has taught even the humblest Chinese that individuals and states are supposed to be virtuous, and that when they are not they deserve rejection. But there is nothing in the Hindu tradition of separate castes of separate origins that suggests a single standard by which all men may be judged. So, although many kinds of strife are within the Indian tradition, protests against injustice simply are not. By a similar token, one can understand why Russians are more reluctant than Europeans to question the moral standing of their rulers. Like most Europeans, most Russians are Christians, and hence most believe that all men are equally subject to God's standard. But the Russian Orthodox Church's tradition of recognizing the Tzar as its spiritual leader (a tradition continued by the Orthodox hierarchy's subjection to the KGB) tended to place the state above judgment. Of course, traditions can change. In Russia, three generations of explicitly atheistic, hateful, communist rule have given the state a hellish reputation, and have engendered much cynicism. In China, by contrast, the communist state's low repute apparently has not dampened the people's tendency to judge men and governments by absolute, even utopian, standards.

Culture explains important habits. Why do Swedes freely take part in a kind of socialism not entirely different from that which communists imposed on East Europeans and Russians only by guns? Because the homogeneous Swedish people had come to think of their leaders as wise, benevolent, and impartial people. In Sweden, contentiousness is in bad taste. By contrast look at Israel, filled with people from all over the world who have survived by their wits. To the possibility that the laws might be impartial Israelis do not give a second thought, and life in Israel is contentiousness itself. The analyst should be readier to believe reports of an anti-establishment campaign coming from a place like Israel than from one in the Swedish mold.

Now consider what broad cultural categories do *not* explain. Politics in the Islamic world differs from politics in Christian lands, in part because Mohammed never said anything like Christ's "Render unto Caesar the things that are Caesar's and unto God the things that are God's." While Christians were elaborating the doctrine of "the two swords" (spiritual and temporal) the Prophet Mohammed was conquering with sword in hand. Thus it is easy to understand why in Christian societies people argue about the legitimacy of regimes largely in terms of the state's achievement of secular goals, and why, for Christians, a government's legitimacy is always a matter of degree. But in the context of Islam, political legitimacy is largely an all-or-nothing spiritual matter. This partly explains why in the Islamic world political opponents do not tolerate each other much. But it does not fully explain the prevalence of despotic government from West Africa to East Timor. To understand that, one must also refer to a pre-Islamic tradition in that part of the world according to which government is the private business of the rulers, to be exercised for their own benefit. Islam does not command (but does not forbid) the royal family of Saudi Arabia to treat the country's vast revenues from oil as private wealth to be expended on palaces. Thus a hypothetical anti-Saudi plotter in the Middle East might quarrel with the royal family's stewardship of Mecca. He might also envy the family's position. The analyst should realize that there is not likely to be a connection between the two sentiments, and there is even less likelihood that if the plotter replaced the house of Saud he would treat the country's wealth more according to Western notions of good government.

Corruption

Cultural circumstances often impart very different meanings to familiar concepts. Take "corruption." One does not have to travel far to note that while in some places people demand money "under the table" to act illegally, in other places they demand it in order to perform their jobs. In former Soviet Georgia, one of the more powerful curses is "May you have to live on your salary!" When the government, by cutting off avenues of personal advancement, has left individuals only the power to slack off, they gain back some of their independence by wielding that prerogative. Through "legal" corruption individuals get to work for themselves. Nurses and doctors in Soviet hospitals had to be paid privately to deliver more than perfunctory care. The Soviet Aeroflot airline seldom sold first-class tickets, even for hard currency, because the crew and airline employees used the first-class cabin for lounging and for paying off private favors. The black market in the former Soviet Union can provide any good or service because someone first took for himself materials and labor that legally belonged to the state. The analyst who judges people who do such things as dishonest misunderstands retail-level secession from the political system.

Then there is the kind of wholesale corruption the foremost exponent of which may be the Philippines. This amounts to using every position of public trust to accumulate as much private wealth as possible. Thus employees of ministries have as their first duty to enrich the Minister, and the better they do this the greater the latitude the Minister gives them to enrich themselves. Loot flows upward, and the power to loot flows downward. Whereas in the classic Leninist model communists had exercised unlimited partisan political power behind the façade of a government, in the Philippines apolitical elites use the government as a tool for unlimited looting. Had St. Augustine foreseen the Philippines in the late twentieth century, he surely would have mentioned them as the archetype of one particular type of government: *magnum latrocinium*— thievery writ large.[20] By the 1980s this way of life had become so entrenched that only ignorance could justify an analyst's hope that corruption in Corazon Aquino's band would be less pervasive than Ferdinand Marcos' had been. The analyst should know that this kind of corruption devours all politics, and that it necessarily leaves governments helpless against well-organized enemies, foreign or domestic.

The corruption prevalent in Syria is of yet another kind. The dictator of that country, Hafez Assad, enriches his chief lieutenants and binds them to himself by granting them the franchise to import luxury goods and hard currency, and to traffic in drugs. Assad strictly limits the number of such operators.[21] Becoming associated with one of them is a high privilege. But Assad makes sure of his barons' loyalties by constantly surveilling them with his secret police, and occasionally breaking one of them for "corruption"—i.e., for suspicion of insufficient loyalty to him. The analyst should know that regimes like Assad's do not suffer from corruption. They live by it and count on it to produce loyal cadres. Thus in the 1980s Panama's Manuel Noriega built a regime on the loyalty of thuggish barons whom he paid by franchising the drug trade to them. The regime proved so strong that nothing short of outright invasion could shake it.

More subtly political, and yet more difficult to manage, is the corruption prevalent in places like Mexico and Italy. In these countries franchising illegal activities is small potatoes compared to the franchising of legal ones. The ruling party (or factions within it, or parties within a governing coalition) determine who gets permission to build a building or to take out a major loan, who gets a major contract, who fills which major post. On any given day the Italian press is filled with stories about interparty and intraparty struggles over nominations to various posts in state-owned or state-influenced enterprises—*lottizazione*. And indeed "private" entrepreneurs are constantly made aware of the need to accommodate those who hold government power. The primary criterion for granting privilege is political loyalty, and everyone knows who the privileged minorities are.

But these regimes are publicly committed to treating all citizens alike. So they must reconcile the general public. Every method for doing this has its drawbacks, however. First, the whole society can be brought into the system of special privileges, and the regime can hope that those less privileged than others won't make too big a fuss—that the general public will work more or less faithfully like Swedes rather than rebelliously take retirement, like Argentines. Second, the government can allow the existence of a vast unregulated, untaxed "second economy" as in Greece, and hope that the official system is not left wholly without the wherewithal to satisfy its political clienteles. In these subtle circumstances, the term "corruption" takes on contradictory meanings: On the one hand it is the very mechanism for determining who gets what, when, and how. On the other hand, it is the complex of private actions for escaping that mechanism.

In sum, then, the analyst must decide whether any given instance of corruption is tearing down the system or maintaining it. Strictly speaking, "corruption" means activities that tend to rot a given regime. To the extent that the principles of a regime are themselves rotten, behavior according to the Ten Commandments, or Confucius' Annalects, can corrupt it. As Alexandr Solzhenitsyn predicted it would, the simple act of speaking the truth corrupted a Soviet system founded on citizens telling lies to one another. Any economic activity outside the control of the Communist party also corrupted the system. A system built on any given principle will be corrupted by the partial acceptance of behavior according to an antagonistic principle. Thus Machiavelli explains the fall of one of his princes by telling us that he did not know how to be bad enough.[22] *Political analysis consists in part of knowing what will preserve a given regime, and what will corrupt it.*

Finally, consider that words that are staples of discourse within Western civilization have taken on sharply different meanings in the process of being adopted by non-Western cultures.[23] Japanese dictionaries give ideographs for familiar Western terms, like "rights" and "economics." But, because of fateful choices by the translators who introduced these concepts to Japan at the time of the Meiji Construction, these Japanese words now carry etymological baggage very different from those in the West. For "rights" the translators chose an ideograph that meant "arbitrary prerogative," and for "economics" they chose one that meant "advantage."[24] Over time, the impact of etymology decreases and that of usage rises. Nevertheless, the Japanese can be forgiven if, when they speak of rights with regard to economics, their minds are not quite where Americans' are. But a political analyst who does not put the words he hears in proper context is not worthy of the name.

Accidents of History

The character of regimes often is due to battles won and lost, and of individual decisions that could have gone either way. Why is Jordan so different from nearby Iraq? In part because Jordan's King Hussein is a Hashemite, the hereditary chief of a Bedouin tribe who rules by virtue of the tribal loyalty of the Arab Legion—a Bedouin army that admits no Palestinians. Not incidentally, King Hussein has survived innumerable attempted assassinations. But his Hashemite cousin, who ruled Iraq until 1958, did not. Why does Morocco have a king whose dynasty reaches back into the eighteenth century? Because during the nineteenth century, when France occupied and modernized the country, the Moroccan monarchs played a double game. Like other colonial potentates, they were happy to act as agents for French rule. But they also made themselves the leaders of nativist resentment. So, unlike other potentates, they emerged from colonialism both as able administrators and as independent patriots. Also, Morocco's King Hassan, unlike the Shah of Iran, never was tempted to carry out a "White Revolution" or to turn himself into a Western liberal. He rules in part by ancient legitimacy, in part through Islamic piety, in part through "corruption," in part as the bringer of the goods of modernity, and in part by killing his enemies. His regime is as deeply rooted as any in that part of the world could be. But, of course, one bullet could utterly change that.

There is no substitute for political analysts knowing details, for their distinguishing between the accidental and the underlying reality, and for their capacity to determine what is contingent on what.

Who Counts

The most immediate question in politics is "Who counts?" In all the civilized cities of Aristotle's time, politics was the business of heads of independent households loosely organized into tribes, and flowing in and out of *ad hoc* parties. Kings, tyrants, and would-be leaders of assemblies had to contend with them. During the Christian Middle Ages in Europe, society was a tangled web of long-term obligations and exemptions. A carpenter in Dijon who owned a vineyard would have been a citizen, a vassal, a guild member, and a parishioner. His relationship to one authority was offset by his relationship to others. Later, during the "age of absolutism," Louis XIV could say without exaggerating, "The state is I." Only kings counted, for nearly all purposes. In most modern countries people count according to their proximity to rulers who dispense society's goods. By intentional contrast, the U.S. Constitution does not contain the word "Sovereignty,"[25] and is a unique attempt in the modern world to base a government of enumerated powers on citizens who retain unenumerated rights. The U.S. government has no presumptive right to run society. Nearly all modern states, however (the U.S. included) purport to represent all adults equally. Theoretically, everyone counts alike. But to figure out who really counts, one must look deeper.

The major exceptions prove the rule: In Eastern Europe in 1989–90 the Communist parties controlled the most massive apparati for mobilizing people that the world had ever known. They controlled where people could live and work; who would and would not rise in every field. They controlled what people could read. And of course schools and workplaces were primarily centers of political control. The Communist parties had even succeeded in breaking down the family. Individuals stood alone against Leviathan. So it is significant that at the moment (and to the extent that) these apparati ceased being backed by armed men willing to kill, they were able to mobilize only an average of 10 percent of the population in free elections. This proves that the massive social and political control apparatus had never really counted, except as an adjunct to the power to kill. Failure to understand this was not limited to U.S. intelligence analysts and the U.S. press, but was common to observers throughout the world who lacked basic understanding. This is not to say that political–economic control structures don't count. Quite the contrary. But it is essential to realize *why* they count, and *how far* they count. For that, only a basic education in comparative politics will do. Here we can only give examples of what that entails.

The primary means of modern political organization is the party. But parties differ widely. The Republican and Democratic parties of the U.S. consist of people who have managed to get themselves elected. Party officials are their creatures, not the other way around. This is so also in Brazil and Switzerland. It is almost so in France, where the single-member-district electoral system, combined with a second-round runoff, gives local voters the power to weed out the choices of local party leaders. But where voters can choose only among party lists, the party leaders who make up the lists are very powerful. There, governments are made and broken by deals among party leaders. There being no primary elections, the party leaders are chosen formally by party officials—their employees. In reality, party leaders chose themselves. But even within any given country, different parties have different relationship with their members. In Italy and France, for example, Communist members of parliament used to turn over their state paychecks to the Party, which would then issue them new ones for a lesser amount. This was to emphasize that they worked for the Party, not for the state.

In countries where the ratio of government or government-directed spending to GNP is high (for example Sweden, Israel, or Greece), party leaders have lots of money to give or withhold from their followers. This adds to the party leaders' power. Being "in" with the right people never hurts anywhere. Although officials and associates of parties in all welfare states benefit themselves and their clienteles, the officials of socialist parties (and of Third World ruling parties as well) tend to be employed by agencies, enterprises, and institutes financed by state funds. Indeed, they often live in Party housing and shop in Party stores. Even after the general collapse of European communism, the communist cadres in Italy's Emila Romagna region still lived this way.

The political party as a subculture in society was developed by European socialists in the late nineteenth century, and the practice of it surely reached its peak in the countries from Russia to Angola wherein communists seized power. But, as the Third World shows, the practice can also exist independent of ideology. Look at Mexico's oil industry, in which party barons in the guise of managers and union leaders, armed with the power of monopoly, of hiring and firing, of eminent domain, and indeed of police powers, built a feudal domain. Even in Western countries, government employees tend to be highly partisan. In some cities (e.g., Detroit and New York), public employees are the biggest constituency and the biggest beneficiaries of government. Regardless of the party's name, its purpose tends to become the comfort of its leaders. The maxim "all politics is local" holds all over the world. But it does so with special force in Nigeria. There, the question of who is who, and what he's after, often begins and ends in a town. Abundant corruption flows whence party leaders hail. To enhance one's image in one's town by building things in it seems to be the consuming political passion. Elsewhere in Africa "party" is synonymous with "tribe," and, almost regardless of the party's espousal of socialism or capitalism, the party winds up serving the interests of the tribe. But no matter where one is "coming from," who he is depends largely on what he is after.

What Are They After?

The proverb "Not even a dog moves his tail for nothing" is a solid touchstone for political analysts. Anyone who has understood a political culture, and who has figured out who's who in a country, must still figure out what they want and what they are willing and able to do to get it. To what extent does a party official regard his patronage as an end or as a means? And as a means to what? Here is the greatest source of error, the greatest temptation to mirror-imaging. Here the analyst must be clearest about his epistemology.

Gorbachev's tenure atop the Soviet Union (1985–1991) spawned a host of analyses of his motives. All were consistent with the observed facts. But these conclusions are largely inconsistent with one another. Joshua Muravchik made a good case, backed by Gorbachev's book *Perestroika*, that Gorbachev, like

Milovan Djilas before him, abandoned the Communist faith into which he was born, but no faster than contact with reality forced him to.[26] Zbigniew Brzezinski argued that Gorbachev sought to preserve as much of communism as possible against the inexorable decline of both the Soviet economy and Soviet society.[27] Uri Ra'anan, for his part, pictured Gorbachev as something of a sorcerer's apprentice who let loose forces he did not understand and could not control.[28] Common sense suggests that there may be an element of truth in all these analyses. *But it would be a mistake to regard any of them as true.* None of these analysts knew or had reports from anyone who had dealt with Gorbachev for years, much less had they confidential reports from personal friends, or confidential letters. The analyst must make working hypotheses, but must guard against hypostatizing them.

The analyst must also consider that the *intensity* of motivations may be more important than the means available to pursue them. By the 1980s, once Soviet communists sought only to live tomorrow as much as possible like yesterday, without being willing to kill or be killed for it, they became "paper tigers" and were doomed. Since the Russians wanted their independence more than the communists wanted to deny it to them, the Soviet Union ceased to be possible. Marxism–Leninism, the cult of Lenin, and the history of communism inspired those who seek to tear down the Soviet state and embarrassed those who would preserve it. This ensures that successor states will be built on other principles, whether better or worse.

The analyst would do well to consider the reasons why both political sources and the people about whom they are reporting want what they want. An educated analyst should then be in a position to answer the very political question "Who would be moved by *this*"?

Dynamics

The whole art of analyzing political events consists of fitting reports of new facts into one's knowledge of the fundamentals. We can only give one out of a myriad of examples of the correct way of doing the job.

How should an analyst in 1990 have treated confirmed reports of divisive, potentially explosive intrigue within South Africa's ruling Nationalist party and within the Soviet Communist party? Both sets of reports, let us assume, were rich in detail of conspiracies among various factions in the party, the security forces, and leaders of the opposition. The analyst should have begun by noting how different the Soviet political situation was from that of South Africa. The ruling class in South Africa, "those who count," are 4.5 million white people—less than 20 percent of the population. The whites' property is, and possibly their lives, are at stake, just as with the 5 percent of the former Soviet population who made up the communist Nomenklatura. But this was the only similarity between the two groups. White South Africans never had the choice of "blending in" with the majority, while the Nomenklatura, after 1989, had every incentive to disguise its power. Communism was the sole *raison d'être* of the Soviet Union, and the widespread impression that it had failed deeply demoralized the communists. But white South Africans were not demoralized. Apartheid had failed—but apartheid had been only a means to an end, not the end itself. So, unlike Soviet communists, South African whites confronted the future with a sense of common danger, and feeling morally justified in using all their very considerable material power to preserve their civilization. In sum, while the Soviet ship was sinking, and its "rats" had every incentive to fight one another for a place on the debris, the South African ship was not sinking, and if it ever did, *its* "rats" would have no place to go. Their incentives favored calm cooperation with one another first, and then with their challengers.

Now look at "the other side." In South Africa there are more than 20 million blacks. But fewer than half of these were involved with South African urban society. The rest lived in another century. Even the more-or-less urban blacks retained strong tribal identification. Apartheid had not, after all, *invented* the tribes. So, to be a black leader in South Africa in 1990—a Desmond Tutu, a Nelson Mandela, a Mangosutho Buthelezi—was not at all like being a Lech Walesa in Poland, a Vigutas Landsbergis in Lithuania, or a Boris Yeltsin in Russia, calling on a homogeneous nation to throw off domination by an easily identified, universally hated group. First, South African black leaders could not credibly call for the destruction of a system that made people poor. The black poor who would be rich wanted greater *participation* in the system. Only a tiny number of black party leaders would benefit from tearing it down. Nor could any of them call for power to the people without raising the question "Which people?" All the blacks together far outnumber the whites. But singly, only the seven million Zulus do. And the Zulus, an independent nation before the formation of South Africa, were not eager to submerge themselves among blacks who are as alien to them as the whites and whom they respect less because, before the white man came, they had cringed before the Zulu war machine. Nor could the black leaders, even if united, call for the kind of massive abandonment of the state that was so effective in Eastern Europe. In the Soviet Union and Eastern Europe, communists were a drain on society. South African whites were its engine.

So, black leaders could have threatened to contribute to inconveniencing the whole of white South Africa—uniting the whites. Any black leader could have promised the sort of cooperation that Zulus and whites entered into in Natal in the context of the *Indaba* council. But such cooperation, however beneficial to those who take part, tends to divide black leaders, both tribally and ideologically. For the purposes of our analysis, such cooperation is obviously not the stuff of secret deals that might divide the leaders of the "White Tribe."

In sum, accurate though reports of intrigue among whites might have been, analysts had every reason to believe that this intrigue would not amount to much—least of all civil war.

In the Soviet Union, however, the entire population was on the other side. Communists are thoroughly interspersed in a society that is deeply disunited about everything except hatred for communism and communists. The race among communist leaders to lower their red flags and raise others—whether the green flag of environmentalism or various nationalist flags—was no secret. Nor was it a secret that anticommunist groups of various kinds, realizing their own lack of access to the wealth and power of the state, were tempted to admit communist leaders who were eager to join them. So there was a kind of natural attraction between social groups bent on revolution, and apparatchiks eager to get out of revolution's way. However, when well-connected Party bureaucrats lend strength to groups that have no intention of cooperating with one another, they may well be setting the stage for civil war. This logic applied most forcefully to the security forces of the Soviet Union. To survive, they must be on the winning side. But since who will win was a matter of opinion, there was every incentive for officials in different units to court their separate deals and then to fight on different sides. So, analysts had every reason to believe reports of intrigue among Soviet military and security forces, and to expect that, as they pursued these deals, they were assembling the stuff of civil conflagration—and striking the sparks. Hence there should have been no surprise that on August 19, 1991, a significant number of Soviet military units defected to Boris Yeltsin's anti-communist Russian side. The only legitimate surprise was that the KGB's elite Alpha force was among them.

The End-Product of Politics

For the intelligence analyst, all of the abovementioned political distinctions are important insofar as they affect the regime's ability to muster society's moral and material resources for political and military conflict. The political bases of success and failure in war include: the extent to which those who are capable of doing the fighting identify with the regime; the extent to which the regime channels society's resources into things military; and the quality of the people who rise to positions of leadership. Switzerland has been free of foreign domination not since the Alps thrust up, but only since the fifteenth century, when the diverse people of that country developed the most consistent and widespread devotion to arms since republican Rome.

MILITARY ANALYSIS

Armies and navies should be easier to analyze than polities, because they must be judged by the simple standard: Whom can they beat?* But history is full of questionable recipes for figuring out who can beat whom.† Also, through the ages rulers have poured out countless treasure to soothsayers and other "scientific" analysts in vain attempts to learn whether there would be war, and how opposing armies would perform. In our own day this expensive habit continues under the guise of "systems analysis," and its principal tool is the computer. We for our part have argued at length elsewhere[29] that there is no good recipe for foretelling the performance of forces or the likelihood of their being employed, because war depends on the clash of unpredictable wills making innumerable high-pressure decisions.

Every high-school athlete knows the cliché "It's not the size of the dog in the fight, but the size of the fight in the dog. . . ." Nevertheless, analysis of military contests is as feasible as the analysis of other contests. Just as football scouts take note of the weight and speed of offensive linemen, and only then venture opinions about a team's capacity to run the ball, military intelligence analysts can speak intelligently about a foreign army's capacity for breakthroughs on the ground only by referring to the analogues of guards and tackles: surface-to-surface missiles, attack aircraft, and artillery. Good military analysis sticks to the basics.

Military intelligence analysts, being human, cannot see the future. They do their jobs if they describe the setting in which the future will occur (the scenery, the cast, the props), and they are excellent if they do this from the point of view of the enemy. But if the commander asks the intelligence analyst to predict what the enemy *will* do, he takes the analyst into an area where the commander himself has more to say than any intelligence officer. That is because how the

---

*Armies, like polities, have peculiar personalities that reflect their commanders. The French Army of the Ancien Régime reflected Turenne and Condé. The U.S. Nuclear Submarine Service was Hyman Rickover writ large. The modern Soviet Navy is an extension of the mind of Sergei Gorshkov. But to say this is to say something different from Plato's and Aristotle's teaching that any polity is the reflection of the people who "set the tone" for it. Classical political analysis has the complex task of figuring out how well a given polity conforms to *its* political model, and whether, given the people's character and circumstances, it is capable of approximating any worthier model. When one analyzes an armed force, however, the model according to which it is built is purely incidental to the only question that matters: How will it cope with its likely enemies?

†Note, for example, Stalin's five permanently operating principles of warfare: solidity of the home front; morale of armies; quantity and quality of weaponry; level of technology; quality of leadership. Howard Bruce Franklin, ed., *The Essential Stalin: Major Theoretical Writings, 1905–52.* Many have seen such a recipe in Clausewitz' principle of concentration of force at the crucial point, and others yet have seen it in the "air power" theories of Giulio Douhet.

enemy actually performs depends in part on what one's own side actually does. How then can military analysts set the scene?

The Human Element

To look no further than a soldier's uniform and simply to count him is a hangover from World War I, when the military art was wrongly supposed to be a variant of industrial mass-production: to marshal greater numbers of men and move tons of ordnance at particular times and places. In those days, Europe's military and social discipline had produced soldiers of roughly equivalent reliability and proficiency. Indeed, the military environment of the Western front required steadfastness unto death, but little else.* Yet certainly the wars both international and civil that followed the Great War showed that differences in allegiance, motivation, and style remained as important as they had ever been. In the Russo–Polish War of 1919–20, the higher motivation of the Polish units was key, and in the Spanish Civil War, military analysts learned to look to the ideological character of the units, as well as to the training they had received in new tactics. In Korea, in December 1950, the U.S. Marines and the U.S. Army, products of the same society, governed by the same code of military justice, performed very differently because while the Marines had been trained to actually carry their full complements of weapons and ammunition, and to behave in a military manner regardless of discomfort, the Army had been allowed to slack off. Morale amongst both groups had been high—but it was morale of a different sort: The Army had used its supply system to bring the men turkeys for Thanksgiving, while the Marine supply system had brought the stuff of war.[30]

But perhaps the most stark of all examples of how easy it is to misperceive the human element are to be found in Italy and the Soviet Union during World War II. When Mussolini listened to his troops marching past the reviewing stand, shouting the Fascist salute, he thought they were his. And they were happy enough to be his—on the parade ground. But on the battlefield they proved soon enough that they had no intention to get shot for him. In 1941 a host of military analysts predicted that the Russian armies would not hold together against the Germans, because they knew that Stalin had purged the officer corps and, they supposed, deprived it of coherence. Stalin, however, was confident that the troops would hold because he placed great stock in the elaborate control

---

*Note the popular turn-of-the-century belief, so well expressed by Rudyard Kipling, that the military system run by "sergeant whatshisname" could "make soldiers out of mud." "Pharaoh and the Sergeant" (1897), *Works of Rudyard Kipling*. Nevertheless, by 1918, differences in quality of troops (produced by training and equipment) became very important. The German offensive in that year almost won the war, in part due to the troops' superior tactics for infiltration.

mechanisms of communism. Both Stalin and the analysts turned out to be wrong. Stalin's control mechanisms could not prevent mass surrenders in the summer of 1941. But later the troops became Stalin's more than they had ever been, even though Stalin eased his controls somewhat, because Nazi brutality drove them into his arms.

So, the analyst must ask: Loyalty to whom, and on what basis? For what purpose? Under what circumstances?

Conscripts are always primarily loyal to their families. The military analysts of old—Thucydides, Livy, Machiavelli—always noticed that "citizen armies" were far more loyal than domestic professionals, never mind foreign mercenaries. But they also noted the particulars of this loyalty. Conscripts may be led silently to the slaughter if the iron discipline necessary to do it is backed by their families.* But, as the U.S. learned in Vietnam, it is very difficult to use any conscript army for purposes not fully backed by the community. Difficult, but not impossible. Soviet conscripts in Afghanistan in 1979–89 (those in combat units) experienced no disloyalty, perhaps because they were treated as professionals,[31] and because it was not yet safe for Soviet citizens to openly express their opposition to what their government was doing. By the same token, observers reported a lack of enthusiasm among German conscripts, and in German society, for World War II. Nevertheless, the control organs of the Nazi party were able to keep this level of dissatisfaction from causing problems, even once it became clear that Hitler was going to take the country to hell with him.

The analyst must tackle military control mechanisms in a straightforward manner, not as imponderables. Adolf Hitler did that in 1934 when he judged that the SA brownshirts, though they shouted "Heil Hitler" and beat up his enemies, were primarily loyal to their commander, Ernst Rohm. So Hitler disbanded the SA, and always kept at his command competing security organizations who were eager to kill one another. Because the KGB's Vladimir Kryuchkov did not have a competing set of killers at hand on August 19, 1991, the defection of the KGB's Alpha force doomed him and his regime. The analyst must judge these matters as successful practitioners do. The trick is to make sure that the designated killers maintain a separate identity from those they might be called on to kill. Xenophon's *Hiero or Tyrannicus* stresses the necessity of *foreign* bodyguards. Lenin used a Latvian regiment to fire on crowds in St. Petersburg and to put down the uprising among sailors at Kronshtadt. All

---

*During the year-long battle for Verdun in World War I, the French troops who would approach the battlefield along the "sacred road" were forbidden to speak either to one another or to the troops who were marching in the opposite direction, lest the fact that they were all very likely to be hit cause panic. Charles de Gaulle writes with compassion of how the "bonds of discipline" tightened upon the doomed troops as they approached the front. *La France et Son Armee*, Ch. 7.

modern tyrants have paid those who are supposed to control military units much more than they have paid the soldiers. Yet the controllers are most effective only insofar as they can get close enough to the regular troops, and especially the officer corps, to gather information. The only way they can do that is to convince some regulars secretly to side with them. This is a tricky business, because it is much easier to buy people than to make sure they stay bought and don't make a better deal for themselves elsewhere.

Now consider the *personality* of the military organization. Like individuals, organizations are more or less fat or lean, inner-directed or outer-directed, quick or slow to seize opportunities, lazy or industrious, dogged or feckless. No one acquainted with the U.S. military before and after the tenure of Robert McNamara as Secretary of Defense would dispute that the personalities of organizations can change. Whereas prior to 1961 officers who wished to rise knew to imitate brash, dashing, get-it-done-and-we'll-talk-about-it-later figures such as Air Force Gen. Curtis LeMay and Adm. Arleigh (31-Knot) Burke, after 1961 the path up led through systems analysis. After the tenure of Caspar Weinberger (1981–87), it also led through successive screenings to eliminate those who question the value of women in the armed forces. For better or worse, by 1990 an Arleigh Burke would hardly have made Lieutenant (j.g.), much less Chief of Naval Operations.

Analysts should be attentive to this sort of radical change in personality because it happens often. When the Nazis took over the German armed forces, they drove professional caution out of the senior officer corps and replaced it with faith in the Führer. This boldness at first made German arms more formidable. But unquestionable faith in victory, and a truly fearless leader, proved to be the Wehrmacht's Achilles' heels. After World War II the West German Bundeswehr seemed preoccupied above all to prove how very different it was from its predecessor. This meant, in part, subjecting officers and men alike to sensitivity sessions on "Innere Führung," inner leadership—whatever *that* meant. Meanwhile, the East German Army kept old traditions alive, including the old uniform, hard physical training, and the goose step.* The combination of these two armies is certain to produce yet another personality.

Some professional personalities are so complex that the analyst may legitimately wonder which aspect will predominate when. The Soviet officer corps,

---

*Donald Abenheim, *Reforging the Iron Cross*, recounts how in 1955–60 the West German Bundeswehr integrated the "healthy" elements of the Reichswehr by a complex process of interviews. As of October 3, 1990, the Bundeswehr had issued 105,000 sets of uniforms to the East German armed forces. It planned to reduce the number of East German "integrees" to 25,000 long-term personnel and ultimately to retain only 4,000 officers by the same techniques it had used a generation earlier.

the world's leading proponent of the proposition that there is such a thing as military science, has lived by tables that relate tons of ordnance (or nuclear equivalent), delivered on kilometers of front, to ratios between attackers and defenders, and believes religiously in "school solutions" for military problems. On the other hand, no group of officers in the world has written so much about initiative, deception, creativity. The analyst must ask how the several aspects of an organization's personality will combine.

The Material Element

Too often military analysis has been reduced to counting men and machines, assuming that God is on the side of the stronger battalions, and that equality of forces portends stalemate. This, of course, is the very negation of military analysis, the chief point of which is to figure out ways in which men and machines can *make a difference*.

Given that since the 1960s the decisive weapons of our time have been ballistic missiles, it is not surprising that military analysis has too often reduced itself to counting missile warheads. In the 1960s the Rand Corporation produced thousands of copies of "bomb damage computers"—slide rules that correlate the yield of a nuclear weapon, how far away from the target it would explode, the blast resistance of the target, and the probability that the target would be destroyed. Armed with that tool, and with the numbers and characteristics of U.S. and Soviet missiles and silos, analysts in the CIA, the Pentagon, and the arms control community, plus the "beltway bandit" study contractors who surround Washington, and academics as well, produced countless "analyses" of U.S.–Soviet nuclear exchanges. The results of these analyses were predetermined by the assumptions that went into them: who would launch what kinds of weapons at which targets, when, with how much warning, etc. One extreme case, a 1978 ACDA study, showed that U.S. and Soviet forces were about equal because each would be able to destroy its own preferred "mix" of targets.[32] Never mind that one set of targets represented an attempt to fight a war while the other optimized civilian damage. Some "studies" have concluded that the U.S. could be decapitated in one blow. Others, that (given all the right assumptions) U.S. nuclear forces would prevail in the long run. The clash of such analyses was domestic politics thinly disguised. This sort of analysis reached its *pons asinorum* in the 1980s with regard to the SDI program. What percentage of attacking warheads would "the system" intercept? Billions of dollars were spent fruitlessly creating scenarios pitting nonexistent measures against nonexistent countermeasures in imaginary conditions.[33] The prize? Bragging rights about defense policy. The various answers, of course, were predetermined by the various definitions of offensive and defensive systems.

Domestic politics aside, quantitative facts are useful insofar as analysts relate them to a military job to be done, and to a plan for doing that job in a given set of circumstances. As regards missiles and warheads, the circumstances have included more and more variables. Even in the 1960s and 1970s not all warheads were created equal. Some were optimized for city-killing, others were optimized for killing missiles in silos. In the 1980s as missiles moved out of silos, nuclear yield and accuracy became less important than real-time intelligence on the location of mobile missiles, and on-line retargeting of offensive warheads. The 1990s added the variable of antimissile defenses. By the 1990s there was no excuse for military analysts to treat ballistic missiles any more deterministically than any other military hardware.

There is a natural temptation to endow any and all military numbers with more significance than they deserve. In 1813, even Napoleon was satisfied by figures that showed the French Army's rapid recovery from the losses of the previous year's Russian campaign. But the figures did not show, among other things, that the new gun carriages had been built out of freshly cut wood, because the seasoned wood had been used up. So, many of the new guns on which Napoleon counted never made it to the battle of Leipzig because the carriages fell apart as the wood shrank.

The most common figure in naval analysis, ship tonnage, is to be taken with a grain of salt. Comparatively small 3,900-ton frigates that launch nuclear tipped cruise missiles can sink 100,000-ton aircraft carriers. Just as importantly, two ships of similar tonnage can be very different. In 1982 the 4,100-ton British destroyer H.M.S. *Sheffield* sank off the Falklands after being hit by a single Exocet cruise missile whose warhead failed to explode. In 1987 the 3,650-ton U.S.S. *Stark* took *two* Exocets (one of which exploded), and stayed afloat in the Persian Gulf. U.S. ships are built more robustly than British ships. American Virginia-class cruisers outweigh Soviet Sovremenny-class destroyers by 50 percent, although the latter have more and bigger teeth. But U.S. ships are incomparably more comfortable than Soviet ships. Why? Because Soviet ships carry more weapons, and more kinds of weapons per ton, than their American counterparts while American ships have more living space. So the analyst must ask: A ton of what? For what purpose?

The way in which an item of hardware is used often is more significant than the numbers in which it is present. France's defeat in 1940 has left the false impression that the Germans who overran it were superior in tanks. In fact, German units involved in the battle had some 2,500 tanks, while the French units they overran had about 3,200. But while the Germans had grouped their tanks into armored divisions ten of which acted as spearheads for the rest of the army, the French had only recently put together three armored divisions (plus a fourth during the debacle). Moreover, when the commander of one of these had the chance to strike at the exposed flank of the German spearhead, he deployed his tanks in fixed positions parallel to it instead. Thinking that his duty was to prevent the Germans from coming through his sector, the French commander wound up guarding the flank of the German advance. This was entirely to be expected because over the previous decade the French Army had given proof positive (in its violent rejection of Charles de Gaulle's ideas) that it did not *want* to understand tanks as autonomous spearheads.[34]

Of course de Gaulle's and Von Manstein's understanding of tanks was outdated by the advent of antitank weapons. Tanks now cannot enter hilly ground or built-up areas occupied by infantry equipped with antitank weapons unless their way is cleared by infantry, or by long-range artillery and missiles. Thus, today an analysis of the "tank balance" must look not just at armored units and their quality, but also at these other devices. By the same token it makes no sense to count airplanes against airplanes (even were they to be identical) without also considering the state of air defenses on either side, and the state of intercept control equipment. The analyst is obliged to take into account the natural interplay between offense and defense, measure and countermeasure. In the field of electronic warfare this interplay means quite literally the difference between shooting at real targets or at synthetic ghosts.

As the SDI episode shows so well, the analyst must discipline himself to dealing with real rather than hypothetical contests. Analysts who play such abstract contests are tempted to use hypothetical "absolute" countermeasures and "absolute" weapons. But the only thing such devices kill is realism. In short, the worth of any weapon lies in the complete context of its use.

All of this is to say that good Order of Battle books are naturally the *beginning* of military analysis rather than its end. At best, a good tally of the material elements in warfare makes possible the clarification of the *possibilities* inherent in them. Any given material fact can be either an asset or a liability. The classic asymmetry in ancient history is that between Athens' naval superiority over Sparta, and Sparta's superiority over Athens in numbers of infantry and cavalry. During the Cold War, the United States built 14 aircraft carrier battle groups to none for the Soviet Union, while the Soviet Union built some 400 land-based, cruisemissile–equipped naval bombers to none for the U.S. What threats and opportunities such asymmetries portend depends almost entirely on how both sides use them.

The Operational Factor

"What is to be our war?" asked King Archidamus of his fellow Spartans. There really was only one answer: Try to bring the Athenians to a big land battle. Pericles, for his part, did not hesitate to tell his fellow Athenians that Athens' strength at sea and weakness on land dictated a protracted war of limited engagements on the periphery of Spartan power. Pericles was right, of course—as were the Spartans. Neither side could lose, as long as it waged its own kind of war. Either side would win if the other matched weakness against strength. In the first half of the Peloponnesian War, Athens stuck to the basics while Sparta briefly forgot them, and Athens won. In the second half, Sparta took advantage of Athens' departure from the basics, and *it* won. Our point here is that both sides analyzed each other correctly in large part because each side understood itself well. *Each side faltered not when it misunderstood the other, but when it forgot what it itself was about.*

The foundation of good operational analysis is the question "How do *we* win?" (and secondarily, "How do *they* win?") The analyst must look at the enemy's Order of Battle and ask how best the enemy might use it to his own advantage. The enemy might certainly wish for a better correlation of forces. He might well have designed his forces to fight another country in other circumstances. But, given what he's got, how can he use it to put us at his mercy? As for ourselves, what or whom do we have to destroy, kill, or hold at risk so that once we've done it the enemy will be at our mercy? And, as we pursue this concept of operations, what opportunities do we give the enemy? That is, what if he decides to fight *his* way rather than ours? In short, good operational analysis begins and ends with, and sticks very close to, the idea of victory. Those who do, like the Israelis of 1973, may be mistaken. But they will always be in the ball park.

It is easy to see the various ways by which one may lose contact with the idea of victory. In 1940 the French concept of victory envisaged the Germans exhausting their infantry and tanks against prepared positions, and then succumbing to a French counterattack. But what if the Germans refused to lend themselves to the concept? What if they concentrated their forces against the most lightly defended points, broke through, and *drove* behind French lines? Even since the mid–1960s, U.S. strategic war games have aimed at restoring "stability" and preventing "escalation," under the assumption that the large-scale use of nuclear weapons would be tantamount to the end of the world. But if it were *not*? What if the nuclear aggressor, much as he shouldn't be, were interested in victory and actually used his nuclear warheads to achieve it? This is the reverse image of Japan's analysis (or lack thereof) in 1941. Japan planned a formidable set of opening moves in the war, and could be confident that by early 1942 it would be the mistress of the western Pacific. But then what? If the Americans refused to accept what Japan had done, how could the Japanese arsenal be used to force America to recognize it? Japan had only such long-run options as America would consent to give it. Had the Japanese analyzed their own plans better, they would have paid greater attention to the panoply of options that America's arsenal and productive capacity provided. *The military analyst dare not lose sight of the only concept that endows warfare with any sense: victory.*

Arsenals that make sense in one operational context make no sense at all in another. Noisy submarines are at an enormous disadvantage roaming the open ocean. But a noisy submarine can become quieter than its quiet quarry when it is sitting on the bottom of a sea lane waiting, and its quarry is moving in. "Stealth" airplanes are indeed nearly invisible to radar—as long as they know where the radar is and fly so as to show them their "slim" profiles. But against mobile radars in unpredictable locations, or against radars that point in a variety of directions, stealth does not give an airplane much of an advantage.

Finally, concepts of operations begin to make sense only when the material bases for implementing them exist. Thus, in 1940 the French Air Force's concept of "assault bombing" (not so different from the Luftwaffe's concept of close air support) was irrelevant because the French had nothing like the German Stuka dive bomber. Similarly, President Carter's Presidential Decision No. 59 of July 1980, directing that henceforth the U.S. would target primarily Soviet missile silos, was largely a "declaratory" policy because the U.S. strategic arsenal had not been built for that purpose.[35]

Knowledge and Action

Military analysis sheds light on the enemy's options. As evidence accumulates, analysis can narrow the range of possibilities about what the enemy has actually chosen to do. But no analytical tool exists that can surely sort out the enemy's options.

Choosing to wait for more information may be costly. During the night of October 5, 1973, the Israeli estimators waited for word from their "best source" in Egypt. The estimators' criteria for certainty were fulfilled only hours before the Egyptian attack itself came. To be sure, the Israeli Defense Force had not stood motionless during September, as the data had poured in to the effect that Egypt and Syria were at least putting themselves in position to launch an attack. The Israelis had gradually built up their forces at the front and increased their readiness—but not to the extent they would have had they believed that the Arabs *would* (as distinguished from *could*) attack.

Contrast this with David Kahn's rendition of the process by which intelligence analysis *and* command judgment prepared the Wehrmacht to successfully defend a small salient of the eastern front in 1942: The German command tailored the buildup of its defensive forces to the growth of the evidence of the Soviet attack.[36] When the attack came, the German troops did not care whether it was a feint or not. They were in a position to defeat the forces they had first suspected and then gradually seen poise themselves to strike on a certain axis.

Analysis cannot decide what action any given level of information requires, any more than a physician can tell someone recovering from a heart attack when it is safe to resume sexual activity. For both sorts of clients the rule of thumb must be "when the desire overcomes the fear of death." Like the physician, the military analyst can help his client make responsible choices.

ECONOMIC ANALYSIS

The wealth of families and, derivatively, of nations, is the natural end of economics.* But intelligence serves another end: victory in conflict. Hence, analysts of economic intelligence must look at economic facts from the noneconomic perspective of conflict.

The adage that armies travel on their bellies means in practice that military forces somehow reflect the economy that sustains them. The problem is to know the economy and, more important, to know the specifics of the "somehow." There is another adage, too—that politics consists of satisfying those who count. The problem is to figure out how effectively that is being done, always keeping in mind that people are satisfied by various mixtures of economic and noneconomic goods. Moreover, all of this must be done from the perspective of how well the regime in question can fight its battles.

Political Economics

Money is the mother's milk of politics. But money gotten through the government's favor, directly or indirectly, is doubly nutritious because it is the fruit of political success and breeds yet more success. Even in the United States, the most law-bound of political systems, the people who dance at inaugural balls have economic reasons for rejoicing. They will benefit disproportionately from government spending. Economic intelligence analysts would be well-advised to do school papers explaining how each of the guests expects his bank account to grow. The best-placed will act as unofficial consultants and gatekeepers of government regulators, grantors, managers. Thus the chiefs of whole industries, whole social groups, will make sure that these best-connected people stumble into innumerable good deals. On the rung below are the government officials and contractors, and below them their employees. There can be no doubt that most actions of modern government tend to foster the economic fortunes of some groups at the expense of others. In the U.S., for example, the Clean Air

---

*The two ancient treatments of economics (Book I of Aristotle's *Politics* and Xenophon's *Oeconomicus*) deal strictly with the family. Adam Smith's eighteenth-century treatment, written after two centuries of mercantilism by European monarchs, tried to restore the proper, private, focus of economics.

Act of 1990 benefited large businesses over small, and especially disadvantaged small dry-cleaners. In the rest of the world, the economic stakes in the great game of politics are higher. Much higher.

This is why intelligence analyses that contain macroeconomic speculation about how the fate of a regime is tied to rises and falls in "the economy" as a whole are a waste of time. Unless the analyst can explain who precisely profits from and who pays for any arrangement, whose fortunes are rising and whose are falling, and precisely what the winners and losers count for in their regime, the analyst might as well not touch the subject of economics.

Can any regime benefit from widespread poverty? Of course. Regimes that aim to reform society positively *require* poverty. Experience from Moscow to Managua has shown that empty bellies and ration coupons are indispensable to encouraging the people's attendance and attention at the endless meetings where they must listen to strange theories and confess their (but mostly their neighbors') sins. Can poverty destroy social reform? Not by itself. True, by 1988 the Nicaraguan economy was producing, on a per capita basis, only about as much as it had in 1946. But life in Nicaragua in 1988 was far grimmer than it had been in 1946. Whereas back then Nicaragua's dictators and their beneficiaries had numbered in the hundreds of thieves, by 1988 the Sandinista regime had to steal enough to keep hundreds of thousands of nonproductive people in lifestyles superior to those of the rationed masses. And these thousands who served on the committees for the defense of the revolution in every city block, every workplace, had friends (amounting to perhaps a fourth of the population overall) who had to be kept loyal enough to join in demonstrations. So the amount that the regime had to take out of what the overall economy produced was far greater than it had been in 1946. The result was that empty shelves were the lot of the rationees, while for the rationers and their friends, life was better than it had ever been. This was the opposite of a political catastrophe because it made the rationees dependent on the rationers. If the three-fourths of the population who were the milk-cows of the Sandinistas could have gotten their daily material needs in less odious ways than by humoring them, they would have. How long could the Nicaraguan economy have continued to support the regime on the basis of declining production on the part of the rationees? Quite as long as the rationers counted for everything and the rationees counted for nothing, and as long as the economy continued to generate enough to satisfy the rationers who held the guns. In satisfying them, the regime was bolstered by aid from the Soviet Union and Western Europe as well. But this aid began to decline in 1988, and by 1990 the regime had been voted out of office.

Yet the regime did not die because those who counted in the Sandinista regime abandoned it. They never did, even after it left office. The regime died because it changed its own rules, and allowed a free election in which each of the many hungry rationees, who had counted for nothing, would count for as much as one of the regime's well-fed pillars. Of course, this numerical contest went directly against the logic of the regime. But why the regime agreed to play by these rules is beyond our scope. Perhaps the Sandinista leaders believed their own propaganda, to the effect that they were beloved by the majority of the population. Be that as it may, *the regime was safe so long as it rested itself on the minority it had enriched, and it died the moment it tried to rest itself on the majority it had impoverished.* Its attempt to mix totalitarian economics with democratic politics did not work. Sobered by their defeat, the Sandinistas went back to fundamentals. Before going out of office, they legislated permanent ownership for their supporters of everything they had seized. Then they handed over most offices on condition that they retain the Army and police. To seal the deal, they allowed some businessmen close to the elected President to share in their privileges. By 1991 the Sandinista regime's economic and military power had made up for its political shortcomings.

But can the reverse work? Is it possible to mix free market economics with communist politics? Consider the Soviet economy in the context of the Soviet political system. The emergence of the "Nomenklatura"—the wealthy, self-perpetuating, ruling elite—and the contemporaneous depression of the Soviet economy are logically linked and symbiotic.[37] Their relationship may be expressed by a paraphrase of Lenin's comment on justice: "[Wealth?] For what class?" The answer is the popular, cynical Soviet saying "Only the best for the Proletariat." The powerful but nonproductive appropriated wealth so exclusively that incentive to do useful work decreased dramatically.

Lenin's intention, borrowed from Marx's *Critique of the Gotha Programme*, was for the Proletariat (i.e., the Party) to crush its enemies out of existence, and to remove the economic bases that might allow them to ever rise again. And so by fire and sword, as well as by administrative fiat, the regime made very sure that the communist bureaucracy was the only path to economic success. This produced a relatively well-heeled ruling class of perhaps 15 million people whose *average* per-capita income was about half that of the average in the United States. The average for the remaining 265 million Soviet citizens who *did not* have an "in" must have been only about one-twelfth that in the U.S. However, until circa 1987 the average non–well-connected Soviet was bearing his lot quietly. The dissatisfaction that wrecked the regime came from the ranks of the privileged.

Ever since the beginning of serious unrest in the Soviet Union, Mikhail Gorbachev and his surrogates criss-crossed the world asking for money and advice, ostensibly to improve the Soviet economy. But how? *More importantly,*

427

for whom? Soviet and post-Soviet leaders talked much of introducing the free market, and attributed their hesitation to fear of harming the mass of manual workers. But even avowedly anticommunist, post-Soviet leaders have not simply abolished economic regulation and let the free market create itself. Why? It is difficult to avoid the conclusion that they were more concerned about their own power to reward and to control than they were about the lot of the workers. True, Soviet workers generally produced goods that they themselves were loath to buy, and that are unsaleable on the world market. But would a market without subsidies, without barriers to the formation of businesses, without currency controls, and without restraints on imports, really impoverish the mass of workers? There is reason to doubt it. The subsidies for food and rent do not come from heaven. They are among innumerable bureaucratic *fiats* that arbitrarily fix how much everything in the society is worth, *and above all who gets to distribute it, and who has access to it.* It is impossible to tell what the relative free market value of the work of Soviet railroad men, street sweepers, farmers, and bread bakers would be. But it is obvious that since these occupations produce necessary goods and services, a free market could not find them worthless. Consumers might prefer Western goods. But without products to sell on Western markets, they would be thrown back on to their own market.

Were that market free, people might be willing to do more for access to food. So, at one extreme, those in the food business might get richer in the goods of their own society. What would people be willing to do with less of? Whom, given the chance, would they patronize less? This opposite extreme is even more obvious: communists in general, and communist administrators in particular, regardless of the new labels they had chosen for themselves. In a market that allowed workers to exchange their labors for those of others, what would the average Russian give for the work of a communist?* The managerial class who rose to power as communists know the answer. *They themselves, not food or rent or oil, are the subsidized commodity par excellence.*

Economic analysts should realize that the flight from the ruble and the rise of barter arrangements are above all attempts to escape the control of politicians and managers who, working people know, will take a cut for themselves and their friends. How then should an analyst approach former Communist leaders' requests for money to aid in "privatization"? The discipline of economics explains how people who already enjoy property rights and equality under the law go about creating wealth. The eighteenth-century classics are crystal clear: Commerce is possible only among equals.[38] But the problem in the former

---

*The *New York Times* (8 September 1990, p. 1) reported frustrated shoppers in Moscow bread lines crying out "Don't sell bread to him, he's a communist!"

Soviet Union is precisely the presence of lots of people who are determined indefinitely to prolong their unearned inequality. Strictly in economic terms, the most elegant solution would be for all these people magically to disappear or at least to live by useful labor. Yet every "plan" somehow involves their accepting Western subsidies to do one thing or another while others remain their subjects. The merits of such plans ought to be evaluated in terms of the political and economic advantages that they confer to various individuals and groups. That is, they ought to be evaluated politically.

There are innumerable ways of adulterating markets for particular advantage. Anyone driving through the Japanese countryside may notice nets spread over rice paddies—to keep the birds off. This laborious penny-pinching makes sense when one notices the price of rice in Japanese grocery stores: $6 per pound. That in turn is possible because tariffs keep out rice grown in Arkansas, without benefit of bird nets, that sells in U.S. grocery stores for 40 cents a pound. That exclusion means noncompetitive living for some Japanese rice farmers, a pillar of Japan's ruling Liberal Democratic party. One hundred million Japanese pay the difference. But among these are electronics workers and others on whose behalf the Party enforces other price-raising market restrictions. Those who count at the polls periodically prove they do not mind, because they all feel like winners—which they are, although they all also lose something.

The primary question of political–economic intelligence must be "How is free economic activity trammeled, for whose benefit, and what does this do to the regime?"

We do not mean to give the impression that political–economic intelligence must see only shades of gray. The capitalist mentality, however adulterated, sees people—both at home and abroad—as customers to be courted and suppliers to be paid. Japanese rice farmers want American rice growers to be rich enough to buy Japanese cars so that Japanese auto workers will be wealthy enough to pay outrageous prices for Japanese rice without balking. The political implications— both domestic and foreign—are obvious: peace and prosperity. People do get greedy, and the capitalist world is full of the bones of geese who had laid golden eggs. But in command economies (modern communists are but one variant of the species; cf. the twelfth-century Mongols) success consists not of giving customers the greatest satisfaction for the least possible inputs, but rather of maximizing the inputs one may command—i.e., of building a bureaucratic empire.[39] This involves looking at possible sources of labor and materials as enemy units that must somehow be compelled into one's enterprise, and looking at customers as people who can help in this compulsion. This mindset, too, can be adulterated. Stalin himself wrote passionately about the need to tailor rewards to performance.[40] In the American South of the 1850s, some slaveowners even paid cash wages to their slaves.[41] But regimes in which property is a mere function of political power have their own peculiar prehensile propensities in domestic, as in foreign, policy.

It is the job of political–economic intelligence to understand how regimes may thus buttress or undermine themselves. The essence of the matter is as Machiavelli stated it: To prosper, a regime must satisfy its constituents. But if any try to do it with their own supporters' coin, they will end up undermining themselves.[42] The absolute amount of wealth is less significant politically than the extent to which the wealth is distributed *according to the principles of the regime*. The key question that analysts must ask about any economic arrangement is: How consistent is it with the principles of the regime?

Guns and Butter

For some regimes military preparations are a bundle of direct costs and opportunity costs, borne for the same reason that individuals bear taxes and insurance payments. For others, military expenditures seem more like ends than means. Regardless of geography, or of any other basis of comparison, regimes that profess allegiance to Marxism–Leninism or to Islam spend for military purposes at much higher rates than regimes that do not.[43] Some people believe not just that political power grows out of the barrel of a gun, but that economic power does, too. In other words, some regimes do not see a choice between guns and butter because they are accustomed to compelling butter by the gun.

Thus, just as the Soviet economy grew from the 1920s through the mid–1940s by compelling a higher and higher percentage of the population and natural resources of the Soviet Union, and from the late 1940s to the 1960s by compelling the resources of the empire and of a growing population, in the 1970s it grew by virtue of huge transfers of inputs from the West.[44] It is conceivable that the Kama River truck factory, the Togliattigrad auto complex, and the other "turnkey" factories delivered in the 1970s in exchange for signatures at concessionary loan rates would have been forthcoming even if the Soviet military had not been so intimidating. But it was, and détente was a sophisticated attempt to bribe the Soviets not to use their guns.* Likewise, the high military spending of a petty tyranny like Tanzania generated the means by

---

*See Henry Kissinger, *The White House Years*. The sophistication lay in the notion of a "network of interests" in which the Soviet leaders would be enmeshed, and in confidence that time spent in this network would have a Pavlovian pacifying effect. The premise of the "grand bargain" elaborated by Harvard University's Graham Allison and Soviet economist Grigory Yavlinsky before the Soviet government self-destructed in 1991 was that Western governments would pay the Soviet government some $100 billion, in exchange for which the Soviet government would "privatize," become less threatening militarily, and not decompose dangerously. This was still a kind of ransom. After August 1991, it evaporated.

which the rural population was herded into communes, where the socialist ruling class were able not just to experiment with it more easily, but also to milk it more effectively.

Making Guns

Let us turn to how analysts are to regard the other aspect of military economics: how a regime organizes itself to produce military goods. First, what is the relationship between the overall economy and the military economy? The standard, garden-variety error is to assume that governments merely devote a certain percentage of a homogeneous "pie." But military economics is inherently different from civilian economics because of the standardized nature of the product, because the "customer" is highly concentrated, and because every regime has its own peculiar ways of deciding how much it will spend and on what. Thus, the military's slice is of a very different kind from others in the same pie.

How different? We know that the Soviet system gave the military customer choices among the *products* of competing factories and design bureaus, and that the perquisites of working for the military–industrial complex were strong, positive incentives for labor and management to satisfy the customer. In a sense, the Soviet military system was an island of consumer sovereignty in a sea of producer monopolies. By contrast, the American military slice of the pie seems less efficient than the rest of the American economy, possibly because the U.S. military customer chooses the contractor on the basis of *proposals*, and is so involved in developing the product that it deprives itself of choice—an island of producer–consumer identity in a sea of competition. Such generalities, however, should matter less to the analyst than whether any given system, under a specific set of circumstances, could make a certain number of items of a certain quality, and at what price. The analyst must also ask whether the customer will be willing to pay that price. The basis of such specific judgments about any one country must be specific knowledge of the military economic system of that country. We can only give a few examples of what to look for.

Let us begin with a "miracle." German military production rose from a base index level of 98 in 1941 to a peak index level of 322 in July 1944, with an increase in the labor force of only 30 percent, and despite the huge Allied bombing campaign.[44] Why? According to Albert Speer, the man credited with the miracle, his plan (a copy of the one by which Walter Rathenau had organized German war production in World War I) consisted of "division of labor from plant to plant," of "standardization," and of "exchange of technical experiences." In other words, each factory was assigned only one product, and told to turn out maximum quantities indefinitely. Products were planned to be compatible, and companies were encouraged to share trade secrets. The Speer system was predictable in its requirements, rewards, and punishments. It had the least effect on those industries that, like the automobile industry, were already organized to mass-produce single products, and the greatest effect on ones that were not. It reduced vertical integration in German companies, and effectively turned all of German industry into one company with him as Chairman of the Board rather than CEO. As regards personnel, the idea was one often stated but not so often realized: to give everyone an interest in doing his job well by, among other things, giving him the authority to do it. Speer not only doubled the efficiency of production, but also introduced wholly new product lines like radars, rockets, and jets.

The main lesson the analyst must draw from this "miracle" is that the method has been attempted many times in vastly different circumstances, with different results. In fact, it was Rathenau's model, not Karl Marx's (Marx had *no* model for a socialist economy), that inspired the Bolsheviks to believe they could surpass the productive achievements of capitalism by organizing the Soviet economy as they did, as well as lesser imitators. The economic reasons why *"The tractor factory"* at Stalingrad, and similar ventures, failed to turn out cheaper and better products is beyond our scope. Perhaps the Rathenau–Speer system can only be made to work by Germans born in the late nineteenth century.

The military economy that produced the mighty Soviet arsenal of the 1980s was not organized that way at all. The Soviet military economy was centered in the General Staff. The General Staff alloted the Army, the Aerospace Defense Force (PVO), the Strategic Rocket Forces, the Navy, and the Long-Range Aviation a budget for each of their many missions. This budget, however, apparently consisted not of rubles, but rather of quality labor and materials. Then individual "mission consumers" shopped among producers of finished goods, who were eager to get the resources that came with the contracts. But, to get the contracts, factories and design bureaus had to impress the customer with actual product prototypes, and with a reputation for quality production. And, in fact, the Soviet military economy developed numerous pockets of excellence—for example, metallurgy, high energy lasers, superconductive powders, and gallium arsenide photoelectric equipment.[45]

In sum, both the Nazi and the Soviet military economies succeeded differently in getting consumers and producers to play their proper economic roles, despite the political systems in which they worked.

The analyst should note how well any given military–industrial complex deals with certain basic temptations. The first is to spend more on administration and less on hardware, becoming a welfare program for both producers and customers. The second is to become a welfare program for scientists—to spend more on R&D and less on production, stretching out the time over which projects must gestate. The third is to become an extension of the regime's "pork barrel." These temptations are important not only because they are drains on efficiency, but chiefly because they are signs that the system is not well-focused on the mission. In the end, the only reason for assigning an analyst to a foreign military economy is to find out what missions it can support and what missions it can't.

Integrated Analysis

PALESTINIAN TERRORISM IN SYRIA

Every topic with which an intelligence analyst might deal will have political, military, and economic aspects. How might the analyst integrate the disparate principles we have outlined above? Here is one example.

Terrorism is neither mere criminal activity by its perpetrators nor mere acts of war by impersonal soldiers. Above all, terrorism is anything but "senseless violence." Though they often grasp their masters' goals but dimly, terrorists are warriors. But they brand themselves as criminals by striking noncombatants. Far from insensible to matters of this world, they are at the end of logistical and command chains that pay well and provide insurance, coordination, refuge, and (most of all) a sense of purpose. Let us now lay out a framework in which an analyst might fit intelligence about one among many kinds of terrorists: Palestininans. We further narrow our subject by focusing on one among the many countries with which (and against which) Palestinian terrorists operate: Syria.

Who Is Involved?

The recruits to Palestinian terrorism, the men who pull the triggers, are poor devils, children of squalor for whom association with the terrorist enterprise is a huge step up in physical comfort, economic prospects, social standing, and the intellectual level on which they live their lives. Given all that, it is not surprising that, almost to a man, captured Palestinian terrorists declare that ideology is their primary motivation.[47] But for them ideology is not primarily a set of abstract beliefs. Rather, it is the consciousness of having joined a church whose tenets they grasp hazily but hold tenaciously.

The senior officers are of a different sort. Middle-class in origin, they spent their formative years in universities or young officers' clubs. They have the intellectual patina of the coffeehouse, and the junior executive's drive to please powerful patrons. In matters of ideology they display a ready versatility of conviction worthy of college presidents. Thus Abu Nidal and Ahmed Jibril, once avid proponents of Maoism, after 1979 became avid proponents of the Koran. Yassir Arafat has been a Communist in Moscow, a strict Koran man in Teheran, a progressive secular pan-Arabist in Baghdad, and of course a liberal in the presence of Americans. Everywhere, however, he is a pederast (which seems to bother none of his interlocutors).[48] Pan-Arabism did not prevent the vast majority of Palestinian terrorist leaders from aligning themselves with Persian Iran against Arab Iraq during most of the 1980s, nor did this prevent them from supporting Iraq in 1990–91. Nor does any ideology push them to, or prevent them from, endless murderous intrigue against one another. Rather, they are pushed hither and yon, as pawns, by the leaders of Arab states.

For the likes of Syria's Hafez Assad, Palestinian terrorism is just one more tool for manipulating external and internal powers. All the leaders of the Arab states in the vicinity of Palestine belong to minorities of their populations and lack both legitimacy and the military or economic power to strike their enemies. Assad is archetypical. He is a member of the Alewite sect, who make up 10 percent of Syria's population and *all* of his regime, and who are despised as "worse than the Jews" by Sunni and Shia Muslims alike. Syria has only 11 million people, and is surrounded by much-more-numerous and none-too-friendly Sunni Muslim nations—Turkey, Iraq, and Jordan (backed alternatively by Egypt, by Iraq, and then by Egypt, and implicitly by Israel as well). So for Assad, hostility to Israel is far more than a personal predilection. It is a means of justifying his own rule by being more Muslim than the Muslims, more Arab than the Arabs. It is also a means of mastering and using for his own ends thousands of Palestinians whom he otherwise would have to integrate within his country or that others might use against him. Moreover, by using Palestinians to strike Israel (and Arab enemies as well), Assad could hope to escape their direct retaliation. The threat of indirect violence earns him respect that would not otherwise be his. Finally, by turning his Palestinians loose against America and the Western powers, he makes these enemies treat him as a major player, much reducing their capacity to act in the Mid-East. He also earned the massive military support of the Soviet Union until it collapsed. We do not contend that these are the only foundations of his regime. But if Israel and the "Palestinian problem" were not there, Assad would have every incentive to invent them. More to the point, he has every incentive to keep using them, but without provoking a conflagration that might consume him.

What Do They Want?

In sum, the soldiers want a job, a bit of recognition for their work, and the thrill of "victories." The officers want to solidify their political support by making the kinds of deals that will give them control of bigger armies, which they then hope to parlay into power over a ministate. From 1971 to 1982 they had one in Lebanon. In the future they hope to have one on the West bank of the Jordan. The political masters want to continue the game, conscious that, as Mussolini said, "He who stops is lost." And in fact the evidence shows that the rhythm of Palestinian terrorism is set neither by the yearnings of the trigger-pullers nor by the machinations of the Abu Nidals or Arafats, but rather by the calculations of the Assads, Qaddafis, and Saddam Husseins.

Consider the coincidences between the occurrence of terrorist acts, and Hafez Assad's interest in the maintenance of Arab–Israeli strife in general as well as in combating Palestinians (e.g. Yasser Arafat) whom he does not control.[49] In 1981, Austria's Bruno Kreisky attempted a mediation between Arafat and Israel. In August of that year a synagogue in Vienna was shot up; two people were killed and 18 wounded. In December of that year the same sort of thing happened at Vienna's airport—three dead and 47 wounded. In 1982, Italy's Bettino Craxi took the lead: In October a Rome synagogue was shot up—one dead, 36 wounded. In 1985, reports of Craxi's efforts on Arafat's behalf were accompanied by a machine gun–grenade attack on Rome airport—16 dead, 75 wounded. The high points of the United States' activities on behalf of a Mid-East settlement were 1983 (the year of the attempt to build a Lebanon that could negotiate with Israel), 1985 (the year of President Reagan's plan for a comprehensive settlement in the area), and 1988 (the year that the U.S. began to negotiate directly with the PLO). In 1983, some 270 U.S. Marines were killed in Lebanon, and the U.S. Embassy there was destroyed. In 1985–86 a TWA jet was hijacked in Athens, the passengers and crew were mistreated for a week, and one American was killed. Then a bomb blew up a night club outside the U.S. Air Force base near Torrejon, Spain—16 dead. In December 1988, Pan Am flight 103 was blown up over Lockerbie, Scotland.*

The same reasoning seemed to underlie terrorist attacks against Arabs. The hijacking of Kuwait Airways flight 422 in Bangkok was a last-ditch attempt to break the will of the Kuwaiti regime to bankroll Iraq. Why? Syria wanted Iraq to lose the war because Saddam Hussein was Assad's competitor. And indeed, no sooner did the war end than Iraq began to lavishly supply the only people in the world who were willing to take on Assad, namely the forces of Lebanese

---

*In 1990 the U.S. government set aside massive evidence that implicated Ahmed Jibril's Syrian based PFLP, and pursued a more slender path that, on Nov. 14, 1991, led to the indictment of the government of Libya. The case against Jibril rested on the capture in Germany of one of his bomb-makers, along with an identical copy of the Toshiba cassette player bomb that destroyed PA103, and an altimeter-fuze set for 31,000 feet, the altitude at which PA103 blew up. The "Libyan" path rests on a fragment of an electronic chip found in a shirt that have been in the suitcase that held the bomb. Libya had bought a supply of timers containing that chip. But the chip is a standard component of many modern devices. As Robert H. Kupperman argued in The New York Times, 16 Nov. 1991, it is difficult to avoid the conclusion that the U.S. government set out to exonerate Syria when it sought to make Syria play the role in the Arab world that the U.S. had set for Iraq until its invasion of Kuwait in 1990.

Christian Gen. Michel Aoun. And by 1989 Aoun was indeed building up to a major campaign to drive Syria out of Lebanon. But Assad funneled arms and money to Aoun's Christian rival, Samir Geaga. This was neither more nor less than Assad had done in 1983 and 1986 when he fueled the Intra-Palestinian "camp war" which saw his Palestinian henchman rout those loyal to Arafat out of refugee camps in northern and central Lebanon, respectively.

Sometimes the terror is more subtle: In February 1990 a Palestinian radio in Syria took credit for the murder of a dozen Israeli tourists on a bus in Egypt. Syria's war on Arafat had given Egypt primary influence over the PLO, to the point that Egypt was almost negotiating with Israel on the PLO's behalf. Syria, for a variety of reasons (including the growing power of Iraq), wanted better relations with Egypt. Nevertheless, this act of terror served two purposes: It cooled relations between Egypt and Israel, and let Egypt know emphatically (but without harming Egyptians) that no Palestinian deal with Israel could take place without Syria's leave.

These were not the only Palestinian terrorist acts of the 1980s, and Assad was far from being the only sponsor. But these acts, all of which originated in Damascus or in Syrian-controlled territory, show something about what one of the major figures in the area wanted, and how he went about getting it.

But then note the change that took place at the end of 1989 and into 1990: no major act of terrorism by the forces of Abu Nidal, Abu Abbas, Abu Mussa, Ahmed Jibril, or Fadlallah. Indeed, it was easy to hear talk in Damascus that these dastardly people might not be welcome in Syria anymore, or in Syrian-controlled Lebanon. Assad met with Egypt's President Mubarak, and indeed with Arafat, with pomp and circumstance, and spoke publicly of reconciliation with Iraq's Saddam Hussein. To the West, and especially to the French and Americans, he offered his good offices in the release of hostages held in Syrian-controlled territory in Lebanon; and by 1990 Damascus was the scene of one dramatic release after another. The Syrian government seemed to be saying loudly: Palestinian terrorism? Here? Perish the thought!

What was happening?

Assets and Liabilities?

The terrorists were bumped from center stage by a Syrian government whose balance of assets and liabilities had itself changed drastically due to events beyond its control. Syria is among the best-armed nations on earth. With some 3,000 tanks for 11 million people it has 10 times as many *per capita* as the United States, and 1.5 times as many per capita as the Soviet Union, its air defense system is second only to that of the Soviet Union; and its air force includes state-of-the-art Soviet fighters.[50] Yet it would be useless to detail Syria's Order of Battle because it is overshadowed by one fact: Each of Syria's neighbors—

Turkey, Iraq, Israel, and even Jordan (if allied with Egypt)—could crush it. So, with the exception of prostrate Lebanon, Syria does not start wars. Its military, far from being a sword, is not even much of a shield. Indeed, Syria has always been scrupulously careful that no terrorist act against Israel proper be launched directly from its territory. But in 1990 another, even more dire, threat loomed: Iraq. Saddam Hussein had won his war against Iran, and saw in Assad the only Arab leader who had sided against him, and the only rival for military supremacy in the Arab world. Assad trembled.

Not only is Syria weak. It is poor. It has no significant oil reserves. Its population, while reasonably skilled and industrious, is hampered by a feudal economic system. Those few Syrians who can, keep their money outside the country. Subsistence is the norm, and severe privation is not exceptional. What *is* Syria's sword? Its shield? Where is its source of wealth? Where the money has come from is clear: Saudi Arabia—and, since 1981 (though to a lesser extent), Iran. The Iranians paid Syria for services rendered in the war against Iraq, and for a share of the action in Lebanon. But why has Saudi Arabia paid? Because Syria has been the principal "front-line state" against Israel—and has proved it by sponsoring the showiest of all anti-Israeli acts. Also, it is the Saudi royal family's policy to pay protection money to those who have demonstrated a capacity for assassination. Yet, by 1990 the Iranian connection had become a big liability for Syria, and Saudi Arabia was worrying more about Iraq than about Israel.

So Abu Nidal, Ahmed Jibril, et al., have been among the Syrian regime's principal sources of treasure, as well as its sword. But what about the shield? What has kept Israelis, or Americans, or Iraqis from crushing an Assad regime that, while bristly on the outside, is actually quite vulnerable? The answer is that for a generation Syria was under the Soviet Union's wing. After the 1982 Lebanese War, when Israel mauled the Syrian Air Force, wrecked its air defense system, and nearly forced Syria out of Lebanon, the Soviet Union helped to stop Israel in the name of "world peace," and stationed so many Soviet advisers in Syria, especially to run the air defense system, that a war against Syria might have been tantamount to a war against the Soviet Union itself. Behind this shield the Syrian regime could continue to collect money to finance the terror by which it manipulated friends and enemies alike, and which helped it collect money. All the Syrian regime had to do was to prevent the resolution of the Arab–Israeli conflict, and make sure that *its* Palestinians were the most terrifying of all, for the game to go on *ad infinitum*.

But then came the great Soviet crash of 1989–91. And, without the security of the Soviet shield, terrorism ceased to be a viable *offensive* weapon for Assad. Indeed, the worth of the 10,000-odd, Syrian-controlled irregulars in Lebanon, and the 200-odd trained hit men in the Syrian-controlled terrorist groups, barely outweighed the trouble they might bring on Assad's head. The terrorists in the Syrian camp do not themselves *have* assets and liabilities worth counting. Rather, they themselves *are* nothing but entries on the regime's balance sheet. If and when they showed up as net liabilities, they would die more quickly than did the regime's liabilities in Hama in February 1982. Meanwhile, in January 1990, as their value to the regime sank, they began a gradual exodus to Iraq—getting out while the getting was good. By 1991, Syria was so heavily engaged against Iraq that it fairly huddled under the protection of the United States, and even of Israel. Assad had sheathed his terrorist sword. After Saddam survived the Gulf War of 1991 Assad lived in the knowledge that his American protectors had every opportunity to use his sponsorship of terrorism as an excuse to throw him to any wolves of their choosing.

Threats and Opportunities

In the 1970s and 1980s, as terrorists entered Western Europe through Eastern Europe, after training in the Soviet Crimea or in Czechoslovakia, and especially after Pope John Paul II was shot by a Turkish professional hit man who had spent much time in (and received money and arms from) Bulgaria, the world's intelligence analysts debated about the extent of the Soviet Union's patronage of terrorism. By 1990 events had resolved the debate: With the fall of Eastern European communist regimes, those countries instantly and completely ceased to be involved with terrorism. The case of Syria is not entirely different. True, Assad sponsored terrorism for his own reasons. But once he became conscious of being without Soviet backing, and once Iraq emerged as a mortal threat, his calculations with regard to terrorism changed.

By 1991 Assad's calculations depended on what the United States, Israel, European countries, Egypt, and others chose to do. On one extreme, the U.S., Israel, Egypt, and allies might demand that Assad hang a large list of terrorists (including some regulars of his own army and secret police), and withdraw from Lebanon. If he did not, he would be left to the mercy of Saddam Hussein. Nor would it be difficult to make him the target of any number of Palestinian factions. Assad has no scruples that would prevent his complying. A midrange policy might involve demands and pressures on Assad to extradite, or imprison, or disarm and disband, or exile any number of terrorists. But the U.S. government chose the other extreme. Ever eager for Arab allies, the U.S. government made what a White House source called a "no-deal deal" with Assad. The U.S. government fully acquiesced in his annexation of Lebanon. As regards terrorism, it exonerated Assad as it had once exonerated Saddam Hussein. Secretary James Baker even supplied Syrian officials with evidence of Syrian-based terrorists' plans to strike the U.S. Ambassador to Jordan—and soon heard that Syria had passed the information to the terrorists. Since the U.S. government did not take this as a reason for ceasing its support of Assad, it was reasonable to expect that Assad would resume anti-Western terrorism to the extent that the "traffic" would bear it. As one might have expected, the opening of a U.S.-sponsored Mid-East peace conference in October 1991 was accompanied by a rise in terrorist activity, including a rare attack on Israel from across the Syrian border. Since Assad gained much and lost nothing from the incident, there was every reason to believe that although the rules of the game had changed a bit, Assad was back in it.

CONCLUSION

If one analyzes intelligence as we have suggested here, one will not always be right. But one will always be "in the ball park"—providing of course that one wishes to be.

One illustration will suffice. At a meeting of experts on China, a Taiwanese admiral noted that the chief of the Guangdong military district, the son of the legendary Marshal Chen Ye, had become so powerful and independent-minded that the central government's writ in Guangdong ran no farther than he wanted it to. Other Taiwanese thought that sooner or later there would be fighting among armed factions on the mainland. An American asked the Deputy Assistant Secretary of Defense for International Security Policy (East Asia), who had previously served as the CIA's chief analyst for East Asia, whether the U.S. ought to prepare, at least intellectually, for the choices it would have to make in case any of the parties to such strife asked for America's help. The official acknowledged that the question was interesting, but closed "I'm not about to order a study of the subject." Why not? For whatever reason, his mind was not pleased to dwell on that possibility. By contrast, the Taiwanese relished such thoughts.

"Where your treasure is, there will your heart be also," taught Christ. Wherever the analysts' and policy-makers' collective values are, there will they also focus their minds.

13

Intelligence, Talent, and Lessons

A prudent man should always enter the paths taken by great men
and imitate those who have been most excellent, so that if one's
own skill does not match theirs, at least it will have the odor of it;
and he should proceed like those prudent archers who, aware of
the strength of their bow when the target they are aiming at seems
too distant, set their sights much higher, not in order to reach such
a height but rather in order to strike their target.
                                                – *Machiavelli*, The Prince

We invest in the chef, not in the restaurant.
                                                – *Richard Larry*

To do intelligence well, a government
does not have to seed the world with resident spies of every stripe, to spend
significant portions of its GNP on technical devices, to hire Julius Caesars as
analysts, to create a corps of counterintelligence specialists with Aristotelian
minds, and to find covert actioneers like T. E. Lawrence. But to be serious about
intelligence any government has to understand the basic lessons taught by

exemplary successes and failures, and it has to make a reasonable effort to apply them, with its limited means, to the situation in which it finds itself. And it has to hire the right kinds of people.

If we have made anything clear thus far, it is that intelligence is a people-intensive business. Good performance depends on certain human talents. Collectors have the access they have—and build the machines they build—because they are who they are. Counterintelligence people are roused by some events and not others because they are who they are. Some covert-action officers can move a particular mountain with seeming ease, but can't budge a nearby molehill, because they are who they are. Analysts, like other human beings, have a tendency to notice the things they understand and that their lives have taught them to value, while neglecting or misinterpreting others.

Is the intelligence business different from other human enterprises in its dependence on the proper personnel? We contend that it is, in that it requires an unusually wide variety of talents, that many of these talents are rare, and that most are not of the sort that can be taught—especially by governments. Thus, building an effective intelligence service comes down to figuring out what sorts of people are best fit for which tasks, finding them, and giving them the proper incentives to perform the tasks to which they have been assigned. Conversely, the worst way to build an intelligence service is to set a bureaucracy on its rails and let it roll on, perpetuating itself. The need for intelligence to be open to talent rather than driven by bureaucratic priorities is especially relevant to countries like the United States, which have established, large, well-connected intelligence bureaucracies that tend to see no difference between what is good for business and what benefits their senior officers.

Our task here is to identify the kinds of talent that each major category of intelligence task requires, and to indicate where such talent might be found. Let us look at the many different kinds of talents required for collection, covert action, counterintelligence, and analysis. Then let us sum up what it means for a government to take intelligence seriously.

Collection

Collectors should be as diverse as their sources and subjects. One can imagine an intelligence official asking his secretary "Have we got a one-armed female Chinese physician around age 50 with a Cantonese accent and good knowledge of economics?" The knowledge of economics would be needed to help elicit the subject matter that the intelligence service is after, while the personal characteristics would be needed for access to a kind-hearted, ailing Cantonese official. One might imagine another official who has asked his assistant to "Get me somebody I can send to get to the bottom of the violence between Zulu and Xhosa workers in [the black townships of South Africa's] Natal province" and sees an innocent-looking young white man walk into his office. The official might upbraid his assistant: "Whatever made you think that this guy could get anywhere near those people and come out alive, much less with information? Get me somebody a lot darker and a lot meaner!" There is no end to the specificity of the characteristics that might favor access and understanding.

Picking a cast to match diverse sources is the least creative part of a collection manager's job. That job, as we have seen, is to engineer access. He must position and cover the cast, manage it, and help guide every part of it to its target. That requires imagination.

Only imagination limits the pretexts that people can use to get next to others. What kind of mind would choose a German auto-mechanic's shop in Colombia as a cover base for collection on drug traffickers? The kind who would put Perrier and granola bars into vending machines in college faculty clubs and schoolteachers' lounges. Who would think of using an elevator-repair business as a long-term cover for bugging in Vienna? The sort of mind that might have invested money in biotechnology stocks in the late 1970s. To manage the widespread networks of "stringers"—to keep them interested and to judge the usefulness of their skills and contributions—requires the motivational talents (and the ice-cold judgments) of a major-league baseball manager who watches talent develop long before he can recruit it, and who then evolves different relationships with players, activates them when necessary, and phases them out as the team's needs change. But surely the greatest creativity is required to design individual operations that place his people—covered and located as they are, with the talents and shortcomings they actually have—in contact with particular sources. The possible stratagems, the seemingly fortuitous coincidences, the support arrangements, have to be made up on the spot. For this one needs the sort of fellow who, when working on a car, does not ask "which tools does the job require?" but "What have I got?" It requires the engineer rather than the scientist; or better, the kid who grew up making radio sets out of junk parts.

The manager of technical collection systems must be a gadgeteer with street smarts—the sort who does not get carried away making gadgets better and better, but who has an idea a minute about new uses to which he can put the pieces he has. In business this mentality would lead not to refining products to a fare-thee-well but to developing new product lines. He would be the sort of entrepreneur who constantly worried about leapfrogging and being leapfrogged by his competitors. But, like old-fashioned businessmen who would relate all their activities to the nature of the market for their products, be that the market for cars or ladies' clothing, he ought to have a fixation on the primary end-use of his product. The end product of intelligence is success in war.

A government must weave its collection nets well ahead of need: Identify the kinds of people and the kinds of physical phenomena about which it wants to know, and then, within its means, build the human and technical structures that will maximize access to the targets. A good collection system must be both diverse and flexible in order to accommodate constantly changing human and physical intelligence targets.

As Germany's World War I intelligence chief, Colonel Nicolai, used to say, "The function of gathering information is inherently aristocratic"[1]—that is, it is something best performed by a few good people. This means that the best way of organizing intelligence collection is for a small core of permanent collectors, who know what they want, to engage part-time collectors in various walks of life to cover particular beats with their peculiar, uncommon talents and access. As needs for information become urgent, existing networks can be activated. As new needs loom beyond the horizon, new ones can be built. Decisions regarding intelligence-collection machines commit money and years of development. The results are by nature rigid. There is every temptation in the world to simply improve current machines. Yet, since the worth of the machines derives from their relationship to the things they must observe (and these change), the very definition of a good decision in this field is one detached from current commitments that makes explicit bets on the future. In sum, collection must be driven by, in the words of early CIA officer Archibald B. Roosevelt, "a lust of knowing."[2] And it must be steered by the practical distinction between useful knowledge and voyeurism.

Today, as always, collection is the part of intelligence that deploys the most people and money. It is also the field that requires the most expertise specific to intelligence. Because it is the part that must be changed most often to match changing circumstances, it most requires creative judgment. Yet, whatever the insufficiencies of collection, few of history's catastrophes have occurred primarily as a result of lack of evidence. After all is said and done, secrets seem to get out, if only because the amount of evidence about any enterprise seems to be roughly proportional to the scale of the enterprise.

Covert Action

Those who are sent out to move people must be able to blend in. Not necessarily to the point of being inconspicuous, but to the extent of not clashing with their hosts. Physical diversity is less important for the talent pool of covert actioneers than it is for the talent pool of collectors, while genuine sympathy for the people with whom they work is essential. Like the collector, the covert-action specialist must be inventive. But this inventiveness must be less oriented to quietly getting around obstacles, less to subtlety, and more to rallying human forces. Thus, while the collector wends his way to the target, surrounds it as a chess player stalks his quarry, the covert-action man must be of the sort who can't sit still, who can't wait to actually fight, to organize. That requires a committed imagination.

Covert action is not for 9-to-5 employees, or for people who are comfortable playing by any set of rules. It is for competitive people who tend to draw lines between "our side" and "theirs," who develop strong, genuine loyalties, and who hurt inside when "our team" suffers any reverses. Such team players can be found in athletics, business, the law, and (certainly) labor unions and politics. Few if any people, however, can muster what is akin to love for, and intimate involvement with, just any cause, or for many causes in rapid succession. One may even doubt the integrity of a hypothetical full-time, all-purpose operative ready to marry any cause, with or against any kind of people. Hence it probably makes more sense for those who manage covert action, as it does for those who manage human collection, to maintain a diverse "stable" of people with peculiar affinities, affections, access, and skills who may be called upon in particular circumstances. It is probably much easier and more effective to teach the tradecraft of covert action to individuals who already have everything else required to operate successfully in a given country for a given cause, than to take someone who possesses only knowledge of covert action (if indeed there is such a thing apart from involvement with particular causes) and try to endow him with affinities, affections, access, and skills that he does not have.

Anyone connected with covert action, however, must live by the maxim "There is more than one way to skin a cat." He will constantly run into avenues that are blocked, people who for one reason or another will not play the roles that his plan called on them to play. So he will have to modify his plan constantly, and adjust the other players' courses in midstream while not losing sight of the objective. Hence the covert-action specialist must be like someone who starts businesses on a shoestring, or like the very creative accountants who organize "workouts" or "reorganizations" of businesses on either side of the edge of bankruptcy. Such people keep one eye fixed on the bottom line (profit and loss) while the other eye juggles assets and liabilities, and figures out ways of bringing new people, new procedures, new products, to bear on the problem. All in all, feverish people are needed for feverish work.

Competence in covert action is totally dependent on competent policy-making. We have shown that success or failure in covert action is seldom due to technical factors. The exception that proves the rule is the failure to perform adequate counterintelligence checks on the people with whom one is working. But that is seldom the failure of an honest effort. Normally it is a conscious decision to dispense with any obstacle to the enterprise. In other words, some covert enterprises are so ill-conceived that they could not proceed if they were properly thought through. Alas, unwillingness to think through what one must do to succeed is one of the principal reasons why governments sometimes engage in covert activity. Not willing to decide whether to do something wholeheartedly or not, they compromise and do it both halfheartedly and secretly. A competent covert activity—except in accidental cases—is an adjunct to overt government policy, rather than a substitute for it.

Covert politics and covert military activities, like overt ones, depend on convincing friends that they are going to win and persuading enemies that they are going to lose. But since both friends and enemies look beyond the boundaries of covert activities for signs of which way the wind is blowing, it is imperative for governments that run covert actions to commit the necessary resources and energy to make them succeed. Covert action is neither magic nor dirty tricks. It succeeds when the military, political, and economic fundamentals are done well, and fails when they are not.

Counterintelligence

CI specialists must have ice water in their veins. Diversity is essentially unimportant for their job. It would be best if the breadth of knowledge required for good CI work could be concentrated in a single mind. Since that cannot be, it should be concentrated in as few minds as might be practical. These broadly informed minds must be rigorous in their procedure, and so disciplined as to be able to accept some explanations for data without being wedded to them, rejecting others without despising them, and ready to reverse their own judgments when new evidence requires it. In short, CI people should be a very bright, dispassionate, monkish lot.

While collectors and covert actioneers must be acquainted with specific people and places for years, CI specialists must be familiar with broad subject areas for decades. In the CI business there is no substitute for long memories. Hence there is every reason why CI people should be bureaucrats. But they must be very special bureaucrats. Whereas the essence of bureaucratic culture is self-justification, the business of CI is the constant questioning of everyone's premises, including its own. What kinds of people develop that kind of intellectual honesty? The "scientific method" of inquiry is a fine abstract guide. Scholars are supposed to be taught to follow trails of evidence even unto unpleasant conclusions, but few ever write on the theme "My work of the past two years was a big mistake." More appropriate may be religious training in the examination of one's conscience for the purpose of identifying and rooting out one's faults, or the practices of financial auditors who specialize in spotting the false asset, the papered-over liability.

The history of counterintelligence—the art of knowing and managing how one is being observed, and of knowing how one knows—shows that information makes a difference in conflict *insofar as it is unequal*. How much information either side in a conflict might have collected matters far less than the disparities in understanding that may exist. Whether at the level of a particular weapons system and its countermeasures, or that of an empire, to know the other side well is worthwhile primarily to the extent that one has shaped the other side's view of one's own condition and plans. How much better off the Germans defending the "Atlantic wall" in 1944 would have been if they had been unable to collect the reconnaissance photographs and the signals by which British counterintelligence deceived them about the time and place of the Allied invasion. All the rest of the true knowledge that German intelligence collected weighed far less in the balance than did those germs of deception. Our point is that while shortcomings in collection, or known losses of secrets, may be more or less important, anything that allows a hostile service to inject the germ of deception, or that makes surprise possible, is potentially devastating. Better a little secure knowledge than floods of data that might be contaminated.

So the great lesson again is, in the words of Sun Tzu, to treat counterintelligence with generosity, to give it the benefit of the doubt. Counterintelligence only begins with security. Its essence is to avoid surprise and deception by hypothesizing what the other side knows, and testing the hypotheses. It is also to manage one's own exposure to foreign intelligence so as to foster certain conclusions and discourage others. This sort of analysis requires methodical doubt about one's own security, about the competence of one's own intelligence operations, an ability to hypothesize the enemy's hand at any point, and a willingness to abandon one's most cherished hypotheses if they don't check out. Whereas collection demands creativity, counterintelligence demands cold intellectual rigor—a willingness to follow trails of evidence, wherever they may lead. Whereas collection demands lots of money, counterintelligence demands the commitment of something even more precious: the willingness to see one's self, one's friends, and one's works as hostile intelligence might see them, and the willingness to explore one's own weaknesses.

Counterintelligence is the natural guardian of the integrity of intelligence, and the great weapon against hostile intelligence. But who guards the guardians, and to what ends does the sword strike? Since counterintelligence is a means to ends set by statesmen, there can be no purely counterintelligence criteria for judging whether an intelligence operation that produced a particular item of information is secure enough, or at what point our own key secrets are well-enough guarded. Statesmen and military commanders will believe whom they will believe, and bear the risks they think worthwhile. CI can only maintain its own standards and make its reports. By the same token, CI can deceive hostile intelligence only to help clear the path for well-defined plans and policies— insofar as statesmen have them. To push foreign minds hither or yon makes sense only to the extent that it makes sense for blockers in the game of football to push defenders to one side or another: In both cases one must coordinate the blocking with the moves of the ball-carrier.

Finally, since CI's primary function in intelligence is akin to quality control, and quality control is as inherently unpopular in any organization as it is necessary, one must make provisions to keep counterintelligence officers independent and eager to perform their magisterial function. But a vigorous CI must be counterbalanced by high-intelligence officials, military commanders, and policy-makers who, while respecting the importance of methodical doubt, are able to put counterintelligence into the perspective of action.

Analysis

The analyst in any given field must be an expert in that field and in his own country's policy with regard to it. The diversity among analysts must be intellectual and occupational. Thus good intelligence analysts should be as easy — and as difficult — to find as good policy-makers. As we have seen, the two minds are two sides of the same purposeful coin.

Facts in any field, as we have also seen, have meaning only to those who know the field and want to do something in it. Policy-makers clearly have to balance cool objectivity about the outside world with the driving ambition to shape events. Analysts must be the kind of people who share that ambition intellectually but who factor it into their dispassionate assessment of the outside world. Being one step removed from the outcome of policy, they have both a greater opportunity and a greater responsibility to balance involvement with detachment.

So the analyst must be a very special person, one whose expertise comes from a background of practical, responsible involvement but who is comfortable being without personal responsibility for the outcome of events, and who has a penchant for reflection on his subject. To find such an ideal subordinate one should look among successful leaders who enjoyed thinking about their field as much as they enjoyed acting in it. Publications in the professional literature might be adequate evidence of reflectiveness. Then one should offer them the chance to be an analytical subordinate at a higher level, with the understanding that if he does well he would have the chance to return to the field whence he came, in an operational capacity, with a generous promotion.

The job of intelligence analysts is to make data shed as much light as possible on subjects of interest. Hence the art of analysis largely boils down to two imperatives: Understand the context, and understand one's own plans and purposes within it. If the analyst can do both, he will surely organize the data correctly. In that case, whether the subject be the capacity of an individual weapon, the plans of an army, or the staying power of a dictator, the analyst's mistakes in fitting the latest report into the picture are unlikely to lead him, or those who listen to him, utterly astray. No human being can predict the future. But a good analyst can uncover in the present the qualities of his subject that must surely shape the future.

There is no such thing as expertise in intelligence analysis distinct from expertise in the subject being analyzed. Substantive expertise consists of knowing the right questions to ask about a particular problem, as well as having a great reservoir of answers from analogous historical situations. In politics, the point of departure is knowledge of who the players are, what they want, and what they are up against. It is a difficult point to reach, but once an analyst understands the characters involved, their priorities, he will be as a spectator to a drama the gist of which he already understands. Accidents or *dei ex machina* may decide the struggle without warning. The personages may mistakenly act against their own interest. But rarely will they step out of character, and never can they change the stage setting.

In military affairs the point of departure, the Order of Battle, is easy enough for the analyst to reach. But that is where the real challenge begins. "War," said Sparta's King Archidamus, "is carried on in the dark." Analysts of weapons systems can sketch out the limited number of ways in which this or that measure and countermeasure could interact. But battles are decided by the unpredictable interplay of innumerable weapons wielded by men of uncertain motivation, and wars end when people on one side decide that their objectives, their regime, are not worth any more of *this*. So military analysts, even more than political analysts, can only set scenes and write likely scripts. The greatest service they can perform is to underline their assumptions.

Economics depend on variable human motivation even more than do politics or military affairs. That is why it will not do for analysts to build models that forecast future output by "crunching" numbers concerning past performance and present inputs. Economic rewards are the most obvious of these motives. In free economies these flow from the capacity of organizations to win the preference of customers. In command economies rewards flow from control of the means of compulsion. But economic man is not driven primarily by rational calculations of economic rewards. If he were, it would be impossible to explain the conscious, long-term, counterproductive economic behavior of peoples— like the Argentines—who are perfectly free to behave otherwise. Surely the causes of the most dramatic economic events in the world (e.g., the doubling of the U.S. GNP in World War II) and the decline of Russia into hunger are not economic. And indeed economic intelligence is properly focused on how economic goods affect political balances of power and military capacities. Economic goods are never shared equally, are never used with equal efficiency. They are quintessentially discretionary means. The point of economic intelligence analysis is to determine in any given circumstances whose ends they serve.

Good intelligence analysis views foreign political, military, and economic realities as threats or opportunities. But it can do this only in relation to the priorities and plans of one's own government—what they are or what they might be. Even as a meteorologist, when asked whether good weather is coming, must ask "Good for what?" the intelligence analyst can do meaningful work only for a government that knows what it is doing.

Talent Seeks Talent

Since the talents required to staff an intelligence service are many, varied, and relatively rare, intelligence services are likely to be badly staffed unless special efforts are made to "do it right." Intelligence is naturally subordinate to the active parts of statecraft. Since subordinates tend to reflect their superiors, it is entirely to be expected that intelligence officers will reflect the chief executives, the generals, and the ambassadors who hire them. Some statesmen are willing to leave their eyes and ears—and part of their cognitive function—to a bureaucracy, as if it were a "black box." They have no basis for questioning its product. In effect they abdicate part of their responsibilities. Others work to make sure that intelligence people reflect only their own views. This is mirror-imaging with a vengeance. Only statesmen who value the burdens and opportunities of dealing with the world *as it is* would go to the trouble of finding and managing the complex of talents we have described.

Our theme about intelligence as a whole has been that it is an integral part of statecraft. According to the old saying, intelligence is "the eyes and ears of the King." But *only* the eyes and ears—not the heart, the mind, the arms, the legs. A defective set of eyes and ears may indirectly harm the other parts, but even the most acute vision and hearing cannot compensate for an unsound body. In the long run, governments get the intelligence they deserve.

449

Notes

PREFACE

1. "Comparative Historical Experience of Doctrine and Organization," in Godson, ed., *Intelligence Requirements for the 1980s, vol. 2, Analysis and Estimates.* "Covert Action and Foreign Policy," in Godson, ed., *Covert Action.* "Wartime Collection," in Godson, ed., *Collection.* "What Is Domestic Security?" in Godson, ed., *Intelligence Requirements for the 1980s, vol. , Domestic Intelligence.* "Covert Action as an Instrument of Policy," in Godson, ed., *Intelligence Requirements for the 1980s, vol. 7, Intelligence and Policy.* "Reforms and Proposals for Reform," in Godson, ed., *Intelligence Requirements for the 1980s, vol. 1, Elements of Intelligence.* "Space Intelligence and Deception," in Dailey and Parker, eds., *Soviet Strategic Deception.*

CHAPTER 1: NATURE AND IMPORTANCE OF INTELLIGENCE

1. Plutarch, *Lives*, Fabius, pp. 212–230.
2. *Protivovozdushnaya Oborona.* See *Slovar Osnovnykh Voennykh Terminov.*
3. U.S. House of Representatives, Select Committee to Study U.S. Intelligence Operations (Washington, DC: USGPO, 1975), p. 147.
4. Thucydides, *The Peloponnesian War*, see Pericles' funeral oration.
5. Conquest, *Inside Stalin's Secret Police.*
6. Bill, ed., *The Eagle and the Lion.* Note the more effusive praise by Richard Falk (*New York Times*, February 16, 1979, p. 27, op-ed), and the statements by President Jimmy Carter to the press on Jan. 18, 1979 that he expected U.S.–Iranian relations to remain friendly.
7. Douglas E. Streusand, "Post-Mortems of the Iranian Revolution," *Strategic Review*, vol. 16, no. 3 (Washington, DC: United States Strategic Institute, 1988), pp. 70–72.

8. Voslensky, *The Nomenklatura*.

9. Starr, *Political Intelligence in Classical Greece*.

10. MacArthur, *Reminiscences*, p. 374.

11. Orlov, *Manual of Intelligence and Guerilla Warfare*, pp. 155–187. Orlov was a senior Soviet intelligence officer who defected in Spain in the 1937. This book is a recreation of a high-level intelligence course he had taught in Moscow before defecting.

12. Bakeless, *Turncoats, Traitors and Heroes*, pp. 74–75.

13. Bakeless, op. cit., p. 187.

14. David Kahn, "Spies Learn Little We Need to Know," *Newsday*, July 26, 1985, p. 87.

15. Daniel Raviv and Yossi Melman, *Every Spy a Prince*, pp. 182 and 215.

16. *New York Times*, February 28, 1984.

17. Lewin, *Ultra*, passim.

18. Steven Fielding Diamond, *Class and Power in Revolutionary Nicaragua* (Ph.D. Dissertation, Univ. of London, December, 1990).

19. Weinberg, pp. 21–22.

20. Hinsley, *British Intelligence in the Second World War*, pp. 62–120.

21. Ibid.

22. Amrom Katz, "Verification and SALT: The State of the Art and the Art of the State" (Washington, DC: Heritage Foundation, 1979).

23. Morgan, *Assize of Arms*.

24. Ledeen and Lewis, *Debacle*.

25. Leon Sloss, "Impact of Deception on U.S. Nuclear Strategy," in Parker and Daily, p. 442; and Michael Mihalka, "Soviet Strategic Deception 1955–1981," *Journal of Strategic Studies*, March 1982, pp. 75–79.

26. "The seekers . . . have over the years categorized everything they've seen in order to establish precise operational patterns. What does not fit the pattern causes immediate suspicion." Burrows, *Deep Black*, p. 273.

27. Machiavelli, *Discourses* XXVII.

28. U.S. Congress, Joint Committee on the Investigation of the Pearl Harbor Attack, *Pearl Harbor Attack*, 79th Congress, 2nd Session (Washington, GPO, 1946).

29. Kahn, *Hitler's Spies*, p. 63.

30. Andrew & Gordievsky. *KGB: The Inside Story*, pp. 598–99.

31. Tuchmann, *The Zimmerman Telegram*, passim, and Kahn, *The Codebreakers*, pp. 266–297.

32. Jacques Massu, *La Vraie Bataille d'Alger*, pp. 135–150 and 199–214. General Massu was the overall French commander in a battle the outcome of which he understood as largely dependent on intelligence. He won it.

33. Kautilya, *Arthasastra*, pp. 33 and 31 respectively.

34. Kahn, *Hitler's Spies*, pp. 366–367.

35. Robert Murphy, *Diplomat Among Warriors* (NY: Pyramid Books, 1985), p. 147: "During the last daylight hours of November 7, many in Algiers learned of a huge Allied convoy steaming majestically through the Mediterranean, said to be bound for Malta, which was in dire need of supplies. Only a few possessing our secret even suspected that these ships would soon turn sharply toward Algiers and unload their military cargo."

36. John J. Dziak, *Chekisty*.

37. Andrew and Gordievsky, *Inside the KGB*, pp. 325–331.

38. U.S. House of Representatives, Committee on Armed Services, *Report of the Technology Transfer Panel*, 98th Congress, 2nd Session (Washington, DC: USGPO, 1984), and U.S.

Department of Defense, *Soviet Acquisition of Militarily Significant Western Technology* (Washington, DC: September 1985). Also see Wolton, *Le KGB en France.*

39. Lord, *Incredible Victory.*
40. *New York Times,* May 11, 1984.
41. U.S. Congress, *Report of the Congressional Committees Investigating the Iran Contra Affair,* 100th Congress, 1st Session (Washington, DC: USGPO, 1987).
42. Vernon A. Walters, *Silent Missions.*
43. Publius (Alexander Hamilton, James Madison, and John Jay), *The Federalist Papers #64.*
44. Thucydides, *The Peloponnesian War.*
45. Mattingly, *Renaissance Diplomacy.*
46. Mattingly, op. cit., pp. 256–268.
47. Niccoló Machiavelli, *Discourse upon Our Language.*
48. Robert B. Holtman, *The Napoleonic Revolution.*
49. U.S. House of Representatives, Committee on Internal Security, *Subversive Involvement in the Origin, Leadership, and Activities of the New Mobilization Committee to End the War in Vietnam, and Its Predecessor Organizations,* 91st Congress, 2nd Session (Washington, DC: USGPO, 1970).
50. Joseph Finder, *Red Carpet,* p. 6.
51. Miles Copeland, *The Game of Nations,* pp. 85–86.

CHAPTER 2: A NEW WORLD DISORDER

1. Francis Fukuyama, "The End of History?" *The National Interest,* Summer 1989.
2. For example, in 1989 the Soviet Union produced 140 Intercontinental Ballistic Missiles (ICBMs) to 12 for the United States—a ratio of 11.7 to 1. As regards tanks, the category of Soviet armaments that suffered the biggest drop in production in 1989 (51 percent), the ratio of Soviet to U.S. production is 3.2 to 1. As regards armored personnel carriers, the 1989 ratio was 10 to 1. Testimony of Paul Wolfowitz, Undersecretary of Defense for Policy, before the U.S. House of Representatives, Committee on Armed Services, February 28, 1990. Copy of prepared remarks distributed at the hearing.
3. John Dunlop, "Crackdown," *The National Interest,* Spring 1991.
4. Richard Pipes, "Gorbachev's Soviet Union Breakdown or Crackdown," *Commentary,* March 1990.
5. *Jane's Defense Weekly* (London: Jane's Publishing Group), vol. 13, no. 9, p. 386.
6. Andrew and Gordievsky, *KGB: The Inside Story.*
7. Steven Emerson, "Where Have All His Spies Gone?" *New York Times Magazine,* August 12, 1990.
8. According to Andrew and Gordievsky. Also see Rummel, *Lethal Politics,* p. 45: "10,850,000 census-based, unnatural, nonbattle deaths . . . during the civil war period."
9. cf. George A. Carver, "Intelligence and Glasnost," *Foreign Affairs,* Summer 1990.

CHAPTER 3: VAIN SPYING

1. Robert Wilmer Rowan, *Thirty-Three Centuries of Espionage,* p. 621.
2. For firsthand accounts by Jedburgh alumni see Colby, *Honorable Men;* and Singlaub, *Hazardous Duty.*
3. Sejna, *We Will Bury You.*
4. Rositzke, *The CIA's Secret Operations,* p. 48.

5. Bower, *The Red Web*.
6. Richard Pipes, "Introduction to Ryszard Kuklinski," *Orbis*, vol. 32, no. 2, Winter 1988, p. 6; and Ryszard Kuklinski, "Crushing Solidarity," ibid., p. 7.
7. Yet another account of the massive amount of accurate, raw information about the Korean invasion is provided by John Singlaub, who had set up the agent networks in 1947 along with Newton S. Miler. See Singlaub, *Hazardous Duty*, ch. 5.
8. Angelo Codevilla, "The Opening to the Left in Italy," *Politeia*, 1964; Ledeen, *Western European Communism and American Foreign Policy*.
9. Gilligan, *CIA Life: 10,000 Days with the Agency*, p. 176.
10. De Forest and Chanoff, *Slow Burn*, pp. 31–34 and 85.
11. Snepp, *Decent Interval*, pp. 367–382 and 431–436.
12. Comment to the author by the U.S. station chief in Rome, October 1982.
13. *New York Times* and *Washington Post*, September 20, 1982.
14. The letters GRU are the initials of the Glavnoye Razvedyvatel' noye Upravleniye, the Main Intelligence Directorate of the General Staff (i.e., Soviet military intelligence).
15. Hood, *Mole*.
16. Penkovsky, *The Penkovsky Papers*.
17. *Newsweek*, November 4, 1985.
18. Burrows, *Deep Black*, p. 67.
19. *Washington Post*, September 16, 1971.
20. For an insightful discussion of this point see Burrows, *Deep Black*, pp. 132–134.
21. For a full discussion of the intellectual outlook underlying these choices in the 1960s see MacDougall's Pulitzer Prize–winning *The Heavens and the Earth*, especially the chapter entitled "Hooding the Falcons."
22. For some of the history of Rhyolite and its subsequent names see Lindsey, *The Falcon and the Snowman*; Burrows, *Deep Black*; and Woodward, *Veil*. The technical characteristics are to be found in *Aviation Week and Space Technology*.
23. Whaley, *Strategem: Deception and Surprise in War*. Forty-eight percent of land battles in World War I were in some sense a "surprise" to the defense. In World War II, with much better technical collection, that figure rose to 68%.

CHAPTER 4: FRAGMENTED COUNTERSPYING

1. U.S. Navy, Division of Operations, *The History and Aims of the Office of Naval Intelligence* (Washington, DC: USGPO, 1920), p. 11.
2. The two contrasting references on the Nosenko case are Epstein, *Legend, The Secret World of Lee Harvey Oswald*, and Mangold, *Cold Warrior*.
3. See Winks, *Cloak and Gown*, pp. 130–140, for Joseph Curtiss' activities in Istanbul beginning July, 1943; and pp. 259–264 for the founding of the X-2 branch of the OSS on June 15, 1943, with its first station in London. Not until 1944 would X-2 formally establish itself in Instanbul.
4. Winks, *Cloak and Gown*, pp. 354–356.
5. Bentley, *Out of Bondage*. The book is a résumé of her testimony before various committees of the U.S. Congress. See also Peter Wright, *Spy Catcher*, p. 182; and Lamphere and Shachtman, *The FBI–KGB War*, pp. 38–41.
6. This is also the view of Andrew and Gordievsky, *KGB: The Inside Story*, p. 367.
7. Colby, in *Honorable Men: My Life in the CIA*, not to mention lesser officers, claims that the CI staff simply nullified the efforts of the Directorate of Operations to recruit

Communists, or at least "badly distorted" the "balance between the Staff and the division." Others make the same charge in venomous language. See Mangold, *Cold Warrior*, especially references to the names Donald Jameson and Leonard McCoy.

8. Epstein, *Deception*, p. 100.
9. For an account of the FBI's organization for counterintelligence see Elliff, *The Reform of FBI Intelligence Operations*.
10. The best description of the Sigler case is in Corson et al., *Widows*.
11. Hurt, *Shadrin*, and Corson et al., *Widows*, pp. 197–234.
12. Lamphere and Shachtman, *The FBI-KGB War*, ch. 11.
13. Ibid.
14. Mangold, *Cold Warrior*, chs. 9, 7, 19, and 10 respectively. This book will stand as the definitive argument *contra* Golitsyn.
15. The Orlov case is fully discussed in Corson et al., *Widows*, as well as in Mangold, *Cold Warrior*, ch. 17.
16. Epstein, *Legend, The Secret World of Lee Harvey Oswald*.
17. Ibid.
18. Interview with Sen. Malcolm Wallop, a member of that Committee. 10 March 1990.
19. *Newsweek*, November 4, 1985.
20. Godson, ed., *Intelligence Requirements for the 1980s, vol. 3, Counterintelligence*; and Godson, ed., *Intelligence Requirements for the 1990s*, pp. 127–164.
21. Corson et al., *Widows*, pp. 7–17.
22. Ibid., pp. 48–52 and 103–104.
23. Woodward, *Veil*, p. 202.
24. *Glavnoe Upravleniye Strategicheskoy Maskirovki* (GUSM) (Chief Directorate for Strategic Deception). See Viktor Suvorov, *Inside the Aquarium*, for a firsthand account of a GRU officer's career.
25. Angelo Codevilla, "Space, Intelligence, and Deception," in Dailey and Parker, eds., *Soviet Strategic Deception*, p. 479.
26. Henry Hurt, "CIA in Crisis: The Kampiles Case," *Reader's Digest*, June 1979, pp. 65–72; and William Burrows, *Deep Black*, p. 24.
27. *Aviation Week and Space Technology*, August 14, 1989, p. 30.
28. Lindsey, *The Falcon and the Snowman*.
29. *Washington Post*, May 28, 1986; and *New York Times*, May 30, 1986.
30. Walter Pincus, "Soviets May be Easing . . . both sides modify . . . ," *Washington Post*, April 16, 1985, p. A13.
31. Interview with Nicolas Sigaldo Ros, *Covert Action*, vol. 1, no. 2, October 1978, pp. 16–21.
32. *The Washington Times*, 12 September 1991.
33. *Washington Post*, March 5, 1977 and June 2, 1977.
34. Stansfield Turner, *Secrecy and Democracy*, p. 50.
35. Edward J. Epstein, *Legend, The Secret World of Lee Harvey Oswald*. The pro-Nosenko books, of which Mangold's *Cold Warrior* is the most comprehensive, do not dispute that Oswald had spied for the Soviets while in the Marine Corps.
36. Turner, *Secrecy and Democracy*, p. 162.
37. I am indebted to Edward J. Epstein's *Deception* for this discussion.
38. *New York Times*, November 8, 1985, p. 10.
39. *Washington Post*, April 3, 1986.
40. *New York Times*, March 13 and 14, 1982; and especially Philip Taubmann, "Recanter's Tale: Lesson in Humility for State Dept," April 2, 1982.

41. Financial report filed by federal prosecutors in Federal District Court, Miami, January 18, 1991; *New York Times*, January 19, 1991.
42. Michael Wines, *New York Times*, August 13, 1990; and Paul Gigot, *Wall Street Journal*, December 20, 1990.
43. Ledeen, *Perilous Statecraft*
44. *New York Times*, 12 March 1991.
45. Quoted in Barron, *Breaking the Ring*, p. 24.
46. The analyst is William R. Harris, an employee of the Rand Corporation. An unclassified version of his work may be found in Godson, ed., *Intelligence Requirements for the 1980s, vol. 3, Counterintelligence* (NY: Crane, Russak & Co., 1980).
47. *New York Times*, January 16, 1979, pp. 8–9. Copies of part of Swearingen's file of allegations were found among the cadavers in Jonestown.
48. United States v. United States District Court, 407 U.S. 297 (1972).
49. Berlin Democratic Club et al. v. Donald H. Rumsfeld et al., 410 F. Supp. 144 (1976).
50. The documents were obtained by French intelligence and described in *Le Monde*, April 2, 1985, and further excerpted in Wolthon, *Le KGB en France*. They were also analyzed by Philip Hanson in "Soviet Industrial Espionage: Some new Information," a discussion paper published by the Royal Institute of International Affairs, London, 1987.
51. *Washington Post*, September 19, 1985. For more on Soviet technology transfer see: CIA, *Soviet Acquisition of Militarily Significant Western Technology: An Update* (Washington, DC: USGPO, 1985); CIA, *Soviet Acquisition of Western Technology* (Washington, DC: USGPO, 1982); and Department of Commerce, *Enforcement of U.S. Export Controls* (Washington, DC: USGPO, 1985).
52. Epstein, *Deception*.

CHAPTER 5: GETTING IT WRONG

1. "We have scattered throughout the various departments of our government documents and memoranda concerning military and naval and air and economic potentials of the Axis which, if gathered together and studied in detail by carefully selected trained minds, with a knowledge both of the related languages and technique, would yield valuable and often decisive results." William Donovan, "Memorandum of Establishment of Service of Strategic Information," June 10, 1941.
2. Winks, *Cloak and Gown*, p. 61.
3. Powerful though unintended support for this thesis may be found in Harold P. Ford, *Estimative Intelligence: The Purposes and Problems of National Intelligence Estimating*. Ford is a veteran CIA analyst, and the book has been well-received by the "old boys" of CIA. For our purposes, note that perhaps three out of every four words in the book deal with personalities and bureaucratic arrangements. The book willy-nilly supports the conclusion that the founding generation of CIA analysts looked at the outside world through the optic of its own social and bureaucratic concerns, and that that optic was so thick as to be largely mirror-like.
4. E. Drexel Godfrey, "Ethics and Intelligence," in *Foreign Affairs*, January 1978, pp. 622–642. Godfrey had served in the CIA between 1957 and 1970, and had headed the Current Intelligence Shop. He was a professor of political science before and after his time at the CIA.
5. This is a recurring theme in pro–CIA literature. Thus Rep. Bud Shuster (R-PA) answered Senator Moynihan's proposal to put intelligence analysis in the operating departments.

Daniel P. Moynihan, "The State Department Can Do the Job," and Bud Shuster, "Independence Means Integrity," *New York Times* op-ed, May 19, 1991.

6. Thomas Hughes, *The Fate of Facts in a World of Men*.
7. Smith, *The Unknown CIA*, p. 187.
8. Kent, *Strategic Intelligence*.
9. Dulles, *The Craft of Intelligence*, p. 222.
10. Smith, *The Unknown CIA*, p. 77.
11. *New York Times Magazine*, November 2, 1980, p. 42.
12. Abel, *The Missile Crisis*, pp. 17–24.
13. Godson, ed., *Intelligence Requirements for the 1980s, vol. 2, Analysis and Estimates*, p. 78.
14. Gen. Daniel Graham, *Shall America Be Defended*, p. 104.
15. Machiavelli, *Discourses on Livy*, Book III, Ch. 48.
16. Richard Pipes, "Intelligence in the Formulation of Foreign Policy," in Godson, ed., *Intelligence Requirements for the 1980s, vol. 7, Intelligence and Policy*, p. 41.
17. Leary, ed., *The Central Intelligence Agency, History and Documents*, p. 137.
18. Op. cit., p. 138. Also, note that Ford, in *Estimative Intelligence* (see note 3 preceding), gives this report the same importance and interpretation that we do.
19. Board of National Estimates, National Intelligence Council, National Intelligence Officers.
20. Thus NIE 11-4 is about Soviet Union's internal politics. For more on the NIEs and their numbering see Prados, *The Soviet Estimate*, pp. 14, 22, et al.
21. Amendment No. 2896 to S. 2477, Congressional Record, U.S. Senate, September 24, 1986, S13566-71; and *New York Times*, October 2, 1986.
22. Willmoore Kendall, "The Functions of Intelligence," in *World Politics*, July 1949. pp. 540–552. Kendall, then a professor of politics at Yale and an alumnus of the OSS, was perhaps the only member of the founding generation whose writings on intelligence touched first principles.
23. Kenneth de Graffenreid, Special Assistant to the President and Senior Director of Intelligence Programs, National Security Council, 1981–87. Interview with the author, November 16, 1989.
24. U.S. Congress, Subcommittee on Priorities and Economy in Government of the Joint Economic Committee, 94th Congress, 2nd Session, *Allocation of Resources in the Soviet Union and China—1976*, Pt. 2, Testimony given May 24, 1976 (Washington, DC: USGPO, 1976), p. 39.
25. Rositzke, *The CIA's Secret Operations*.
26. Szulc, *Fidel: A Critical Portrait*. Also see Tad Szulc, *New York Times Magazine*, April 1986.
27. Rowen and Wolf, Jr., eds., *The Impoverished Superpower*, especially Richard E. Ericson, "The Soviet Statistical Debate" and Anders Aslund, "How Small Is Soviet National Income?" An important sidelight to this debate is the spurious contention that the CIA intentionally *overestimated* Soviet GNP in order to "pump up" the image of a Soviet military threat. On this point see Haynes Johnson, *Washington Post*, July 20, 1990. The CIA did overestimate Soviet GNP, but largely by overestimating *civilian consumption*. At the same time, it seriously *underestimated* Soviet military spending.
28. Statement by George Kolt, Director of Soviet Analysis, Directorate of Intelligence, Central Intelligence Agency, July 16, 1990, before the U.S. Senate Committee on Foreign Relations (copy handed out at the hearing). This paragraph refers to this statement.

29. Rosefielde, *False Science*, and Rowen and Wolf, Jr., eds., *The Impoverished Superpower*.
30. William T. Lee, *The Estimation of Soviet Defense Expenditures for 1955-75: An Unconventional Approach* (NY: Praeger, 1977).
———, "CIA Estimates of Soviet Defense Spending," testimony before the U.S. House of Representatives, Select Committee on Intelligence, September 3, 1980, pp. 17-72.
———, testimony before the U.S. Senate Committee on Foreign Relations, July 16, 1990 (copy handed out at the hearing).
    Also see Rosefielde, *False Science*.
31. Joseph Alsop, "A Cautionary Tale," *Washington Post*, March 7, 1977.
32. *New York Times*, March 7, 9, 13, and 25, 1990.
33. *New York Times*, April 23, 1990.
34. See 95th Congress, 2nd Session, *Report of the Senate Select Committee on Intelligence Subcommittee on Collection, Production and Quality*, February 16, 1978., esp. pp. 9-14.
35. William T. Lee and Richard Staar, *Soviet Military Policy Since World War II* pp. 80-90.
36. William Beecher, "United States May Reply to Soviet Rays," *Boston Globe*, October 10, 1976, p. 7.
37. Codevilla, *While Others Build*, p. 85.
38. Godson, ed., *Intelligence Requirements for the 1980s, vol., Analysis and Estimates*, p. 212.
39. Ambrose and Immerman, *Ike's Spies*, pp. 257-258. cf. Harold Ford, *Estimative Intelligence*, p. 78.
40. Ambrose and Immerman, *Ike's Spies*, pp. 257-258.
41. Colby, *Lost Victory*. The agency applied these standards pell mell around the world. The local leaders who have carried out such "white revolutions from above" have generally failed badly. The most outstanding case was that of the Shah of Iran, who quite literally destabilized himself by behaving as a foreigner in his own country. See Ledeen and Lewis, *Debacle: The American Failure in Iran*. Also see Grace Goodell, "How the Shah Destabilized Himself," *Policy Review*, Spring, 1981.
42. Stockdale and Stockdale, *In Love and War*, pp. 431-432.
43. *Washington Post*, November 25, 1983.
44. Ralf Dahrendorf, *Society and Democracy in Germany*, pp. 401, 406, 408.
45. Godson, ed., *Intelligence Requirements for the 1990s*, pp. 111-119.
46. *New York Times*, April 30, 1990, and *Jane's Defence Weekly*, vol. 13, no. 14, 7 April 1990, p. 619. The actual "discovery" consisted of a telephone call from an East German Army reserve lieutenant to the West German Defense Ministry, which then contacted its East German counterpart. In Romania, too, 25 SS-23s turned up, for a total of 72 that the CIA had wrongly certified as having been destroyed.

CHAPTER 6: SORCERERS' APPRENTICES

1. The PCI's representatives at that meeting were Luigi Longo (later Party Secretary) and Eugenio Reale. Reale's papers, including a set of notes from the meetings at Sklarska Poreba, are in the archives of the Hoover Institution, Stanford University.
2. Powers, *Richard Helms: The Man Who Kept the Secrets*, p. 3.
3. See the statement by Jules Moch, Minister of the Interior, on November 16, 1948. Assemblee Nationale, *Journal Officiel*, 1948, pp. 6991-7008. See also Vernon L. Van Dyke, "The Position and Prospects of the Communists in France," *Political Science Quarterly*, March 1948. Charles de Gaulle of course believed that he, not any American, was his country's guarantor against chaos and communism.

4. Thomas Bedell Smith, *The Essential CIA* (1975), p. 9. This is a privately printed book whose only exposure to a broad public was in Powers, *Richard Helms: The Man Who Kept the Secrets*, p. 318 ff,9.

5. Vernon Walters, *Silent Missions*.

6. The CIA's Kermit Roosevelt was in charge. But the man handing out the cash to the military was Brig. Gen. H. Norman Schwarzkopf (father of the General of the same name who commanded U.S. troops in the Gulf War of 1991). Without the General's connections in the military, the operation would have been far more difficult. Kermit Roosevelt, *Countercoup: The Struggle for the Control of Iran*.

7. Richard Harkness and Gladys Harkness, *The Saturday Evening Post*, November 1954.

8. Lansdale, *In the Midst of Wars*.

9. Angelo Codevilla, "The Opening to the Left: Expectations and Results," in Ranney and Sartori, *Eurocommunism: The Italian Case*.

10. On the U.S. involvement in Chile see Phillips, *The Night Watch*; U.S. Senate Select Committee to Study Governmental Operations with Respect to Intelligence Operations, vol. 4 (Washington, DC: USGPO, 1976), and Powers, *The Man who Kept the Secrets*.

11. *Saturday Evening Post*, May 20, 1967.

12. The only comprehensive work on the Congress is Coleman, *The Liberal Conspiracy*—a sympathetic treatment.

13. Joseph Burkholder Smith, *Portrait of a Cold Warrior*.

14. Powers, *The Man Who Kept the Secrets*, p. 57.

15. Malcolm Wallop, "Covert Action: Policy Tool or Policy Hedge," *Strategic Review*, Summer 1983. Wallop wrote about the covert action of the 1980s, but his analysis applies as far back as the 1960s.

16. Gabriel Almond and Sidney Verba, *The Civic Culture*, and Lucian Pye, *Political Culture and Political Development*.

17. Rostow, *The Stages of Economic Growth; a Non-Communist Manifesto*.

18. Colby, *Lost Victory*.

19. Sterling Seagrave, *Yellow Rain*.

20. *New York Times*, January 6, 1961.

21. The Army's clandestine training mission was under Maj. Gen. John A. Heintgen. In April 1961 the program became overt under Brig. Gen. Andrew J. Boyle.

22. U.S. Congress, *CIA The Pike Report*, p. 197.

23. For two differing slants on the same facts see John Stockwell, *In Search of Enemies*, passim, and Cord Meyer, *Facing Reality*, pp. 250–270.

24. Letter from Rep. Robert Michel (R-IL) to the Honorable George Shultz, Secretary, Department of State, 18 October 1985. *Washington Post*, 23 October 1985, p. 1.

25. U.S. Congress, Report of the Congressional Committees Investigating the Iran–Contra Affair, with Supplemental, Minority, and Additional Views, 100th Congress, 1st Session. Washington, DC: USGPO, 1987. (Hereafter referred to as Iran–Contra Report.)

26. U.S. Congress, Iran–Contra Report, op cit., "Background on U.S.–Nicaraguan Relations," p. 27.

27. U.S. Congress, Iran–Contra Report, op cit., p. 32.

28. U.S. Congress, Iran–Contra Report, p. 395.

29. U.S. Congress, Iran–Contra Report, p. 406.

30. Woodward, *Veil*, pp. 97–98, and 158–159.

31. *Newsweek*, December 21, 1981, p. 16.
32. *New York Times*, "An Anti-Qaddafi Plot by U.S. Fails," March 12, 1991.
   For a discussion of the morality of assasination see *Wall Street Journal*, editorial page, February 25, 1991, and Seabury and Codevilla, *War: Ends and Means*, pp. 227–229.
33. *Washington Post*, December 4, 1986, and *Time*, December 15, 1986.
34. *The Federalist* #51.

CHAPTER 7: INTELLIGENCE AND THE GULF WAR

1. *New York Times*, June 13, 1991.
2. *Los Angeles Times*, January 17, 1991; *Washington Post*, January 18, 1991; and *New York Times*, February 13, 1991.
3. *New York Times*, January 19, 1991.

CHAPTER 8: REFORM

1. Kenneth de Graffenreid, "Intelligence and the Oval Office," in Godson, ed., *Intelligence Requirements for the 1980s, Intelligence and Policy*, pp. 9–31.
2. Herbert Meyer from *Fortune* magazine, special assistant to the DCI; Henry Rowen from the Rand Corp., Chairman of the Council of National Intelligence Officers; and Constantine Menges, NIO for Latin America. Kenneth de Graffenreid, from the Senate Intelligence Committee, became Director of Intelligence Programs at the National Security Council— the President's go-between to the intelligence community. But of course William Casey filled that role.
3. *Periscope* (Journal of the Association of Former Intelligence Officers), no. 3, 1990, p. 3.
4. *Wall Street Journal*, February 15, 1991, p. A-10.
5. "Report of the Jacobs Panel," U.S. Senate Select Committee on Intelligence, May 23, 1990 (21 pp. plus appendices).
6. Vince Cannistraro, "The CIA Dinosaur," *Washington Post* (op-ed) September 1991.
7. See the testimony of former CIA chief of station Tom Polgar before the Senate Intelligence Committee on 19 September 1991. *The New York Times*, 21 September 1991. p. 1.

CHAPTER 9: ACCESS TO SECRETS

1. Chester G. Starr, *Political Intelligence in Classical Greece*, p. 9.
2. Kautilya, *Arthasastra*, 11–13.
3. *New York Times*, December 6, 1989, and February 16 and 18, 1990.
4. Jacques Abtey and Fritz Unterberg Gibhardt, *2ᵐᵉ Bureau contre Abwehr*, pp. 19–22. When German troops entered Paris in 1940, Oplinsky "threw off the mask" and acknowledged what he had done.
5. Angelo Codevilla, "Space Intelligence and Deception," in Daily and Parker, eds, *Soviet Strategic Deception*, pp. 467–486.
6. John Dunlop, "Crackdown," *The National Interest*, Spring 1991.

CHAPTER 10: QUALITY CONTROL

1. Nikolai Brusnitsin, *Openness and Espionage*, pp. 28–29.
2. Aldouby and Ballinger, *The Shattered Silence: The Eli Cohen Affair*, pp. 325–326; and

Daniel Raviv and Yossi Melman, *Every Spy a Prince* (Boston: Houghton Mifflin, 1989), pp. 143–149.

3. Peter Wright, *Spy Catcher*, pp. 91–135.
4. Raviv and Melman, *Every Spy a Prince*, pp. 122–123.
5. U.S. Department of Defense, *Soviet Military Power 1988*, pp. 59–62.
6. Hansard, *Parliamentry Debates*, 5th series, vol. 639, 1961, cols. 1613–1614.
7. Brusnitsin, *Openness and Espionage*, pp. 4–5.
8. Malcolm Wallop and Angelo Codevilla, *The Arms Control Delusion* (San Francisco: ICS Press, 1987).
9. Yaacov Caroz, *The Arab Secret Service*, pp. 125–126.
10. *New York Times*, July 12 and 13; August 7, 11, and 13; September 29; and October 15, 1985; and *Washington Post*, July 12, 14, and 19; and September 28, 1985.
11. Abtey and Gibhardt, *2ᵐᵉ Bureau contre Abwehr*, pp. 41–48 and 167–171.
12. Arendt, *The Origins of Totalitarianism*. For a somewhat divergent view see Andrew and Gordievsky, *KGB: The Inside Story*.
13. Kevin Toolis, "Informer: The Life and Death of an IRA Man," *New York Times Magazine*, February 3, 1991.
14. Abtey and Gibhart, *2ᵐᵉ Bureau contre Abwehr*, pp. 182–195.
15. Andrew and Gordievsky, *KGB: The Inside Story*, pp. 227–228.
16. The following discussion borrows from Angelo Codevilla, "Space, Intelligence and Deception," in Dailey and Parker, eds., *Soviet Strategic Deception*.
17. Lees, *The Rape of Serbia*.
18. *The Nation*, April 11, 1981, p. 423. Note that Establishment Americans have taken tacit credit for the events of September 1965, e.g. James Reston in *New York Times*, June 12, 1966.
19. Peper Dole Scott, "The United States and the Overthrow of Sukarno," *Intelligence and Parapolitics*, vol. 2, 1986, p. 15.
20. Raviv and Melman, *The Imperfect Spies*, p. 199.
21. Leggett, *The Cheka*, pp. 295–296.
22. Caroz, *The Arab Secret Service*, p. 25.
23. Caroz, Op cit., pp. 68–69.
24. Arthur Koestler, *The Invisible Writing*, p. 254.
25. Machiavelli, *Discourses*, Book III, Ch. 6.
26. Ibid.

CHAPTER 11: SUBVERSION AND POLICY

1. Stevenson, *A Man Called Intrepid*, and Angelo Codevilla's review thereof in *Strategic Review*, Spring 1978.
2. Schultz and Godson, *Dezinformatsia*, pp. 133–149.
3. Harry Hopkins' pro-Soviet sentiments were never a secret. See Sherwood, *Roosevelt and Hopkins*, especially p. 80.
4. Andrew and Gordievsky, *KGB: The Inside Story*, pp. 286–290.
5. *New York Times*, January 15 and February 14, 1991.
6. *New York Times*, December 15, 1984.
7. *New York Times*, August 20, 1989.
8. *Washington Post*, July 18 and 24, and August 11, 1989.

9. Machiavelli, *The Prince*, ch. 19.
10. *New York Times*, March 21, 1991.
11. chapters 7, 12, 13, 14, 15, and 24.
12. Machiavelli, *The Prince*, ch. 7.
13. Quoted in Macaulay's *History of England*. vol I., p. 359. See also pp. 200, 215, 358, 363.
14. Edward Mead Earle, "The Influence of Power upon History," *Yale Review*, Summer 1946, p. 586.
15. Norman Cohn, *Pursuit of the Millennium*, esp. ch. 13.
16. On the neutron bomb campaign see Schultz and Godson, *Dezinformatsia*, pp. 74–79 and 126–130.
17. See especially the *New York Times'* lead editorial of October 15, 1986.
18. Raviv and Melman, *Every Spy a Prince*, pp. 324–330. For a different view see Michael Ledeen, *Perilous Statecraft* (NY: Scribners, 1988), pp. 151–163.
19. This is what happened to the emperor Akhbar from 1578 to 1581. See Streusand, *The Formation of the Mughal Empire*, pp. 166–170.
20. Vaksberg, *The Prosecutor*, p. 124.
21. Machiavelli, *The Prince*, ch. 19, contains a discussion of this topic.
22. Andrew and Gordievsky, *KGB: The Inside Story*, pp. 167–172.
23. This discussion follows the argument set forth in Angelo M. Codevilla, "Covert Action and Foreign Policy," in Godson, ed., *Intelligence Requirements for the 1980s, vol. 3, Covert Action*, pp. 97–104.
24. Thucydides, *The Peloponnesian War*; Machiavelli, *Prince* and *Discourses*; Montesquieu, *The Greatness of the Romans and Their Decline*; Publius, *The Federalist Papers*.
25. The expression is Montesquieu's. See *The Greatness of the Romans and Their Decline*.
26. See Abraham Lincoln's arguments against Stephen Douglas in Angle, ed., *Created Equal? The Lincoln-Douglas Debates*. See especially Lincoln's speech at Peoria. Lincoln's formulation for this "original sin" is "You work, I eat." Also see Harry V. Jaffa, *Crisis of a House Divided*.
27. Machiavelli, *The Prince*, ch. 4.
28. Solzhenitsyn, *The Gulag Archipelago*, vol. 3.
29. ———, "Misconceptions About Russia Are a Threat to America," *Foreign Affairs*, Spring 1980.
30. See David Brooks, "Hard Currency Gods," *The Wall Street Journal*, 21 May 1991. p. A20.
31. Denning, *A New Life of Toyotomi Hideyoshi*.
32. De Gaulle, *Memoires de Guerre*, vol. 1, p. 9.
33. Deacon, *Kempei Tai: A History of the Japanese Secret Service*, p. 9.
34. Machiavelli, *The Prince*, ch. 20; *Discourses*, Bk III, ch. 26.
35. ———, *Discourses*, Bk III, ch. 21.
36. *Idem.*, Bk II, ch. 30.

CHAPTER 12: GETTING IT RIGHT

1. See Ernest May, *Knowing One's Enemies*.
2. F. E. H. Hinsley, *British Intelligence in the Second World War*, vol. 1, pp. 64–66.
3. Kautilya, *Arthasastra*, p. 27.
4. See the discussion of the command and control of the 1980 Iran rescue mission in Seabury and Codevilla, *War: Ends and Means*, p. 93.

5. Kahn, *Hitler's Spies*, p. 277.
6. *New York Times*, March 7, 9, 13, and 25, 1990.
7. Hinsley, *British Intelligence in the Second World War*, vol. 1, pp. 173-176.
8. Wright, *A Study of War*. Compare Seabury and Codevilla, *War: Ends and Means*.
9. Kennedy, *The Rise and Fall of the Great Powers*.
10. Machiavelli, *Discourses*, Bk III, ch. 39.
11. Churchill, *The Second World War*, vol. 2, p. 121.
12. Thucydides, *The Peloponnesian War*, Book VI.
13. Stettinius, *Roosevelt and the Russians*, pp. 609-610.
14. Churchill, *Marlborough*, Book I, vol 2, pp. 701-769.
15. Hart, *The Tanks*; and Cruttwell, *A History of the Great War, 1914-1918*, p. 547.
16. This was the theme of De Tocqueville's *Democracy in America*.
17. It has been reported that Amin even slaughtered his own son and ate his heart. See Smith, *Ghosts of Kampala*, pp. 110-112. Also see Johnson, *Modern Times*, p. 535.
18. De Soto, *The Other Path*.
19. Huntford, *The New Totalitarians*.
20. St. Augustine, *City of God*, Bk XIV.
21. Alan Cowell, "Trouble in Damascus," *New York Times Magazine*, April 1, 1990.
22. Machiavelli, *The Prince*, ch. 8.
23. Bozeman, *Culture and Politics*.
24. Tetsuyo Najita, unpublished paper at Conference on Political Culture and Modernization, The Hoover Institution, April 5-6, 1990.
25. See Chief Justice John Marshal's opinion in Chisolm v. Georgia, 2 U.S. 363 (1793), and President James Monroe's *The People The Sovereigns*, republished by James River Press, 1987.
26. Joshua Muravchik, "Mikhail Gorbachev's Intellectual Journey," *The New Republic*, March 5, 1990.
27. Brzezinsky, *The Grand Failure*.
28. Uri Ra'anan, *The Soviet Empire: The Challenge of National and Democratic Movements*, for "Testimony" before U.S. Senate Committee on Foreign Relations, July 24, 1990 (copy distributed at the hearing).
29. Seabury and Codevilla, *War: Ends and Means*, especially ch. 3.
30. Cohen and Gooch, *Military Misfortunes*, ch. 7.
31. Alex Alexiev, *Inside the Soviet Army in Afghanistan.*
32. "Arms Control and Disarmament Agency Study on U.S. and Soviet Strategic Capabilities Through the Mid-1980s," August 17, 1978, in *Documents on Disarmament 1978* (Washington, DC: GPO, 1980), pp. 512-520.
33. Codevilla, *While Others Build*, especially chs. 4 and 5.
34. De Gaulle, *Vers L'Armee de Metier*. Also see de Gaulle's account of his unsuccessful struggle to have his ideas adopted, in *Memoires de Guerre*, Vol. 1, L'Appel.
35. For a good description of Presidential Decision #59 and the concept of declaratory policy, see Nolan, *Guardians of the Arsenal*. Also see Angelo M. Codevilla, "Who Guards the Guardians?" in *National Review*, March 6, 1990.
36. David Kahn, "An Intelligence Case History: The Defense of Osuga, 1942," *Aerospace Historian*, December 1981, pp. 242-251.
37. Hammerow, *From the Finland Station: The Graying of Revolution in the Twentieth Century*, describes the phenomenon, but persists in seeing it as dysfunctional, unintention-

al, and largely unwelcome to such as Stalin, Mao Tze-tung, and Fidel Castro. He is mistaken.

38. Montesquieu, *L'Esprit des Lois*, BK I.
39. Mikhail Bernstam, "Economic Systems, Demographic Change, and International Conflicts," in Saunders and Freedman, eds., *Demographic Change and Western Security*.
40. Hammerow, *From the Finland Station*, pp. 327–328.
41. Fogel and Engerman, *Time on the Cross*.
42. Machiavelli, *The Prince*, ch. 16.
43. Payne, *Why Nations Arm*. Also see Wolf and Zycher, *Military Dimensions of Communist Systems: Findings and Implications*.
44. Gur Ofer, "Soviet Economic Growth 1928–1985," *Journal of Economic Liturature*, vol. 25, no. 4, December 1987, pp. 1767–1833.
45. Speer, *Inside the Third Reich*, pp. 207–213.
46. "Communist Entrepreneurs, N.Y." See *New York Times*, May 4, 1990, p. C-1.
47. Schlomo Gazit and Michael Handel, "Insurgency, Terrorism and Intelligence," in Godson ed., *Intelligence Requirements for the 1980's, vol. 3, Counterintelligence*.
48. Livingstone and Halevy, *Inside the PLO*, pp. 91–92. Also see Pacepa, *Red Horizons: Chronicles of a Communist Spy Chief*, p. 36; and Xavier Raufer in *Notes et Etudes* de L'institut de Criminilogie de Paris, March 13, 1990. I thank Christian de Bongain for many of the insights in this section.
49. Raufer, *Notes et Etudes*, No. 13, March 1990.
50. International Institute for Strategic Studies, *The Military Balance* (London: IISS, 1990).

Chapter 13: Intelligence, Talent, and Lessons

1. "Der Nachrichtendienst ist immer ein Herrendienst." Literally, "The information-gathering service is always a lordly service." Reinhard Gehlen, Chief of Intelligence for Foreign Armies East during World War II, and later Chief of the Bundesnachrichtendienst, popularized the expression.
2. Archibald B. Roosevelt, *For Lust of Knowing* (Boston: Little, Brown, 1988). Roosevelt, who spoke 16 languages, wrote that a collector "must be able to empathize with true believers of every stripe in order to understand and analyze them. He must, like Chairman Mao's guerillas, be able to swim in foreign seas. But then he must be able to pull himself to shore and look back calmly, objectively, on the waters that immersed him."

Bibliography

———. *Operation Zapata: The "Ultrasensitive" Report and Testimony of the Board of Inquiry on the Bay of Pigs*. Frederick, MD: University Publications of America, Inc., 1981.

———. *Slovar Osnovnikh Voennykh Terminov*. Moscow: Voenizdat, 1965.

ABEL, ELIE. *The Missile Crisis*. NY: Lippincott, 1966.

ABENHEIM, DONALD. *Reforging the Iron Cross*. Princeton, NJ: Princeton Univ. Press, 1988.

ABTEY, JACQUES & FRITZ UNTERBERG GIBHARDT. *2ᵐᵉ Bureau contre Abwehr*. Paris: La Table Ronde, 1967.

AGEE, PHILIP. *Inside the Company: CIA Diary*. Harmondsworth, Eng.: Penguin Books, 1975.

ALDOUBY, ZWY, AND JERROLD BALLINGER. *The Shattered Silence: The Eli Cohen Affair*. NY: Coward, McCann & Geoghegan, 1971.

ALEXIEV, ALEX. *Inside the Soviet Army in Afghanistan*, Santa Monica, CA: Rand, 1988.

ALMOND, GABRIEL & SIDNEY VERBA. *The Civic Culture*. Princeton: Princeton Univ. Press, 1963.

AMBROSE, STEPHEN E., AND RICHARD H. IMMERMAN. *Ike's Spies*. NY: Doubleday, 1981.

ANDREW, CHRISTOPHER. *Her Majesty's Secret Service: The Making of the British Intelligence Community*. NY: Viking Penguin, 1986.

ANDREW, CHRISTOPHER, AND OLEG GORDIEVSKY. *KGB: The Inside Story*. NY & London: Harper Collins, 1990.

ANGLE, PAUL, ED. *Created Equal? The Lincoln–Douglas Debates*. Chicago: Univ. of Chicago Press, 1958.

ARENDT, HANNAH. *The Origins of Totalitarianism*. NY: Harcourt Brace, 1951.

BAILEY, GEOFFREY. *The Conspirators*. NY: Harper & Bros., 1960.

BAKELESS, JOHN. *Turncoats, Traitors and Heroes*. Philadelphia: Lippincott, 1959.

BAMFORD, JAMES. *The Puzzle Palace*. NY: Penguin Books, 1983.

BARRON, JOHN. *Breaking the Ring*. Boston: Houghton Mifflin, 1987.

———. *KGB Today; The Hidden Hand* NY: Berkley Books, 1985.

———. *MiG Pilot: Lt. Victor Belenko's Final Escape*. NY: Readers Digest Press, 1979.

BEMIS, SAMUEL FLAGG. *The Diplomacy of the American Revolution*. Bloomington and London: Indiana Univ. Press, 1967.

BENNETT, RALPH. *Ultra in the West: The Normandy Campaign 1944–45*. NY: Charles Scribner, 1980.

BENTLEY, ELIZABETH T. *Out of Bondage*. NY: Devin Adair, 1951.

BIBLIOGRAPHY

BERNET, PHILIPPE. *SDECE Service 7, L'Extraordinaire Histoire du Colonel LeRoy-Finville et de ses Clandestins*. Paris: Presses de la cité, 1980.

BILL, JAMES A., ED. *The Eagle and the Lion*. New Haven: Yale Univ. Press, 1988.

BITTMAN, LADISLAV. *The Deception Game*. NY: Ballantine Books, 1981.

———. *The KGB and Soviet Disinformation: An Insider's View*. Washington, DC: Pergamon–Brassey's, 1985.

BLACK, J. B. *The Reign of Elizabeth, 1558–1603*. Oxford: The Clarendon Press, 1959.

BLACKSTOCK, PAUL. *The Strategy of Subversion*. Chicago: Quadrangle Books, 1964.

BLAUFARB, DOUGLAS S. *The Counterinsurgency Era: U.S. Doctrine and Performance, 1950 to the Present*. NY: The Free Press, 1977.

BOWER, TOM. *The Red Web: MI6 and the KGB Master Coup*. London: Aurum Press, Ltd., 1989.

BOYLE, ANDREW. *The Fourth Man*. NY: The Dial Press, 1979.

BOZEMAN, ADDA. *Culture and Politics*. Princeton: Princeton Univ. Press, 1961.

BROWN, ANTHONY CAVE. *The Last Hero: Wild Bill Donovan*. NY: Times Books, 1982.

———, ED. *The Secret War Report of the OSS*. NY: Berkley Pub. Corp. 1976.

BRUSNITSIN, NIKOLAI. *Openness and Espionage*. Moscow: Military Publishing House [Voenizdat], 1990.

BRZEZINSKY, ZBIGNIEW. *The Grand Failure*. NY: Scribners, 1989.

BURROWS, WILLIAM. *Deep Black*. NY: Random House, 1987.

CAROZ, YAACOV. *The Arab Secret Service*. London: Corgi, 1978.

CASEY, WILLIAM. *The Secret War Against Hitler*. NY: Regnery Gateway, 1987.

CECIL, ROBERT. *A Divided Life: A Personal Portrait of the Spy Donald Maclean*. London: The Bodley Head, 1988.

CENTRAL INTELLIGENCE AGENCY. *Intelligence in the War of Independence*. Washington, DC: CIA Office of Public Affairs, n.d.

CHAMBERS, WHITTAKER. *Witness*. NY: Random House, 1952.

CHURCHILL, WINSTON. *Marlborough, His Life and Times*. London: Harrap, 1963.

———. *The Second World War*. Boston: Houghton Mifflin, 1949.

CLINE, RAY. *Secrets, Spies, and Scholars: Blueprint of the Essential CIA*. Washington, DC: Acropolis Books, 1976.

CODEVILLA, ANGELO. *The Cure That May Kill: Unintended Consequences of the INF Treaty*. London: Institute for Defence and Strategic Studies, 1988.

———. *While Others Build*. NY: Free Press, 1988.

COHEN, ELIOT, AND JOHN GOOCH. *Military Misfortunes*. NY: Free Press, 1990.

COHN, NORMAN. *The Pursuit of the Millennium*. NY: Oxford Univ. Press, 1970.

COLBY, WILLIAM, WITH PETER FORBATH. *Honorable Men: My Life in the CIA*. NY: Simon & Schuster, 1978.

COLBY, WILLIAM, WITH JAMES McCARGER. *Lost Victory*. Chicago, New York: Contemporary Books, 1989.

COLEMAN, PETER. *The Liberal Conspiracy: The Congress for Cultural Freedom and the Struggle for the Mind of Post War Europe*. NY: Free Press, 1989.

CONQUEST, ROBERT. *Inside Stalin's Secret Police*. Stanford: Hoover Institution Press, 1985.

COPELAND, MILES. *The Game of Nations: The Amorality of Power Politics*. London: Weidenfeld & Nicolson, 1969.

CORSON, WILLIAM, SUSAN TRENTO, AND JOSEPH TRENTO. *Widows*. NY: Crown, 1989.

COURRIERE, YVES. *La Guerre D'Algerie, Tome III: L'heure des Colonels*. Paris: Fayard, 1974.

CRUTTWELL, C. R. M. F. *A History of the Great War, 1914–1918*. Oxford: Clarendon, 1940.

DAHRENDORF, RALF. *Society and Democracy in Germany*. NY: Doubleday, 1969.

DAILEY, BRIAN B., AND PATRICK P. PARKER, EDS. *Soviet Strategic Deception*. Stanford: Hoover Institution Press, 1987.

DEACON, RICHARD. *Kempei Tai: A History of the Japanese Secret Service*. NY and Toronto: Beaufort Books, 1983.

DENNING, WALTER. *A New Life of Toyotomi Hideyoshi*. Tokyo: 1904.

DEPARTMENT OF DEFENSE. *Soviet Military Power, An Assessment of the Threat*. Washington, DC: USGPO, 1988.

465

BIBLIOGRAPHY

DOUGLAS, WILLIAM. *Developing Democracy*. Washington: Heldref Publ., 1972.

DOUHET, GIULIO. *Il Dominio dell'Aria*. Rome: Istituto nazionale fascista di cultura, 1927.

DRACHOVITCH, M., AND LAZITCH, EDS. *The Comintern: Historical Highlights*. NY: F. A. Praeger, 1966.

DRACHOVITCH, M., ED. *The Revolutionary Internationals, 1864–1943*. Stanford: Stanford Univ. Press, 1966.

DULLES, ALLEN. *The Craft of Intelligence*. NY: New American Library, 1965.

DZHIRKVELOV, ILYA. *Secret Servant: My Life with the KGB and the Soviet Elite*. London: Collins, 1987.

DZIAK, JOHN J. *Chekisty: A History of the KGB*. Lexington, MA: Lexington Books, 1988.

ELLIFF, JOHN T. *The Reform of FBI Intelligence Operations*. Princeton: Princeton Univ. Press, 1979.

EPSTEIN, EDWARD J. *Deception: The Invisible War Between the KGB and the CIA*. NY: Simon & Schuster, 1989.

————. *Legend, The Secret World of Lee Harvey Oswald*. NY: Reader's Digest Press, 1978.

FELIX, CHRISTOPHER. *A Short Course in the Secret War*, rev. ed. NY: Bantam, 1988.

FINDER, JOSEPH. *Red Carpet*. NY: Scott Foresman & Co., 1983.

FOGEL, ROBERT W. AND STANLEY L. ENGERMAN. *Time on the Cross*. Boston: Little Brown, 1974.

FORD, HAROLD P. *Estimative Intelligence: The Purposes and Problems of National Intelligence Estimating*. Washington, DC: Defense Intelligence College, 1989.

DE FOREST, ORRIN, AND DAVID CHANOFF. *Slow Burn*. NY: Simon & Schuster, 1990.

FRANKLIN, HOWARD BRUCE, ED. *The Essential Stalin: Major Theoretical Writings, 1905–52*. Garden City, NY: Anchor Books, 1972.

GADDIS, JOHN LEWIS. *Strategies of Containment; A Critical Appraisal of Post War American National Security Policy*. NY: Oxford Univ. Press, 1982.

DE GAULLE, CHARLES. *La France et Son Armee*. Paris: Plon, 1938.

————. *Memoires de Guerre*, vol. 1, *L'Appel*. Paris: Plon, 1954.

————. *Vers L'Armee de Metier*. Paris: Berger–Levrault, 1944.

GEISMAR, PETER. *Fanon*. NY: Dial Press, 1971.

GEROLYMATOS, ANDRE. *Espionage and Treason. A Study of Proxenia in Political and Military Intelligence Gathering in Classical Greece*. Amsterdam: J. C. Gieben, 1986.

GERTH, HANS H. & MILLS, C. WRIGHT, EDS. *From Max Weber: Essays in Sociology*. NY: Oxford University Press, 1946.

GILLIGAN, TOM. *CIA Life: 10,000 Days with the Agency*. Guilford, CT: Foreign Intelligence Press, 1991.

GLEES, ANTHONY. *The Secrets of the Service; British Intelligence and Communist Subversion, 1939–1951*. London: Jonathan Cape Ltd., 1987.

GODSON, ROY. *American Labor and European Politics; The AFL as a Transnational Force*. NY: Crane, Russak & Co., 1976.

————, ED. *Collection*. Washington, DC: National Strategic Information Center, 1983.

————, ED. *Covert Action*. Washington, DC: National Strategic Information Center, 1980.

————, ED. *Intelligence Requirements for the 1990s*. Lexington, MA: Lexington Books, 1989.

————, ED. *Intelligence Requirements for the 1980s, vol. 7, Intelligence and Policy*. Lexington, MA: Lexington Books, 1986.

————, ED. *Intelligence Requirements for the 1980s, vol. 6, Domestic Intelligence*. Lexington, MA: Lexington Books, 1986.

————, ED. *Intelligence Requirements for the 1980s, vol. 2, Analysis and Estimates*. New Brunswick: Transaction Books, 1980.

————, ED. *Intelligence Requirements for the 1980s, vol. 3, Counterintelligence*. Washington, DC: Consortium for the Study of Intelligence, 1981 or NY: Crane, Russak & Co., 1980.

————, ED. *Intelligence Requirements for the 1980s, vol. 1, Elements of Intelligence*. Washington, DC: National Strategy Information Center, 1983.

GRAHAM, DANIEL. *Shall America Be Defended*. New Rochelle, NY: Arlington House, 1979.

GRAHAM, LAWRENCE S., AND DOUGLAS WHEELER, EDS. *In Search of Modern Portugal: The Revolution and Its Ramifications*. Madison: Univ. of Connecticut Press, 1983.

HAIDUCU, MATEI PAVEL. *J'ai Refuse de Tuer; Un Agent Secret Roumain Revele les Dessous de "L'Affaire."* Paris: Plon, 1984.

HAMMEROW, THEODORE. *From the Finland Station: The Graying of Revolution in the Twentieth Century,* NY: Basic Books, 1990.

HANDEL, MICHAEL, ED. *Intelligence and Military Operations.* London: Frank Cass, 1990.

HART, BASIL LIDELL. *The Tanks: History of the Royal Tank Regiment and Its Predecessors,* 2 vols. London: 1959.

HASWELL, C. J. D. *Spies and Spymasters: A Concise History of Intelligence.* London: Thames & Hudson, 1977.

HERRINGTON, STUART. *Silence Was a Weapon; The Vietnam War in the Villages: A Personal Perspective.* Novato, CA: Presidio Press, 1982.

HILLEL, SHLOMO. *Operation Babylon,* tr. Ina Friedman. Garden City, NY: Doubleday, 1987.

HINSLEY, F. E. H. *British Intelligence in the Second World War; Its Influence of Strategy and Operations.* NY: Cambridge Univ. Press, 1979.

HINSLEY, F. E. H., AND C. A. G. SIMKINS. *British Intelligence in the Second World War: Volume V, Security and Counterintelligence.* London: HMSO, 1990.

HOLTMAN, ROBERT B. *The Napoleonic Revolution.* NY: Lippincott, 1967.

HOOD, WILLIAM. *Mole.* NY: W. W. Norton & Co., 1982.

HUGHES, THOMAS. *The Fate of Facts in a World of Men.* NY: Foreign Policy Association, 1976.

HUNTFORD, ROLAND. *The New Totalitarians.* NY: Stein & Day, 1972.

HURT, HENRY. *Shadrin: The Spy Who Never Came Back.* NY: Reader's Digest Press, 1981.

JAFFA, HARRY V. *Crisis of a House Divided.* NY: Doubleday, 1959.

JOHNSON, PAUL. *Modern Times.* NY: Harper & Row, 1983.

JONES, ROSEMARY DEVONSHIRE. *Francesco Vettori; Florentine Citizen and Medici Servant.* London: The Athlone Press, 1972.

KAHN, DAVID. *Hitler's Spies.* NY: Macmillan, 1978.

——— *The Codebreakers: The Story of Secret Writing.* London: Weidenfeld & Nicolson, 1967.

KATZ, AMROM. *"Verification and SALT: The State of the Art and the Art of the State."* Washington, DC: Heritage Foundation, 1979.

KATZ, BARRY M. *Foreign Intelligence: Research and Analysis in the Office of Strategic Services 1942–1945.* Cambridge, MA: Harvard Univ. Press, 1989.

KAUTILYA. (R. SHAMASASTRY, ED.) *Arthasastra.* Mysore, India: Mysore Printing and Pub. House, 1961.

KENNEDY, PAUL. *The Rise and Fall of the Great Powers.* NY: Random House, 1987.

KENT, SHERMAN. *Strategic Intelligence.* Princeton: Princeton Univ. Press, 1949.

KIPLING, RUDYARD. *Works of Rudyard Kipling.* NY: Harcourt, 1910.

KIRKPATRICK, LYMAN. *The U.S. Intelligence Community: Foreign Policy & Domestic Activities.* NY: Hill & Wang, 1973.

KISSINGER, HENRY. *The White House Years.* Boston: Little Brown, 1979.

KOESTLER, ARTHUR. *The Invisible Writing.* London: Hutchinson, 1969.

LAMPHERE, ROBERT J., AND TOM SHACHTMAN. *The FBI–KGB War: A Special Agent's Story.* NY: Random House, 1986.

LANDSDALE, EDWARD. *In the Midst of Wars.* NY: Harper & Row, 1972.

LEARY, WILLIAM M., ED. *The Central Intelligence Agency, History and Documents.* University, AL: Univ. of Alabama Press, 1984.

LEDEEN, MICHAEL. *Western European Communism and American Foreign Policy.* New Brunswick: Transaction Books, 1987.

——— *Perilous Statecraft.* NY: Scribner, 1988.

LEDEEN, MICHAEL, AND WILLIAM LEWIS. *Debacle: The American Failure in Iran.* NY: Knopf, 1981.

LEE, WILLIAM T., AND RICHARD STAAR. *Soviet Military Policy Since World War II.* Stanford: Hoover Institution Press, 1986.

LEES, MIKHAEL. *The Rape of Serbia: The British Role in Tito's Grab for Power 1943–44.* NY: Harcourt Brace Jovanovich, 1990.

LEGGETT, GEORGE. *The Cheka: Lenin's Political Police.* Oxford: Clarendon Press, 1981.

LEVCHENKO, STANISLAV. *On the Wrong Side: My Life in the KGB.* Washington, DC: Pergamon–Brassey's, 1988.

LEVINE, MICHAEL. *Deep Cover: The Inside Story of how DEA Infighting, Incompetence, and Subterfuge Lost Us the Biggest Battle of the Drug War.* NY: Delacorte Press, 1990.

LEWIN, RONALD. *Ultra Goes to War: The First Account of World War II's Greatest Secret Based on Official Documents.* NY: McGraw–Hill, 1978.

LINDSEY, ROBERT. *The Falcon and the Snowman.* NY: Pocket Books, 1979.

LIVINGSTONE, NEIL C., AND DAVID HALEVY. *Inside the PLO.* NY: Morrow, 1990.

MACARTHUR, DOUGLAS. *Reminiscences.* NY: McGraw–Hill, 1964.

MACDONALD, CALLUM. *The Killing of SS Obergruppenführer Reinhard Heydrich.* NY: Free Press, 1989.

MACDOUGALL, WALTER. *The Heavens and the Earth.* NY: Basic Books, 1985.

MCCORD, WILLIAM. *The Springtime of Freedom; Evolution of Developing Societies.* NY: Oxford Univ. Press, 1965.

MACAULAY, THOMAS BABBINGTON. *Macaulay's History of England.* Philadelphia, 1874.

MADER, JULIUS. *Who's Who in the CIA.* Berlin: Julius Mader, 1066 Berlin W 66, Mauerstrasse 69, 1968.

MARCHETTI, VICTOR, AND JOHN MARKS. *The CIA and the Cult of Intelligence.* NY: Knopf, 1974.

MANGOLD, TOM. *Cold Warrior.* NY: Simon & Schuster, 1991.

MASSU, JACQUES. *La Vraie Bataille d'Alger.* Paris: Plon, 1971.

MASTERMAN, J. C. *The Double-Cross System in the War of 1939–1945.* New Haven and London, Yale Univ. Press, 1972.

MATTINGLY, GARRETT. *Renaissance Diplomacy.* Boston: Houghton Mifflin, 1971.

MAY, ERNEST R. *Knowing One's Enemies.* Princeton: Princeton University Press, 1984.

———, *"Lessons" of the Past: The Use and Misuse of History in American Foreign Policy.* London, NY: Oxford Univ. Press, 1975.

MEYER, CORD. *Facing Reality: From World Federalism to the CIA.* NY: Harper & Row, 1980.

MOCH, JULES. *Recontres Avec Leon Blum.* Paris: Plon, 1970.

MONROE, JAMES. *The People, The Sovereigns.* Republished by James River Press, 1987.

MONTAGU, EWEN. *Beyond Top Secret Ultra.* London: Peter Davies Ltd., 1977.

———. *The Man Who Never Was.* London: Evans, 1953.

MONTALDO, JEAN. *Les Finances du PCF.* Paris: Allein Michel, 1977.

———. *Les Secrets de la Banque Sovietique en France.* Paris: Allein Michel, 1979.

MORGAN, JOHN H. *Assize of Arms: The Disarmament of Germany.* NY: Oxford Univ. Press, 1946.

MURPHY, ORVILLE T. *Charles Gravier, Comte de Vergennes: French Diplomacy in the Age of Revolution: 1719–1787.* Albany: State Univ. of New York Press, 1982.

MURPHY, ROBERT. *Diplomat Among Warriors.* NY: Pyramid Books, 1985.

MYAGOV, ALEKSEI. *Inside the KGB.* New Rochelle, NY: Arlington House, 1976.

NICOLAI, COL. W. *The German Secret Service,* trans. George Renwick. London: Stanley Pau & Co., Ltd., 1924.

NOLAN, JANNE E. *Guardians of the Arsenal.* NY: New Republic Books, 1989.

ORLOV, ALEXANDER. *Manual of Intelligence and Guerilla Warfare.* Ann Arbor: Univ. of Michigan Press, 1963.

PACEPA, ION MIHAI. *Red Horizons: Chronicle of a Communist Spy Chief.* Washington, DC: Regnery Gateway, 1987.

PACKENHAM, ROBERT. *Liberal America and the Third World.* Princeton: Princeton Univ. Press, 1973.

PAYNE, JAMES L. *Why Nations Arm.* Oxford: Basil Blackwell, 1989.

PENKOVSKY, OLEG. *The Penkovsky Papers.* NY: Doubleday, 1965.

PHILBY, HAROLD (KIM). *My Silent War.* NY: Grove Press, 1968.

PHILLIPS, DAVID ATLEE. *The Night Watch; Twenty-Five Years of Peculiar Service.* NY: Atheneum, 1977.

PIPES, RICHARD. *Survival Is Not Enough.* NY: Simon & Schuster, 1986.

PLUTARCH. *Lives,* Fabius. NY: Modern Library, 1969.

POSSONY, STEFAN. *Lenin: The Compulsive Revolutionary.* London: Allen & Unwin, 1966.

POWERS, THOMAS. *The Man Who Kept the Secrets: Richard Helms and the CIA.* NY: Knopf, 1979.

PRADOS, JOHN. *The Soviet Estimate.* NY: Dial Press, 1982.

PYE, LUCIAN. *Political Culture and Political Development*. Princeton: Princeton Univ. Press, 1965.

RA'ANAN, URI. *The Soviet Empire: The Challenge of National and Democratic Movements*. Lexington, MA: Lexington Books, 1990.

RADOSH, RONALD. *American Labor and United States Foreign Policy*. NY: Random House, 1969.

RANELAGH, JOHN. *The Agency: The Rise and Decline of the CIA*, revised and updated. NY: Simon & Schuster, 1987.

RAUFER, XAVIER. *Le Nebuleuse: le Terrorisme du Moyen-orient*. Paris: Librairie Artheme Fayard, 1987.

RAVIV, DANIEL, AND YOSSI MELMAN. *The Imperfect Spies: The Complete History of Israel's Intelligence Community*. London: Sidgewick & Jackson, 1989. [American title: *Every Spy a Prince*: . . .]

ROBERTSON, K. G. *British and American Approaches to Intelligence*. London: Macmillan, 1987.

ROOSEVELT, ARCHIBALD B. *For Lust of Knowing*. Boston: Little Brown, 1988.

ROOSEVELT, KERMIT. *Countercoup: The Struggle for the Control of Iran*. NY: McGraw-Hill, 1979.

ROSE, CLIVE. *The Soviet Propaganda Network: A Directory of Organizations Serving Soviet Foreign Policy*. NY: St. Martin's Press, 1988.

ROSEFIELDE, STEVEN. *False Science Underestimating the Soviet Arms Buildup: An Appraisal of the CIA's Direct Costing Effort, 1960-1980*. Chapel Hill: Univ. of North Carolina Press, 1982.

ROSITZKE, HARRY. *The CIA's Secret Operations: Espionage, Counterespionage, and Covert Action*. NY: Reader's Digest Press, 1977.

ROSTOW, WALT WHITMAN. *The Stages of Economic Growth; A Non-Communist Manifesto*. Cambridge, Eng.: Cambridge Univ. Press, 1971.

ROWEN, HENRY S., AND CHARLES WOLF, JR., EDS. *The Impoverished Superpower*. San Francisco: ICS Press, 1990.

RUMMEL, R. J. *Lethal Politics*. New Brunswick: Transaction Publishers, 1990.

RUNCIMAN, STEVEN. *The Medieval Manichee*. NY: Viking, 1961.

SARTORI, GIOVANNI, AND AUSTIN RANNEY, EDS. *Eurocommunism: The Italian Case*. Washington, DC: American Enterprise Institute, 1978.

SAUNDERS, M. L., AND PHILLIP TAYLOR. *British Propaganda During the First World War, 1914-18*. London: Macmillan, 1982.

SCHULTZ, RICHARD, AND ROY GODSON. *Dezinformatsia: Active Measures in Soviet Strategy*. NY: Pergamon-Brassey, 1984.

SCOTT, HARRIET FAST, AND WILLIAM SCOTT. *The Armed Forces of the USSR*, 3rd. rev. ed. Boulder, CO: Westview Press, 1984.

————. *The Soviet Art of War*. Boulder, CO: Westview Press, 1982.

SEABURY, PAUL, AND ANGELO CODEVILLA. *War: Ends and Means*. NY: Basic Books, 1989.

SEAGRAVE, STERLING. *Yellow Rain*. NY: M. Evans, 1981.

SEALE, PATRICK, AND MAUREEN MCCONVILLE. *Philby: The Long Road to Moscow*. NY: Simon & Schuster, 1973.

SEJNA, JAN. *We Will Bury You*. London: Sidgwick & Jackson, 1982.

SHAFER, D. MICHAEL. *Deadly Paradigms: The Failure of U.S. Counterinsurgency Policy*. Princeton: Princeton Univ. Press, 1988.

SHERWOOD, ROBERT E. *Roosevelt and Hopkins*. NY: Harper, 1948.

SHEVARDNADZE, EDUARD. *The Future Belongs to Freedom*. NY: Free Press, 1991.

SHEVCHENKO, ARKADY. *Breaking with Moscow*. NY: Knopf, 1985.

SINGLAUB, JOHN K. *Hazardous Duty*. NY: Simon & Schuster, 1991.

SMITH, EARL E. T. *The Fourth Floor*. NY: Random House, 1962.

SMITH, GEORGE IVAN. *Ghosts of Kampala*. London: Weidenfeld & Nicolson, 1980.

SMITH, JOSEPH BURKHOLDER. *Portrait of a Cold Warrior*. NY: Putnum, 1976.

SMITH, RICHARD HARRIS. *OSS: The Secret History of America of America's First Central Intelligence Agency*. Berkeley: Univ. of California Press, 1972.

SMITH, RUSSELL JACK. *The Unknown CIA*. Washington, DC: Pergamon-Brassey's, 1989.

SNEPP, FRANK. *Decent Interval*. NY: Random House, 1977.

SOKOLOVSKY, V. D. *Soviet Military Strategy*, 3rd ed. NY: Crane Russak, 1975.

SOLEY, LAWRENCE. *Radio Warfare*. NY: Praeger, 1989.

BIBLIOGRAPHY

SOLZHENITSYN, ALEXANDR. *The Gulag Archipelago*, vol. 3 NY: Harper & Row, 1978.

DE SOTO, HERNANDO. *The Other Path*. NY: Harper & Row, 1989.

SPEER, ALBERT. *Inside the Third Reich*. NY: Macmillan, 1970.

STAFFORD, DAVID. *Britain and European Resistance, 1940–1945; A Survey of the Special Operations Executive, with Documents*. Toronto: Univ. of Toronto Press, 1980.

STARR, CHESTER G. *Political Intelligence in Classical Greece*. The Hague: Ludguni Batavorum, 1974.

STETTINIUS, EDWARD. *Roosevelt and the Russians*. NY: Doubleday, 1949.

STEVENSON, WILLIAM. *A Man Called Intrepid*. NY: Harcourt Brace Jovanovich, 1976.

STOCKDALE, JAMES B., AND SYBIL STOCKDALE. *In Love and War*. NY: Harper & Row, 1984.

STOCKWELL, JOHN. *In Search of Enemies: A CIA Story*. NY: W. W. Norton, 1979.

STRAUSS, LEO. *Natural Right and History*. Chicago: Univ. of Chicago Press, 1959.

STREUSAND, DOUGLAS. *The Formation of the Mughal Empire*. New Delhi: Oxford Univ. Press, 1989.

SUVOROV, VICTOR. *Inside the Aquarium*. NY: Macmillan, 1986.

SZULC, TAD. *Fidel: A Critical Portrait*. NY: William Morrow, 1986.

THOMPSON, J. W., AND S. K. PADOVER. *Secret Diplomacy; Espionage and Cryptography, 1500–1815*. NY: Frederick Ungard, 1963.

THOMPSON, ROBERT. *Defeating Communist Insurgency; The Lessons of Malaya and Vietnam*. NY: Praeger, 1966.

TREVERTON, GREGORY. *Covert Action: The Limits of Intervention in the Postwar World*. NY: Basic Books, 1987.

TROY, THOMAS F. *Donovan and the CIA; A History of the Establishment of the Central Intelligence Agency*. Frederick, MD: University Publications of America, 1981.

TUCHMANN, BARBARA. *The Zimmermann Telegram*. NY: Macmillan, 1966.

TURNER, STANSFIELD. *Secrecy and Democracy*. NY: Houghton Mifflin, 1985.

U.S. CONGRESS. Report of the Congressional Committees Investigating the Iran–Contra Affair, with Supplemental, Minority, and Additional Views, 100th Congress, 1st Session. Washington, DC: USGPO, 1987. (Hereafter referred to as Iran–Contra Report.)

U.S. CONGRESS. House Select Committee on Intelligence. *CIA The Pike Report*. Nottingham: Spokesman Books, 1977.

U.S. DEPARTMENT OF DEFENSE. *Soviet Military Power: An Assessment of the Threat, 1988*. Washington, DC: 1988.

U.S. NAVY DEPARTMENT, DIVISION OF OPERATIONS. *The History and Aims of the Office of Naval Intelligence*. Washington, DC: 1920.

VAKSBERG, ARKADY. *The Prosecutor: Andrei Vishinsky and the Moscow Show Trials*. NY: Grove Widenfeld, 1991.

VIERICK, GEORGE SYLVESTER. *Spreading Germs of Hate*. NY: Horace Liveright, 1930.

VOEGELIN, ERIC. *The New Science of Politics*. Chicago: Univ. of Chicago Press, 1953.

VOSLENSKY, MICHAEL. *The Nomenklatura*. Garden City, NY: Doubleday, 1984.

WALTERS, VERNON. *Silent Missions*. NY: Doubleday, 1978.

WEBER, MAX. *The Sociology of Religion*. Boston: Beacon, 1963.

———. *Wirtschaft und Gesellschaft* Tuebingen: J.C.B. Mohr, 1925.

WEINBERG, GERHARD L. *The Foreign Policy of Hitler's Germany: Diplomatic Revolution in Europe, 1933–1936*. Chicago: Univ. of Chicago Press, 1970.

WELCHMAN, GORDON. *The Hut Six Story: Breaking the Enigma Codes*. NY: McGraw–Hill, 1982.

WHALEY, BARTON. *Strategem: Deception and Surprise in War*. Cambridge: Massechussetts Institute of Technology Center for International Studies, 1969.

WINKS, ROBIN W. *Cloak and Gown*. NY: Morrow, 1989.

WOLF, CHARLES, AND BENJAMIN ZYCHER. *Military Dimensions of Communist Systems: Findings and Implications*, R-3629 USDP Santa Monica: Rand, [January] 1989.

WOLFE, BERTRAM. *Three Who Made a Revolution*. NY: Penguin, 1966.

WOLTON, THIERRY. *Le KGB en France*. Paris: Bernard Grasset, 1986.

WOODWARD, BOB. *Veil*. NY: Simon & Schuster, 1987.

BIBLIOGRAPHY

WRIGHT, PETER. *Spycatcher: The Candid Autobiography of a Senior Intelligence Officer.* NY: Viking, 1987.

WRIGHT, QUINCY. *A Study of War.* Chicago: Univ. of Chicago Press, 1942.

WRISTON, HENRY MERRITT. *Executive Agents in American Foreign Relations.* Baltimore: The Johns Hopkins Press, 1929.

ZEMAN, ZBYNEK A. B. *The Merchant of Revolution; The Life of Alexander Israel Helphand (Parvus),* 1867–1924. London and New York: Oxford Univ. Press, 1965.

ZONIS, MARVIN. *Majestic Failure.* Chicago: U. of Chicago Press, 1991.

Index

473

CPSIA information can be obtained at www.ICGtesting.com
Printed in the USA
LVOW08s0246260713

344649LV00012B/656/A